T0368399

LAST AND NEAR-LAST WORDS OF THE FAMOUS, INFAMOUS AND THOSE IN-BETWEEN

Joseph W. Lewis, Jr., M.D.

authorHOUSE®

AuthorHouse™
1663 Liberty Drive
Bloomington, IN 47403
www.authorhouse.com
Phone: 1 (800) 839-8640

Published by AuthorHouse 10/28/2016

ISBN: 978-1-5246-4788-9 (sc)
ISBN: 978-1-5246-4787-2 (e)

Print information available on the last page.

This book is printed on acid-free paper.

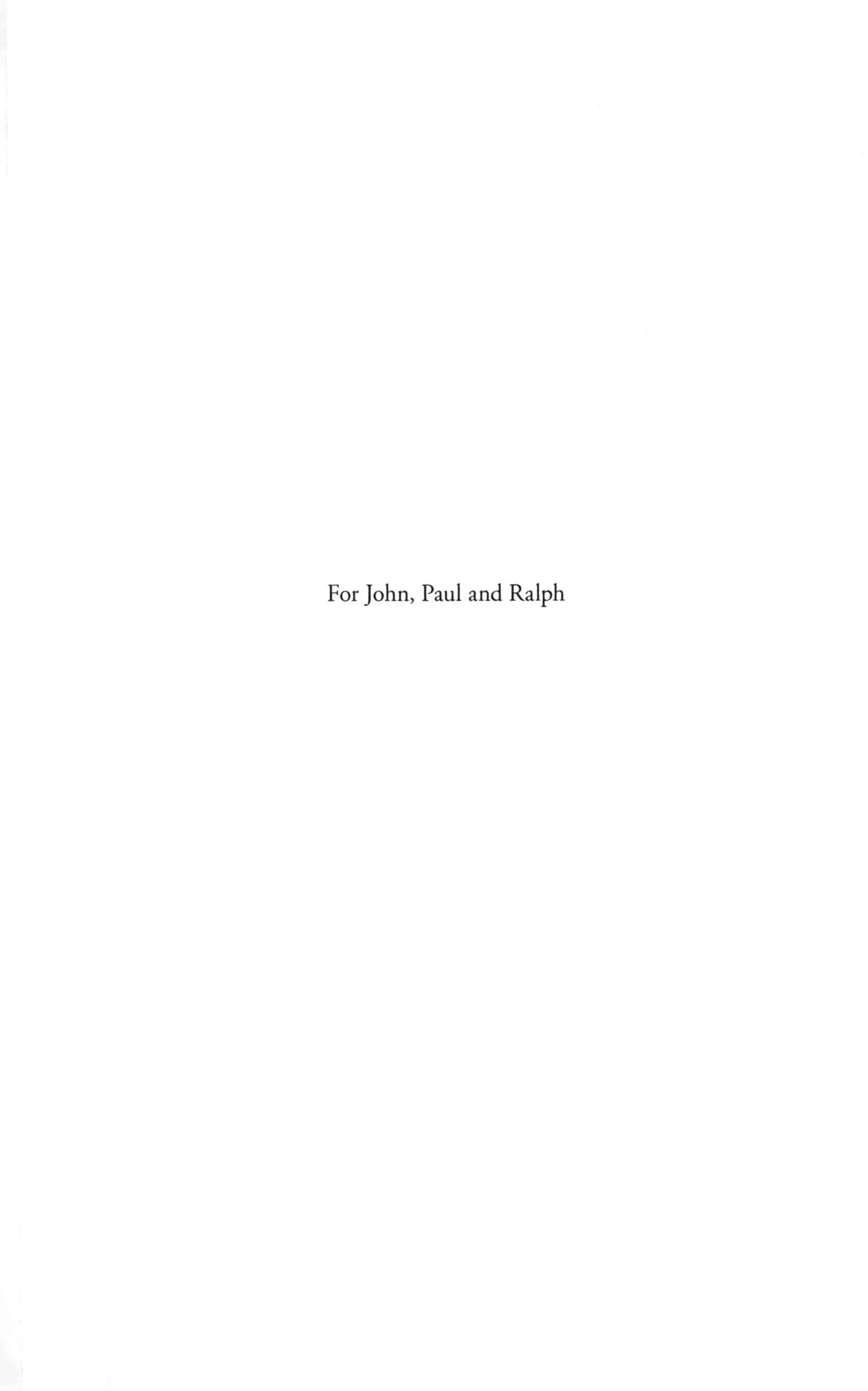

For John, Paul and Ralph

My Ten All-time Favorite Last Words

Behan, Brendan (1923-1964). Irish writer, playwright and poet. Dying from complications of alcoholism and diabetes, Behan remarked to his wife: "You made one mistake. You married me." He then spoke to his nurse, a nun: "Thank you, sister. May you be the mother of a bishop."

Brillat-Savarin, Paulette (fl. late 18th-early 19th century). Dying short of her 100th birthday, the sister of the French epicure Anthelme Brillat-Savarin exclaimed: "Quick! Serve the dessert! I think I am dying."

Fox, Henry, Baron Holland (1705-1774). English Member of Parliament. Fox spoke to an attendant concerning a friend and political rival George Selwyn who had a fondness for viewing corpses and executions: "If Mr. Selwyn calls again, show him up; if I am alive, I shall be delighted to see him, and if I am dead, he would like to see me."

Goethe, Catharina (1731-1808). Mother of the German writer and statesman Johann von Goethe. Declining an invitation to a party: "Say that Frau Goethe is unable to come. She is busy dying at the moment."

Haller, Albrecht von (1708-1777). Swiss physician, anatomist and philosopher. Palpating his own pulse, Haller told a colleague. "Now I am dying. The artery ceases to beat"

Mahy, Thomas de, Marquis de Favras (1744-1790). French nobleman who supported the monarchy during the French Revolution. Condemned to die, Mahy criticized the official document outlining his sentence as he was led to the guillotine: "I see that you have made three spelling mistakes."

Marx, Karl (1818-1883). German-born political and economic theorist who espoused a fundamental philosophy for emerging socialist and communist governments. Dying of a chronic chest ailment, Marx allegedly chided his housekeeper who urged him to speak his last words so they could be recorded for posterity: "Get out of here and leave me alone. Last words are for fools who haven't said enough already."

Maugham, W. Somerset (1874-1965). Parisian-born British novelist and playwright. Toward the end, Maugham jokingly made known his views on the end of life: "Dying is a very dull and dreary affair. And my advice to you is to have nothing whatever to do with it."

O'Carolan, Turlough (1670-1738). Irish composer, singer and harpist. At the end, O'Carolan wished for a last drink of whiskey, saying: "It would be hard indeed if we two dear friends should part after so many years, without one sweet kiss."

Saroyan, William (1908-1981). Pulitzer Prize-winning American writer. Before he died of cancer, Saroyan quipped: "Everybody has got to die, but I have always believed an exception would be made in my case. Now what?"

Introduction

Of the estimated 108 billion humans who have inhabited the earth, only a small number of those souls have had their last words preserved for posterity. Undoubtedly, most of our predecessors uttered final statements, but limitations of recording, transmission and interest restricted preservation of their utterances until recent times. I have put together a collection of 3676 farewells from a varied population ranging from convicted criminals to the most holy. Many are famous, some are notorious and others blur into a less well-defined subgroup of relative unknowns. Although the majority of entries consist of last spoken words, a few wills, epitaphs, final diary notes and last letters are included in this compilation. A brief sketch of each individual in alphabetical format includes birth and death dates, country of origin and a short biographical sketch. In some instances, an expanded summary is included to better illuminate the circumstances of a last expression when indicated. All italics used in quotations were present in the original source material.

Table 1 highlights the primary careers or avocations of the included individuals and their distribution in the compilation. In actuality, only 3674 utterances came from humans; one last greeting came from Alex, a dying African Grey parrot and the other from NASA's Mars Phoenix Lander, as its batteries depleted. In those individuals with multiple fields of interest, I tried to select the calling that best described the person. For the sake of analysis, martyred saints and clergy were separated from their non-martyred counterparts, because their last words were generally dissimilar. Those who succumbed to martyrdom tended to offer words that committed their souls to the divine, generally imploring: "Into Thy hands I commit my spirit." In contrast, saints and clergy who escaped a gruesome ending often spoke about their oncoming death in terms such as: "This is the end" or "I feel death coming." Most deathbed statements seemed to reflect the circumstances at the conclusion of their lives, but a few souls made it known during their lifetime what they wished to say at the end. James Hog, the 19th century Scottish esquire, said throughout his life that he wanted to utter the following words at his death: "Lord Jesus, receive my spirit. Thou art my only hope." Unfortunately, Hog was unable to speak when the end was at hand. By pointing to a printed alphabet with a reed in his mouth, he spelled a slightly different final message: "I am looking to the Savior. My only hope is in Jesus." The esquire then died peacefully.

The British Broadcasting Corporation television science fiction program *Doctor Who* reminds us: "What's the use of a good quotation if you can't change it?" Verifying the accuracy and authenticity of last statements, at times, can be daunting. Of the 3676 entities in this survey, 616(16.8%) had alternative expressions that were presented as final words. Fryderyk Chopin, the noted pianist and composer, had at least 16 different purported last goodbyes. Undoubtedly, some of these pronouncements were made at different times during his last days and were recorded and construed by the listener as the musician's last words. In other individuals, the differences in ultimate statements were minor and did not alter the gist of the utterances. On his deathbed, the French poet François de Malherbe criticized a priest attempting to describe heaven in "vulgar and trite phrases:" "Ah, for God's sake, say no more of heaven, for your bad style would give me a disgust to it." Other authors have recorded the poet's last words as variations on that theme: "Hold your tongue; your miserable style puts me out of conceit with heaven;" "Hold your tongue! Your wretched style disgusts me;" "Hold your tongue; your wretched style only makes me out of conceit with them;" "Hold your tongue, father! Your low style entirely makes me out of conceit with them;" "Hold your tongue! Your wretched chatter disgusts me;" "Do not speak of it any more. Your bad style leaves me disgusted," and "Your ungrammatical style is putting me off them." Although the meaning of de Malherbe's parting words remains quite clear, the variations probably represent nothing more than embellishments and differences in translation.

Table 1. Occupations or Life Pursuits of Quoted Individuals

Categories	Number	Percentage
Entertainers	365	10.0
Criminals	353	9.6
Clergy	351	9.5
Writers/ Journalists	342	9.4
Politicians/ Statesmen	305	8.3
Military	291	7.9
Rulers	240	6.6
Martyrs*	165	4.5
Poets	131	3.6
Aristocrats	124	3.4
Businessmen/ Women	99	2.7
Scientists/ Inventors	95	2.6
Revolutionaries	87	2.4
Saints	80	2.2
Artists/ Sculptors	77	2.1
Activists	65	1.8
Scholars/ Educators	64	1.7
Philosophers	62	1.6
Medical Practitioners	60	1.5
Athletes	53	1.4
Aviators	52	1.3
Legal Profession	47	1.2
Explorers	41	1.1
Socialites	41	1.1
Frontiersmen/ Women	16	0.5
Lawmen	13	0.4
Philanthropists	13	0.4
Students	8	0.2
Miscellaneous	36	1.0
Total	3676	100

* Includes martyred clergy, saints and other

Some final utterances should be considered near-last words rather than absolute end of life articulations. In some instances, the statements recorded as "last words" were made months or even years before death. The deathbed pronouncement attributed to Charles Lamb, the English literary critic, was: "... My bedfellows are cough and cramp, we sleep 3 in a bed... Don't come yet to this house of pest and age." Actually, these words were found in a letter to an acquaintance Edward Moxon, written 20 months before Lamb's death. As the critic succumbed to a streptococcal infection (erysipelas), he spoke quite different words with his last breath- the names of his two friends: "Moxon... Proctor." Final words attributed to King Farouk of Egypt and the actor Charlie Chaplin were, in fact, spoken 12 and 30 years respectively before their deaths. Whether these statements were repeated at the time of their demise is uncertain. Occasionally, final utterances do not support the facts reported at the time of death. The English poet and satirist Charles Churchill supposedly exclaimed at the end: "Thank God! I die in England," although many biographers place the location of his death in Boulogne, France. Discrepancies like these, however, need not detract from the enjoyment of "death bed statements" no matter when or where uttered.

Aggrandizement, either self-proclaimed or concocted by others, may attempt to add luster to an otherwise mundane circumstance. The noted German writer and statesman Johann von Goethe supposedly left the world calling literally or figuratively, for "Light, more light." The editors Bryan Bennett and Negley Harte in their book *The Crabtree Orations 1954-1994* opine: "The 'seldom quoted remark: 'light, more light' is an oft misquoted version of Goethe's dying words. It was felt more appropriate to have Goethe's last words radiant with transcendental promise: 'Mehr Licht'- more light, but others closer to the great man's dying breath claimed that the sentence, barely audible, went on beyond the first two words and was: 'Mir liegt der Leberkäs schwer am Magen'- the liver sausage is lying heavily on my stomach.'" I believe most would prefer to remember the great man's last utterance in the context of "more light" rather than a complaint about indigestion from a liver sausage.

Embellishment or falsification of a person's last comments can be proffered without much bother. A noted example occurred when a mentally deranged bricklayer attempted to shoot president-elect Franklin Roosevelt on his 1933 trip to Miami, Florida. Instead of striking Roosevelt, the bullet mortally wounded the Democratic mayor of Chicago, Anton "Tony" Cermak. The wounded man allegedly responded: "I'm glad it was me and not you, Mr. President." Later, a Hearst reporter John Dienhart, a friend of the mayor, admitted that he had fabricated the parting quote, saying: "I couldn't very well have put out a story that Tony would have wanted it the other way around." Cermak's actual last words "Kiss me" were spoken to his wife immediately before he died in hospital.

Galileo, the controversial Italian philosopher, mathematician and astronomer, was forced by the Inquisition to recant his belief that the earth rotated around the sun. He supposedly remained steadfast in his "heretical" conviction by stating at the end: "Yet it moves." J.J. Fahie, in his 1903 biography *Galileo His Life and Work*, discounted the quote, saying that the consequences of persisting in this heliocentric view would have been too severe for the scientist. According to Boller and George in their book *They Never Said It*: "It was a French writer, writing more than a century after Galileo's death, who first put the words in the great scientist's mouth."

Of the 3676 collected quotes, 2515 (68.4%) had qualities that allowed categorization of these final statements (Table 2). Although some last words conveyed a variety of feelings, I chose the single thought that best represented the crux of the expression. The most commonly verbalized sentiment was a perception that death was near, such as "I am dying" or "It's a good day to die." Less common quotes varied from statements of emotion or feeling, how one planned to meet the end, greetings to friends or relatives, pleas for help, a mention of food or an entreaty for more time to complete earthly endeavors. The desire to die with courage and dignity most commonly was made by soldiers. Not surprisingly, the majority of apologies and protestations of innocence came from condemned criminals. Martyred individuals tended to utter words that committed their souls to the divine. Obscenities found their way into final declarations infrequently (only 87 of 3676 individuals or 2.4%). When expletives were uttered in concluding statements, they tended to be voiced by entertainers and criminals. Before his execution, the convicted murderer Stephen Johns summarized his perception of final statements made by felons: "... I have, over the past many years, heard many 'last words' of those killed by the State and its citizens. They range from 'I'm sorry' to 'kiss my fat a** ...'" He should know. In this collection, no clergy, saint or martyr was caught uttering any profanity at the time of death.

Table 2. Categorization of Final Statements

Category of Last Words	Number	Percentage
Death Prediction	752	29.9
See How I Die	210	8.3
Expression of Feeling	182	7.2
Let Me Die	166	6.6
Name Mention	166	6.6
Greeting	121	4.8
Into Thy Arms	98	3.9
Love	92	3.7
Yes or No	92	3.7
Food or Beverage	79	3.1
Burial Arrangements	73	2.9
Innocent	63	2.5
Expression of Thanks	59	2.4
Forgive/Pardon Me	57	2.3
Ask for More Time	47	1.9
Mercy	46	1.8
Peace	38	1.5
Tired/Need Rest	37	1.5
Apology	35	1.4
Need Sleep	33	1.3
Pray	28	1.1
Help	21	0.8
Pain	13	0.5
Confess	7	0.3
	2515	100

I hope this compilation of last words will shed some light on a select group of individuals as they faced their approaching demise. Some serenely committed their souls to a higher being, while other railed against the ending. Undoubtedly, a few final pronouncements surfaced as misquotes or stemmed from dubious origins, but most have stood the test of time and scrutiny. As I completed this undertaking, the last words of Andrew Bradford, the American colonial publisher, came to mind: "Oh Lord, forgive the errata!"

A Compilation of Last and Near-last Statements

Abbey, Edward (1927-1989). American writer and environmental activist. Dying from surgery for esophageal bleeding, Abbey left a note for those who might ask about him later: "No comment." His last spoken words: "I did what I could."

Abbot, Robert (1560-1617). Archbishop of Salisbury, England. On his deathbed: "Come Lord Jesus, come quickly! Finish in me the work that Thou hast begun. Into Thy hands I commend my spirit, for Thou hast redeemed me, Thou God of truth. Save Thy servant who hopeth and trusteth in Thee alone. Let Thy mercy be showed upon me. In Thee, O Lord, have I hoped. Let me not be confounded forever!"

Abbott, Charles (1762-1832). English barrister who later became Lord Chief Justice of the King's Bench. Suffering from a fever, Abbott spoke to an imaginary jury: "Gentlemen, you are all dismissed."

Alternative: * "Gentlemen of the jury, you will now consider your verdict."

Abbott, Darrell "Dimebag" (1966-2004). American guitarist and member of the heavy metal rock band Damageplan. Before performing with his group in a Columbus, Ohio venue, Abbott said to his brother: "Van Halen [the name of a different American rock band]!" Several minutes later, he was killed by gunshots to the head fired by a deranged audience member.

Abbott, Emma (1850-1891). American operatic soprano. Dying of pneumonia: "I shall sing my next song in heaven... I am not afraid to die."

Abd-ar-Rahman III (891-961). Caliph of Córdoba, Spain and first ruler of the Muslim Umayyad Dynasty. In a note found after his death: "I have now reigned fifty years in victory or peace, beloved by my subjects, dreaded by my enemies and respected by my allies. Riches, honor, power and pleasure have waited on my call, nor does any earthly blessing appear to have been wanting in my felicity. In this situation I have diligently numbered the days of pure and genuine happiness and they amount to FOURTEEN! O man! Place not thy confidence in this present world."

Abélard, Pierre (1079-1142). French philosopher and theologian. Before dying, Abélard enigmatically pronounced: "I don't know! I don't know!"

Abercromby, Ralph (1734-1801). Scottish-born English general who was mortally wounded in a battle with the French army near Alexandria, Egypt. A subordinate placed a support under the stricken man's head, saying that it was only a soldier's blanket. Abercromby replied: "Only a soldier's blanket? Make haste and return it to him at once!"

Abernethy, John (1764-1831). English surgeon and educator. Commenting about his own abdominal ailment: "It is all stomach. We use our stomachs ill when we are young, and they use us ill when we are old." On his deathbed, he queried: "Is there anybody in the room?"

Abimelech (died c. 1233 BCE). King of Shechem, near Nablus in present-day Israel. As Abimelech laid siege to Thebez, a city in the central mountainous region of Israel, a woman pushed a millstone onto his head. With his skull grievously injured, the king ordered one of his men to: "Draw your sword and kill me, lest men say of me: 'A woman killed him.'" His armor-bearer complied.

Accoramboni, Vittoria (1557-1585). Italian noblewoman, the Duchess of Bracciano. When her husband died, Accoramboni quarreled with a relative over the division of his property. The relative subsequently arranged Accoramboni's murder. To her assassins: "Jesus! I pardon you."

Achterberg, Gerrit (1905-1962). Dutch poet. When asked by his wife if he wanted some potatoes for their meal, Achterberg replied: "Yes, but not too many." He then suffered a heart attack and died.

Adam of Baghdad (died 2010). Iraqi child. As Muslim radicals killed Christian worshipers in a Baghdad church, the three year-old Adam wandered through the bloody carnage repeating: "Enough, enough, enough." Adam eventually was slain.

Adam, Alexander (1741-1809). Scottish schoolmaster. After suffering a stroke, Adam imagined that he appeared before his old class: "That Horace was very well said... *you* did not do it so well. But it grows dark, very dark. The boys may dismiss."

Alternative: * "But it grows dark, boys- you may go; we must put off the rest till to-morrow."

Adams, Abigail (1744-1818). Wife of John Adams, the second U.S. president. Dying of typhoid fever (some say typhus): "If I cannot be useful, I do not wish to live." Later: "Do not grieve, my friend- my dearest friend. I am ready to go, and John, it will not be long."

Adams, Allen (died 1886). American criminal. Adams was sentenced to die by hanging for the murder of his boss. On the gallows: "Go ahead and do what you ___ please. Don't squeeze me to death, ___ you. It don't take a hundred men to hang me." When asked for last words: "None of your business. What in the ___ do you want to take a man's life in this way for, you ___ ___ cutthroats. Hurry up, old man, or [Sheriff] Clark will want another drink of whiskey. If you don't look out, I may fall through and sue the city for damages." Robert Elder in his book *Last Words of the Executed* opines: "The blanks in his speech, presumably, represent profanity the newspaper didn't wish to print."

Adams, Frederick (1786-1858). American physician, theologian and violin maker. On his deathbed: "If there is a Christian's God, I am not afraid to trust myself in his hands."

Adams, Henry (1838-1918). American author, historian and great-grandson of President John Quincy Adams. As death neared, to his secretary: "Dear child, keep me alive." To his housekeeper: "Goodnight, my dear." Adams later died in his sleep.

Adams, John (1735-1826). Second U.S. president. On the 50th anniversary of the signing of the Declaration of Independence, the weakened Adams was asked if he realized the significance of the day. He replied: "Oh, yes; it is the glorious Fourth of July. It is a great day. It is a good day. God bless it. God bless you all." He then drifted into unconsciousness for several hours. When he aroused around noon, Adams was widely quoted as saying: "Thomas Jefferson still survives." Witnesses, however, reported that the dying man only mumbled: "Thomas Jefferson..." Adams was unaware that his friend Jefferson had died earlier in the day at his home near Charlottesville, Virginia. Before dying, Adams gasped to his granddaughter Susanna: "Help me, child! Help me!"

Adams, John Quincy (1767-1848). Sixth U.S. president. After leaving office, Adams later became a member of the U.S. House of Representatives. While attending a session of congress on February 21, 1848, he suffered a stroke. As the stricken man was taken into the Speaker's office, he mumbled: "Thank the officers of the House." Later he said: "This is the last of earth. I am content." Adams died two days later.

Adams, Marian "Clover" (1843-1885). American socialite, Washington D.C. hostess and wife of the historian Henry Adams (above). After the death of her father, Clover became severely depressed and committed suicide by swallowing potassium cyanide. In a letter to her sister: "If I had one single point of character or goodness I would stand on that and grow back to life. Henry is more patient and loving than words can express. God might envy him- he bears and hopes and despairs hour after hour... Henry is beyond all words tenderer and better than all of you even" The letter remained on Adams' desk unsent.

Adams, Maude, born Maude Kiskadden (1872-1953). American actress, best-known for her performance in J.M. Barrie's play *Peter Pan*. While reclining on her sofa, Adams exclaimed: "Life is still full of joy. Thumbs up for joy and adventure."

Addams, Jane (1860-1935). Social reformer, temperance advocate, pacifist and first American woman to win the Nobel Peace Prize. Following cancer surgery, to her physician: "When I was a child, I had an old doctor friend who told me the hardest thing in the world was to kill an old woman. He seems to have been right." When asked immediately before her death if she wanted water: "Always. Always water for me." Some, however, reported that Addams' last words possibly were a response to spirits proffered as a stimulant.

Addison, Joseph (1672-1719). English journalist, essayist, poet and politician. Dying of "dropsy" and asthma, to his "dissipated" stepson, Lord Warwick: "I have sent for you that you may see how a Christian can die."

Alternative: * "See in what peace a Christian can die."

Adenauer, Konrad (1876-1967). First chancellor of the Federal Republic of Germany. To his family: "Stick together. See as much as possible of one another." Before lapsing into a coma: "No reason to weep."

Adoniram, Judson (1788-1850). American Baptist missionary to Burma. Before dying during a sea voyage: "I go with the gladness of a boy bounding away from school. I feel so strong in Christ."

Agape, Saint (died 304). Thessalonican martyr. When Agape was asked if she would obey the heathen law imposed by the Romans, she replied: "Not any laws that command the worship of idols and devils." Agape was burned to death for her answer.

Agassiz, Louis (1807-1873). Swiss-born American zoologist, geologist and paleontologist. Sensing death's arrival: "All is finished. The game is finished."

Alternative: * "The play is finished."

Agatha, Saint (died c. 251). Sicilian Christian martyr. After refusing the sexual advances of the Roman administrator Quintianus, Agatha was beaten, burned and had her breasts cut off: "Cruel tyrant, do you not blush to torture this part of my body, you that sucked the breasts of a woman yourself?" Agatha then was imprisoned, where she died: "Lord, you who created me, and protected me from my infancy, and made me act with courage in my youth. You who took away from me love of the world, kept my body free from pollution; who made me overcome the hangman's tortures, the sword, fire and chains; who gave me the virtue of patience in the midst of tortures. I beg you to receive my soul now; for it is time that you order me to leave this world here, and to come to your mercy."

Alternatives: * "Cruel man, have you forgotten your mother and the breast that nourished you that you dare to mutilate me this way?"

* "Lord, my Creator, you have ever protected me from the cradle; you have taken from me the love of the world and given me patience to suffer. Receive now my soul"

Agesilaus II (c. 444-c. 360 BCE). King of Sparta. When asked if he wished a monument erected in his honor: "If I have done any honorable exploit, that is my monument. But if I have done none, all your statues will signify nothing."

Agesistrata (died 241 BCE). Mother of Agis of Sparta (below). Because she approved of her son's reforms, Agesistrata was hanged. "I pray the gods that all this may redound [to have an effect] to the good of Sparta."

Agis IV (died 241 BCE). King of Sparta. For his attempts to reform wealth and land distribution in his country, Agis became very unpopular and was sentenced to die. To an officer who was crying openly: "Weep not, friend, for me, who die[s] innocent, by the lawless act of wicked men. My condition is much better than theirs."

Alternative: * "Weep not for me: suffering, as I do, unjustly, I am in a happier case than my murderers."

Agnes of Rome, Saint (c. 292-c. 304). Roman noblewoman, martyred for her refusal to renounce her Christian faith and marry a Roman official's son. To the executioner: "I am now glad. I rejoice that thou art come. I will willingly receive into my bosom the length of this sword that thus married unto Christ, my spouse. I may surmount and escape all the darkness of this world. O eternal Governor, vouchsafe to open the gates of heaven, once shut up against all the inhabitants of the earth, and receive, O Christ, my soul that seeks thee!" Agnes was killed by a sword blow.

Alternatives: * "Destroy the body that draws the admiration of those eyes from which I shrink."

* "Jesus Christ is my only Spouse."

Agnew, Andrew (1793-1849). Scottish nobleman and politician. Dying of a respiratory ailment: "Did the doctors really say I was not to get up? If they said so, then I won't get up, but I feel well." When asked if he wished his pillows lowered: "No, I will keep them as the doctors left them."

Agrestis, Julius (died 69). A Roman centurion who served under Emperor Vitellius. Charged with treason for allegedly misrepresenting facts about the destruction of Cremona in 69 CE, Agrestis tried to affirm his loyalty by taking his own life. To the emperor: "I perceive you require a remarkable proof, and since neither my life nor death can benefit you, I shall give you what you may believe." Agrestis then fell on his sword.

Agrippa, Henricus (1486-1535). German philosopher, physician, alchemist and occultist. According to F.R. Marvin in his *Last Words (Real and Traditional) of Distinguished Men and Women*, Agrippa "...was always accompanied by a devil in the shape of a black dog. When he perceived that death was near, he wished, by repentance, to free his soul from the guilt of witchcraft, and so took off the collar from his dog's neck:" "Be gone, thou wretched beast, which hast utterly undone me."

Agrippina (c. 16-59). Roman noblewoman. By eliminating rivals, Agrippina orchestrated the placement of her son Nero as emperor of Rome. When she later tried to assert her authority in court, Nero conspired to kill her. To her assassins: "Strike here. Level your rage against the womb which gave birth to such a monster!"

Alternatives: * "Smite my womb!"
* "Strike here... strike here for this bore Nero."
* "Strike here where Nero's head once rested."

Agustin I, born Agustin de Iturbide (1783-1824). Emperor of Mexico. Overthrown after a short term of leadership, Augustin went into exile but later returned to his homeland. Arrested as a traitor, he was sentenced to die before a firing squad: "I am no traitor! Such a stain will never attach to my children or to their descendants."

Alternatives: * "Mexicans! In the very act of my death, I recommend to you the love of the fatherland, and the observance to our religion, for it shall lead you to glory. I die having come here to help you, and I die merrily, for I die amongst you. I die with honor, not as a traitor; I do not leave this stain on my children and my legacy. I am not a traitor, no."

* "Mexicans! I die with honor, not as a traitor; do not leave this stain on my children and my legacy. I am not a traitor, no."
* "Mexicans! I die because I came to help you; I die gladly, because I die among you. I die not as a traitor, but with honor."
* "... I am no traitor, and such a stain will never attach to my children or to their descendants. Preserve order and render obedience to your commanders. From the depths of my heart, all my enemies."

Ahab (c. 875-853 BCE). Israeli king and husband of Jezebel (below). While fighting the Syrians, Ahab was struck by an arrow. He ordered his charioteer to: "Turn about and carry me out of the battle, for I am wounded." He later died of his injury (I Kings 22: 34).

Ainsworth, William (1805-1882). British editor and historical novelist. From his last letter: "Dr. Holman [his physician] thought me much wasted since I last saw him and so I am in no doubt. Your affectionate cousin, W. Harrison Ainsworth."

Aitken, William "Max" Lord Beaverbrook (1879-1964). Canadian-born British politician, businessman and publisher. Aitken's last public statement: "... But this is my final word. It is time for me to become an apprentice once more. I have not settled in which direction. But somewhere, sometime, soon." In the final stage of cancer, Aitken was advised to rest: "But maybe I wouldn't wake up."

Akbar, Mohammed (1542-1605). Indian ruler. To his son and assembled noblemen: "I cannot bear that any misunderstanding should subsist between you and those who have for so many years shared in my toils and been the companions of my glory." Akbar begged forgiveness of anyone who had been wronged, passed his empire to his son and then died.

Akiba ben Joseph, also Akiva (c. 50-c. 135). Judean rabbi and scholar. For his refusal to stop teaching the Torah, Akiba was condemned by Roman authorities. Before his execution by flaying, a Torah supposedly was burned before him, provoking the response: "The paper burns, but the words fly free." As his flesh was stripped from his body, Akiba recited the Shema [a Jewish declaration of faith from Deuteronomy 6:4]: "Hear, O Israel, Adonai [the Lord] is our God; Adonai is one."

Alternative: * "Hear, O Israel, Jehova, Our Lord, Jehova is one."

Alacoque, Saint Margaret Mary (1647-1690). French Roman Catholic nun and mystic. As she was anointed: "I need nothing but God and to lose myself in the heart of Jesus."

Alban, Saint (died c. 304). British martyr who was beheaded for hiding a priest during the Roman persecution of Christians. When commanded to worship idols: "My name is Alban, and I worship the only true and living God, who created all things." Then: "The sacrifices you offer are made to devils; neither can they help the needy, nor grant the petitions of their votaries." The executioner was so impressed by the martyr's faith that he converted to Christianity on the spot and refused to behead Alban. An alternate executioner accomplished the decapitation.

Alternative: * "These sacrifices, which are offered to devils, are of no avail. Hell is the reward of those who offer them."

Albert I (1875-1934). Belgian king. Out for a drive, the monarch asked his chauffeur to stop at a cliff face: "… If I feel in good form, I shall take the difficult way up. If I do not, I shall take the easy one. I shall join you in one hour." When the king failed to return promptly, his lifeless body was found nearby. The circumstances of his death remain unclear.

Albert Victor (1864-1892). Duke of Clarence and Avondale who was the grandson of English Queen Victoria. Dying of pneumonia, Albert spoke deliriously of his younger brother who later would become king: "Something too awful has happened! My darling brother George is dead." Hours later, he repeated over and over "Who is that?" until he lost consciousness and died.

Albert, Prince Francis (1819-1861). German-born husband of England's Queen Victoria. Dying of suspected typhoid fever, Albert spoke to the queen: "Good little wife." Victoria answered: "It is your little woman." They embraced and he died.

Albertoni, Saint Louisa (1473-1533). Prosperous Roman philanthropist who used her wealth to aid the poor. On her deathbed, Albertoni prayed: "Father, into Thy hands I commend my spirit."

Alcott, Amos (1799-1888). American writer, philosopher, educator and father of Louisa Alcott (below). Alcott suffered a career-ending stroke in 1882. On his deathbed, to his daughter: "I am going up. Come with me." When Louisa responded that she wished she could. Alcott replied: "Come soon." Ironically, she died two days later.

Alcott, Louisa (1832-1888). American author, best-known for her novel *Little Women*. Alcott experienced poor health following a case of typhoid fever, acquired while serving as a Civil War nurse. Asking her physician about the nature of her terminal illness: "Is it not meningitis?"

Alderson, Edward Hall (1787-1857). British judge. When told his medical condition was no better: "The worse, the better for me."

Aldrich, Thomas (1836-1907). American novelist and poet. "In spite of it all, I am going to sleep. Put out the lights"

Alex (1976-2007). An African Grey parrot used in studies by Dr. Irene Pepperberg, an American researcher in comparative psychology. When Pepperberg put Alex in his cage for the night, the bird responded with its usual parting words: "You be good. See you tomorrow. I love you." Alex unexpectedly died overnight.

Alexander I (1777-1825). Russian czar. Terminally ill with a fever, possibly typhus, Alexander remarked: "What a beautiful day." To his wife: "I am dying of fatigue." To his physicians who proposed treating his illness with leeches: "Now gentlemen, do your work. Give me the remedies that you judge necessary."

Alexander II (1818-1881). Russian czar who freed the serfs and reorganized the legal system. Fatally injured by an anarchist's bomb, Alexander pleaded to be taken back to his palace: "Quicker- home- carry me to the Palace- to die- there." In transit, the czar inquired about the safety of those with him but lost consciousness as he entered the palace. Some say his final words were: "I am sweeping through the gates, washed in the blood of the Lamb." Because of the magnitude of Alexander's injuries, it is unlikely that he made this statement.

Alexander III (1845-1894). Russian czar. Succumbing to kidney and heart failure, Alexander was found out of bed despite orders for strict bed rest. When queried by his doctor about his activity, the czar replied: "No! No, doctor, but it was done in obedience to the Czar's own command." Shortly before dying, to his family: "I feel the end approaching. Be calm. I am quite calm." After receiving the Last Rites, to his priest: "How good!"

Alexander III, also Alexander the Great (356-323 BCE). King of Macedon and creator of one of the largest empires in ancient history. Fatally ill with a fever, Alexander bemoaned his fate saying: "I am dying with the help of too many physicians." An apocryphal story relates that later the king was asked on his deathbed who would succeed him. Because his reply was indistinct, some heard the word "Krateros," the name of one of his generals. Others though Alexander said "Kratistos," to the strongest. These words carry little credence, because Alexander probably was unable to speak during the terminal part of his illness.

Alexander I (1888-1934). Montenegrin-born Yugoslavian king. Assassinated by a Bulgarian revolutionary, Alexander allegedly cried: "Safeguard Yugoslavia." More likely, the king died instantly.

Alexander VI (c. 1431-1503). Spanish-born Pope from 1492 until his death. Mortally ill with a fever, Alexander believed Satan in the form of an ape was running around his sickroom. When a cardinal offered to catch the imaginary creature, the Pope replied: "Let it alone, for it is the devil!" Supposedly he deliriously said to his vision: "I come. I come. It is just. But wait a little."

Alexandra Feodorovna (1872-1918). German-born empress consort of Nicholas II of Russia. Imprisoned in August 1917 by the new provisional government, Alexandra and her family were kept in captivity for nearly a year. During the early morning hours of July 17, 1918, the family was moved to the basement of the house where they had been confined. Alexandra remarked: "Well, then, is there no chair? Can't we sit down?" Shortly after a chair was provided, she and her family were shot to death.

Alexis I (1629-1676). Russian czar. Dying shortly after his second marriage, Alexis said: "I would never have married had I known that my time would be so brief. If I had known that, I would not have taken upon myself double tears."

Alfieri, Vittorio (1749-1803). Italian poet. Dying from "gout in the stomach," to his mistress Princess Louise of Stolberg: "Clasp my hand, dear friend, I am dying."

Alfonso XII (1857-1885). Spanish king. Dying of tuberculosis, to his wife: "I don't deserve to be cared for as you have cared for me. I know that when I have gone, you will care for Spain as I have myself."

Alfonso XIII (1886-1941). Spanish king who died in exile. As he expired, Alfonso kissed a crucifix and said: "Spain! My God."

Alfonso of Spain (1907-1938). Eldest son of Alfonso XIII and Prince of Asturias, a municipality in northwestern Spain. After his marriage to a commoner, Alfonso relinquished his right of succession to the Spanish throne. After suffering minor injuries in an automobile accident in Miami, Florida, he screamed to his treating doctors: "I am going to die! I am going to die!" Unbeknownst to them, the count was a hemophiliac. He turned to a friend and said: "*¡Mi madre*! *¡Mi madre*! Where is my mother? I'm all alone in this country. Don't leave me, Jack!"

Alford, Henry (1810-1871). English clergyman, theologian and hymnodist. On his deathbed, Alford requested the Bishop of Dover for his funeral service: "Will you move a vote of thanks for his kindness in performing the ceremony?"

Alfred the Great (849-899). Saxon king who fought the Vikings and reformed the laws of the country that would become England. "I desire to leave to the men that come after me a remembrance of me in good works."

Alternative: * To his son: "Thus, my dear son, set thee now beside me and I will deliver thee true instructions. My son, I feel that my hour is coming. My countenance is wan. My… my days are almost done. We must now part. I shall to another world, and thou shalt be left alone in all my wealth. I pray thee, for thou art my dear child, strive to be a father, and a lord to thy people. Be thou the children's father and the widow's friend. Comfort thou the poor and shelter the weak; and with all thy might, right that which is wrong. And, son, govern thyself by law. Then shalt the Lord love thee and God above all things shall be thy reward. Call thou upon Him to advise thee in all thy need, and so He shall help thee, the better to compass that which thou wouldst."

Alger, Horatio (1832-1899). American author whose stories reflected an ability to rise over adverse circumstances. When Alger told his sister and nurse that he wished to travel to New York, he was assured that his bags would be packed. His response: "Splendid! I'll sleep now. I shall have a nap. Later I can pack and leave on the evening train. But I'm tired. Let me rest." He did not live long enough to make the trip.

Ali ibn Abi Talib (c. 600-661). Muslim leader or caliph who was the cousin of the prophet Muhammad. Because of a feud among the faithful, Ali was stabbed in the head with a poisoned sword by a fanatic while attending the Morning Prayer. To his sons: "If I die of this stab of his, kill him with one similar stroke. Do not mutilate him! I have heard the Prophet, peace be upon him, say: 'Mutilate not even a rabid dog.'" His son Hassan decapitated the assassin several days later.

Alternative: * "By the Lord of the Ka'bah, I have won."

Alice, Grand Duchess of Hesse (1843-1878). Daughter of English Queen Victoria and mother of the future Empress Alexandra of Russia. Dying of diphtheria contracted from her daughters: "Now I will go to sleep again." Her last words upon awakening: "From Friday to Saturday- four weeks- may- dear papa..."

Alleine, Joseph (1634-1668). English Puritan nonconformist preacher. Toward the end: "If I should die fifty miles away, let me be buried at Taunton [a town in Somerset, England where he preached]." Near death: "This vile body shall be made like Christ's glorious body. Oh, what a glorious day will the day of the resurrection be! Methinks I see it by faith… O this vain foolish world… I care not to be in it longer than my Master hath doing or suffering work for me. Were that done, farewell to earth." Alleine's burial wish was fulfilled.

Allen, Clarence (1930–2006). American criminal who claimed Native American heritage. Condemned to die by lethal injection for multiple murders: "My last words will be *Hoka hey*. It's a good day to die. Thank you very much. I love you all. Goodbye." *Hoka hey* was used by Native Americans as a battle cry meaning a good day to die.

Allen, Ethan (1738-1789). American Revolutionary War leader and politician. When told by his doctor (some say clergyman) that the angels were waiting for him, Allen replied: "Waiting are they? Waiting are they? Well, let 'em wait!"

Allen, Gracie (1895-1964). American entertainer who paired with her husband George Burns in a long-running comedy act. To the attendants placing Allen in an ambulance after she suffered a heart attack: "I'm sorry, boys. I'm all wet."

Allen, James "Red Dog" (1954-1993). Native American rapist and murderer, executed by lethal injection in the Delaware Correctional Center: "I'm going home, babe."

Allen, Loraine (1763-1783). Daughter of the American Revolutionary War hero, Ethan Allen (above). On her deathbed, Loraine questioned her

Deist father: "I am about to die; shall I believe in the principles you have taught me, or shall I believe what my mother has taught me?" He replied: "Believe what your mother has taught you." Mrs. Allen had instilled Christian values in her daughter.

Allende, Salvador (1908-1973). President of Chile who died possibly from a self-inflicted gunshot (some say from an assassin's bullet) during a military coup. His farewell radio address: "...Long live Chile! Long live the people! Long live the workers! These are my last words, but I am sure my sacrifice will not be in vain. I am sure that this sacrifice will constitute a moral lesson that will punish cowardice, perfidy, and treason."

Alleray, Legrand d' (died 1793). French parliamentarian. Alleray and his wife were falsely accused of an illegal correspondence during the Reign of Terror of the French Revolution. When a judge suggested that the couple could make a life-saving evasive answer to the charges, d'Alleray replied: "I thank you for the efforts you make to save me, but it would be necessary to purchase our lives by a lie. My wife and myself prefer rather to die. We have grown old together without ever having lied; we will not do so now to save a remnant of life. Do your duty; we will do ours. We will not accuse you of our death; we will accuse the law only."

Allingham, William (1824-1889). Irish poet. In his last days, Allingham was asked if he had any last minute requests: "No. My mind is at rest... And so, to where I wait, come gently on. I thank you. I thank everyone." His last words: "I am seeing things that you know nothing of."

Alternative: * "I see such things as you cannot dream of."

Alphege, Saint, also Ælfheah (c. 954-1012). English clergyman who became the Archbishop of Canterbury. Invading Danes captured Alphege and killed him when a ransom for his release went unpaid: "I have not the money which you ask for... I cannot consent to enrich the enemies of my country. You will urge me in vain. I am not the man to provide Christian flesh for pagan teeth, by robbing my flock to enrich their enemies."

Alsop, Stewart (1914-1974). American journalist and political commentator. Final words of his autobiography *Stay of Execution*: "There is a time to live, but there is also a time to die. That time has not yet come for me. But it will. It will come for all of us." Later, dying of leukemia: "A dying man needs to die, as a sleepy man needs to sleep, and there comes a time when it is wrong, as well as useless, to resist."

Altgeld, John (1847-1902). German-born American lawyer who became governor of Illinois. Collapsing and later dying of a stroke after a speech, Altgeld spoke about his wife: "You've got to be careful of her, you know." To his final visitor: "How d'you do, Cushing, I am glad to see you."

Ambrose of Milan, Saint (c. 340-397). German-born Bishop of Milan. During his terminal illness, Ambrose told his colleagues: "I have not lived among you in such a way that I would be ashamed to live still longer, but neither do I fear to die, since we have a good Lord." Just before expiring, he said: "I see the Lord Jesus at my bedside, smiling at me."

Amelia, Princess (1783-1810). Daughter of King George III of England. Dying of tuberculosis, Amelia told her parents: "Remember me, but do not grieve for me."

Alternative: * "I could not wish for a better trust than in the merits of the Redeemer."

American Union Soldier, name unknown, who served during the U.S. Civil War (died 1864). During the June 3rd, 1864 suicidal attack against Robert E. Lee's troops at the Battle of Cold Harbor, Virginia, many Union soldiers pinned last notes to the inside of their jackets: "Cold Harbor. June 3rd. I am dead."

Ames, Edward (1806-1879). American Methodist Episcopal Bishop. "When I can do no more work, I care not how soon I die. All right."

Ames, Fisher (1758-1808). Member of the U.S. House of Representatives. "I have peace of mind. It may arise from stupidity, but I think it is founded on a belief of the gospel. My hope is in the mercy of God through Jesus Christ."

Ampère, André (1775-1836). French physicist and pioneer in the study of electromagnetism. The unit of electrical current bears his name. Toward the end of Ampère's life, a friend wished to avoid weighty discussions because of the scientist's delicate health: "My health! My health! What does my health signify? There ought to be no consideration here, between us two, about anything but the eternal truths, about the men and things which have been useful or hurtful to humanity."

Anacharsis (fl. 6th century BCE). Scythian philosopher. Anacharsis moved from his native land to Athens where he became familiar with Greek culture and law. Returning to his homeland, he attempted to introduce reforms based on his Grecian experience but was met with indifference. Because of this adverse reaction "to the admission of foreign usages," the Scythian king mortally wounded Anacharsis with a poison arrow. The philosopher's last words: "In Greece, where I traveled to learn the literature and manners of the country, I was allowed to remain in safety; but in my own soil, envy has been the cause of my death."

Anastasia, Albert (1902-1957). American gangster who ran the notorious organized Mafia crime group "Murder, Inc." Words spoken before being shot in a New York barber shop by members of a rival gang: "A quick haircut!"

Anaxagoras (c. 500-428 BCE). Greek philosopher and schoolmaster. To a former student who implored the philosopher to take nourishment: "O Pericles! Those who need a lamp take care to feed it with oil." When asked what would be a satisfactory memorial, Anaxagoras replied: "Give the boys a holiday."

Anaxarchus (c. 380-c. 320 BCE). Greek philosopher and advisor to Alexander the Great (above). Having insulted a ruler of Cyprus in the presence of Alexander, Anaxarchus later was condemned to die by pounding in a mortar with metal pestles. "Just pound the bag of Anaxarchus, you do not pound himself."

Alternative: * "Pound, pound the pouch containing Anaxarchus. You pound not Anaxarchus."

Anaxibius (died 388 BCE). Spartan military leader. Anaxibius was killed in an ambush by Athenian soldiers during the Corinthian War: "Men, it is good for me to die on this spot, where honour bids me; but you hurry and save yourselves before the enemy can close with us." He and a small band of comrades fought to the death.

Alternative: * "Friends, my honour commands me to die here; but do you hasten away and save yourselves before the enemy close with us."

Andersen, Hans Christian (1805-1875). Danish writer, noted for his children's stories "The Little Mermaid" and "The Ugly Duckling." Dying of cancer, Andersen consulted a composer about his funeral music: "Most of the people who will walk after me will be children, so make the beat keep time with little steps." On his deathbed, to his hostess who inquired how he felt: "Don't ask me how I am! I understand nothing more."

Anderson, Michael (1959-2003). American astronaut, killed when the Space Shuttle Columbia disintegrated upon reentering the earth's atmosphere. Before the fatal flight: "… There's always that unknown…"

Anderson, Newton "Hacksaw Red" (1976-2007). American criminal who murdered two individuals during a home burglary. Prior to his execution by lethal injection: "For all those that want this to happen, I hope you get what you want, and it makes you feel better, and gives you some kind of relief. I don't know what else to say. For those that I have hurt, I hope, after a while, it gets better... I am sorry. That's it. Goodbye." The red-headed Anderson acquired his nickname for an earlier attempt to saw his way out of a jail cell.

Anderson, Sherwood (1876-1941). American writer. Taken ill on a cruise, Anderson was hospitalized in the Panama Canal Zone where he died from peritonitis caused by a colon perforation from an ingested toothpick. In response to a companion's earlier joke that he "[couldn't] bear to go down the coast with me," Anderson replied: "You expect pretty costly tribute from your admirers, don't you my girl? I'll let them examine me here at the Canal and do what they have to do and then I'll catch the next boat."

Anderson, Violette (1882-1937). English-born American lawyer. Anderson was the first African American female to argue a case before the U.S. Supreme Court. Dying of colon cancer, Anderson was unable to preside at the annual meeting of her college sorority: "Tell the girls to keep on going ahead. Put over the boule [council] with a bang. Don't let my passing throw the slightest shadow of gloom. The organization has a grand mission before it."

André, John (1750-1780). British spy who conspired with Benedict Arnold (below) to deliver West Point, New York to the British during the American Revolutionary War. Believing that he would die in front of a firing squad, André raised the handkerchief from his eyes and saw the hangman's noose: "I am reconciled to my death but I detest the mode." He then asked his executioners: "All I request of you, gentlemen, is that while I acknowledge the propriety of my sentence, you will bear me witness that I die like a brave man." Seconds before he perished, André whispered: "It will be but a momentary pang."

Alternative: * "Must I die in this manner?"

Andrew, Saint (fl. 1st century). Brother of Saint Peter (below) and an apostle of Jesus Christ. When Andrew refused to worship Roman gods, he was condemned to die by crucifixion: "Oh, cross, most welcome, and long looked for; with a willing mind, joyfully and desirously I come to thee, being the scholar of Him who did hang on thee, because I have been always thy lover and have coveted to embrace thee."

Andrews, Roy (1884-1960). American explorer and naturalist who became director of New York's American Museum of Natural History. Dying of a heart attack: "There's that pain again! I can feel it in my arm and in my head."

Andronicus I (c 1110-1185). Emperor of Constantinople. Because of his harsh rule, Andronicus was hated by many of his subjects. Overthrown by a rebellious crowd, he was tortured over several days and killed by the sword: "Lord, have mercy on me! Why wilt Thou break a bruised reed?"

Andronicus of Ephesus, Saint (died c. 304). A prominent citizen of Ephesus, an ancient Greek city. When Andronicus refused to deny his Christian faith to the Romans, he was tortured and then thrown to wild animals. Because the beasts shunned the martyr, he later was killed with a sword blow. "My body is before you; do with it what you will... Commence your torments as soon as you please, and make use of every means that your malignity can invent, and you shall find in the end that I am not to be shaken from my resolution."

Anne of Austria (1601-1666). Queen Consort of French King Louis XIII. Dying of breast cancer: "Monsieur de Montaigu, consider what I owe to God, the favor He has shown to me, and the great indulgence for which I am beholden to Him." She then looked at her hands noted for their beauty: "Observe how they are swelled; time to depart."

Anne Stuart (1665-1714). Queen of England from 1702 until her death. "Suffering under an excess of apoplexy," the queen handed the symbolic staff of office to Lord Shrewsbury saying: "For God's sake, use it for the good of my people." Then she allegedly raved: "Oh, my brother! Oh, my poor brother! What will become of you? Oh, my poor brother!" Because of his Catholic faith, her half-brother James Stuart was denied succession to the English throne.

Annenberg, Moses "Moe" (1877-1942). Prussian-born American newspaper publisher. Dying of a brain tumor, to his son: "Walter, who knows what is the scheme of things? My suffering has all been for the purpose of making you a man."

Annesley, Samuel (c. 1620-1696). English clergyman, best-known for his collected sermons *Morning Exercises*. "... I will die praising Thee, and rejoice that there are others that can praise Thee better. I shall be satisfied with Thy likeness! Satisfied! Satisfied! O my dearest Jesus, I come."

Annunzio, Gabriele d' (1863-1938). Italian writer, poet and soldier. Suffering from a stroke, Annunzio told his chauffeur: "Stop- I turn home. I'm bored... I'm bored."

Anonymous Death Notes:

* **Anonymous French Aristocrat** (died 1794). Declining a glass of rum before the guillotine blade fell: "I lose all sense of direction when I am drunk."
* **Anonymous San Francisco Dishwasher** who committed suicide by hanging: "That's all folks!"
* **Anonymous Suicide Note Left by a Banker**: "Sorry to be a nuisance this way..."
* **Anonymous Suicide Note of a Doctor**: "Waiting. Feeling very happy. First time I ever felt without worry, as if I were free. My heart must be strong. It won't give up. Pulse running well. I feel fine. When will it be over?"
* **Anonymous Suicide Note of a Hollywood Failure**: "I tried so hard to make a comeback. Exit, Act III."
* **Anonymous Suicide Note of an American Worker**: "My small estate I bequeath to my mother; my body to the nearest accredited medical school; my soul and heart to all the girls; and my brain to Harry Truman."
* **Anonymous Suicide Note** Scribbled on the wall of an empty London house: "Why suicide? Why not?"

Anselm, Saint (c. 1033-1109). Religious leader born in present-day northern Italy who later became Archbishop of Canterbury. "Yes, if it be His will I shall obey it willingly. But were He to let me stay with you a little longer till I had resolved a problem about the origin of the soul, I would gladly accept the boon, for I do not know whether anyone will work it out when I am gone. If I could but eat, I think I should pick up a little strength. I feel no pain in any part of my body, only I cannot retain nourishment and that exhausts."

Alternative: * "I shall gladly obey his call; yet I should also feel grateful if He would grant me a little longer time with you, and it could be permitted me to solve a question… on the origin of the soul."

Anselmi, Albert (1883-1929). Sicilian-born American gangster. To avenge a purported betrayal, Anselmi and his partners-in-crime, John Scalise and Joseph Giunta, allegedly were beaten and shot to death by the Chicago crime boss Al Capone: "Not me, Al. Honest to God, Jonnie. It was his idea. His and Joe's. Believe me, Al, I wouldn't..."

Ansgar, Saint (801-865). French-born monk. Because Ansgar brought Christianity to Northern Europe, he was called the "Apostle of the North." As he died: "Into Thy hands do I commend my spirit, for Thou hast redeemed me, Oh, Lord!"

Anthony of Padua, Saint (c. 1195-1231) Portuguese priest who served in France and Italy. Dying of "dropsy:" "I see my God. He calls me to Him."

Anthony of the Desert, Saint (died 356). Egyptian monk who preferred a hermit's life in the desert. "And let this word of mine be kept by you, so that no one shall know the place, save you alone, for I shall receive it [my body] incorruptible from my Saviour in the resurrection of the dead. And distribute my garments thus: To Athanasius, the bishop, give one of my sheepskins, and the cloak under me, which was new when he gave it [to] me, and has grown old by me; and to Serapion, the bishop, give the other sheepskin; and do you have the hair-cloth garment. And for the rest, children, farewell, for Anthony is going, and is with you no more."

Anthony, Susan (1820-1906). American activist who played a central role in the women's suffrage campaign. Dying of heart disease and pneumonia, Anthony spoke of her followers: "They are passing before me- face after face, hundreds of them. I know how hard they have worked. I know the sacrifice they have made."

Antiochus IV (c. 215-164 BCE). Despotic Syrian king. Antiochus, known for his persecution of the Jews, ordered the death of a 15-year-old boy because he refused to worship idols. When the youngster was hung by the feet, scalded with hot water and thrown to the wild animals, the king collapsed and died muttering: "My bowels burn with the fire of hell."

Antoinette, Marie (see Marie Antoinette).

Antoninus Pius (86-161). Roman Emperor. When a tribune of the night watch came to ask for the password, the dying Antoninus gave the word that reflected his life: "Equanimity."

Antonius, Marcus, also Mark Antony (c. 83-30 BCE). Roman general and politician. Defeated in battle by his rival Octavian, Antonius contemplated suicide. After ordering his slave Eros to kill him, the servant fell on his own sword instead: "It is well done, Eros. You show your master how to do what you had not the heart to do yourself." Antonius then stabbed himself. Before dying he was taken to his lover Cleopatra (below): "You must not pity me in this last turn of fate. You should rather be happy in the remembrance of our love and in the recollection that of all men I was once the most powerful and now at the end have fallen not dishonorably, a Roman by a Roman vanquished."

Antrim, Henry (see Billy the Kid).

Apollonia, Saint (died 249). Egyptian Christian martyr and patron saint of dentistry. When Apollonia refused to renounce her Christian faith to a "seditious mob," she was led to a bonfire and her teeth were knocked out. Given another chance to recant, she said: "Take your hands off me and give me a little time to think it over." After she was released, Apollonia jumped into the flames, which failed to kill her. She then was beheaded.

Appel, George (died 1928). American criminal, convicted of murdering a New York City policeman. Before his execution in Sing-Sing's electric chair: "Well, folks, you'll soon see a baked Appel."

Apphianus of Lycia, Saint (died 306). Martyred religious leader, born in present-day Turkey. During the Roman Christian persecutions, Apphianus was apprehended and commanded by the governor of Palestine to give his name, his father's name and place of residence. His reply: "I am a Christian;

my father is God." Despite torture, he gave no further information and was thrown into the sea to drown.

Appleton, Jesse (1772-1819). American clergyman. Dying of a painful throat ailment, Appleton uttered these last words: "Glory to God in the highest! The whole earth shall be filled with His glory."

Appleton, Thomas (1812-1884). American writer, poet, artist and fine arts patron. Dying of pneumonia: "How interesting this all is!"

Aquinas, Saint Thomas (c. 1225-1274). Italian clergyman, theologian and philosopher. Aquinas became ill while traveling. After receiving the Eucharist: "I receive you, the price of my redemption. I receive you, Companion of my life on this earth. All my studies, all my vigils, and all my labors have been for love of you. I have preached you and taught you. Never have I said anything against you. If anything was not well said, that is to be attributed to my ignorance... I submit all to the judgment and correction of the Holy Roman Church, in whose obedience I now leave this world."

Alternatives: * As Thomas received the Last Rites: "I receive Thee, ransom of my soul. For love of Thee have I studied and kept vigil, toiled, preached and taught..."

* "I now receive you who are the price of my soul's redemption, I receive you who are the food for my final journey, and for the love of whom I have studied, kept vigil, and struggled; indeed, it was you, Jesus, that I preached and you that I taught."
* "He who walks in the presence of God and is always ready to give an account of his actions to Him certainly will never be separated from Him by sin."
* "Be assured that he who shall always walk faithfully in His presence, always ready to give Him an account of all his actions, shall never be separated from Him by consenting to sin."

Arago, François (1786-1853). French scientist, best-known for his studies of magnetism and optics. Several hours before his death, to a colleague:

"I intend to resign my situation of perpetual secretary to the Academy [of Science], since I can no longer discharge it's duties."

Aram, Eugene (1704-1759). English schoolmaster and convicted murderer. Aram was hanged for the killing of a man suspected of having an affair with his wife. On the scaffold when asked if he wished to say anything: "No."

Arany, János (1817-1882). Hungarian poet and writer. "What is the time? Never mind, it's not important..."

Aratus of Sicyon (271-213 BCE). Greek statesman. Because of the enmity that developed between Aratus and King Philip V of Macedon, the statesman was poisoned. As Aratus wasted away, he coughed up blood, saying to a friend: "These, Oh Cephalon, are the wages of a king's love."

Archer, Thomas (1653-1685). Martyred Scottish clergyman. Archer was convicted of treason for his Covenanter beliefs and sentenced to die by hanging. While on the scaffold, Archer decried the "evil and hazard of popery." Then: "Fear of death does not fright or trouble me. I bless the Lord for my lot." After praying, he sang Psalm 73, verse 24 to the end.

Archibald, Alexander (1772-1851). American theologian, educator and author. On his deathbed: "As an aged man, I would say to my fellow pilgrims who are also in this advanced stage of the journey of life, endeavor to be useful as long as you are continued upon earth..."

Archimedes (287-212 BCE). Greek mathematician, philosopher and inventor. After the conquest of Syracuse, the commanding Roman general wished to meet Archimedes. The soldier entrusted with the summons found the mathematician sitting on the ground solving geometry problems. When confronted, Archimedes responded: "Do not disturb my circles!" Enraged, the soldier fatally stabbed Archimedes despite orders to avoid any harm. Some say the soldier was unaware of the Greek's identity.

Alternatives: * "Wait until I have finished my problem."
* "When I have finished this problem."
* "I really cannot go until I have finished my problem."

* "Don't disarrange my circles!"
* "Man, do not disturb my figures."
* "Stand away, fellow, from my diagram."
* "Don't disturb my equation."

Ardley, John (died 1555). English Protestant martyr who refused to recant his religion. When the Bishop of London described the pain that would be inflicted by burning at the stake, Ardley replied: "I am not afraid to try it, and I tell you, Bishop, if I had as many lives as I have hairs on my head, I would give them all up sooner than I would give up Christ."

Aretino, Pietro (1492-1556). Italian writer, satirist and poet. After receiving Last Rites where he was anointed with oil, Aretino quipped to his priest: "Keep the rats away now that I am all greased up."

Alternative: * "Well, now that I am oiled, protect me from the rats."

Armistead, Lewis (1817-1863). Confederate general during the U.S. Civil War. As his unit breached the Union line during the Battle of Gettysburg, Pennsylvania, Armistead commanded his troops to: "Give them [the Union artillery] the cold steel, boys! Give them the cold steel!" Shortly thereafter, he was mortally wounded by enemy fire. Before he died, Armistead spoke of his friend, the Union General Winfield Hancock, who also was injured: "... Say to General Hancock for me that I have done him and done you all a grievous injury, which I shall always regret."

Alternatives: * "Come on boys, give them the cold steel! Who will follow me?"
* "Give them the cold steel, men!"

Armour, Philip (1832-1901). American industrialist who founded one of the largest meat-packing businesses in history. Suffering from pneumonia: "I am not afraid to die."

Armstrong, Herbert (1869-1922). English solicitor, hanged for the arsenic poisoning of his wife Katherine (also Katerine or Katharine). On the gallows: "Kitty I'm coomin to ye!" Before the trap opened: "I am innocent of the crime for which I have been condemned to die."

Arnauld, Marie Angélique (1591-1661). Abbess of the Cistercian Convent at Port-Royal, France. To her grieving Sisters: "How human you still are." Before dying: "Jesus, oh Jesus, you are my God, my justice, my strength, my all."

Arnaz, Desi (1917-1986). Cuban-born American bandleader and costar of the *I Love Lucy* television series. Dying of lung cancer, Arnaz had a last telephone conversation with his former wife, Lucille Ball (below): "I love you too, honey. Good luck with your show."

Arndt, Johann (1555-1621). German Lutheran clergyman and theologian. Dying of a throat ailment and fever: "Now I have overcome all."

Arnold, Benedict (1741-1801). American Revolutionary War general. While commanding the American fort at West Point, New York, the pusillanimous Arnold plotted to surrender it to British forces. The turncoat survived the war as a British officer and spent his last days in England. Dying of "dropsy," Arnold requested: "Let me die in the old [Continental Army] uniform in which I fought my battles for freedom. May God forgive me for putting on any other."

Arnold, Jack (died 2005). American Presbyterian minister. While delivering a sermon, Arnold predicted: "And when I go to heaven..." The 69 year-old minister then collapsed and died of an apparent heart attack.

Arnold, Thomas (1795-1842). English educator and author. When Arnold perceived that his end was fast approaching, he said to his son: "Thank God, Tom, for giving me this [chest] pain! I have suffered so little pain in my life that I feel it is very good for me; now God has given it to me, and I do so thank Him for it. How thankful I am that my head is untouched." When told about the immediate danger of his heart condition, the educator replied: "Ah, very well."

Arnould, Sophie (1740-1802). French operatic soprano. When her priest commented on the "bad times" she had gone through, Arnould replied: "Ah, the times were good. It was I who was so unhappy."

Arsentiev, Francys (1958-1998). American mountaineer. After summiting Mt. Everest, Arsentiev and her husband were forced to spend the night in the "Death Zone" without supplemental oxygen. To her rescuers: "I am an American. Please don't leave me." When the climbers assured Arsentiev they would return for her, she asked: "Why are you doing this to me?" Both she and her husband perished on the mountain.

Arvers, Félix (1806-1850). French poet, best-known for his poem *Un Secret*. To his confessor: "Ah, Coquereau, I forgot to mention one of the greatest faults of my life. I have spoken badly of Charles X."

Asano, Naganori (1667-1701). Japanese feudal lord. Because of disagreements with a protocol officer, Asano tried to kill the official. Ordered to perform seppuku (abdomen cutting and disembowelment) for his transgression, Asano composed his death poem before committing suicide: "I wish I could enjoy/ the rest of Spring/ as the cherry blossoms are yet in bloom/ in spite of the spring breeze/ which is attempting to blow off all their petals."

Ascham, Roger (c. 1515-1568). English scholar, humanist and writer. Ascham was a tutor to Princess Elizabeth who later became queen. "I am suffering much pain. I sink under my disease. But this is my confession, this is my faith, this prayer contains all that I wish for: 'I desire to depart, hence, and be with Christ.'"

Ashby, Turner (1828-1862). Confederate officer who fought in the U.S. Civil War. During a Union army attack at Good's Farm, near Harrisonburg, Virginia, Ashby urged his troops: "Forward, my brave men!" Waving his sword, he exhorted: "Charge men! For God's sake charge!" Ashby was felled by a shot to his heart.

Askew, Anne (1521-1546). English Protestant martyr. When Askew refused to abandon her Protestant religion and name fellow worshipers, she was imprisoned as a heretic and tortured on the rack. Because her joints were dislocated by the action, she was carried to the stake in a chair. Before her immolation, Askew spoke these words: "I came not thither to deny my Lord and Master."

Asplund, Carl (1871-1912). Swedish-born farmer. Asplund and three of his sons perished during the sinking of the *Titanic* ocean liner. To his wife as she boarded a lifeboat: "Go ahead. We will get into one of the other boats." His wife and two other children survived the disaster.

Astor, John Jacob I (1763-1848). German-born American businessman. Astor had large real estate properties in New York and could be quite severe with tenants. Shortly before his death, one of his renters fell behind in payments, thus enraging the old man. An agent sent to collect the debt mentioned the problem to one of Astor's sons who covered the shortfall. When the money was presented to the dying Astor, he said: "There! I told you she would pay if you went the right way to work with her!"

Astor, John Jacob IV (1864-1912). American great-grandson of John Jacob Astor I, businessman and passenger on the ill-fated RMS *Titanic*. As the ship sank after striking an iceberg in the North Atlantic, Astor assisted his wife into a lifeboat saying: "The ladies have to go first." As his wife tried to get out of the boat, he told her: "Get in the lifeboat to please me. Goodbye, dearie. I'll see you later." When Astor was advised to jump into the water by a crewmember who survived: "No thank you, I think I'll have to stick." When the crewman asked to shake his hand: "With pleasure." Astor did not survive.

Astor, Nancy (1879-1964). American-born activist who became the first woman to serve in the British Parliament. When Lady Astor awoke during her last moments and found her children gathered at the bedside, she asked her son: "Jakie, is it my birthday or am I dying?" His reply: "A bit of both, Mum."

Astor, William Backhouse (1792-1875). American businessman and son of John Jacob Astor I. "I might have lived another year if I had not caught this cold, but I am satisfied to go now. I am eighty-four years old [*sic*]- long past the allotted time of man- and at my age, life becomes a burden."

Astros, Paul-Thérèse-David d' (1772-1851). French Roman Catholic cardinal. "Neither life nor death, nor any being can separate us from Him."

Atahualpa (c.1497-1533). Incan ruler. Condemned to die by the conquering Spaniard, Francisco Pizarro, Atahualpa asked: "What have I done, or my children, that I should meet such a fate? And from your hands too, you, who have met with friendship and kindness from my people, who have received nothing but benefits from my hands." He then asked Pizarro to: "Show compassion to my children and receive them under your care."

Atatürk, Mustafa Kemal (1881-1938). Founder and long-term leader of the modern Turkish republic. Before drifting into a coma, Atatürk queried a friend (some say his physician): "What time is it?" Then: "Goodbye."

Athanasios Diakos (1788-1821). Greek revolutionary fighter. Athanasios was captured by the Turks during the Greek War of Independence. Offered a pardon if he would join the Ottoman army and convert to Islam, he defiantly declared: "I was born a Greek; I shall die a Greek." Athanasios was impaled on a spear and roasted to death.

Attalus (died 177). Roman martyr from what is modern-day France. When the Roman Emperor Marcus Aurelius (below) decreed death for all Christians unwilling to renounce their faith, Attalus was roasted in an iron chair. When asked the name of his God, he replied: "Where there are many gods, many names are used to distinguish them; but where there is but one God, there is no name necessary." Attalus then was thrown to the beasts but they failed to attack him. He subsequently was beheaded.

Alternatives: * "God is not like us mortals; He hath no name."
* "God has not a name as man has."

Attlee, Clement (1883-1967). British Prime Minister and leader of the Labour Party until the mid-1950s. Dying of pneumonia, to his aide, Charlie Griffiths: "Hullo, Griff. How are you getting on?"

Atworth, Robert (1968-1999). American criminal, executed by lethal injection for robbery and murder: "... Remember this; if all you know is hatred, if all you know is blood-love, you'll never be satisfied. For everybody out there that is like that and knows nothing but negative, kiss my proud white Irish a**. I'm ready, warden, send me home."

Atzerodt, George (1835-1865). German-born conspirator in the Abraham Lincoln assassination. As part of the plot, Atzerodt was supposed to kill Vice-President Andrew Johnson but lost his nerve and failed to follow through with his task. To the hangman: "Goodbye, gentlemen. May we all meet in the other world. God take me now."

Audebert, Ann (died 1549). French martyr. Audebert, an apothecary's widow "who designed on an account of her faith to retire to Geneva," was seized and sent to Paris for alleged heresy. When a rope was placed around her waist to lead her to the stake, the martyr likened it to a wedding girdle "wherein she would be married to Christ." As the flames consumed her, Audebert cried: "I was once married to a man on a Saturday, and now I shall be married to God on the same day of the week."

Audubon, John (1785-1851). Haitian-born American ornithologist, naturalist and artist who was renowned for his paintings of American birds. Dying in a demented state, Audubon asked his daughter: "It is you, my mother, who loved me so? Is it you, Mama?" To a relative: "Yes, yes, Billy! You go down that side of Long Pond, and I'll go this side, and we'll get the ducks."

Augustine of Hippo, Saint (354-430). African theologian and philosopher. Dying of a fever: "Oh, Lord, shall I die at all? Shall I die at all? Yes! Why, then, oh Lord, if ever, why not now?" His final words: "Thy will be done. Come, Lord Jesus."

Alternative: * "Into Thy hands, I commend my spirit."

Augustus Caesar (see Caesar, Augustus).

Aurangzeb (1618-1707). Mogul emperor of Hindustan who ascended the throne by murdering a number of close relatives who blocked his path. A final letter to his favorite son: "The agonies of death come fast upon me. I am going. Whatever good or evil I have done, it was for you. No one has seen the departure of his own soul, but I know that mine is departing."

Alternative: * "Soul of my soul, now I am going alone. I grieve for your helplessness. But what is the use? Every torture that I have inflicted, every sin that I have committed, every wrong that I have done, I carry the consequences with me. Strange that I came with nothing into the world and now go away with this stupendous caravan of sin. Wherever I look I see only God. I have greatly sinned, and I know not what torment awaits me. Let not Muslims be slain, and the reproach fall upon my useless head. I commit you and your sons to God's care and bid you farewell. Your sick mother, Udaipur, would fain die with me. Peace."

Aurelius, Marcus (121-180). Roman Emperor and philosopher. When a tribune asked for the watchword, Aurelius answered: "Go to the rising sun, for I am setting. Think more of death than of me"

Alternatives: * "Go to the rising star, for I am setting."
* "Go to the rising sun, for my sun is setting."

Austin, Ernest (1890-1913). Australian criminal, hanged for the rape and murder of a child: "I say straight out that I highly deserve this punishment. I did not know what I was doing at the time. I have asked the Lord to forgive me for all my faults and He has done so... I ask you all to forgive me... May you all live long and die happy. God save the King." As a cap was placed over his head before the trapdoor opened: "God save the king. Send a wire to my mother and tell her I died happy... Goodbye all. Goodbye all."

Austin, Jane (1775-1817). English author who wrote *Sense and Sensibility* and *Pride and Prejudice*. Austen died of a chronic wasting illness. When her sister Cassandra asked if she needed anything: "I want nothing, but death." Then: "God grant me patience; pray for me, oh, pray for me!"

Austin, Stephen (1793-1836). American colonizer who helped to establish the Republic of Texas. Although Austin died of pneumonia before Texas was annexed by the U.S., he deliriously fanaticized: "Texas recognized! [Doctor] Archer told me so. Did you see it in the papers?"

Alternative: * "The independence of Texas is recognized! Don't you see it in the papers? Doctor Archer told me so."

Austin, Tom (died 1694). English criminal, executed for multiple murders. On the gallows, when asked for last words: "Nothing, only there's a woman yonder with some curds and whey, and I wish I could have a penny-worth of them before I am hanged, 'cos I don't know when I shall see any again."

Avaroa, Eduardo (1838-1879). Bolivian military officer. During the Battle of Topáter when Chile invaded Bolivia in 1879, Avaroa's badly outnumbered forces were told to surrender. Avaroa contemptuously replied: "Surrender? Your grandmother should surrender, you b*******!"

Averill, Jim (1851-1889). Accused American cattle rustler. Averill managed a cattle ranch and small store in Sweetwater, Wyoming. He and his wife Ella "Cattle Kate" ran afoul of local ranchers who suspected the pair of cattle rustling. To these cowboys preparing to hang them: "Stop your fooling, fellows!" The cowboys were not fooling.

Avery, Isaac (1828-1863) Confederate officer during the U.S. Civil War. Killed at the Battle of Gettysburg, Pennsylvania, Avery scribbled a note to a colleague: "Tell father I died with my face to the enemy."

Aymond de Lavoy (died 1543). French martyr who preached at St. Faith's in the town of Anjou. Aymond was accused of teaching "false doctrine" and was condemned to die: "My flesh lusteth against the spirit, but shortly I shall cast it away: I beseech you pray for me. O Lord my God, into Thy hands I commend my soul!" He was strangled and then burned.

Azeglio, Massimo (1798-1866). Italian statesman, writer and painter. Moments before dying of a fever, to his estranged wife: "Ah, Luisa, you always arrive just as I am leaving."

Baal, Thomas (1965-1990). American criminal who killed a woman during a robbery that netted $20. Executed by lethal injection: "Send my love to my mama and my papa."

Baba, Meher, born Merwan Sheriar Irani (1894-1969). Indian mystic and spiritual leader. Baba's last words were spoken in 1925 after a cobra was killed in his compound: "How fortunate you are that you have heard my voice so many times today! This incident with the snake took place to allow you to hear me speak for the final time." To emphasize his feelings that spoken words had little meaning, the mystic lived in silence thereafter, communicating only by hand gestures and an alphabet board.

Alternative: * "Don't worry; be happy."

Babar, Muhammad (1483-1530). Emperor of the Mughal Empire in India. To his son Humayun: "I give your brothers to your keeping. Be faithful to them and to all the people."

Alternative: * "Do nothing against your brothers, even though they may deserve it."

Babcock, Maltbie (1858-1901). American clergyman who wrote the hymn "This Is My Father's World." After taking poison and slashing his wrist during his terminal illness, Babcock told his wife (some say hospital attendants): "I have swallowed corrosive sublimate [mercuric chloride]."

Babel, Isaac (1894-1941). Russian short-story writer. Arrested by the Soviet secret police and falsely accused of treason, Babel died while imprisoned: "I am only asking for one thing- let me finish my work."

Babington, Anthony (1561-1586). English conspirator. After plotting to assassinate Protestant Queen Elizabeth I, Babington was hanged, drawn and quartered. "The murder of the Queen has been represented to me as a deed lawful and meritorious. I die a firm Catholic."

Babylas of Antioch, Saint (died c. 253). Martyred bishop of Antioch in present-day Turkey. When Babylas refused to worship Roman gods, he was imprisoned and beheaded. At the end, he quoted Psalm 116:7: "Return unto thy rest, my soul, for the Lord hath dealt bountifully with thee."

Bacon, Francis (1561-1626). English philosopher, scientist, statesman and writer. While performing an experiment to determine whether snow could preserve meat, Bacon developed pneumonia. Dying at the estate of the Earl of Arundel, he left a note for his absent host: "My very good Lord,—I was likely to have had the fortune of Caius Plinius the elder, who lost his life by trying an experiment about the burning of Mount Vesuvius; for I was also desirous to try an experiment or two touching the conservation and induration of bodies. As for the experiment itself, it succeeded excellently well; but in the journey between London and Highgate, I was taken with such a fit of casting as I know not whether it were the Stone, or some surfeit or cold, or indeed a touch of them all three. But when I came to your Lordship's House, I was not able to go back, and therefore was forced to take up my lodging here, where your housekeeper is very careful and diligent about me, which I assure myself your Lordship will not only pardon towards him, but think the better of him for it. For indeed your Lordship's House was happy to me, and I kiss your noble hands for the welcome which I am sure you give me to it. I know how unfit it is for me to write with any other hand than mine own, but by my troth my fingers are so disjointed with sickness that I cannot steadily hold a pen." At the end, Bacon suffered from "a gentle fever, accidentally accompanied with a great cold, whereby the defluxion of rheum fell so plentifully upon his breast, that he died by suffocation."

Alternatives: * "... Thy creatures, O Lord, have been my books, but Thy Holy Scriptures much more. I have sought Thee in the courts, fields and, gardens, but I have found Thee, O God, in Thy Sanctuary, Thy Temples..."

* From Bacon's will: "For my burial, I desire it may be in St. Michael's Church, St. Albans; there was my mother buried, and it is the parish church of my mansion-house of Gorhambury, and it is the only Christian Church within the walls of Old Verulam. For my name and memory, I leave it to men's charitable speeches, to foreign nations and the next ages." Bacon's burial wishes were followed.

Bacon, John (1740-1799). British sculptor. The self-composed inscription for Bacon's tombstone: "What I was as an artist seemed to me of some importance while I lived, but what I really was as a believer in Christ Jesus is the thing of importance to me now."

Baer, Maximilian "Max" (1909-1959). American professional boxer and World Heavyweight Champion. Suffering chest pains in a Hollywood, California hotel, Baer asked the front desk to call a physician. When the clerk replied that a house doctor would be sent up, the boxer joked: "House doctor? No, dummy, I need a people doctor." Dying of a heart attack shortly thereafter, Baer said: "Oh God, here I go!"

Baesell, Norman (died 1944). American Army officer who accompanied band leader Glenn Miller (below) on a proposed flight from England to France. As Miller boarded the plane, the musician asked: "Hey, where the hell are the parachutes?" Baesell riposted "What's the matter, Miller, do you want to live forever?" Despite inclement weather, the pilot took off and the aircraft was never heard from again.

Bagehot, Walter (1826-1877). English economist and journalist. To his sister when his pillow was adjusted: "Let me have my own fidgets."

Bailey, Raymond (1932-1958). Australian criminal, executed by hanging for a triple murder: "Get a move on, I haven't much time."

Bailli, Roche de "La Riviere" (died1605). French physician in ordinary to King Henry IV of France. Sensing death's approach, Bailli bequeathed all his possessions except his bed to his servants who quickly removed them. Later, when his visiting physicians asked what had happened to his furnishings, Bailli replied: "I must hasten away since my baggage has been sent off before me." He died shortly thereafter.

Bailly, Jean (1736-1793). French astronomer and Parisian mayor at the beginning of the French Revolution. Bailly was condemned for his involvement in the July 17, 1791 massacre when the National Guard fired on demonstrating civilians. As he left prison on a cold, drizzly day (some say snowy), Bailly spoke to his weeping friends: "Be calm. I have rather a difficult journey to perform and I distrust my constitution... I hope, however, to reach the end properly." Approaching the guillotine, the condemned man began to shiver. When someone cried out that the mayor was trembling. Bailly replied: "I tremble but it is from the cold."

Alternatives: * "My friend, it is only from cold."
* "I am cold, my friend."

Bainham, James (died 1532). English Protestant martyr. Burned at the stake as a heretic, Bainham's parting words to his accusers were: "God forgive thee, and show thee more mercy than thou showest me." As the flames consumed him: "O ye papists behold, ye look for miracles, and here now you may see a miracle; for in this fire I feel no more pain, than if I were in a bed of down: but it is to me as a bed of roses."

Baker, Edward (1811-1861). British-born American lawyer, politician and Union Army officer during the U.S. Civil War. Baker, a close friend of Abraham Lincoln, was killed by a volley at the Battle of Ball's Bluff, Loudoun County, Virginia. Shortly before dying, he told a comrade: "The officer who dies with his men will never be harshly judged." Noting that a Confederate soldier had been hit across the field, Baker remarked: "See, he falls." He was mortally wounded shortly thereafter.

Baker, James (1823-1862). Union Army officer during the U.S. Civil War. While charging the Confederate lines at the Battle of Corinth, Mississippi, Baker was mortally wounded: "Thank God, when I fell, my regiment was victoriously charging."

Baker, Josephine (1906-1975). American-born jazz singer, dancer and actress who performed primarily in France. To a younger man who took her home instead of nightclubbing: "Oh, you young people act like old men. You are no fun." Baker died of a stroke later that night.

Baker, Lena (1900-1945). African American maid. In a violent dispute with her employer, Baker allegedly killed him in self-defense. Before her execution by electrocution: "What I done, I did in self-defense, or I would have been killed myself. Where I was I could not overcome it. God has forgiven me. I have nothing against anyone. I picked cotton for Mr. Pritchett, and he has been good to me. I am ready to go. I am one in the number. I am ready to meet my God. I have a very strong conscience." She was given an unconditional posthumous pardon 60 years later.

Baker, Theodore (died 1887). American criminal. Arrested for the murder of his lover's husband in 1885, Baker was dragged from his jail cell and hanged by vigilantes. He was cut down in an unconscious state by a sheriff and allowed to recover from his injury. The following year he was convicted of the murder and sentenced to die by hanging. At the gallows, Baker said: "Gentlemen, I am sorry it ends this way. Let her go."

Bakker, Jan de (see Pistorius, Johannes).

Bakker, Tammy Faye (see Messner, Tammy Faye Bakker).

Balboa, Vasco de (1475-1519). Spanish explorer and first European to see the Pacific Ocean. Balboa and four of his accomplices were beheaded on alleged charges of rebellion and treason. On the scaffold: "That [charge] is false! I always have served my king loyally and sought to add to his domains!"

Alternative: * "That is a gross falsehood. As sure as my last moments are near at hand, I never had even a thought except of the most loyal and faithful devotion to my king, nor had any other desire than to increase his dominions, with all my power and ability."

Baldwin, Elias "Lucky" (1828-1909). American financier. Baldwin drew his nickname from shrewd investments in mining operations in the "Old West." His last words possibly reflected his declining fortunes: "By gad, I'm not licked yet."

Baldwin, James (1924-1987). American writer and civil rights activist, known for his novel *Go Tell It on the Mountain* and essay *Notes of a Native Son*. Dying of stomach cancer: "I'm bored."

Baldwin, Stanley (1867-1947). British prime minister between the World Wars. "I am ready now."

Balfour, Arthur (1848-1930). British prime minister at the turn of the 20th century. To his brother and sister sitting by his deathbed: "Thank you for all that you have done."

Balfour, Clara (see Hemans, Felicia).

Ball, Lucille (1911-1989). American comedienne and actress who starred with her husband Desi Arnaz in the long-running *I Love Lucy* television sitcom. While Ball convalesced from aortic aneurysm surgery, her daughter asked if she needed anything. Her reply: "My Florida water."

Balzac, Honoré de (1799-1850). French writer, best-known for his collection of short stories and interlinked novels *La Comédie humaine.* Speaking of one of his characters who worked miracles, Balzac on his deathbed quipped: "Only Bianchon can save me."

Alternatives: * "If Bianchon were here, he would save me."
* "Send for Bianchon!"
* Words written by the novelist on a note his wife sent to a friend: "I can no longer read or write. De Balzac."

Bancroft, George (1800-1891). American historian, politician and writer. To a friend: "I cannot remember your first name." When told it was George like his own: "Then what is your last name?"

Bankhead, Tallulah (1902-1968). American stage and screen actress. Dying from complications of pneumonia and emphysema, Bankhead's parting words reflected her drug and alcohol abuse: "Codeine... bourbon."

Bannister, John (1760-1836). English actor, theatre manager and artist. "My hope is in Christ."

Barbal, Saint Jaime Hilario (see Hilario, Saint Jaime).

Barber, Thomas (c. 1814-1855). American abolitionist and farmer. Barber was gunned down without provocation by a gang of pro-slavery men. Before falling from his horse, Barber muttered: "That fellow hit me."

Barbirolli, John (1899-1970). British symphonic conductor. After awakening with chest pain, Barbirolli spoke to his wife: "Anyway, I can get a good rest in the morning. There's no rehearsal till three."

Barham, Richard, whose pen name was Thomas Ingoldsby (1788-1845). English clergyman, author and poet who wrote *The Ingoldsby Legends*. The last line of his final poem "As I Laye A-Thynkynge:" "Here is rest."

Baring, Maurice (1874-1945). English writer, journalist and poet. When asked for his lunch order: "Whatever you would like me to have."

Barker, Arizona "Ma" born Arizona Clark (1873-1935). Matriarch of an American criminal gang. Barker's family participated in a series of bank robberies, kidnappings and other crimes. When her house was surrounded by FBI agents, she admonished her son to begin a shootout that resulted in her death: "All right! Go ahead."

Barkley, Alben (1877-1956). U.S. vice-president under Harry Truman and later a junior senator from Kentucky. While giving a speech, Barkley fell back and died of a heart attack after uttering these words: "... And now I am back again as a junior senator and I am willing to be a junior. I'm glad to sit in the back row, for I would rather be a servant in the House of the Lord than sit in the seats of the mighty."

Barksdale, William (1821-1863). American lawyer, politician and Confederate officer in the U.S. Civil War. Mortally wounded during the Battle of Gettysburg, Pennsylvania, Barksdale spoke to his aide as he fell from his horse: "I am killed. Tell my wife and children that I died fighting at my post." Left for dead, Barksdale was treated by a Union surgeon who heard his last words: "Tell my wife I am shot, but we fought like hell."

Barnardo, Thomas (1845-1905). Irish physician and philanthropist who worked to improve the care of indigent children. Dying of a heart attack, to his wife: "My head is so heavy. Let me rest it on your face."

Barnato, Barney (1852-1897). English-born South African millionaire. Barnato made his fortune in diamond and gold mines in his adopted country. Before falling from a ship taking him to England, he inquired: "What is the time?" Because Barnato suffered financial reversals, some have suggested suicide as a motive for his fatal plunge.

Barnave, Antoine (1761-1793). French statesman. Because of his intercession for the royal family during the French Revolution, Barnave was condemned to die. He uttered these words before the guillotine blade fell: "This, then, is my reward."

Barnes, Djuna (1892-1982). American writer, best-known for her cult-novel *Nightwood*. Dying a recluse: "There should be a law! This business of helping them [old people] stay alive- it's inhuman! I'm already lost! Do you know that? I've already died and they brought me back. It's terrible."

Barnes, Robert (c. 1495-1540). Martyred English reform minister who was burned at the stake for heresy. "… Wherefore, I trust in no good work that ever I did, but only in the death of Christ. I do not doubt but through him to inherit the kingdom of heaven... We must do [good works], because they are commanded us of God, to show and set forth our profession, not to deserve or merit; for that is only the death of Christ…"

Barneveldt, Jan van Olden (1547-1619). Martyred Dutch statesman and patriot. Because of his opposition to certain Calvinist doctrines, Barneveldt was accused of treason and sentenced to die. Before his beheading, he asked "Oh, God, what then is man?" On the scaffold, the elderly man turned his eyes upward and said: "O God! What does man come to? This then is the reward of forty years' service to the state!" To the executioner: "Be quick about it. Be quick."

Barney, Jeffrey (1958-1986). American criminal, executed by lethal injection for the rape and murder of a minister's wife: "I'm sorry for what

I done. I deserve it. I hope Jesus forgives me." As the drugs took effect: "I'm tingling all over."

Barnum, Phineas T. (1810-1891). American impresario, writer, politician and co-founder of the Ringling Bros. and Barnum & Bailey Circus. On his deathbed, Barnum allegedly asked about his show: "How were the circus receipts today at Madison Square Garden?" To his wife shortly before he died: "Nancy, I want you to know that my last thoughts were of you."

Alternative: * "I am glad."

Barre, Jean-François (1745-1766). Martyred French nobleman. Barre was beheaded and his body burned for allegedly desecrating a crucifix. This offence and other minor improprieties were trumped up against him to bolster the fight for religious intolerance prevalent at the time. His last words: "I did not think they would put a young gentleman to death for such a trifle."

Barron, Clarence (1855-1928). American publisher of the "Wall Street Journal." To his secretary: "What is the news? Are there any messages?" He died moments later.

Barrymore, Ethel (1879-1959). American stage, screen and television actress. Dying of heart disease, Barrymore asked her maid: "Is everybody happy? I want everybody to be happy. I know I'm happy."

Alternative: * "Are you happy? I'm happy."

Barrymore, John (1882-1942). American actor and brother of actress Ethel Barrymore (above). On his deathbed, Barrymore asked his friend Gene Fowler, a journalist and writer: "Tell me, Gene, is it true that you're the illegitimate son of Buffalo Bill?" These words may reference an interview Fowler had with Buffalo Bill Cody about the frontiersman's love life. When asked about death, Barrymore replied: "Die? I should say not, dear fellow. No Barrymore would allow such a conventional thing to happen to him." Delirious from complications of cirrhosis, he exclaimed: "This is wonderful! What a wonderful place!" Gene Fowler, in his Barrymore biography *Good Night, Sweet Prince*, asserts that the actor's last words were spoken to his brother Lionel. When Barrymore roused, Lionel asked what he said: "You heard me, Mike."

Barth, Karl (1886-1968). Swiss theologian. While working late on a lecture, Barth received a telephone call from a friend. He concluded the conversation by reflecting on the unsettled world condition: "... but keep your chin up! Never mind! He [God] will reign!" His wife found him dead the next morning at his desk with his hands folded in prayer.

Alternative: * On the eve of his death, Barth had a final conversation with a fellow minister: "... God does reign. Hence, I myself do not fear. Let us remain confident even at the darkest hour... God will not let us fall, not a single one of us, nor all of us together! Things are indeed being governed."

Barthou, Jean-Louis (1862-1934). French foreign minister. While visiting Marseille, France, Barthou and King Alexander I of Yugoslavia were shot by a Bulgarian revolutionary. The Frenchman remarked: "I can't see what's happening now. My eyeglasses, where are my eyeglasses?" As he died: "I am suffering. I am thirsty."

Bartók, Béla (1881-1945). Hungarian-born pianist, composer and ethnomusicologist. Dying of leukemia, Bartók told his physician: "I am only sad that I have to leave with a full trunk," referring to his last works.

Barton, Clarissa "Clara" (1821-1912). American nurse, humanitarian and founder of the American Red Cross. After a long illness: "Let me go! Let me go!"

Barton, Rocky Lee (1956-2006). American criminal, executed by lethal injection for the murder of his wife: "I'm sorry for what I done. I'm sorry for killing your mama. I'm not asking you to forgive me. Not a day goes by that I'm not trying to forgive myself. Don't let your anger and hate for me destroy your lives." Then: "As Gary Gilmore said [below, before his execution]: 'Let's do it.'"

Bartow, Francis (1816-1861). American lawyer, politician and Confederate officer during the U.S. Civil War. Mortally wounded during the First Battle of Bull Run, near Manassas, Virginia, Bartow told his men: "They have killed me, boys, but never give up the field."

Basedow, Johann (1724-1790). German educator and writer. Dying of a "hemorrhage:" "I desire to be dissected for the benefit of my fellow-men."

Bashkirtseff, Marie, also Bashkirtseva (1858-1884). Russian-born diarist and artist. Dying of tuberculosis, Bashkirtsev addressed a sputtering candle by her bedside: "We shall go out together."

Basquiat, Jean-Michel (1960-1988). American Neo-Expressionist painter. Suffering from depression and drug abuse, Basquiat died of a heroin overdose. To a friend: "I'm so sick of this... I love you."

Bass, Sam (1851-1878). American stagecoach, train and bank robber. Fatally wounded as he attempted to rob a bank, Bass was asked by his assailants about accomplices: "It's agin my trade to blow [snitch] on my pals. If a man knows anything, he ought to die with it in him." Immediately before expiring, Bass said: "Let me go... The world is bobbing around me."

Alternative: * "The room is jumping up and down."

Bastiat, Frédéric (1801-1850). French economist, writer and politician. Dying of tuberculosis: "I am not able to explain myself."

Bateman, Thomas (1778-1821). English physician who made important observations in the field of dermatology. "I surely must be going now, my strength sinks so fast… What glory! The angels are waiting for me! Lord Jesus, receive my soul! Farewell."

Bates, Ellas Otha (see Diddley, Bo).

Batouty, Gamil El (see Habashy, Ahmed Mahmoud El).

Battalino, Robert (died 1949). American criminal, condemned to die in a Colorado gas chamber for murdering a former employer. To the warden: "I hate your guts."

Battie, William (1703-1776). English physician who specialized in the field of mental illness. Dying of a stroke, to his attendant: "Young man, you have heard, no doubt, how great are the terrors of death. This night will probably offer you some experience. But you may learn, and may you profit by the example, that a conscientious endeavor to perform his duties through life will ever close a Christian's eyes with comfort and tranquility."

Baudelaire, Charles (1821-1867). French poet and writer known for his controversial collection of poems, *The Flowers of Evil.* Suffering from a stroke, Baudelaire could only verbalize one phrase: "Holy Name."

Baum, L. Frank (1856-1919). American writer, best-known for his children's novel *The Wonderful Wizard of Oz.* Suffering from a stroke, to his wife: "Now we can cross the Shifting Sands together." He undoubtedly referred to the Shifting Sands described in his imaginary Land of Oz.

Baxter, Charles (1814-1847). American military officer who served during the 1846-48 Mexican-American War. To his physician who was writing to the wounded man's father: "Then say to him that the New York Regiment was there, and that I fell where I should have fallen, at the head of it." He died moments later.

Baxter, John (1958-2002). American executive in the scandal-plagued Enron Corporation. When Baxter discovered irregularities in the energy firm's business dealings, he became despondent and ended his life with a gunshot to the head. The suicide note left for his wife read: "Carol, I am so sorry for this. I feel I just can't go on. I have always tried to do the right thing but where there was once great pride now it's gone. I love you and the children so much. I just can't be any good to you or myself. The pain is overwhelming. Please try to forgive me. Cliff."

Baxter, Richard (1615-1691). English clergyman, hymnodist and writer. Baxter told friends visiting his deathbed: "I am the vilest dunghill worm that ever went to heaven. Lord! What is man; what am I, vile worm, to the great God!" When a companion tried to comfort him, Baxter continued: "I was but a pen in God's hands; and what praise is due to a pen?" Close to death, Baxter exclaimed: "I have pain- there is no arguing against sense- but I have peace. I have peace! I am almost well." As Baxter neared his end: "Death! Death! Oh, I thank Him! I thank Him! The Lord teach you to die!"

Bayard, George D. (1835-1862). Union officer during the U.S. Civil War. Bayard was mortally wounded by shrapnel at the Battle at Fredericksburg, Virginia. He dictated his will before the skirmish: "My black mare and sorrel horse I give to you, father. There are about sixty dollars in my pocketbook. There are papers in my trunk to be turned over to the Department to settle. Once more, goodbye, beloved father, mother, sisters, all. Ever yours, George D. Bayard." [Addendum]: "My sabre goes to father." After his injury, a telegram was sent to his family: "I have been badly hurt, come on." To a fellow officer before expiring: "Tell [General] McClellan that my last regret, as a military man, is that I did not die serving under him."

Bayard, Pierre de (c. 1473-1524). French soldier who was mortally wounded by a gunshot while fighting in northern Italy in the service of King Francis I. After Bayard was helped from his horse, he told his troops: "Pity not me. I die as a man of honor ought, in the discharge of my duty. They indeed are objects of pity who fight against their king, their country and their oath." Moments before dying, Bayard exclaimed: "Let me die facing the enemy."

Alternatives: * "Weep not, for I die in the bed of honor. I have lived long enough. The only thing that distresses me is that I can no longer serve my prince."

* To a former comrade fighting on the opposing side: "Sir, there is no need to pity me. I die as a man of honour ought, doing my duty; but I pity you, because you are fighting against your king, your country, and your oath."

Beall, John (1835-1865). Confederate soldier during the U.S. Civil War. Separated from his unit, Beall carried out clandestine actions against Union forces during the last part of the war. After his capture, Beall was convicted of spying and subsequently hanged: "I protest against this execution of the sentence. It is absolute murder- brutal murder. I die in the defense and service of my country." When a cap was drawn over his eyes: "I beg you to make haste."

Beamer, Todd (1968-2001). American businessman. Beamer was a passenger on United Airlines Flight 93, commandeered by terrorist hijackers during the September 11, 2001 tragedies. His last words were made via a cell phone call before he and others tried to retake the plane: "Are you guys ready? Let's roll." The aircraft crashed near Shanksville, Pennsylvania, killing all aboard.

Beard, George (1839-1883). American physician who specialized in neurological and mental disorders. To his doctors: "You are good fellows, but you can do nothing for me. My time has come." His last utterance: "I should like to record the thoughts of a dying man for the benefit of science, but it is impossible."

Alternative: * "Tell the doctors it is impossible for me to record the thoughts of a dying man. It would be interesting to do so, but I cannot. My time has come. I hope others will carry on my work."

Beard, James (1903-1985). American culinary expert and cookbook author. Trying to converse with a friend, as he died of heart failure: "I can't [speak] anymore."

Beardsley, Aubrey (1872-1898). English illustrator whose drawings often emphasized the exotic and decadent. Dying of tuberculosis, Beardsley sent a letter to his publisher entitled "Jesus is our Lord and Judge:" Dear Friend, I implore you to destroy all copies of *Lysistrata* [his illustrated version of Aristophanes' comedy] and bad drawings. Show this to Pollitt [an English art collector] and conjure him to do same. By all that is holy *all* obscene drawings. In my death agony. Aubrey Beardsley." His request was not fulfilled.

Alternatives: * "I am imploring you- burn all the indecent poems and drawings."
* "Burn all my bawdy pictures."

Beaton, David (c. 1494-1546). Scottish Archbishop of St. Andrews who later was appointed cardinal. Beaton was targeted for assassination by radicals for his involvement in the martyrdom of reformer George Wishart (below). When attacked, he cried: "I am a priest! I am a priest!" As he fell dying: "Fie! Fie [an antiquated expression of disgust]! All is gone."

Beauchamp, Jereboam (1802-1826). American lawyer. Beauchamp accused a Kentucky politician of fathering an illegitimate child by his future wife Anna Cooke. He eventually stabbed the implicated man to death, was convicted of his murder and sentenced to die. Before the execution, Beauchamp's wife smuggled a knife into the prison, and both tried to commit suicide. The wife died of her injuries, but Beauchamp was rushed to the gallows and hanged before he could expire from his self-inflicted wound. To his wife as she died: "Farewell, child of sorrow! Farewell, child of misfortune and persecution! For thee I have lived; for thee I die." Before his hanging: "I want to go to my wife."

Beaufort, Henry, Cardinal of Winchester (c. 1377-1447). French-born English clergyman and statesman. The well-to-do Beaufort queried on his deathbed: "Why should I die, having so much riches? If the whole realm would save my life, I am able either by policy to get it, or by riches to buy it. Fie! Will not death be hired; will money do nothing?" Later, he said: "... But I see now the world faileth me, and so am I deceived, praying you all to pray for me." At the end, the cardinal's tormented mind caused him to say: "Away! Away! Why thus do you look at me?"

Alternative: * "And must I die? Will not all my riches save me? What! Is there no bribing death?"

Beaumont, Joseph (1794-1855). English minister. Beaumont collapsed and died during a Sunday service while repeating lines from the hymn "Eternal Power:" "Thee while the great archangel sings,/ He hides his face behind his wings,/ And ranks of shining hosts around/ Fall worshiping and spread the ground."

Beaverbrook, Lord (see Aitken, William "Max").

Beazley, Napoleon (1976-2002). American criminal, executed by lethal injection for the robbery and murder of a businessman: "The act I committed to put me here was not just heinous, it was senseless. But the person that committed that act is no longer here- I am. He then apologized for his crime and discussed the pros and cons of capital punishment. Beazley concluded: "... No one wins tonight. No one gets closure. No one walks away victorious."

Beck, Ludwig (1880-1944). Chief of the German General Staff during WWII. After the failure of the Stauffenberg plot to assassinate Adolf Hitler, Beck attempted to shoot himself for his involvement in the affair. After two unsuccessful tries, he implored a soldier to complete the task: "If it doesn't work this time, then please help me." The soldier succeeded with a gunshot to the back of the general's neck.

Beck, Martha (c. 1920 -1951). Obese American serial murderer and lover of Raymond Fernandez (below), also a convicted murderer. The so-called "Lonely Hearts Killers" answered personal ads from elderly women and then swindled them of their savings. Victims offering any resistance were killed. Prior to her execution in the electric chair at New York's Sing-Sing prison, Beck opined: "What does it matter who is to blame? My story is a love story, but only those tortured with love can understand what I mean. I was pictured as a fat, unfeeling woman. True, I am fat, that I cannot deny, but if that is a crime, how many of my sex are guilty. I am not unfeeling, stupid or moronic. The prison and the death house have only strengthened my feeling for Raymond, and in the history of the world, how many crimes have been attributed to love? My last words are and my last thoughts will be: He who is without sin cast the first stone." When asked by the chaplain if she had repented: "I know my sin was great, but the penalty is great too. That makes things even, I guess." While strapped in the electric chair: "So long."

Becket, Saint Thomas à (c. 1118-1170). Archbishop of Canterbury. When Becket ran afoul of English King Henry II, the archbishop was slashed to death by a group of the monarch's henchmen. Because of his prominence, many versions of his last words exist. To his assassins: "No one shall set the sea between me and my Church. I did not come here to run away: anyone who wants me may find me... I am prepared to die for Christ and His Church. I charge you in the name of the Almighty not to hurt any other person here, for none of them has been concerned in the late transactions... In vain you menace me. If all the swords in England were brandishing over my head, your terrors could not move me." As he died: "I humbly commend my spirit to the God who gave it."

Alternatives: * "For the name of Jesus and the protection of the church I am ready to embrace death."

* "I am ready to die for my Lord, that in my blood, the Church may obtain peace and liberty. But in the name of the Almighty God I forbid you to harm any of my men, whether clerk or lay."
* "... I go to death in the Lord's name. I commend my soul, and the cause of the church, to God and the Saints. I will not fly on account of your swords, but I forbid you to touch my friends."
* "To God and Blessed Mary... I commend myself! Into Thy hands, O Lord, I commend my spirit! I accept death for the Name of Jesus and his church."
* "I do commend my cause to God, the Virgin, St. Denis of France and St. Alphege of England, and all the tutelar [guardian] saints of Canterbury."
* "Lord, receive my spirit."

Beckford, William (1760-1844). British writer. Dying of influenza, Beckford sent a note to his daughter: "Come quick, quick!" She heeded the request and arrived before he expired.

Bécu, Jeanne, Madame du Barry (1743-1793). Mistress of French King Louis XV. Bécu was sentenced to die for allegedly helping citizens escape the French Revolution. To the executioner as she approached the guillotine:

"You are going to hurt me! Please don't hurt me. Just one more moment, executioner, a small moment, I beg you!"

Beddoes, Thomas (1803-1849). English physician, dramatist and poet whose works showed a preoccupation with death. Suffering from depression, Beddoes committed suicide by poisoning. Portions of his suicide note written to a friend read: "… I am food for what I am good for- worms... I ought to have been among other things a good poet. Life was too great a bore on one peg, and that a bad one." A portion of one leg had been amputated earlier after Beddoes fell from a horse.

Bede the Venerable (c. 673-735). English theologian, historian and writer. To the priests as he distributed his meager worldly possessions: "… The time of my dissolution draws nigh; for I desire to die and be with Christ…" As Bede dictated a translation of the gospel of St. John, his amanuensis commented that only one sentence remained: "Write quickly." When told it was finished, Bede said: "It is well, you have said the truth. It is finished. Receive my head into your hands, for it is a great satisfaction to me to sit facing my holy place where I was wont to pray, that I may, also sitting, call upon my father." He died singing the *Gloria Patri*: "Glory be to the Father, and to the Son, and to the Holy Ghost."

A different version relates that Bede was reminded of a missing chapter. His reply: "It is easily done. Take thy pen and write quickly." When told that a sentence was needed, the scholar said: "Write it quickly." When advised that the passage was finished, Bede replied: "You speak truth. All is finished now. Glory to God." In a similar account, Bede asked how many chapters required translation. His scribe mentioned only one but admonished the scholar that he was too weak to continue. Bede replied: "No, take your pen and write quickly." When advised that the task was completed, Bede replied, "Thou hast said truly *consummatum est* (it is finished)." He died shortly thereafter.

Alternative: * "Glory be to the Father and to the Son and to…"

Bedell, William (1571-1642). Bishop of Kilmore, Ireland. "... I have fought a good fight. I have finished the course of my ministry and life together...

O, Lord, I have waited for thy salvation…I have kept the faith once given to the saints; for the which cause I have also suffered these things; but I am not ashamed; for I know whom I have believed, and I am persuaded that He is able to keep that which I have committed to Him against that day."

Alternative: * "Be of good cheer. Be of good cheer. Whether we live or die we are the Lord's."

Bédoyère, Charles de (1786-1815). French general in Napoleon's army. Because he received conflicting orders during the Battle of Waterloo in present-day Belgium, Bédoyère actions were construed as treasonous. Before a firing squad, he pointed toward his heart and said: "Above all do not miss me!"

Alternative: * "This is what you must not miss."

Bee, Barnard (1824-1861). Confederate officer during the U.S. Civil War. Seeing his colleague, General Thomas Jackson (below, standing firmly during the First Battle of Bull Run, near Manassas, Virginia, Bee attempted to rally his men by shouting: "Look men! There is Jackson standing like a stone wall! Let us determine to die here, and we will conquer! Follow me!" Although Bee perished in the skirmish, his rallying call bestowed on Jackson one of the most memorable military sobriquets.

Beecher, Henry (1813-1887). American minister and social reformer. After suffering a stroke, Beecher was asked by his physician if he could raise his arm. He replied: "Well, high enough to hit you, doctor." Later, when asked if he heard the comment made that his illness was terminal: "You were saying that I could not recover." He died shortly thereafter.

Alternative: * "Now comes the mystery."

Beecher, Lyman (1775-1863). American minister who was a co-founder of the American Temperance Society. As he died, Beecher recited a portion of 2 Timothy 4:7-8:"'I have fought a good fight. I have finished my course. I have kept the faith, henceforth there is laid up for me a crown which God the righteous judge will give me at that day.' *That* is my testimony. Write it down. That is my testimony."

Beeter, Lawrence (birth and death dates unclear). British soldier who served during WWII. After a missile slammed into his position, Beeter exclaimed: "Maybe they only had one rocket." Shortly thereafter, a second projectile hit the bunker complex, killing Beeter.

Beethoven, Ludwig van (1770-1827). German-born composer, pianist and conductor. Sensing death's approach, Beethoven told his friends three days before expiring: "Plaudite, amici, comedia finita est!" ["Applaud, friends, the comedy is ended!"] The following day, he uttered his final recorded words: "Pity, pity, too late." This statement was not a lament that death would cut short his musical aspirations but rather a reference to the late arrival of a shipment of wine from Mainz. That evening, Beethoven lapsed into a coma and died from complications of cirrhosis two days later.

Alternatives: Beethoven's final words are subject to historical debate and vary with many biographies. A number of his utterances were made in the days before his death but were recorded as his last words:

* Apropos his deafness: "I shall hear in Heaven."
* To his friend, the composer Johann Hummel who was at his deathbed: "Is it not true, Hummel, that I have some talent after all?"
* "Too bad! Too bad! It's too late!"
* "There, do you hear the bell? Don't you hear it ringing? The curtain must drop. Yes! My curtain is falling."
* "Clap now, my friends, the comedy is done."
* After receiving Last Rites of the Roman Catholic Church, to the priest: "I thank you, Reverend Sir. You have brought me comfort." Shortly thereafter, he apparently lost consciousness.
* Other biographers have Beethoven saying nothing at the end but simply shaking his fists defiantly at the heavens as a thunderstorm raged outside his window.

Behan, Brendan (1923-1964). Irish writer, playwright and poet. Dying from complications of alcoholism and diabetes, to his wife: "You made one mistake. You married me." To his nurse, a nun: "Thank you, sister. May you be the mother of a bishop."

Alternative: * To his nurse, presumably the same nun: "Ah, bless you sister, may all your sons be bishops."

Behiter, Joseph (1901-1934). American criminal, condemned to die in the Nevada gas chamber for the murder of a woman. To an attendant: "Don't strap me to the chair too tightly. It might keep the gas from my lungs."

Behringer, Earl (1964-1997). American criminal, executed by lethal injection for the murder of two college students: "It's a good day to die. I walked in here like a man and I am leaving here like a man. I had a good life. I have known the love of a good woman, my wife. I have a good family. My grandmother is the pillar of the community. I love and cherish my friends and family. Thank you for your love." To the family of one of the murdered female students: "I am sorry for the pain I caused you. If my death gives you any peace, so be it. I want my friends to know it is not the way to die, but I belong to Jesus Christ. I confess my sins. I have..."

Belasco, David (1853-1931). American playwright who wrote extensively for the Broadway stage. "I'm fighting for my life, doctor!"

Bell, Alexander Graham (1847-1922). Scottish-born inventor who developed the first practical telephone. As Bell lay dying from complications of diabetes, his deaf wife pleaded that he should not leave her. He responded by signing: "No." While dictating during his last hours, Bell's amanuensis (some say his wife) asked the inventor about the rush to finish: "But I have to. So little done. So much to do!"

Bell, Charles (1774-1842). Scottish anatomist and surgeon. While traveling from Edinburgh to London, Bell became seriously ill near Worcester in the Midlands. Dying of a probable heart attack, he said: "This is a sweet spot. Here I should like to rest till they come to take me away." To his wife: "Hold me in your arms." He died later that night after hearing the 23rd Psalm.

Bellamy, Edward (1850-1898). American socialist writer, best-known for his novel *Looking Backward.* To relatives who wished to stay with him during the night: "What can happen to me? I can only die."

Bellamy, Joseph (1719-1790). American clergyman and writer. As he lay dying, a friend asked Bellamy what he would do if he went to hell. The minister replied "I will tell them there forever Jesus is precious."

Bellini, Vincenzo (1801-1835). Sicilian composer, primarily of *bel canto* operas. Suffering from amebic dysentery complicated by a liver abscess, the dying composer reflected: "… Had I just quitted this world, they [his friends] would go on their way, light-hearted as before, giving not a thought to me, and perhaps one day would hear my music without even saying 'Poor Bellini.'" Later, in a delirious state, Bellini told his doctor: "Can't you see all my family have arrived?" He then began naming all members, starting with his mother and father.

Belloc, Hilaire (1870-1953). French-born British writer, historian and poet. Late in life, Belloc nodded off and fell into a fireplace. The burns he sustained ultimately proved fatal. Before dying, he quipped: "Better burn the writer than his work."

Bellone, Constantia (birth and death dates unclear). Waldensian (a Christian movement that began in the late 12th century) martyr. When a priest asked Bellone if she would renounce the devil and attend mass, she refused and replied: "I was brought up in a religion by which I was always taught to renounce the devil, but should I comply with your desire and go to mass, I should be sure to meet him there in a variety of shapes." Enraged, the priest then ordered his underlings to cut pieces of flesh from her body. Because Bellone remained steadfast in her beliefs despite the torment, the priest ordered a firing squad to kill her. As they raised their weapons, she said: "What horrid and lasting torments will you suffer in hell for the trifling and temporary pains which I now endure."

Alternative: * "I was brought up in a religion which required me to renounce the devil. But should I yield to your solicitations and go to mass, I should be sure to see *him there*, in a variety of shapes… Oh! man...

you a messenger of the gospel! You a servant of the Lord Jesus! Oh! what horrid and lasting torments will you suffer in hell for the trifling pains and temporary agony I now endure!"

Belmont, Alva (1853-1933). American socialite and woman's rights champion. Possibly reflecting on her antagonizing aristocratic airs, to a friend: "It makes no difference now. The important thing is learning how to live. Learn a lesson from my mistakes. I had too much power before I knew how to use it, and it defeated me in the end. It drove all sweetness out of my life except for the affection of my children. My trouble was that I was born too late for the last generation and too early for this one. If you want to be happy, live in your own time."

Belushi, John (1949-1982). American comedian and actor, best-known for his performances in the movies *Animal House* and *The Blues Brothers*. Dying of an overdose of cocaine and heroin, Belushi spoke to the woman who supplied him with the drugs: "Just don't leave me alone."

Benchley, Robert (1889-1945). American writer and humorist. Immediately before his death from a stroke, Benchley made a note on the title page (some say at the end) of an essay, entitled "Am I Thinking?" by James Robinson. He penned: "NO. (And supposing you were?)."

Bender, Tony, birth name Anthony Strollo (1899-1962). American mobster who was a member of several New York crime gangs. When his wife recommended an overcoat before leaving the house, Bender responded: "I'm only going out for a few minutes. Besides, I'm wearing thermal underwear." He was never seen again.

Benedek, Ludwig von (1804-1881). Hungarian-born commander of the Austrian army that was defeated at the 1866 Battle of Königgrätz, present-day Czech Republic. Benedek retired from military service and died 14 years later. A telegram to his wife: "Relieved to hear you feel better. I had a very bad night. Am now strong. Your poor Louis."

Benedict, Lewis (1817-1864). U.S. Civil War Union officer killed at the Battle of Pleasant Hill, Louisiana. His last order: "Colonel, rally your men and advance as soon as possible." Moments later, he was mortally wounded.

Benjamin, Judah (1811-1884). West Indian-born lawyer and politician. Benjamin became a U.S. senator from Louisiana and later a successful barrister in Britain. Last letter to a friend: "… For more than two months, I have alternated between my bed and my armchair; but if we can only get rid of this glacial temperature and dry east wind, I shall get some strength. What I require is warmth. Will it never come?"

Benjamin, Park (1809-1864). British Guiana-born American journalist. When his wife asked if he knew her: "Why should I not know you, Mary?"

Bennett, Arnold (1867-1931). English novelist and journalist, best-known for his self-help book *How to Live on 24 Hours a Day.* Dying of typhoid fever, to his mistress: "Everything's gone wrong, my girl."

Benny, Jack, born Benjamin Kubelsky (1894-1974). American comedian, actor, musician and vaudevillian. Near death from pancreatic cancer, Benny called the name "Lyman Woods." His valet knew that Woods was a long-deceased vaudeville actor and questioned his employer about it. Benny replied: "I just saw Lyman Woods and he spoke to me. He is going to help me through. He showed me the way; it was beautiful! I was with Lyman. He told me it was beautiful and it was. It was."

Benson, George (1861-1901). British Royal Artillery officer, killed at the Battle of Bakenlaagte, South Africa during the Boer War. A proponent of night marches with surprise attacks, Benson's last words reflected his vision of death: "Ah, [Colonel] Sampson, old boy, we shall do no more night marching. It is all by day now. Goodbye and God bless you."

Benson, Robert (1871-1914). English Roman Catholic clergyman and author. To spare his brother the "shock" of watching death's approach: "Arthur! Don't look at me. Nurse, stand between my brother and me! Jesus, Mary and Joseph, I give you my heart and soul."

Bentham, Jeremy (1748-1832). English philosopher, political theorist, writer and lawyer who promulgated the theory of utilitarianism. In his will, Bentham stated that his body should be dissected and preserved *post mortem.* On his deathbed, to his doctor: "I now feel that I am dying. Our care must be to minimize pain. Do not let any of the servants come into the room, and keep away the youths. It will be very distressing to them and they can be of no service. Yet I must not be alone. You will remain with me, and you only; and then we shall have reduced the pain to the least possible amount." Three days after his death, the specified dissection took place in London's Webb Street School of Anatomy and his clothed skeleton was placed in a corridor of the University College. Because his head was not suitable for display, a wax replica was placed instead.

Benton, Thomas (1782-1858). U.S. senator. Dying of cancer, to his housekeeper: "I am comfortable. I am content." He asked her to put her ear to his chest and said: "Do you hear that, Kitty? That is the death rattle."

Berengar of Tours (c. 999-1088). French theologian and canon of Tours Cathedral who died on January 6, the day of Epiphany. Some of Berengar's works were condemned by his contemporaries as heresy. Perhaps those censures colored the canon's last words: "I shall not long hesitate between conscience and the Pope, for I shall soon appear in the presence of God to be acquitted, I hope; to be condemned, I fear."

Alternative: * "Today, on the day of his Epiphany, my Lord Jesus Christ will appear to me, either for glory, as I in my repentance should like, and as I hope, or for condemnation, as others would like, and as I fear."

Bérenger, Madame de Bois (died 1794). French aristocrat arrested during the French Revolution. Beranger and her immediate family were condemned to die for "conspiracy." To her mother before their execution: "Dearest madam, be consoled: why are you not happy? You die innocent, and in the same innocence all your family follow you to the tomb, and will partake with you, in a better state, the recompense of virtue."

Alternative: * "Be composed, my dearest parent, nor let an emotion of regret accompany you to the tomb. You have all your family with you; to you they look up for consolation; since your virtues are about to receive the recompense they merit in the mansions of innocence and peace."

Bérenger, Pierre (1780-1857). French poet and songwriter. To a priest: "... My life has been that of an honest man. I remember no action for which I have cause to blush before God."

Beresford, Louisa, Marchioness of Waterford, born Louisa Stuart (1818-1891). Parisian-born artist. To her goddaughter: "Oh darling Adelaide! goodness and beauty, beauty and goodness, those are ever the great things!"

Berg, Alban (1885-1935). Austrian composer who employed elements of romanticism and atonality in his music. As he lay dying of septicemia from an infected insect sting on his lower back, Berg responded to his wife's admonition to rest: "But I have so little time!" He added: "Today is the 23rd. It will be a decisive day!" Probably imagining that he directed a piece of music, the delirious musician repeated: "An up-beat! An up-beat!" Throughout his life, Berg fixated on the number 23. His earlier prediction about the decisiveness of the 23rd was slightly off the mark; the composer died the following day, December 24, 1935.

Berg, Morris "Moe" (1902-1972). American professional baseball player, linguist and WWII spy for the United States. Dying of injuries received in a fall in his apartment, to his nurse: "How'd the [New York] Mets do today?" The Mets beat the St. Louis Cardinals 7 to 6.

Bergerus, Joachimus (died c. 1602). Councilor to Emperor Maximilian. "Farewell. O farewell, all earthly things, and welcome heaven! Let none hereafter make any mention of earthly things to me."

Bergman, Ingrid (1915-1982). Swedish stage and screen actress, well-known for her role in the 1942 movie *Casablanca*. Dying of cancer, Bergman was told that a visitor wished to see her: "Do I look all right? Give me my brush and makeup."

Berlioz, Hector (1803-1869): French composer and conductor. The sensual textures of Berlioz's scores and the huge ensembles required to perform some of them often confused French audiences and critics alike. As a result, his music, at times, enjoyed a greater acceptance abroad than in his homeland. Perhaps the remembrance of this reaction induced Berlioz to speak these words shortly before his death from a stroke: "They are finally going to play my music."

Alternatives: * Speaking to his dead wife: "Oh, Mère Recio, it is finished."

* After quoting from Macbeth's final soliloquy in Shakespeare's play of the same name: "'Life's but a walking shadow, a poor player, that struts and frets his hour upon the stage, and then is heard no more; it is a tale told by an idiot, full of sound and fury, signifying nothing.' That is my signal."
* Speaking about a contemporary Russian composer: "One thousand greetings to Balakirev."

Bern, Paul (1889-1932). German-born American film director, screenwriter and producer who married the actress Jean Harlow (below). Several months after their nuptials, Bern was found dead in his bathroom from a gunshot wound to the head. The suicide supposedly was precipitated by his "impotence." Bern's suicide note read: "Dearest Dear, Unfortuately [*sic*] this is the only way to make good the frightful wrong I have done you and to wipe out my abject humiliation. Paul" In a postscript: "You understand that last night was only a comedy."

Bernadotte, Folke (1895-1948). Swedish nobleman and statesman who helped secure the release of thousands of concentration camp inmates during WWII. While serving as a United Nations mediator in Jerusalem, Bernadotte was assassinated by Jewish radicals. When wished "good luck," he replied: "I'll need it."

Bernard of Clairvaux, Saint (1090-1153). French abbot who was a member of the Cistercian Order. When fellow monks prayed for his recovery, Bernard asked: "Why do you thus detain a miserable man? You are the stronger; you prevail against me. Spare me. Spare me and let me depart.... I am already no longer of this world... May God's will be done."

Alternatives: * "I know not to which I ought to yield, to the love of my children, which urges me to stay here, or to the love of God, which draws me to Him."
* "Thy kingdom come, Thy will be done."

Bernard, Claude (1813-1878). French physiologist who helped pioneer the application of scientific methodology in medicine. When a rug was placed over his legs, Bernard responded: "This time it will serve me for the voyage from which there is no return- the voyage of eternity."

Bernard, Francis (1712-1779). English-born American colonial governor of New Jersey and the Province of Massachusetts Bay. Dying of a stroke, Bernard spoke in a bewildered way about an imagined danger: "Never fear; if you will but have patience. I don't doubt that we shall get through; but take care how you ever get in such a scrape again."

Bernhardt, Sarah, born Henriette Rosine Bernard (1844-1923). French stage and film actress. When told that reporters were awaiting word of her death, Bernhardt said: "All my life reporters have tormented me enough. I can tease them now a little by making them cool their heels." As her death throes dragged on, she commented: "How slow my death agony is."

Alternative: * "I'll keep them dangling. They've tortured me all my life, now I'll torture them."

Berrigan, Philip (1923-2002). American clergyman and peace activist. Succumbing to cancer, Berrigan declared: "I die with the conviction, held since 1968 and Catonsville [Maryland where he and others had destroyed draft records], that nuclear weapons are the scourge of the earth; to mine for them, manufacture them, deploy them, use them, is a curse against God, the human family, and the earth itself."

Berry, Hiram (1824-1863). Union officer in the U.S. Civil War. Shot during the Battle of Chancellorsville, Virginia, Berry spoke to his men: "I am dying. Carry me to the rear."

Berryman, John (1914-1972). American poet, scholar and educator. The suicide of Berryman's father weighed heavily on his mind and found its way into some of his works. Troubled by depression and alcoholism, Berryman left a suicide note for his wife: "I am a nuisance." At that point, he failed to consummate the act and penned his last poem that ended: "... here's the terror of tomorrow's lectures/ bad in themselves, the students dropping the course,/ the Administration hearing/ & offering me either a medical leave of absence/ or resignation- Kitticat [his wife's nickname], they can't fire me." Two days later, Berryman told his wife that he was going to clean out his university office and added: "You won't have to worry about me anymore." He then jumped from a bridge to his death.

Besant, Annie (1847-1933). British theosophist, women's rights activist and writer. "I wonder why so many pretty little animals die so young."

Bessarion, Basilios (1403-1472). Greek scholar and patriarch of Constantinople. On his deathbed, Bessarion prayed: "Thou art just, O Lord, and just are Thy decrees, but Thou art good and merciful, and Thou wilt not recall our failings."

Bestuzhev-Ryumin, Michael (1801-1826). Russian revolutionary. Because he openly advocated overthrow of the monarchy, Bestuzhev was condemned to hang. When the first rope broke, he commented: "Nothing succeeds with me. Even here I meet with disappointment."

Bethune, Mary (1875-1955). American educator and civil rights activist. Dying of a heart attack, to her family: "Life is wonderful. I am wonderful."

Bevan, Aneurin (1897-1960). Welsh-born leader of Britain's Labour Party and champion of workers' rights. Battling cancer, Bevan lamented: "I want to live because there are a few things I want to do." Realizing there was little hope, he refused further treatment saying: "I will not become a surgeon's plaything."

Beveridge, William (1637-1708). English bishop and writer. At the end of his life, Beveridge was afflicted with a dementia that prevented him from recognizing family and friends. However, when asked on his deathbed whether he knew Jesus, he replied “Oh yes, I have known Him these forty years. Precious Savior! He is my only hope.”

Bhatti, Shahbaz (1968-2011). Pakistani politician who was a member of the National Assembly. Because of threats received for his pro-Christian beliefs, Bhatti had a premonition of death: “They say there’s a terrorist plot to assassinate me. They’ve told me to be careful, but didn’t tell me anything else. I haven’t been given any extra security. It’s just the same as it has been since I became a minister. I have struggled for a long time for justice and equality. If I change my stance today, who will speak out? I am mindful that I can be assassinated any time, but I want to live in history as a courageous man.” He was gunned down the day following this statement.

Bhutto, Benazir (1953-2007). Pakistani prime minister and daughter of Zulfikar Bhutto (below). Bhutto, an opposition candidate in the 2008 parliamentary elections, was assassinated as she left a political rally. Moments before her vehicle was attacked, she shouted to the crowd: “Long live Bhutto!” She later died of her injuries.

Bhutto, Zulfikar (1928-1979). President and later prime minister of Pakistan. Deposed in 1977, Bhutto was tried on charges that he had authorized the murder of a political rival. Before his hanging, the chief of the security detail heard Bhutto implore: “This to me? God help me, for I am innocent!” His final words were muffled by the hood over his head.

Bickersteth, Edward (1786-1850). English clergyman. To his child who asked for a blessing: “The Lord bless thee, my child, with overflowing grace, now and forever.”

Biddle, Nicholas (1750-1778). American naval officer who served during the Revolutionary War. While engaging a British man-of-war, Biddle’s ship took a broadside that wounded him. He refused to retire below and ordered: “Bring me a chair. Carry me forward and there the surgeon will dress my wound… I am only slightly wounded.” As his injury was tended, another volley destroyed the ship with only four survivors. Biddle went down with his vessel.

Bidwell, Daniel (1819-1864). Union officer during the U.S. Civil War. At the Battle of Cedar Creek, Virginia, Bidwell was mortally wounded by a Confederate shell: "Doctor, I suppose there is no hope of recovery?" When told there was none: "Oh, my poor wife. Doctor, see that my record is right at home. Tell them I died at my post doing my duty."

Biederwolf, Edward (1867-1939). American evangelist and writer. To his wife at the end of a protracted, painful illness: "I am soon going to exchange my cross for a crown."

Bierce, Ambrose (1842-c. 1914). American writer and journalist, best-known for his satirical lexicon *The Devil's Dictionary.* In 1913, Bierce traveled through the southern U.S. and eventually crossed into Mexico. In a letter to his family: "If you hear about my being stood up against a Mexican stone wall and shot to rags, please know that I think it's a pretty good way to depart this life. It beats old age, disease, or falling down the cellar stairs." Later that year, Bierce traveled to Chihuahua, Mexico, which was occupied by the revolutionary army of Pancho Villa. He wrote to a friend: "Pray for me- real loud." Bierce's last letter to his secretary: "Trainloads of troops leaving Chihuahua every day." To this day, his fate remains unknown.

Biggs, John (birth and death dates unclear). English smuggler and robber. "I never was a murderer, unless killing fleas and such-like harmless little cruelties fall under the statute. Neither am I guilty of being a whoremaster, since females have always had the ascendency over me, not I o'er them. No, I am come here to swing like a pendulum for endeavoring to be too rich, too soon."

Bilac, Olavo (1865-1918). Brazilian poet and journalist. "Give me coffee, I'm going to write."

Billy the Kid, also known as Henry McCarty, William Bonney and Henry Antrim (1859-1881). American Old West robber and murderer. Sheriff Pat Garrett (below) tracked the outlaw to a house near Fort Sumner, New Mexico and confronted him in a darkened room. When Billy asked: "Who is it? Who is it?" Garrett shot him dead.

Alternative: * "Who is there? Who is there?"

Bilney, Thomas (c. 1495-1531). English martyr. Because of his reformist views, Bilney was branded a heretic and condemned to die. As he was being tied to the stake for burning, the assembled crowd groused about who had caused his death. When some of the assembled clergy threatened to withhold alms to the people if they were blamed for his martyrdom, Bilney said: "I pray you, good people, be never the worse to these men for my sake, as though they should be the authors of my death. It was not they." As the flames consumed his body, Bilney spoke Jesus' name several times and cried: "*Credo*; *credo*." ["I believe; I believe."]

Birney, David (1825-1864). American lawyer and Union officer during the U.S. Civil War. In the Siege of Petersburg, Virginia, Birney was stricken with a febrile illness, possibly malaria or typhoid fever, and was sent home to convalesce. Dying several months later, Birney deliriously recalled his military service: "Boys, keep your eyes on that flag."

Biron, Louis, Duc de Lauzun (1747-1793). French soldier and politician. Accused of treason during the Reign of Terror in the French Revolution, Biron was condemned to die by beheading. To the executioner's messenger who interrupted his last meal: "I beg a thousand pardons, my friend, but permit me to finish this last dozen of oysters..." Biron then offered the man a glass of wine commenting: "Take this wine; you must need courage in your profession." Before the guillotine blade fell, Biron said: "I have been false to my God, to my order and to my King. I die full of faith and of repentance."

Alternative: * "Citizen, allow me to finish."

Bishop, Arthur (1952-1988). American criminal, executed by lethal injection for multiple murders: "I want to offer again my most profound and heartfelt apologies to my victims' families. I am truly sorry. I have tried my best to empathize with their grief and devastation and I hope they come to know of my concerns and prayers for them."

Alternative: * "Give my apologies to the families of my victims."

Bishop, Bernice (1831-1884). Hawaiian aristocrat and philanthropist. Dying of cancer, to a friend: "Happiness is not money. Having so much, I feel responsible and accountable. Pray, and bid all my friends pray, for I need help from on high." She became comatose and died a week later.

Bishop, Jesse (1933-1979). American criminal, executed in the Nevada gas chamber for a murder committed during a robbery: "I've always wanted to try everything once... Let's go!"

Alternative: * "This is just one more step down the road of life that I've been heading all my life. Let's go!"

Bismarck, Otto von (1815-1898). Prussian statesman and military leader. On his deathbed, Bismarck said: "I do not want a lying official epitaph. Write on my tomb that I was the faithful servant of my master, the Emperor William, King of Prussia." Later, possibly referencing Mark 9:24: "Dear Lord, I believe. Help Thou my unbelief and receive me into Thy heavenly Kingdom." To his daughter who wiped perspiration from his forehead: "I thank you, my child."

Bixby, Wilfred "Bill" (1934-1993). American film and television actor. Dying of prostate cancer, Bixby spoke to his wife and a friend: "Thanks for the laughter."

Bizet, Georges (1838-1875): French composer, best known for his opera *Carmen*. Dying of a severe streptococcal infection and possible rheumatic fever, Bizet uttered these words to a family maid: "My poor Marie, I am in a cold sweat. It is the sweat of death. How are you going to tell my poor father?"

Alternative: * "My arms, Maria, I have a cold sweat, a sweat of death..."

Black Elk (1863-1950). Native American Lakota chieftain and cousin of Crazy Horse (below). Black Elk participated in the Battle of Little Big Horn and the Wounded Knee Massacre. He later toured with Buffalo Bill Cody's Wild West Show (below). To his daughter: "It seems like I will go any time now, so if your car is all right, go after your younger brother. I want to see him." Black Elk died a few minutes later.

Black, Hugo (1886-1971). American politician and jurist who became an associate justice of the U.S. Supreme Court. After suffering a stroke, Black relinquished his position on the bench. When his wife asked if he would like to see a telecast covering his resignation, he replied: "It doesn't make a difference."

Blackie, John (1809-1895). Scottish writer and translator. Blackie expressed his love of Psalms and the Scottish literature in his last breath: "The Psalms of David and the songs of [Robert] Burns, but the Psalmist first... Psalms, poetry..."

Blackwell, Alexander (c. 1700-1747). Scottish physician and adventurer. While in Sweden, Blackwell was accused of meddling with the succession to the throne and was condemned to die. Inadvertently placing his head on the wrong side of the block, he told the executioner: "I am sorry for the mistake, but this is the first time I've been beheaded."

Blair, John (1759-1823). American clergyman. To his children: "Lord Jesus, into Thy hands I commend my spirit! I should like once more to speak to this congregation, but shall not be able to do that."

Blair, William (1766-1822). English surgeon and writer. To a friend: "Reach me that blessed Book, that I may lay my hand on it once more. I rest in Christ."

Blake, Daniel (died 1763). English burglar and murderer. Blake was a menial in a household that he burgled from time to time. When confronted by the butler, Blake killed him. Before his hanging: "Be careful to attend divine worship; profane not the Sabbath; repent of your sins, and make a timely peace with God. Behold the consequence of my iniquities! Fear God, and honour your parents, for neglecting which I must suffer a disgraceful death."

Blake, William (1757-1827). English poet, painter, printmaker and mystic. Dying of "jaundice and torments of the stomach," Blake said to his wife: "I am going to the country that all my life I have longed to see. I am happy, hoping for salvation through Jesus Christ." Shortly before he died, the poet sang of the visions of heaven. When his wife asked whose songs he sang, Blake remarked: "My beloved, they are not mine. No, they are not mine."

Blanc, Maurice (died 1547). French martyr. Because of alleged heretical thoughts, Blanc, an inhabitant of Mérindol in southern France, was tied to a tree and executed by a firing squad: "Lord God! These men take away my life full of misery, but thou wilt give unto me life everlasting by thy Son Jesus Christ, to whom be glory."

Blanchard, Sophie (1778-1819). French aeronaut and wife of balloonist Jean Pierre Blanchard. While ascending during a Parisian exhibition, fireworks attached to Blanchard's balloon ignited the contained hydrogen gas. As she plummeted to her death: "*A moi*!" (Help! [literally translated: To me!]).

Blanche of Castile (1188-1252). Consort of Louis VIII of France and mother of Louis IX. Praying: "Help me, ye saints of God! Fly hither, ye angels of the Lord and receive my soul and bear it before the All-High!"

Blandina, Saint (died 177). French Christian slave and martyr during the reign of Marcus Aurelius (above). Because Blandina refused to renounce her Christian faith, she was imprisoned and tortured. After her body was scourged and burned, Blandina was thrown to wild animals and later stabbed to death. Before dying, she moaned: "I am a Christian and there is nothing vile done by us."

Blandy, Mary (1720-1752). English criminal. Blandy poisoned her father with arsenic because he objected to her entanglement with a married man. On the scaffold before her hanging, she pleaded: "Gentlemen, I beg you will not hang me high for the sake of decency. I am afraid I shall fall."

Blaurer, Ambrosius (1492-1564). German-born Protestant Reformation leader. "Oh, my Lord Jesus Christ, this made You in Your great thirst desire nothing, but You were given gall and vinegar."

Blavatsky, Helena (1831-1891). Russian-born mystic and founder of the American Theosophical Society. Shortly before dying from complications of kidney failure and influenza, Blavatsky exhorted: "... Keep the link unbroken. Do not let my last incarnation be a failure." Her last words: "I do my best, doctor."

Blaylock, Celia "Mattie" (c. 1850-1888). American frontier woman and one-time companion of Marshal Wyatt Earp (below) who left her for another companion. Blaylock suffered from chronic headaches treated with the opiate laudanum. She died of a suicidal overdose of alcohol and laudanum saying: "I think I can sleep."

Bliss, Philip (1838-1876). American composer, conductor and evangelist. Bliss and his wife were involved in a train accident in Ohio. Unhurt, he entered the burning wreckage searching for his trapped wife. When urged to save himself, he replied: "If I cannot save her, I will perish with her." Neither survived the accident.

Bloch, Marc (1886-1944). French economic historian and resistance fighter. During WWII, Bloch joined the French Resistance and was captured by the Vichy police who turned him over to the Gestapo. When he and other prisoners were scheduled to be shot, a boy said "This is going to be bad." Bloch tried to reassure him saying: "No, son, it's not bad." As Bloch fell mortally wounded, he said: "Long live France."

Blomfield, Charles (1786-1857). Church of England bishop. Succumbing to a "fit," Blomfield told his attendant: "I am nearer to my end than they think." At the end: "I am dying."

Blood, Thomas (c. 1618-1680). Irish adventurer and criminal. Blood was best known for his 1671 attempt to steal the Crown Jewels. Inexplicably King Charles II pardoned the thief who died of natural causes nine years later. "I do not fear death."

Blount, Thomas (died 1400). English conspirator. Remaining loyal to deposed King Richard II, Blount and others plotted against Henry IV who had ascended the throne. Captured and sentenced to die, Blount was hanged but cut-down before expiring. The executioner then disemboweled the condemned man who was asked if he wished a drink: "No, you have taken away wherein to put it, thank God!" Blount asked to be put out of his misery and was beheaded.

Alternatives: * "No, for I do not know where I should put it."
* "*Te Deum laudamus* [God, we praise You!]!" Blessed be the day on which I was born, and blessed be this day, for I shall die in the service of my sovereign lord, the noble King Richard."

Blücher, Gebhard (1742-1819). Prussian field marshal. Blücher figured prominently in Napoleon's defeat at Waterloo. Dying of natural causes four years later, to an aide: "Nostitz, you have learned many a thing from me. Now you are to learn how peacefully a man can die."

Blum, Léon (1872-1950). French prime minister. Suffering what would be a fatal heart attack, Blum said: "It's nothing. Don't worry about me."

Blum, Robert (1807-1848). German politician and revolutionary leader. During the Vienna Uprising of 1848, Blum joined the rebellious forces and was arrested. Before the firing squad, he refused the traditional blindfold: "I want to look death in the eye. I die for freedom. May my country remember me. I am ready. Let there be no mistake and no delay."

Bluntschli, Johann (1808-1881). Swiss politician and jurist. Before dying, Bluntschli paraphrased Luke 2:14:"Glory be to God in the highest. Peace on earth, good will to all men."

Bo Diddley (see Diddley, Bo).

Boas, Franz (1858-1942). German-born American anthropologist and ethnologist. "It isn't necessary to wear oneself out repeating that racism is either a monstrous error or a shameless lie. The Nazis themselves have recently had to appreciate the accuracy of the facts that I have brought together on the European immigrants of America." While in the middle of this speech on racial issues, Boas unexpectedly collapsed and died.

Bocarmé, Hippolyte, Visart de (1818-1851). Belgian nobleman and murderer. Using a nicotine extract, the insolvent Bocarmé poisoned his wealthy brother-in-law for money. He subsequently was sentenced to die by the guillotine: "I trust the blade is sharp."

Boerhaave, Hermann (1668-1738). Dutch physician and philosopher. After a prolonged period of suffering, Boerhaave prayed that God should end his life. Later, he contritely remarked to a friend: "He that loves God ought to think nothing desirable but what is pleasing to the Supreme Goodness."

Bogart, Humphrey (1899-1957). American motion picture actor, best-known for his roles in the films *Casablanca* and *The Maltese Falcon*. Despite an extensive operation and chemotherapy for esophageal cancer, Bogart succumbed to the disease. A widely attributed deathbed statement, "I should never have switched from Scotch to Martinis," probably was not his last, if uttered at all. When his wife, the actress Lauren Bacall, left on an errand, Bogart said: "Goodbye, kid. Hurry back." He lapsed into a coma and died shortly thereafter."

Böhme, Jacob (1575-1624). German mystic, theologian and philosopher. To his son: "Do you hear that beautiful music, my son?" When answered in the negative: "Open the door then, so we can hear it better." Later, when told that the time was two o'clock: "Then my time has not yet come; three hours hence is my time." Around the appointed hour, Böhme said: "Now I go hence into paradise," and died.

Boileau, Nicolas (1636-1711). French critic and poet, best-known for his treatise on rules of composition, *L'Art poétique*. On his deathbed: "It is a great consolation to a poet on the point of death that he has never written a line injurious to good morals."

Alternative: * "It is a great consolation to a poet about to die that he has never written anything injurious to virtue."

Boleyn, Anne (c. 1507-1536). Second wife of English King Henry VIII. Boleyn supposedly was condemned for "treason" by her husband, because she did not give him a male heir. When the Lieutenant of the Tower told her "… that it [the beheading] would be no pain, it was so subtle," Boleyn clasped her throat and exclaimed: "I hear the executioner is very good, and I have a little neck." On the scaffold, she made a short speech to the crowd (one of many versions): "Good Christian people, I am come hither to die, according to law, for by the law I am judged to die, and therefore I will speak nothing against it. I come here only to die, and thus to yield myself humbly to the will of the King, my lord. And if, in my life, I did ever offend the King's Grace, surely with my death I do now atone. I come hither to accuse no man, nor to speak anything of that whereof I am accused, as I know full well that aught I say in my defense doth not appertain to you. I pray and beseech you all, good friends, to pray for the life of the King, my sovereign lord and yours, who is one of the best princes on the face of the earth, who has always treated me so well that better could not be, wherefore I submit to death with good will, humbly asking pardon of all the world. If any person will meddle with my cause, I require them to judge the best. Thus I take my leave of the world, and of you, and I heartily desire you all to pray for me. Oh Lord, have mercy on me! To God I commend my soul." With her neck on the block, Boleyn pleaded: "O God, have pity on my soul. O God, have pity on my soul. O God, have pity...!"

Alternatives: * "The executioner is, I believe, an expert... and my neck is very slender."
* "It is small, very small indeed"

Bolingbroke, Henry St. John (1678-1751). English statesman and political philosopher. To Lord Chesterfield, a British nobleman: "God, who placed me here, will do what He pleases with me hereafter, and He knows best what to do. May He bless you."

Bolivar, Simón (1783-1830). South American liberator and political leader. Because of displeasure with his empire building, Bolivar prepared to leave Columbia for exile in Europe. His life, however, was cut short by complications of tuberculosis. One week before dying he made a farewell proclamation to the Columbian people: "... I have been the victim of my persecutors, who have brought me to the brink of the grave. I forgive them... If my death will help to end factions to consolidate the Union, I shall go to my grave in peace." To his physician during his final days: "The three greatest fools of history have been Jesus Christ, Don Quixote, and... me." As he prepared to depart: "Let's go! Let's go! People in this land do not want me! Come, boys! Take my baggage on board the frigate." Bolivar died before he could leave.

Bolles, Donald (1928-1976). American investigative journalist. Bolles made an arrangement to meet John Adamson, an informant who supposedly would supply incriminating evidence on fraudulent Arizona real estate deals. After a bomb exploded in his car, the mortally-wounded journalist muttered: "They finally got me... the Mafia... Emprise... find John Adamson." Adamson was charged with Bolles murder.

Bolton, Robert (1572-1631). English clergyman and writer. Dying of a "quartan ague [a fever every fourth day]," Bolton responded to a friend who asked if he felt pain: "Truly no. The greatest I feel is your cold hand."

Bonaparte, Elizabeth (1785-1879). American-born wife of Jerome Bonaparte, the youngest brother of Napoleon I (below). On being told nothing was more certain than death, Elizabeth replied: "Except taxes."

Alternative: * "Nothing is so certain as death, except taxes."

Bonaparte, Joséphine (1763-1814). Empress of France and first wife of Napoleon I. Napoleon divorced Josephine to marry the Austrian princess Marie-Louise. Dying of pneumonia, Josephine opined: "I can say with truth to all at my last moments that the first wife of Napoleon never caused a tear to flow." Her final words were: "Bonaparte... Elba... Marie-Louise!"

Alternatives: * "... I may say with truth to all who attend me in my last moments, that never, no, never, did the first wife of Napoleon Bonaparte cause a tear to flow."

* "Napoleon... Elba... Marie-Louise!"
* "Bonaparte... the island of Elba... the King of Rome."

Bonaparte, Letizia Ramolino (1750-1836). Mother of Napoleon I. Speaking of her birthplace: "I leave my heart to Corsica."

Bonaparte, Louis-Napoleon (see Napoleon III).

Bonaparte, Mathilde (1820-1904). French princess who was the niece of Napoleon I. Dying on the anniversary of one of her uncle's greatest victories, Mathilde said as she gazed at the sky: "Ah, it is the sun of Austerlitz."

Bonaparte, Napoleon (see Napoleon I).

Bonaparte, Napoleon Eugène (see Napoleon IV).

Bonaparte, Napoleon François (see Napoleon II).

Bonaparte, Pauline (1780-1825). Corsican-born princess who was a sister of Napoleon I. Succumbing to cancer, Pauline looked in a mirror and said: "She may be dying, but she was always beautiful."

Alternative: * "I always was beautiful."

Bonchamps, Charles-Melchior (1760-1793). French politician. Bonchamps led a group of Royalists in an insurrection against Republican forces during the French Revolution. Mortally wounded at the Battle of Cholet in northwestern France, Bonchamps called for the release of captured Republican forces: "Pardon for the prisoners, Bonchamp[s] commands it." This demand saved the lives of many prisoners.

Bonhoeffer, Dietrich (1906-1945). German theologian, hanged for his dissident anti-Nazi activities and alleged involvement in an attempted assassination of Adolf Hitler: "This is the end. For me, the beginning of life."

Boniface, Saint (c. 680-754). English martyr and missionary to Frisia. In this southeastern coastal region of the North Sea, Boniface "destroyed the divinity of the heathen temples... and built churches with great zeal."

Attacked by hostile Frisians, Boniface refused to defend himself. To his comrades: "Stop fighting, lads! Give up the battle! For we are taught by the trusty witness of Scripture, that we render not evil for evil, but contrariwise good for evil. Already the long desired day is at hand, and the voluntary time of our departure is near... Endure firmly here the sudden moment of death that ye may be able to reign with Christ for all time." As he died: "I thank Thee Lord Jesus, Son of the living God." Fifty-three lost their lives in the encounter.

Alternatives: * "Cease, my children, from strife. The Holy Scripture commands us to return good for evil. This is the day I have long desired, and the hour of our deliverance is at hand. Strengthen yourselves in the Lord, put your hope in Him, and He will speedily grant unto you an eternal reward in His heavenly kingdom."

* "My children, cease your resistance; the long-expected day is come at last. Scripture forbids us to resist evil. Let us put our hope in God: He will save our souls."

Bonin, William "The Freeway Killer" (1947-1996). American serial killer, executed by lethal injection in California's San Quentin Prison. His final note: "... I would suggest that when a person has a thought of doing anything serious against the law, that before they did, that they should go to a quiet place and think about it seriously."

Bonnet, Charles (1720-1793). Swiss naturalist and philosopher. When Bonnet told his wife that he suspected a servant of stealing some of his papers, she humored him, saying she would have the man admit his guilt. He replied: "So he repents? Let him come and all will be overlooked."

Bonney, William (see Billy the Kid).

Bonnot, Jules (1876-1912). French anarchist and murderer. After a series of robberies, Bonnot killed a policeman during a shootout. He was traced to a building where he wrote: "I am a famous man. My name has been trumpeted to the four corners of the globe... I believe it useful to submit these few lines... Should I regret what I have done? Yes, perhaps, but I will carry on... Jules Bonnot." He was killed in the ensuing raid.

Boone, Daniel (1734-1820). American frontiersman and explorer. Dying of natural causes, to his family: "Do not grieve. I have lived to a good old age and am going to a world of happiness. I am going. My time has come."

Booth, Catherine (1829-1890). British-born temperance activist and wife of William Booth (below), founder of the Salvation Army. Dying of breast cancer, Catherine remarked: "The waters are rising, but so am I. I am not going under but over. Do not be concerned about dying; go on living well, the dying will be right." To her husband: "Pa."

Booth, Edwin (1833-1893). American actor, brother of the assassin John Wilkes Booth (below). To his grandson who asked how he was doing: "How are you yourself, old fellow?"

Booth, John Wilkes (1838-1865). American actor who assassinated Abraham Lincoln. After Booth shot President Lincoln in Ford's Theatre, Washington, D.C., he was tracked to a tobacco barn in nearby Virginia. When told that the barn would be set ablaze if he did not surrender, Booth said to his pursuers: "Well, my brave boys, you can prepare a stretcher for me… Captain, make quick work of it; shoot me through the heart." After being mortally wounded, he uttered his last words: "Tell my mother I died for my country. I did what I thought was for the best." As he looked at his hands: "Useless . . . useless..."

Alternative: * As Booth lay dying: "Kill me! Kill me!"

Booth, Junius Brutus (1796-1852). British-born actor and father of Edwin and John Wilkes Booth. When Booth collapsed on a steamboat near Cincinnati, Ohio, he said to those trying to help: "Pray! Pray! Pray!"

Booth, William (1829-1912). English evangelist and founder of the Salvation Army. During his last days, Booth admonished his son to help care for the homeless: "Mind you, if you don't, I'll come back and haunt you!" His last words, again, to his son and successor: "I'm leaving you a bonnie handful. Railton [Booth's second in command] will be with you."

Boothby, Robert (1900-1986). British politician and writer. Dying of a heart attack, to his wife: "I love you so much; look after the dogs."

Borgia, Cesare (c 1475-1507). Italian nobleman, statesman, mercenary and brother of Lucrezia Borgia (below). During the Siege of Viana, about 150 miles northeast of Madrid, Spain, Borgia was killed by a spear: "I had provided in the course of my life, for everything except death. And now, alas, I am to die, though entirely unprepared."

Alternative: * "I have taken care of everything in the course of my life, only not for death, and now I have to die completely unprepared."

Borgia, Lucrezia, also Lucretia (1480-1519). Italian political schemer and illegitimate daughter (some say niece) of Rodrigo Borgia who became Pope Alexander VI. Dying from complications of childbirth, a last letter to Pope Leo X (below): "Most Holy Father and Honored Master. With all respect I kiss your Holiness' feet and commend myself in all humility to your holy mercy. Having suffered for more than two months, early on the morning of the 14th of the present, as it pleased God, I gave birth to a daughter and hoped then to find relief from my sufferings. But I did not and shall be compelled to pay my debt to nature. So great is the favor which our merciful Creator has shown me, that I approach the end of my life with pleasure, knowing that in a few hours, after receiving for the last time all the holy sacraments of the church, I shall be released. Having arrived at this moment, I desire as a Christian, although I am a sinner, to ask your Holiness, in your mercy, to give me all possible spiritual consolation and your Holiness's blessing for my soul. Therefore I offer myself to you in all humility and commend my husband and my children, all of whom are your servants, to your Holiness's mercy. In Ferrara, June 22, 1519, at the fourteenth hour. Your Holiness's humble servant, Lucretia D'Este"

Boris Godunov (c. 1551-1605). Russian czar, noted for his social and educational reforms. Dying of a stroke: "I leave Russia to God's will and to the council."

Börne, Ludwig (1786-1837). German satirist and political writer. "Pull back the drapes! I'd gladly see the sun! Flowers! Music!"

Bosco, Saint John (1815-1888). Italian Roman Catholic priest and educator. Fearing an inability to bestow his blessings on visitors, Bosco implored a fellow priest: "When I can no longer speak and someone comes to ask my blessings, lift up my hands and make it with the sign of the cross. I will make the intention. Jesus, Mary and Joseph, I give you my heart and soul!"

Bossuet, Jacques-Bénigne (1627-1704). French bishop and writer. Dying from complications of chronic kidney stones: "May the will of God with regard to me be done. I feel my insignificance... I feel the machine is worn out. Let us pray but little at a time, on account of the great pain I suffer." When his fellow clergymen praised him, Bossuet admonished them: "Cease such discourse. Speak of pardon alone, the only word that man ought to use." Toward the end: "Lord, I suffer grievously, but I am not confounded, for I know in Whom to trust. Thy will be done."

Alternative: * "I suffer the violence of pain and death, but I know whom I have believed."

Bottomley, Horatio (1860-1933). Expelled member of the English Parliament and swindler. Because he participated in a financial scheme to defraud investors, Bottomley was sentenced to jail for seven years. Dying in poverty: "Nurse, I want some milk. I must have milk. I will have milk."

Alternative: * "Goodbye and God bless you. I'll see you again tomorrow."

Bouhours, Dominique (1628-1702). French grammarian, essayist and priest. "I am about to- or I am going to- die: either expression is correct."

Alternative: * "'Tis or I am going to die; one of these expressions is used."

Boulanger, Lili (1893-1918). French composer who was the first woman to win the prestigious *Prix de Rome* competition. Dying possibly of Crohn's disease: "I offer to God my sufferings so that they may shower down on you as joys."

Boulanger, Nadia (1887-1979). French composer, musical pedagogue and older sister of Lili Boulanger (above). When the composer and conductor Leonard Bernstein visited Boulanger near the end, he asked what music was playing in her head. She replied: "A music with neither beginning nor end." She lapsed into a coma and died a month later.

Bourbon, Louis de (1438-1482). Prince-Bishop of Liège, Belgium. Bourbon was assassinated on the order of the adventurer William de la Marck-Arenberg, who wished to place his son in the bishopric: "Mercy, Lord of Arenberg. I am your prisoner."

Bourg, Anne du (1521-1559). Martyred French magistrate. Accused of defending Calvinism, du Bourg was branded a heretic and condemned to die by hanging. Before his execution, he declared: "Six feet of earth for my body, and the infinite heavens for my soul, is what I shall soon have" At the gallows: "My friends, I am not here as a thief or a murderer, but for the sake of the gospel." Before hanging: "My God, forsake me not, that I may not forsake Thee."

Bourg, Edme-Théodore (1785-1852). French man of letters. Bourg's suicide note to his children read. "At four o'clock or at 4:15 I will carry out my design, if everything goes right. I am not afraid of death, since I am seeking it, since I desire it! But prolonged suffering would be frightful. I walk; all ideas vanish. I think only of my children. The fire is dying out. What a silence all around! Four o'clock. I hear the chimes. Soon comes the moment of sacrifice. I put my snuff box in my desk drawer. Goodbye my dearest daughters! God will pardon my sorrows. I put my spectacles in the drawer. Goodbye, once more, goodbye, my darling children! My last thought is yours, for you are the last flutterings of my heart."

Bowditch, Henry (1808-1892). American physician and abolitionist who was the son of Nathaniel Bowditch (below). When asked if he were in pain, Bowditch replied: "No, dear... wish that the end would come."

Bowditch, Nathaniel (1773-1838). American mathematician and astronomer. After accepting a drink of water: "How delicious! I have swallowed a drop- a drop from 'Siloa's brook that flowed fast by the oracle of God! [from John Milton's *Paradise Lost*]'" Later, he blessed his children and addressed a son: "My dear, it is coming! I am ready."

Alternative: "Good-bye, my son; my work is done; and if I knew I were to be gone when the sun sets in the West, I would say, Thy will, O God, be done. '... So live that, sinking in thy last long sleep, calm thou mayst smile, while all around thee weep [from Sir William Jones' Persian translation].'"

Bowdre, Charlie (1848-1880). American outlaw who was a member of Billy the Kid's gang. Cornered by Sheriff Pat Garrett (below) and his posse in a dilapidated house in Stinking Springs, New Mexico, Bowdre was shot dead: "I wish- I wish- I wish. I'm dying."

Bowen, Joshua (1849-1878). American criminal. Bowen was convicted of murdering a local gang member he thought was an informant. Before his hanging, Bowen asked an older man in the crowd: "Do you believe I killed your son, Brother?" When answered in the affirmative, the condemned man allowed: "You believe a doggone lie! I didn't do it! It was my blasted brother-in-law, John Wesley Hardin." Regardless, the trap was duly opened.

Bowles, Samuel (1826-1878). American journalist and publisher. To his nurse: "You may be sure that in another world there will always be one soul praying for you."

Boyer, John (1845-1871). French Sioux Native American criminal. Boyer was hanged for the murder of two men suspected of raping his mother and sister: "Look at me! I no cry; I no woman; I man. I die brave!"

Bozzaris, Marcos (c. 1788-1823). Greek patriot who was killed during the defeat of the Turks at Karpinisi in south central Greece: "O, to die for Liberty is a pleasure, not a pain."

Braddock, Edward (1695-1755). British soldier who led an ill-fated military unit in the French and Indian War. Mortally wounded by French and Native American troops near modern-day Pittsburg, Pennsylvania, Bradford exclaimed: "Is it possible? All is over." Hoping that he would live to fight again: "We shall know better how to deal with them the next time." As Bradford died: "Who would have thought it?"

Bradford, Andrew (1686-1742). American colonial publisher who printed the first newspaper in Philadelphia, Pennsylvania. "Oh Lord, forgive the errata!"

Alternative: * "Oh Lord, forgive the misprints!"

Bradford, John (1510-1555). Martyred English reformer. When the Catholic Queen Mary I came to power, Bradford, a member of the Church of England, was arrested, convicted of heresy and condemned to burn at the stake. As the flames were stoked, he quoted Matthew 7:14: "Strait is the way, and narrow is the gate, that leadeth to salvation, and few there be that find it." Bradford then turned to a similarly-convicted man tied to the stake with him and said: "Be of good comfort, brother, for we shall have a merry supper with the Lord this night. If there be any way to heaven on horseback or in fiery chariots, this is it."

Alternatives: * "Strait is the gate, and narrow is the way, that leadeth to eternal salvation, and few there be that find it."

* "Strait is the gate, and narrow is the way, that leadeth unto life, and few there be that find it. And now, O Lord Jesus, receive my spirit"

Bradford, William (1590-1657). English-born governor of the Plymouth Colony, Massachusetts. Shortly before he died, Bradford proclaimed: "The good Spirit of God has given me a pledge of my happiness in another world and the first fruits of eternal glory."

Brady, Hugh (1768-1851). American military officer who served in the Northwest Indian War and War of 1812. Severely injured in a carriage accident, Brady spoke to his minister when told he would not survive: "Mr. Duffield, let the drum beat; my knapsack is slung; I am ready to die."

Brady, James "Diamond Jim" (1856-1917). American tycoon and philanthropist. Noted for his lavish lifestyle and large collection of diamonds, Brady made this parting comment to his physician: "Someday, doctor, you'll understand how much I appreciate your interest in me."

Bragg, Robert (died 1977). American first officer on Pan Am Flight 1736. The American aircraft was struck by a KLM 747 jet attempting to take-off on a fog-shrouded Canary Island runway with the loss of 583 lives. Recorded cockpit conversation moments before the Boeing 747 jumbo jets collided (see also Veldhuyzen van Zanten, Jacob): Victor Grubbs, the Pan Am captain, exclaimed about the approaching KLM aircraft: "There he is... look at him! G******, that son of a b**** is coming! Bragg then shouted: "Get off! Get off! Get off!" moments before the sound of the crash was recorded.

Brahe, Tycho (1546-1601). Danish nobleman, astronomer and colleague of fellow astronomer Johannes Kepler (below). In a delirium: "Let me not seem to have lived in vain."

Brahms, Johannes (1833-1897). German-born composer and pianist. As Brahms lay dying of pancreatic cancer, one of his physicians gave an injection of morphine to relieve his abdominal pain. When the analgesic wore off, the composer was offered a glass of Rhine wine. In response to this act of kindness, Brahms said: "Ah, that was good." He expired several hours later.

Alternatives: * "Thanks, thanks."
* "Oh, that tasted fine. You're a kind man."
* "Ah, that tastes nice. Thank you."
* "That was good. You are a kind man."

Brainerd, David (1718-1747). American missionary to Native Americans in New York, New Jersey and Pennsylvania. Suffering from the ravages of tuberculosis, Brainerd tried to convey the extent of "bodily pain and anguish" associated with death: "It is another thing to die than people have imagined." Hoping that death would come: "I am almost in eternity. I long to be there. My work is done. I have done with all my friends. All the world is nothing to me. I long to be in heaven, praying and glorifying God with the holy angels. All my desire is to glorify God."

Alternative: * "Oh! Why is the chariot so long in coming? Why tarry the wheels of his chariot? Come, Lord Jesus; come, quickly!"

Bramblett, Earl (1942-2003). American criminal, electrocuted for the murder of four members of a Virginia family: "I didn't murder the Hodges family. I've never murdered anybody. I'm going to my death with a clear conscience. I am going to my death having had a great life because of my two great sons, Mike and Doug."

Branch, Elizabeth (1672-1740). English murderer. Elizabeth and her daughter Mary had a history of cruelty to their servants. When a serving maid tarried on an errand, the mother and daughter beat her to death. Before her hanging, Elizabeth delivered a lengthy discourse recounting her regrets, culminating thusly: "...I declare I had no design of killing the deceased, as the Lord is my judge, and before whom I must shortly appear. I beg of you to pray for me unto God that my sins may be forgiven me, and that I may be received to mercy."

Branch, Mary (c. 1716-1740). English murderer. Mary and her mother Elizabeth (above) viciously murdered a serving maid. Before her hanging: "Good people, pity my unhappy case, who, while young, was trained up in the paths of cruelty and barbarity; and let all present take warning by my unhappy end, so as to avoid the like crimes. You see I am cut off in the prime of life, in the midst of my days. Good people, pray for me."

Brandsma, Titus (1881-1942). Dutch clergyman, imprisoned and executed by the Nazis for his opposition to the printing of their propaganda. Near death, Brandsma gave his rosary to a nurse who said: "But I can no longer pray." He responded: "Well if you can't say the first part, surely you can still say 'Pray for us sinners.'" She then administered a lethal injection to the priest.

Brandt, Karl (1904-1948). German physician and administrator of the Nazi euthanasia program during WWII. Condemned for his war crimes during the Nuremburg Trials, Brandt was sentenced to be hanged: "It is no shame to stand on this scaffold. I served my fatherland as others before me."

Brant, Joseph (1742-1807). Native American Mohawk leader. To his adopted nephew: "Have pity on the poor Indians. If you can get any influence with the great, endeavor to do them all the good you can."

Brasidas (died 422 BCE). Spartan general, mortally wounded during the Peloponnesian War. "These men [Athenians] do not mean to face us. See how their heads and spears are shaking. Such behavior always shows that an army is going to run away. Open me the gates as I ordered and let us boldly attack them at once." The Spartans succeeded in defeating the superior Athenian force.

Brecht, Bertolt (1898-1956). German writer, poet and playwright. Brecht's ever-popular *The Threepenny Opera* was produced in collaboration with the composer Kurt Weill. Speaking about his 58th birthday: "At least one knows that death will be easy. A slight knock at the windowpane, then..." While receiving intensive treatment for complications of a heart attack at age 58: "Leave me in peace."

Breitinger, Johann (1701-1776). Swiss philologist and writer. Dying of a stroke: "Whether we live or die, we are the Lord's."

Bremer, Fredrika (1801-1865). Finnish-born Swedish writer and women's rights activist. Dying of a respiratory infection, Bremer repeated: "Light, eternal light!" At the end, to her nurse: "Ah, my child, let us speak of Christ's love- the best, the highest love."

Brereton, William (died 1536). Groom of the Privy Chamber of English King Henry VIII. Embroiled in the conspiracy to condemn Anne Boleyn (above), Brereton unjustly was sentenced to die by beheading. "I have deserved to die, if it were one thousand deaths." When prompted to place his head on the block: "But the cause wherefore I die, judge ye not. If ye judge, judge the best."

Brewster, David (1781-1868). Scottish physicist who invented the kaleidoscope. Dying of pneumonia: "I shall see Jesus, and that will be grand. I shall see him who made the worlds." At the end: "I have had the Light for many years, and oh! How bright it is! I feel so safe, so satisfied."

Alternative: * "I shall see Jesus who created all things. Jesus who made the worlds. I shall see Him as He is... I shall see Jesus and that will be grand..."

Bridgman, Laura (1829-1889). At age two years, the New Hampshire-born Bridgman developed a case of scarlet fever that left her blind, deaf and mute. Despite these disabilities, she was able to secure an education through the diligence of her family and a school for the blind. Dying of pneumonia, she traced the letters "M-O-T-H" in a friend's hand. When queried if she meant "mother," Bridgman nodded her head twice and died shortly thereafter.

Briggs, George (1796-1861). Member of the U.S. House of Representatives and staunch opponent of slavery. As he lay dying from an accidental gunshot wound, Briggs spoke to his son who had re-entered the room: "It will come- pretty soon. You won't leave me again, will you?"

Brillat-Savarin, Paulette (fl. late 18th-early 19th century). Dying short of her 100th birthday, the sister of the French epicure Anthelme Brillat-Savarin exclaimed: "Quick! Serve the dessert! I think I am dying."

Brindley, James (1716-1772). English engineer who specialized in canal building. To his workers constructing a canal that was not progressing satisfactorily: "Then puddle it, puddle it, and puddle it again." Puddle is a watertight material used in the construction of canals. After having his lips wetted: "It's enough. I shall need no more."

Brisbane, Albert (1809-1890). American writer and supporter of the utopian movement. To his wife: "*Mon amie*, turn me over... towards you."

Brisbane, Arthur (1864-1936). American journalist and son of Albert Brisbane (above). Perhaps paraphrasing the German polymath Gottfried

Leibniz's sentiment coined in a 1710 essay: "This is the best of all possible worlds."

Briscoe, Joe (died 1876). Irish-born American buffalo hunter. Briscoe was mortally wounded in a campfire fight with fellow hunter Pat Garrett (below). Before dying, he asked Garrett: "Won't you come over here and forgive me?"

Brochu, Emy (died 2012). Canadian woman, killed while texting and driving. A last text message to her boyfriend Mathieu Fortin before fatally crashing her car into a merging truck: "I love you too and I'll try to make you happy Mr Fort..."

Brock, Kenneth (died 1986). American criminal, executed for the murder of a convenience store worker: "I have no last words. I am ready."

Brocklesby, Richard (1722-1797). English physician. To his attendants who were helping him undress for bed: "What an idle piece of ceremony this buttoning and unbuttoning is to me now."

Broderick, David (1820-1859). American abolitionist and U.S. senator. Broderick and former California Chief Justice David Terry fought a duel over inflammatory statements made about slavery and election issues. Before succumbing to his wound, Broderick said: "I die! Protect my honor!"

Alternative: * To Colonel E.D. Baker, a U.S. senator: "Baker, when I was struck, I tried to stand firm, but the blow blinded me and I could not."

Brontë, Anne (1820-1849). English writer and poet who was the sister of Charlotte, Emily and Branwell Brontë. Dying of tuberculosis, a friend inquired if Anne were comfortable. "It is not you who can give me ease, but soon all will be well, through the merits of our Redeemer." To her only surviving sister: "Take courage, Charlotte, take courage!"

Brontë, Charlotte (1816-1855). English poet and writer, best-known for her novel *Jane Eyre.* Dying from complications of pregnancy, Charlotte awoke from a coma to the sound of her husband, the Rev. Arthur Nicholls, praying nearby. She responded: "Oh, I'm not going to die, am I? He will not separate us. We have been so happy."

Brontë, Emily (1818-1848). English poet and writer, best-known for her novel *Wuthering Heights*. Ill with tuberculosis, Emily steadfastly refused a physician's care. However, in her death throes, she told her sisters: "If you will send for a doctor, I will see him now." To a sister who wanted to put her to bed: "No, no!" Emily died sitting on a couch.

Brontë, Maria (1783-1821). English mother of the Brontë family. Dying of cancer: "Oh, God! My poor children."

Brontë, Patrick (1777-1861). Irish-born Anglican rector and writer who was the patriarch of the Brontë clan. Patrick managed to outlive his wife, daughters and son. "While there is life, there is will."

Brontë, Patrick Branwell (1817-1848). English painter, writer and brother of the Brontë sisters. Dying of tuberculosis, Patrick managed to whisper "Amen" as prayers for the dying concluded.

Brooke, Gustavus (1818-1866). Irish actor who performed in the British Isles and Australia. Before drowning in a shipwrecked vessel bound for Australia, Brooke refused to enter the overcrowded lifeboats: "No, no! Goodbye. Should you survive, give my last farewell to the people of Melbourne."

Brooke, Stopford (1832-1916). Irish-born biographer and clergyman. As he left his study for the last time: "It will be a pity to leave all that."

Brookings, Robert (1850-1932). American businessman, philanthropist and founder of the think tank, the Brookings Institution. "I have done everything I wanted to do. This is the end."

Brooks, Elbridge (1816-1878). American clergyman. When asked how he felt: "My head is pillowed upon the bosom of the dear God." To a colleague before he died: "Thanks be to God, who giveth us the victory."

Brooks, Gordon (died 1979). Flight engineer on Air New Zealand's DC 10 that crashed into Mt. Erebus in Antarctica killing all 257 on board. Brooks spoke before the Ground Proximity Warning System alarmed: "I don't like this." When the warning device sounded, the engineer reported: "Five hundred feet...four hundred feet," immediately before the crash.

Brooks, Phillips (1835-1893). American Episcopal bishop and writer of the hymn "O Little Town of Bethlehem." As death approached, Brooks mused: "There is no other life but the eternal." In a confused state before he died: "Take me home. I must go home."

Alternative: * To his housekeeper: "Katie, you may go. I shall not need you anymore. I am going home."

Broughton, William (1788-1853). English-born Australian bishop. "Let the earth be filled with His glory."

Broun, Heywood (1888-1939). American journalist and newspaper editor. Dying of pneumonia, Broun told his wife: "I've been pretty sick, Connie, but now I'm going to be all right."

Brown, Abel (1810-1844). American clergyman and abolitionist who helped slaves gain freedom through the Underground Railroad. Dying in a delirious state, Brown felt that he was surrounded by a mob: "Must I be sacrificed? Let me alone, every one of you!"

Brown, James (1933-2006). American soul singer and songwriter, often called "The Godfather of Soul." Dying from complications of pneumonia: "I'm going away tonight…" Brown took several deep breaths and died quietly.

Alternative: * "I don't think I'll be going with you"

Brown, John (1800-1859). Militant American abolitionist. On October 16, 1859, Brown led a raid on the Harpers Ferry Armory, West Virginia in an attempt to arm slaves and foment a rebellion against slavery. He was captured during the abortive siege and sentenced to die. On his execution day, he wrote: "I, John Brown, am now quite certain that the crimes of this guilty land will never be purged away but with blood. I had, as I now think, vainly flattered myself that without very much bloodshed it might be done." On the scaffold, Brown was asked if he would like a signal before the trap was sprung. His reply: "No. I am ready at any time, but do not keep me needlessly waiting."

Alternative: * "No, but don't keep me waiting longer than necessary."

Brown, John, Jr. (died 1997). American criminal, executed by lethal injection for a murder committed during a robbery. At the end, Brown said: "Let my baby sister know I love her and the rest of my family, for supporting me. I love you very much. I'm ready to go now." As the drugs took effect, he exclaimed: "Wow."

Brown, Karla Faye (1959-1998). American criminal, executed by lethal injection for her part in two murders committed during a 1983 robbery. Brown's last words reflected her jailhouse conversion to Christianity: "Yes sir, I would like to say to all of you, the Thornton family and Jerry Dean's family, that I am so sorry. I hope God will give you peace with this. Baby, I love you. Ron, give Peggy a hug for me. Everybody has been so good to me. I love all of you very much. I am going to be face to face with Jesus now. Warden Baggett, thank all of you so much. You have been so good to me. I love all of you very much. I will see you all when you get there. I will wait for you."

Brown, Moses (1742-1804). American naval officer who captained the ironclad *Merrimac* at the turn of the nineteenth century. Later, while guiding a merchant ship back to the U.S., Brown suffered a stroke. In sight of the coast, he asked to be carried on deck for a last look at his homeland: "I have seen enough. Carry me below." He died an hour later.

Brown, Owen (1824-1889). American abolitionist who was the son of John Brown (above). Brown participated in the Raid at Harpers Ferry but managed to escape his pursuers. Dying of "typhoid pneumonia" three decades later: "It is better to be in a place and suffer wrong than to do wrong."

Brown, Reece (died 1856). American abolitionist. During the Kansas-Missouri discord over slavery, a group of proslavery activists hacked the Free State settler to death. To his wife, as he died: "They murdered me like cowards."

Browne, John (died1511). English martyr who lived during the reign of King Henry VIII. At his trial for heresy, Browne's feet were burned to the bones to secure a confession of his errors. He refused crying: "... If I should deny my Lord in this world, He would hereafter deny me..." The next day at the stake: "O Lord, I yield me to Thy grace. Grant me mercy for my trespass. Let never the fiend my soul chase. Lord, I will bow, and Thou shalt beat, let never my soul come in hell-heat. Into Thy hands I commend my spirit. Thou hast redeemed me, O Lord of Truth!"

Browning, Elizabeth (1806-1861). English poet and wife of Robert Browning (below). Dying of a painful respiratory ailment, to her husband who had asked how she was: "Beautiful."

Alternative: * "It is beautiful."

Browning, Robert (1812-1889). English poet. Browning responded to a good review of a volume of his poetry *Asolando*: "How gratifying!" To his son: "I'm dying dear boy, my dear boy."

Brownson, Nathan (1742-1796). American physician and politician who was a delegate to the Continental Congress from 1776-8. Brownson's final statement: "The scene is now closing; the business of life is nearly over. I have, like the rest of my fellow-creatures, been guilty of foibles, but I trust to the mercy of my God to pardon them, and to his justice to reward my good deeds."

Brownson, Orestes (1803-1876). American clergyman and philosopher. Brownson became frustrated that he could not make his son understand his point in an argument. When his daughter-in-law knocked to deliver the evening meal, he said: "If that is Henry, I'm too tired to make it plainer tonight." He lost consciousness and died several days later.

Bruce, David (1855-1931). Australian-born British physician. Bruce, with the help of his wife, pioneered the understanding and treatment of numerous tropical diseases: "If any notice is taken of my scientific work when I am gone, I should like it to be known that Mary is entitled to as much credit as I am." The couple died within days of each other.

Bruce, Lenny, born Leonard Alfred Schneider (1925-1966). American comedian and social critic. Before dying of a drug overdose, Bruce allegedly asked: "Do you know where I can get any s*** [narcotics]?"

Bruce, Robert (1554-1631). Scottish clergyman and theologian. Becoming ill during breakfast, Bruce realized the gravity of his situation: "Now, God be with you, my dear children; I have break-fasted with you, and shall sup with my Lord Jesus Christ this night." Bruce died shortly thereafter.

Bruch, Max (1838-1920). German composer and conductor, best-known for his works for cello and violin. To his daughter: "Can I not go to my home once again by flying there in a zeppelin?"

Brueys, François-Paul (1753-1798). French naval commander. Brueys was mortally wounded during the Battle of the Nile against the English fleet led by Horatio Nelson (below): "An admiral ought to die giving orders."

Brummell, George "Beau" (1778-1840). English men's fashion maven. Penniless and insane from the effects of advanced syphilis at the time of his demise, Brummell was told that he should pray. His reply: "I do try."

Brune, Guillaume (1763-1815). One of Napoleon's generals who was murdered by a royalist mob during the Second White Terror in 1815: "Good God! To survive a hundred fields and die like this..."

Alternative: * "To live through a hundred battles, and to die hanging from a lantern in Provence!"

Brunerie, Guillaume, Dode de la (1775-1851). French general. Brunerie characterized his last illness as "the enemy:" "The doctors still assess that the enemy is retreating. I believe, on the contrary, that we are, as it were, on the eve of a battle. God knows what tomorrow will bring."

Bruno, Giordano di (1548-1600). Italian philosopher and martyr, accused of heresy by the Inquisition. Concerning his denunciation, Bruno asserted: "You are more afraid to pronounce my sentence than I am to receive it." Asked to kiss a crucifix as he was burned at the stake, the martyr refused saying: "I die a martyr and willingly my soul shall mount up to heaven in this chariot of smoke."

Alternatives: * "Perhaps this sentence gives you more alarm than it gives to me."
* "I die a martyr and willingly. My soul shall mount up with the smoke to paradise!"

Brutus, Marcus (85-42 BCE) Roman senator and co-conspirator in Julius Caesar's assassination. Two years after the death of Caesar, Brutus' legions were defeated by Marcus Antonius at the Battle of Philippi. Escaping the battlefield: "Yes, indeed, we must fly but not with our feet, but with our hands." He then committed suicide by falling on his sword, crying: "Oh wretched valor thou wert but a name, and yet I worshipped thee as real indeed. But now it seems thou wert but fortune's slave."

Alternative: * "We must indeed flee, but it shall be with our hands."

Bryan, William Jennings (1860-1925). American politician, statesman, anti-evolution activist and prosecution witness in the 1925 Tennessee Scopes "Monkey Trial." Dying from complications of diabetes, to his son: "Seems there's hardly time for resting... none at all for dying."

Bryant, Charles "Black-Faced Charlie" (died 1891). American outlaw. In Bryant's youth, a gun was fired near his face, resulting in a permanent black stippling of the skin. He later joined the Dalton outlaw gang and participated in numerous robberies and murders. He eventually was captured and died in a shoot-out while being transported to a federal court in Wichita, Kansas. Bryant's last request: "I can't die with my boots on! Please pull them off."

Bryant, William (1794-1878). American poet and magazine editor. After stumbling and striking his head on the sidewalk, Bryant appeared dazed: "Whose house is this? What street is this? Would you like to see Miss Fairchild [his niece]?"

Alternative: * "Whose house is this? What street are we in? Why did you bring me here?"

Brynner, Yul (1920-1985). Russian-born American actor, best-known for his appearance in the movies, *The Ten Commandments* and *The King and I.* Dying of lung cancer related to his tobacco abuse, Brynner spoke to his son who had stopped smoking: "About time!"

Buber, Martin (1878-1965). Austrian-born Jewish philosopher. "I am not afraid of death, but of dying."

Buchalter, Louis "Lepke" (1897-1944) Convicted American murderer who headed the Murder, Inc. organization. Electrocuted in New York's Sing Sing prison, Buchalter was one of the highest ranking members of organized crime to be executed. "All I want to say is I'm innocent and I'm here on a framed-up charge. Give my love to my family and everything."

Buchanan, George (1506-1582). Scottish scholar, historian and writer who was a tutor of King James VI. Summoned by the king to appear in court for an objectionable comment he had made, the ailing Buchanan dispatched a reply: "Before the days mentioned by your Majesty shall be expired, I shall be in that place where few kings enter!" James allegedly wept when he received the message. Near death, Buchanan expressed his lack of interest for his mortal remains: "It matters little to me, for if I am once dead, they may bury me or not bury me as they please. They may leave my corpse to rot where I die if they wish." Buchanan was interred in Greyfriars Kirkyard, Edinburg, Scotland.

Alternative: * "Tell the people who sent you that I am summoned to a higher tribunal."

Buchanan, Robert (1841-1901). English poet and writer. An avid bicycle rider, Buchanan suggested to his daughter: "I should like to have a good spin down Regent Street." He suffered a stroke moments after speaking and remained mute until his death eight months later.

Büchner, Georg (1813-1837). German dramatist, writer and poet. Dying of typhus: "We have not too much pain; we have too little, for through pain we enter into God! We are death, dust, ashes. What right have we to complain?"

Buck, Pearl (1892-1973). American author, best-known for her novel *The Good Earth.* Buck's literary endeavors earned her a 1932 Pulitzer Prize and the 1938 Nobel Prize in Literature. Dying of lung cancer, her final words reflected her early years spent in China: "Look at me. Look at the way I'm living here. There are children hungry and crying in China, and I have all this here. This isn't what I want."

Buckland, Francis (1826-1880). British surgeon, scientist and inspector of fisheries. Dying of pulmonary bleeding: "I am going on a long journey. I shall see many strange animals on the way. God is so good, so good to the little fishes, I do not believe He would let their inspector suffer shipwreck at last."

Buddha, Siddhartha Gautama (c. 563-c. 483 BCE). Nepalese-born (some say Indian) spiritual teacher who laid the foundation for Buddhism. "... Behold now, brethren, I exhort you, saying 'decay is inherent in all component things, but the truth will remain forever!! Work out your salvation with diligence.'"

Alternatives: * "Never forget it; decay is inherent in all things."

* "Beloved, that which causes life, causes also decay and death. Never forget this; let your minds be filled with this truth. I called you to make it known to you."
* "Impermanent are all created things; strive on with awareness."
* "Beloved Bickus [his followers], the principle of existence, and mutability carries with it the principle of destruction. Never forget

this; let your minds be filled with this truth; to make it known to you I have assembled you."

* "All compound things are subject to breaking up. Strive on with mindfulness."

Budgell, Eustace (1686-1737). English writer and politician. After losing his fortune on poorly conceived investments, Budgell decided to end his life by drowning. He filled his pockets with stones and hired a boatman to take him onto the Thames River. After his death, a note was found which read: "What Cato did, and Addison approved, cannot be wrong." Cato, an adversary of Caesar, committed suicide (see Cato, Marcus Porcius). The writer, Joseph Addison (above), was Budgell's cousin.

Buffalo Bill (see Cody, William).

Bugeaud, Robert, Marquis de la Piconnerie (1784-1849). French general and later governor-general of Algeria. Dying of cholera: "It is all over with me."

Bull, Ole (1810-1880). Norwegian violinist and composer. Dying of cancer, to his second wife Sara: "Please play Mozart's *Requiem*." Fryderyk Chopin (below) made a similar request for his own funeral.

Bullard, Eugene (1894-1961). American-born military aviator. Bullard was the first African American to fly a combat aircraft. He flew 20 sorties during WWI while a member of the French air corps. Dying of abdominal cancer, to a friend: "Don't fret honey, it's easy."

Bumby, John (1808-1840). English missionary to New Zealand. Bumby drowned in a frigid river when his canoe overturned. As he clung to the vessel: "O dear, dear, dear me! We are dead."

Bundy, Theodore "Ted" (1946-1989). Convicted American serial killer. Before his execution by electrocution in the Florida State Prison: "... I'd like you to give my love to my family and friends."

Bunker, Chang and Eng (1811-1874). Thai-born Siamese twins, conjoined at the sternum and upper abdomen. The Bunker brothers spent most of their lives touring as medical curiosities. Dying of suspected pneumonia, Chang complained of chest pain and said: "[My] breathing was so bad that it would kill me to lie down." Nevertheless, Eng persuaded his twin to recline and they both drifted off to sleep. When Eng awoke and found his brother dead, he said to his children: "I must go also. My last hour is come. Move Chang nearer to me. Straighten his limbs. May God have mercy on my soul." Before a surgeon could attempt to separate the twins, Eng also expired.

Bunsen, Christian von (1791-1860). Prussian diplomat and theologian. During his terminal illness, to his wife: "Love, love- we have loved each other- live in the love of God and, and we shall be united again! In the love of God we shall live on, forever and ever! We shall meet again; I am *sure of that*! Love- God is love- love eternal!" Refusing nourishment during his last days: "God sees it is no longer needful for me." Near the end, to a visitor who had taken his hand: "Very kind, very glad."

Bunyan, John (1628-1688). English clergyman and writer, best-known for his allegory *The Pilgrim's Progress.* Catching a chill on a journey home from London: "Weep not for me, but for yourselves. I go to the Father of our Lord Jesus Christ, Who will, no doubt, through the mediation of His Blessed Son, receive me, though a sinner, where I hope we ere long shall meet to sing the new song and remain everlastingly happy, world without end. Amen!" Then: "Take me, for I come to Thee."

Burbank, Luther (1849-1926). American horticulturist who developed over 800 strains and varieties of plants. Dying from complications of a heart attack: "I don't feel good." To his doctor: "I'm a very sick man."

Burckhardt, Jacob (1818-1897). Swiss art and cultural historian. Burckhardt died uttering the enigmatic words: "Farewell my dear little cat's table."

Burgess, George (1809-1866). American clergyman and writer. While on a voyage to Haiti, Burgess died suddenly, saying: "I will lie down now."

Burke, David (1952-1987). Burke, a recently fired US Airways employee, smuggled a pistol aboard a subsidiary Pacific Southwest Airlines flight from Los Angeles to San Francisco. The supervisor who had terminated Burke also was aboard the plane. After Burke fired several shots in the aircraft cabin, a flight attendant told the pilots: "We have a problem." When the captain asked what kind of problem, Burke who entered the cockpit replied: "I'm the problem." He then shot the pilots, causing the plane to crash with no survivors. In the wreckage, an air-sickness bag was found with words supposedly written by Burke to his supervisor: "Hi Ray. I think it's sort of ironical that we ended up like this. I asked for some leniency for my family. Remember? Well, I got none and you'll get none."

Burke, Robert (c 1820-1861). Irish explorer who died of starvation as his expedition attempted to cross the Australian continent. Burke's last journal entry from the bush: "I hope we shall be done justice to. We have fulfilled our task, but we have been aban-. We have not been followed up as we expected, and the depot party abandoned their post... King [the only expedition survivor] has behaved nobly. He has stayed with me to the last and placed the pistol in my hand, leaving me lying on the surface as I wished. R. O'H. Burke Cooper's Creek, June the 28th"

Burn, Andrew (1742-1814). British Royal Marine officer. On his deathbed, Burn was asked if he would like to see anyone: "Nobody, nobody but Jesus Christ. Christ crucified is the stay of my poor soul."

Burness, Frank (died 1904). American criminal, condemned to die in the electric chair for the murder of a schooner captain: "I deserve to die, and the sooner they put an end to my troubles the better. I've got an uncontrollable temper, and if released would only commit more violent crimes. I'd kill a man for 5 cents as quick as for anything else."

Burnett, Frances (1849-1924). English-born American writer, best-known for her novel *Little Lord Fauntleroy.* Dying of heart failure: "With the best that was in me I have tried to write more happiness into the world."

Burney, Charles (1726-1814). British composer and musical historian, best-known for his reference *A General History of Music.* Dying of a "last fatal seizure:" "All of this will soon pass away as a dream."

Burns, George (1795-1890). Scottish shipping tycoon who helped develop the Cunard Cruise Ship Line. "Lord Jesus, come, come... I am waiting. I am ready. Home, home. Give me patience to wait Thy time, but Thou knowest what I suffer."

Burns, James (1823-1864). Scottish Presbyterian minister and hymnodist. "... I have been dying for twenty years, now I am going to live. Christ hath abolished death and brought life and immortality to light through the Gospel." Near death, Burns remarked on the sound of the sea: "A weary sound- it cannot rest. There is a point of sympathy between me and it just now..." His last utterance was the Greek word for a day of Sabbath rest: "Sabbatismos."

Burns, Robert (1759-1796). Scottish poet and member of the local militia. While visiting friends several days before his death, Burns responded to a woman who asked if he would like the blinds pulled: "Thank you, my dear, for your kind attention; but oh, let him shine; he will not shine long for me." On his deathbed, Burns quipped to a friend: "John, don't let the awkward squad fire over me." The "awkward squad" was composed of new military recruits who were not yet seasoned adequately to join the regular troops of the Dumfries militia. Awakening from a stuporous state: "I am much better today. I shall be soon well again, for I command my spirits and my mind. But yesterday I resigned myself to death." The day before dying (some say in a delirium at his death), Burns spoke his brother's name: "Gilbert." On the day he died, Burns responded to a bill sent for his militia uniform: "That d***** rascal Matthew Penn!" At the poet's funeral, the volunteer squad fired three volleys over his grave without incident as the dirt was shoveled in.

Burnside, Ambrose (1824-1881). Union Army general, governor of Rhode Island and U.S. senator. Stricken with a heart attack, to his physician: "Something must be done at once!"

Burr, Aaron (1756-1836). American military officer, lawyer and U.S. vice president who killed Treasury Secretary Alexander Hamilton in an 1804 duel. Burr, an avowed atheist, was asked on his deathbed about the existence of God and whether he could be saved. His alleged response: "On that subject I am coy." Later, he spoke the word "Madame" to his attendant as she took his glasses. The utterance was interpreted as a desire to pass the spectacles to his former wife, Madame Eliza Jumel.

Burr, Raymond (1917-1993). Canadian-born actor, best-known for his roles in the television series *Perry Mason* and *Ironside.* Dying of cancer, to a friend: "I think the worst is over. One day we'll be together again."

Burris, Gary (1956-1997). American criminal, executed for a murder committed during a robbery. Before he died, Burris quoted a popular expression from the television series *Star Trek*: "Beam me up!"

Burroughs, John (1837-1921). American naturalist and essayist. Suffering a heart attack in Ohio on a train bound from California to his home state of New York, Burroughs asked: "How far are we from home?"

Burrows, William (1785-1813). American naval officer. Burrows commanded the USS *Enterprise* in her action against HMS *Boxer* during the War of 1812. Wounded, he refused to be carried below until the *Boxer* surrendered. His last words: "Now I am satisfied. I die contented."

Burton, Richard, born Richard Jenkins, Jr. (1925-1984). Welsh stage and screen actor. Before dying of a stroke, Burton penned lines from Shakespeare's plays *Macbeth* and *The Tempest*:

"The multitudinous seas incarnadine,
Making the green one red.
Tomorrow and tomorrow and tomorrow...
Our revels now are ended...
Cap a pi..."

Burton, Richard Francis (1821-1890). British explorer and writer. Dying of a heart attack, to his wife who would not give him any medicine unless a doctor was present: "Oh Puss, chloroform, ether or I am a dead man."

Alternative: * "Quick, Puss, chloroform! Ether! Or I am a dead man."

Burton, Robert (1577-1640). British writer and scholar who suffered from melancholy: "Be not solitary, be not idle." Often quoted as Burton's last words, this admonition actually appeared in his best-known work *The Anatomy of Melancholy* published nearly two decades before his death: "... Observe this short precept, give not way to solitarinesse and idlenesse. *Be not solitary, be not idle.*" Burton supposedly hanged himself.

Bushemi, John (1917-1944). American photographer. Mortally wounded by a mortar shell while photographing an American landing at Eniwetok Atoll during the WWII Pacific campaign, Bushemi directed: "Be sure to get those pictures back to the office."

Bushnell, Horace (1802-1876). American clergyman and theologian. To his family: "Well, now we are all going home together, and I say, the Lord be with you- and in grace and peace and love- and that is the way I have come along home."

Busoni, Ferruccio (1866-1924): Italian pianist, conductor and composer. Dying of a kidney ailment, Busoni took his wife's hand and said: "Dear Gerda, I thank you for every day we have been together."

Bustia, Cipriana (fl. 17th century). Italian martyr. When Bustia was asked to renounce his religion in favor of the Catholic Church, he refused saying: "I would rather renounce life or turn dog." After he died of starvation in prison, his body was thrown into the street and eaten by dogs.

Butler, Arthur (1844-1910). British educator, literary translator and mountaineer. Butler wished to be buried in Wantage, Oxfordshire, his childhood home: "... where the larks sing..."

Butler, Benjamin (1818-1893). Union general during the U.S. Civil War and later a member of the U.S. House of Representatives. To his valet: "That's all, West. You need do nothing more." When the servant returned a half-hour later, Butler was dead.

Butler, Benjamin Franklin (1795-1858). U.S. attorney general under President Andrew Jackson. The day before he died, Butler exclaimed: "I have peace, perfect peace." He then quoted Isaiah 26:3: "Thou dost keep him in perfect peace, whose mind is stayed on Thee." As he expired: "I die a happy man. I die a happy man. Rock of Ages cleft for me."

Butler, Joseph (1692-1752). English clergyman, Bishop of Durham. When a colleague read from John 6:37, the bishop commented: "I am surprised that though I have read that Scripture a thousand times over, I never felt its virtue till this moment, and now I die happy." Some say Butler's parting words were directed to his chaplain: "O, this is comfortable!"

Butler, Richard (1743-1791). American Revolutionary War hero. Following the war, Butler fought in the Northwest Territory against Native American forces and was killed during the Battle of the Wabash, near present-day Fort Recovery, Ohio. To a family member: "Edward, I am mortally wounded. Leave me to my fate and save my brother [Thomas]!" Butler's sibling survived the conflict and died 13 years later.

Butler, Dr. Samuel (1774-1839). English scholar and Bishop of Lichfield, Canterbury. Dying of "water on the heart:" "Doctor, shall I rally or shall I send for my son?" When told it might be better to send for his Father in heaven, he replied: "Thank you. You are a sensible man."

Butler, Samuel (1835-1902). English writer, best known for his novel *The Way of All Flesh*. Concerning the purchase of a house, to his clerk: "Have you brought the cheque book, Alfred?" Butler then removed his glasses, saying: "I don't want them anymore." He then fell back dead.

Butt, Archibald (1865-1912). American military officer who perished during the RMS *Titanic* sinking. Helping a fellow passenger into a lifeboat:

"Goodbye, Miss Young. Good luck to you, and don't forget to remember me to the folks back home."

Buxton, Thomas (1786-1845). English politician, abolitionist and social activist. Buxton, through his leadership in Parliament, agitated for penal reform and abolition of slave trading. During his last days: "I feel my faculties and powers obscured, but my faith is strong." Before dying: "Christ is *most merciful- most merciful* to me. I do put my trust in Him."

Byles, Mather (1707-1788). American clergyman, poet and nephew of Cotton Mather (below). To a friend: "I feel as if I had about got to that land where there are no bishops."

Byng, Julian (1862-1935). British military officer and statesman. Dying, Byng spoke his wife's nickname: "My Pog."

Byrd, John Jr. (1963-2002). American criminal, executed by lethal injection for the murder of a convenience store worker. Byrd told his family that he loved them and exhorted them to fight the death penalty. Before the lethal drugs were administered: "... The corruption of the state shall fall. Governor Taft [of Ohio], you will not be re-elected. The rest of you, you know where you can go." Immediately before he died: "What you are witnessing, for whosoever is here for this state-sanctioned murder, a cowardice way of hiding behind the state seal - you don't know what you're doing." Byrd was wrong about Taft's re-election.

Byron, George Gordon, also Lord Byron (1788-1824). English poet who fought alongside the Greeks in their quest for independence from the Turks. Dying of fever in Missolonghi, a town in western Greece, Byron said to those attending him: "Those d***** doctors have drenched me so that I can scarcely stand. I want to sleep now. Shall I sue for mercy? Come, come, no weakness; let me be a man to the last." To his physicians: "Your efforts to preserve my life will be [in] vain. Die I must. I feel it... One request let me make it to you. Let not my body be hacked or be sent to England. Here let my bones molder. Lay me in the first corner without pomp or nonsense." Regardless, his body was embalmed and shipped back to England for interment. His heart supposedly was buried in Missolonghi.

Most agree that Lord Byron's last words were some variation of: "Now I shall go to sleep."

Alternatives: * "I must sleep now."
* "There are things that make the world dear to me. For the rest, I am content to die. I have given her [Greece] my time, my means, my health, and now I give her my life. What could I do more?" Later in the evening: "Now I shall go to sleep."
* "Shall I sue for mercy? Come, come, no weakness; let's be a man to the last."

Cabrini, Saint Frances Xavier (1850-1917). Italian-born religious sister who founded hospitals, schools and orphanages in the U.S. Dying of dysentery, Cabrini was asked what she would like to eat: "Bring me anything you like. If I don't take it, I may take something else."

Cadogan, William (1751-1797). English clergyman. To his physician: "I am going- I am dying- it is well- I die in the faith of the Lord Jesus Christ, and in love with all mankind." To a loyal servant: "I thank you for all your faithful services. God bless you." Before dying, Cadogan began praying, saying at times: "Not my will, but Thine be done."

Cadoudal, Georges (1771-1804). French politician, executed by guillotining for plotting against Napoleon. Advised to repeat the "Hail Mary, full of grace" for protection at the hour of death, Cadoudal replied: "For what? Isn't this the hour of my death?"

Caesar, Augustus (63 BCE-14 CE). First Roman emperor. Shortly before his death, Augustus spoke to his friends: "Do ye think I have acted my part on the stage of life well? If all be right, with joy your voices raise, in loud applauses to the actor's praise." To his wife immediately before dying: "Livia, mindful of our union, live on and farewell."

Alternatives: "Did I play my role well? If so, then applause, because the comedy is finished!"
* "Do you think I have played my part pretty well through the farce of life?"

* "Have I played the part well? Then applaud as I exit"
* "The play is over, applaud!"

Caesar, Julius (100-44 BCE). Roman general and political leader, assassinated by Marcus Brutus (above) and other conspirators. Perhaps the most often-quoted last words of Caesar have come from William Shakespeare's play *The Tragedy of Julius Caesar*: "*Et tu, Brute*? Then fall, Caesar." In actuality, Caesar may have perished with only a groan.

Alternatives: * "Why, this is violence!"
* "Impious Casca [one of the assailants], what doest thou."
* "You too, my child?"
* "Thou, too, Brutus, my son?"
* "You too, my son!"
* "What! Art thou, too, one of them! Thou, my son!"

Cajetan, Saint (1480-1547). Italian priest and humanist. When encouraged to lie on a mattress, Cajetan replied: "My Savior died on a cross. Allow me at least to die on wood."

Calamity Jane, born Martha Jane Canary (c. 1852 -1903). American frontierswoman who claimed marriage to "Wild Bill" Hickok (below). On her deathbed, Calamity asked the date and was told August 2nd. She responded: "It's the twenty-seventh anniversary of Bill's death." As she expired: "Bury me next to Bill." Her dying wish was fulfilled.

Calconis (died c.108). As the pagan Calconis observed the martyrdom of two Christians from Brescia, a city in northern Italy, he blurted out: "Great is the God of the Christians." For his outcry, Calconis was struck down and killed on the spot.

Caldclough, James (died 1739). English highwayman who committed a series of robberies. Before his hanging, Caldclough made a plea that others should not repeat his mistakes, concluding: "... Were I able to make satisfaction to those whom I have wronged, I would do it; but alas! I cannot, and therefore I pray that they will forgive me. I hope my life will be at least some satisfaction, as I have nothing besides to give; and, as I die in charity with all mankind, may the Lord Jesus receive my soul."

Calderón, Don Rodrigo (c. 1580-1621). Spanish courtier. Implicated in the murder of a soldier, Francisco de Juaras, Calderón was beheaded in Madrid. His last words: "All my life I have carried myself gracefully." Before dying, he said that he "gave his soul in the name of Jesus." Because of Calderón's inflated self-esteem, Jonathon Green in his book *Famous Last Words* commented: "His death gave rise to the Spanish proverb to be haughtier than Don Rodrigo on the scaffold."

Caldwell, Merritt (1806-1848). American educator and writer. Dying of tuberculosis: "Farewell! My dear wife. Glory to Jesus! Jesus, my life. Jesus, my trust. Jesus! Jesus!"

Calhoun, John (1782-1850). U.S. vice president, South Carolina senator and spokesman for Southern interests before the U.S. Civil War. Dying of tuberculosis, Calhoun was asked if he wanted to be saved: "I won't be told what to think!" On his deathbed, he exclaimed: "The South! The poor South! God knows what will become of her." When asked by his son how he felt: "I am perfectly comfortable." Later, his doctor tried to feel a pulse but found none. He gave Calhoun a drink of wine as a stimulant but still found no evidence of cardiac activity. When he conveyed this information to Calhoun, the statesman waited silently for the end.

Caligula (12-41). Roman emperor. Because of Caligula's cruelty and extravagance, a plot was hatched to assassinate him. Stabbed by his own soldiers, the dying Caligula exclaimed: "I still live!" The assassins then finished their work.

Callas, Maria, born Sophia Cecelia Kalos (1923-1977). American-born operatic soprano, renowned for her *bel canto* singing and dramatic prowess. After suffering a heart attack, the 53-year-old Callas was given several spoonfuls of coffee. "I've had enough. I feel better."

Callicrates (died 479 BCE) Spartan warrior. Wounded by a Persian invader's arrow before the start of the Battle of Plataea in central Greece,

Callicrates remonstrated: "I grieve, not because I have to die for my country, but because I have not lifted my arm against the enemy, nor done any deed worthy of me, much as I have desired to achieve something."

Calvin, John, also Jean Cauvin (1509-1564). French theologian prominent during the Protestant Reformation. Calvin told visiting friends: "I come to you, brethren, for the last time. I am never again to sit at table... The intervening wall [between the dining room and bedroom], though it make me absent in body, will not prevent me from being present with you in spirit" Perhaps thinking of Isaiah 53:10, Calvin said: "Thou Lord bruisest me, but I am abundantly satisfied, since it is from Thy hand."

Cambronne, Pierre-Jacques-Étienne (1770-1842). French general who refused to surrender to the British during the Battle of Waterloo. Dying almost three decades later: "Ah, mademoiselle! Man is thought to be something, but he is nothing."

Cameron, James (1801-1861). American commander of the 79th New York Highlanders during the U.S. Civil War. Cameron was killed at the Battle of Bull Run, near Manassas, Virginia. As he led a charge: "Scots, follow me."

Alternative: "Come on boys! The rebels are in full retreat!"

Camões, Luís de (c. 1524-1580). Portuguese poet and writer. Mortally ill with the plague around the time Portugal's army was soundly defeated by the Spanish: "I am happy in that I die in the bosom of my country. Nay, in that I am dying with her."

Alternative: * "... So I shall conclude my life and all will see how I was so attached to my country that I was not satisfied to die in it, but to die with it."

Camp, Henry (1839-1864). Union officer during the U.S. Civil War. Mortally wounded at the Battle of Darbytown Road, near Richmond, Virginia, Camp exhorted his troops: "Come on, boys! Come on!"

Campan, Jeanne-Louise (1752-1822). French educator, writer and lady-in-waiting to Marie Antoinette. After making a demand on one of her caregivers, Campan apologized: "How imperious one is when one has no time for politeness!"

Campbell, Archibald (1629-1685). Scottish nobleman, the Ninth Earl of Argyll. Convicted of treason for espousing civil and religious freedom, Campbell was beheaded: "I die not only a Protestant, but with a heart-hatred of Popery, Prelacy and all superstition whatsoever." The nobleman then knelt and embraced the block, nicknamed the "maiden," saying: "This is the sweetest maiden I ever kissed, it being the mean to finish my sin and misery, and is my inlet to glory, for which I long." He gave the signal for execution after repeating: "Lord Jesus, receive my spirit."

Alternative: * "Lord Jesus, receive me into Thy glory."

Campbell, Donald (1921-1967). British land and water speed record holder. While attempting a new water speed record in his rocket-powered watercraft called Bluebird, Campbell lost control and died in a spectacular crash. His last radio intercom transmission: "The nose is up. Pitching a bit down here as I drive over my own wash. Stabilising, up blind tract... rather close to Peel Island, tramping like mad [rocking from side to side]... er... full power, and er, tramping like hell here. Can't see very much, the water's dark and green. I can't get over the top. She's lost a bit of her bloody track. I can't see anything. Hello, the bow's up! I've gone! Oh..."

Alternatives: "... Full nose up... Pitching a bit down here... coming through our own wash... er getting straightened up now on track... rather closer to Peel Island... and we're tramping like mad... and er... Full power... er tramping like hell... Over... I can't see much and the water's very bad indeed... I'm galloping [I can't get] over the top... and she's actually giving a hell of a bloody row in here. I can't see anything... I've got the bows out... I'm going ... U-hh."

* "... The water is dark green, and I can't see anything... She's tramping! She's tramping! I'm on my back! She's going!"

Campbell, Edmund "Heck" (died 1875). American criminal. Campbell was tried in the courtroom of "The Hanging Judge" Isaacs Parker at Fort Smith, Arkansas for the murder of a farmer and his mistress. On the gallows: "I did not shoot anybody. I am innocent and ready to die."

Campbell, George (1850-1881). American lawman. To Marshal Dallas Stoudenmire, who mistakenly shot him in the Battle of Keating's Saloon in El Paso, Texas: "You big son-of-a-b****, you murdered me!"

Campbell, Richard (c. 1730-1781). American Revolutionary War officer. When told that his troops had routed the British during the Battle of Eutaw Springs, South Carolina, Campbell allowed: "I die contented."

Campbell, Willielma (1741-1786). Scottish philanthropist. Campbell distributed her wealth among evangelical causes in her native country. To a visitor: "If this be dying, it is the easiest thing imaginable."

Campbell-Bannerman, Henry (1836-1908). British Prime Minister who resigned from office due to poor health. On his deathbed: "This is not the end of me."

Campion, Saint Edmund (1540-1581). English Jesuit martyr. Because of his writings against the Anglican Church and alleged conspiracy against Queen Elizabeth I, Campion was hanged, drawn and quartered. Asked whether he prayed for Queen Elizabeth or Mary: "Yea, for Elizabeth, your Queen and my Queen, unto whom I wish a long quiet reign with all prosperity."

Canaris, Wilhelm (1887-1945). German military officer who headed the Nazi intelligence service during WWII. Because of his clandestine opposition to Hitler and the Nazi party, Canaris eventually was accused of treason and sentenced to die. Before his hanging, the condemned man tapped a coded message to a Colonel Lunding in an adjacent cell: "I die for my country and with a clear conscience. You as an officer will realize that I was only doing my duty to my country when I endeavored to oppose Hitler and to hinder the senseless crimes by which he had dragged Germany to ruin. I know that all I did was in vain, for Germany will be completely defeated. I knew that she would be as far back as 1942... Do what you can for wife [and] daughters. They've broken my nose. I die this morning. Farewell."

Candy Darling, born James Slattery (1944-1974). American transsexual actress, best-known for her roles in Andy Warhol movies. Dying of cancer, Candy Darling directed a deathbed letter to her friends: "To whom it may concern: By the time you read this I will be gone. Unfortunately before my death I had no desire left for life. Even with all my friends and my career on the upswing I felt too empty to go on in this unreal existence. I am just so bored by everything. You might say bored to death. It may sound ridiculous but is true. I have arranged my own funeral arrangements with a guest list and it is paid for..." She then said goodbye to specific friends and concluded: "... I am sorry, did you know I couldn't last, I always knew it. I wish I could meet you all again. Goodbye for Now
Love Always
Candy Darling
Tinkerbell HI! [a magazine writer]

Candy, John (1950-1994). Canadian-born comedian and actor. While shooting a movie in Mexico, Candy complained: "I'm so tired, all I want to do is go home and be with my family." He died of a heart attack shortly thereafter.

Canitz, Friedrich von (1654-1699). German statesman and poet. Viewing the sunrise: "Oh, if the appearance of this earthly and created thing is so beautiful and so quickening, how much more shall I be enraptured at the sight of the unspeakable glory of the Creator Himself?"

Cano, Alonso (1601-1667). Spanish sculptor, artist and architect. When Cano put aside an ornate crucifix presented to him, he was asked if it were not the image of the Lord: "So do I believe, father, yet vex me not with this thing, but give me a simple cross, that I may adore it, both as it is in itself and as I can figure it to my mind."

Canonchet (died 1676). Native American Narragansett chief. Canonchet was captured during the King Philip's War that pitted Native American troops against English colonists. When offered his life if he made peace with the English, he chose death by firing squad instead: "I like it well. I shall die before my heart is soft, and before I have said anything unworthy of myself."

Capel, Arthur (c. 1604-1649). One of the leaders of the second English Civil War and supporter of the executed king, Charles I. Convicted of treason, Capel spoke before his beheading: "God Almighty, staunch this blood. God Almighty, staunch, staunch, staunch this issue of blood. This will not do the business. God Almighty, find out another way to do it." To the executioner: "I will try first how I can lie; am I well now?" When answered in the affirmative: "... Here lie both my hands out... When I lift up my hands thus, then you may strike." After a short prayer, Capel raised his right arm and the deed was done.

Capote, Truman, born Truman Steckfus Persons (1924-1984). American author and screenwriter, best-known for his books *In Cold Blood* and *Breakfast at Tiffany's*. Dying of liver cancer, Capote repeated: "Mama... Mama... Mama... Mama..."

Captain Jack, also Kintpuash (c. 1837-1873). Native American chief and murderer. Captain Jack resisted relocation of his tribal members from their ancestral land and later killed an Army general and clergyman during a peace commission meeting. He was tracked down and sentenced to die by hanging. When a clergyman told Captain Jack heaven is a beautiful place, he responded: "Well, preacher, I tell you what I'll do with you. I will give you just twenty-five head of ponies if you will take my place today, as you say it is such a nice place, because I do not like to go right now." After his hanging, Captain Jack's head was severed and taken to Washington D.C. where it supposedly was exhibited. In 1984, it was returned to relatives.

Captain Lightfoot (see Martin, Michael).

Cardozo, Benjamin (1870-1938). Associate U.S. Supreme Court justice. To a fellow jurist: "They tell me I am going to get well, but I file a dissenting opinion."

Carême, Antonin (c. 1784-1833). French master chef. After suffering a stroke, Carême continued to plan a meal: "Tomorrow, bring me some fish. Yesterday, the quenelles of sole were very good, but your fish was not right. You hadn't seasoned it well. Listen..." He continued to direct the preparations but died within the half-hour.

Carew, George (c. 1504-1545). English naval officer. Carew and many of his men perished when his ship, the *Mary Rose*, sank during the French invasion of Portsmouth, England. Before the tragedy, he called to his uncle on a sister ship: "I have the sort of knaves whom I cannot rule."

Carey, William (1761-1834). British Baptist missionary to India. When asked about the prospects of death, Carey replied: "... I tremble." Then, to a friend: "After I am gone, Brother Marshman will turn the cows into the garden." To a fellow missionary: "Mr. Duff, you have been speaking about Dr. Carey; when I am gone, say nothing about Dr. Carey; speak about Dr. Carey's Savior." Carey asked for the following words on his tombstone:
"William Carey, born August 17, 1761: died...
A wretched, poor, and helpless worm,

On thy kind arms I fall."

Cargill, Donald (c. 1619-1681). Martyred Scottish Covenanter. In 1680, Cargill unwisely excommunicated King Charles II and other prominent Scottish government leaders. For his trouble, he was sentenced to death and hanged the following year. Cargill allegedly said to the assembled crowd: "The Lord knows I go on this ladder with less fear and perturbation of mind, than ever I entered the pulpit to preach… Welcome Father, Son, and Holy Ghost; into Thy hands I commit my Spirit."

Alternative: * "The Lord knows I go up this ladder with less fear, confusion or perturbation of mind, than ever I entered a pulpit to preach."

Carlyle, Jane (1801-1866). Scottish-born writer who was the wife of Thomas Carlyle (below). Last letter to her husband who had asked her to purchase a particular picture: "… I offered five shillings on the spot, but he would only come down to six shillings. I will go back for it, if you like, and can find a place for it on my wall." When given a dose of laudanum for shortness of breath: "Good night, and thank ye!"

Carlyle, Thomas (1795-1881). Scottish writer, historian and philosopher. On his deathbed: "I am as good without hope and without fear; a sad old man gazing into the final chasm." To his doctor: "... For me you can do nothing. The only thing you could do, you must not do- that is help me to make an end of this. We must just go on as we are." Carlyle's last words: "So this is death- well..."

Carmichael, John (1728-1785). Scottish-born American clergyman. Dying of pneumonia: "Oh that I had a thousand tongues that I might employ them all in inviting sinners to Christ."

Carnegie, Andrew (1835-1919). Scottish-American businessman and philanthropist who was a dominant force in the expansion of the U.S. steel industry. Dying of pneumonia, to his wife Louise who wished him good night: "I hope so, Lou."

Carnot, Marie-François-Sadi (1837-1894). President of France. Stabbed in the abdomen by an Italian anarchist, Carnot lost consciousness but revived a short time later. When asked if he knew his condition: "Yes, I am dying." When told he was surrounded by friends: "I am very touched by your presence and I thank you for what you are doing for me." He was dead within a half-hour.

Alternative: * "I am glad to find my friends here."

Caroline of Brandenburg-Ansbach (1683-1737). German-born consort of English King George II. On her deathbed, Caroline told her grieving husband: "Do not weep; you know you can marry again." He replied that he would only take mistresses: "My God, that doesn't prevent it." When she asked one of her attendants to remove the candles from her bedside, her husband asked if they hurt her eyes. Caroline replied: "No, Sire, but I would spare you the affliction of seeing me die." Gasping for breath, she referred to her estranged son Frederick Louis: "At least I shall have one comfort in having my eyes eternally closed. I shall never see that monster again." At the end: "I have now got an asthma. Open the window. Pray." Caroline died after a few prayers were read.

Alternative: * "Pray louder that I may hear."

Caroline of Brunswick (1768-1821). German-born consort of English King George IV. Despised by her husband, Caroline became ill after his unsuccessful divorce attempt. To a lady attendant: "The doctors do not understand my malady. It is here [pointing to her heart]. But, I will be silent. My lips shall never make it known: injustice and cruelty have triumphed"

Carradine, John (1906-1988). American film and theater actor. Shortly before he became ill, Carradine had climbed to the top of Milan's stately cathedral, the Duomo. His questionable last words were: "Milan: What a beautiful place to die."

Alternative: * "Oh, to die in Italy!"

Carrillo, Felipe Puerto (1872-1924). Governor of the Yucatan state, Mexico. Because Carrillo resisted a rebel force aligned against the government, he was convicted by a military tribunal and executed by firing squad: "Don't abandon my Indians!"

Carroll, Charles (1737-1832). U.S. senator and last-surviving signer of the Declaration of Independence. When exhorted by his physician to eat, Carroll replied: "Thank you, doctor, not just now... I feel no desire for food." When lifted to his bed: "Thank you. That is nicely done." Again, when offered food, to his daughter: "Mary, put it down; I want no food." When the doctor helped change his position, Carroll thanked him and died quietly several hours later.

Carroll, Lewis, penname of Charles Dodgson (1832-1898). English mathematician who created the novel *Alice's Adventures in Wonderland.* Dying of pneumonia: "Take away those pillows. I shall need them no more."

Carson, Christopher "Kit" (1809-1868). American frontiersman who participated in numerous Old West expeditions and military conflicts. Dying of a ruptured aneurysm: "Doctor, I'm going. *Adiós compadre* [Goodbye comrade]."

Alternatives: * "Goodbye doctor. *Adiós compadre*!"
* "Farewell, comrade. Farewell."
* "I just wish I had time for one more bowl of chili."

Carstares, William (1649-1715). Scottish minister. Dying of a stroke: "I have peace with God through our Lord Jesus Christ."

Carter, Richard (died 1692). English admiral. Mortally wounded during the decisive Battle of Barfleur against a French fleet off the northern coast of France: "Fight the ship. Fight the ship as long as she can swim."

Carteret, John (1690-1763). English statesman. After listening to a reading of the draft of the Treaty of Paris: "It has been the most glorious war, and it is now the most honorable peace this nation ever saw."

Caruso, Enrico (1873-1921). Italian operatic tenor. Dying from complications of a chest infection, Caruso spoke to his wife Doro: "Let me sleep." Shortly thereafter, he cried: "Doro, I can't get my breath!"

Carver, George Washington (c. 1864-1943). American agricultural chemist and educator who espoused alternative planting to enrich depleted soil. Dying from complications of a fall, to his secretary: "I think I'll sleep now."

Cary, Alice (1820-1871). American poet. Dying of tuberculosis, Cary spoke to her sister Phoebe (below), also a well-respected poet: "I want to go away."

Cary, Phoebe (1824-1871). American poet. Dying of hepatitis five months after her sister Alice's death: "Oh, God, have mercy on my soul."

Casals, Pablo (1876-1973). Spanish cellist, composer and conductor. As he was driven to a San Juan hospital in an ambulance, Casals complained: "The driver's a maniac! He'll kill us all!" Casals died while in hospital.

Casanova, Giacomo (1725-1798). Italian lothario and writer who chronicled his many romantic adventures. As death from a urinary tract infection approached, Casanova wrote: "Life is a wench that one loves, to whom we allow any condition in the world, so long as she does not leave us." After taking the sacraments: "I have lived as a philosopher and die as a Christian."

Casaubon, Isaac (1559-1614). Swiss-born classical scholar and writer. When asked in which religion he preferred to die, Casaubon took umbrage saying: "Then you think, my lord, that I have been all along a dissembler in a matter of the greatest moment!"

Casement, Roger (1864-1916). Irish patriot. Because Casement organized a group of volunteers to fight with Germany against England during WWI, he was convicted of treason and condemned to hang. At his trial (some say from prison), he said: "Where all your rights become only an accumulated wrong; where men must beg with bated breath for leave to subsist in their own land, to think their own thoughts, to sing their own songs, to garner the fruits of their own labors... then surely it is braver, a saner and truer thing, to be a rebel... than tamely to accept it as the natural lot of men… How would you feel yourselves as Englishmen if that man was to be submitted to trial by jury in a land inflamed against him and believing him to be a criminal, when his only crime was that he cared for England more than for Ireland." In his last letter, to his sister: "It is a cruel thing to die with all men misunderstanding…" On the gallows: "I die for my country… Into Thy hands, O Lord, I commend my spirit. Jesus receive my soul."

Caserio, Sante-Geronimo (1873-1894). Italian assassin of French President Marie-François-Sadi Carnot (above). Before dying by the guillotine: "Courage comrades! Long live anarchy!"

Casey, Hugh (1913-1951). American major league baseball pitcher. After being named in a paternity suit, Casey shot himself in the neck but was able to call his estranged wife over the telephone: "So help me God, I am innocent of those [paternity] charges."

Cassady, Neal (1926-1968). American drifter and drug abuser. After attending a wedding party in Mexico, Cassady set off walking along railroad tracts toward the closest station. He apparently decided to count the number of railroad ties on the journey back to the station. Found beside the tracks by locals, he was taken to a nearby hospital. Cassady's last words: "Sixty-four thousand, nine hundred and twenty-eight."

Castillo, David (1964-1998). American criminal, executed by lethal injection for the murder of a liquor store clerk: "Keep it brief here. Just want to say, uh, family, take care of yourselves. Uh, look at this as a learning experience. Everything happens for a reason. We all know what really happened, but there are some things you just can't fight. Little people always seem to get squashed. It happens. Even so, just got to take the good with the bad. There is no man that is free from all evil, nor any man that is so evil to be worth nothing. But it's all part of life, and my family, take care of yourselves. Tell my wife I love her. I'll keep an eye on everybody, especially my nieces and nephews. I'm pretty good. I love ya'll. Take care. I'm ready"

Castlereagh, Viscount (see Stewart, Robert).

Catesby, Robert (c. 1572-1605). English conspirator. Catesby and Guy Fawkes were two of the collaborators in the infamous Gunpowder Plot, hatched to blow up England's Houses of Parliament and kill King James I. Catesby died resisting arrest: "Stand by me, Tom [Thomas Winter, also a co-conspirator], and we will die together." Winter was captured and later hanged, drawn and quartered.

Catherine II, also Catherine the Great, (1729-1796). Empress of Russia. During her reign, Catherine made Russia one of the great European powers. After suffering a stroke, the only word she could say was "Water."

Catherine de Medici (see Medici, Catherine de).

Catherine of Aragon (1485-1536). Spanish-born first wife of English King Henry VIII. Dying of cancer, Catherine penned this note to Henry: "My most dear lord, King and husband, the hour of my death now drawing on, the tender love I ouge [owe] thou forceth me, my case being such, to commend myselv to thou, and to put thou in remembrance with a few words of the healthe and safeguard of thine allm [soul] which thou ougte to preferce before all worldley matters, and before the care and pampering of thy body, for the which thoust have cast me into many calamities and thineselv into many troubles. For my part, I pardon thou everything, and I desire to devoutly pray God that He will pardon thou also. For the rest, I commend unto thou our doughtere Mary, beseeching thou to be a good father unto her, as I have heretofore desired. I entreat thou also, on behalve of my maides, to give them marriage portions, which is not much, they being but three. For all mine other servants I solicit the wages due them, and a year more, lest they be unprovided for. Lastly, I makest this vouge [vow], that mine eyes desire thou aboufe all things.
Katharine the Quene"
Catherine's last words: "Lord, into Thy hands I commend my spirit."

Alternative: * "The hour of my death is now approaching. I cannot choose but out of the love I bear you advise you of your soul's health, which you ought to prefer before all consideration of the world of flesh whatsoever. For which yet you have cast me into many calamities and yourself into many troubles. But I forgive you all and pray God to do so likewise... Lastly, I want only one true thing, to make this vow: that, in this life, mine eyes desire you alone. May God protect you."

Catherine of Genoa, Saint (1447-1510). Italian noblewoman and mystic. Nearing death, Catherine experienced a vision of the devil: "Drive away that beast that wants to eat..." The rest of her words were indistinct.

Catherine of Siena, Saint (1347-1380). Italian nun, theologian and mystic, known for her visions of Christ, Mary and the saints. Dying of a stroke: "No, I have not sought vain glory, but only the glory and praise of God."

Catlin, George (1796-1872). American artist who specialized in painting scenes of Native Americans. Possibly referring to his Indian Gallery that eventually was placed in the Smithsonian American Art Museum: "What will become of my gallery? What will become of my gallery?"

Cato, Marcus Porcius, also Cato the Younger (95-46 BCE). Roman philosopher and statesman. Cato committed suicide after Julius Caesar's victory over his allies at the Battle of Thapsus in modern-day Tunisia. In his last moments: "Now I am master of myself." To his agent: "Have my friends yet embarked? Does anything yet remain that could be done to serve them?" Then: "Shut the door." Cato later stabbed himself.

Cauchy, Augustin-Louis (1789-1857). French mathematician, astronomer, physicist and educator. Dying of a fever, to the archbishop of Paris: "Men pass away, but their deeds abide."

Alternative: * "No, I do not suffer much... Jesus, Mary and Joseph!"

Caumont de la Force, Armand (died 1572). Protestant Frenchman, caught up in the St. Bartholomew's Day Massacre. As he and his father François lay dying of stab wounds: "Ah, my father! Oh, my God! Oh, my God, I am gone!"

Cavaignac, Louis Eugène (1802-1857). French general, prominent in his country's conquest of Algeria. Expressing a last wish, Cavaignac asked if the pianist Fryderyk Chopin (below) could be summoned to perform for him. Moving to the room where the musician played, his mother tried to direct him back to bed. Cavaignac's last words: "Don't fear, mother. I heard the music of the spheres sung by angels; it did me good."

Cavell, Edith (1865-1915). English nurse, executed for harboring and aiding the escape of allied troops during WWI. Cavell was captured and executed before a German firing squad. To the chaplain who attended her at the execution: "They have all been very kind to me here. But this I would say, standing, as I do, in view of God and Eternity... I realize that patriotism is not enough. I must have no hatred or bitterness towards anyone." When the chaplain said she would be remembered as a martyr, Cavell replied: "Don't think of me like that. Think of me only as a nurse who tried to do her duty. We shall meet again." Before the firing squad, Cavell said to the chaplain: "Ask Mr. Gahan [the Anglican minister who had given her Communion the preceding day] to tell my loved ones that my soul, I believe, is safe, and that I am glad to die for my country."

Cavendish, Henry (1731-1810). Franco-English scientist who discovered the element hydrogen. Dying of a bowel problem, to his valet: "Mind what I say, I am going to die. When I am dead, *but not till then,* go to my brother Frederick, and tell him of the event. Go!" Approximately an hour later, Cavendish summoned his attendant and said: "Repeat to me what I have ordered you to do. Give me the lavender water. Go." When the valet returned, he found Cavendish dead. Some say the dying man asked his attendant to notify Lord George Cavendish.

Cavendish, Spencer (1833-1908). British statesman, the 8th Duke of Devonshire. Dying of pneumonia: "The game is over and I am not sorry."

Cavour, Camillo Benso de (1810-1861). Italian patriot who played a significant role in his country's unification. Dying of suspected malaria, Cavour told his physicians: "Gentlemen, cure me promptly. I have Italy on my hands and time is precious..." Later he said: "Italy is made- all is safe!" At the end: "I have confessed and received absolution... I wish Turin to know I die a good Christian. My mind is at ease. I have never harmed anyone…" To his priest: "Brother, brother, a free church in a free state."

Caxton, William (c. 1422-c. 1491). British printer and writer who introduced the printing press to England. Caxton printed his last words: "God then give us His grace and find in us such a house that it may please Him to lodge therein, to the end that in this world He keeps us from adversity spiritual and in the end of our days He brings us with Him into His realm of heaven for to be partners of the glory eternal, which grant to us the Holy Trinity. Amen."

Cayce, Edgar (1877-1945). American self-proclaimed psychic. Dying of a stroke, Cayce asked his wife: "Who is that man? He looks like a musical conductor. It's beautiful music." When she asked what he was conducting, Cayce replied: "Oh, I don't know. I don't know much about music."

Cazotte, Jacques (1719-1792). French writer. Cazotte, a self-professed prophet, made some disparaging statements about the French Revolution. Condemned to death by guillotining during the Reign of Terror, he said to his family: "My dear wife, my dear children, do not weep: do not forget me, but above all, remember never to offend God." Before the blade fell: "I die as I have lived, faithful to God and my King."

Ceauşescu, Elena (1916-1989). Wife of Romanian Communist leader Nicolae Ceauşescu. Deposed because of his repressive governing, Ceauşescu and his wife attempted to flee Romania. They were captured, accused of genocide and sentenced to die by firing squad. Before the execution, Elena spoke to her husband who was humming the left-wing anthem "The Internationale:" "Stop it, Nicu. Look, they're going to shoot us like dogs... I can't believe this. Is the death penalty still in force in Romania?" Apparently, it was.

Cecil, William, Lord Burghley (1520-1598). English statesman and longtime advisor to Queen Elizabeth I. Recovering from a convulsion: "Now the Lord be praised! The time is come." To those present: "Love and fear God and love one another." Passing his affairs to his steward: "I have ever found thee true to me and now I trust thee with all."

Cecilia, Saint (fl. 3rd century). Roman martyr who became the patron saint of music. Challenging her Christian faith, Cecilia was ordered to sacrifice to Roman gods. She declined saying: "Are these the gods that you worship, or are they blocks of wood and pieces of stone?" Cecilia was condemned and attempts were made to scald her to death in her bath. When this failed, she was struck three times in the neck, but the blows failed to kill her outright. She lived for three days saying to her bishop: "I asked for a delay of three days so that I might commend all of us to your beatitude and have you consecrate my house as a church." Cecilia's request for house consecration subsequently was fulfilled.

Cermak, Anton (1873-1933). Czech-born Democratic mayor of Chicago. In Miami, Florida, a mentally deranged bricklayer, Giuseppe Zangara (below), attempted to assassinate president-elect Franklin Roosevelt but inadvertently shot Cermak. The wounded mayor allegedly said "I'm glad it was me and not you, Mr. President." Later, a Hearst reporter, John Dienhart who was a friend of the mayor, admitted that he had fabricated the quote, saying: "I couldn't very well have put out a story that Tony would have wanted it the other way around." Cermak's actual last words were spoken to his wife in the hospital several days later: "Kiss me."

Alternative: * "I'm glad it was me instead of you, Frank[lin]. The country needs you."

Cervantes, Miguel de (1547-1616). Spanish writer, best-known for his novel *Don Quixote de la Mancha*. A last letter to his benefactor, the count of Lemos: "Your Excellency may remember an ancient couplet commencing 'With foot already in the stirrup,' and I may commence in the same words; for I may truly say that, with my foot already in the stirrup, and even now experiencing the anguish of death, I address this letter to you. Yesterday I received Extreme Unction. Today I am writing this. My time is short; my pains increase; my hopes vanish; yet do I greatly desire that my life might be prolonged till the return of your Excellency to your native country. But, as Heaven has decreed otherwise, we must bow to its will, and all that remains will be to acquaint your Excellency with the deep sentiments of affection towards you which I bear with me to my grave." Returning from an Italian tour, the count arrived in Spain after Cervantes' death.

Alternatives: * The conclusion of the preface to *Labours of Persiles and Sigismunda*, written shortly before Cervantes died: "... But, adieu to gaiety; adieu to humour; adieu to my pleasant friends! I must now die, and I wish for nothing better than speedily to see you well contented in another world."

* "... Goodbye, all that is charming. Goodbye, wit and gaiety. Goodbye, merry friends, for I am dying and wish to see you contented in another life."

Cézanne, Paul (1839-1906). French Post-Impressionist painter. Dying from complications of diabetes and pneumonia, Cézanne spoke the name of the curator of the local museum who failed to display his works: "Pontier! Pontier!" At the end, he repeated his son's name "Paul."

Chaffee, Roger (1935-1967). American astronaut. During a prelaunch test of an Apollo spacecraft in 1967, the module in which Chaffee, Gus Grissom and Ed White were confined caught fire. Grissom shouted: "Fire!" followed by Chaffee's last words: "We've got a bad fire! Let's get out – we're burning up! We're on fire! Get us out of here!" All three died in the capsule.

Alternative: * "... "I'm reporting a bad fire. I'm getting out. Oh! Oh!"

Chaliapin, Feodor (1873-1938). Russian operatic basso. Dying of leukemia, to his wife: "Masha, why is it so dark in this theatre? Tell them to turn on the lights."

Chamberlain, Neville (1869-1940). British Prime Minister during the early stages of WWII. Dying of bowel cancer: "Approaching dissolution brings relief."

Chambers, Robert (1802-1871). Scottish writer and publisher. Asked how he was feeling: "Quite comfortable, quite happy, nothing more."

Chamfort, Sébastien-Roch-Nicolas (1741-1794). French writer and orator. Although he embraced the tenets of the French Revolution, Chamfort changed his allegiance during the Reign of Terror. Briefly imprisoned for his views, the playwright later was threatened with another period of incarceration. Depressed, he attempted suicide in the fall of 1793. When a gunshot to the face failed to produce the desired result, Chamfort stabbed himself in the neck and then the chest. Amazingly he survived but died the following April. At his death: "My friend, I'm finally taking leave of this earth, a place where one's heart must either break or be hard as bronze."

Alternatives: * "… And so I leave this world, where the heart must either break or turn to lead."

* "… At last I am about to leave this world, where the heart must be broken or be brass."

Championnet, Jean (1762-1800). French general who served under Napoleon I. Dying in bed, Championnet expressed remorse that he was not killed during battle: "My friends, take care to console my mother. Would that I had been able to die like Joubert." General Joubert (below) commanded the French Army in Italy and was killed by a bullet to the heart while leading his troops.

Chanel, Gabrielle "Coco" (1883-1971). French fashion designer. To the concierge in her building: "In about three or four minutes, I'm going to die." To a servant helping her get into bed: "You see, this is how you die."

Alternative: * "So this is how they let you die."

Channing, William (1780-1842). American Unitarian minister. To a friend: "I have received many messages from the Spirit." To his nephew: "You need not be anxious concerning tonight. It will be very peaceful and quiet with me."

Chaplin, Charles "Charlie" (1889-1977) English-born comic actor and filmmaker, best-known for his silent movies made during the first half of the 20th century. When the attending priest said: "May the Lord have mercy on your soul," Chaplin quipped: "Why Not? After all, it belongs to him." Although widely quoted as Chaplin's last utterance, those words were spoken by the main character in the comedian's 1947 "black movie" *Monsieur Verdoux*.

Chapman, Annie, born Eliza Smith (1841-1888). English murder victim of Jack the Ripper. Chapman spoke as she left a pub to "earn" eight pence for her rooming house bill: "I haven't enough now, but keep my bed for me. I shan't be long."

Chapman, Gerald (1891-1926). American robber and bootlegger who murdered a policeman. Chapman was the first criminal dubbed "Public Enemy No. 1" by the press. Condemned to hang for his crime, he allowed: "Death itself isn't dreadful, but hanging seems an awkward way of entering the adventure."

Chapman, Graham (1941-1989). English physician, actor and comedian, best-known for his association with the Monty Python comedy series. Dying of cancer, Chapman spoke to his adopted son who had arrived at the hospital: "Hello."

Alternative: * To a nurse after a needle stick: "Sorry for saying f***."

Chapman, John (1862-1933). American writer, essayist and lawyer. Dying of cancer, the semiconscious Chapman stroked his wife's fingers as if they were a harp. He said: "I want to take it away! I want to take it away!" Asked if he meant the pillow: "No, no! The mute, the mute! I want to play on the open strings!"

Chapman, Raymond (1891-1920). American professional baseball player. Struck in the head by a pitched ball, Chapman spoke to a friend: "John, for God's sake, don't call Kate. I don't want her to worry, but if you do, tell her I'm all right." He died after emergency surgery.

Charlemagne (742-814). King of the Franks and Holy Roman Emperor from 800 until his death. Suffering from a chill that progressed to pneumonia and pleurisy, Charlemagne told his doctors: "Leave me. I'll die well enough without your remedies!" Speaking about two of his deceased children: "Patience, I'll soon join them." His last words: "Lord Jesus, into Thy hands I commend my spirit."

Charles I (1887-1922). Austro-Hungarian Emperor. After the end of WWI, Charles was deposed and exiled to Madeira. His empire subsequently was dismantled. Dying of pneumonia, to his wife: "I can't go on much longer... Thy will be done... Yes, yes... As you will it... Jesus!"

Alternative: * "Oh, God, Thy will be done... Into Thy hands I commend my spirit and the care of my wife and children... I offer Thee my life as a sacrifice for my people." Then, to his wife: "I love you so much... Jesus."

Charles I (1600-1649). King of England, Scotland and Ireland. Defeated by Parliamentarian forces in the English Civil War, Charles was tried for treason, convicted, and sentenced to death. To the bishop who accompanied him to the block: "... I lay not my blood on you, or on my people, and demand no other compensation for any punishment than the return of peace and a revival of the fidelity which the kingdom owes my children. My friend, I go from a corruptible Crown to an incorruptible..." When a spectator stumbled against the axe: "Touch not the axe! That may hurt me." Pressing the bishop's hand: "*Remember*!" To his executioner: "When I put out my hands this way, then… Stay [wait] for the sign." When Charles extended his arms in the form of a cross, the axe fell. The executioner then held up the severed head crying: "Behold the head of a traitor!"

Alternative: * "I go from a corruptible to an incorruptible Crown, where no disturbance can be, no disturbance in the world. Remember!"

Charles II (1630-1685). King of England, Scotland and Ireland. Dying of "apoplexy," Charles' last words have a number of variations. To his brother: "Let not poor Nelly [his mistress, Nell Gwynne] starve." On the morning of his death four days after the stroke: "I have been a most unconscionable time dying, but I beg you to excuse it." Then: "Open the curtains that I may once more see daylight." By noontime, Charles was dead.

Alternatives: * "Don't forget poor Nell."

* "You must pardon me, gentlemen, for being a most unconscionable time a-dying."
* "I fear, gentlemen, I am an unconscionable time a-dying; but I hope you will excuse it."
* "Draw back the curtain, that I might once again behold the light of day."
* "That clock must be wound tomorrow."

Charles V (1337-1380). King of France. Dying of kidney failure: "Withdraw, my friends, withdraw and go away a little, so I can rest from the bother and labor I did not shirk."

Charles VII (1403-1461). King of France. Charles regained the throne after his father abdicated to the English King Henry V. Dying of a jaw infection: "I thank God that I, the greatest of sinners, should die on this day [the feast of St. Mary Magdalene, July 22nd]."

Charles VIII (1470-1498), King of France. Dying of an accidental head injury: "My God, the Virgin Mary, my lord St. Claude, and my lord St. Blaise, they help me!" Later: "I hope never again to commit a mortal sin, nor even a venial one, if I can help it."

Charles IX (1550-1574). King of France. Under an oath of safety, a group of French Protestants was allowed into Paris to attend the wedding of the King of Navarre. Charles' mother, Catherine de Medici, urged him to order the slaughter of thousands of these Protestants- the St. Bartholomew's Day massacre. Apparently this act greatly troubled the dying monarch, because he lamented to his medical attendants: "Asleep or awake, I see the mangled forms of the Huguenots passing before me. They drip with blood. They point at their open wounds. Oh! That I had spared at least the little infants at the breast! What blood! I know not where I am. How will all of this end? What shall I do? I am lost forever! I know it. Oh, I have done wrong. God pardon me!" After receiving Communion, to his nurse: "If Jesus my Savior should number me among His redeemed!" As he expired, Charles held his mother's hand and said: "Mother."

Alternatives: * Dying of tuberculosis: "Nurse, nurse, what murder! What blood! Oh, I have done wrong. God pardon me!"

* "Ah my nurse, my dearest nurse, what blood and murders! I have had but wicked counsel. Oh my God, forgive me for all that and so it please Thee, have mercy on me."
* "Blood, blood, rivers of blood! So much blood! Ah, nurse, what bad advice I listened to! Ah, God forgive me! I don't know where I am

anymore. What will become of me and my people? I am lost, lost! Thank God I have no son to succeed me!"

Charles X (1757-1836). King of France. Dying of cholera, to his grandchildren: "God protect you, my children. Walk in the ways of righteousness. Do not forget me. Pray for me sometimes."

Alternatives: * "May God protect you, my children. Walk in the paths of justice. Do not forget me. Pray for me sometimes."

* "I forgive, from my heart, those who have made themselves my enemies, more particularly, those who have been led away by the advice of others. I have forgiven them for a long time before God. To my grandson will devolve the happiness of and glory of pardoning them before men."

Charles II (1661-1700). King of Spain. Charles suffered from multiple physical deformities, possibly due to inbreeding among his ancestors. He died several days shy of his 39th birthday: "Now I am as one of the dead."

Charles III (1716-1788). King of Spain. When asked if he forgave his enemies, Charles responded: "It did not need this extremity for me to forgive them. They were all of them forgiven in the moment of doing me injury."

Charles V (1500-1558). Spanish king and Holy Roman Emperor from 1519 until his abdication in 1556. After relinquishing power, Charles retired to a monastery and died of possible malaria two years later. As he received the sacrament: "Lord God of truth, our Redeemer, into Thy hands I commit my spirit... Jesus." Charles' spoke as he gazed at a crucifix: "Now, Lord, I go!" A moment later, he added, "Ay, Jesus!" and expired.

Charles IX, King of Sweden (see Karl IX, King of Sweden).

Charles XI, King of Sweden (see Karl XI, King of Sweden).

Charles XII, King of Sweden (see Karl XII, King of Sweden).

Charles Ferdinand, Duc de Berry (1778-1820). French aristocrat. Attacked by a deranged man as he left the Paris Opera House, Charles Ferdinand cried: "I've been stabbed." Before dying the following day: "I forgive him."

Alternative: "Blessed Virgin, have mercy."

Charlotte Augusta (1796-1817). Princess of Wales. Having suffered a miscarriage after a prolonged period of labor, Charlotte bled profusely. To her physicians: "Is there any danger?" When told to compose herself: "I understand the meaning of that answer." After receiving a stimulant of wine and brandy, she said to one of her doctors, Baron Stockmar: "They have made me tipsy." When Stockmar left the room for a few moments, Charlotte cried: "Stocky! Stocky!" She died approximately five hours after the delivery of her dead infant.

Alternative: * "You make me drunk. Pray leave me quiet. I feel it affects my head."

Charlotte Augusta Matilda (1766-1828). English-born Queen Consort of Frederick I, King of Württemberg, Germany. On her deathbed: "I hear your voice, but I don't see you anymore."

Charmion (died 30 BCE). One of Egyptian Queen Cleopatra's maids-in-waiting. After the defeat of Cleopatra's army by Octavian, the queen considered suicide. When Roman soldiers broke into the royal mausoleum, they discovered the queen and one of her maids dead; her attendant Charmion was found clinging to life. A soldier angrily asked: "Was this well done of your lady, Charmion?" She replied: "Extremely well and as became the descendant of so many kings." She then fell dead.

Charteris, Francis (died 1732). Scottish aristocrat whose womanizing earned him the sobriquet of "The Rape-Master General." Charteris said around the time of his death: "I would gladly give £30,000 (some say Lira) to have it proved to my satisfaction that there is no such place as hell."

Chase, Harold "Hal" (1883-1947). American major league baseball player and disgraced gambler. "I knew it years ago and I know it more clearly now, that my life has been one great mistake after another."

Chastelard, Pierre de (1540-1562). French poet. Enamored of Mary, Queen of Scots, Chastelard was discovered in her apartment and subsequently sentenced to death for treason. Gazing toward the palace window as he awaited execution by hanging: "Farewell, thou who art so beautiful and so cruel, who killest me and whom I cannot cease to love."

Chateaubriand, François-René (1768-1848). French statesman and writer. During the revolution that deposed Louis Philippe I (below) and established the Republican government, street fighting was not uncommon. Told that a disturbance was occurring in the streets, Chateaubriand wistfully said: "I want to go there."

Chaucer, Geoffrey (c.1343-1400). English poet and writer, best-known for his collected stories *The Canterbury Tales.* Chaucer died repeating a "moral ode:" "A balade made by Geffrey Chaucyer upon his dethe-bedde lying in his grete anguysse."

Chávez, Georges (see Dartnell, Jorge Chávez).

Chávez, Hugo (1954-2013). President of Venezuela. Dying of cancer and a "heart attack," Chávez mouthed the words: "I don't want to die... please don't let me die."

Chekhov, Anton (1860-1904). Russian writer, playwright and physician, best-known for his short stories. Terminally ill with tuberculosis, Chekhov commented after receiving a glass of champagne ordered by his physician: "I am dying. I haven't drunk champagne for a long time."

Alternative: * "It has been some time since I have drunk champagne."

Chénier, André (1762-1794). Turko-French poet and political activist. Chénier was accused of being an enemy of the state by Robespierre (below) and was executed during the last days of the French Revolution.

Approaching the guillotine, the poet said: "I leave nothing for posterity; and yet," touching his forehead (some say his heart), "I had something there." Ironically, Robespierre, himself, was guillotined three days later.

Alternative: * The novelist Alexandre Dumas related that Chénier touched his forehead and said: "And yet, I did have something here." A friend nearby touched his heart and exclaimed: "No, it was there!"

Chenoweth (died 1856). Northwest U.S. Native American Cascades chief. Chenoweth and other tribal warriors fought in the Cascades Massacre that resulted in the deaths of immigrant settlers and U.S. soldiers. After they were captured, all were sentenced to die by hanging. When the "rope did not work well," Chenoweth muttered: "I am not afraid to die." He then was shot dead by a soldier.

Cherokee Bill **(see Goldsby, Crawford).**

Chesterton, Gilbert "G.K." (1874-1936). English novelist, journalist and poet. Dying from complications of heart and kidney afflictions: "The issue is now quite clear: it is between light and darkness and everyone must choose his side." To his wife and secretary successively: "Hello, my darling... hello, my dear."

Chevalier, Maurice (1888-1972). French actor and singer. Dying after surgery for a kidney ailment: "There's fun in the air."

Chickering, Hannah (1817-1879). American prison reformer. Dying of a chronic painful illness: "Say only that I was at peace. More than this, if repeated, might indicate a deeper spiritual experience than I ever had."

Childers, Robert (1870-1922). Irish patriot, writer and politician. Childers fought for a free Irish republic during the Irish Civil War and was condemned to death for treason. To the firing squad: "Take a step or two forward, lads. It will be easier that way."

Chin, Vincent (1955-1982). Chinese-born American draftsman. Chin was beaten to death by two Detroit auto workers who associated him with the

Asian incursion into the struggling U.S. automotive industry. Chins's last words were: "It's not fair."

Chiniquy, Charles (1809-1899). Canadian Roman Catholic priest. Because of conflicts with the Catholic Church, Chiniquy converted to the Protestant faith. Near death, the Roman Catholic archbishop wished to offer him the services of the ministry: "I am thankful to the Archbishop, but I have definitely retired from the Church of Rome. I am perfectly happy in the faith of Jesus Christ. God and Jesus suffice me. I long for the moment of leaving."

Choate, Joseph (1832-1917). American lawyer and diplomat who was ambassador to Great Britain at the beginning of the 20th century. Dying of a heart attack, to his wife: "I am feeling very ill. I think this is the end."

Choate, Rufus (1799-1859). American lawyer and U.S. senator. Dying suddenly, Choate's words were similar to those spoken by his cousin Joseph above: "I don't feel well. I feel faint."

Chopin, Fryderyk (1810-1849): Polish-born pianist and composer who died of tuberculosis. When asked by his physician if he were suffering, Chopin allegedly replied immediately before he died: "No longer."

Alternatives: * Probably spoken two days before dying: "She [George Sand, his lover] told me I would die in no arms but hers."

* "Mama!"
* "Mother, my poor Mother!"
* "I am happy! I feel death drawing near. Pray for me. We will see one another again in heaven."
* To cellist Auguste Franchomme and Princess Czartoryska: "You will play Mozart together in my memory."
* "Play Mozart in memory of me- and I will hear you."
* To Princess Marceline and Mlle. Gavard: "When you play music together think of me, and I shall hear you."
* "I am already at the source of happiness."
* "Now I am already at the source of Blessedness!"

* As he lay dying, Chopin called: "Jesus, Mary, Joseph," kissed a crucifix and said "Now I am at the source of blessedness!"
* After receiving something to drink: "*Cher ami*"
* "Who is near me?" in response to the presence of Adolph Gutmann, one of his pupils.
* To the abbé who gave him Extreme Unction: "Thanks! Thanks! Thanks to you I shall not die like a pig."
* "Without you I should have croaked like a pig."

These alleged terminal phrases varied depending on which person claimed to have heard Chopin's last words. In all probability, his last utterance, again, was "No longer" or "No more" in response to the question about pain.

Chopin had a morbid fear that he might be buried alive (taphephobia). His last written words were directed toward that end: "As this earth will smother me, I adjure you to have my body opened so that I may not be buried alive." Controversy has arisen concerning the word "earth" in Chopin's writing. Herbert Weinstock, in his biography *Chopin The Man and His Music*, writes: "In Chopin's original scrawl, this word looks like terre (earth), which it has always been taken to be. Nicolas Slonimsky [former editor of *Baker's Biographical Dictionary of Musicians*] reads it as toux (cough), a deciphering I find it all but impossible to make. Nor do I agree with Mr. Slonimsky that the traditional reading 'makes no sense.' Certainly earth would smother a man buried alive."

Alternatives: * "The earth is suffocating. Swear to make them cut me open, so that I won't be buried alive."

* "As this cough will choke me, I implore you to have my body opened, so that I may not be buried alive."

Christian III (1503-1559). King of Denmark and Norway. To his councilors: "Now I will sing, and you must sing with me, that it may be said that the king sang himself to the grave." He began chanting Psalm 103 and expired as he sang: "As a father pitieth..."

Christian IV (1577-1648). King of Denmark and Norway. Taking the hand of his minister: "Now comes the fight."

Christian IX (1818-1906). King of Denmark. At a party, Christian said: "I'll go into the next room and fetch a cigar. I'll be back in a moment." When his daughter offered to obtain one, he replied: "No, certainly not." After the king returned, he was in obvious distress. Taken to bed, Christian announced: "I think I can sleep a little." He died several minutes later.

Christian X (1870-1947). King of Denmark. Dying of a heart attack, Christian said: "My task on this earth is over. I am at peace with my God and myself. I am so tired."

Christian, Fletcher (1764-1793). English mutineer sailor aboard HMS *Bounty*. In 1789, Master's mate Christian and 22 others seized control of William Bligh's merchant vessel 1,300 miles west of Tahiti. Christian and fellow mutineers sailed to Pitcairn Island in the South Pacific and settled there. In 1808, a ship called on the island and its crew found one of the original mutineers alive. John Adams, the survivor, claimed that he had heard Christian's last words: "... Now I see before me the entrance only to the grave. God forgive me! I have been a great sinner. Pray for me, Adams. I feel so very cold- I shiver, and I can hardly see the large tree, which I know is not a fathom from me. Good-night, Adams- good-night! Ha!- it was another shot, and someone else is..." Adams claimed that Christian was murdered in a dispute between Tahitians and the mutineers.

Christopher, Saint (fl. 3rd century). Canaanite Christian martyr. Emperor Decius (some say the King of Samos) ordered his archers to slay Christopher for failure to renounce his Christian faith. Legend relates that an arrow inadvertently struck the emperor/king in his eye. Before his eventual beheading, Christopher advised: "I know O King that I shall be dead on the morrow. When I am dead, do thou tyrant make a paste of my blood, rub it upon thine eyes and thou shalt recover thy sight." The ruler followed the martyr's recommendation and had his sight restored.

Chrysippus (c. 280-c. 207 BCE). Greek Stoic philosopher. After he gulped down "a draught of Bacchus," Chrysippus observed a donkey eating some of his figs. He burst out laughing and died suddenly after exclaiming: "Give him a bumper [a glass filled to the rim] of wine!"

Alternative: * "Now give the ass a drink of pure wine to wash down the figs."

Chrysogonus, Saint (died c. 304). Roman Christian martyr. Chrysogonus was beheaded, because he refused to worship Roman gods during the persecutions ordered by Emperor Diocletian: "I adore the One God in heaven, and I spurn your proffered dignities as clay."

Alternative: * "I adore one God in heaven and spurn your honors as dirt."

Chrysostom, Saint John (c. 347- 407). Patriarch of Constantinople. Because he promulgated unpopular clerical reforms, Chrysostom was banished from Constantinople. Dying during his exile, Chrysostom spoke after taking the Eucharist: "Glory be to God for all Things. Amen."

Chuang Tzu (c. 369-c. 286 BCE). Chinese philosopher. When Chuang Tzu neared death, his disciples told the master they would like to give him a grand burial. He replied that either the heaven [burial above ground] or earth [below ground] would be very suitable. When they expressed fears that the birds of the field would consume his corpse, Chuang Tzu's replied: "Above ground, I shall be food for kites [a bird that feeds mostly on carrion]; below I shall be food for mole-crickets and ants. Why rob one to feed the other?"

Alternative: * "Above, the crows and kites will eat me; below, the mole-crickets and ants will eat me; to take from those and give to these would only show your partiality."

Chubbuck, Christine (1944-1974). American television news reporter. Suffering from depression and suicidal thoughts, Chubbuck wounded herself on the air with a gunshot to the head. Her last words: "And now, in keeping with Channel 40's policy of always bringing you the latest in blood and guts, in living color, you're about to see another first- an attempted suicide." She later died of her injury.

Chudleigh, Elizabeth (1720-1788). English noblewoman, the Duchess of Kingston. After downing several glasses of wine to the consternation of her attendants, Chudleigh allowed: "I will lie down on the couch. I can sleep and after that I shall be entirely recovered." Instead, she died.

Church, Frank (1924-1984). U.S. senator. Dying of pancreatic cancer, Church answered a cousin who asked how he was doing: "John, it is very, very interesting."

Churchill, Charles (1732-1764). English poet and satirist. Because of his dissolute lifestyle, Churchill's supposed last words reflected the disappointment he held for himself: "What a fool I have been." Some say his last statement was: "Thank God! I die in England." These words may be spurious, because many biographers place his death in Boulogne, France.

Churchill, Jennie (1854-1921). American-born socialite and mother of Winston Churchill (below). After breaking an ankle in a fall, gangrene forced the amputation of Churchill's leg above the knee. Dying of bleeding from the surgical site, she cried out: "Nurse! Nurse! I'm pouring blood."

Churchill, John, Duke of Marlborough (1650-1722). English general and diplomat. Dying from complications of a stroke, Churchill was asked if he wished to hear prayers. His reply: "Yes! And I joined in them." When queried if he wished to be lifted to bed, Churchill answered "Yes." He never awoke from his sleep.

Churchill, Randolph (1911-1968). English politician and writer who was Winston Churchill's only son. Dying of a heart attack, Churchill was asked if he believed in God: "No, I don't think I do. But I believe that when you die all the goodness in you comes together as a force."

Churchill, Winston (1874-1965). English prime minister who led Great Britain during WWII. On his 75th birthday: "I am ready to meet my maker. Whether my maker is prepared for the great ordeal of meeting me is another matter." Dying of a stroke at age 90, before lapsing into a coma: "I'm so bored with it all."

Alternative: * "Everything is so boring."

Chytræus, David, also Chyträus (c. 1530-1600). German theologian and historian. Known as one of the fathers of the Lutheran Church, Chytræus commented on the completion of his final manuscript: "I have concluded the history of this century and put the finishing touches to it, and not another word will I write." His death ensured the accuracy of his last words.

Cicero, Marcus (106-43 BCE). Roman statesman, orator and lawyer. Murdered during the unrest that followed the assassination of Julius Caesar one year earlier, Cicero exclaimed to his assailants as he pointed to his neck: "Here! Veteran! If you think it right, strike."

Alternative: * "There is nothing proper about what you are doing, soldier, but do try to kill me properly."

Cilley, Jonathan (1802-1838) Member of the U.S. House of Representatives. Cilley was mortally wounded in a duel with a fellow congressman over a disputed newspaper article: "I am shot."

Clanton, William "Billy" (1862-1881). American cattle rustler who was wounded in the O.K. Corral shootout. When told that he would die, Clanton demanded: "Get a doctor and put me to sleep. Pull off my boots. I always told my mother I'd never die with my boots on." As he was laid out: "They murdered me! Clear the crowd away from the door and give me air. I've been murdered." After receiving an analgesic injection: "Drive the crowd away."

Clare, John (1793-1864). English poet. Clare suffered from depression and insanity that forced his institutionalization. Dying of "apoplexy:" "I have lived too long. I want to go home."

Clark, George (1752-1818). American Revolutionary War officer. When told that a friend had died: "Everybody can die but me."

Clark, Guy (died 1832). American criminal, hanged for the brutal murder of his wife. On the way to the gallows, the sheriff urged Clark to hurry: "Nothing will happen until I get there."

Clarke, Adam (c. 1762-1832). Irish-born English Methodist preacher and scholar. Dying of cholera, Clarke was asked if he trusted in the Lord: "I do! I do!" To his son: "Am I blue? Are you going?" He died peacefully.

Claude, Jean (1619-1687). French clergyman, theologian and educator. "I am so oppressed that I can attend only to two of the great truths of religion- the mercy of God and the gracious aids of the Holy Spirit... My whole resource is the mercy of God. I expect a better life than this; our Lord Jesus Christ is my only righteousness."

Claudel, Paul (1868-1955). French poet, dramatist and diplomat. Worlds away from his elegant writings, Claudel asked on his deathbed "Doctor, do you think it could have been the sausage?"

Claudius, Matthias (1740-1815). German poet and essayist. "Lead me not into temptation. O deliver me from evil… Goodnight, goodnight."

Clay, Henry (1777-1852). American politician and unsuccessful presidential candidate. Dying of tuberculosis, Clay started the childhood prayer: "Now I lay me down to sleep." To his son: "Sit near me, my dear son. I do not wish you to leave me for any time today." Later: "Give me some water… I believe, my son, I am going." He then requested his son to: "… button [my] shirt collar" and died.

Cleburne, Patrick (1828-1864). Irish-born American Confederate officer during the U.S. Civil War. Killed at the Battle of Franklin, Tennessee, Cleburne spoke to General John Hood before leading his troops against Union soldiers: "General, I have my division in two lines and am ready. General. I am more hopeful of the success of our cause than I have ever been since the war commenced."

Clemenceau, Georges (1841-1929). French premier during WWI. On his deathbed: "I wish to be buried standing- facing Germany." Delirious from his terminal illness, Clemenceau asked a friend: "What has happened, Pietri?" When told that he had an "attack," the statesman replied: "This time it will be a long one."

Clemens, Olivia (1845-1904). American wife of Samuel Clemens (Mark Twain). Dying of heart failure, her husband asked why she didn't call on her beliefs in religion for a respite. Her reply: "I don't have any of them anymore. You made certain of that." As Samuel sang and played the piano upstairs, Olivia spoke to her maid: "He is singing a good-night carol to me." She died before her husband returned downstairs.

Clemens, Samuel, pen name of Mark Twain (1835-1910). American humorist and writer. Deathbed memorandum: "Death, the only immortal, who treats us all alike, whose pity and whose peace and whose refuge are for all. The soiled and the pure, the rich and the poor, the loved and the unloved." Dying of a heart attack, to his daughter: "Goodbye... If we meet..."

Alternative: * "Goodbye, dear. Then, if we meet..."

Clement XI (1649-1721). Pope from1700 until his death. At the end: "See how all the honors of the world come to an end. Only that is great which is great in God's sight. Make it your endeavor to be a saint."

Clement XII (1652-1740). Pope from 1730 until his dissolution. During his deathbed confession, Clement said: "I have no fault of any kind." When chided that even a pope might have some indiscretion to repent, he steadfastly replied: "No, neither on that point do we feel any remorse of conscience."

Clement XIV (1703-1774). Pope from 1769 until his death. When cardinals prompted Clement to name 11 more princes to the church before he died, he responded: "We cannot and we will not do it. The Lord will judge our reasons." When the cardinals repeated their request, the annoyed pope declared: "I'm on my way to eternity and I know why!" Some say Clement's last words expressed more than sarcasm, rather a suspicion that poison may have caused his death.

Clément, Jacques (1567-1589). French Dominican friar and conspirator, killed after he fatally stabbed King Henry III of France. Before dying, Clement was asked if he dared look an angry king in the face: "Yes, yes, yes! And kill him too."

Clemente, Roberto (1934-1972). Puerto Rican-born American professional baseball player. When Clemente planned to accompany a plane-load of supplies bound for earthquake-stricken Nicaragua, he was told that the aircraft was unsafe. He replied: "If you're going to die, you're going to die." The plane crashed en route and his body was never found.

Cleopatra (69-30 BCE). Egyptian Queen. After the defeat of her army by Octavian and the suicide of her co-combatant and lover Marcus Antonius, Cleopatra ended her life by the bite of a poisonous snake. When she saw the reptile, she remarked: "So, here it is." Some historians feel she died of a self-administered poison.

Alternative: * "Here thou art, then!"

Cleveland, Grover (1837-1908). Twenty-second and later twenty-fourth U.S. president. Dying of a heart attack: "I have tried so hard to do right."

Cliff, Montgomery (1920-1966). American stage and screen actor. The night before his death from a heart attack, Cliff was asked if he wanted to watch *The Misfits*, a movie in which he had starred. His reply: "Absolutely not!" He was found dead the next day.

Clifford, Thomas, Baron Clifford of Chudleigh (1630-1673). English politician. Suffering from "the stone" and depression, Clifford was found hanging from his bed tester (canopy supporter), "vomiting out a great deale of bloud." As he died: "Well, let men say what they will, there is a God, a just God above."

Clive, Robert (1725-1774). British soldier and statesman. Clive suffered from depression during the last part of his life. He became addicted to opium, which he used to treat chronic abdominal pain. When a friend asked if he would make a pen, Clive replied: "To be sure." He then took a penknife and fashioned a writing quill. Later he used the same knife to fatally lacerate his throat (jugulation). Some, however, say he died of an opium overdose.

Close, Del (1934-1999). American actor, improviser, comedian and teacher. Dying from complications of emphysema: "Thank God. I'm tired of being the funniest person in the room."

Cobain, Kurt (1967-1994). American pop musician and lead singer of the band Nirvana. Struggling with depression and drug abuse, the 27 year-old Cobain shot himself in the head. The conclusion of his suicide note:

"... I have a goddess of a wife [Courtney Love] who sweats ambition and empathy and a daughter [Frances] who reminds me too much of what I used to be, full of love and joy, kissing every person she meets because everyone is good and will do her no harm. And that terrifies me to the point to where I can barely function. I can't stand the thought of Frances becoming the miserable, self-destructive, death rocker that I've become.

"I have it good, very good, and I'm grateful, but since the age of seven, I've become hateful towards all humans in general. Only because it seems so easy for people to get along that have empathy. Empathy! Only because I love and feel sorry for people too much I guess. Thank you all from the pit of my burning, nauseous stomach for your letters and concern during the past years. I'm too much of an erratic, moody baby! I don't have the passion anymore, and so remember, it's better to burn out than to fade away. Peace, love, empathy. Kurt Cobain

Frances and Courtney, I'll be at your altar. Please keep going Courtney, for Frances. For her life, which will be so much happier without me.

I LOVE YOU, I LOVE YOU!"

Cobbe, Frances (1822-1904). Irish suffragist, antivivisectionist and writer. Cobbe's final letter: "I am touched by your affectionate words, dear Blanche [Atkinson, a writer], but *nobody* must be sorry when that time comes, least of all those who love me."

Cobden-Sanderson, Thomas (1840-1922). English bookbinder and book designer. Cobden-Sanderson's last diary entry: "Every day, every day my Guide says to me 'Are you ready?' And I say to my Guide 'I am ready.' And my Guide says 'March.' And to the end one day more I march. Oh every day, every day, am I ever on the ever-diminishing way to the end."

Cochin, Augustin (1823-1872). French politician and writer. Cochin's final letter: "... The Republic has been killed by her own children. The odious 1793, the foolish 1848. 1870 has carried her to her grave. She was killed by Robespierre, by Marat [both below] and then by all the word-mongers who have dealt in plots, in debts and foolish actions and who have three times ascended this chariot of the people."

Cochise (c. 1812-1874). Native-American Apache chieftain. Dying of an abdominal ailment, Cochise asked Thomas Jeffords, an Indian agent friend: "Do you think you will ever see me again?" Jeffords replied that he didn't think so and predicted that the chief would be dead by the following evening. Cochise agreed, saying: "I think so too, about tomorrow morning, at ten o'clock. I will pass out, but do you think we will ever meet again?" When his friend said: "I don't know," Cochise responded: "Well, I have been giving it a good deal of thought since I have been sick here, and I think we will." Jeffords asked where and the chief replied: "I don't know, somewhere up there," pointing to the sky. Cochise died the following morning before medical help arrived.

Alternative: * "... I don't know. It is not clear to my mind, but I think we will, somewhere up there."

Cocteau, Jean (1889-1963). French writer, playwright poet and filmmaker, best-known for his novel *Les Infants Terribles* and the movie *Beauty and the Beast.* Informed about the death of the French singer Edith Piaf, Cocteau commented: "The boat is going down."

Cody, William "Buffalo Bill" (1846-1917). American soldier, bison hunter, showman and folk hero. Suffering from kidney failure, Cody was told by his physician that he had about 36 hours to live. The showman replied: "Thirty-six hours? That's all? Well, let's forget about it and play High Five [a card game]."

Alternative: * "Well, let's forget about it and play High Five. I wish Johnny would come." Cody mentored Johnny Baker and treated him as a surrogate son. Baker did not arrive in time for the showman's death.

Coffin, Charles (1823-1896). American journalist and U.S. Civil War correspondent. When asked how his head felt: "If it were not for this pain, I should get up and write." Coffin died of a stroke.

Coffin, Robert (1892-1955). American poet, writer and educator who won the 1936 Pulitzer Prize for Poetry. Suffering a heart attack during a lecture, Coffin said: "The cold air caught my breath. Just let me sit down for a moment."

Coghill, George (1872-1941). American anatomist and naturalist. After his nurse asked him to swallow a dose of peppermint water: "Why, that's what we used to give to babies."

Cohn, Harry (1891-1958). American film producer who was president of the Columbia Pictures Corporation. Dying of a heart attack, before reaching the hospital: "It's no use. It's too tough. It's just too tough."

Coke, Edward (1552-1634). English Lord Chief Justice, noted for his ruling that common law superseded the wishes of the Crown. His last words were from Matthew 6:10: "Thy kingdom come, Thy will be done."

Colbert, Auguste (1777-1809). French general in the service of Napoleon I. Colbert was mortally wounded by a British sharpshooter during the Battle of Cacabelos in northwest Spain. Earlier, Colbert responded to an aide who advised him to stay out of the line of fire: "You are then very much afraid of dying today?"

Colbert, Jean-Baptiste (1619-1683). Finance minister of French King Louis XIV. To his wife who asked if he had answered a letter from the king: "It is the King of Kings that I should be thinking about."

Colburn, James (1960-2003). American criminal, executed by lethal injection for a murder and attempted rape: "The statement that I would like to make is, none of this should have happened and now that I'm dying, there is nothing left to worry about. I know it was a mistake. I have no one to blame but myself. It's no big deal about choosing right from wrong. I pray that everyone involved overlooks the stupidity. Everybody has problems and I won't be a part of the problem anymore. I can quit worrying now, it was all a mistake. That's all I want to say." As the drugs took effect: "It's going to be like passing out on drugs."

Cole, Nathaniel "Nat King" (1919-1965). American popular singer. Shortly before his death from lung cancer, Cole said: "My future is now in the hands of Jesus and God. I'm ready for whatever happens." The last word spoken to his nurse was his wife's name "Maria," although some say he used her nickname "Skeez."

Cole, Thomas (1801-1848). English-born American artist, founder of the Hudson River School movement. Dying of pneumonia: "I want to be quiet."

Coleman, Roger (1958-1992). American criminal, electrocuted for the rape and murder of his sister-in-law: "An innocent man is going to be murdered tonight. When my innocence is proven, I hope Americans will realize the injustice of the death penalty as all other civilized countries have..."

Coleridge, Samuel Taylor (1772-1834). English poet and philosopher, best-known for *The Rime of the Ancient Mariner* and *Kubla Khan*. Addicted to opium, Coleridge spent many years living with his physician. On his deathbed: "My mind is quite unclouded. I could even be witty."

Coleridge-Taylor, Samuel (1875-1912). British conductor and composer. Dying of pneumonia, Coleridge-Taylor spoke to his wife: "I look forward to meeting such a crowd of musicians [in heaven]." Because his father was African, he fretted about his obituary: "All the papers will call me a Creole."

Colette, Sidonie-Gabrielle (1873-1954). French writer, best-known for her novel *Gigi*. Pointing to a box of butterflies and fluttering her hands like wings, Colette said to her husband, Maurice Goudeket: "Look, Maurice, look!"

Coligny, Gaspard de (1519-1572). French admiral. Coligny, a supporter of the Protestant cause in France during the mid-1500s, was captured by Catholic forces during the St. Bartholomew's Day massacre. When his assassins asked if he were Coligny, the admiral replied: "I am indeed. Young man, you should have respect unto my gray hairs! But work your will; you can abridge my life only by a few short days." At the initial sword strikes to his arms, Coligny spoke to Maure, preacher to the queen of Navarre: "Oh, my brother, I now perceive that I am beloved of my God, seeing that for His most holy name's sake I do suffer these wounds." Coligny then was run through with a sword, his body was thrown from the window and his severed head was sent by the French king and queen to the pope (some say to Philip II of Spain).

Alternatives: * "Young man thou sightest to respect my years, and my infirmity of the body, but it is not thou that canst shorten my days."
* "Young man, you ought to consider my age and infirmity, but you will not make my life any shorter."

Colley, Thomas (died 1751). English criminal who drowned an elderly woman suspected of witchcraft. The conclusion of a final written declaration before his hanging: "... I am fully convinced of my former error, and with the sincerity of a dying man, declare that I do not believe there is such a thing in being as a witch; and pray God that none of you, through a contrary persuasion, may hereafter be induced to think that you have a right in any shape to persecute, much less endanger the life of a fellow creature. I beg of you all to pray to God to forgive me, and to wash clean my polluted soul in the blood of Jesus Christ, my savior and redeemer. So exhorteth you all, the dying Thomas Colley."

Collier, James (1947-2002). American criminal, executed by lethal injection for a double murder: "The only thing I want to say is that I appreciate the hospitality you guys have shown me and the respect. And the last meal was really good. That is about it. Thank you guys for being there and giving me a little bit of spiritual guidance and support." Although Collier asked for a T-bone steak and jumbo shrimp for his last meal, he was served chicken-fried steak and fried fish.

Collingbourne, William (died 1484). English administrator and critic of King Richard III. In 1484, Collingbourne penned the rhyme: "The cat, the rat and Lovell our dog rule all England under the hog." Because this was directed against Richard (the hog) and three of his supporters, William Catesby, Richard Ratcliffe and Francis Lovell, he was accused of treason. Collingbourne was hanged, drawn and quartered over an hour's period. As the executioner ripped out his bowels (some say heart), the condemned man allegedly muttered: "Oh, Lord Jesus, yet more trouble!"

Collins, Anthony (1676-1729). English philosopher, essayist and deist. "I have always endeavored, to the best of my ability, to serve God, my king and my country. I go to the place God has designed for those who love Him."

Alternative: * "The Catholic faith is, to love God and to love man. This is the best faith, and to its entertainment I exhort you all."

Collins, James "Jim" (died1979). Air New Zealand pilot. On November 28, 1979 an Air New Zealand DC-10 jetliner made a scheduled sightseeing flight to Antarctica. When the plane approached Mt. Erebus, the ground proximity warning system alarmed, prompting the flight engineer Gordon Brooks to exclaim: "I don't like this." Seconds later Collins asked for "Go-around power please." Before evasive action could be taken, the jetliner slammed into the mountain killing all 257 on board. The accident apparently was caused by faulty position entries in the plane's computer.

Collins, Joel (died 1877). American outlaw, a member of the Sam Bass gang that robbed stage coaches and trains. Tracked by the law and cavalry after robbing a train near Big Springs, Nebraska, Collins tried to resist arrest. To his partner: "Pard, if we are to die, we might as well die game [to die fighting]." They did not survive the shootout.

Alternative: * "I'm going down with my six-guns."

Collinson, Harry (died 1991). Chief planning officer for Derwentside District Council, northern England. On June 20, 1991, Collinson was supervising the demolition of an unauthorized cottage built by Albert Dryden. When the builder brandished a pistol, Collinson spoke to an accompanying TV cameraman: "Can you get a shot of this gun?" Dryden shot the planning officer dead while being televised. The assailant later was sentenced to life imprisonment.

Colquhoun, Janet (1781-1846). Scottish noblewoman and religious writer. Seeking her grandson: "Where is he? I cannot see him!"

Colt, Samuel (1814-1862). American inventor and firearms manufacturer. Dying from suspected rheumatic fever (some say malaria): "It's all over now."

Columba, Saint (died 597). Irish monk and missionary. Concluding his last transcription of a Psalter, Columba put down his pen and said: "Here I must stop, at the end of this page. What follows, let Baithen [a fellow monk] write." Then to a trusted companion, a message for the community: "Dear children, this is what I command [some say commend] with my last words- let peace and charity, a charity mutual and sincere, reign always among you! If you act thus, following the example of the saints, God who strengthens the just will help you, and I, who shall be near Him, will intercede on your behalf, and you shall obtain of Him not only all the necessities of the present life in sufficient quantity, but still more the rewards of eternal life, reserved for those who keep His law."

Alternative: * "Here I cease. Have peace and love."

Columbus, Christopher (1451-1506). Italian-born navigator, sailor and explorer, best-known for his four voyages from Spain across the Atlantic Ocean to the Americas. After partaking of the Holy Sacraments: "Into Thy hands, O Lord, I commend my spirit."

Combe, Andrew (1797-1847). Scottish physician who was a strong proponent of phrenology. Dying of tuberculosis, Combe was asked how he was doing: "Happy! Happy!"

Combe, George (1788-1858). Scottish phrenologist and older brother of the physician, Andrew Combe (above). "From my present sensations I should say I was dying, and I am glad of it."

Comer, Robert (1956-2007). American criminal, executed by lethal injection for a double murder. Comer's last words were directed to the Oakland Raider professional football team: "Yes. Go Raiders." The team had a losing season in 2007-2008.

Comte, Auguste (1798-1857). French philosopher who laid the foundations for modern sociology and developed the belief of positivism. Referring to his impending death from cancer: "What an irreparable [some say incomparable] loss."

Condé, Henri de (1552-1588). French aristocrat and military leader. Dying of poison allegedly given by his wife: "Hand me my chair. I feel extremely weak." Some say his death was caused by a previous battle injury.

Confucius, also Kong-Fu-Tse (c. 551-479 BCE). Chinese philosopher. Confucius spoke of his death: "The great mountain must crumble, the strong beam must break, and the wise man wither away like a plant." He then went into his house and spoke to an aide: "... I am a man of Yin and last night I dreamt that I was sitting with offerings before me between the two pillars [where a burial ceremony would take place]. No intelligent monarch arises; there is not one in the kingdom that will make me his master. My time is come to die."

Alternatives: * "The great mountain must crumble, the strong heart must break, and the wise man wither away like a plant. In all the provinces of the empire there arises not one intelligent monarch who will make me his master. My time has come to die."
* "I have taught men how to live."

Conner, Johnny (1975-2007). American criminal, executed by lethal injection for the murder of a convenience store worker. Connor directed his last words to the daughter of his victim: "Shed no tears for me. When I get to the gates of heaven, I'm going to be waiting for you. I will open my arms for you. What's happening now, you are suffering. I didn't mean to hurt y'all.... This is destiny. This is life. This is something I have to do... To Allah I belong and to Allah I return."

Conner, Kevin (died 2005). American criminal, executed by lethal injection for a triple murder: "Everybody has to die sometime, so ... let's get on with the killing."

Conrad, Joseph, born Józef Konrad Korzeniowski (1857-1924). Polish/ Ukrainian-born British writer, best-known for his novels with nautical settings. To his wife moments before dying of a heart attack: "You, Jess! I'm better this morning! I can always get a rise out of you."

Alternative: * "Here..."

Conradin von Hohenstaufen (see Konradin von Hohenstaufen).

Consalvi, Ercole (1757-1824). Italian Vatican statesman and cardinal, noted for his negotiations at the Congress of Vienna that restored the position of the Papal States. "My mind is at rest."

Constant, Benjamin (1767-1830). Swiss-born French political activist and writer. Delaying corrections of proofs for his *History of Religions*: "The rest tomorrow."

Constantine I, also Constantine the Great (c. 272-377). Emperor of Rome who was baptized into the Christian faith shortly before his death. At the end, Constantine proclaimed: "Now, now I know in very truth that I am blessed; now I have confidence that I am a partaker of divine light... I have the assurance that I have been found worthy of eternal life. My only anxiety now is to hasten my journey to God."

Constantine XI (c. 1404-1453). Byzantine Emperor. As he defended Constantinople from the Turks, Constantine allegedly shouted: "So there is no Christian who wishes to free me from this life?" A few moments later enemy soldiers obliged him.

Alternative: * "The city is taken, and I am still alive."

Cook, Anthony (1959-1993). American criminal, executed for the murder of a law student: "... I believe that the State of Texas is making a mistake tonight. Tell my family I love them. I'm ready."

Cook, Frederick (1865-1940). American arctic explorer who claimed to have been the first person to reach the North Pole. Suffering from a stroke, Cook learned that President Franklin Roosevelt had pardoned his earlier conviction for mail fraud in a Texas oil scheme. He awoke from a comatose state saying: "Great... happy day... pardon..."

Cook, James (1728-1779). British naval explorer and cartographer. During his exploration of the Hawaiian Islands, one of his ship's small boats was purloined by locals. Cook exclaimed: "I am afraid these people will oblige me to use some violent measures; for they must not be left to imagine that they have gained an advantage over us." During an ensuing fight, Cook ordered his men to cease firing but was clubbed and stabbed to death by the natives.

Cooke, Jay (1821-1905). American banker whose firm supplied significant financial support to the federal government during the U.S. Civil War. Hearing the prayer for the dead, Cooke exclaimed: "Amen. That was the right prayer."

Cooke, Samuel "Sam" (1931-1964). American pop singer and song writer. During an altercation at a Los Angeles motel, Cooke allegedly was shot in self-defense by the manager of the establishment: "Lady, you shot me!"

Cooke, Terence (1921-1983). Roman Catholic archbishop of New York. Dying of leukemia, to his grieving housekeeper: "Maura, you were always so good and kind to me. You've got to be very brave, just like my sister."

Cooke, William (1846-1876). Union officer during the U.S. Civil War and an adjutant to General Custer at the Little Big Horn massacre. Cooke's transcription of Custer's orders to Captain Frederick Benteen who covered one of his flanks: "Benteen- Come on. Big village. Be quick. Bring packs. W.W. Cooke P.S. Bring pacs [*sic*]." Cooke was killed during the skirmish.

Cookman, Alfred (1828-1871). American Methodist minister. Dying of a painful myalgia, to his sister-in-law: "This is the sickest day of my life, but all is well. I am so glad I have preached full salvation. What would I do without it now? If you forget everything else, remember my testimony- washed in the blood of the Lamb! Jesus is drawing me closer and closer to His great heart of infinite love." To his wife: "I am Christ's little infant..." To his son: "My son, your pa has been all day *sweeping close by the gates of death*. How sweet and quiet everything seems. I feel like resting now."

Alternative: * "I am sweeping through the gates, washed in the blood of the Lamb!"

Coolidge, Calvin "Silent Cal" (1872-1933). Thirtieth U.S. president. A taciturn man, Coolidge spoke to a carpenter working on his home: "Good morning, Robert." An hour later, his wife found the president dead on their bedroom floor.

Cooper, Ashley, Lord Shaftesbury (1801-1885). English philanthropist. To a friend: "When I feel age creeping on me and I know I must soon die- I hope it is not wrong to say it, but I cannot bear to leave the world with all the misery in it." When handed an article by his valet: "Thank you."

Alternative: * "I am just touching the hem of His Garment."

Cooper, Astley Paston (1768-1841). British surgeon and anatomist. After a final consultation with physicians about his ailment: "My dear sirs, I am fully convinced of your excellent judgment and of your devotion to me, but your wishes are not to be fulfilled. God's will be done! God bless you both. Bransby [presumably his biographer and nephew, Bransby Blake Cooper], my dear, kiss me. You must excuse me, but I shall take no more medicine." When death neared: "Goodbye, God bless you."

Cooper, Gary, born Frank James Cooper (1901-1961). American screen actor, best-known for his performances in *Sergeant York* and *High Noon*. Dying of cancer, Cooper opined: "It is God's will."

Alternative: * "We'll pray for a miracle, but if not, and that's God's will, that's alright too."

Cooper, Gladys (1888-1971). British stage, film and television actress. Looking into a mirror: "If this is what viral pneumonia does to one, I really don't think I shall bother to have it again." Cooper died later that night.

Copeland, John Jr. (c. 1836-1859). African American abolitionist. Convicted of treason and hanged for his involvement in the Harpers Ferry raid (see Brown, John above): "If I am dying for freedom, I could not die for a better cause. I had rather die than be a slave."

Copernicus, Nicolaus (1473-1543). Polish astronomer, known for his magnum opus *On the Revolutions of Heavenly Bodies*. In this book, Copernicus formulated the novel idea that the sun was the center of our solar system. Dying of a stroke (some say a fever), the astronomer deliriously exclaimed: "The book- tell me- they surely have not burned it- you know I wrote no word but truth- oh, how could they burn my book!" To assuage his distress, a copy was placed in his hands. As he expired: "Now, oh Lord, set Thy servant free."

Copleston, Edward (1776-1849). English clergyman and academic. "I expect soon to die and I die in the firm faith of the redemption wrought by God in man through Christ Jesus, assured that all who believe in Him will be saved."

Copley, John (1738-1815). American-born British artist. Dying of a stroke, to his daughter who asked how he felt: "Happy, happy, supremely happy!"

Copley, John, Lord Lyndhurst (1772-1863). American-born British lawyer and politician, son of John Copley (above). To his daughter as he pointed to a family picture painted by his father: "See, my dear, the difference between me *here* and *there*."

Coppola, Ann (1921-1962). Wife of the American mobster "Trigger Mike" Coppola (not to be confused with Frank Coppola below). After many years of physical and mental abuse by her husband, Coppola ended her life with an overdose of alcohol and barbiturates. Her suicide note read: "Mike Coppola- Someday, somehow, a person, or God, or the law shall catch up with you, you yellow-bellied b******. You are the lowest and biggest coward I have ever had the misfortune to meet." She then wrote in lipstick over her hotel bed: "I have always suffered; I am going to kill myself. Forget me."

Coppola, Frank (1944-1982). American criminal, electrocuted for the murder of a woman during a robbery: "I felt I owed it to myself to take control of my own destiny. What the hell? We all have to die. At least, I can say when… Take care of my family." As he entered the death chamber: "Fire it up."

Corbet, Miles (1595-1662). English politician who was one of the signers of King Charles I's death warrant. After the Restoration, Corbet was convicted of regicide and sentenced to die by hanging: "For this for which we are to die I was no contriver of it; when the business was motioned I spoke against it, but being passed in parliament I thought it my duty to obey. I never did sit in that which was called the high court of justice but once."

Corbet, Richard (1582-1635). English bishop and poet. To his chaplain and confidant: "Goodnight, Lushington."

Corbulo, Gnaeus (c.7-67). Roman general accused of plotting to overthrow Emperor Nero. Ordered to commit suicide for his failure, Corbulo lamented: "Well deserved," as he fell on his sword.

Corday, Charlotte (1768-1793). French assassin. Corday surmised that the assassination of Jean-Paul Marat (below), a member of the revolutionary Jacobin faction, might lead to stability in France. After securing a meeting, she encountered Marat in his bathtub from which he often sought solace from a persistent skin ailment. Corday thrust a knife into his chest, fatally injuring him. At her trial: "I killed one man to save a hundred thousand; a villain to save innocents, a savage wild beast, to give repose to my country..." Corday subsequently was sentenced to die by decapitation. To the artist who painted her portrait before the execution: "Monsieur, I know not how to thank you for the trouble you have taken; I have only this (a lock of her hair she had trimmed) to offer you. Keep it, in memory of your kindness and my gratitude." As she approached the guillotine, the condemned woman said to the executioner who blocked her view: "I have the right to be curious; I've never seen one before." As she placed her neck on the block: "This toilette of death, though performed by rude hands, leads to immortality." After her head was severed by the blade, the executioner held it by the hair and slapped it. Rumor has it that a blush was seen on Corday's countenance.

Alternatives: * "One man have I slain to save a hundred thousand."
* "This is the toilette of death, arranged by somewhat rude hands, but it leads to immortality."

Corder, William (1803-1828). British criminal who killed his lover at the Red Barn, Suffolk, England. The notorious crime subsequently was dubbed "The Red Barn Murder." Convicted of her slaying, Corder spoke moments before his hanging: "I am guilty. My sentence is just: I deserve my fate. And may God have mercy on my soul."

Alternative: * "I am justly sentenced and may God forgive me."

Corey, Giles (c. 1611-1692). English-born colonial Salem, Massachusetts farmer. Accused of witchcraft, Corey refused to answer the charge. In an attempt to "press" the truth from him, he was placed beneath a board and heavy weights were added "*peine forte et dure* [strong and hard punishment]." In an attempt to hasten his death, Corey begged: "More weight."

Cornell, Lieutenant J.G. (died 1814). U.S. naval officer. Serving aboard the American ship USS *Essex* during the War of 1812, Cornell sustained a mortal wound during battle. When the surgeon turned from an injured man, Cornell said: "No, no, doctor, none of that. Fair play's a jewel. One man's life is as dear as another's. I would not cheat any poor fellow out of his turn." Later, when approached by David Farragut, a shipmate, he spoke his last words: "O Davy, I fear it's all up with me." The ship's doctor opined that Cornell might have been saved, if he had been treated earlier.

Cornstalk, also Hokoleskwa (c. 1720-1777). Native American Shawnee chief. Falsely implicated in the murder of a militiaman (some say a hunter), Cornstalk faced his accusers and was shot dead: "My son, the Great Spirit has seen fit that we should die together and has sent you here to that end. It is His will and let us submit; it is all for the best." His son and another Shawnee also were killed.

Corot, Jean-Baptiste (1796-1875). French landscape and portrait painter. Dying of a "stomach disorder," probably cancer, Corot pointed his fingers toward a wall as if painting: "Look how beautiful it is! I have never seen such admirable landscapes."

Alternative: * "In spite of myself I go on hoping- I hope with all my heart there will be painting in heaven."

Corrigan, Michael (1839-1902). Archbishop of New York. Dying of heart failure and pneumonia while convalescing from a fall: "I feel very weak."

Cortés, Agustín (1898-1927). Martyred Mexican clergyman. Caught up in the turmoil of the Cristero War, Cortés was sentenced to die. Before a firing squad: "We live for God, and for Him we die."

Coryat, Thomas (c. 1577-1617). British traveler and travelogue writer. Dying of dysentery in India, Coryat deliriously begged for a drink: "Sack! Sack! Is there any such thing as sack? I pray you give me some sack [a strong, cheap wine]."

Cosgrove, Kevin (1955-2001). American businessman. Cosgrove was caught in the September 11, 2001terror attacks on the World Trade Center in New York City. He made a call to 911 from the doomed South Tower immediately before it collapsed: "My wife thinks I'm all right, I called and said I was leaving the building and that I was fine, and then bang... Hello? Hello! We're looking in, we're overlooking the Financial Center. Three of us, two broken windows." Shortly thereafter, Cosgrove yelled "Oh God! Oh...," as the tower collapsed.

Costello, Louis "Lou" born Louis Cristillo (1906-1959). American actor and member of the Abbott and Costello comedy team. Dying of a heart attack, to his nurse after asking her to move him onto his side: "I think I'll be more comfortable."

Alternative: * To his agent who brought a strawberry soda: "That was the best ice-cream soda I ever tasted."

Cottolengo, Saint Benedict Joseph (1786-1842). Italian priest who ministered to the sick and poor. Dying, Cottolengo quoted Psalm 122:1: "I rejoiced when it was said unto me, 'Let us go unto the House of the Lord!'"

Cotton, John (1585-1652). English-born American Puritan minister. When a friend promised to pray that God would grant him the light of His countenance, Cotton replied: "God hath done it already, brother." To his attendant: "The God that made you, and bought you with a great price, redeem your body and soul unto himself."

Courtright, Timothy "Jim" (1848-1887). American sheriff. Courtright had an argument with a Ft. Worth, Texas saloon owner and was shot during a subsequent gunfight. To lawman John Fulford who went to Courtright's aid: "Ful, they've got me."

Couzens, James (1872-1936). U.S. senator and businessman. To his wife and son before undergoing an operation that would end his life: "Don't worry. They can't kill an old dog like me. I'll see you later, Mother. Don't worry."

Covency, Joseph (c. 1805-1897). Irish-born American atheist. To his children who implored him to repent: "Die as I lived. I disbelieve in God, the Bible, and the Christian Religion." In a *New York Times* article written the day after his death, Covency was referred to as "one of the most noted infidels in the United States."

Cowan, Frederick (1943-1977). American laborer and Nazi fanatic. Expressing his pent-up hatred, Cowan killed four coworkers at a New Rochelle, New York moving company and a police officer who responded to the massacre. During the ensuing standoff, the assailant demanded food via a telephone link to a police official. Cowan said these last words shortly before he shot himself: "I get mean when I'm hungry... All I want is the food and I'm not going to hurt anybody at this point. Tell the mayor that I'm sorry to be causing the city so much trouble." As police tried to keep him on the line, Cowan abruptly hung up saying: "Just get the godd*** food!"

Coward, Noël (1899-1973). English playwright, actor and composer. To friends as they left for the night: "Good night my darlings, I'll see you tomorrow." The next morning, the valet found the ailing Coward and offered to summon his friends: "No, it's too early; they will still be asleep." He died of a heart attack shortly thereafter.

Cowper, John (1737-1770). British clergyman, brother of William Cowper (below). On the day of Cowper's death, his brother asked how he had fared during the night. John's reply: "A sad night, not a wink of sleep… I endeavored to spend the hours in the thoughts of God and prayer; I have been much comforted, and all the comfort I got came to me in this way."

Cowper, William (1731-1800). British poet and hymnodist. Dying of "dropsy," the melancholy Cowper asked his attendant who offered some sustenance: "What does it signify?"

Coy, Bernard (c. 1901-1946). American bank robber. While attempting to escape from Alcatraz Prison in San Francisco Bay, Coy was shot and killed. His last words: "It don't matter; I figure I licked the Rock [a nickname for Alcatraz] anyway."

Crabbe, George (1754-1832). English poet, writer and clergyman. To his family: "All is well at last. You must make an entertainment. God bless you. God bless you!"

Craib, Karola (died 2011). German-born American newspaper food writer. Dying of cancer, Craib left a note for her daughter: "Never eat margarine."

Craigie, Pearl, whose pen name was John Oliver Hobbes (1867-1906). American-born English writer. Taken ill in London during a holiday trip to Scotland, Craigie's last telegram read: "Excellent journey. Crowded train. Reached here by nine. Fondest love, Pearl."

Crane, Hart (1899-1932). American poet and writer, best-known for his poem *The Bridge*. While on a ship in the Caribbean, the despondent Crane told his girlfriend: "I'm not going to make it, dear. I'm utterly disgraced." When his friend tried to cheer him up, he said: "All right, dear. Goodbye." Minutes later he jumped overboard and was lost. Some say he called: "Goodbye, everybody!" before leaping.

Crane, Stephen (1871-1900). American poet and writer, best-known for his novel *The Red Badge of Courage*. Dying from complications of tuberculosis, Crane spoke to a friend and collaborator, Robert Barr: "Robert - when you come to the hedge- that we all must go over- it isn't bad. You feel sleepy and- you don't care. Just a little dreamy curiosity [some say 'anxiety']- which world you're really in- that's all."

Cranmer, Thomas (1489-1556). Martyred English Archbishop of Canterbury. Cranmer had supported the independence of the English Church from Rome and the ascension of Lady Jane Grey to the throne after the death of King Edward VI. When Mary I took the throne instead, the Catholic monarch insured that the Protestant Cranmer would be tried for treason. Despite numerous recantations of his views against Catholicism, Cranmer was consigned to the stake. As the flames grew, he thrust his hand forward, crying: "This was the hand that wrote it [the recantation]; therefore it shall suffer first punishment." As Cranmer died: "My unworthy right hand! This hand hath offended. Lord Jesus, receive my spirit... I see the heavens open and Jesus standing at the right hand of God."

Alternative: * "This hand having sinned in signing the writing must be the first to suffer punishment. This hand hath offended."

Crantor of Soli (c. 335-c. 275 BCE). Greek philosopher who was a follower of Plato. Facing death, Crantor reflected about his burial: "Sweet in some corner of native soil to rest."

Crates the Cynic (c. 365-c. 285 BCE). Theban disciple of the Greek philosopher Diogenes. Taking stock of himself as death approached, Crates complained: "Ah! Poor hump-back! Thy many long years are at last conveying thee to the tomb. Thou shalt soon visit the palace of Pluto."

Cratesicleia (died 222 BCE). Mother of Spartan King Cleomenes. After the death of her son, his enemy Ptolemy of Alexandria ordered the murder of Cratesicleia and her grandchildren. As Cratesicleia watched the slaughter, she cried: "O children, whither are ye gone?"

Crawford, Francis (1854-1909). Italian-born American novelist. Dying of a heart attack: "I love to see the reflection of the sun on the bookcase."

Crawford, Joan, born Lucille Fay LeSueur (1904-1977). American film and television actress. Dying of a heart attack complicating pancreatic cancer, Crawford admonished an attendant who had begun to pray aloud: "D*** it! Don't you dare ask God to help me."

Crawford, William (1732-1782). American Revolutionary War soldier. Crawford led an ill-fated expedition against Native American combatants and British troops in northern Ohio. Taken captive, he was killed in retaliation for a previous massacre: "My fate is then fixed and I must prepare to meet death in its worst form." Crawford then was tortured by burning at the stake and scalping: "Almighty God, be with me now. Have mercy upon me God. I pray you end this suffering so that I might be with you where there is no pain and suffering. Oh god, dear God, help me!"

Crazy Horse (c. 1842-1877). Native American Sioux chieftain. Crazy Horse joined Sitting Bull to defeat George Custer's army at the Battle of the Little Bighorn. Later imprisoned at Fort Robinson, Nebraska, Crazy Horse was stabbed by a soldier during his attempted escape. To a relative who tried to restrain him: "Cousin, you killed me! You are with the white people!" Later, to his father [some say a friend]: "I am hurt bad. I am going to die. Tell the people they cannot depend on me anymore." Just before dying, Crazy Horse spoke unintelligible words in his native language.

Cream, Neil (1850-1892). Scottish-born physician who poisoned a number of people in England, Canada and the United States. Condemned to hang for murder by a London, England court, Cream's last words were: "I am Jack..." Speculation has arisen that Cream was confessing to the Jack the Ripper murders committed in London around 1888, although he was not in England at that time.

Crevel, René (1900-1935). French writer and member of the Surrealist Movement. Despondent because of problems with his professional life and health (tuberculosis), Crevel committed suicide by inhaling gas from his kitchen stove. He left a note which read "Please cremate my body. Loathing."

Alternative: * "Everything disgusts me."

Crippen, "Dr." Harvey (1862-1910). American-born homeopathic physician, hanged for the alleged murder of his wife Cora. Ethel "Le Neve" Neave, his lover at the time the time of his wife's death, was acquitted of involvement in the sordid affair. The conclusion of Crippen's last note: "... In this farewell letter to the world, written as I face eternity, I say that Ethel le Neve loved me as few women love men and that her innocence of any crime, save that of yielding to the dictates of her heart, is absolute. To her I pay this last tribute. It is of her that my last thoughts have been. My last prayer will be that God may protect her and keep her safe from harm and allow her to join me in eternity..." Recent DNA analysis raised questions whether the body found in Crippen's basement actually was his slain wife.

Crisp, Donald (1882-1974). British actor. Suffering from complications of a stroke, Crisp was asked if dying were difficult: "Not as difficult as playing comedy."

Crisp, Quentin, born Denis Pratt (1908-1999). British writer and actor. "You crawl out of your mother's womb; you crawl across open country under fire and drop into your grave."

Crittenden, John (1787-1863). U.S. senator, representative and attorney general. To his son Thomas: "Tom, come and raise me up and arrange my pillow. That's right, Tom."

Crittenden, William (1823-1851). American mercenary soldier, son of John Crittenden (above). Captured while on an expeditionary incursion into Cuba, Crittenden was executed by firing squad. When ordered to kneel: "I will kneel only to my God."

Alternatives: * "No! An American kneels only to his God, and always faces his enemy."

* "A Kentuckian never turns his back on an enemy and kneels only to his God."

Crockett, David "Davy" (1786-1836). American frontiersman, politician and soldier. While defending the Alamo in San Antonio, Texas, Crockett was killed by the attacking Mexicans led by Santa Anna (below): "I'm warning you boys, I'm a screamer!" Because no defenders survived the assault, these purported final words are questionable. Santa Anna, Antonio López de

Croker, John (1780-1857). Irish-born English politician and writer. To a friend who commented death was an awful thing: "I do not feel it so. The same Hand which took care of me when I came into this world will take care of me when I go out of it." To a servant as he fainted away: "Oh, Wade..."

Croll, James (1821-1890). Scottish scientist who wrote about climate change as a function of variations in the earth's orbit. After abstaining from alcoholic beverages during his lifetime, Croll requested spirits on his deathbed: "I'll take a wee drop o' that. I don't think there's much fear o' me learning to drink now."

Alternative: * "I don't think there's much fear of me becoming a drunkard now."

Crome, John (1768-1821). British landscape painter. Dying of a fever, Crome made motions with his arm as if painting. He said: "There- there- there's a touch- that will do- now another- that's it. Beautiful!" To his son: "John, my boy, paint, but paint for fame; and if your subject is only a pig-stye- dignify it." Moments before dying, he remembered the 17th century Dutch artist saying: "Oh, Hobbema, my dear Hobbema! How I have loved you!"

Cromwell, Oliver (1599-1658). English military leader and politician who helped overthrow the English monarchy and establish a transitory republican commonwealth. Cromwell brought about the end of the Irish Confederate Wars and later became Lord Protector of England. On his deathbed four years later, he said: "I would be willing to live, to be further serviceable to God and His people, but my work is done! Yet God be with his people!" He then asked his chaplain if it were possible to fall from grace. When reassured in the negative, Cromwell replied: "Then I am safe, for I am sure that I once was in a state of grace." When entreated to rest: "It is not my design to drink or to sleep, but my design is to make what haste I can to be gone." The following day, Cromwell advised his doctors: "You physicians think I shall die. I tell you I shall not die this hour. I am sure on't. I speak the words of truth upon surer grounds than Galen or Hippocrates furnish you with." Later, to friends: "Go on cheerfully. Banish sadness altogether and treat my death as no more to you than that of a serving man." As the statesman drifted into a coma: "My own faith is all in God." When Royalists returned to power, Cromwell's remains were exhumed, placed in chains and his head was impaled on a pole outside Westminster Hall for a number of years.

Alternative: * "Then I am safe, for at one time I am confident that I was chosen."

Cromwell, Thomas, Earl of Essex (c.1485-1540). English statesman during the reign of King Henry VIII. Running afoul of Henry and his marital affairs, Cromwell was condemned to die by beheading. On the scaffold, he prayed: "Oh, God, I prostrate myself to my deserved punishment; Lord, be merciful to Thy prostrate servant." Before the blade fell, his final prayer: "… Grant me, merciful Savior, that when death hath shut up the eyes of my Body, yet the eyes of my Soul may still behold and look upon Thee, and when death hath taken away the use of my tongue, yet my heart may cry and say unto thee, Lord into thy hands I commit my Soul, Lord Jesus receive my spirit. Amen."

Crosby, Frances "Fanny" (1820-1915). American poet and prolific hymnodist who was sightless from infancy. When Crosby's nephew checked on her during her last hours, she said: "All right, Governor." Later that night, Crosby died of a stroke.

Crosby, Harry "Bing" (1903-1977). American popular singer and actor. While vacationing in Spain, Crosby played a full round of golf and commented: "That was a great game of golf, fellers." He later collapsed and died of a heart attack.

Alternative: * "Let's go get a Coke."

Crosby, Howard (1826-1891). American Presbyterian minister and scholar. "My heart is resting sweetly with Jesus and my hand is in His."

Alternative: * "I place my hand in the hand of Jesus."

Cross, Edward (1832-1863). American journalist and Union officer during the U.S. Civil War. Cross was mortally wounded by a Confederate sharpshooter at the Battle of Wheatfield during the 1863 Gettysburg campaign: "I think the boys will miss me."

Crowfoot (c.1830-1890). Native American chief of the Blackfoot tribe. Dying of tuberculosis: "A little while and I will be gone from among you, whither I cannot tell. From nowhere we come, into nowhere we go. What is life? It is a flash of a firefly in the night. It is a breath of a buffalo in the winter time. It is as the little shadow that runs across the grass and loses itself in the sunset."

Crowley, Aleister (1875-1947). British occultist, magician poet and writer. Dying of bronchitis and a heart ailment, Crowley's last words were "I am perplexed."

Alternatives: * "Sometimes I hate myself."
* "... Satan, get out!"

Crowley, Francis "Two Gun" (1911-1932). American bank robber and murderer. After a 1931 crime spree, Crowley declared: "I hadn't anything else to do, that's why I went around bumping off cops." Before his electrocution at Sing Sing prison. New York: "My last wish is to send my love to my mother."

Crumpton, Boudinet "Bood Burris" (died 1891). American criminal, hanged for the shooting death of a companion while intoxicated: "Men, the next time you lift a glass of whiskey, I want you to look into the bottom of the glass and see if there isn't a hangman's noose in it, like the one here."

Alternative: * "To all you who are present, especially you young men, the next time you are about to take a drink of whiskey, look closely into the bottom of the glass and see if you cannot observe in there a hangman's noose. There is where I first saw the one which breaks my neck."

Cuauhtémoc (c. 1495-1525). Aztec emperor. Fearing a revolution at the hands of Cuauhtémoc, the Spanish conquistador Hernán Cortés condemned the Aztec leader to die by hanging: "I knew what it was to trust to your false promises, Malinche [Cortés' Indian nickname]; I knew that you had destined me to this fate, since I did fall by my own hand when you entered my city of Tenochtitlan. Why do you slay me so unjustly? God will demand it of you!"

Alternative: * "Oh Malinche! Now I understand your false promises and the kind of death you have had in store for me. For you are killing me unjustly. May God demand justice from you, as it was taken from me when I entrusted myself to you in my city of Mexico!"

Cuffee, Paul (1759-1817). American Quaker businessman, sea captain and abolitionist. To his family when they offered nourishment: "By no means, but let me pass quietly away." Later in the evening: "I can no longer strive against nature. All is well." To his sister-in-law: "Feed my sheep and my lambs."

Cullen, William (1710-1790). Scottish physician, chemist, inventor and educator. "I wish I had the power of writing or speaking, for then I would describe to you how pleasant a thing it is to die."

Cummings, Bruce (1889-1919). English biologist and writer. Dying of "disseminated sclerosis," Cummings referenced the journal documenting his progressive failing health: "The kindness almost everybody has shown the *Journal*, and the fact that so many have understood its meaning have entirely changed my outlook. My horizon has cleared. My thoughts are tinged with sweetness and I am content."

Cummings, Edward E. "E.E" (1894-1962). American poet, writer, artist and playwright. When his wife asked him to stop cutting wood on a hot day, Cummings replied: "I'm going to stop now, but I'm just going to sharpen the axe before I put it up, dear." He then died of a stroke.

Cunard, Maud "Emerald" (1872-1948). American-born English socialite. When offered a teaspoon of champagne by her maid, Cunard replied: "No. Open a bottle for the nurse and yourself."

Curie, Marie (1867-1934). Polish-born scientist. Curie and her husband Pierre discovered the element radium. Curie was awarded the Nobel Prize in Physics in 1903 and the Nobel Prize in Chemistry eight years later. Dying of leukemia, probably related to her previous radiation exposures, Curie was offered an analgesic by her nurse (some say a doctor): "I don't want it. I want to be left alone."

Curley, James (1874-1958). American politician who served as governor of Massachusetts, mayor of Boston and a member of the U.S. House of Representatives. Dying after surgery for stomach cancer, Curley was jounced when his stretcher hit a rough spot in the floor: "I wish to announce the first plank in my campaign for reelection... we're going to have the floors in this godd***** hospital smoothed [some say straightened] out."

Curran, John (1750-1817). Irish politician and wit. Curran's physician remarked that his patient was coughing with more difficulty: "That is surprising, since I have been practicing all night."

Curtis, George (1824-1892). American writer and civil rights activist. To a younger brother who asked if he could do anything: "Nothing, but to continue to love me."

Curtis, Ian (1956-1980). Founding member of the British rock band Joy Division. Despondent over his poor health and failing marriage, Curtis hanged himself. His suicide note read: "At this moment I wish I were dead. I just can't cope anymore."

Cushing, Harvey (1869-1939). American neurosurgeon, dubbed the "father of modern neurosurgery." Dying of a heart attack, Cushing said to his nephew who was treating him (some say adjusting his bedclothes): "Pat, you have the touch. You're a good doctor."

Cushman, Charlotte (1816-1876). American-born stage actress. Dying of breast cancer and pneumonia, Cushman spoke after milk punch was offered to her: "Punch, brothers! Punch with care!" from a quote by Mark Twain in an 1876 article "A Literary Nightmare."

Custer, George Armstrong (1839-1876). American army officer who fought in the U.S. Civil War and the Indian Wars. Custer's troops were outnumbered and decimated by Native American tribes at the Battle of the Little Bighorn, Montana ("Custer's Last Stand"). Before starting on his ill-fated mission, he wrote a last letter to his wife: "My Darling, I have but a few moments to write as we start at twelve, and I have my hands full of preparations for the scout. Do not be anxious about me. I hope to have a good report sent you by the next mail. A success will start us all toward Lincoln... Your devoted Autie [his nickname]."

As Custer divided his men into three groups before the attack, he remarked about his foes: "Custer's luck! The biggest Indian Village on the Continent!" Before the battle, his hubris was apparent: "Hurrah, boys, we've got them! We'll finish them up and then go home to our station." As the fighting deteriorated, Custer told one of his men: "Orderly, I want you to take a message to Colonel Benteen. Ride as fast as you can and tell him to hurry. Tell him it's a big village and I want him to be quick, and to bring ammunition packs... Now orderly, ride as fast as you can to Colonel Benteen. Take the same trail we came down. If you have time and there is no danger, come back; but otherwise stay with your company." Custer's last order written by his adjutant and passed to the orderly for dispatch read: "Benteen- come on- Big Village- be quick- bring packs." Because no troops survived the battle, his climactic last words were lost.

Alternatives: * "Courage, boys! We'll get them! And, as soon as we do, we'll go home to glory."

* "Hurrah boys! Let's get these last few reds then head on back to camp. Hurrah!"
* "We've caught 'em napping."

Cuthbert, Saint (c. 634-687). English bishop who for many years lived a hermit's existence. To a fellow holy man: "... Study diligently, and carefully observe the Catholic rules of the Fathers, and practise with zeal those institutes of the monastic life which it has pleased God to deliver to you through my ministry. For I know that although during my life some have despised me, yet after my death you will see what sort of man I was and that my doctrine was by no means worthy of contempt."

Cutler, Benjamin (1798-1863). American clergyman. Suffering from a cough and shortness of breath, Cutler asked two acquaintances to raise him in bed: "Lift me up, lift me right up." His head slumped forward and he died.

Cutter, Charles (1846-1864). American Union army soldier, mortally wounded during the U.S. Civil War. Cutter's last words were recorded by the poet Walt Whitman (below) who volunteered in a Washington D.C.

hospital. Whitman asked Cutter if he needed anything: "Oh, nothing. I was only looking around to see who was with me."

Cuvier, Clementine (c. 1805-1827). Daughter of the Frenchman Georges Cuvier (below). Active in the spiritual life of her community, Cuvier told a lady friend: "You know we are sisters for eternity. There is life. It is only there that there is life." To her betrothed who was weeping: "What is the matter with you? I am grieved to see you ill- all is right, since it is the will of God." Shortly before her death, she called her relatives to her bedside but was unable to speak further.

Alternative: * "You know you are my sister in Christ-for eternity- there is nothing else deserves the name."

Cuvier, Georges (1769-1832). French naturalist whose research led to the establishment of the fields of comparative anatomy and paleontology. To the attendant applying leeches as a type of bloodletting: "Nurse, it was I who discovered that leeches have red blood." Unable to swallow during his last hours, Cuvier handed a proffered glass of lemonade to his sister-in-law (some say daughter) saying: "It is delightful to see those whom I love still able to swallow."

Cyprian, Saint (died 258). Martyred Bishop of Carthage. When Rome decreed that all Christian clerics should renounce their religious beliefs or be executed, Cyprian refused, saying: "... I am a Christian and cannot sacrifice to the gods... I heartily thank Almighty God, who is pleased to set me free from the chains of this body." Condemned to die by beheading, he uttered: "Thanks be to God."

Cyrus the Great (c. 600-c. 529 BCE). Founder of the Persian Empire. Many accounts of Cyrus' death relate that he fell defending his empire or while acquiring new territories. More than likely, he passed peacefully in his Persian capital. To his sons: "When I am dead, my children, do not enshrine my body in gold, or in silver, or in any other substance; but restore it to the earth as soon as possible; for what can be more desirable than to be mixed with the earth, which gives birth and nourishment to everything excellent and good? I have always hitherto borne an affection to men, and I feel that I should now gladly be incorporated with that which is beneficial to men. And now my soul seems to be leaving me, in the same manner as, it is probable, it begins to leave others. If, therefore, any one of you is desirous of touching my right hand, or is willing to see my face, while it has life, let him come near to me; but when I shall have covered it, I request of you, my sons, let no man, not even yourselves, look upon my body. Summon, however, all the Persians, and the allies, to my tomb, to rejoice for me, as I shall then be safe from suffering any evil, whether I be with the divine nature, or be reduced to nothing. As many as come, do not dismiss until you have bestowed on them whatever favors are customary at the funeral of a rich man. And remember this, as my last admonition: by doing good to your friends, you will be able also to punish your enemies. Farewell, dear children, and say farewell to your mother as from me; farewell, all my friends, present and absent."

Alternatives: * "... And remember this as my last and dying words. If you do kindness to your friends, you will be able to injure your enemies... Farewell."

* "Remember my last saying. Show kindness to your friends, and then you shall have it in your power to chastise your enemies. Goodbye, my dear sons, bid your mother goodbye for me. And all my friends, who are here or far away, goodbye"

Cyrus the Younger (c. 423-401 BCE). Persian prince and military leader. During a campaign of conquest in the Babylon region, Cyrus rode his horse through the enemy lines shouting: "Clear the way, villains, clear the way!" He later died in battle.

Czolgosz, Leon (c. 1873-1901). American-born anarchist who assassinated President William McKinley in 1901. Before his electrocution at Auburn Prison in New York, Czolgosz allowed: "I killed the President because he was the enemy of the good people, the good working people. I am not sorry for my crime. I am sorry I could not see my father."

D'Annunzio, Gabriele (1863-1938). Italian writer, poet and WWI military leader. After suffering a stroke, D'Annunzio spoke about an earlier trip to Rome: "I want to see again in the springtime the city that I love. I have been thinking about this trip with joy and with trembling." He lay down to rest and died.

Alternative: * To his chauffeur: "Stop! Turn home! I'm bored. I'm bored."

Dahl, Roald (1916-1990). British writer, poet and military aviator. Dying of a bone marrow disorder, to his family: "... It's just that I will miss you all so much." When a nurse administered an injection: "Ow, f***!"

Dahlgren, John A. (1809-1870). American naval leader and armament inventor. To his wife as he took a glass in hand: "The clear ring of the ice was refreshing. Madeline; I will take nothing more until you go to your breakfast, which you must require."

Dahlgren, Ulric (1842-1864). Union Army officer during the U.S. Civil War. Dahlgren was ambushed by enemy soldiers while approaching Richmond, Virginia to assassinate Confederate President Jefferson Davis and his cabinet. Before he died: "Surrender, you d***** rebels, or I'll shoot you."

Dahmer, Jeffrey (1960-1994). American serial killer, convicted of murdering 15 young men. While serving 15 life sentences, Dahmer was beaten by a fellow prisoner. Before dying, he told his assailant: "I don't care if I live or die. Go ahead and kill me."

Dalí, Salvador (1904-1989). Spanish surrealist painter. Dying of heart failure, Dalí possibly thought of one of his best-known works, *The Persistence of Memory*, which featured melting timepieces: "Where is my clock?"

Dalton, Frank (1859-1887). American deputy U.S. marshal. While trying to arrest a horse thief in Indian Territory near the Arkansas River, Dalton was shot in the chest. In the resultant gun battle, the thief was killed, but his accomplice shot Dalton again: "Please don't fire. I'm preparing to die."

Dalton, Robert "Bob" (1867-1892). American bank and train robber who was a member of the notorious Dalton gang. Bob, accompanied by two brothers and two accessories, attempted to rob two banks in Coffeyville, Kansas simultaneously. When the plan went awry, Bob was mortally wounded. To his brother, Emmett, who was the sole survivor: "Don't mind me, boy. I'm done for. Don't surrender. Die game [fighting]."

Damien De Veuster, Saint (1840-1889). Belgian missionary. Damien spent many years with lepers in Hawaii and eventually died of the disease himself. His parting words: "Well, God's will be done. He knows best. My work, with all its faults and failures, is in his hands, and before Easter I shall see my Savior."

Damiens, Robert (1715-1757). Disgruntled Frenchman who failed in his attempt to assassinate King Louis XV. Condemned for his crime, Damiens was tortured, drawn and quartered. As he was taken from his cell on his last day, he said: "The day will be hard." His last words: "Oh death, why art thou so long in coming? May God have pity on me and Jesus deliver me!" Frederick Marvin in his book *Last Words (Real and Traditional) of Distinguished Men and Women* describes Damiens' last day in vivid detail: "The punishment inflicted upon Damiens for his attack upon the king was horrible. The hand by which he attempted the murder was burned at a slow fire; the fleshy parts of his body were then torn off by pincers; and finally, he was dragged about for an hour by four strong horses, while into his numerous wounds were poured molten lead, resin, oil and boiling wax. Towards night, the poor wretch expired, having by an effort of will almost superhuman, kept his resolution of not confessing who were his accomplices if, indeed, he had any. His remains were immediately burned, his house was destroyed, his father, wife and daughter were banished from France forever, and his brothers and sisters compelled to change their names."

Damrosch, Walter (1862-1950). German-born American conductor and composer. Suffering from dementia, Damrosch imagined that he had returned from a tour. To a friend: "Just back from Japan. They loved us in Tokyo. Rave reviews everywhere. Marvelous! Marvelous!"

Dancourt, Florent (1661-1725). French actor and playwright. Near death, Dancourt ruminated about the sins of his early days. When his daughter said: "Father, a man who dies well is half saved," he replied: "May God's will be done. My grave is dug. My last bed is made. You have to lie on the bed you have made."

Daniel, Jack (1846-1911). American distiller and founder of the operation that bears his name. Daniel allegedly injured a toe when he angrily kicked a safe that did not open properly. Infection set in, and he died of blood poisoning, saying: "One last drink, please."

Danks, Hart (1834-1903). American hymnodist and popular songwriter, best-known for his melody "Silver Threads Among the Gold." An unfinished note left by Danks referred to his estranged wife: "It is hard to die alone- since I kissed you, mine alone- you have never grown older."

Dante Alighieri (1265-1321). Italian poet and philosopher, best-known for his epic poem *Divine Comedy*. Dying of a fever, possibly of malarious origin, Dante offered some sage civic advice: "... Dedicate your strength and your spirit to your prince and your country, and leave to God the mysterious balance of fortune. Every banner that is not borne by a traitor leads to virtue."

Danton, Georges-Jacques (1759-1794). French lawyer who figured prominently in the early stages of the French Revolution. Later accused of disloyalty by Robespierre, Danton was sent to the guillotine. During his trial, the accused man was asked his name and place of residence. His reply: "My name is Danton; my dwelling will soon be in annihilation; but my name will live in the Pantheon of history!" At the guillotine, Danton remarked: "... I leave it all in a frightful welter [confusion]. Not a man of them has an idea of government. Robespierre will follow me; he is dragged down by me. Ah! Better be a poor fisherman [possibly a reference to St. Peter] than meddle with the governing of men." When told that he could not embrace a fellow prisoner, the doomed man exclaimed: "Fool! Not to see that our heads must in a few seconds meet in that basket." To his executioner: "Sanson, you will show my head to the people; it is worth seeing."

Alternatives: * "… You will show my head to the people. It will be worth the trouble."

* … "Be sure you show the mob my head. It will be a long time ere they see its like."
* … "You will show my head to the people; it will be worth the display!"

Darius III (c. 380-330 BCE). Persian ruler. When Alexander the Great invaded Darius' domain, the Persian was unsuccessful in repelling the attacking forces. After dissatisfied provincial governors arranged Darius' assassination, the mortally wounded leader was found by a Macedonian soldier called Polystratus. Darius allegedly requested: "But Alexander, whose kindness to my mother, my wife and my children, I hope the gods will recompense, will doubtless thank you for your humanity to me. Tell him, therefore, in token of my acknowledgment, I give him this right hand." Darius took Polystratus' hand and died.

Darnell, Linda, born Monetta Darnell (1923-1965). American screen actress. Darnell perished from burns sustained during a house fire. Before dying, she whispered to her daughter Lola: "I love you, baby; I love you."

Dartnell, Jorge Chávez, also called Georges Chávez (1887-1910). French-born Peruvian aviator. On September 23, 1910 Dartnell became the first aviator to fly over the Alps, but crashed his Bleriot airplane on landing. In a delirious state from his injury, he mumbled: "Higher, always higher," before expiring. His last words became the motto of the Peruvian Air Force.

Darwin, Charles (1809-1882). English naturalist whose book *On the Origin of Species* became a landmark in the science of evolution. Darwin's last words: "I am not the least afraid to die. I am only sorry that I haven't the strength to go on with my research"

Alternative: * "It's almost worthwhile to be sick to be nursed by you."

Darwin, Erasmus (1731-1802). English scientist, poet and physician who was the grandfather of Charles Darwin (above). Realizing that death was imminent, Darwin implored his wife: "My dear, you must bleed me instantly." When she hesitated, he asked his daughter: "Emma, will you? There is no time to be lost." She said: "Yes, my dear father, if you will direct me." Before any intervention could be made, Darwin died.

David (c.1040-970 BCE). King of Israel. As David lay dying, he addressed his son and heir-apparent, Solomon (1 Kings 2: 8-9). This scripture passage references the man who had sided with another son, Absalom, who wished to succeed David: "... And there is also with you Shim'e-i the son of Gera, the Benjaminite from Bahu'rim, who cursed me with a grievous curse on the day when I went to Mahana'im [a settlement east of the Jordan River]; but when he came down to meet me at the Jordan, I swore to him by the Lord, saying: 'I will not put you to death with the sword.' Now therefore hold him not guiltless, for you are a wise man; you will know what you ought to do to him, and you shall bring his gray head down with blood to Sheol [a place for the dead]." With that pronouncement, King David died. When Solomon succeeded his father, he placed a death decree on Shim'e-i.

David, Jacques-Louis (1748-1825). French artist. David directed corrections on a copy of one of his paintings: "Too dark... too light...The dimming of the light is not well-enough indicated... This place is blurred... However, I must admit that's a unique head of Leonidas ["Leonidas at Thermopylae"]." Apparently the exertion was too great, because David died suddenly.

Davidson, Lucretia (1808-1825). American poet. Dying of consumption (some say anorexia nervosa): "Death, which once looked so dreadful to me, is now divested of all its terrors."

Davidson, William (1781-1820). Jamaican-born English cabinetmaker and insurrectionist. Davidson joined the Cato Street Conspiracy to murder members of the British cabinet and the prime minister. Convicted of treason, Davidson and four co-conspirators were hanged and decapitated:

"God bless you all! Good-bye." After reciting the Lord's Prayer, he concluded with: "God save the king."

Daviess, Joseph (1774-1811). American lawyer and military officer. Shot in the chest during the Battle of Tippecanoe, near present-day Lafayette, Indiana, Daviess commanded that his body should not be seized by the Native American combatants: "Under no circumstances let me fall into the hands of savages." Daviess was buried on the Tippecanoe battlefield.

Davis, Cushman (1838-1900). Union army officer during the U.S. Civil War who later became a U.S. senator. "Oh, that I might live five more years for my country's sake."

Davis, David (1815-1886). Advisor to President Abraham Lincoln and member of the U.S. Supreme Court. Dying from complications of diabetes, Davis spoke his son George's nickname: "Geordie!"

Davis, Elizabeth "Bette" (1908-1989). American stage and screen actress. Dying of breast cancer, Davis spoke of her estranged daughter, Barbara Davis Hyman: "Tell B.D. I'm sorry. I loved her. I really did love her."

Davis, Jefferson (1808-1889). American politician who became president of the Confederacy during the U.S. Civil War. Dying from complications of bronchitis and malaria, Davis declined medication offered by his wife: "Please excuse me, I cannot take it."

Davis, Jerome (1838-1910). Union Army officer during the U.S. Civil War and later a missionary to Japan. On his deathbed: "I thought I was passing away, but now I feel as bright as a button."

Davis, Sammy, Jr. (1925-1990). American dancer, singer and actor. Dying of throat cancer, Davis allegedly said to his son: "Don't cry for me. I'll be dancing in heaven." Because Davis' larynx was removed several weeks before his death, it is questionable whether he uttered those words.

Davis, Thomas (1814-1845). Irish politician, poet and writer. Dying of tuberculosis, the conclusion of a last letter to a colleague: "I have had a bad attack of scarlatina [scarlet fever], with a horrid sore throat; don't mention this to anyone, for a delicate reason I have... In four days I hope to be able to look at light business for a short time."

Davis, Varina (1826-1906). American author who was the second wife of Confederate leader Jefferson Davis. Dying of pneumonia, to her daughter: "My darling child, I am going to die this time, but I'll try to be brave about it. Don't you wear black. It is bad for your health, and will depress your husband." Shortly before expiring, Davis said: "O Lord, in Thee have I trusted. Let me never be confounded!"

Davis, William (1957-1999). American criminal, executed by lethal injection for a murder committed during a robbery. Before dying, Davis spoke about his religious beliefs and then apologized to the victim's family and his relatives for his actions: "... I love [my family] dearly from the bottom of my heart, and one day I would like to see them on the other side. Some I will; some I won't. I would like to thank all of the men on Death Row who have showed me love throughout the years, but especially the last two or three weeks, and I hold nothing against no man. I am so thankful that I have lived as long as I have. I hope that I have helped someone. I hope that donating my body to science that some parts of it can be used to help someone, and I just thank the Lord for all that he has done for me. That is all I have to say, Warden... Oh, I would like to say in closing, what about those cowboys [presumably the Dallas Cowboys football team]?"

Davy, Humphry (1778-1829). English chemist who discovered various elements including sodium, calcium and potassium. Dying of heart failure, to his brother: "I am dying, and when it is all over, I desire that no disturbance of any kind be made in the house. Lock the door, and let everyone retire quietly to his apartment."

Day, Dorothy (1897-1980). American journalist and social activist who was one of the founders of the Catholic Worker movement. To her daughter: "How good life can be at certain moments."

Alternative: * Others relate that Day said: "Rise, clasp my hand and come." The English poet Francis Thompson wrote in an earlier work "The Hound of Heaven:" "The soul fleeing from God to every creature./ Resisting grace./ Returning to God./ Rise, clasp My hand and come."

Dayan, Moshe (1915-1981). Israeli soldier and foreign minister. Dying of a heart attack, to his daughter who had admonished him to be strong: "You are such an idiot! Philosophy s***! Thank God I'm leaving this place!"

Dead, born Per Yngve Ohlin (1969-1991). Swedish singer in the Norwegian black metal band Mayhem. With a history of self-mutilation and depression, Dead slit his wrists and shot himself in the head with a shotgun. His suicide note read: "Excuse all the blood. The knife was too dull to finish the job so I had to use the shotgun."

Dean, James (1931-1955). American actor, best-known for his performance in the film *Rebel Without a Cause*. As Dean drove with his mechanic Rolf Wütherich to a sports car competition in Salinas, California, a vehicle turned in front of his car, resulting in a violent crash. Before impact, Dean exclaimed to his companion: "That guy's got to stop... He'll see us." The actor died of multiple, massive injuries. Ironically, Wütherich perished in an automobile accident 26 years later.

Dearing, James (1840-1865). Confederate general in the U.S. Civil War. While engaged in a close pistol duel with Union officers at the Battle of High Bridge during the Appomattox Campaign, Dearing was mortally wounded. Before dying, he pointed to one of his subordinates, Colonel Elijah White, and said of his general's stars: "These belong on his collar."

De Barry, Gerald (1926-1964). Swiss-born American zoologist. De Barry received a fatal envenomation by a puff adder when he fell into the reptile's pen during a dizzy spell: "Don't blame the snake, it wasn't his fault. It was only trying to protect itself."

Debs, Eugene (1855-1926). American labor union leader and unsuccessful U.S. presidential candidate. Dying of heart failure, Debs wrote down lines from William Hensley's poem *Invictus* during his last days: "It matters not how strait the gate/ How charged with punishments the scroll,/ I am the master of my fate,/ I am the captain of my soul."

Decatur, Stephen (1779-1820). American naval officer, a hero of the War of 1812 and Barbary Wars. Mortally wounded in a duel with a fellow naval officer, Decatur uttered these words before he died: "I did not believe it possible to endure so much pain. I am a dying man. I do not so much regret my death as I deplore the manner of it. Had it found me on the quarter-deck it would have been welcome." To a friend: "You can do me no service; go to my wife, and do what you can to console her."

Alternative: * "I am mortally wounded, I think."

Decius, Gaius (c. 200-251). Military leader and Emperor of Rome. After his son was killed in battle with the Goths at Abrittus (modern-day Bulgaria), Decius spoke to his troops: "The loss of one soldier is not important to the Roman state. Let no man mourn the emperor's son!" Decius was killed a few moments later.

Deering, John (1898-1938). American criminal, executed by firing squad for a murder committed during a robbery. Referencing the donation of his body to the University of Utah: "At least I'll get some high class education." Before the firing squad: "Good-bye and good luck! Okay, let it go." Deering volunteered to have an electrocardiogram connected to his body to determine how long his heart would beat after shots were fired. Cardiac activity was noted for 15 seconds following a round to the heart.

Defoe, Daniel (1660-1731). English writer, best-known for his novel *Robinson Crusoe.* Dying of "lethargy:" "I don't know which is more difficult in a Christian life, to live well or to die well." Defoe published similar words in the *Compleat Tradesman* seven years prior to his death: "I know not whether of the two is most difficult, in the course of a Christian life; to live well, or to die well."

De Gaulle, Charles (1890-1970). French military leader during WWII who later president of France. Dying of a heart attack, to his wife: "... Yvonne, I hurt on my right side! Call a doctor! Oh, how it hurts!"

Alternative: * Pointing to his neck: "I feel a pain right here."

DeGraff, Peter (died 1894). American criminal, executed for the murder of his lover, Ellen Smith. DeGraff fostered a child with the simple-minded Smith but eventually tired of her attention. He subsequently lured her to a deserted area and put a bullet through her heart. Captured one year later, DeGraff was sentenced to die by hanging. On the gallows: "That thing you call corn liquor, cards, dice and other games of chance, pistols and bad women, are the things which brought me to this place. Yes, I shot that woman. I was drunk at the time. I put the pistol to her breast and fired it. The only words she said after I shot were: 'Lord have mercy on me.'"

Alternative: * "I stand here today to receive my just reward. I again say to the people here, beware of bad women and whiskey... don't put your hands on cards, bad women and dice. Hear my parting words."

Dekker, Edouard (1820-1887). Dutch writer and staunch critic of the colonial administration of the former Dutch East Indies. To his postal chess opponent: "That you are still not crushed, I admit, but that will come a little later. And if this is too difficult for you, let it go if you like. The game can wait."

De Koven, Reginald (1859-1920). American composer, primarily of comic operas. De Koven's last telegram read: "House sold out for Friday night, box office *Vox Dei* [God's voice] hurrah!"

Delacroix, Eugène (1798-1863). French Romantic painter. Dying of a chronic chest ailment: "Oh, if I get well, I will do wonderful things! My mind is bubbling with ideas!"

Delahanty, Edward (1867-1903). American major league baseball player. Removed from a train near Niagara Falls for disorderly behavior, Delahanty was found on a nearby bridge in an inebriated state. When approached by a watchman with a light, the ballplayer said: "Take that light away, or I'll knock your d***** brains out!" The athlete then fell into the water shouting for help; his body was recovered several days later.

De La Mare, Walter (1873-1956). English poet and short story writer. Dying of a heart attack, De La Mare was asked if he would like some fruit or flowers: "Too late for fruit, too soon for flowers." When asked if he were comfortable: "I'm perfectly all right."

DeLancey, William (1778-1815). American-born British army officer. DeLancey was mortally wounded by a cannon shot during the Battle of Waterloo. Miraculously, his wife later was able to reach his side before he perished. DeLancey's last words were a request: "Magdalene, my love, the spirits." She handed him a bottle of lavender spirits and he died.

Delane, John (1817-1879). British editor and journalist. Dying from a chronic, painful illness: "It is better for me to die than to live."

Delaney, Joe (1958-1983). American professional football player. Despite a fear of water, Delaney rushed into a pond to aid three struggling boys. When asked if he could swim: "I can't swim good, but I've got to save those kids. If I don't come up, get somebody." Only one of the youngsters survived.

Delaney, Mary (1700-1788). English artist and writer. Delaney's physician prescribed bark to help with fevers from "an inflammation on the lung." Her response: "I have always had a presentiment that if bark were to be given, it would be my death. You know I have at times a great defluxion [discharge of fluid or inflammation] on my lungs- it will stop that and my breath with it." When her attendant said she would withhold the bark: "Oh, no, I never was reckoned obstinate and I will not die so." Delaney expired shortly thereafter.

Delano, Jane (1862-1919). American nurse who founded the American Red Cross Nursing Service. This organization trained nurses in disaster relief and prepared many for service in WWI. Dying from complications of mastoiditis: "What about my work? I must get back to my work."

De la Torre, Lisandro (1868-1939). Argentinian provincial senator and lawyer. In 1935, one of De la Torre's protégés was murdered by a dissident, but the bullet probably was meant for the senator. Depressed by this event and his later financial problems, De la Torre took his own life by a gunshot to the chest. In a suicide note/will, he outlined plans for his cremation and funeral, concluding: "... If you do not disapprove, I would wish my ashes scattered to the winds. It seems to me an excellent way to return to nothingness, comingling with all that dies in the Universe."

Delk, Monty (1967-2002). American criminal, executed by lethal injection for a murder committed during a robbery: "I've got one thing to say: Get your warden off this gurney and shut up. I am from the island of Barbados. I am the warden of this unit. People are seeing you do this." After shouting profanities, Delk continued: "You are not in America. This is the island of Barbados. People will see you doing this."

Delle, Jeremy Wade (1975-1991). American teenager. Delle, a despondent 15 year-old Texas high school student, was late for an English class and was told by his teacher to obtain an admittance slip. When he returned, Delle replied: "Miss, I got what I really went for." He pulled a gun from his clothing, placed the barrel in his mouth and committed suicide in front of his classmates.

De Molay, Jacques (c. 1244-1314). French nobleman who was the last Grand Master of the Knights Templar order. After Pope Clement V disbanded the Knights, Philip IV of France charged De Molay and fellow prisoner Geoffroi [Geoffrey] de Charney with heresy and other trumped-up offences. Before his sentencing, De Molay professed his innocence: "To say that which is untrue is a crime both in the sight of God and man. Not one of us has betrayed his God or his country. I do confess my guilt, which consists in having, to my shame and dishonor, suffered myself, through the pain of torture and the fear of death, to give utterance to falsehoods imputing scandalous sins and iniquities to an illustrious Order, which hath nobly served the cause of Christianity. I disdain to seek a wretched and disgraceful existence by engrafting another lie upon the original falsehood." Astounded by this "exhibition of firmness and courage," the Knights were returned to prison to await Philip's reaction. When the king demanded that they should be burned to death, De Molay exclaimed: "France, remember our last moments. We die innocent. The decree which condemns us is an unjust decree, but in heaven there is an august tribunal to which the weak never appeal in vain. To that tribunal within forty days

I summon the Roman Pontiff. Oh, Philip, my master, my King! I pardon thee in vain, for thy life is condemned. At the tribunal of God, within a year, I await thee." Clement died about one month later and Philip followed in November of the same year!

Alternative: * "Let evil swiftly befall those who have wrongly condemned us. God will avenge us."

Demonax (died c. 170). Cyprian-born Greek philosopher. Asked about burial instructions: "Don't borrow trouble! The stench will get me buried." When asked whether his remains might be exposed to wild animals after his demise, Demonax replied: "I see nothing out of the way in it if even in death I am going to be of service to living things." His remains were placed in a tomb.

Alternative: * "You may go home, the show is over."

De Mornay, Philippe (1549-1623). French writer, Protestant leader and soldier. In his last hours, to his pastor: "If I die, I fly to heaven; the angels carry me to my Savior's bosom. I know that my Redeemer liveth; I shall see Him with these eyes." When asked if he were consoled with the Holy Spirit: "Yes, indeed. I am assured of it; the love of God is in my heart."

Demosthenes (384-322 BCE). Athenian orator who took poison to prevent his capture by the Macedonians: "... For my part, O Gracious Neptune, I quit thy temple with my breath within me; but Antipater [Alexander the Great's successor] and the Macedonians would not have scrupled to profane it with murder."

Demps, Bennie (1950-2000). American criminal, executed by lethal injection for the murder of a fellow inmate. When attendants had difficulty inserting a needle for the lethal infusion: "They butchered me back there, I was in a lot of pain... They cut me in the groin; they cut me in the leg. I was bleeding profusely. This is not an execution, it is murder."

Denmark, Barbara (died 2012). Florida resident. During an argument with her grandson, the 69 year-old Denmark was stabbed multiple times.

When the dying woman said "I love you," the young man halted his attack, called 911and surrendered himself to authorities.

Dennis, John (1657-1734). English critic and playwright. Informed on his deathbed that someone had published a series of verses using his name: "By God! They could be no one but that *fool* Savage's!"

Denver, John (1943-1997). American popular singer, songwriter and pilot. Denver was killed when his newly-acquired experimental airplane crashed into the Pacific Ocean near Pacific Grove, California. His last cockpit communication after transmitting a four digit code: "Do you have it now?"

De Reszke, Jean (1850-1925). Polish operatic tenor. Dying of influenza, to his wife: "Let me lie quietly. I am very tired." Delirious, De Reszke sang arias from Richard Wagner's opera *Tristan und Isolde* and later a chromatic scale. He did not speak or sing further and died several days later.

De Rosa, Anthony (died 1752). English criminal of Portuguese descent. Although De Rosa seemed to have an airtight alibi, he was convicted of a murder committed during a robbery. At his hanging: "I am as innocent as the child unborn. Would you have me own myself guilty of what I know no more of than you do? I know if I be guilty, and deny it, I must send my soul to the bottom of hell, which I hope I know better than to do."

De Sade, Marquis Donatien (1740-1814). French libertine, revolutionary and writer. After many years of debauched living, De Sade was committed to the Charenton insane asylum. Instructions for burial were set forth in the last section of his will: "The ground over my grave should be sprinkled with acorns so that all traces of my grave shall disappear so that, as I hope, this reminder of my existence may be wiped from the memory of mankind." His memory, however, lives on in the word "sadism."

Desaix de Veygoux, Louis (1768-1800). French general who was mortally wounded in Napoleon's victory at the Battle of Marengo, Italy. Desaix's alleged last words: "Go tell the First Consul that I die regretting not having done enough to live in posterity." Because he was shot through the heart, it is unlikely that Desaix uttered this statement.

Descartes, René (1596-1650). French philosopher, mathematician and scientist. Several days before he died of pneumonia (some postulate poisoning), Descartes said: "My soul, thou hast long been held captive; the hour has now come for thee to quit thy prison, to leave the trammels of this body; suffer, then, this separation with joy and courage." On the day of his death, Descartes asked his valet to help him from bed. He fainted but aroused saying: "Ah, dear Schluter, this is the fatal stroke that must part us."

Alternatives: * "Ah, my dear Schlüter, this is the fatal stroke! I must leave now."

* To his physicians who wished to bleed him: "Sirs, save the French blood."

DeShields, Kenneth (1960-1993). American criminal, executed by lethal injection for the murder of a Democratic committeewoman. "It ain't worth it. It ain't worth taking a life. I just like to say I don't hate anybody. What I did was wrong. I just hope everybody is satisfied with what's about to happen."

De Smet, Pierre-Jean (1801-1873). Belgian missionary to Native American souls. Suffering from a chronic wasting illness, De Smet remarked on the looseness of his clothing. When reminded that he was once overweight, he replied: "Too fat for comfort. It's better to be thin. I am a lazy old fool after all."

Desmoulins, Lucie-Simplice (1760-1794). French revolutionary, journalist, lawyer and politician. For his criticism of the French Revolution leader Robespierre and association with Georges-Jacques Danton (above), Desmoulins was condemned to die by the guillotine: "The monsters who assassinate me will not long survive my fall." Speaking of a lock of his wife's hair clenched in his fist: "Convey my hair to my mother-in-law." As he viewed the blade: "Behold, then, the recompense reserved for the first apostle of liberty."

Desmoulins, Lucile (1771-1794). French revolutionary who was the wife of Lucie-Simplice Desmoulins (above). Lucile was condemned to die for her attempts to free her imprisoned husband. To a fellow prisoner slated for the guillotine: "Monsieur, they say that you insulted Marie-Antoinette when she was in the tumbrel [an open cart used to transport prisoners], and I readily believe it. But you would do better to conserve some of your boldness to confront another queen, the queen of death, whom we shall soon be meeting."

De Soto, Hernando (c. 1497-1542). Spanish conquistador who was the first European to explore the Mississippi River. Dying of a fever: "A draught of water. Quick! Quick! For the love of heaven."

Despard, Edward (1751-1803). Irish-born English revolutionary. Despard and others were convicted of a plot to seize the Tower of London and kill King George III. Before his hanging and decapitation, Despard proclaimed his innocence and the hope that justice would prevail, concluding: "... I have little more to add, except to wish you all health, happiness and freedom, which I have endeavored, as far as was in my power, to procure for you, and for mankind in general."

Devereux, Robert (1565-1601). English nobleman, the Earl of Essex. Accused of treason for leading a coup d'état against the government of Queen Elizabeth I, Devereux was beheaded in the Tower of London. His last words: "Executioner, strike home! Come, Lord Jesus! Come, Lord Jesus and receive my soul! Oh, Lord, into Thy hands I commend my spirit!" Reportedly, three blows were required to sever his head.

Alternative: * "In humility and obedience to Thy commandment, in obedience to Thy ordinance and to Thy good pleasure, Oh God, I prostrate myself to my deserved punishment. Lord, be merciful to Thy prostrate servant. Lord, into Thy hands I commend my spirit."

Dewey, George (1837-1917). U.S. Admiral of the Navy who defeated the Spanish Pacific squadron at the Battle of Manila Bay in 1898. Words deliriously spoken on his deathbed: "Gentlemen, the battle is done. The victory is ours!"

Diaghilev, Sergei (1872-1929). Russian-born ballet impresario. Dying from complications of diabetes, to a friend: "Catherine, how beautiful you are! I am happy to see you. How sick I am! I am very sick... I feel as if I were drunk."

Alternative: * "Ah, Catherine, how beautiful you look! I am ill! Very ill indeed... I feel so hot- lightheaded."

Diana, Princess of Wales, born Diana Spencer (1961-1997). English noblewoman, the former wife of Prince Charles, heir apparent to the throne. Mortally injured in an auto accident in Paris, Diana allegedly asked moments after the crash: "My God. What's happened?"

Alternative: * "Leave me alone."

Diane de France, Duchess of Angoulême (1538-1619). French noblewoman and illegitimate daughter of King Henry II of France. "My God, I am going to beg pardon for my sins. Help Thy humble servant in this moment which is to be decisive for me for all eternity."

Díaz, Ángel (1951-2006). Puerto Rican-born American criminal, executed by lethal injection for murdering a Florida strip club manager: "The state of Florida is killing an innocent person. The state of Florida is committing a crime, because I am innocent. The death penalty is not only a form of vengeance, but also a cowardly act by humans. I'm sorry for what is happening to me and my family who have been put through this."

Dickens, Charles (1812-1870). English novelist and social critic whose novels famously portrayed Victorian London. After suffering a stroke, Dickens was told by his sister-in-law to lie down. His response: "Yes, on the ground!" He died shortly thereafter.

Dickerson, Almeron (1800-1836). American military officer. Dickerson was one of the last combatants to perish during the Alamo massacre. To his wife: "Great God, Sue, the Mexicans are inside our walls! All is lost. If they spare you, save my child." His wife and child survived the carnage.

Dickinson, Charles (1780-1806). American lawyer, killed in a duel with Andrew Jackson. Dickinson and Jackson had a dispute over a wager (some say disparaging words about Mrs. Jackson), which eventually led to a duel with pistols. The future president sustained a nonlife-threatening gunshot to the chest and was able to return fire, mortally wounding his opponent. Before dying, Dickinson exclaimed: "Great God! Have I missed him?"

Dickinson, Emily (1830-1886). American poet. Dying of Bright's disease, Dickinson said: "I must go in; the fog is rising." This statement possibly reflects words used earlier by the poet's mother, summoning her indoors: "It's already growing damp." Dickinson uttered her last words when offered a glass of water: "Oh, is that all it is?"

Diddley, Bo, whose birth name was Ellas Otha Bates (1928-2008). American rock and roll singer, guitarist and songwriter. Responding to a gospel song "Walk Around Heaven" sung at his deathbed: "Wow." As he died: "I'm going to heaven."

Diderot, Denis (1713-1784). French encyclopedist, writer and philosopher. Suffering from "dropsy," Diderot was told by his wife not to eat an apricot that he had in his hand: "But what the devil do you think that will do to me?" Diderot ate it anyway and died suddenly.

Alternatives: * "What possible harm could it do to me?"
* "But how the devil do you think this could harm me?"
* "The first step toward philosophy is incredulity."

Dieneces (died 480 BCE). Dauntless Spartan warrior. At the Battle of Thermopylae in east-central Greece, Dieneces was told that enemy Persian archers would blacken the sky with their arrows. His response before perishing: "... If the Medes [Persians] darken the sun, we shall have our fight in the shade."

Diesel, Rudolf (1858-1913). German engineer who developed the engine that bears his name. Diesel's final letter: "Greetings and a kiss. In fondest love, Your father." In late September 1913, Diesel disappeared on a sea voyage from Belgium to England. Ten days later, his body was found floating in the English Channel. Some feel the engineer possibly committed suicide during a bout of depression.

Dietrich, Marlene (1901-1992). German-born actress and singer. Dying of kidney failure, Dietrich ruminated about the afterlife: "… I lost my faith during the war and can't believe they are all up there, flying around or sitting at tables, all those I've lost. All, all, all. I suppose I'm jealous. I can't believe, but I can't. If it were true, Rudi [her husband who died almost 16 years earlier] would be there and would give me a message." Her last spoken word was her daughter's name "Maria."

Digby, Everard (c. 1578-1606). English nobleman. For his involvement in the scheme to blow up the Houses of Parliament and dethrone James I, Digby was condemned to be hanged, drawn and quartered. Following disembowelment, the executioner held up the condemned man's heart and cried: "Here is the heart of a traitor." Allegedly, Digby managed to say: "Thou liest!"

Dillinger, John (1903-1934). American gangster who specialized in bank robberies. Surveilled by the FBI, Dillinger was spotted leaving a Chicago movie theater on July 22, 1934. When he tried to escape, his pursuers shot the gangster multiple times. Apocryphal stories circulated that Dillinger muttered "You got me," but it is unlikely that he was able to utter a sound.

Dillon, Wentworth, Earl of Roscommon (c. 1633-c. 1685). Irish-born poet and writer. Immediately before death, Dillon recited lines from his own translation of the *Dies Irae*, the Latin hymn, the "Day of Wrath:" "My God, my Father and my Friend, do not forsake me in the end."

DiMaggio, Giuseppe "Joe" (1914-1999). American professional baseball star. Dying from complications of lung cancer, DiMaggio spoke about his former wife Marilyn Monroe (below): "I'll finally get to see Marilyn."

Diogenes the Cynic (c. 412-323 BCE). Greek philosopher who was one of the founders of Cynic philosophy. When Diogenes was asked where he would like to be buried, the philosopher replied that his body simply should be placed "in an open field." When disciples argued that animals would eat his corpse, Diogenes said: "If that be the case, it is no matter whether they eat me or not, seeing I shall not be sensible to it."

Alternative: * When asked how he would like to be buried: "Face downward, because everything will shortly be turned upside down."

Disney, Walter "Walt" (1901-1966). American movie producer. Dying of lung cancer, Disney opined: "Fancy being remembered around the world for the invention of a mouse!" When told that he was better off than Hitler because he had not killed anyone: "No, but I wanted to. Donald Duck for instance! There were times when I really wanted to wipe out that little monster!" Later he requested: "Raise my bed, so I can look out the window and see my studio."

Disraeli, Benjamin (1804-1881). English Prime Minister during the reign of Queen Victoria. When told during his last hours that Victoria wished to visit, Disraeli quipped: "No, it is better not. She would only ask me to take a message to Albert [the Queen's late consort]." His last words: "I have suffered much. Had I been a Nihilist, I should have confessed all. I had rather live, but I am not afraid to die." Disraeli moved his lips without speaking and died several minutes later.

Alternatives: * "Why should I see her? She will only want to give a message to Albert."

* "What's the use? She would only want me to take a message to dear Albert."

Dix, Dorothea (1802-1887). American reformer of mental health care, hospitals and prisons. To her doctor: "Don't give me anything. None of those anodynes to dull the senses or relieve pain. I want to feel it all. And... please tell me when the time is near. I want to know."

Dixon, Henry (1822-1870). English sportswriter and lawyer whose pen name was The Druid. When told that he was near death: "Oh God, I thank Thee! I could not bear much more."

Dod, John (c. 1549-1645). English clergyman and writer. "I desire to dissolve and be with Christ."

Dodd, Westley (1961-1993). American criminal, condemned to die for child molestation and multiple murders: "I was once asked by somebody, I don't remember who, if there was any way sex offenders could be stopped. I said 'No.' I was wrong. I was wrong when I said there was no hope, no peace. There is hope. There is peace. I found both in the Lord, Jesus Christ. Look to the Lord, and you will find peace."

Dodd, William (1729-1777). English clergyman and writer. For debts related to his extravagant lifestyle, Dodd resorted to forged notes to cover his shortfalls. Convicted of this misdeed, Dodd was sentenced to die by hanging. At the gallows, he said to the hangman: "Come to me." Although not well-documented, the condemned man possibly asked the executioner to pull down on his legs to ensure a quick death. The hangman later went through that motion.

Doddridge, Philip (1702-1751). English nonconformist clergyman and hymnodist. Shortly before dying of tuberculosis: "… I am full of confidence and this is my confidence- there is hope set before me; I have fled, I still fly, for refuge to that hope." At the end, to his wife: "… So sure am I that God will be with you and comfort you, that I think my death will be a greater blessing to you, than ever my life hath been."

Dodge, Grace (1856-1914). American social activist and philanthropist. Because she was too ill to receive guests, Dodge asked about visitors: "And were they happy?"

Dodgeson, Charles Lutwidge **(see Carroll, Lewis).**

Dolet, Étienne (1509-1546). French scholar and printer. Condemned for works branded heretical, Dolet mused on the way to his execution: "Dolet is not doleful, but these compassionate people are doleful for him." He was strangled and burned for his views.

Alternative: * "'Tis not Dolet who's doleful."

Dollfuss, Engelbert (1892-1934). Austrian chancellor, shot by the Nazis in an attempted coup d'état. To the police who came to his aid: "Children, you are so good to me. Why aren't the others like you? I only wanted peace. We never attacked; we only had to defend ourselves. May the Lord forgive them. Give my regards to my wife and children."

Domenec, Michael (1816-1878). Spanish-born American clergyman. Taken ill while visiting his birthplace near Barcelona, Domenec spoke to the archbishop who offered his residence to the ailing man: "A thousand thanks, sir. You know my mission is not to incommode anybody."

Dominic de Guzmán, Saint (1170-1221). Spanish Roman Catholic priest who founded the Dominican Order. When asked where he wished to be buried: "Under the feet of my friars." To his disciples: "Do not weep. I may be more useful to you where I am going than I could be here." Dominic then prayed: "Come to my aid, saints of God, and bear my soul into the presence of the Most High."

Alternative: * "Let not my departure in the flesh trouble you, my sons, and doubt not that I shall serve you better dead than alive!"

Domitian (51-96). Roman emperor whose tyrannical rule brought him in conflict with members of the Senate. Before dying in a palace coup, Domitian commanded an aide to: "Hand me the dagger under my pillow, and call the servants." The personal weapon of the emperor had been removed in preparation for his assassination.

Don Carlos (1545-1568). Pretender to the Spanish throne of King Philip II. When Don Carlos' actions became erratic after suffering a head injury, he was imprisoned and possibly poisoned by his father: "God be propitious to me, a sinner."

Donia, Pier Gerlofs (c. 1480-1520). Frisian freedom fighter and folk hero. Near the end, Donia was asked where he wished to go after death: "To my Lord."

Donizetti, Gaetano (1797-1848). Italian composer, primarily of *bel canto* operas. Dying of central nervous system syphilis, Donizetti spoke of his wife during one of his more lucid moments: "I shall be miserable until she intercedes with God for my death and our eternal reunion." Immediately before he lost his ability to speak, he told a friend: "Donizetti... Donizetti... But don't you know, don't you know that poor Donizetti is dead?"

Donn-Byrne, Brian (1889-1928). American-born Irish writer and poet. Shortly before dying in an auto accident from a defective steering mechanism: "I think I'll go for a drive before dinner. Anyone come along?"

Donne, John (1572-1631). English clergyman and poet. Dying of a stomach ailment: "I were miserable if I might not die." Later he prayed: "Thy Kingdom come, Thy Will be done."

Alternative: * "I repent of my life except that part of it which I spent in communion with God and in doing good."

Donop, Carl von (1732-1777). Hessian soldier who fought with the British in the American Revolutionary War. Mortally wounded during the Battle of Red Bank near Philadelphia: "It is finishing a noble career early; but I die the victim of my ambition, and of the avarice of my sovereign."

Alternative: * "See here, Colonel, see in me the vanity of all human pride! I have shone in all the courts of Europe, and now I am dying here on the banks of the Delaware in the house of an obscure Quaker."

Dooley, Thomas (1927-1961). American medical missionary who worked primarily in Southeast Asia. Dying of cancer, Dooley commented on the birthday cake brought into his hospital room: "I'll have a piece of that in about two hours."

Doorman, Karel (1889-1942). Dutch admiral. While defending the Java Sea against invading Japanese vessels during WWII, Doorman's flagship was attacked. Before it sank, the admiral issued a rallying signal in Dutch, reported variously as: "I attack, follow me!" or "All ships follow me!"

Dorman, Isaiah (died 1876). American former slave who interpreted for General George Custer (above) at the Battle of Little Big Horn. Wounded during the skirmish, Dorman implored the Sioux: "My friends, you have already killed me; don't count coup on me." Sitting Bull told his men to spare Dorman, but when the chief left, they savagely mutilated his body. Counting coup was an action of bravery such as striking or touching the enemy, practiced by warriors with risk of injury or death.

Dornacker, Jane (1947-1986). American radio broadcaster. While Dornacker transmitted a live traffic report for a New York City radio station, her helicopter plunged into the Hudson River when the engine failed. Her last words: "Hit the water! Hit the water! Hit the water!" The pilot suffered serious injuries but survived.

Dorney, Henry (1613-1683). English writer. To his wife: "I am almost dead; lift me up a little higher."

Dos Passos, John (1896-1970). American artist and writer, best-known for his novel *U.S.A. Trilogy*. To his wife: "I think I'd like to read the paper now." When she returned with the periodical, Dos Passos was unconscious and later died of heart failure.

Dostie, Anthony Paul (1821-1866). American abolitionist, killed by a New Orleans, Louisiana mob: "I am dying. I die for the cause of liberty. Let the good work go on."

Dostoevsky, Feodor (1821-1881). Russian writer, best-known for his novels *Crime and Punishment*, *The Idiot* and *The Brothers Karamazov*. Dying of a pulmonary hemorrhage, to his wife: "My poor darling, my dearest... what am I leaving you with? My poor girl, how hard it will be for you to live! Call the children."

Alternative: * "Did you hear? Hold me not back. My hour has come. I must die"

Douglas, Alexander (1767-1852). Scottish nobleman. Because of his interest in Egyptian mummies, Douglas bought a sarcophagus that eventually would hold his mummified remains. Sensing that the sarcophagus might be too small for his large frame, he instructed: "Double me up! Double me up!" Indeed, his feet had to be cut off to ensure a fit.

Douglas, Howard (1776-1861). British general, engineer and politician. Reflecting on his knowledge of military fortifications: "All that I have said about armour-ships will prove correct. How little do they know of the undeveloped power of artillery!"

Douglas, James (c. 1286-1330). Scottish soldier and nobleman. Charged with carrying Robert the Bruce's embalmed heart (below) to Jerusalem during one of the Crusades, Douglas was killed by the Moors in Andalusia. As he went down, he threw the relic contained in a silver case toward the Holy Land, shouting: "Now pass thee onward as thou wast wont, and Douglas will follow thee or die." The heart never reached Jerusalem but eventually was carried back to Scotland.

Alternatives: * "A Douglas! A Douglas! I follow or die!"
* "Pass first in fight, as thou wert wont to do, and Douglas will follow thee or die."

Douglas, John Sholto, Marquis of Queensbury (1844-1900). Italian-born Scottish nobleman and boxing promoter. "Fight on, my merry men."

Douglas, Norman (1868-1952). Austrian-born British writer. Dying of a drug overdose: "Get these f****** nuns away from me!"

Alternative: "Love, love, love."

Douglas, Stephen (1813-1861). American politician who lost to Abraham Lincoln in the 1860 presidential election. Dying of typhoid fever, Douglas was queried by his wife for words for their sons: "Tell them to obey the laws and support the Constitution of the United States." When his doctor asked why all the windows were open: "So that we can have fresh air." When the doctor told his wife that he didn't look comfortable, Douglas remarked with his last breath: "He is very comfortable."

Douglass, Frederick (1818-1895). American abolitionist, diplomat and emancipated slave. While preparing to leave for a meeting at a near-by Baptist church, Douglass fell to his knees and said to his wife: "Why, what does this mean?" He then died of a heart attack.

Doumer, Paul (1857-1932). French president. While attending a Parisian book fair, Doumer was shot by a mentally unstable Russian émigré. The president exclaimed: "Is it possible?"

Alternative: * Other sources state that Doumer felt his mortal blow resulted from a car accident, not an assassin's bullet: "Ah, a road accident... a road accident."

Dowson, Ernest (1867-1900). English poet and writer. Suffering from the ravages of alcoholism and tuberculosis, to the lady who was nursing him: "You are like an angel from heaven. God bless you!"

Doyle, Arthur Conan (1859-1930). Scottish physician and writer, creator of the Sherlock Holmes short stories. Dying of a heart attack, to his nurse: "There ought to be a medal struck for you, inscribed 'To the best of all nurses.'" To his wife: "You are wonderful."

Drake, Francis (c. 1540-1596). English privateer, slaver and explorer. Dying of dysentery aboard his ship while sailing the Caribbean, Drake deliriously asked an aide to: "Help me dress and buckle on my armor, that I might die like a soldier!"

Draper, Daniel (1810-1866). English Methodist missionary to Australia. Draper drowned during a violent storm on a voyage from England to Australia. A survivor recounted the cleric's last words: "The captain tells us there is no hope; that we must all perish. But, I tell you there is hope, hope for *all*. Although we must all die, and never again see land, *we may all make the port of Heaven...* Oh God, may those that are not converted be converted now, hundreds of them. In a few moments we must all appear before our Great Judge. Let us prepare to meet Him." As the ship went down, the hymn "Rock of Ages Cleft for Me" was sung.

Dreiser, Theodore (1871-1945). American writer, best-known for his novel *An American Tragedy.* Dying of heart failure, to his wife: "You are beautiful."

Drew, Andrew (1885-1913). American aviator. Drew, a former pupil of the aviation pioneer, Orville Wright (below), spoke to a partner in his flight school before an ill-fated jaunt: "Let's take just one little joy ride, and then I'll go eat with you." After the partner demurred, Drew took off, but his biplane caught fire in flight and crashed.

Drew, Robert (1959-1994). American criminal, convicted of murder during an altercation while hitchhiking. Despite conflicting reports of the crime, Drew eventually was executed by lethal injection in a Texas prison. His last words: "I don't know why Marta Glass [an anti-death penalty activist] wasn't allowed in here. I love you all. Keep the faith. Remember the death penalty is murder. They are taking the life of an innocent man. My attorney, Ron Kuley... [unintelligible], will read my letter at a press conference after this is over. That is all I have to say. I love you all."

Drew, Samuel (1765-1833). English theologian, historian and writer. The day before his death, Drew spoke to his nurse: "Thank God, to-morrow I shall join the glorious company above." When told the following noon that he would meet the Lord before the day was finished, Drew replied: "Yes, my good sir, I trust I shall." He died later that evening.

Drexel, Saint Katharine (1858-1955). American Roman Catholic nun and philanthropist. To a priest who arrived several weeks before his usual annual visit: "You've come early."

Drucci, Vincent "The Schemer" (1898-1927). American thief and murderer. After Drucci was captured by the police, he taunted and scuffled with the officer who took him into custody, saying: "You take your gun off me or I'll kick hell out of you! I'll take you and your tool [gun]! I'll fix you!" During the ensuing fight, the gangster was mortally wounded.

Drummond, Henry (1851-1897). Scottish evangelist, explorer and writer. Dying of cancer, Drummond recited a few lines of his favorite hymn by

Charles Wesley (below): "I'm Not Ashamed to Own My Lord." Then to a friend: "There's nothing to beat that, Hugh."

Drummond, William (c. 1617-1677). Scottish-born American colonist who became embroiled in Nathaniel Bacon's Rebellion against the colonial governor of Virginia. Drummond was convicted of treason and hanged: "I expect no mercy from you. I have followed the lead of my conscience and done what I could to rescue my country from oppression."

Drusus, Marcus (died c. 91 BCE). Roman statesman. Through his bold political dealings, Drusus made many enemies and ultimately was stabbed by an assassin. Before dying, he cried: "When will the republic find again a citizen like me?"

Du Barry, Comtesse Jeanne (see Bécu, Jeanne, Madame du Barry).

Du Bois, William (1868-1963). American civil rights leader and one of the founders of the National Association for the Advancement of Colored People. At age 95, to his wife: "Now sit here beside me. Rest your little self. Don't bother with supper or anything else. Just stay here with me." Several moments later, he called her name "Shirley" and died.

Dubos, John Baptiste (1670-1742). French writer, diplomat, historian and theologian. Dubos' parting words: "Death is a law and not a punishment. Three things ought to console us for giving up life: the friends whom we have lost, the few persons worthy of being loved whom we leave behind us, and finally the memory of our stupidities and the assurance that they are now going to stop."

Dubroff, Jessica (1988-1996). American aviator. With the assistance of a certified flight instructor and her father, the seven-year-old Dubroff attempted to become the youngest person to fly across the U.S. While waiting to depart the Cheyenne, Wyoming airport during a thunderstorm, Dubroff spoke to her mother by telephone: "Mom, do you hear the rain? Do you hear the rain? Mom, I just want to take-off in the plane." Moments after take-off, her plane plummeted to the ground killing all aboard.

Ducos, Jean-François (1765-1793). French patriot, condemned to die by the guillotine during France's Reign of Terror. To the executioner who was cutting his hair: "I hope that the edge of your guillotine is sharper than your scissors." As he placed his head in the device: "The Convention has forgotten one decree: a decree on the indivisibility of heads and bodies."

Alternatives: * "What a pity the Convention did not decree the unity and indivisibility of our persons!"

* "It is about time that the convention should decree the inviolability of heads."

Dudley, John (c. 1502-1553). English military leader and politician. Dudley was beheaded for his conspiracy to place his daughter-in-law, Lady Jane Grey (below), on the throne following the death of English King Edward VI: "I have deserved a thousand deaths."

Duff, George (1764-1805). British naval officer. Duff was killed by a cannonball fired from a French vessel at the Battle of Trafalgar. His last letter to his wife before the battle: "My dearest Sophia, I have just had time to tell you that we are going into action with the Combined Fleets. I hope and trust in God that we shall all behave as becomes us and that I may yet have the happiness of taking my beloved wife and children in my arms. Norwich [his son serving as a midshipman on the same ship to whom the letter was entrusted] is quite well and happy. I have, however, ordered him off the quarter-deck. Yours ever and most truly, Geo. Duff."

Du Guesclin, Bertrand (c. 1320-1380). French soldier who fought during the Hundred Years' War. To those around his deathbed: "Remember that your business is only with those who carry arms. The churchmen, the poor, the women and children are not your enemies. I commend to the king my wife... my brother. Farewell, I am at an end."

Duke, James "Buck" (1856-1925). American tobacco tycoon whose endowment helped to establish Duke University in North Carolina. To his attorney: "I have not provided sufficient funds for carrying out the complete plans I have in mind for the university. I want to arrange to give an additional seven million to complete the building program."

Dulles, John Foster (1888-1959). U.S. Secretary of State under Dwight Eisenhower. Dying of colon cancer, to a friend: "Bill, just remember this. If the United States is willing to go to war over Berlin, there won't be war over Berlin."

Dumas, Alexandre père (1802-1870). French novelist, author of *The Three Musketeers* and *The Count of Monte Cristo.* Dying of a stroke, Dumas showed two coins to his son and said: "Alexandre (below), everybody has said that I was prodigal. You yourself wrote a play about it. And so, do you see how you were mistaken? When I first landed in Paris, I had two 'louis' in my pocket. Look! I still have them." Complaining about his novel *The Count of Monte Cristo*: "I shall never know how it all comes out."

Alternatives: * "My son, fifty years ago I set out for Paris to make my fortune. I had in my possession but one golden louis. They say I have been prodigal with my money. Why? I have that louis still."

* When his son asked for forgiveness: "What for, my boy?"
* "Tell me, Alexandre, on your soul and conscience, do you believe that anything of mine will last?"

Dumas, Alexandre fils (1824-1895). French novelist and playwright who wrote *The Lady of the Camellias.* To his daughters: "Go and have lunch and leave me to get some rest."

Dumas, Thomas-Alexandre (1762-1806). Haitian-born general under Napoleon I and father of the writer Alexandre Dumas père (above). Dying of stomach cancer, Dumas lamented: "Oh, must a general who at thirty-five was at the head of three armies die at forty in his bed, like a coward? Oh, my God! My God! What have I done that you should condemn me so young to leave my wife and children?" Changing his mind about summoning his son: "No. The poor child is sleeping; don't wake him up."

Dunant, Henri (1828-1910). Swiss businessman and social activist. Dunant's book *A Memory of Solferino* documented the aftermath of the Battle of Solferino in Italy. His observations led to the formation of the International Committee of the Red Cross. He was awarded the Nobel Peace Prize in 1901. In his final days, Dunant made known his burial requests: "I wish to be carried to my grave like a dog without a single one of your ceremonies which I do not recognize. I trust to your goodness faithfully to respect my last earthly request. I count upon your friendship that it shall be so. Amen. I am a disciple of Christ as in the first Century and nothing more." Dunant's final words: "Where has humanity gone?"

Dunbar, Paul (1872-1906). American poet and writer. Dying of tuberculosis, Dunbar muttered a portion of Psalm 23: "When I walk through the valley of the shadow..."

Duncan, Isadora (1877-1927). American-born dancer. Duncan's fondness for long flowing scarves led directly to her death. As she entered an open sports car in Nice, France one evening, her scarf became tangled in the car's wheel. As the car accelerated, Duncan was pulled from the vehicle and thrown to the pavement. Death was instantaneous. Her last words spoken to a friend before entering the vehicle allegedly were: "Farewell, my friends! I go to glory!" This statement may have been a fabrication designed to protect the dancer's image. Presumably, Duncan had no premonition that her life was in danger when she parted company with her friends. Later versions of Duncan's words implied that she had planned a romantic evening with her driver, saying: "I am off to love."

Alternatives: * "Goodbye, my friends, I go in glory!"
* "Adieu, my friends. I go off to glory!"

Dupetit-Thouars, Aristide (1760-1798). French naval officer who fought against the British in the Battle of the Nile. After a cannonball shot away his arms and a leg, Dupetit-Thouars told his lieutenant: "I might lose my head along with my blood and do something foolish if I keep the command. It is time I gave it up." He then "blew his brains out with his pistol."

Dupin, Aurore (see Sand, George).

Dupin, Sophie Delaborde (1773-1837). French writer and mother of the author George Sand, the pen-name of Aurore Dupin. "Please tidy my hair."

Alternative: * "Comb my hair."

DuPont, Alfred (1864-1935). American industrialist and philanthropist who rose to prominence in his family's gunpowder business. "Thank you, doctors; thank you, nurses. I'll be all right in a few days."

Durocher, Marie-Rose (1811-1849). Canadian Roman Catholic mother superior and educator. Farewell note to her sisters: "I beg pardon, my sisters, for lacking sweetness and kindness in your regard. I beg pardon for having hurt anyone in conversation at recreation, for having spoken harsh or offensive words. I beg pardon for having lacked charity in not having towards you the heart of a mother. I beg pardon for my irregularities in spiritual exercises. I beg pardon for my shortcomings."

Duse, Eleonora (1858-1924). Italian actress. While performing in Pittsburg, Pennsylvania, Duse developed pneumonia. Not wishing to die in a foreign country, she pleaded: "We must stir ourselves! Move on! Work! Work! Cover me! Must move on! Must work! Cover me." She died in the U.S. but was buried in Italy.

Alternatives: * "We must start off again! Work again! Cover me up."
* "At dawn we must leave. Hurry, we must leave."

Duveen, Joseph (1869-1939). English art dealer. Dying of cancer, Duveen outlived some of his medical prognosticators who at times had given him only months to live. On his deathbed, Duveen told his nurse: "Well, I fooled 'em for five years."

Dwyer, R. Budd (1939-1987). American politician. Dwyer was convicted of receiving a bribe in an insurance dispute. He called a press conference the day before his sentencing and produced a handgun before the assembled news media. He then said: "Please leave the room if this will offend you." When several people approached the distraught man, he responded: "No, no! Don't! Don't! Don't! Stay back! This could hurt someone!" Dwyer placed the gun barrel in his mouth and pulled the trigger, ending his life.

Dyer, Mary (c. 1611-1660). English-born American Quaker, one of the so-called Boston martyrs. Banned from Boston by a law that outlawed Quakers, Dyer was arrested when she returned to the city and was sentenced to die. Before her hanging, Dyer refused to return to the "orthodox fold," saying: "Nay, I cannot. For in obedience to the will of the Lord God I came, and in his will I abide faithful to the death."

Eads, James (1820-1887). American civil engineer and inventor. While working on a project to transport ocean-going ships across Latin America, Eads said: "I cannot die. I have not finished my work."

Eagels, Jeanne (1890-1929). American Broadway and screen actress who died of a possible drug overdose. "I'm going to Dr. Caldwell's for one of my regular treatments."

Earhart, Amelia (1898-disappeared 1937). American aviator and explorer. Earhart, the first woman to fly solo across the Atlantic Ocean, planned a flight around the globe in 1937. A letter to her husband before her last flight read: "Please know that I am quite aware of the hazards. I want to do it because I want to do it. Women must try to do things as men have tried. When they fail, their failure must be but a challenge to others." To a newspaper correspondent: "I have a feeling that there is just about one more good flight left in my system and I hope this trip is it. Anyway when I have finished this job, I mean to give up long-distance 'stunt' flying."

Having successfully flown with intermediate stops from the U.S. to New Guinea, Earhart and her navigator Fred Noonan departed midnight GMT on July 2, 1937 for the next leg over the Pacific Ocean. She planned to communicate with a Coast Guard ship *Itasca*, stationed off Howland Island, approximately 2,500 miles away. At the proposed rendezvous time, Earhart radioed: "KHAQQ [her call sign] calling *Itasca*. We must be on you but cannot see you but gas is running low. [We have] been unable to reach you by radio. We are flying at 1000 feet." Approximately one hour later: "KHAQQ to Itasca. We are on the line 157-337. [We] will repeat message. We will repeat this on 6210 KCS [kilocycles]. Wait… We are running on N ES S [course] line." No further communication was received and to date, her disappearance remains a celebrated mystery.

Early, Jubal (1816-1894). Confederate general who served during the U.S. Civil War. Several weeks after falling down a flight of stairs, Early remarked to a friend: "I want to tell you goodbye, Major. Don't leave the room. I want to talk to you about certain arrangements." These "arrangements" became a mystery, because Early died suddenly.

Earp, Morgan (1851-1882). American lawman and member of the Arizona Earp clan (below). Following the 1881 O.K. Corral shootout in Tombstone, Arizona, the Earps received a number of death threats. Five months later, Morgan was ambushed while playing billiards. When his brothers tried to assist him: "Don't. I can't stand it. This is the last game of pool I'll ever play." When he asked who fired the shot, his brother Wyatt promised to seek revenge: "That's all I'll ask, but Wyatt, be careful." Earlier, the brothers had made a pact that they would report any vision of the next world experienced near death. As he died, Morgan complained to Wyatt: "I can't see a d***** thing."

Earp, Warren (1855-1900). American lawman and gunfighter, the youngest of the Earp brothers. In an alcohol-fueled argument, the volatile Warren had a dispute with an acquaintance named Johnnie Boyett, possibly over a prostitute. Earp issued a challenge: "Boyett, get your gun and we'll settle this right here. I've got mine, go and get yours." Boyett obliged him, producing two handguns. Earp changed his mind and said: "I have not got arms. You have a good deal the best of this." Apparently, Boyett feared for his life and shot Earp dead.

Alternative: * "Johnnie, go get your gun this time! We're going to shoot it out!"

Earp, Wyatt (1848-1929). American gunfighter and lawman. Wyatt was best-known for his participation in the October 26, 1881 gunfight at the O.K. Corral. Dying of a prostate ailment 48 years later, Earp joked with his wife and a friend: "What are you two coyotes cooking up?" His last request: "Water."

Alternative: * Some say his last utterance was an enigmatic: "Suppose, suppose..."

Eastman, George (1854-1932). American industrialist and philanthropist who founded the Kodak photographic company. Suffering from a chronic painful spinal disorder, Eastman feared that he would become an invalid. After discussing changes in his will with friends, he said: "I have a note to write." The industrialist then retired and shot himself through the heart. His suicide note read: "To my friends, my work is done. Why wait?"

Eaton, Margaret "Peggy" (c. 1799-1879). American matron who was involved in the "Petticoat Affair" that disrupted President Andrew Jackson's cabinet. Expiring decades later: "I am not afraid to die, but this is such a beautiful world to leave."

Eaton, Theophilus (1590-1658). English-born American settler who became governor of the New Haven colony. When his wife suggested they should return to England, Eaton replied: "You may, Ann. Some time thou mayst go, but I shall die here. Goodnight." Later that night, he uttered a groan and was asked how he was: "Very ill." Eaton turned his head and died.

Eaton, William (1764-1811). American military officer and politician. When asked if he would like his head moved to see the sunrise, Eaton replied: "Yes sir, I thank you."

Eddy, Mary Baker (1821-1910). American theologian and founder of the Christian Science movement. Dying of pneumonia, her last thought: 'God is my life."

Eddy, Nelson (1901-1967). American singer and movie star. While performing in a Florida nightclub, Eddy stopped suddenly and said: "Something has happened. I'm so dry." To the audience: "Will you bear with me a minute? I can't seem to get the words out." To his piano accompanist: "Would you play 'Dardanella?' Maybe I'll get the words back... My face is getting numb. Is there a doctor here? I can't see! I can't hear!" He died of a massive stroke shortly thereafter.

Edelstein, Morris (1888-1941). American politician who became a member of the U.S. House of Representatives. When a fellow congressman made disparaging remarks about Jewish bankers, Edelstein vehemently retorted: "As a member of this House I deplore such allegations, because we are living in a democracy. All men are created equal regardless of race, creed, or color; and whether a man be Jew or Gentile he may think what he deems fit." Edelstein then suffered a heart attack and died.

Edgeworth, Richard (1744-1817). English inventor, writer and politician. "I die with the soft feeling of gratitude to my friends and submission to the God who made me."

Edison, Thomas (1847-1931). American inventor of the light bulb, phonograph, motion picture camera and others. Dying from complications of diabetes, Edison was asked about his thoughts on eternity: "It doesn't matter. No one knows." Asked if he were uncomfortable: "No. Just waiting." Waking from a coma, to his wife as he gazed out a window: "It is very beautiful over there." Whether he remarked about the hereafter or his surroundings remains a mystery.

Edmund, Saint (died c. 869). King of East Anglia. For failing to renounce his Christian religion, Edmund was flogged, shot with arrows and beheaded by the conquering Danes. During his torture, Edmund cried: "Jesus! Jesus!" Before the axe fell: "O Lord, who of Thy high mercy didst send Thy Son to earth to die for us, grant me patience unto the end. I yearn to change this world's life for Thy blessed company."

Edward I (1239-1307). King of England. The weakened Edward accompanied his troops northward to suppress a Scottish bid for independence. Contracting dysentery on the way, he allegedly charged his followers to: "Carry my bones before you on your march, for the rebels will not be able to endure the sight of me, alive or dead." His remains, however, were carried south and buried in Westminster Abbey.

Alternative: * "Wrap my bones in a hammock and have them carried before the army, so that I may still lead the way to victory."

Edward VI (1537-1553). King of England and Ireland. Dying of possible tuberculosis, Edward spoke to those at his bedside: "Lord God, deliver me out of this miserable and wretched life, and take me among Thy chosen: howbeit not my will, but Thy will be done. Lord, I commit my spirit to thee. O Lord! Thou knowest how happy it were for me to be with Thee: yet, for Thy chosen's sake, send me life and health, that I may truly serve thee. O my Lord God, bless thy people, and save thine inheritance! O Lord God, save thy chosen people of England! O my Lord God, defend this realm from papistry, and maintain Thy true religion; that I and my people may praise Thy holy name, for Thy Son Jesus Christ's sake!" Turning to the assembled: "Are you so nigh? I thought ye had been further off." When asked what he had said, the king replied: "I was praying to God." Before dying: "I am faint; Lord, have mercy upon me, and take my spirit"

Edward VII (1841-1910). King of the United Kingdom and British Dominions. Dying of a heart attack, Edward refused a move to his bed, saying: "No, I shall not give in. I shall go on. I shall work to the end." When told that one of his horses had won a local race, he uttered his last words: "Yes, I have heard of it. I am very glad."

Edward VIII (1894-1972). King of the United Kingdom and British Dominions who later became the Duke of Windsor. To marry the divorcée, Wallis Simpson, Edward was forced to abdicate the throne in favor of George VI. Dying of throat cancer decades later: "I want to die in my own bed." When his wife said she would stay up with him: "No darling, I shall soon be asleep. Get some rest please." Later he asked his attendant: "Am I going to die?" At the end: "Mama, Mama, Mama, Mama."

Edward, Duke of Kent (1767-1820). Father of the future Queen Victoria of England. Dying of pneumonia, to his wife: "Do not forget me."

Edward, Prince of Aquitaine (1330-1376). English nobleman and military leader. Edward failed to ascend the English throne, because he predeceased his father Edward III by one year. Dying of a lingering illness, his last words possibly reflected his involvement in the massacre of French citizens in Limoges in 1370: "I give Thee thanks, O God, for all Thy benefits, and with all the pains of my soul I humbly beseech Thy mercy to give me remission of those sins I have wickedly committed against Thee; and of all mortal men whom willingly or ignorantly I have offended I ask forgiveness with all my heart."

Alternative: * "I thank Thee, O Lord, for all Thy benefits. With all my power I ask for Thy mercy, for Thou wilt forgive me for all the sins that I, in my wrong-doing, have committed against Thee. And I ask with my whole heart the grace of pardon from all men whom I have knowingly or unwittingly wronged."

Edwards, Edgar, also Edgar Owen (died 1903). English murderer, condemned to hang for a triple slaying. Edwards spoke to a chaplain before his execution: "I've been looking forward to this lot!"

Edwards, Edward (1812-1886). English library historian and pioneer of free public libraries. To his landlady who finished washing his feet. "I am much obliged to you- very..."

Edwards, Jonathan (1703-1758). American clergyman, theologian and philosopher. After receiving a vaccination for smallpox, Edwards developed a fever and died shortly thereafter. After bidding goodbye to his children: "Now where is Jesus, my never-failing friend?" At the end: "Trust in God, and ye need not fear."

Egbert, Henry (1839-1899). American military leader. Egbert was killed in Manila while leading a charge against insurgents during the Philippine-American War. When his commanding officer tried to comfort him: "Goodbye, General. I'm done. I'm too old."

Eichmann, Adolf (1906-1962). Nazi official who participated in the extermination of Jews in death camps during WWII. Captured by Israeli agents after a long period of hiding in Argentina, Eichmann was convicted in a Jerusalem court and hanged for his crimes. His last statement on the gallows: "Long live Germany. Long live Argentina. Long live Austria. These are the three countries with which I have been most connected and which I will not forget. I had to obey the laws of war and my flag. I am ready. Gentlemen, we shall all meet again soon. So is the fate of all men. I have believed in God all my life, and I die believing in God."

Alternative: * "... I greet my wife, my family, and my friends. I am ready. We'll meet again soon. So is the fate of all men. I die believing in God."

Einstein, Albert (1879-1955). German-born physicist, best-known for his theories of relativity and the law of the photoelectric effect. Einstein was awarded the1921 Nobel Prize in Physics. After declining surgery for a bleeding abdominal aortic aneurysm, he said: "I want to go when I want. It is tasteless to prolong life artificially. I have done my share. It is time to go. I will do it elegantly." While reviewing some research papers, to his son: "If only I had more mathematics!" When told to rest, Einstein replied: "Your presence won't stop me from going to sleep." His nurse reported that his last words were spoken in German. Because she was unfamiliar with that language, his parting statement remains a mystery.

Alternative: * Some assert that Einstein's last utterance was: "Is the universe friendly?" but this quote was made to a reporter much earlier.

Eisenhower, Dwight (1890-1969). Supreme commander of allied forces in Europe during WWII and thirty-fourth U.S. president. Dying of congestive heart failure, Eisenhower requested: "Lower the shades!" To his son and one of his doctors: "Pull me up! Two big men! Higher!" As death neared: "I want to go. God, take me."

Alternative: "I've always loved my wife, my children, and my grandchildren, and I've always loved my country. I want to go. God, take me."

Eldon, John (1751-1838). Lord Chancellor of England. When an acquaintance mentioned the weather, Eldon replied: "It matters not where I am going whether the weather be cold or hot."

Elijah of Tishbe (fl. 9th century BCE). Hebrew biblical prophet. On his deathbed, Elijah was asked for a double share of his spirit by Elisha, one of his disciples. The prophet replied (2 Kings 2: 10-12): "You have asked a hard thing. Yet, if you see me as I am being taken from you, it shall be so for you. But if you do not see me, it shall not be so." The scripture continues: "And as they still went on and talked, behold, a chariot of fire and horses of fire separated the two of them. And Elijah went up by a whirlwind into heaven..."

Eliot, Andrew (1718-1778). American clergyman. "Come, Lord Jesus, come quickly- why are Thy chariot wheels so long in coming?"

Eliot, George, the pen-name of Mary Ann Evans (1819-1880). English novelist who wrote *Silas Marner* and *The Mill on the Floss*. Dying of a kidney ailment, Eliot spoke to her husband: "Tell them I have a great pain in the left side."

Eliot, John (1604-1690). English-born missionary to Native American Indians. Dying of a fever: "... The Lord Jesus, whom I have served for eighty years, forsakes me not. Oh, come in glory! I have long waited for that coming. Let no dark cloud rest on the work of the Indians. Let it live when I am dead." To a minister friend: "Brother, you are welcome to my very soul, but retire to your study, and pray that I may have leave to be gone." His last words: "Welcome joy!"

Elisabeth of Brunswick-Wolfenbüttel (1715-1797). Queen Consort of Frederick the Great of Prussia (below). On her deathbed: "I know you will not forget me."

Elisabeth, Empress of Austria (1837-1898). German-born consort of Franz Joseph I of Austria (below). During a visit to Geneva, Switzerland, Elisabeth was stabbed in the chest by an anarchist. Unaware of the severity of her wound, the Empress boarded a boat on Lake Geneva where she collapsed. After a momentary recovery, she responded: "Thank you. Whatever happened to me?" She died shortly thereafter.

Alternative: * "Why, what has happened?"

Elizabeth I (1533-1603). Queen of England and Ireland who was the daughter of Henry VIII and Anne Boleyn. In her final hours, Elizabeth reflected about her impending death: "All my possessions for one moment of time." Later: "I have been a great queen, but I am about to die and must yield an account of my stewardship to the great King of Kings." After her advisor Robert Cecil suggested she must rest, the queen angrily replied: "Must! Is *must* a word to be addressed to princes? Little man, little man! Thy father, if he had been alive, durst not have used that word. But alas, alas, thou art grown presumptuous, because thou knowest that I shall die." When her ministers suggested Lord Beauchamp as a possible successor, Elizabeth exclaimed: "I will have no rascal's son in my seat; none but a king shall sit upon the throne and who should that be our cousin, the King of Scots." She gradually lost consciousness and succumbed.

Elizabeth Charlotte, Duchesse d'Orléans (1652-1722). German-born French noblewoman. On her deathbed, Elizabeth wrote her final letter: "Thank God, I am prepared to die, and I only pray for strength to die bravely. It is not bad weather although today a fine rain is setting in. But I do not think any weather will help me. Many complain of coughs and colds, but my malady lies deeper. Should I recover you will find me the same friend as ever. Should this be the end, I die with full faith in my Redeemer." To her son: "Why do you weep? Must one not die?" To a lady of the court who wished to kiss Elizabeth's hand: "You may kiss my lips; I am going to a land where all are equal."

Elizabeth Ka'ahumanu (see Ka'ahumanu, Elizabeth).

Elizabeth of Aragon, Saint, also Saint Elizabeth of Portugal (1271-1336). Spanish-born Queen Consort of King Denis of Portugal. Having experienced a vision of the Virgin Mary: "Draw up a chair for the radiant lady in white who is coming." As she died: "Mary, mother of grace."

Élizabeth of France (1764-1794). Sister of French King Louis XVI. In the wake of the French Revolution, Élizabeth was condemned to die. Before the guillotine blade fell, the executioner's assistant tore part of her cape to remove a religious medal around her neck. Élizabeth exclaimed: "I pray you, gentlemen, in the name of modesty, suffer me to cover my bosom."

Alternative: * "In the name of your mother, cover me, sir!"

Elizabeth of Hungary, Saint (1207-1231). Daughter of King Andrew II of Hungary. Elizabeth was noted for her work with the poor and infirm. Her dying words: "This is the moment when the Almighty God calls His friends to Himself."

Alternative: "The time has already arrived wherein God has called those that are His friends to the heavenly espousals!"

Elizabeth of the Trinity (1880-1906). French Carmelite nun and writer. Dying of Addison's disease: "I am going to Light, to Love, to Life."

Elizabeth of Wied (1843-1916). German-born Queen Consort of King Carol I of Romania. Dying of pneumonia, Elizabeth told her physicians: "Stop giving me injections! Let me go!"

Elizabeth, Empress of Russia (1709-1762). Daughter of Czar Peter the Great (below) and ruler of Russia from 1741 until her death. To her nephew and successor, Peter III: "Be kind to your subjects. Live in peace with your wife. Cherish your son."

Elizalde, Jaime Jr. (1971-2006). American criminal, executed by lethal injection for a double murder: "... We talk about a reprieve or stay from the Supreme Court, but the real Supreme Court you must face up there and not down here. Keep your heads up and stay strong. I love you all. That is it. Stay strong. Thank you."

Ellery, William (1727-1820). American statesman who was a delegate to the Continental Congress and a signer of the Declaration of Independence. "I know that I am dying."

Ellington, Edward "Duke" (1899-1974). American pianist, composer and jazz band leader. Dying of lung cancer, to his wife: "Kisses, kisses... More kisses... Smile kisses."

Alternative: * "Music is how I live, why I live and how I will be remembered."

Elliott, Ebenezer (1781-1849). English poet. To a relative: "You see a strange sight, sir, an old man unwilling to die!" As the end approached, Elliott's mind wandered: "I thought I was on the Common, and a child knocked me down with a flower... What a strange head your sister has, like a flower top-heavy."

Elliott, John (1868-1942). American social activist and educator. Elliott created social programs that helped individuals and neighborhoods improve their living conditions. "The only thing in life I have found worth living for, and working for, and dying for, is love and friendship."

Ellis, Anthony (1953-1992). American criminal, executed by lethal injection for a murder-robbery: "I just want everyone to know that the prosecutor and Bill Scott [an inmate, who testified against him] are sorry sons of b******." Before he died, Ellis told his family that he loved them.

Ellis, Havelock (1859-1939). English psychologist and student of human sexuality. To his nurse: "You must go to bed. You are so tired, and I feel better. Perhaps I may sleep a little. I shall ring if I need you."

Ellsworth, Elmer (1837-1861). Union officer in the U.S. Civil War. Possibly the first casualty of that conflict, Ellsworth was killed trying to take down a Confederate flag flying conspicuously in Alexandria, Virginia. The last lines of a letter for his parents written one day before his death: "... I am perfectly content to accept whatever my fortune may be, confident that He who noteth even the fall of a sparrow will have some purpose even in the fate of one like me. My darling and ever-loved parents, good-bye! God bless, protect and care for you. Elmer." After confiscating the flag, Ellsworth shouted "My God!" as he was gunned down.

Eloi, Saint (died c. 659). French Bishop of Noyon (northeastern France). "And now, O Christ, I shall render up my last breath in confessing loudly Thy name; receive me in Thy great mercy and disappoint me not in my hope; open to me the gate of life and render the Prince of Darkness powerless against me. Let Thy clemency protect me, Thy might hedge me and Thy hand lead me to the place of refreshment and into the tabernacle Thou hast prepared for Thy servants and them that stand in awe of Thee."

Elphinstone, Arthur (1688-1746). Scottish military leader and nobleman. Elphinstone, an avowed Jacobite, was taken prisoner in the Battle of Culloden and sentenced to die by decapitation for high treason. As he presented the executioner with a fee of three guineas, Elphinstone prayed: "O Lord, reward my friends, forgive my foes, bless King James, and receive my soul!"

Elwes, John (1714-1789). English politician. Despite his amassed wealth, Elwes pursued a parsimonious lifestyle. Because of his miserly ways, he was thought to be the inspiration for Ebenezer Scrooge in Charles Dickens' novel *A Christmas Carol.* On his deathbed, to his son: "John, I hope I have left you as much as you wished."

Emmanuelle, Sister (1908-2008). Belgian-born Roman Catholic nun, noted for her missionary work with the poor. Dying at age 99 years, Sister Emmanuelle recorded a note to her publisher: "When you hear this message, I will no longer be there. In telling of my life- all of my life- I wanted to bear witness that love is more powerful than death. I have confessed everything, the good and the less good, and I can tell you about it. Where I am now, life does not end for those who know how to love."

Emmet, Robert (1778-1803). Irish patriot. Convicted of treason for his involvement in an abortive revolt against British rule, Emmet was hanged and then beheaded. On the scaffold, he said: "My friends, I die in peace, and with sentiments of universal love and kindness towards all men." When the executioner asked if he were ready, Emmet replied: "Not yet." When asked a second time: "Not yet." When asked a third time, the impatient executioner tilted the plank on hearing: "Not..."

Alternatives: * "I die at peace with mankind."
* "My cause was a noble one and I die at peace with all the world."

Emmett, Belinda (1974-2006). Australian actress and singer. Dying of breast cancer at age 32, to her sister who was crying: "Are you alright?"

Emmett, Christopher (1971-2008). American criminal, executed for the robbery and murder of a coworker in 2001: "Tell my family and friends

I love them, tell the governor he just lost my vote. Y'all hurry this along; I'm dying to get out of here."

Emmons, Nathaniel (1745-1840). American theologian who founded the Massachusetts Missionary Society: "I am ready."

Empedocles (c. 490-c. 430 BCE). Sicilian-born Greek philosopher, poet and mystic. "I am your deathless god- a mortal never more."

Engel, George (1836-1887). German-born American anarchist and labor union activist. Eight union leaders were condemned to hang for their involvement in Chicago's Haymarket Square riot that resulted in numerous deaths and injuries. Engel, one of the instigators, shouted before his execution: "Hurrah for anarchy! This is the happiest moment of my life."

Enghien, Duc d,' Louis de Bourbon (1772-1804). French nobleman and military leader. After Napoleon I falsely accused Enghien of treachery against the government, a commission hastily ordered his execution by firing squad: "I die for my king and for France... May God preserve my king, and deliver my country from the yoke of the foreigner!" Refusing the traditional blindfold: "A loyal soldier, who has been so often exposed to fire and sword, can see the approach of death with naked eyes and without fear." Before the fatal volley was fired, Enghien admonished the soldiers: "Grenadiers! Lower your arms, otherwise you will miss me or only wound me."

Epaminondas (c. 418-362 BCE). Theban general and statesman. Epaminondas was victorious over the Spartans at the Battle of Mantinea during the Peloponnesian War. Mortally wounded by a javelin blow to the chest, the general remarked when told of the victory: "... All is well… Then I die happy." When some of his comrades lamented that he had no offspring to perpetuate his line, the general retorted: "You are mistaken. I leave two daughters; the Victory at Leuctra and that at Mantinea." After the javelin point was extracted, Epaminondas died suddenly.

Alternatives: * "I have lived long enough, since I die unconquered."
* "Now it is time to die."

Epicurus (c. 341-c. 270 BCE). Greek philosopher who founded the philosophy of Epicureanism. Epicurus endured chronic pain from underlying kidney stones. On his deathbed, he wrote to a friend: "I have written this letter to you on a happy day to me, which is also the last day of my life. For I have been attacked by a painful inability to urinate, and also dysentery, so violent that nothing can be added to the violence of my sufferings. But the cheerfulness of my mind, which comes from the recollection of all my philosophical contemplation, counterbalances all these afflictions. And I beg you to take care of the children of Metrodorus [a disciple], in a manner worthy of the devotion shown by the young man to me, and to philosophy." His last words: "Now farewell. Remember all my words."

Epipodius, Saint (died 179). Lyonnais (east-central France) martyr. When Epipodius refused to renounce Christianity, he was placed on a rack where his flesh was lacerated by hooks. Before he was beheaded, the martyr responded: "The frame of man being composed of two parts, a body and soul, the first, being mean and perishable, should be brought into subjection to the latter. Your idolatrous feasts may gratify the mortal, but they injure the immortal part… Your pleasures lead to eternal death, our pains to eternal pleasure."

Erasmus, Desiderius (1466-1536). Dutch humanist, theologian and writer. Dying from a protracted case of dysentery, Erasmus pleaded: "O Lord Jesus, have pity upon me. Deliver me; make an end. Lord, pity me!" Retaining his sense of humor, Erasmus spoke to three visitors: "Why, then, do they not rend their garments and put ashes upon their heads?"

Alternatives: * "Dear God, O Jesus, have mercy on me! O Lord, deliver me! Lord, put an end to my misery! Lord, have mercy upon me!"
* "O Lord, I entreat Thy mercy! Lord Jesus, deliver me. O Lord, have compassion upon me!"

Ericsson, John (1803-1889). Swedish-born American engineer who designed the ironclad *Monitor* for the Union Navy during the U.S. Civil

War. Dying of Bright's disease: "I am resting. This rest is more magnificent, more beautiful than words can tell."

Ernest Augustus, Duke of Brunswick (1887-1953). Austrian-born royalty. To his wife, Princess Viktoria: "Now I must jump the final hurdle, but God will help me over it."

Erskine, Ralph (1685-1752). Scottish clergyman. Shortly before dying, Erskine raised and clapped his hands, exulting: "I shall be forever a debtor to free grace. Victory! Victory! Victory!"

Erskine, William (1770-1813). British army officer and politician. In a fit of delirium, Erskine jumped from a window in Lisbon, Portugal in 1813. Before dying, he asked: "Now why did I do that?"

Esparza, Guadalupe (1964-2011). American criminal, executed by lethal injection for the rape-murder of a child. To the family of Alyssa Vasquez, whom he killed: "... I hope you will find peace in your heart. My sympathy goes out to you. I hope you find it in your heart to forgive me..." To the witnesses at his execution: "... Say goodbye to my family and pray for me. Pray for my soul; may I rest in peace. I don't know why all this happened. I don't know why. Jesus take me home..."

Espinosa, Felipe (c. 1836-1863). Mexican-American mass murderer. After witnessing the death of family members during a U.S. Navy shelling in the Mexican-American War, Espinosa vowed to kill Americans for revenge. After murdering over two dozen people, he was tracked down and shot: "Jesus, favor me!" To his accomplice: "Escape. I am killed!"

Estrampes, Francisco (1827-1855). Cuban-born American revolutionary. Estrampes and a small armed group invaded Cuba to foment revolution but were quickly caught. Before his garroting, Estrampes cried: "Liberty forever! Death to tyranny!"

Etty, William (1787-1849). English artist. Etty spoke of dying as "a great mystery:" "Wonderful, wonderful, this death!" Consoling his servant: "You will have me there," pointing to his portrait.

Eucles (died 490 BCE). Greek soldier. Eucles ran from the plain of Marathon to the Greek senate in Athens announcing the defeat of an invading Persian army by a small Greek force. His last words before dying on the spot: "Rejoice! For we rejoice!" Some authors, however, assert that Pheidippides (below), a Greek runner, possibly delivered the message.

Eugene IV (c. 1383-1447). Pope from 1431 until his death. Eugene looked back on his controversial papacy in a disconsolate manner and lamented: "O Gabriel, Gabriel [his given name], better would it have been for you to have been neither pope, nor cardinal, nor bishop but to have finished your days as you commenced them, following peaceably in the monastery the exercises of your order." To those assembled at his deathbed: "Pray only that God will perform His will. We have often begged in our prayers for what would have been better not to have prayed... I do not desire to live long, but to die quickly, and that my soul may return to God."

Alternative: * "Oh Gabriele, how much better would it have been for thee, and how much more would it have promoted thy soul's welfare, if thou hadst never been raised to the Pontificate, but hadst been content to lead a quiet and religious life in the monastery:"

Eugene, Prince of Savoy (1663-1736). Parisian-born Austrian general and diplomat. Dying of pneumonia: "That is enough for today. We will reserve the rest for tomorrow- if I live that long."

Eugénie de Montijo (1826-1920). Spanish-born Empress Consort of Napoleon III On her deathbed, to a friend: "It will soon be over."

Euler, Leonhard (1707-1783). Swiss-born mathematician, astronomer and physicist. Succumbing to a "brain hemorrhage:" "I am dying."

Evans, Christmas (1766-1838). Welsh minister. Evans' given name derived from his birth on Christmas day. On his deathbed, to the attending ministers: "... Look at me in myself; I am nothing but ruin. But look at me in Christ; I am heaven and salvation! Goodbye! Drive on!"

Evans, Daniel (1854-1875). American frontier murderer. Accused of killing a traveling companion, Evans was tried before the "Hanging Judge" Isaac Parker and sentenced to die by the rope. Because five other men had been given similar punishment at that time, Evans said at the gallows: "There are worse men here than me."

Evans, Saint Philip (died 1679). Welsh priest, condemned with clergyman John Lloyd (below) for treason. Before his hanging: "... I die for God and religion's sake; and I think myself so happy that if I had never so many lives, I would willingly give them all for so good a cause..." Then, to his fellow martyr: "Adieu, Mr. Lloyd! Though for a little time, for we shall shortly meet again... Into your hands, Lord I commend my spirit."

Evarts, Jeremiah (1781-1831). American missionary and activist for Native American's rights. Dying of tuberculosis: "Wonderful, wonderful, wonderful glory! We cannot understand- we cannot comprehend- wonderful glory- I will praise Him, I will praise Him! Who are in the room? Call all in. Call all. Let a great many come. I wish to give directions. Wonderful! Glory! Jesus reigns!"

Evereruard, Charles d' (1613-1703). French gourmet and courtier. When asked if he could be reconciled with Christ, Evereruard replied: "With all my heart I would fain [gladly] be reconciled with my stomach which no longer performs its usual functions."

Everett, Edward (1794-1865). American politician and educator. Dying of pneumonia, the conclusion of a letter to his daughter: "... I have barely weathered an attack of Pneumonia, which is an old fashioned 'lung fever.' I have turned the corner, and as soon as I can get a little appetite, shake off my carking [worrisome] cough, and get the kidneys to resume their action, and subdue the numbness of my limbs, and get the better of my neuralgic pain in the left shoulder, I hope to do nicely."

Evers, Medgar (1925-1963). African American civil rights activist, assassinated in Mississippi by a white supremacist. As a neighbor tried to staunch the bleeding: "Let me go! Let me go!" While being transported to a local hospital: "Sit me up! Turn me loose!"

Ewell, Richard (1817-1872). Confederate general during the U.S. Civil War. Ewell lost the lower part of his left leg during the 1862 Battle of Groveton, northern Virginia but returned to service the following year. Dying of pneumonia at age 54, he felt his illness was caused by wearing a pair of light-weight pants in mid-winter: "After all my fighting against the United States so long, it is strange that an old pair of infantry pantaloons should kill me at last."

Fairbanks, Douglas Sr., born Douglas Elton Thomas Ulman (1883-1939). American actor, director and producer. After complaining of severe chest pains, Fairbanks' physician advised strict bed rest. When the actor awoke later in the day, his nurse inquired how he was feeling: "I've never felt better." Fairbanks died later that night of a heart attack.

Fall, Bernard (1926-1967). Austrian-born American war correspondent who died covering the Vietnam conflict. While on patrol with a unit of Marines, Fall dictated his impressions into his recorder immediately before a landmine detonated: "… Shadows are lengthening and we've reached one of our phase lines after the fire fight and it smells bad- meaning it's a little bit suspicious...Could be an amb…"

Falletti, Giulietta (1785-1864). French-born Italian prison reformer. "May the will of God be done in me and by me in time and for eternity."

Fannin, James (1804-1836). American military officer. While leading a contingent of men during Texas' struggle for independence, Fannin's group was surrounded by a Mexican force and summarily executed. Before a firing squad: "Don't shoot me in the head and see that my body is decently buried." He died from gunshots to the head and his body was burned.

Fanon, Frantz (1925-1961). Martinique-born French physician, writer and activist who championed Algerian independence. Dying of leukemia, Fanon quipped that frequent blood transfusions were turning his dark-complected skin white: "They [his doctors] put me in the washing machine again last night."

Faraday, Michael (1791-1867). British scientist and educator, known for his work with electromagnetism. While watching a rainbow from his window, to his wife: "He hath set His testimony in the heavens." When asked what his occupation might be in eternity, Faraday replied: "I shall be with Christ, and that is enough."

Farinato, Paolo (c. 1525-1606). Italian artist and architect. Dying, Farinato told his ill wife: "Now I am going." She replied: "I will bear you company, my dear husband." She died later that same day.

Farley, Chris (1964-1997). American comedian. Farley who struggled with drug abuse pleaded with a prostitute as she left his room: "Please don't leave me. Please don't leave me." The comedian died shortly thereafter of a drug overdose.

Farnsworth, Elon (1837-1863). Union Army officer in the U.S. Civil War. When his commander ordered a suicidal charge into the Confederate lines during the Battle of Gettysburg, Farnsworth replied: "General, if you order the charge, I will lead it, but you must take the responsibility." After some indistinct chatter with his superior, he said: "I will obey your order."

Farouk (1920-1965). King of Egypt, deposed during the 1952 Egyptian Revolution. Farouk died of a heart attack while in exile 12 years later. Some have recorded these words as his last: "There will soon be only five Kings left: the Kings of England, Diamonds, Hearts, Spades and Clubs." Farouk actually uttered them to British Lord Boyd-Orr shortly before his abdication.

Farquhar, George (1677-1707). Irish dramatist. Note to his friend, Robert Wilks [an actor and collaborator]: "Dear Bob, I have not anything to leave thee to perpetuate my memory but two helpless girls. Look upon them sometimes and think of him that was to the last moment of his life, thine, George Farquhar."

Farragut, David (1801-1870). Union naval officer who figured prominently in the U.S. Civil War. Farragut is best-known for his order given during the Battle of Mobile Bay, to the effect: "Damn the torpedoes, full speed ahead." While standing on the deck of a dismantled sloop-of-war six years later, Farragut prophesied: "This is the last time I shall ever tread the deck of a man-of-war."

Faulkner, William (1897-1962). American novelist who won the 1949 Nobel Prize in Literature. When Faulkner was hospitalized after falling from a horse, his brother asked to be informed when he wished to leave the medical facility. Faulkner replied: "Yes, Jim, I will." He died of a heart attack shortly thereafter.

Faure, François (1841-1899). French statesman who died of a stroke while serving as president: "You see, my poor Bridier, what a poor thing man is, even when he is President of the Republic."

Fauré, Gabriel (1845-1924). French organist and composer. Late in life, Fauré suffered a severe hearing loss but was able to continue composing. He uttered these words immediately before dying of complications from hardening of the arteries: "Have my works received justice? Have they not been too much admired or sometimes too severely criticised? What of my music will live? But then, that is of little importance." To his sons: "After I'm gone, you'll hear people say 'When all's said and done, that's all there is to it!' Supporters will fall away, maybe... You mustn't be upset by this. It's fate. It happened with Saint-Saëns [one of his teachers] and with other composers... They all go through a period of oblivion... None of that is important. I did what I could. Now let God be my judge."

Alternative: * "There is always a moment of oblivion. All that is unimportant, I did what I could. May God be the judge."

Fawcett, Henry (1833-1884). British economist, statesman and educator. Despite losing his sight in a hunting accident at age 25, Fawcett became a respected economist and Member of Parliament. Dying of pleurisy: "The best things to warm my hands with would be my fur gloves. They are in the pocket of my coat in the dressing room."

Fawcett, John (1740-1817). English minister, theologian and hymnodist, best-known for his hymn "Blest Be the Tie that Binds." "Come, Lord Jesus, come quickly! O receive me to Thy children."

Fawsitt, Amy (1836-1876). English-born stage actress. Dying of suspected tuberculosis: "I am hungry."

Febronia, Saint (died 304). Assyrian martyr. Febronia was arrested during Emperor Diocletian's suppression of the Christian movement promulgated throughout the Roman Empire. Steadfastly refusing to renounce her faith, she was burned and various parts of her body were scarified. Before she died: "My Lord! My God! See what I suffer and receive my soul into Thy hands!" Eventually, Febronia had her hands, feet and head hacked off.

Alternative: * "Lord, my God, look at my dire affliction; may my soul come into your hands!"

Feldman, Andrea (1948-1972). American actress. Feldman was best-known for her performances in a series of Andy Warhol films. After inviting ex-boyfriends to her parent's apartment, the mentally unstable actress jumped from a 14th floor window. Among numerous goodbye notes left by Feldman: "I'm going for the big time. Heaven," and "I was unique as an antique, you're going to miss me, farewell."

Félix, Rachel (1821-1858). French actress. Dying of tuberculosis, Félix wrote for an autograph seeker: "In a week from now, I shall begin to be food for worms and for writers of biographies. Rachel" When the visitor objected: "Take it, take it, it will, perhaps, be the last thing I shall ever write." Her last letter read: "My poor Rebecca, my dear sister, I am going to see thee! I am indeed happy."

Felix of Thibiuca, Saint (247-303). North African priest, martyred during the Diocletian persecutions. Before his beheading for refusing to surrender Christian writings: "God, I thank you. I have passed fifty-six years in this world. I have preserved my chastity; I have observed the Gospels; I have preached the Faith and the Truth. Lord God of Heaven and Earth, Jesus Christ, I bend my neck as a sacrifice for you, who abides forever."

Fénelon, François (1651-1715). French writer and Roman Catholic archbishop. Dying of "an inflammation on his lungs," Fénelon proclaimed: "I am on the cross with Christ." As he died: "Lord, if I am still necessary to Thy people, I refuse not to labor for the rest of my days. Thy will be done."

Alternatives: * "Father, if it be possible, let this cup pass from me; nevertheless, not as I will, but as Thou wilt."
* "Not my will, but Thine be done."

Fennell, Frederick (1914-2004). American conductor and composer, best-known for his work with wind ensembles. At the end, Fennell told his daughter that he was "frustrated and disappointed." When she asked why: "Why? There's no drummer here yet. I can't die without a drummer!" When told that heaven's best drummer was coming: "I hear him. I hear him. I'm OK now."

Ferdinand I (1865-1927). King of Romania. Dying of cancer, Ferdinand remarked to his wife: "I am so tired."

Ferdinand, Duke of Alva (1508-1582). Spanish military leader and statesman. When the neglected Ferdinand learned that King Philip II would visit, he lamented: "Too late."

Ferdinand, Franz (see Franz Ferdinand).

Ferguson, Samuel "Champ" (1821-1865). Confederate guerrilla fighter during the U.S. Civil War. At war's end, Ferguson was found guilty of multiple murders and was sentenced to hang. His response to the verdict: "I am yet and will die a Rebel... I killed a good many men, of course, but I never killed a man who I did not know was seeking my life... I had always heard that the Federals would not take me prisoner but would shoot me down wherever they found me. That is what made me kill more than I otherwise would have done. I repeat that I die a Rebel out and out, and my last request is that my body be moved to White County, Tennessee, and be buried in good Rebel soil." His burial wish was fulfilled.

Fergusson, Robert (1750-1774). Scottish poet. In the last year of his short life, Fergusson sustained a head injury that led to insanity. Shortly before dying, he rambled to his mother and sister: "What ails ye? Wherefore sorrow for me, sirs? I am very well cared for here, I do assure you, I want for nothing, but it is cold. It is very cold. You know, I told you, it would come to this at last, yes, I told you so." As they prepared to leave: "Oh, do not go yet, mother. I hope to be soon, oh, do not go yet, do not leave me!"

Fernandez, Raymond (1914-1951). American criminal. Fernandez and his common-law wife Martha Beck (above) committed a series of murders for which they were condemned to die in the electric chair. The so-called "Lonely Hearts Killers" answered personal ads from elderly women and then swindled them of their savings. If the victims offered any resistance, they were killed. Fernandez left these last words: "People want to know if I still love Martha. But of course I do. I want to shout it out. I love Martha. What do the public know about love?"

Alternative: * "I am going to die. That is all right. As you know, that's something I've been prepared for since 1949. So tonight I'll die like a man." As he approached death, Fernandez lost his resolve, struggled and had to be dragged to the electric chair.

Fernando, Gratien (1915-1942). Sri Lankan revolutionary. Fernando, one of the instigators of the Cocos Islands Mutiny, tried by insurrection to end British colonial rule in Sri Lanka. His revolt was suppressed and he was sentenced to hang: "Loyalty to a country under the heel of a white man is disloyalty."

Ferrar, Robert (c. 1500-1555). Martyred English bishop. Disgruntled cannons of Ferrar's diocese brought charges of mismanagement and abuse of authority against him. He was found guilty and burned at the stake. As Ferrar was chained to the post: "If I stir through the pains of my burning, believe not the doctrine I have taught."

Ferrer, Francisco (1859-1909). Spanish revolutionary and pedagogue who developed schools for lower class students. During a period of unrest in Spain during the first decade of the 20th century, Ferrer was accused of insurrection and sentenced to die. To the firing squad: “I desire to be shot standing, without a bandage over my eyes. Look well, my children, it is not your fault. I am innocent. Long live the school.”

Ferrier, Kathleen (1912-1953). English opera singer. Dying of cancer, Ferrier spoke to her nurse: “Wouldn’t it be lovely if I could go to sleep and not wake up again?” Parodying Mozart’s serenade *Eine Kleine Nachtmusik*, she quipped: “Now I’ll have *eine kleine* pause.”

Ferry, Noah (1831-1863). Union officer during the U.S. Civil War. When his men broke ranks during the Battle of Gettysburg, Ferry shouted: “Rally, boys! Rally for the fence!” He was felled by a gunshot to the head.

Fersen, Axel von (1755-1810). Swedish nobleman. Fersen was implicated in the poisoning of the Swedish crown prince Carl August. During the prince’s funeral procession, Fersen was killed by an inflamed mob before guards could rescue him. His last words: “Save me!” Fersen posthumously was absolved of any complicity.

Alternative: * “Give me salvation.”

Fessenden, Reginald (1866-1932). Canadian-born inventor who performed pioneering research in radio wave transmission. Fessenden held over 500 patents. Following afternoon tea: “That was a nice little party. I’m sure this summer is helping me with all this rest and sunshine and the sunshine lamps. I ought to be able to find out something that will be helpful not only to me but to others.”

Fetterman, William (1833-1866). Army officer in the U.S. Civil War and battles on the western Great Plains. Boasting that he could suppress Native American aggression against settlers in his territory, Fetterman led a group of 80 soldiers to their death in an ambush near Ft. Phil Kearny, Wyoming, staged by the Sioux warrior called Red Cloud: “Give me 80 men and I’ll ride through the whole Sioux nation.”

Feynman, Richard (1918-1988). American physicist who was awarded the1965 Nobel Prize in Physics for his quantum electrodynamics research. Dying of cancer: "I'd hate to die twice. It's so boring."

Alternative: * "This dying is boring."

Fichte, Johann (1762-1814). German philosopher. To his son who tried to give him medicine: "Leave it alone; I need no more medicine; I feel that I am well."

Field, Cyrus (1819-1892). American businessman and director of the company that laid the first trans-Atlantic telegraph cable. On his deathbed, the delirious Field muttered: "Hold those ships! Don't let them sail yet! I must make further experiments first."

Field, Eugene (1850-1895). American poet, journalist and writer, best-known for his children's poetry. Fields told his family: "Goodnight" and died unexpectedly in his sleep.

Field, John (1782-1837). Irish pianist and composer. Dying of cancer and pneumonia, Fields was asked by a priest if he were a Protestant: "No." Then a Catholic: "No." Then a Calvinist: "Not exactly that. I am not a Calvinist, but a *Claveciniste* [a French word meaning harpsichordist]." When a friend tried to wipe his forehead, Field said: "Thank you- but don't kiss me: it is the sweat of death. I'm dying, and it's for the best."

Alternative: * "I am a pianist."

Field, Katherine "Kate" (1838-1896). American explorer, journalist and lecturer. Dying of pneumonia on a steamer cruising among the Hawaiian Islands, Field asked a companion: "What did you say is the name of your expedition, and what are you going for?" When she was answered, Field uttered her last words: "The Amherst Eclipse Expedition!"

Fields, W. C., born William Claude Dukenfield (1880-1946). Irreverent American comedian. While Fields was hospitalized for alcohol-related bleeding at the end of his life, a visiting friend found him perusing a Bible.

When queried about this out-of-character behavior, the comedian quipped: "I'm looking for loopholes." His apocryphal last words were spoken to his mistress, the film actress Carlotta Monti: "Grab everything and run. The vultures are coming... God d*** the whole f******' world and everyone in it but you, Carlotta!"

Alternative: * "I have spent a lot of time searching through the Bible for loopholes."

Filiaggi, James (1965-2007). American criminal, executed by lethal injection for the murder of his ex-wife: "We all got to go sometime, some sooner than others. I'm going to be busy getting the Browns to the Super Bowl. Working magic. I love you guys." The Cleveland Browns professional football team did not make it to the Super Bowl that season.

Alternative: * "I know I flipped some Worlds upside-down. For me, it's fine. But the State needs to learn, this [the death penalty] ain't the answer. This is no deterrent to crime. Some are falsely convicted, railroaded. The State needs to wake up, maybe they will follow the Europeans. God is the only one who knows."

Fillmore, Millard (1800-1874). Thirteenth U.S. president. Dying of a stroke, Fillmore spoke to his nurse (some say his doctor) who attempted to feed him a bowl of soup: "The nourishment is palatable."

Alternatives: * "The food is palatable."
* "It tastes good."

Filmer, Henry (died 1543). English Protestant preacher who was condemned to die at the stake for his reformist views. Before he was burned, Filmer proclaimed: "Be merry, be merry my brethren, and lift up your hands unto God; for after this sharp breakfast, I trust we shall have a good dinner in the kingdom of Christ, our Lord and Redeemer."

Filipović, Stjepan (1916-1942). Yugoslavian partisan who was executed for his opposition to German aggression during WWII. Before his death by hanging, Filipović cried: "Death to fascism, freedom to the people!"

Finch, Barbara (died 1959). California housewife. Dr. Bernard Finch, Barbara's husband, was involved in a romance with a neighbor, Carole Tregoff. To remove Mrs. Finch from the love triangle, the doctor and his mistress conspired to murder her. During a struggle, Dr. Finch shot his wife dead. He alleged her last words were: "I'm sorry...I should have listened to you...I love you...take care of the kids..." Both conspirators were convicted of murder but later were paroled.

Alternative: "Wait... I'm sorry... I should have listened... Don't leave me... take care of the kids..."

Fink, Mike (c. 1770-1822). American brawler and keel boatman on the Ohio and Mississippi Rivers. Fink and a friend named Carpenter indulged in a game where each would shoot, at a distance, a cup of whiskey off the other's head. On the last occasion, Carpenter shot the cup from Finks head but grazed his scalp in the process. The boatman angrily said: "Carpenter, my son, I taught you to shoot differently from that last shot! You've missed once, but you won't again!" Fink proceeded to shoot his companion in the forehead. When a witness to the incident accused him of murder, Fink responded: "I didn't mean to kill my boy!" The accuser shot the boatman dead on the spot.

Finney, Charles (1792-1875). American clergyman, educator and abolitionist. Suffering a heart attack: "Perhaps this is the thirst of death... I am dying."

Finucane, Brendan "Paddy" (1920-1942). Decorated British RAF pilot, killed during the Battle of Britain. When his plane was damaged by a German land gun, the aviator turned his stricken plane toward the sea. Finucane's last radio transmission before crashing into the English Channel: "This is it, chaps."

Firstbrook, Thomas (died 1876). American laborer. Fatally injured in a sawmill accident, Firstbrook shouted before he died: "Victory, victory, victory! I am sweeping through the gates, washed in the blood of the Lamb."

Fischer, Adolf (1858-1887). German-born American anarchist and labor union activist. Eight union leaders, including Fischer, were accused of inciting the riot at Chicago's Haymarket Square that resulted in numerous deaths and injuries. Prior to his execution, Fischer spoke to his hangman: "Don't draw it too tight. I can't breathe... Long live anarchy... This is the happiest moment of my life."

Fischer, Robert "Bobby" (1943-2008). American chess grandmaster. Dying of kidney failure: "Nothing is as healing as the human touch."

Alternative: * "Nothing soothes pain like [the] human touch."

Fish, Hamilton "Albert" (1870-1936). American child molester and serial killer who allegedly cannibalized some of his victims. Convicted of murder, Fish was executed in the Sing Sing Prison electric chair. While being positioned in the device, the felon told prison officials: "What a thrill that will be if I have to die in the electric chair. It will be the supreme thrill. The only one I haven't tried." Fish's last words before the switch was thrown: "I don't even know why I am here."

Fisher, Saint John (c. 1469-1535). English Roman Catholic clergyman. Fisher was beheaded for his opposition to Henry VIII as the proclaimed head of the Church of England. On the scaffold, he prayed: "O Lord, in Thee have I trusted. Let me never be confounded."

Fisher, Lavinia (1793-1820). American criminal. During the early 1800s, Fisher and her husband allegedly joined a gang of highway robbers active around Charleston, South Carolina. A different legend relates that Fisher and her mate killed a number of guests at their inn for their money and possessions. Regardless of the circumstances, the pair was sentenced to die by hanging. In a quirk of fate, the condemned woman escaped the hangman's pull by jumping to her death from the gallows. As she leapt, Lavinia cried: "If you have any message for the Devil, give it to me, for I am about to meet him!"

Alternatives: * "If you have a message you want to send to hell, give it to me. I'll carry it."

* "If anyone has a message for hell, give it to me. I'll deliver it."

Fish-Harnack, Mildred (1902-1943). American educator. In 1929, Fish-Harnack and her husband moved to the German capital where she took a teaching position at the University of Berlin. Because of their involvement with the resistance movement during WWII, the Nazi regime condemned both to die. Before she was guillotined, Fish-Harnack lamented: "And I loved Germany so much." She was the only known American woman executed for treason by the Third Reich.

Fisk, James, Jr. "Big Jim" (1834-1872). American businessman. Fisk was shot by his ex-partner who failed in an attempt to extort money from him. As Fisk lay injured, he moaned: "For God's sake, will nobody help me?" Later the dying man said to his doctors: "I'm as strong as an ox, and it takes four times as much [pain] medicine to affect me as an ordinary man."

Fisk, Willbur (1792-1839). American minister and scholar. When Fisk's wife asked if he recognized her: "Yes, Love, yes!"

Fithian, Charles (died 1931). American criminal, electrocuted for a murder committed during a robbery: "I want to make a complaint... The soup I had for supper tonight was too hot."

Fitzgerald, Edward (1809-1883). British poet, best-known for his translation of Persian verses that he called *The Rubáiyát of Omar Khayyám*. Before Fitzgerald's sudden death: "I will go to bed."

Fitzgerald, F. Scott (1896-1940). American writer, best-known for his novel *The Great Gatsby*. Fitzgerald at the time of his death lived with the nationally syndicated columnist Sheilah Graham. He told her: "I'm going to Schwab's to get some ice cream." When she reminded him that he might miss the doctor and offered chocolate instead, Fitzgerald replied "Good enough. They'll be fine." He collapsed shortly thereafter and died of a heart attack.

Fitzgerald, George (died1786). Irish eccentric and duelist who was convicted of murdering a colonel in the Mayo Volunteers. When the rope broke at his hanging, Fitzgerald joked: "You see, I am once more among you unexpectedly." While waiting for a replacement, he advised the sheriff to procure a rope from a different shop. Before the second attempt, Fitzgerald tried to procrastinate, asking for time to pray. The second rope did not break, but the criminal's neck did.

Flagstad, Kirsten (1895-1962). Norwegian operatic soprano. Dying of cancer, Flagstad spoke to her daughter: "I know this is the end, Elsa, but you mustn't be sad. It is best so. You must be a brave, strong girl and take it calmly and naturally." To a friend: "No, you mustn't cry. You must be strong, like Elsa. There's nothing to cry about. I have sung my song."

Flaubert, Gustave (1821-1880). French writer, best-known for his novel *Madame Bovary*. Dying of advanced syphilis and a stroke, Flaubert spoke somewhat incoherently: "Rouen... we're not far from Rouen... Hellot [a physician]... I know the Hellots..."

Flavel, John (1627-1691). English clergyman and writer. "I know that it will be well with me."

Flavus, Subrius (died 65). A member of the Roman Praetorian Guard who conspired against Emperor Nero. When Flavus was told to offer his neck "resolutely" for beheading, he responded: "I wish that your stroke may be as resolute."

Flecker, James (1884-1915). English poet, writer and playwright. Dying of tuberculosis, Flecker prayed: "Lord, have mercy on my soul."

Flegenheimer, Arthur (see Schultz, Dutch).

Fleming, Alexander (1881-1955). British physician who discovered the antibiotic penicillin. Fleming was awarded the 1945 Nobel Prize in Medicine for his research. Dying of a heart attack: "I'm covered in a cold sweat. And I don't know why I've got this pain in my chest. It's not the heart. It's going down from the esophagus to the stomach."

Fleming, Ian (1908-1964). English writer who created the James Bond spy novels. Dying of a heart attack, to the ambulance drivers transporting him to hospital: "I am sorry to trouble you, chaps. I don't know how you get along so fast with the traffic on the roads these days."

Fleming, Marjory (1803-1811). Precocious Scottish diarist and poet. Dying of meningitis at eight years of age, Fleming cried: "Oh mother, mother..."

Fletcher, Andrew (c. 1653-1716). Scottish politician, writer and patriot. Dying of "a flux contracted by drinking ye waters of the river Seine at Paris," Fletcher was asked by Lord Sunderland if he had any requests. The dying man replied: "I have a nephew who has been studying the law. Make him a judge when he is fit for it." His last words: "Lord, have mercy on my poor country that is so barbarously oppressed."

Flint, Frank "Silver" (1855-1892). American professional baseball player. Dying of alcoholism shortly after retiring from baseball, Flint spoke to his former teammate Billy Sunday, now a minister: "There's nothing in the life of years ago I care for now. I can hear the bleachers cheer when I make a hit that wins the game. But there is nothing that can help me out now. And if the Umpire calls me out now, won't you say a few words over me, Billy?"

Flora, Saint (died 851). Christian martyr of Córdoba, Spain. Flora was born to a Muslim father and a Christian mother. After her father died, she was raised in her mother's faith. When brought before a Muhammadan judge, Flora refused to renounce her beliefs. Before her beheading for apostasy, she said: "I am the woman of pagan extraction, whom you punished with stripes some time ago because I would not deny Christ. Hitherto, through weakness of the flesh I have hid myself, but now, trusting in the divine grace, I fear not to declare that Christ is the true God, and to denounce your false prophet as a wretch, an adulterer and a magician."

Flowers, Theodore "Tiger" (1895-1927). American professional boxer. Before undergoing a "minor" procedure to remove a mass close to the right eye, Flowers recited a child's prayer: "If I should die before I wake, I pray thee, Lord, my soul to take." He did not survive the surgery.

Floyd, Charles (1782-1804). American explorer who was the only casualty of the Lewis and Clark Expedition. Dying of an abdominal complaint, possibly appendicitis: "I am going away. I want you to write me a letter."

Floyd, Charles "Pretty Boy"(1904-1934). American bank robber and murderer. Trapped by the FBI in an Ohio field, Floyd was shot by one of the agents. When asked if he were "Pretty Boy," the robber allegedly asked: "Who the hell tipped you off? I'm Floyd, all right. You got me this time."

Alternatives: * "I'm done for. You've hit me twice."
* "I'm going."

Flynn, Errol (1909-1959). Tasmanian-born Hollywood actor. Flynn spoke during an interview shortly before dying: "I've had a hell of a lot of fun and I've enjoyed it… every minute of it." While visiting a friend, Flynn retired for a rest: "I shall return." The actor died of a heart attack shortly thereafter.

Foch, Ferdinand (1851-1929). French general selected as supreme commander of Allied forces during WWI. Foch's last words: "Let me go."

Alternative: * "Let us go."

Folger, Abigail (1943-1969). American socialite and great-granddaughter of Folgers Coffee Company's founder. Folger was stabbed multiple times by members of the Manson Family during their rampage on August 9, 1969. As she lay dying, Folger cried: "You can stop now; I'm already dead."

Fontaine-Martel, Madame de (died 1733). French socialite. Fontaine-Martel's last words were recorded by the writer Voltaire: "My consolation at this hour, I am sure that somewhere in the world, someone is making love... what is the time?" When told it was two o'clock, she replied: "God be praised, whatever time it is, somewhere lovers keep their tryst."

Alternatives: * "God be blessed. Whatever the hour there is always a rendezvous going on."
* "What o'clock is it?" Without being told: "Blessed be God, whatever the hour may be, there is somewhere a rendezvous!"

Fontenelle, Bernard de (1657-1757). French writer and scientist. Fontenelle perceived his approaching death: "I feel nothing, apart from a certain difficulty in continuing to exist."

Alternatives: * "I do not suffer, my friends. I only feel a certain difficulty of living."
* "I suffer nothing, but feel a sort of difficulty of living longer."

Foot, Solomon (1802-1866). American politician who became a member of the U.S. House of Representatives and Senate. Dying of a painful month-long illness, Foot spoke to a colleague: "Oh, yes, we shall meet again in heaven, and the time will not be long. Farewell, dear friend. God bless you forevermore." Then to his wife: "What, can this be death? Is it come already? I see it! I see it! The gates are wide open! Beautiful! Beautiful!"

Foote, Andrew (1806-1863). Union admiral who served during the U.S. Civil War. When told by his physician there was no hope for recovery from his kidney failure: "Well, I am glad to be done with guns and war." To his attendant: "We will have them, North and South." When queried what was meant by the statement, the admiral answered: "The colored people, yes, we will have them. We must have charity, charity, charity..." Foote lost consciousness and died.

Fooy, Sam (died1875). Native American criminal, convicted of robbing and murdering a school teacher. In the late summer of 1875, six men including Fooy were tried in Fort Smith, Arkansas before "The Hanging Judge" Isaac Parker and sentenced to death by the rope. Before his execution, Fooy spoke to newsmen about a dream he had the previous night: "… When the drop came, I felt no pain, but fell asleep and woke up in a beautiful garden- the most beautiful place I ever saw, with running waters and stars dancing on the waves." On the gallows: "I am anxious to get out of this world, as the people who have come here today are to see me. I will not delay you." The crowd and the condemned men then sang two hymns. Before the trap was sprung, one of the six men called out: "Lord Jesus receive me."

Forbes, Archibald (1838-1900). British war correspondent. On his deathbed, Forbes spoke deliriously about the tumultuous 1879 Zulu Wars in South Africa: "Those guns, man, those guns! Don't you hear those guns?"

Ford, Arthur (1896-1971). American psychic who founded the movement Spiritual Frontiers Fellowship. Dying of a heart ailment, Ford lamented: "Oh, God, I can't take any more! God, help me!"

Ford, Henry (1863-1947). American automobile manufacturer who pioneered the assembly line concept. Dying of a stroke, Ford spoke to his maid: "I'll sleep well tonight. We're going early to bed."

Ford, Paul (1865-1902). American writer. Ford was shot by his disinherited brother who then committed suicide. Before succumbing to his wound, the writer managed to say: "All right, I want to die bravely."

Fordyce, George (1736-1802). Scottish physician. Dying of heart failure, Fordyce told his daughter who was reading to him: "Stop. Go out of the room... I am going to die." He expired shortly thereafter.

Forrest, Nathan (1821-1877). Confederate general during the U.S. Civil War. Dying from complications of diabetes, Forrest spoke to his minister: "Just here I have an indescribable peace. All is peace within. I want you to know that between me and the face of my heavenly Father not a cloud intervenes. I have put my trust in my Lord and Savior." Days later he uttered his last command: "Call my wife."

Forrest, Thomas (see Forret, Thomas).

Forrestal, James (1892-1949). U.S. Secretary of Defense under President Harry Truman. Hospitalized for severe depression, Forrestal allegedly penned a portion of Sophocles' poem *Ajax*, which chronicled the suicide of that mythical Greek hero: "Woe to the mother in her close of day./ Woe to her desolate heart and temples gray/ When she shall hear/ Her loved one's story whispered in her ear!/ 'Woe! Woe!' will be the cry-/ No quiet murmur like the tremulous wail/ Of the lone bird, the querulous night..."

Without completing the word "nightingale," he apparently jumped to his death from his 16th story window at the Bethesda Naval Hospital. Some accounts have Forrestal copying a different passage from *Ajax* and jumping from the 13th floor. Unsubstantiated conspiracy theories opine that the former Secretary was murdered.

Alternative: * "Frenzy hath seized thy dearest son,/ Who from thy shores in glory came/ The first in valor and in fame;/ Thy deeds that he hath done/ Seem hostile all to hostile eyes.../ Better to die, and sleep/ The never waking sleep, than linger on,/ And dare to live, when the soul's life is [gone]..."

Forret, Thomas, also Thomas Forrest (died 1540). Martyred Scottish clergyman. Condemned as a heretic for his preaching, Forret was strangled and burned at the stake. His last words: "God, be merciful to me, a sinner! Lord Jesus, receive my spirit!" He then quoted the beginning of Psalm 51: "Have mercy upon me, O God, according to Thy loving-kindness."

Alternative: "... Pity me, O God! Receive me in Thy infinite mercy."

Forster, Edward "E.M." (1879-1970) English writer, best-known for his novels *A Passage to India* and *A Room with a View*. Before dying of a stroke, Forster commented about a garrulous friend who had left his bedside: "He's really nice, that old bore."

Forster, Georg (1754-1794). German naturalist, explorer and writer who was the son of Johann Forster (below). Dying of a suspected stroke, Forster penned a last letter to his children: "It's true isn't it, my children, that two words are better than none? I haven't strength to write more. Goodbye. Keep away from illness. A kiss for my little darlings."

Forster, Johann (1729-1798). Polish naturalist, writer and explorer on one of Captain James Cook's Pacific voyages. "This is a beautiful world."

Fosdick, Harry (1878-1969). American Protestant minister and educator. To his daughter: "I'll be waiting for you at the bottom steps of the Pearly Gates." When she asked why the bottom steps, Fosdick explained with a wink: "Because you'll need someone to guide you up and by St. Peter."

Fossey, Dian (1932-1985). American zoologist who studied gorillas in their natural habitat in Rwanda, Africa. The last line of an unfinished letter written before she was murdered in her cabin on December 26, 1985: "Camp will be bulging by the time I leave for America in March, but right now it is awfully quiet…" Her last diary entry: "When you realize the value of all life, you dwell less on what is past and concentrate more on the preservation of the future." Fossey possibly lost her life, because she tried to protect gorillas from poachers.

Foster, John (1770-1843). English clergyman and essayist. The last line of a note written to a friend: "... I commend you to the God of mercy, and very affectionately bid you- farewell."

Foster, Stephen (1826-1864). American songwriter who wrote "Beautiful Dreamer," "Oh! Susanna" and many other popular tunes of the day. After lacerating his neck on a washbasin broken during a fall, the alcoholic Foster lamented: "I'm done for" and begged a friend for a drink. Admitted to New York's Belleview Hospital, Foster complained to a companion that "Nothing has been done for me. I can't eat the food they bring me." He died while hospitalized. A scrap of paper with the words: "Dear friends and gentle hearts," was found in his wallet. In 1949, Bob Hilliard and Sammy Fain wrote a popular song incorporating those words.

Foster, Vincent (1945-1993). American attorney who was a member of President William Clinton's White House staff. Suffering from depression, Foster apparently shot himself in the head. The last lines of his suicide note read: "… I was not meant for the job or the spotlight of public life in Washington. Here, ruining people is considered sport."

Fothergill, Samuel (1715-1772). English Quaker minister. "All is well with me. Through the mercy of God, in Jesus Christ, I am going to a blessed and happy eternity. My troubles are ended. Mourn not for me."

Fothergill, William (1865-1926). British gynecologic surgeon and educator. Dying suddenly after delivering a speech at a banquet: "I have enjoyed tonight one of the best dinners I can remember."

Four Bears, also Mato-Tope (died1837). Native American Mandan chieftain. Dying of smallpox that killed approximately ninety percent of the Mandans, Four Bears condemned the white man for bringing the scourge to his people, concluding: "... I do not fear death, my friends. You know it, but to die with my face rotten, that even the wolves will shrink with horror at seeing me, and say to themselves, that is The Four Bears, the friend of the whites. Listen well what I have to say, as it will be the last time you will hear me. Think of your wives, children, brothers, sisters, friends, and in fact all that you hold dear- are all dead, or dying, with their faces all rotten, caused by those dogs the whites. Think of all that, my friends, and rise all together and not leave one of them alive. The Four Bears will act his part."

Fourcroy, Antoine François, Comte de (1755-1809). French chemist. Upon learning he had been made a count, Fourcroy interrupted his writing and exclaimed: "I am dead." He expired shortly thereafter.

Fourier, Joseph (1768-1830). French mathematician and physicist. Dying of heart disease, Fourier exclaimed to his doctor: "Quick, quick! Some vinegar! I am fainting!"

Fox, Charles (1749-1806). British statesman. When told that his days were numbered, Fox responded: "God's will be done. I have lived long enough and I shall die happy." When his wife asked what he had said, the dying man replied with a figure of speech meaning that it was not important: "It don't signify, dearest Liz." His last coherent words were: "God bless you- bless you- and you all. I die happy- I pity you!"

Alternative: * A different response to his wife's question (above): "Trotter [who published Fox's memoirs] will tell you."

Fox, George (1624-1691). English preacher and founder of the Quaker movement. After collapsing at a meeting, Fox told those attempting to help him: "All is well. The Seed [word or power] of God reigns over all and over death itself. And though I am weak in body yet the power of God is over all and the Seed reigns over all disorderly spirits." Later, when asked how he was doing: "Never heed, the Lord's presence is over all weakness and death. The Lord reigns, blessed be the Lord."

Fox, Henry, Baron Holland (1705-1774). English Member of Parliament. Concerning a friend and political rival George Selwyn who had a fondness for viewing corpses and executions: "If Mr. Selwyn calls again, show him up; if I am alive, I shall be delighted to see him, and if I am dead, he would like to see me."

Fox, Henry Watson (1817-1848). English missionary to the Madras region of India. On his deathbed, Fox proclaimed: "Jesus, Jesus must be first in the heart." When asked if this were true in his case, he replied: "Yes, He is."

Fox, Margaret (1614-1702). English preacher, writer and wife of George Fox (above). To her daughter: "Rachel, take me in thy arms. I am in peace."

France, Anatole, born François-Anatole Thibault (1844-1924). French writer, journalist, playwright and poet who was awarded the 1921 Nobel Prize in Literature. "So this is what it is like to die. It takes a long time. Maman [mother]!"

Frances of Rome, Saint (1384-1440). Roman mystic and activist for the sick and poor. In a rapture as she died: "The heavens open! The angels descend! The archangel has finished his task. He stands before me. He beckons me to follow him."

Francis I (1494-1547). King of France. Dying of a disease that left him with "his stomach abscessed, his kidneys shriveled, his entrails putrefied, his throat corroded and one of his lungs in shreds," the monarch said: "I am ready to go. I have had my full life and I am glad to die. Into Thy hands, O Lord, I commend my spirit. Jesus."

Francis of Assisi, Saint (c. 1182-1226). Italian Catholic friar who founded the Franciscan Order of Monks. Francis' love of nature was reflected in one of his earlier statements: "God gives special grace to those who love their little brothers and sisters, the birds and beasts." At the end: "Tell me bravely, Brother Doctor, that death, which is the gateway of life, is at hand." To his brothers: "When you see that I am brought to my last moments, place me naked upon the ground just as you saw me the day before yesterday, and let me lie there after I am dead, for the length of time it takes to walk one mile unhurriedly" His parting words were: "Welcome, sister Death."

Alternatives: * "Death, my sister, welcome be thou."

* "Farewell, my children. Remain always in the fear of the Lord. That temptation and tribulation which is to come, is now at hand and happy shall they be who persevere in the good they have begun. I hasten to go to our Lord, to whose grace I recommend you."
* To those at his bedside: "The righteous wait expectant till I receive my recompense."

Francis of Sales, Saint (1567-1622). French-born Roman Catholic Bishop of Geneva. Dying of "apoplexy:" "Weep not, my children, must not the will of God be done?" Asked if he feared Satan: "I place all my trust in the Lord, who will know how to deliver me from all my enemies." As he pressed the hand of a loving attendant: "It is toward evening, and the day is far spent." His last word: "Jesus."

Alternative: * "If I am still necessary for thy people, I refuse not to labour."

Franck, César (1822-1890). Belgian-born French pianist, organist and composer. Franck suffered a protracted illness following a traffic accident in May, 1890. On his deathbed, approximately six months later, the composer deliriously wrestled with a fragment of music repeating: "My children, my poor children." Perhaps musical notes were his poor children.

Franco, Francisco (1892-1975). Spanish general and post-WWII fascist dictator. Complaining to his physicians about the measures they used to keep him alive: "Please let me be... How hard this is to bear! My God, how hard is it to die!"

Alternative: * On his deathbed, many of Franco's followers gathered outside the palace shouting his name. When his physician said they wished to say goodbye, the confused dictator allegedly replied: "Where are they going?"

Francois, Marvin (1946-1985). African American criminal, electrocuted for the murder of six individuals during a drug-related robbery. "I am as a grain of sand on the beach of the black race. The black race has lost its pride and dignity and is slowly dying from within and without. My death ends my tears, and the fortune of watching my race slowly die. If there is such a thing as an Antichrist, it ain't one man, but the whole white race."

Frank, Anne (1929-1945). German-born Dutch Jewish diarist. While living in Amsterdam, Holland, Frank chronicled the two years spent hiding with her family from the Nazis. The last diary entry before her arrest and transfer to a concentration camp read: "...And finally I twist my heart round again, so that the bad is on the outside and the good is on the inside, and keep on trying to find a way of becoming what I would so like to be, and could be, if . . . there weren't any other people living in the world. Yours, Anne." The 15 year-old Frank died of typhus while in captivity.

Frank, Hans (1900-1946). German-born Nazi governor of Poland during WWII. Frank was hanged as a war criminal for his involvement in the Holocaust. At his trial: "A thousand years will pass and the guilt of Germany will not be erased." Frank's last words reflect the renewal of his Roman Catholic faith before his execution: "I am thankful for the kind of treatment during my captivity and I ask God to accept me with mercy."

Frankfurter, Felix (1882-1965). Austrian-born associate justice of the U.S. Supreme Court. Dying of heart failure, Frankfurter spoke to an aide: "I hope I don't spoil your Washington's Birthday."

Franklin, Benjamin (1706-1790). American statesman, scientist, inventor and philosopher. During his last days, Franklin was afflicted with a respiratory ailment complicated by a painful pleurisy. When one of his daughters expressed good wishes for his recovery and long life, the statesman replied tersely: "I hope not!" Toward the end, he asked his nurse to hang a picture of Christ where he could view it: "Ay, Sarah, there is a picture worth looking at. That is the picture of Him who came into the world to teach men to love one another." When told that a change in position might help his breathing, Franklin spoke his last words: "A dying man can do nothing easy."

Alternative: "These pains will soon be over. They are for my good. What are the pains of a moment compared to the pleasures of eternity?"

Francisco de san Roman (see Romanes, Francis).

Franz Ferdinand (1863-1914). Archduke of Austria and nephew of Franz Josef I (below). Franz Ferdinand and his wife Sophie were fatally wounded by a terrorist who fired into their open car in Sarajevo, Bosnia, an event that helped spark WWI. When Sophie saw her husband bleeding from the mouth, she screamed: "In God's name, what has happened to you?" and collapsed. Franz Ferdinand allegedly cried: "Sopherl [a term of endearment]! Sopherl! Don't die! Live for my children!" As he was rushed from the scene, the Archduke said over and over: "It is nothing."

Franz Josef I (1830-1916). Emperor of Austria. After helping Franz Josef into bed, his valet asked when he should return: "Tomorrow morning, half past three." After taking some tea, Franz Josef uttered his last word: "Fine."

Alternative: * Some sources record that Franz Josef died singing "God save the Emperor" or "God Preserve the Emperor."

Franz, Robert (1815-1892). German composer and conductor. Indicating a portrait of his late wife, Franz told guests: "There, take a good look at that! Such a face you will never see again." He then asked them to "greet certain of [my] American friends cordially."

Fraser, Simon (1729-1777). Scottish-born military leader who fought with the British during the American Revolutionary War. Killed by a sniper while in support of General John Burgoyne: "Oh, fatal ambition; poor General Burgoyne! My poor wife"

Fraser, Simon, Lord of Lovat (c. 1667-1747). Scottish nobleman. For his involvement in the Jacobite Rebellion that ended in 1746, Fraser was branded a traitor and sentenced to die. Before his execution, he allegedly quoted a line from Horace's *Odes*: "It is sweet and fitting to die for one's country." He then repeated one of Ovid's sayings: "For those things which were done either by our fathers or ancestors, and in which we had no share, I can scarcely call my own." To a friend: "God save us, why should there be such a bustle about taking off an old grey head that cannot get up three steps [of the scaffold] without three bodies to support it? Cheer up thy heart man! I am not afraid, why should you be?" To a relative: "My dear James, I am going to heaven, but you must continue to crawl a little longer on this evil world." Fraser said a short prayer and the axe fell.

Alternatives: * "It is sweet and glorious to die for my country."
* "'Tis a glorious and pleasant thing to die for our country."

Frederick I Barbarossa (c. 1123-1190). German Holy Roman Emperor. Before the Battle of Iconium in south-central Turkey during the Third Crusade, Frederick spoke to his soldiers: "Why stand ye here and grieve, my children? Christ reigns. Christ commands. Christ conquers. Come with me, my brethren in arms who have left your homes to win heaven by your blood." Ironically, the emperor later drowned in a local stream while bathing.

Frederick II, also Frederick the Great (1712-1786). King of Prussia. Dying at age 74, Frederick frequently expressed thoughts about his forthcoming death: "My life is on the decline. The time which I still have I must employ. It belongs not to me, but to the State." While looking at the sun, he reflected: "Perhaps I shall be nearer thee soon!" On his deathbed, Frederick noticed that one of his dogs shivered from the cold. He asked his valet to: "Throw a quilt over it." Later, he deliriously said before he died: "The mountain is passed; we shall be better now."

Alternatives: * "The finest day of life is that on which one quits it."
* "We are over the hill; we shall go better now."

Frederick III (1831-1888). Emperor of Germany. At age 56, Frederick developed throat cancer and was able to rule only three months. To treat his ailment, a tracheostomy was performed, which, by its nature, prevented speaking. In his last days, communication was facilitated by writing.

When asked if he were tired, Frederick wrote: "Very. Very." Later, the ruler admonished his daughter: "Remain as noble and good as you have been in the past. This is the last wish of your dying father."

Frederick II (1534-1588). King of Denmark and Norway. To his physician: "Let the pulse beat as it may, we know the mercy of God will never fail."

Frederick V (1723-1766). King of Denmark and Norway. Although Frederick pursued a somewhat debauched lifestyle, his last words reflected what he considered a more reserved reign: "It is a great consolation to me in my last hour that I have never willfully offended anyone and there is not a drop of blood on my hands."

Frederick VI (1768-1839). King of Denmark and Norway. "It's getting cold; we must see that the poor folks have fuel."

Frederick VIII (1843-1912). King of Denmark. While visiting Hamburg, Frederick collapsed while strolling incognito. A passerby noticed him and offered to take him to a hospital. The king declined saying: "I am staying at the Hamburger Hof. I feel better. I will go on foot." He never made it.

Frederick Lewis (1707-1751). German-born Prince of Wales. Frederick was the son of George II of England but did not live long enough to ascend the throne. Dying of a lung abscess allegedly after a cricket ball injured his chest, Frederick lamented: "I feel death."

Frederick William I (1688-1740). King of Prussia and father of Frederick the Great. In his last days, the king inspected his coffin saying: "I shall sleep right well there." He then dictated his funeral and burial wishes in great detail. Hearing the Biblical passage (Job 1:21) "Naked I came from my mother's womb, and naked shall I return..." Frederick commented: "No, not quite naked. I shall have my uniform on." As he died, the king remarked: "Herr Jesu, to Thee I live. Herr Jesu, to Thee I die. In life and death, Thou art my gain."

Frederick, Earl, Sr. (1951-2002). American criminal, executed by lethal injection for the murder of a Vietnam War veteran: "I'm sorry it's taken so long to have justice served for y'all, but it's being served now."

Freeman, Edward (1823-1892). English historian and educator. Freeman's final journal entry was written in Valencia, Spain before he died of bronchitis and smallpox: "Very weak. Rail to La Encina and Alicante." Apparently, he was contemplating a move from Valencia to the cities named in his journal. Freeman was buried in Alicante.

Frelinghuysen, Theodore (1787-1862). Member of U.S. Senate and unsuccessful vice presidential candidate. On his deathbed, Frelinghuysen was asked how he felt: "All peace. More than ever before."

Frémont, John (1813-1890). American explorer, soldier and politician who lived for a period in California. Dying of peritonitis in New York City, Frémont spoke to his physician: "If I keep this free of pain, I can go home next week." When queried which home, he said: "California, of course." At the time of his death, Fremont lived on Staten Island and was buried in Sparkill, New York.

French, James (c. 1936-1966). American criminal, sentenced to die by electrocution for the murder of his cellmate. To the press covering his execution: "Hey, fellas! How about this for a headline for tomorrow's paper? 'French Fries!'" To the executioner: "I'd kill your mother, your father, or your daughter. I love to kill. So you'll be doing society one of the best jobs you ever did." When the warden asked for last words: "Everything's already been said."

Alternative: * "How's this for a headline? 'French Fries.'"

Frere, Bartle (1815-1884). British colonial official who spent most of his career in India and Africa. Several years before his death, Frere published a defense of his actions against the Zulu that possibly led to the Anglo-Zulu War. Semiconscious at the end, Frere mumbled last words to his wife: "If they would only read the 'Further Correspondence,' they would surely understand. They *must* be satisfied."

Freud, Sigmund (1856-1939). Viennese psychiatrist who pioneered psychoanalysis. Freud developed throat cancer as a result of his long-standing tobacco abuse. When the end approached, he talked to his friend and physician Max Schur about the euthanasia pact that had been made earlier: "Schur, you remember our 'contract' not to leave me in the lurch when the time had come. Now it is nothing but torture and makes no sense." When Schur agreed, Freud said: "I thank you. Talk it over with Anna [his daughter], and if she thinks it's right, then make an end of it." The physician later gave Freud a narcotic which helped end his life. Some contend his last statement was: "This is absurd! This is absurd!"

Alternative: * "My dear Schur, you remember our first talk. You promised me then you would help me when I could no longer carry on. It is only torture now and it has no longer any sense."

Frick, Henry (1849-1919). American industrialist and philanthropist. Dying of a heart attack, Frick said to his nurse who passed him a glass of water: "That will be all. Now I think I'll go to sleep."

Frick, Wilhelm (1877-1946). Nazi politician who was convicted of war crimes. As Minister of the Interior, Frick authored laws that sanctioned the use of concentration camps during WW II. Before his hanging: "Long live eternal Germany."

Friedell, Egon (1878-1938). Viennese actor, philosopher, historian and writer who openly criticized the Nazi regime. When members of the Gestapo appeared at his residence, Friedell committed suicide by jumping from a window. Before leaping, he warned passersby on the street below: "Watch out please."

Frith, John (1503-1533). Martyred English clergyman. Because of his contrary views on the infallibility of the clergy and transubstantiation, Frith was branded a heretic and condemned to die. As he was burned at the stake: "The Lord forgive thee."

Fritsch, Werner von (1880-1939). German general. While inspecting front-line troops during the Polish invasion at the outset of WWII, Fritsch was wounded in the thigh. When an aide tried to remove his suspenders, the general said: "Please leave it." Fritsch died shortly thereafter.

Froebel, Friedrich (1782-1852). German educator who promulgated the concept of "kindergarten." During his last illness: "I am not going away. I shall hover around in the midst of you." When his doctor discouraged a move near an open window, Froebel replied: "My friend, I have peeked at lovely nature all my life. Permit me to pass my last hours with this enchanting mistress." As he died: "God, Father, Son and Holy Ghost."

Frohman, Charles (1860-1915). American theatrical producer. Before he perished on the torpedoed RMS *Lusitania*, Frohman paraphrased to friends a line from his production of J.M Barrie's *Peter Pan* ("To die would be an awfully big adventure."): "Why fear death? It is the most beautiful adventure that life gives us." Before a wave swept him to his death: "They've done for us; we had better get out."

Alternative: * "Why fear death? Death is only a beautiful adventure."

Frost, Robert (1874-1963). Pulitzer Prize-winning American poet. Frost died of a pulmonary embolus complicating prostate surgery. Accustomed to seeing his physician with an entourage, the poet quipped when the doctor entered his hospital room alone: "Traveling light today, aren't you?" Later, to friends: "I feel as though I were in my last hours."

Froude, James (1818-1894). English historian and writer. Froude's last words quoted a section of Genesis 18:25: "Shall not the Judge of all the earth do right?"

Fry, Elizabeth (1780-1845). English Quaker prison reformer and philanthropist. Dying of a stroke, Fry prayed: "Oh, my dear Lord, help and keep Thy servant."

Fuller, Andrew (1754-1815). English cofounder of The Baptist Missionary Society. As he lay dying, Fuller repeated to colleagues: "I have no religious joys, but I have a hope in the strength of which I think I could plunge into eternity... I have been a great sinner; and if I am saved at all, it must be by great and sovereign grace." At the end, to his eldest daughter: "Come, Mary, come and help me." As he died: "Help me."

Fuller, Arthur (1822-1862). Union army chaplain during the U.S. Civil War and grandfather of Buckminster Fuller (below). Although discharged for failing health, Fuller volunteered to stay with his unit. Taking up a musket during the Battle of Fredericksburg, Virginia, he spoke to the commanding officer: "Captain, I must do something for my country. What shall I do?" Fuller was shot dead by an attacking Mississippi sharpshooter.

Fuller, Buckminster (1895-1983). American inventor and theorist who popularized the concept of the geodesic dome. Fuller visited his comatose wife who was dying of cancer in a Los Angeles hospital. When she showed some sign of arousal, he exclaimed: "She is squeezing my hand!" In the excitement, Fuller suffered a heart attack and died shortly thereafter. His wife followed him in death 36 hours later.

Fuller, Margaret (1810-1850). American writer and women's rights activist. Returning from Italy, Fuller drowned in a shipwreck within sight of the New York shoreline. When urged to abandon the sinking vessel, she was heard to say: "I see nothing but death before me. I shall never reach the shore." Her body was not recovered.

Fuller, Melville (1833-1910). Chief justice of the U.S. Supreme Court. Fuller's last words were prescient: "I am very ill."

Fuseli, John (1741-1825). Swiss-born English artist. Fuseli listened for carriage sounds that signaled the arrival of a friend: "Is Lawrence come? Is Lawrence come?"

Alternative: * When Fuseli's friend Samuel Cartwright approached his bedside: "Is it you, Samuel?"

Gabrilowitsch, Ossip (1878-1936). Russian-born American pianist and conductor. Delirious during his terminal battle with stomach cancer, Gabrilowitsch told his wife Clara, the daughter of Mark Twain: "You must not think I am crazy, but I am not as crazy as you think because I know that I am crazy."

Gacy, John Wayne (1942-1994). American rapist and serial killer, executed for the murder of 33 individuals. Before dying of a lethal injection in an Illinois state correctional facility, Gacy allegedly told a prison official: "Kiss my a**! You can go to hell!."

Alternatives: * "You can kiss my a**!"
* "Kiss my a**! You'll never find the rest!"

Gaddafi, Muammar al (1942-2011). Libyan dictator. During the 2011 Arab Spring civil war, Gaddafi was forced to flee for his life. Cornered in a drainage pipe, he was beaten, stabbed and shot. Before dying, he allegedly pleaded: "Don't shoot me. Don't shoot me."

Alternative: * "What did I do to you? Do you know right from wrong?"

Gadsby, William (1773-1844). English Baptist clergyman. It is reported that this peripatetic minister traveled over 60,000 miles and preached close to 12,000 sermons during his lifetime. On his deathbed, Gadsby exulted: "I shall soon be with him, shouting Victory, Victory, Victory, forever."

Gadsden, Christopher (1724-1805). American Revolutionary War officer, statesman and clergyman. As Gadsen expired, he raised his arms heavenward and said: "I am reaching toward my inheritance."

Gage, Jeremiah (died 1863). Confederate soldier, mortally wounded at the Battle of Gettysburg, Pennsylvania during the U.S. Civil War. A last letter to his mother read: "Gettysburg, Penn July 3rd [1863] My dear mother, This is the last you may ever hear from me. I have time to tell you that I died like a man. Bear my loss as best you can. Remember that I am true to my country and my greatest regret at dying is that she is not free and that you and my sisters are robbed of my worth whatever that may be. I hope this will reach you and you must not regret that my body cannot be obtained. It is a mere matter of form anyhow. This is for my sisters too as I cannot write more. Send my dying release to Miss Mary... you know who. J.S.

Gage Co. A, 11th Miss. Mrs. P.W. Gage Richland, Holmes County, Miss. This letter is stained with my blood." Gage was buried in a Richmond, Virginia cemetery.

Gainsborough, Thomas (1727-1788) British portrait and landscape painter. Dying of cancer, Gainsborough said to his friend William Jackson about Sir Anthony Van Dyke, a painter of the preceding century: "We are all going to Heaven, and Van Dyke is of the company."

Gaitskell, Hugh (1906-1963). British Labor Party leader. To his wife about his team of doctors: "Here come the plumbers!"

Galba, Servius (3 BCE-69 CE). Roman emperor. Galba became unpopular with his subjects and subsequently was attacked by men loyal to his successor, Marcus Otho. Before dying, Galba bared his throat to his assailants and cried: "Strike, if it be for the good of Rome!" He was decapitated and his head was delivered to Otho.

Alternatives: * "What's all this, comrades? I am yours and you are mine. Strike, if it be for the good of Rome!"
* "Do your work, if it is better so for the Roman people."

Galgani, Saint Gemma (1878-1903). Italian mystic who experienced stigmata and was said to levitate occasionally. Dying of tuberculosis: "O Jesus, You see I am at the end of my strength. I can bear no more. If it be Your holy will, take me. Mother [Mary], I commend my soul into your hands. Do ask Jesus to be merciful to me."

Galileo Galilei (1564-1642). Italian astronomer, mathematician and philosopher. Forced to recant his belief that the earth rotated around the sun, Galileo remained steadfast in his "heretical" conviction, supposedly protesting at the end: "And yet it moves." J.J. Fahie, in his 1903 biography *Galileo His Life and Work*, discounted the quote, opining that the consequences of persisting in this heliocentric view would have been too severe. According to Boller and George in their book *They Never Said It*: "It was a French writer, writing more than a century after Galileo's death, who first put the words in the great scientist's mouth."

Alternative: * "It moves, nevertheless."

Gallagher, Jack "Three-Fingered Jack" (died 1864). American frontier robber and killer, not to be confused with Manuel "Three Fingered Jack" Garcia (below). Gallagher and four other criminals were rounded up by a group of vigilantes and hanged without a trial. While awaiting execution, he untied his hands, produced a knife and attempted to slit his throat. When this failed, Gallagher asked for a shot of whiskey. Choking, he spluttered: "I hope forked lightening will strike every one of you b******* dead!" The desperado then jumped from the box on the platform, thus hanging himself.

Gallaudet, Thomas (1787-1851). American scholar who pioneered educational opportunities for the hearing impaired. To his family: "I will go to sleep."

Galli-Curci, Amelita (1882-1963). Italian operatic soprano whose beautiful singing voice was ruined by a complication of goiter surgery. Dying of respiratory failure, Galli-Curci wrote to her friends: "I am learning to make peace with my handicaps. I read a lot. I still have much to learn, and I enjoy fully this final, fascinating cycle of my life that prepares me for the exodus- The Great Adventure."

Gallo, Saint Maria Francesca, also St. Mary Frances of the Five Wounds of Jesus (1715-1791). Neapolitan nun and mystic. Depressed by events of the French Revolution, Maria prayed: "Troubles in the present! Greater troubles in the future! I pray God that I may not live to witness them."

Galois, Évariste (1811-1832). French mathematician. Galois fought in a duel, possibly over a love affair, and was mortally wounded by a gunshot to the abdomen. Before dying, he spoke to his brother: "Don't cry, Alfred! I need all my courage to die at twenty!"

Galsworthy, John (1867-1933). English novelist who won the 1932 Nobel Prize in Literature. Unable to speak at the time of death because of a brain tumor, Galsworthy enigmatically wrote: "I've enjoyed too pleasant circumstances."

Gamba, Francia (died1554). Italian Protestant martyr. Before his planned burning at the stake, Gamba was offered a wooden cross by a monk. He derisively said: "My mind is so full of the real merits and goodness of Christ that I want not a piece of senseless stick to put me in mind of Him." Because of this response, Gamba's tongue was "bored through" before he was set ablaze.

Gambetta, Léon (1838-1882). French statesman. Dying of abdominal cancer, Gambetta bemoaned his fate: "I am dying; there is no use in denying it, but I have suffered so much it will be a great deliverance." When a visitor fainted seeing Gambetta on his deathbed, the statesman asked: "Good heavens, has he hurt himself?"

Alternative: * "I am lost and there is no use denying it. I have suffered so much that death will be a relief."

Gandhi, Indira (1917-1984) Indian prime minister. Gandhi spoke these words the night before she was assassinated by two of her Sikh guards: "… I don't mind if my life goes in the service of the nation. If I die today every drop of my blood will invigorate the nation..." As she approached her guards the following day, she said "*Namaste* [Greetings to you]" before they fired the fatal shots.

Gandhi, Kasturbai, also Kasturba (1869-1944). Indian activist and wife of Mohandas Gandhi (below). When her husband asked what troubled her, Kasturbai replied: "I don't know. I am going now. No one should cry after I am gone. I am at peace."

Gandhi, Mohandas (1869-1948). Indian statesman and father of modern India. Gandhi was assassinated by a Hindu nationalist extremist as he prepared to attend a prayer meeting. Allegedly the wounded leader uttered the phrase "*Hé Ram*! [O, lord Ram!]" Immediately after he was shot. More than likely, Gandhi gasped at the shock and died before he could speak further.

Gandhi, Rajiv (1944-1991). Indian prime minister who took office in 1984 following the assassination of his mother Indira Gandhi (above).

While attending a campaign rally in 1991, Gandhi spoke these words to his security staff shortly before he was killed by a suicide bomber: "Don't worry, relax!"

Ganguly, Suhrid (died1998). Calcutta engineer. The 22 year-old Ganguly was depressed because he couldn't have his telephone repaired without paying a bribe. Before hanging himself, he wrote: "There is no other way to change the system and get an honest right to live."

Garcia, Manuel "Three Fingered Jack" (died 1853). California bandit, not to be confused with Jack "Three-Fingered Jack" Gallagher (above). The outlaw acquired his nickname after losing part of his hand in an earlier fight. Embroiled in a shootout with a California Ranger, Garcia allegedly shouted these words before he was shot: "I will throw up my hands for no gringo dog."

Gardiner, James (1687-1745). Scottish-born British officer who served in a regiment loyal to George II. Gardiner was mortally wounded during the Battle of Prestonpans, east of Edinburgh. As a Highlander charged: "Fire on, my lads, and fear nothing." Before dying, Gardiner allegedly said to his enemy: "You are fighting for an earthly crown; I am going to receive a heavenly one."

Alternative * To an attendant who led Gardiner's horse: "Take care of yourself."

Gardiner, Stephen (c. 1483-1555). English bishop, active during the English Reformation. After becoming Lord Chancellor of England, Gardiner oversaw the persecution of many subjects. His last words: "I have sinned with Peter, but have not wept with Peter."

Alternatives: * "I have sinned like Peter, but have not wept like him."
* "I have denied with Peter, and gone out with Peter, but I have not yet wept with Peter."

Gardner, Ava (1922-1990). American screen actress. Dying of emphysema and pneumonia, Gardner told her housekeeper: "Carmen, I'm tired."

Alternative: * "I'm so tired."

Gardner, John (1958-1992). American criminal, executed by lethal injection for a double murder committed during a robbery: "All I have to say is if more parents would raise their children in God-fearing homes, maybe some of them wouldn't end up in the position I'm in."

Garfield, James A. (1831-1881). Twentieth U.S. president. On his way to deliver a speech, Garfield was shot by a disgruntled federal office-seeker. After two bullets struck home, he exclaimed: "My God! What is this?" The president suffered almost 80 days before succumbing to infection and heart failure. Before dying, Garfield asked an aide: "Old boy, do you think my name will have a place in human history?" When told that he had much more work to do, the president replied: "No, my work is done." Later that day, Garfield suffered a bout of severe chest pain. Before dying, he complained to his Chief of Staff David Swaim: "Oh Swaim! Swaim! I am in terrible agony! Can't you do something to relieve me? Oh, my heart! The terrible pain! Oh, Swaim! Swaim!"

Alternatives: * "Oh Swaim, this terrible pain! Press your hand on it." Later: "Oh, Swaim, can't you stop this?"

* "Oh Swaim, there is a pain here. Swaim, can't you stop this? Oh, oh, Swaim!"

Garibaldi, Giuseppe (1807-1882). Italian military leader and patriot who helped create a united homeland. Seeing a pair of finches on his windowsill, Garibaldi remarked: "Those are the spirits of my little girls, Rosa and Anita, who have come to see their father die. Be kind to them, and feed them -when I am dead."

Alternatives: * "Maybe they are the souls of my little ones come to call me. Feed them when I am gone."

"Let the little birds in. Feed them when I have gone. Perhaps they are the spirits of my little Anita and Rosa, come to bear their father away."

Garland, Samuel (1830-1862). Confederate general during the U.S. Civil War. Mortally wounded near Boonsboro, Maryland while rallying his troops: "I am killed; send for the senior colonel and tell him to take command."

Garnett, Henry (1555-1606). English Jesuit priest. Garnett was executed for his participation in the Gunpowder Plot to kill King James I and members of the English Parliament. Before he was hanged, decapitated and dismembered, the priest implored: "Imprint the cross on my heart... Mary, mother of grace."

Garnett, Robert (1819-1861). Confederate general in the U.S. Civil War. Killed at the Battle of Rich Mountain, Virginia, Garnett exposed himself to Union Army fire, allowing: "The men need a little example."

Garnock, Robert (c. 1660-1681). Scottish Covenanter. Because he fought against government troops, Garnock was accused of treason and sentenced to die. Before hanging, he wrote a testimonial, which concluded: "... Farewell, sweet prison, for my royal Lord Jesus Christ, it is now at an end. Farewell, all crosses of one sort or another, and so farewell, everything in time, reading, praying, and believing. Welcome, eternal life, and the spirits of just men made perfect. Welcome, Father, Son, and Holy Ghost. Into Thy hands I commit my spirit."

Garrett, Johnny (1963-1992). American criminal, executed by lethal injection for the rape and murder of a Roman Catholic nun: "I'd like to thank my family for loving me and taking care of me. And the rest of the world can kiss my ever-loving a**, because I'm innocent."

Garrett, Patrick "Pat" (1850-1908). American frontier lawman who killed Billy the Kid (above). Later in life, the financially strapped Garrett agreed to allow grazing on his land as part of a deal to cover some of his debts. During an argument over the particulars of the agreement, he allegedly told his assailant: "Well, d*** you! If I don't get you off one way, I will another." Garrett was shot dead before he could take action.

Garrick, Eva (see Veigel, Eva Marie).

Garrick, David (1717-1779). English actor and playwright. Dying of "palsy in the kidneys," Garrick spoke to his attendant: "Well Tom, I shall do very well yet and make you amends for all this trouble." The day before his death, the actor noticed a number of men in his room and asked who they were. When told they were physicians who came to see him, Garrick quoted lines of Horatio from *The Fair Penitent*: "Another and another still succeeds and the last fool is welcome as the former." Immediately before dying, Garrick said to his wife: "Oh dear!"

Garrison, William (1805-1879). American writer and abolitionist who was a cofounder of the American Anti-Slavery Society. Dying of kidney failure, Garrison was asked what he wanted: "To finish up."

Garth, Samuel (1661-1719). English physician and poet. On his deathbed, Garth entreated his doctors: "Dear gentlemen, let me die a natural death." After receiving Last Rites, he said: "I am going on my journey: they have greased my boots already."

Gasparin, Agénor de (1810-1871). French politician and writer. Gasparin spoke to his wife who was following him up the stairs: "No, you know I like to have you go before me."

Gassendi, Pierre (1592-1655). French philosopher, scientist and priest. When his clergyman offered to pray the Psalms, Gassendi said: "I pray you, say them softly, because speaking out loud disturbs me." After multiple bloodlettings, to his amanuensis who had placed his hand over the philosopher's heart: "You see what is man's life."

Gates, John (1504-1553). English soldier and courtier. Gates was charged and convicted of treason for his support of Lady Jane Grey's ascension to the English thrown. Before his beheading, to the executioner: "I forgive thee with all my heart." Kneeling down, he said: "I will see how meet this block is for my neck. I pray thee strike not yet, for I have a few prayers to say, and that done, strike on, good leave have thou." When Gates' prayers were completed, his head was detached with one stroke.

Gates, Titus (see Oates, Titus).

Gauguin, Paul (1848-1903). French Post-Impressionist painter. Gauguin spent the last eight years of his life on a Polynesian island. Dying of suspected syphilis and the effects of alcohol abuse, he sent a last note to a missionary asking for help: "Dear M. Vernier, Would it be troubling you too much to ask you to come to see me. My eyesight seems to be going and I cannot walk. I am very ill." The artist died before help arrived.

Gaunt, Elizabeth (died 1685). Martyred English shopkeeper who often offered shelter to oppressed citizens. Falsely accused of participating in the Rye House Plot to kill King Charles II and his brother James, Gaunt was sentenced to die by burning: "I have obeyed the sacred command of God to give refuge to the outcast and not to betray the wanderer."

Gaveston, Piers (c. 1248-1312). English nobleman. Because of Gaveston's ready access to King Edward II, a group of opposition noblemen perceived him as a threat and arranged his execution: "Oh! noble earl, spare me."

Gaye, Marvin, Jr. (1939-1984). American rock singer and musician. In the months prior to his death, Gaye endured a stormy relationship with his father. An argument with the elder Gaye on the day of the singer's demise prompted this response: "Mother, I'm going to get my things and get out of this house. Father hates me and I'm never coming back." Moments later, Gaye was fatally shot by his father. To his brother who held the singer in his arms: "It's good. I ran my race. There's no more left in me."

Gazuyeva, Elza (c. 1978-2001). Chechen suicide bomber. The 23 year-old Gazuyeva approached the Chechnyan regional Russian Army commander she felt was responsible for the death of her husband and relatives, asking: "Do you still remember me?" When the officer told her to get away, Gazuyeva exploded a grenade, killing them both.

Geer, Louis de (1818-1896). Swedish statesman. On his deathbed, Geer prayed: "My God, have pity on me. Do not visit on me suffering beyond my strength. Oh, Christ, Thou hast suffered still more for me!"

Gehrig, Henry "Lou" (1903-1941). Hall of Fame American professional baseball player. Dying of a progressive neurological disease called amyotrophic lateral sclerosis (ALS), Gehrig proclaimed: "I'm going to beat this thing!" Speaking of his appointed post as a police commissioner, Gehrig predicted: "I'll be back on the parole board yet. I've still got a fifty-fifty chance!" He often used the fifty percent phrase when asked how he was doing. On the day of his death, he mouthed these words to his wife: "Fifty-fifty! Eleanor!" and died. In the years following his death, ALS has become known as Lou Gehrig's disease.

Geleazium (fl. Middle Ages). Italian martyr of St. Angelo. Refusing to renounce his Christian faith: "Death is much sweeter to me with the testimony of truth than life with the least denial."

Gellée, Claude, also Claude Lorrain (c. 1604-1682). French Baroque artist. From Gellée's will: "First I commend my soul to God and to His Holy mother and to my Guardian Angel and to all the saints in heaven, praying the Divine Majesty to vouchsafe to receive it into the glory of Paradise." He then left detailed instructions for his burial and the disposition of his property.

Gellert, Christian (1715-1769). German writer, poet and educator. When informed that he had only one hour to live, Gellert responded: "God be praised! Only one more hour!"

Gemelli, Agostino (1878-1959). Italian theologian and physician. Bothered by the lamp in his hospital room: "Please put out that light."

Genghis Khan, born Temüjin (c. 1162-1227). Emperor of the Mongol Empire. Through carefully planned and executed invasions, Genghis Khan conquered most of Eurasia- the largest contiguous dominion in history. Dying in enemy territory, the emperor said to his sons: "... I die in the territory of my enemy, and though the ruler of Hsi Hsia [the Tangut state, also called Xi Xia] has submitted, he has not yet arrived. Hence, after I am dead, conceal my death and kill him when he comes." Genghis Khan's forces subsequently devastated most of Hsi Hsia.

Alternatives: * "Let not my end disarm you, and on no account weep or keen for me, lest the enemy be warned of my death."

* "It is clear to me that I must leave everything and go hence from thee."

Gentry, Kenneth (died 1997). American criminal, executed by lethal injection for the murder of a 23 year-old male. From Gentry's last statement: "... I'd like to thank the Lord for the past 14 years [on death row] to grow as a man and mature enough to accept what's happening here tonight. To my family, I'm happy. I'm going home to Jesus. Sweet Jesus, here I come. Take me home. I'm going that way to see the Lord."

George I (1660-1727). King of Great Britain and Ireland. Stricken with manifestations of a stroke, George realized the end was near: "It's all over with me."

George II (1683-1760). King of Great Britain and Ireland. Dying of a cardiovascular ailment, George asked for his daughter: "Call Amelia!" He died before she could reach him.

George III (1738-1820). King of Great Britain and Ireland. Mentally deranged in his late years, George responded to the moistening of his lips by his nurse: "Do not wet my lips but when I open my mouth. I thank you. It does me good."

George IV (1762-1830). King of Great Britain and Ireland. Dying of "dropsy," George turned to Sir Walthen ("Wally" or "Watty") Waller and asked: "Wally, what is this? It is death, my boy. They have deceived me!"

Alternatives: * "Watty, what is this? It is death, my boy. They have deceived me."

* "My dear boy, this is death!"
* "O God! I am dying! This is death!"
* "Good God, what do I feel? This must be death!"

George V (1865-1936). King of the United Kingdom and British Dominions who ruled during WWI. Suffering from a chronic respiratory ailment, George's last hours seemed to drag on. To relieve his suffering, his physician injected a dose of morphine and cocaine. George's last words allegedly were directed to the person who administered the medication: "God d*** you."

Alternatives: * At an earlier time, George had visited the seaside resort town of Bognor Regis in Sussex for a period of recuperation. When statements were made that he would soon be well-enough to revisit the resort, the king sardonically replied with a vulgarity: "Bugger Bognor."

* "The king's "official" last words printed in newspapers probably relate to an earlier question addressed to his secretary: "How is the Empire?"
* To the members of the Privy Council assembled in his chambers: "Gentlemen, I am sorry for keeping you waiting like this. I am unable to concentrate"

George VI (1895-1952). King of the United Kingdom and British Dominions who ruled during WWII. George spoke his last words to a valet: "I'll see you in the morning." The king died in his sleep.

George I (1845-1913). King of Greece. While walking on the streets of Thessalonica, one of his officers commented on the lack of security. The king replied: "My dear General, don't let me have that sermon over again. I am a fatalist. When my hour comes, it will be no use, even if I immure myself in my house and put a thousand Evzones [an elite unit of the army] on guard outside." He then commented about a writer named Walter Christmas: "Thank God, Christmas can now finish his work [a biography] with a chapter to the glory of Greece, of the Crown Prince and of the Army." Moments later, an anarchist shot him dead.

George II (1890-1947). King of Greece. Dying of a heart attack, George spoke to his maid: "Get me a glass of water."

George, Henry (1839-1897). American economist and writer. Dying of a stroke, George told his wife: "I don't feel well, but I suppose it doesn't amount to much." He died shortly thereafter.

Alternative: * To his wife: "Yes, yes, yes."

Gérard, Balthazar (c. 1557-1584). French-born assassin. Gérard shot the Dutch independence leader William I of Orange in response to a bounty placed on his head by the Spanish King Philip II. When the assassin was captured, he exclaimed: "Like David, I have slain Goliath of Gath." During his extended torture, Gérard uttered the words spoken by Pontius Pilate when he presented a scourged Jesus Christ to the masses: "Behold the man." The doomed man eventually was drawn, quartered and beheaded.

Gerhardt, Paul (1607-1676). German clergyman and hymnodist. Gerhardt's dying words came from one of his hymns: "... Him no death hath power to kill,/ But from many a dreaded ill/ Bears his spirit safe away;/ Shuts the door of bitter woes,/ Opens yon bright path that glows/ With the light of perfect day!"

Geronimo (1829-1909). Native American Apache leader. Criticized by a friend for his refusal to accept the Christian religion, Geronimo replied: "I have been unable to follow The Path in my life, and now it is too late!" Because the U.S. government would not allow him to return to his place of birth, Geronimo lamented: "I want to go back to my old home before I die. Tired of fight and want to rest. I asked the Great White Father [the U.S. president] to allow me to go back, but he said no." Geronimo asked his doctor to summon his surviving children, but they arrived after he died.

Gershwin, George (1898-1937). American pianist and composer. Dying of a brain tumor, Gershwin whispered "Astaire" to his brother Ira as he was wheeled into surgery. He expired postoperatively without regaining consciousness. The Gershwins provided the lyrics and music for the 1937 musical comedies *Shall We Dance* and *A Damsel in Distress* that starred Fred Astaire.

Gerson, Jean Charlier de (1363-1429). French theologian, scholar, writer and poet. Gerson gathered a group of school children around his deathbed and asked them to pray: "Lord, have mercy on Thy poor servant, Jean Gerson." He then implored: "Now, O God! Thou dost let Thy servant depart in peace. The soul that is accompanied to eternity by the prayers of three hundred children may advance with humble hope into the presence of their Father and their God."

Gertrude of Delft, Saint (died 1358). Dutch mystic who devoted her life to austerity, meditation and charity. Before dying, Gertrude said: "I am longing, longing to go home."

Gertrude of Helfta, Saint (1256-1302). German mystic and theologian. "When wilt Thou come? My soul thirsteth for Thee, O loving Father."

Getty, J. Paul (1892-1976). American industrialist who founded the Getty Oil Company. Toward the end, Getty groused about his five marriages that ended in divorce: "I'd give all my wealth for one successful marriage." Before dying of heart failure, he said: "I want my lunch."

Getulius, Saint (died 120). Roman Christian martyr. When ordered to worship Roman gods or die, Getulius replied: "My life will not be extinguished, and I rejoice with joy unspeakable to refuse to sacrifice to the idols. I thank my God, the Father Almighty and Jesus Christ, that I am able to offer Him an acceptable sacrifice." When queried about his statement, Getulius responded: "A broken and contrite heart." He then was beheaded (some say beaten to death).

Ghiyásu-d dín (died 1500). Indian sultan. Ghiyásu-d dín's son had tried twice to poison his father, but the sultan thwarted the attacks with an antidote each time. On the third attempt, the old man freely swallowed the poison saying: "O Lord! I have now arrived at the age of eighty. All this time I have passed in ease and prosperity, and in a state of pleasure such as has been the lot of no monarch. This moment is my last, and I pray thee not to hold my son Nasír answerable for my blood. May my death be deemed a natural death, and may my son be not held answerable for it."

Giacometti, Alberto (1901-1966). Swiss artist and sculptor. Dying of a cardiorespiratory ailment, Giacometti said to his doctor: "Soon again I'll see my mother." To his wife before expiring: "Till tomorrow."

Gianger (died 1552). Son of the Turkish ruler Solyman (also Suleiman) the Magnificent. Solyman murdered Gianger's brother Mustapha and offered the slain man's possessions to him. When Gianger refused and subsequently committed suicide by stabbing, he cried out: "Fie of thee, thou impious and wretched dog, traitor, murderer. I cannot call thee father. Take the treasures, the horse and the armour of Mustapha to thyself."

Gibbon, Edward (1737-1794). English historian who wrote *The History of the Decline and Fall of the Roman Empire.* Gibbon was afflicted by a swelling of his scrotum, which necessitated several operations. As he lay dying of peritonitis, probably related to his previous surgeries, the author said: "This day may be my last. I will agree that the immortality of the soul is at times a very comfortable doctrine. All this is now lost, finally irrevocably lost. All is dark and doubtful." Before trying to sleep, Gibbon asked his valet: "Why do you leave me?"

Gibbons, James (1834-1921). Roman Catholic archbishop of Baltimore, Maryland. After two days in a coma "caused by the infirmities of advanced age," Gibbons revived long enough to say: "I have had a good day!"

Gibran, Kahlil (1883-1931). Lebanese-American writer and poet, best-known for his book of poetic essays *The Prophet.* Dying of cirrhosis, Gibran remarked: "Don't be troubled. All is well."

Gilbert, Ann (1782-1866). English poet and writer. Kissing her daughter twice, Gilbert said: "That's for thank you. That's for goodnight."

Gilbert, Humphrey (c. 1539-1583). English explorer and politician who was a half-brother of Sir Walter Raleigh (below). Returning to England after a voyage to America, Gilbert drowned when his ship sank in a storm near the Azores. His last words were shouted before the vessel went down: "Courage, my lads! We are as near to heaven by sea as by land!"

Alternative: * "The road to heaven is as short by sea as by land!"

Gilbert, William (1836-1911). English lyricist who collaborated with Sir Arthur Sullivan (below) on a number of ever-popular operettas. While aiding a drowning girl at a lake on his estate, Gilbert exclaimed: "Put your hands on my shoulders and don't struggle!" He suffered a heart attack and perished, but the girl survived.

Gilfillan, George (1813-1878). Scottish Protestant clergyman and writer. On his deathbed Gilfillan asked his physician: "I am dying, doctor?" When answered in the affirmative: "The will of the Lord be done..."

Gillis, Lester (see Nelson, George "Baby-Face").

Gilman, Charlotte (1860-1935). American writer and social activist. Dying of breast cancer, Gilman chose to end her life. Her suicide note read: "A Last Duty... When all usefulness is over, when one is assured of an unavoidable and imminent death, it is the simplest of human rights to choose a quick and easy death in place of a slow and horrible one... I have preferred chloroform to cancer."

Gilmore, Gary (1940-1977). American criminal, executed for the murder of two men during separate robberies. Before his death by a firing squad, Gilmore was asked if he had any last words. His reply: "Let's do it." Gilmore then repeated the Latin phrase "*Dominus vobiscum* [The Lord be with you]." The attending Catholic prison chaplain Father Meersman responded: "*Et cum spiritu tuo* [And with your spirit]." The prisoner grinned and replied: "There'll always be a Meersman." After these last words, the squad shot him dead.

Ginsberg, Allen (1926-1997). American poet and prominent leader of the 1950s "Beat Generation." Dying of cancer, Ginsberg allegedly uttered his last goodbye: "Toodle-oo!"

Alternatives: * At the end, Ginsberg whispered a weak: "Aah."
* When asked if he could sleep: "Oh, yes."

Gipp, George "Gipper" (1895-1920). American star halfback on the University of Notre Dame football squad. Dying of a streptococcal throat infection and pneumonia, Gipp allegedly made a last request to his coach, Knute Rockne (below): "What's tough about it? I've no complaint. I've got to go, Rock. It's all right. I'm not afraid. Sometimes, when things are going wrong, when the breaks are beating the boys, tell them to go out and win one for the Gipper. I don't know where I'll be then, Rock, but I'll know about it, and I'll be happy." Controversy remains whether these words actually were spoken to the coach. However, almost eight years later, Rockne recounted to the team: "The day before he died, George Gipp asked me to wait until the situation seemed hopeless- then ask a Notre Dame team to go out and beat Army for him. This is the day, and you are the team." Notre Dame beat Army 12-6; the halfback who scored the winning score allegedly shouted: "That's one for the Gipper!"

Alternative: * "One day when the going is tough and a big game is hanging in the balance, ask the team to win one for the Gipper. I don't know where I'll be, Rock, but I'll know about it, and I'll be happy."

Girard, Catelin (died 1500). French Waldensian martyr. Branded a heretic, Girard was condemned to be burned at the stake. Before he submitted to the flames, the martyr asked the executioner for a rock to illustrate his beliefs. He held out the proffered stone and said: "When it is in the power of man to eat and digest this stone, the religion for which I am about to suffer shall have an end and not before."

Girard, Stephen (1750-1831). French-born banker and philanthropist. Girard's bank helped fund the U.S. government's involvement in the War of 1812. Dying of pneumonia, he rallied to say: "How violent is this disorder! How very extraordinary it is!"

Gissing, George (1857-1903). English writer. An avowed agnostic most of his life, Gissing's last words may reflect a religious conversion before he died or a figure of speech: "Patience... patience... God's will be done."

Giustiniani, Saint Lorenzo [Lawrence] (1381-1456). Patriarch of Venice. When his aides tried to move him to a more comfortable bed: "Not so! My Saviour did not die in a feather bed, but on the hard and painful wood of the Cross....Good Jesus! Behold I come!"

Gladiators. In ancient Rome, the traditional phrase of address before a gladiatorial match could be a combatant's last words: "Ave imperator. Morituri te salutant [Hail Emperor. We who are about to die salute you]."

Gladstone, William (1809-1898). British prime minister. When the end approached, Gladstone spoke to his daughter: "God bless you. God bless you. May a good and silver light shine down upon your path. I am quite comfortable. I am only waiting, only waiting, but it is a long time, the end. Kindness, kindness, nothing but kindness on every side."

Alternative: * After his son read the Liturgy: "Amen."

Glass, Jimmy (c. 1962-1987). American criminal. Glass killed two people when he escaped from a Louisiana jail in 1982. Captured and convicted of the crime, he was condemned to die in the electric chair. Before his execution, Glass joked: "I'd rather be fishing."

Glatman, Harvey (c. 1927-1959). American serial rapist and murderer, known popularly as the "Lonely Hearts Killer." Condemned to die for his crimes, Glatman was executed in California's San Quentin State Prison gas chamber. His last words: "It's better this way. I knew this is the way it would be."

Gleason, John "Jackie" (1916-1987). American comedian and actor. Dying of cancer, Gleason quipped: "If God wants another joke man, I'm ready."

Gleason, Robert (1970-2013). American criminal. While serving a life sentence for murder, Gleason killed two inmates to force his execution. Before dying in the electric chair: "... Put me on the highway going to Jackson and call my Irish buddies. "*Póg mo thóin* [Kiss my a** in Irish Gaelic]! God bless."

Glinka, Mikhail (1804-1857). Russian composer. Dying of probable stomach cancer, Glinka commented on eternal life: "It is nonsense! I do not believe in eternity!"

Gluck, Christoph Willibald (1714-1787). German-born composer, best-known for his operas. In late 1787, the Viennese musician Antonio Salieri (below) showed Gluck a recent composition titled *The Last Judgment* and asked his advice about who should sing the role of Jesus Christ, a tenor or bass. Gluck replied: "If you wait a little while, I shall be able to tell you from personal experience." Some say Salieri asked which of two accompanying melodies he preferred with a similar reply from Gluck who died of a stroke two weeks later. No record exists documenting whether Salieri received any word from his late friend on the other side.

Alternative: * "... Wait a few days, and I shall give you news from the next world."

Goar of Aquitaine, Saint (died 649). French-born hermit and missionary to the Rhine Region. Dying of a fever: "Here shall my Savior be known in all the simplicity of His doctrines. Ah, would that I might witness it, but I have seen those things in a vision. But I faint! I am weary! My earthly journey is finished. Receive my blessing. Go and be kind to one another."

Godet, Frédéric (1812-1900). Swiss Protestant theologian. To his family: "I have carried you in my heart all my life, and I hope I will still be permitted to do the same up there."

Godolphin, Sidney (1610-1643). English military officer, politician and poet. Godolphin was killed by a musket shot during the English Civil War: "Oh God, I am hurt."

Godwin, Earl of Wessex (died 1053). English nobleman. In olden times, a piece of bread often was fed to an accused person to determine guilt or innocence. If one choked on the morsel, guilt was presumed. When Edward the Confessor accused Godwin of murdering his brother, the earl allegedly choked to death on "the testing piece of bread." To King Edward before expiring: "So might I safely swallow this morsel of bread, as I am guiltless of the deed." Actually, Godwin probably died of a stroke.

Alternative: * "I know you suspect me of his death, but may God cause this morsel of bread to choke me if I am guilty of his murder!"

Godwin, Fanny (see Imlay, Frances "Fanny").

Godwin, William (1756-1836). English political philosopher and writer. Godwin's final diary entry read: "Sa [Saturday]. March 26, Constip. Malfy, fin. Call on Hudson, Trelawny calls, cough, snow." "Constip" probably relates to his bowel status. "Malfy" refers to John Webster's play *The Tragedy of the Dutchesse of Malfy*. John Hudson was Godwin's executor. "Trelawny" possibly refers to the English biographer Edward Trelawny. "Cough" was a prominent symptom of Godwin's illness.

Goebbels, Joseph (1897-1945). German Nazi propaganda minister and close advisor to Adolf Hitler. As the Third Reich crumbled, Goebbels asked a colleague to: "Tell Dönitz [Hitler's successor] that we understood not only how to live and fight, but also how to die." To fulfill his statement, Goebbels arranged for the poisoning of his children and later, the death of his wife. Before committing suicide himself, the *Reichsminister* spoke to his adjutant: "[Günther] Schwägermann, this is the worst treachery of all. The Generals have betrayed the Führer. Everything is lost. I shall die, together with my wife and family. You will burn our bodies. Can you do that?" Schwägermann later carried out the order.

Goebbels, Magdalena "Magda" (1901-1945). German wife of *Reichsminister* Joseph Goebbels (above). Before her suicide, Frau Goebbels spoke to her husband's adjutant about a son from her first marriage: "You see, we die an honorable death. If you should ever see Harald again, give him our best and tell him we died an honorable death."

Goering, Hermann (1893-1946). Nazi leader of the German *Luftwaffe* and second in command to Adolf Hitler. Convicted of war crimes, Goering spoke to his wife during her last prison visit: "You may be sure of one thing. They won't hang me. No, they won't hang me." Before his execution, a priest urged Goering to repent. His response: "I am a Christian, but I cannot accept the teachings of Christ. But I feel at ease." Later, the condemned man told his doctor: "Good night." Goering then swallowed a cyanide capsule, thereby escaping the hangman's noose.

Goethals, George (1858-1928). American engineer, military leader and politician who directed construction of the Panama Canal. Dying in New York City, Goethals requested: "Let me stay here. If I stay here, I'll be much nearer to West Point." Goethals graduated from the Academy in 1880.

Goethe, Catharina (1731-1808). Mother of Johann von Goethe (below). Declining an invitation to a party: "Say that Frau Goethe is unable to come. She is busy dying at the moment."

Goethe, Johann von (1749-1832). One of the pillars of German literature, best-known for his play *Faust*. Many of the last words attributed to Goethe reflect his desire to have more light, either literally or figuratively: "Light, more light."

Alternatives: *"Open the second shutter, so that more light can come in."

* "Light, light, the world needs more light."
* "More light, more light!"
* "Let the light enter."
* To his daughter-in-law Ottilie: "Come my little one, and give me your hand."
* "Nothing more."
* Whispered: "The liver sausage is lying heavy on my stomach."

Goffe, Thomas (1591-1629). English clergyman and dramatist. One of Goffe's Oxford confidants, Thomas Thimble, had counseled against marriage to a certain woman, saying: "She will break thy heart." Indeed, she later proved to be a miserable companion. On his deathbed, Goffe acknowledged his friend's sage advice: "Oracle, oracle, Thomas Thimble."

Gogh, Theodoor "Theo" van (1957-2004). Dutch film director, actor, newspaper columnist and publicist. Before he was shot and then stabbed by a Muslim extremist in Amsterdam, van Gogh pleaded: "Mercy, mercy! Can't we talk this over?" Apparently, the Dutchman's assassination was precipitated by a film he had made that contained anti-Islamic sentiments.

Alternative: "Have mercy! Have mercy! Don't do it! Don't do it!"

Gogh, Vincent van (1853-1890). Dutch Post-Impressionist painter. van Gogh suffered from severe depression and ultimately committed suicide by gunshot. His brother who was summoned to his bedside reported that the artist's last words were: "There is no end to sorrow."

Alternatives: * "The sadness will last forever."

* "Now I want to go home. Don't weep. What I have done is best for all of us. No use. I shall never get rid of this depression."

Gogol, Nikolai (1809-1852). Ukrainian-born Russian novelist. Gogol suffered from a severe mental illness during his last years. Delirious from fasting and ill-advised treatments from his doctors, the writer rambled: "Go on! Rise up! Charge, charge the mill." According to John Cournos in his introduction to Gogol's novel *Dead Souls*: "His [Gogol's] last words, uttered in a loud frenzy, were: 'A ladder! Quick, a ladder!' This call for a ladder- 'a spiritual ladder,' in the words of [Dmitry] Merejkovsky [a Russian novelist and poet]- had been made on an earlier occasion by a certain Russian saint, who used almost the same language."

Alternatives: * "Give me! Give me! Come on, give me! The ladder! Quick, pass me the ladder!" Gogol earlier had written about a ladder thrown down from heaven to help the dying ascend.

* "Ah! If people knew how pleasant it was to die, they would not fear death."

Goldberger, Joseph (1874-1929). Hungarian-born physician who researched the cause of pellagra, a vitamin-deficiency disease. Dying of cancer, to his wife: "Mary, don't leave me. You have always been my rock, my strength. Mary, we must have patience."

Goldman, Israel "Charlie" (1888-1968). Polish-born American boxing trainer. Dying of a heart attack, Goldman's last words reflected his profession: "Only suckers get hit with right hands."

Goldsborough, Fitzhugh (1879-1911). American classical violinist and murderer. The deranged Goldsborough shot and killed the writer David Phillips (below) because he felt one of the author's books adversely portrayed his family. As he shot Phillips, Goldsborough shouted: "Here you go!" He then turned the gun on himself and said: "Here I go!"

Alternative: * "There you are! I guess that does for you! I'll finish the job now!"

Goldsby, Crawford "Cherokee Bill" (1876-1896). American murderer, hanged at Fort Smith, Arkansas for his crimes. When asked for any last words, he exclaimed: "No! I didn't come here to make a speech. I came here to die." Before his execution, Goldsby said "Goodbye" and commented: "The quicker this thing's over the better."

Alternatives: * "No! I came here to die, not to make a speech!"
* On the scaffold: "Goodbye, all you chums down that way."

Goldsmith, Oliver (1728-1774). Anglo-Irish writer, author of *The Vicar of Wakefield*. In his last hours, Goldsmith's physician said: "Your pulse is in a greater disorder than it should be from the degree of fever which you have. Is your mind at ease?" Goldsmith acerbically replied "No, it is not!"

Goliath of Gath (died c. 1030 BCE). Giant Philistine warrior. To David, the future king of Israel: "Am I a dog that you come to me with sticks? Come to me, and I will give your flesh to the birds of the air and to the beasts of the field (I Samuel 17:43-4)." David then slung a stone that hit the giant in the head, killing him.

Gompers, Samuel (1850-1924). British-born American labor leader. "God bless our American institutions. May they grow better day by day."

Gonzaga, Saint Aloysius (1568-1591). Italian priest who died while aiding Black Plague victims in Rome. To a colleague hearing his confession: "We are going, Father, we are going." When asked where, Gonzaga replied: "To heaven. Into Thy hands..."

Gooch, Arthur (c. 1908-1936). American criminal, executed by hanging for the kidnapping of two policemen. Gooch was convicted and sentenced to die under the Federal Kidnapping Act ("Lindbergh's Law"), although his victims survived: "It's kind of funny- dying. I think I know what it will be like. I'll be standing there, and all of a sudden everything will be black, then there'll be a light again. There's got to be a light again- there's got to be." Gooch actually strangled to death over a period of 15 minutes because of the inexperience of his hangman.

Gooch, Mary (died 1823). English woman who suffered from "fits." In an attempted double suicide, Gooch and her lover took a dose of laudanum. She asked: "My dear, pray give me that blue muslin handkerchief, that I may have it in my hand when I die. Pray don't you take anything; but let me die, and you will get over it." Her lover survived the venture. Gooch's remains were interred in a nearby crossroads, a common practice at that time for suicide victims.

Good, Sarah (1653-1692). American Salem, Massachusetts witchcraft trial victim. Good and four other women were accused of witchcraft and sentenced to hang. At the gallows, Good responded when told she was a witch: "You are a liar; I am no more a witch than you are a wizard, and if you take away my life, God will give you blood to drink."

Gooden, Robert (1874-1976). English-born Episcopal Bishop of Los Angeles. Gooden asked: "You will pay my bills, won't you?"

Goodman, Benjamin "Benny" (1909-1986). American jazz and classical clarinetist and bandleader. Dying of a heart attack, to a friend: "It's all right."

Goodman, Irwin (1943-1991). Finnish protest rock and folk singer. Dying of a heart attack: "Don't get nervous now."

Goodwin, Thomas (1600-1679). English Puritan theologian, writer and educator. "Ah, is this dying? How I have dreaded as an enemy this smiling friend."

Gordon, Charles "Chinese" (1833-1885). English officer, serving as governor-general of the Sudan. Gordon died defending Khartoum from Mahdist insurgents. Before the town was overrun, he told an aide: "Now leave me to smoke these cigarettes." Before he was killed, Gordon asked: "Where is the Mahdi [the leader of the insurgents]?" His last journal entry read: "... I have done my best for the honour of my country. Good-bye."

Gordon, George (see Byron, George Gordon, Lord Byron).

Gordon, Nathaniel (1826-1862). American pirate and slave trader. Convicted and hanged for slave trading under an 1820 U.S. law that outlawed piracy, Gordon protested: "I did nothing wrong."

Goretti, Saint Maria (1890-1902). Italian maiden, stabbed repeatedly while resisting rape by a 19 year-old boy: "What are you doing, Alessandro [her attacker]? You will go to hell!" Later: "Carry me to bed! Carry me to bed, because I want to be nearer the Madonna!" Asked by a chaplain if she could forgive her attacker: "Yes, yes, I too for the love of Jesus, forgive him and I want him to be with me in paradise. May God forgive him, because I already have forgiven him." Delirious before dying, Maria mumbled: "The Madonna is waiting for me."

Alternatives: * "May God forgive him. I want him in heaven."
* Deliriously: "Alessandro, Alessandro, let me go... No! No! No! You will go to hell! Mama, Mama, help!"

Gorgas, William (1854-1920). U.S. surgeon general. Gorgas' efforts toward eradication of mosquitoes that transmitted yellow fever and malaria facilitated construction of the Panama Canal. Succumbing to a stroke, to his wife: "Well, if this is dying, dying is very pleasant."

Gorguloff, Paul (1895-1932). Russian assassin. The deranged Gorguloff shot French President Paul Doumer to death (above). Before dying on the guillotine, Gorguloff said: "Oh Holy Russia."

Gorky, Arshile (1904-1948). Armenian-born American artist. In his last years, Gorky underwent surgery for cancer, was left by his wife and suffered a fractured spine in a car accident that affected his painting arm. Before hanging himself, the painter scrawled: "Goodbye My Loveds."

Gorky, Maxim, born Alexei Maximovich Peshkov (1868-1936). Russian writer, playwright and social activist. Gorky prophesied: "There will be wars. We have to prepare. We have to button all our buttons."

Gosse, Edmund (1849-1928). English poet, art critic and writer. Gosse penned this last letter before dying in surgery: "You will think of me in this hour with sympathy and hope. There seems good reason to think I will survive the shock. In any case I am perfectly calm, and able to enjoy the love which has accompanied me through such long years and surrounds me still."

Göth, Amon (1908-1946). Austrian-born Nazi war criminal. Shortly before his hanging for killing thousands of prisoners in German-occupied Poland during WW II, Göth shouted: "Heil Hitler!"

Gotō, Aritomo (1888-1942). WWII Japanese admiral. During an evening naval engagement in the South Pacific near Guadalcanal, Gotō's fleet unexpectedly was shelled by American ships. Believing the fire originated from "friendly" forces, the admiral shouted "Idiots! Idiots!" before he fell mortally wounded.

Gottschalk, Louis (1829-1869). American pianist and composer. Dying of a ruptured appendix, to his physician: "I have traveled much and have often been dangerously ill, but never have I found a friend as devoted as you. A father or brother could not have done more. Your efforts are truly superhuman." He made the sign of the cross over the doctor's forehead and kissed his hand. Gottschalk died the following morning.

Gouges, Marie-Olympe de (1748-1793). French writer and feminist. Gouges was condemned by the Revolutionary Tribunal for articles that railed against the revolutionary movement. Before her beheading on the guillotine: "Children of the fatherland, you will avenge my death."

Gough, John (1817-1886). Anglo-American temperance advocate and lawyer. While lecturing, Gough suffered a stroke as he spoke the words: "Young man, keep your record clean."

Gould, Glenn (1932-1982). Eccentric Canadian classical pianist, composer and writer. Dying of a stroke, Gould spoke to a friend: "Ray, where are you?"

Gounod, Charles (1818-1893). French organist and composer, best-known for his melody "Ave Maria" (Bach-Gounod) and operas *Faust* and *Roméo et Juliette.* Several days before he died of a stroke, Gounod told a reporter: "... You must know that some time ago I had an attack of paralysis. Now when I look at you in this way, I can see one half of your face. I know I look robust, but, as St. Paul says in his epistle to Timothy: 'I am now ready to be offered and the time of my departure is at hand. I have fought a good fight. I have finished my course. I have kept the faith [2 Timothy 4:6-7].' I have had several attacks already..." On the day of his death, Gounod said farewell to a friend: "*Au revoir.*"

Gowanlock, John (c. 1857-1885). Canadian frontiersman. Massacred by Cree Indians during the Northwest Rebellion in present-day Alberta, Canada, Gowanlock admonished: "My dear wife, be brave to the end." She survived and chronicled her husband's death.

Grable, Ruth "Betty" (1916-1973). American screen actress, "the girl with the million dollar legs." Dying of cancer, Grable spoke to her family on the mistaken belief that a sister was missing: "Marjorie isn't here."

Gracie, Hélio (1913-2009). Brazilian martial arts master. Dying at age 95, Gracie opined: "I created a flag from the sport's dignity. I oversee the name of my family with affection, steady nerves and blood."

Graham, Barbara "Bonnie" (1923-1955). American criminal, convicted of robbery and murder. Before her execution in the San Quentin, California gas chamber, Graham said: "Good people are always so sure they're right." When a guard told her to take a deep breath of the fumes to make her passing easier, she quipped: "How the hell would you know?"

Graham, Gary (1963-2000). American criminal, executed by lethal injection for a murder committed during a robbery: "... I'm an innocent black man that is being murdered... Keep marching black people, black power... They are killing me tonight. They are murdering me tonight."

Graham, James. Earl of Montrose (1612-1650). Scottish nobleman and military leader, condemned to die by the Scottish Parliament for his support of Charles I. Before he felt the hangman's noose, Graham said: "The covenant which I took, I own it and adhere to it. Bishops, I care not for them. I never intended to advance their interests..." Then: "May God have mercy on this afflicted kingdom."

Graham, James (1792-1861). British politician. Resting after suffering a heart attack, Graham said: "Ah! I thought it was over then."

Graham, John, Viscount of Dundee (c. 1648-1689). Scottish nobleman and soldier. Graham was killed in the Battle of Killiecrankie, Scotland, fought between forces of James VII of Scotland and King William of Orange. When Graham asked about the battle, a soldier told him that it went well for King James. Before dying, the viscount responded: "If it goes well for him, it matters the less for me."

Grainger, Percy (1882-1961). Australian-born pianist, composer and educator. Grainger spoke to his wife Ella immediately before his death from prostatic cancer: "You're the only one I like."

Granados, Carlos (1970-2007). American criminal, executed by lethal injection for the fatal stabbing of his girlfriend's son. "Kathy, you know I never meant to hurt you. I gave you everything and that's what made me so angry. But I never meant to hurt you. I'm sorry."

Grandier, Urbain (c. 1590-1634). French Catholic martyr. Grandier was condemned for his alleged practice of witchcraft and was burned at the stake: "My God, by the light I wait for you... My God, forgive my enemies."

Grant, Cary, born Archibald Leach (1904-1986). English-born Hollywood actor. Dying of a stroke, Grant reassured his wife: "I love you, Barbara... don't worry."

Grant, Joe "Texas Red" (died 1880). American gunslinger. Billy the Kid (above) and the inebriated Grant met in a saloon in Fort Sumner, New Mexico. Billy inspected Grant's pistol and surreptitiously turned the cylinder so the weapon would not fire. When Grant said he wanted to kill a certain individual, Billy replied: "You've got the wrong pig by the ear, Joe." Grant shouted: "That's a lie. I know better." He then turned his gun on Billy and pulled the trigger, but, as expected, the weapon failed to fire. Billy then put a bullet through Grant's brain.

Grant, Ulysses S. (1822-1885). Union general during the U.S. Civil War and eighteenth U.S. president. Dying of throat cancer, Grant resorted to note-writing during his last days. To a visiting clergyman: "I am a great sufferer all the time... all that I can do is to pray that the prayers of all these good people may be answered so far as to have us all meet in another and a better world. I cannot speak even in a whisper." To his physician: "I do not sleep, though sometimes I dose [*sic*] off a little. If up, I am talked to and in my efforts to answer cause pain. The fact is, I think I am a verb instead of a personal pronoun. A verb is anything that signifies to be, to do or to suffer. I signify all three." Just before he died, Grant was asked if he had any needs: "Water."

Grasso, Thomas (died 1995). American criminal, executed for a double murder. After finishing a glutinous last meal, Grasso complained before the lethal injection: "I did not get my Spaghetti-Os, I got spaghetti. I want the press to know this."

Grattan, Henry (1746-1820). Irish politician who opposed the merger of Ireland and Great Britain. "I am perfectly resigned. I am surrounded by my family. I have served my country. I have reliance upon God and I am not afraid of the devil."

Gray, Bryant (died 1863). Union officer in the U.S. Civil War. Dying of pneumonia in a Georgetown hospital, the delirious Gray roused and uttered his last words: "Forward! March!"

Gray, Henry (1892-1928). American murderer. Gray, a married man, plotted with his lover Ruth Snyder to murder her husband. Both were convicted of the crime and sentenced to die in the electric chair. Gray's last words: "I am ready to go. I have nothing to fear."

Gray, Robert (1809-1872). English-born bishop of Cape Town, South Africa. When informed that taking Holy Communion the following day probably would be too late, Gray replied: "Well dear fellow, I am ready when you like."

Gray, Thomas (1716-1771). English poet, scholar and educator. Dying of "gout in the stomach," Gray prophesied to a relative: "Molly, I shall die!"

Greble, John (1834-1861). Union officer in the U.S. Civil War. Mortally wounded during the Battle of Big Bethel, Virginia, Greble relinquished his post: "Sergeant, take command! Go ahead!"

Greely, Horace (1811-1872). American journalist, politician and abolitionist. Greely's purported last utterance was: "It is done." However, Clara Kellogg, an American operatic soprano, claims in her autobiography that Greely's last words were: "I know that my Redeemer liveth" from Handel's *Messiah*, which he had heard her sing earlier.

Green, G.W. (1936-1991). American criminal, executed by lethal injection for a robbery and murder. To the warden: "Lock and load. Let's do it, man." Before expiring, he described life in vulgar terms.

Green, Hetty (1834-1916). American financier. Because of her miserliness, Green was nicknamed "The Witch of Wall Street." Dying of a stroke, the eccentric businesswoman mused: "… I am not worrying. I do not know what the next world is, but I do know that a kindly light is leading me and that I shall be happy after I leave here."

Green, Joseph (1791-1863). English surgeon. After coughing and examining his own pulse, Green excitedly announced: "Congestion... stopped." He died moments later.

Alternative: * "It's stopped."

Green, Roosevelt (1956-1985). American criminal, executed by electrocution for the robbery and murder of a convenience store worker: "I am about to die for a murder I did not commit, that someone else committed ... I love the Lord and hope that God takes me into his kingdom, and goodbye, mother."

Greene, Graham (1904-1991). English writer and literary critic. Greene was nominated for the 1967 Nobel Prize in Literature. Dying of leukemia, he confided to a friend: "Will it be an interesting experience? Will I find out what lies beyond the barrier? Why does it take so long to come?"

Greene, Robert (c. 1560-1593). English poet. Greene directed that his tract *Groats-Worth of Wits* should be published posthumously. One of the last stanzas reflects a wistful yearning: "O, that a year were granted me to live,/ And for that year my former wits restored:/ What rules of live, what counsel would I give?/ How should my sin with sorrow be deplored?/ But I must die of every man abhorred./ Time loosely spent will not again be won,/ My time is loosely spent, and I undone."

Gregg, Maxey (1814-1862). Confederate officer in the U.S. Civil War. Mortally wounded during the Battle of Fredericksburg, Virginia, Gregg directed his dying words to the governor of South Carolina: "If I am to die at this time, I yield my life cheerfully, fighting for the independence of South Carolina!"

Grégoire, Henri (1750-1831). French Roman Catholic priest. Grégoire beseeched Abbé Baradère who administered the Viaticum: "... I see that my last hour is come. Do not desert me in my last moments."

Gregory I, also St. Gregory the Great (c. 540-604). Pope from 590 until his death. "I pray that the hand of Almighty God raise me from the sea of this present life and let me rest on the shores of eternal life... My body is dried up as if already in the coffin. Death is the only remedy for me."

Gregory VII, Saint (c.1020-1085). Pope from 1073 until his death. After retiring to Salerno, Gregory's health declined: "My brethren, I make no account of my good works; my only confidence is that I have always loved justice and hated iniquity, and, for that, I die in exile."

Alternative: * "I have loved righteousness and hated iniquity: therefore I die in exile."

Gregory XII (c. 1326-1417). Pope from 1406-1415. Forced to resign to end the Western Schism, Gregory lamented on his deathbed: "I have not understood the world and the world has not understood me."

Gregory XVI (1765-1846). Pope from 1831 until his death. Realizing that the end was imminent, Gregory asked for Communion. When his *valet-de-chambre* said that this act would upset his followers, the pontiff replied: "Certainly, I am very ill. I feel it and do you want me to appear before God without having taken the bread of life? I wish to die as a monk and not as a sovereign."

Gregory, Isabella (1852-1932). Irish writer and playwright. Gregory, a staunch Protestant, lay dying of breast cancer. When her nurse attempted to convert her to Catholicism, she replied: "Never!"

Grellet, Stephen (1773-1855). French Quaker missionary who ministered in Europe and North America. Dying of a painful illness, Grellet ended his prayers with: "Not my will, but Thine be done."

Grenville, Richard (c. 1541-1591). English admiral. During the Battle of Flores, a small island in the Azores archipelago, Grenville's ship engaged a much larger French fleet. When his vessel expended all of its ordinance, the wounded admiral ordered her to be scuttled. The crew refused and negotiated a surrender. As Grenville lay dying, he railed against some of his men: "Here die I, Richard Grenville, with a joyful and quiet mind, for that I have ended my life as a good soldier ought to do, who has fought for his country, queen, religion and honour. Wherefore my soul most joyfully departeth out of this body, and shall always leave behind it an everlasting fame of a true soldier, who hath done his duty as he was bound to do. But the others of my company have done as traitors and dogs, for which they shall be reproached all their lives and leave a shameful name forever." Ironically, the captured English vessel sank in a violent storm shortly thereafter. Often, the last sentence condemning his men is omitted in declarations of Grenville's last statement.

Grese, Irma (1923-1945). German concentration camp worker during WWII. Condemned to die for war crimes, Grese spoke to the hangmen immediately before the trap opened: "*Schnell* [Quickly]."

Grey, Jane (1537-1554). Queen of England. Lady Jane held the throne nine days but was usurped by Mary I who later arranged her execution. Before the ax fell, the executioner asked Jane for forgiveness. After she acceded to his wish, she implored: "I pray you dispatch me quickly." As she knelt down, Jane asked: "Will you take it [my head] off before I lay me down?" When told "No, madam," she tied a handkerchief over her eyes and felt for the block saying: "What shall I do? Where is it? Where is it?" Guided to the proper spot, Lady Jane uttered her last words: "Lord, into Thy hands I commend my spirit."

Grey, Katherine (1540-1568). Countess of Hertford and younger sister of Lady Jane Grey. Because Elizabeth I disapproved of Katherine's marriage to Edward Seymour and her possible threat to the throne, the queen imprisoned the countess. Near death from tuberculosis at age 27, Katherine said: "Lo, He comes!... Yea, even so, come Lord Jesus!... Welcome, death! O Lord. For Thy manifold mercies, blot out of Thy book all of mine offences." When it was suggested that the local church bell should be tolled at her death, she replied: "Good... Let it be so." As she died, Katherine prayed: "O Lord, into Thy hands I commend my spirit."

Grey, Zane (1872-1939). American writer, best-known for his stories of the "Old West." Suffering heart pains, Grey made a fateful misdiagnosis: "A slight case of indigestion."

Grieg, Edvard (1843-1907). Norwegian pianist and composer. Dying of cardiorespiratory failure, Grieg realized his time was short, stating: "So this will be the end." Later, to his wife: "Well— if it must be so."

Grimaldi, Joseph (1778-1837). English actor and comedian. Because Grimaldi lost the use of his lower extremities later in life, he was carried to and from a local tavern by its proprietor: "God bless you, my boy. I shall be ready for you tomorrow night." The actor died in his sleep.

Grimston, Robert (1816-1884). English sportsman who excelled at cricket. Before he died, Grimston spoke to an acquaintance: "I don't think I shall join you at dinner, but I will punish your dinner for you. I will have a bit of your fish."

Grindecobbe, William (died 1381). English martyr. During the Peasants' Revolt of 1381, Grindecobbe and other rebels took the charters binding serfs to the abbots of St. Albans, a settlement just north of London. Arrested for his act, Grindecobbe was offered a pardon if he surrendered the charters. Later condemned as a traitor, he was hanged, drawn and quartered. Before his execution, Grindecobbe spoke to his followers: "If I die, I shall die for the cause of the freedom we have won, counting myself happy to end my life by such a martyrdom. Do then today as you would have done had I been killed yesterday."

Grissom, Virgil "Gus" (1926-1967). American astronaut. During a prelaunch test of an Apollo spacecraft in 1967, the module in which Grissom, Roger Chaffee (above) and Ed White were confined caught fire. Grissom shouted: "Fire!" but all three died before they could be extricated.

Griswold, Rufus (1815-1857). American anthologist, critic and poet. Dying of tuberculosis, Griswold asserted: "Sir, I may not have been always a Christian, but I am very sure that I have been a gentleman."

***Grøntoft* Wireless Operator** (died 1922). On March 2, 1922 the Norwegian cargo ship *Grøntoft* sank in an Atlantic gale. The distress signal sent by an unnamed wireless operator: "We are sinking stern first. The boats are smashed. Can't hold out any longer. The skipper dictated that. He ought to know. Where did I put my hat? Sorry we couldn't wait for you. Pressing business elsewhere. *Skaal* [Good health]." The Baltic liner *Esthonia* steamed to the presumed location of the stricken ship but found no evidence of survivors.

Grossinger, Asher (1867-1931). Austrian-born restaurateur and hotelier. Grossinger developed a resort complex in the New York Catskill Mountains that flourished until the 1980s. As he died, Grossinger told one of his workers: "Abie, make sure that everybody eats."

Grotius, Hugo, also Hugo de Groot (1583-1645). Dutch jurist and writer who laid the groundwork for international law. Shipwrecked after a visit to Sweden, Grotius washed up on a German shore barely alive. When a clergyman recited a prayer for the dying, Grotius said: "I hear your voice well, but I understand with difficulty what you say."

Groves, Anthony (1795-1853). English missionary to Iraq and India. In declining health, Groves spoke to his son: "Now my precious boy, I am dying; be a comfort to your beloved mother, as your dear brothers Henry and Frank have been to me. And may the Lord Himself bless you and make you His own. May the Lord give you the peace and joy in Himself that He has given me, for these are true riches. What would thousands of gold and silver be to me now? Now I give you a father's blessing."

Grubbs, Victor (see Bragg, Robert).

Guay, Joseph-Albert (1917-1951). Canadian mass murderer. Guay became dissatisfied with his wife and plotted to kill her during an airline flight. He smuggled a bomb aboard a Canada Pacific airliner that killed 23 individuals including his wife. At his hanging: "At least I die famous."

Guesclin, Bertrand du (c. 1320-1380). French military leader during the Hundred Years' War. Before dying of an illness while on a military expedition, Guesclin proclaimed: "Remember that your business is only with those that carry arms. The churchmen, the poor, the women and children are not your enemies. I commend to the King my wife, my brother... Farewell... I am at an end."

Guevara, Ernesto "Che" (1928-1967). Argentine-born revolutionary who aided Fidel Castro's rise to power in Cuba. While conducting guerilla operations in Bolivia, Guevara was captured and later executed. Before the fatal shots were fired, he taunted his executioner: "I know you have come to kill me. Shoot coward, you are only going to kill a man."

Alternatives: * "Know this now, you are killing a man."
* "Kill me! I'm just a man."

* "Do not worry, Captain; it is all over. I have failed. Guevara then added that he was ashamed of being taken alive.

Guggenheim, Benjamin (1865-1912). American businessman who perished during the RMS *Titanic* disaster. As the vessel sank, Guggenheim gave a message for his wife to a steward: "... Tell my wife, Johnson [the steward], if it should happen that my secretary and I both go down and you are saved, tell her I played the game out straight and to the end. No woman shall be left aboard this ship because Ben Guggenheim was a coward. Tell her that my last thoughts will be of her and of our girls, but that my duty now is to these unfortunate women and children on this ship. Tell her I will meet whatever fate is in store for me, knowing she will approve of what I do." He was last seen chatting with associates as the ship began to sink.

Guggenheim, Marguerite "Peggy" (1898-1979). American art collector, socialite and daughter of Benjamin Guggenheim. On her deathbed: "These nurses don't have any idea what's wrong with me. They haven't a clue."

Guiccioli, Teresa (1800-1873). Italian mistress of Lord Byron while he lived in Ravenna, Italy. "The more Byron is known, the better he will be loved."

Guiteau, Charles (1841-1882). Mentally-unbalanced American lawyer who assassinated President James Garfield (above) in 1881. Guiteau was upset that the president had rejected his numerous job applications. On the scaffold prior to his hanging for the crime, Guiteau read a selection from the 10th chapter of Matthew. He followed this passage with a poem written for the occasion entitled "Simplicity," saying: "I am now going to read some verses which are intended to indicate my feelings at the moment of leaving this world. If set to music they may be rendered very effective. The idea is that of a child babbling to his mamma and his papa. I wrote it this morning about ten o'clock." The last stanzas of his poem: "I wonder what I will do when I get to the Lordy,/ I guess that I will weep no more/ When I get to the Lordy!/ Glory hallelujah!/ I wonder what I will see when I get to the Lordy,/ I expect to see most glorious things,/ Beyond all earthly conception/ When I am with the Lordy!/ Glory hallelujah! Glory hallelujah!/ I am with the Lord."

Guiteau dropped the manuscript, which was a signal to commence the execution. He then shouted: "Glory, ready, go," before the trap opened.

Guizot, François-Pierre (1787-1874). French statesman. On the day of his death, Guizot's daughter said they would meet again in eternity. He replied: "No one is more convinced of that than I am." He then asked her to dispense with oratory at his funeral: "God alone should speak by the side of the grave."

Gunther, Mary (died 1910). American defendant. In a courtroom, Gunther was accused of trying to steal another woman's husband. When she heard the charge, she cried: "I never! I wouldn't do such a thing!" Gunther then swooned and died.

Gurney, Joseph (1788-1847). English Quaker activist, banker and philanthropist who fought against slavery and capital punishment. Before dying, Gurney said to his wife: "I think I feel a little joyful, dearest."

Gurney, Samuel (1786-1856). English philanthropist, banker and brother of Joseph Gurney (above). "O Lord, let Thy will be done, notwithstanding my impatience."

Gusenberg, Frank "Tight Lips" (1893-1929). American gangster, wounded in the Chicago St. Valentine's Day Massacre. Before dying of multiple gunshot wounds, Gusenberg responded to a policeman who asked who shot him: "Nobody shot me. I ain't no copper." Later to a police lieutenant: "It's getting dark, Tom. I'm cold, awful cold. Pull the covers up over me."

Alternatives: * "No one. Nobody shot me."
* "All I know is that coppers did it."

Gussman, Charles (1913-2000). American writer who specialized in the television "soap opera" genre. Before dying, Gussman whispered jokingly to his daughter: "And now for a final word from our sponsor..."

Gustav II, also Gustavus Adolphus (1594-1632). King of Sweden. Sustaining a fatal wound in the Battle of Lützen, near Leipzig, Germany during the Thirty Years' War, Gustav feebly said to an aide: "I am gone. Look to your own life."

Alternatives: * "I have enough, brother. Try to save your own life."
* "I am a dead man; leave me and try to save your own lives."
* To his enemies: "I am the King of Sweden and seal with my blood the Protestant religion and the liberties of Germany. Alas, my poor queen. My God. My God."

Gustav III, also Gustavus III (1746-1792). King of Sweden. Because of discord with elements of the Swedish nobility, a plot was hatched to dispatch Gustav. He was shot at a masked ball and died of a wound infection almost two weeks later. At the end, Gustav told his attendants: "I feel sleepy; a few moments rest would do me good."

Alternative: * "It is all over."

Guthrie, James (c. 1612-1661). Scottish clergyman who was hanged as a covenanter. Before his execution, Guthrie proclaimed: "I take God to record upon my soul that I would not exchange this scaffold for the palace or mitre of the greatest prelate in Britain… Now, let Thy servant depart in peace, since mine eyes have seen Thy salvation." On the scaffold: "The covenants, the covenants shall yet be Scotland's reviving..."

Gwenn, Edmund (1877-1959). Welsh-born actor who won an Academy Award for his performance in *Miracle on 34th Street.* When asked if dying were difficult, Gwenn replied: "Yes, it's tough, but not as tough as doing comedy."

Alternatives: * "It is. But not as hard as farce."
* "But it's not as bad as playing comedy."

* "Not nearly as difficult as playing comedy."
* "Dying is easy. Comedy is difficult."
* "It is hard to die… but it is harder to do comedy."

Habashy, Ahmed Mahmoud El (died 1999). Egyptian aviator. On October 31, 1999, EgyptAir Flight 990 departed New York for Cairo but crashed off the coast of Massachusetts with no survivors. The U.S. National Transportation Safety Board later concluded that the disgruntled co-pilot, Gamil El Batouty, purposely sent the aircraft into a fatal dive when Habashy left the flight deck. The cockpit voice recorder captured the co-pilot repeating the phrase "I rely on God" multiple times after starting his suicidal actions. When Habashy returned to the cockpit, he said: "What's happening? What's happening, Gamil? What's happening? What is this? What is this? Did you shut the engines? Get away in the engines. Shut the engines." The co-pilot replied: "It's shut." Habashy continued: "Pull. Pull with me. Pull with me. Pull with me..." No further conversation was recorded.

Hackman, James (1752-1779). English clergyman and murderer. Hackman became infatuated with Martha Ray, the mistress of Lord Sandwich who incidentally originated the finger food that eponymously bears his name. Because of unrequited love, Hackman shot her dead and unsuccessfully tried to kill himself. Convicted of murder, he was executed by hanging. Before his death, he wrote a final note to a friend: "Farewell forever in this world. I die a sincere Christian and penitent, and everything I hope that you can wish me. Would it prevent my example's having any bad effect if the world should know how I abhor my former ideas of suicide, my crime... will be the best judge. Of her fame, I charge you to be careful. My poor sister will..."

Hadley, Samuel (1842-1906). American clergyman and reformed alcoholic who ministered to the homeless of New York City. Dying of complications from an appendectomy, Hadley asked: "My poor bums! My poor bums! Who will look out for them for me?"

Hadrian (76-138). Roman emperor. Hadrian was known for his building projects throughout the Roman Empire. He uttered these verses before he died: "Soul of mine, pretty one, flitting one,/ Guest and partner of my clay,/ Whither wilt thou hie [hasten] away;/ Pallid one, rigid one, naked one,/ Never to play again, never to play?"

Haggard, Mark (1876-1914). WWI Welsh military officer. Reconnoitering a German machine gun emplacement, Haggard ordered his men to: "Fix bayonets, boys." Mortally wounded during the ensuing charge, Haggard uttered a rallying call: "Stick it, the Welsh!"

Hahnemann, Samuel (1755-1843). German physician who developed the discipline of homeopathy. To his wife: "Every man on earth works as God gives him strength and meets from man with a corresponding reward; no man has a claim at the judgment seat of God. God owes me nothing. I owe him much- yea, all."

Hale, Edward (1822-1909). American clergyman and writer. Hale's last journal entry: "It was a lovely day and I spent all the time on the deck from half-past ten till five. Had a very good night."

Hale, George (1868-1938). American astronomer. As he lay dying, Hale mentioned a telescope he helped design: "It is a beautiful day. The sun is shining and they are working on Palomar [an observatory in southern California]."

Hale, Matthew (1609-1676). English jurist. When offered Communion, Hale responded: "No, my heavenly Father has prepared a feast for me and I will go to my Father's house to partake of it."

Hale, Nathan (1755-1776). American soldier and spy during the Revolutionary War. While reconnoitering British troop movements during the Battle of Long Island, Hale was captured and sentenced to die. Before his hanging, the patriot allegedly uttered his immortal words: "I only regret that I have but one life to lose for my country." Some contend that Hale actually may have paraphrased a section of Joseph Addison's *Cato* (see above): "What pity is it that we can die but once to serve our country."

Alternative: * A British officer who witnessed the hanging gave a different recollection of Hale's last words: "It is the duty of every good officer to obey any orders given him by his commander-in-chief."

Halévy, Jacques (1799-1862). French composer, best-known for his opera *La Juive.* Dying of tuberculosis, Halévy asked his daughter to help him turn while reclining: "Lay me down like a gamut." The musician then accompanied each movement with the musical notation: do-re-mi-fa etc. until he reached his final position, at which time he died.

Hall, Ben (1837-1865). Australian robber. When the police found the fugitive and opened fire, Hall spoke to a former Aboriginal friend, Billy Dargin: "Shoot me dead, Billy! Don't let the traps take me alive."

Hall, John (1774-1860). English temperance advocate and writer. "Passing away, passing away... Jesus, Jesus... He is, He is... pray... Amen."

Hall, Radclyffe (1880-1943). English poet and writer, best-known for his novel *The Well of Loneliness.* Dying of colon cancer: "What a life, but such as it is, I offer it to God."

Hall, Robert "Rob" (1961-1996). New Zealand-born mountaineer. While leading a climb up Mt. Everest, Hall and several of his clients perished. He spoke to his wife by satellite phone shortly before he died of exposure: "I love you. Sleep well, my sweetheart. Please don't worry too much."

Hall, Robert (1764-1831). English clergyman. Plagued by "hypochondria" and sporadic mental instability, to a friend: "I am dying. Death is come at last. All will now be useless!" When asked if he suffered: "Dreadfully."

Halleck, Fitz-Greene (1790-1867). American poet. On the night of his death, Halleck said to his sister with whom he lived: "Marie, hand me my pantaloons [trousers], if you please."

Haller, Albrecht von (1708-1777). Swiss physician, anatomist and philosopher. Palpating his own pulse, Haller told a colleague: "It's beating... beating... beating... It's stopped."

Alternatives: * "Now I am dying. The artery ceases to beat"
* "My friend, the artery ceases to beat."
* "My friend, the pulse has ceased to beat."
* "I am calm."

Halliburton, Richard (1900-1939). American explorer and writer. In 1939, Halliburton attempted to sail the Chinese junk *Sea Dragon* across the Pacific Ocean from Hong Kong to San Francisco. The last message from his sinking ship: "Southerly gales, squalls, lee rail under water, wet bunks, hard tack, bully beef, wish you were here — instead of me!"

Halyburton, Thomas (1674-1712). Scottish minister. Halyburton was afflicted by a pulmonary disorder during his waning years. Toward the end, he said: "When I shall be so weakened as not to be able to speak, I will give you, if I can, a sign of triumph, when I am near to Glory." Trying to clear his throat of secretions, the minister was able to say: "I am effectually choked. Pity, pity, Lord…" To his wife: "Be not discouraged. The Lord's way is the best way, and I am composed. Whether I go away in a fit of vomiting or fainting, 'tis all one. I did not know whether I was up or down" During his last six hours, Halyburton spoke only in broken sentences but, from time-to-time, was able to exhort those around him to: "Pray! pray!" The sign he gave before dying was a clapping of his hands.

Alternative: * "When I fall so low, that I am not able to speak, I will show you a sign of triumph when I am near glory, if I be able…"

Hamer, Fannie Lou (1917-1977). American civil rights leader. During her lifetime, Hamer suffered physical and verbal abuse in her quest to secure civil rights for all. Shortly before dying of breast cancer, she spoke to friends: "I'm so tired. I want you all to remember me and keep up the work. I've taken care of business. My house is in place. Everything is in order with God."

Hamerton, Philip (1834-1894). English artist, art critic and essayist. A note written several hours before Hamerton's death read: "If I indulge my imagination in dreaming about a country where justice and right would always surely prevail, where the weak would never be oppressed, nor an honest man incur any penalty for his honesty- that is truly ideal dreaming, because, however far I travel, I shall not find such a country in the world, and there is not any record of such a country in the authentic history of mankind."

Hamilton, Alexander (1757-1804). West Indian-born American founding father and first U.S. secretary of the treasury. During the 1804 New York gubernatorial election, Hamilton backed the candidate who defeated Aaron Burr, the former U.S. vice president. Due to continuing animosity between the two, Burr sought recourse through a pistol duel that resulted in Hamilton's death. Before expiring, the wounded man spoke to his physician: "This is a mortal wound, doctor." He turned to his wife and uttered his last words: "Remember, my Eliza, you are a Christian."

Hamilton, Edith (1867-1963). German-born American writer and historian. To a friend: "You know, I haven't felt up to writing, but now I think I am going to finish that book on Plato [*The Collected Dialogues of Plato*]."

Hamilton, Louis (1844-1868). American military officer under the command of General George Custer. Although ordered to stay behind and guard the rear echelon, Hamilton persuaded Custer to let him participate in the Battle of Washita River, Oklahoma against Black Kettle's Cheyenne tribe. Before he was mortally wounded by a gunshot to the chest, Hamilton exhorted his soldiers: "Now men, keep cool! Fire low and not too rapidly."

Hamilton, Patrick (1504-1528). Scottish Lutheran martyr. Because of his reformist preaching, Hamilton was convicted of heresy and sentenced to die by burning. After refusing to recant his confessions, the minister professed: "My confession I will not deny for dread of your fire, for my confession and my belief are in Jesus Christ. And as to sentence this day pronounced against me, I here, in presence of you all, appeal contrary to the said sentence and judgment, and betake me to the mercy of God." When told to call on the Virgin Mary, he replied: "O, wicked man [the friar who urged him to recant], thou knowest that I am no heretic: I cite thee to appear at the judgment-seat of Christ!" As the flames consumed his body, Hamilton moaned: "How long, O Lord, shall darkness overwhelm this realm? How long wilt Thou suffer this tyranny of men?" As he died, Hamilton implored: "O Lord Jesus, receive my spirit."

Alternative: * "Thou wicked man, thou knowest that I am not an heretic, and that is the truth of God for which I suffer; so much didst thou confess unto me in private; and thereupon I appeal thee to answer before the judgment seat of Christ."

Hamlin, Cyrus (1811-1900). American educator and missionary to Turkey. Hamlin asked to be moved to a chair he had used as a boy: "Put me there."

Hamlin, Henrietta (1811-1850). American wife of Cyrus Hamlin (above) and missionary to Turkey. Dying of a respiratory illness, the delirious Hamlin asked her husband: "What child is this? Is it little Carrie?" When he told her no children were in the room, she replied: "Yes! It is little Carrie, and the room is full of them."

Hammerstein, Oscar II (1895-1960). American lyricist and producer who collaborated with the composer Richard Rodgers to produce a number of enduring Broadway musicals. Dying of cancer, to his weeping son: "God d*** it! I'm the one dying, not you!" To his daughter: "I know I'm going to die. I don't want to die, but I know I'm going to..." He later said: "There's a game that people are playing now as to who would you rather be than yourself if you had your life to live over. I'm actually dying, so I should play the game better than anybody. Yet I can't figure out whether I'd be Albert Einstein or Babe Ruth. Einstein's mind and feeling for people, his sense of music, makes me feel he's the most sensitive and best man of this country. But as soon as I think of that- just the feel and hearing the ball hit the bat and see it go over the fence... So, I don't know." Perhaps Hammerstein's last words naming his favorite ballplayers made the matter clearer: "Ruth... Gehrig... Rizzuto..."

Hamnett, Nina (1890-1956). Unconventional Welsh writer, artist and musicologist, known as the "Queen of Bohemia." Hamnett fell from a window and impaled herself on a wrought-iron fence: "Why don't they let me die?" Questions arose whether the act was a suicide, homicide or accident.

Hampden, John (1594-1643). English soldier, clergyman and statesman. During the English Civil War, Hampden was wounded at Chalgrove Field, Oxfordshire, while battling forces loyal to King Charles I. Dying several days later, he beseeched: "Lord Jesus, receive my soul! Oh, Lord, save my country. O Lord, be merciful, to..." He was unable to finish the sentence.

Alternative: * "Oh, Lord, save my country. Lord, be merciful, too."

Hampton, Wade (1818-1902). Confederate general during the U.S. Civil War who later became governor of South Carolina and later a U.S. senator. "All my people, black and white, God, bless them all."

Hamsun, Knut (1859-1952). Norwegian writer who won the 1920 Nobel Prize in Literature. When Hamsun's wife attempted to move his pillow: "Leave it be, Marie – I'm dying now."

Hancock, Anthony "Tony" (1924-1968). British actor and comedian. Troubled by alcohol abuse and depression, Hancock committed suicide by a drug overdose. One of the notes he left: "Nobody will ever know I existed. Nothing to leave behind me. Nothing to pass on. Nobody to mourn me. That's the bitterest blow of all." A portion of another note read: "Things just seemed to go too wrong too many times."

Hancock, John (1737-1793). American patriot whose distinctive signature appears on the Declaration of Independence. Dying of an "apoplectic stroke" after completing a note that ended: "... I shall look forward to a pleasant time."

Hand, Daniel (1801-1891). American businessman and philanthropist. Hand often repeated: "I have now a very short time for this world, but I take no concern about that; no matter where or when I die, I hope I am ready when called."

Handel, George Frideric (1685-1759). German-born English organist, conductor and composer, best-known for his oratorio *Messiah*. After signing his will, Handel said: "I want to die on Good Friday, in the hope of rejoining the good God, my sweet Lord and Savior, on the day of His Resurrection." According to a colleague, James Smyth, the composer then said goodbye to his friends and told his servant: "... Not to let me [Smyth] come to him anymore, for that he had now done with the world." He died of a stroke on Holy Saturday, the day after Good Friday.

Hanna, Marcus (1837-1904). American industrialist and Ohio senator. Dying of typhoid, Hanna complained when offered a handkerchief: "Yes, I would like one, but I suppose I cannot have it. My wife takes them all."

Hannibal (c. 247-c. 183 BCE). Carthaginian general and statesman. Hannibal conquered a large portion of Italy during the Second Punic War but later was pushed back to Carthage by the Romans. During the last stage of his life, he committed suicide by poisoning while in exile to avoid capture by his old adversaries: "Let us ease the Romans of their continual dread and care, who think it long and tedious to await the death of a hated old man. Yet Titus will not bear away a glorious victory, nor one worthy of those ancestors who sent to caution Pyrrhus, an enemy, and a conqueror too, against the poison prepared for him by traitors."

Alternatives: * "Let me free the Roman people from their long anxiety, since they think it tedious to wait for an old man's death..."

* "It is time now to end the great anxiety of the Romans, who have grown weary in waiting for the death of a hated old man..."

Hansford, Thomas (c. 1646-1676). American martyr. In 1676, Hansford joined Nathaniel Bacon's rebellion against the management policies of Virginia's colonial governor. When the insurrection was quelled, Hansford was hanged for his involvement. "Take notice I die a loyal subject and a lover of my country."

Hanway, Jonas (1712-1786). English philanthropist, merchant and writer. Ever thinking of others, Hanway expressed his last wish: "If you think it will be of service in your practice, or to anyone who may come after me,

I beg you will have my body opened. I am willing to do as much good as is possible." As he died: "Christ..."

Harden, Jacob (1837-1860). American minister and murderer. Because of a loveless marriage, Harden poisoned his wife with arsenic. Convicted of her murder, the preacher was condemned to die by hanging. Before the trap opened: "God have mercy upon me! Lord Jesus, save me in Heaven."

Harden-Hickey, James (1854-1898). American adventurer and writer who was the son-in-law of the wealthy businessman Henry Flagler. While on a cruise in the South Atlantic, Harden-Hickey visited the island of Trinidad and later claimed it as his own. He spent the latter part of his life in an unsuccessful bid to establish the legitimacy of this claim. Depressed by his failure and the inability to sell a Mexican holding, Harden-Hickey took his life by a drug overdose. His suicide note: "My Dearest [his wife, Annie Flagler Harden-Hickey], no news from you, although you have had plenty of time to write. Harvey has written me that he has no one in view at present to buy my land. Well, I shall have tasted the cup of bitterness to the very dregs, but I do not complain. Goodbye. I forgive you your conduct toward me and trust you will be able to forgive yourself. I prefer to be a dead gentleman to a living blackguard like your father." Harden-Hickey earlier had penned a treatise on suicide, *Euthanasia: The Aesthetics of Suicide.*

Hardin, John Wesley (1853-1895). American gunfighter and murderer. While shooting dice in a Texas saloon, Hardin was confronted by a local lawman. Before he was shot dead by the constable, he exclaimed to a fellow player: "Brown, you have four sixes to beat!"

Harding, Florence (1860-1924). Widow of U.S. President Warren Hardin. Dying of kidney failure, Harding spoke to her husband's former secretary George Christian: "I am glad you are here, George. I want you to take care of all this mail and see that every letter is acknowledged, and thank them for their kind interest."

Harding, Warren G. (1865-1923). Twenty-ninth U.S. president. Dying unexpectedly during a west coast trip, the president spoke to his wife who was reading favorable newspaper reports to him: "That's good. Go on, read some more."

Hardy, Oliver "Ollie" born Norvell Hardy (1892-1957). Corpulent member of the American Laurel and Hardy comedy team. Terminally, Hardy suffered a stroke possibly related to a rapid weight loss from dieting. Unable to speak, his wife Lucille felt that he mouthed the words "I love you," before he died.

Hardy, Thomas (1840-1928). English writer and poet, known for his novels *Far from the Madding Crowd* and *Tess of the d'Urbervilles*. Dying of pleurisy, Hardy asked his sister-in-law: "Eva, Eva, what is this?"

Harlan, John Marshall (1833-1911). Associate U.S. Supreme Court justice. Dying of a respiratory ailment, Harlan bid farewell to his family: "Goodbye, I am sorry to have kept you all waiting so long."

Harlan, John II (1899-1971). Grandson of John Marshall Harlan who also became an associate U.S. Supreme Court justice. Near blind and dying of cancer, Harlan asked: "Why did this have to happen to me?"

Harley, John (1786-1858). English actor. "Stricken with a paralysis," Harley repeated a line from Shakespeare's *A Midsummer-Night's Dream*:" "I have an exposition of sleep come upon me."

Harlow, Jean, born Harlean Harlow Carpenter (1911-1937). American screen actress who was nicknamed the "Blond Bombshell." Dying of kidney failure, Harlow asked: "Where is Aunt Jetty? Hope she didn't run out on me..."

Harmison, Frank (died 1889). American gunfighter and vigilante. Members of the Marlow Brothers gang based in north-central Texas were jailed for horse stealing and murder. When the arrested men were transferred to a more secure jail, Harmison and a vigilante band attacked the procession. In the ensuing gun fight, members of both sides were killed. As the vigilantes retreated, one of the Marlows called Harmison a coward. As he reversed his direction toward the outlaws, a companion asked: "Where you going?" Harmison scornfully replied: "Back to see it out!" He was felled by a bullet between the eyes.

Harmsworth, Alfred, Lord Northcliffe (1865-1922). British newspaper and publishing magnate. Dying from complications of endocarditis, Harmsworth made clear his burial plans and obituary: "I wish to be laid as near Mother as possible at North Finchley (north London). I do not wish anything erect from the ground or any words except my name, the year I was born and this year on the stone. In the *Times* I should like a page reviewing my life work by someone who really knows, and a leading article by the best man available on the night."

Harold II, also Harold Godwinson (c. 1022-1066). King of England and son of Godwin, Earl of Wessex (above). Before perishing against forces led by William of Normandy at the Battle of Hastings on the southeastern English coast, Harold cried: "Out! Out! God Almighty! Holy Cross!"

Haroun Al Raschid (c. 765-809). Caliph (Islamic leader) of Baghdad. During a military campaign in the eastern region of his empire, the caliph became indisposed: "Haroun is prince of the believers, those of the race that knows how to die." To his attendant: "Sahl, remember in a moment like this what the poet has said: 'Descended from a race so great, I firmly bear the hardest fate.'"

Harpe, Jean François de La (see La Harpe, Jean François de).

Harpe, Micajah "Big" (c. 1768-1799). American murderer. "Big" Harpe, a very large man, joined with his brother (some say cousin) "Little" in the wanton murder of several dozen men, women and children in the 1790s. "Big" eventually was tracked down by a posse and shot. As his captors hacked at his neck, the wounded man cried: "You are a God-d***** rough butcher, but cut on and be d*****!" After his decapitation, the murderer's head was impaled on a pole at a nearby crossroads.

Harper, Henry (1873-1901). Canadian journalist and civil servant. While ice skating on a river, Harper saw a woman fall through the ice. Urged not to jump into the water, he replied: "What else can I do?" Both drowned.

Harrington, Calvin (1826-1886). American educator. As he died, Harrington recited part of the *Gloria Patri*: "As it was in the beginning, is now, and ever shall be, world without end. Amen."

Harris, Frank (1856-1931). Irish-born American editor and writer. Dying of a heart attack, to his wife: "Nellie, my Nellie- I'm going!"

Harris, George (1959-2000). American criminal who murdered an acquaintance over missing firearms. Before his execution by lethal injection, Harris joked: "Somebody needs to kill my trial attorney."

Harris, Jack (died 1882). Irish-born American saloon/theater owner. Shot by an acquaintance over a long-standing gambling debt, Harris spoke to a doctor attending him: "He took advantage of me and shot me from the dark." The assailant subsequently was indicted for murder but later was acquitted of the crime.

Harris, Joel Chandler (1848-1908). American writer who created the Uncle Remus stories. Dying of nephritis and cirrhosis, Harris' reply when asked how he was doing: "I am about the extent of a tenth of a gnat's eyebrow better."

Harris, Robert (1953-1992). American criminal, executed in the San Quentin, California gas chamber for the murder of two teenage boys. His last words: "You can be a king or a street sweeper, but everybody dances with the Grim Reaper," possibly referring to a line from the movie *Bill and Ted's Bogus Journey*: "... Sooner or later you'll dance with the Reaper."

Harrison, Benjamin (1833-1901) Twenty-third U.S. president and grandson of former President William Harrison. The day before he died of pneumonia, Harrison asked his wife: "Are the doctors here?" Immediately before expiring, he exclaimed: "Doctor... my lungs..."

Harrison, Carter (1825-1893). Member of the U.S. House of Representatives and later mayor of Chicago. Shot by a disgruntled constituent, the mayor spoke to a neighbor who came to his aid: "This is death, Chalmers. I am shot through the heart" When told that he was shot through the stomach,

Harrison exclaimed: "No, through the heart, I tell you!" He then asked to see his fiancée Annie Hall and died shortly thereafter.

Alternatives: * "No, I have been shot in the heart, and I know I cannot live."

* To his son: "I am shot, Preston and cannot live."
* "Give me water. Where is Annie?"

Harrison, George (1943-2001). English musician who played lead guitar in The Beatles rock band. Dying of cancer, Harrison admonished family members gathered at his deathbed: "Love one another."

Harrison, Reginald "Rex" (1908-1990). British actor and film star, best-known for his roles in the films *My Fair Lady* and *Dr. Dolittle.* Dying of pancreatic cancer, to his wife: "What did I do to deserve you?"

Harrison, Thomas (1606-1660). English military leader and conspirator. Harrison was one of the signers of the death decree exacted against King Charles I. After the Restoration of the English monarchy, Harrison was convicted of regicide and sentenced to die. Before he was hanged, drawn and quartered, the condemned man said on the way to his execution: "I go to suffer upon the account of the most glorious cause that ever was in the world" When asked where the cause stood now at the time of his execution, Harrison replied: "Here it is [placing his hand on his heart], and I am going to seal it with my blood." At the gallows, Harrison was asked how he was doing: "Never better in my life." When told that a crown of glory was prepared for him: "O yes, I see it." On the gallows, he said: "He hath covered my head many times in the day of battle. By God I have leaped over a wall, by God I have run through a troop, and by my God I will go through this death and He will make it easy for me. Now into Thy hands, Oh Lord Jesus, I commend my spirit."

Harrison, William (1773-1841). Ninth U.S. president who died in office after serving only one month. Mortally ill with pneumonia, Harrison spoke to his nurse: "Ah, Fanny, I am ill, very ill, much more so than they think." He also complained about the ineffective treatments offered by his physicians: "It is wrong! I won't consent! It is unjust! These applications, will they never cease? I cannot stand it! I cannot bear this! Don't trouble me." Toward the end, Harrison spoke deliriously to one of his doctors, perhaps mistaking him for his Vice President John Tyler: "Sir, I wish you to understand the true principles of the government. I wish them carried out. I ask nothing more."

Hart, Lorenz (1895-1943). American Broadway musical lyricist who, for many years, collaborated with the composer Richard Rodgers. Dying of pneumonia and the effects of alcohol abuse, Hart philosophically asked: "What have I lived for?"

Hartley, Wallace (1878-1912). English musician who sailed on the RMS *Titanic*. Hartley was a member of the small band that played on the deck of the doomed liner before she sank. A surviving passenger heard Hartley tell his colleagues "Gentleman, I bid you farewell…" before they were washed into the ocean. His violin, which survived the accident, was recently auctioned for £900,000 ($1.7 million U.S.).

Harvey, Frederick "Fred" (1835-1901). English-born American restaurateur whose establishments catered primarily to railroad passengers in the southwest U.S. Noted for his generous portions, the dying Harvey allegedly told his sons: "Don't cut the ham too thin, boys." Some say he actually cautioned frugality, saying: "Cut the ham thinner, boys."

Harvey, William (1811-1866). Irish botanist. Dying of tuberculosis, Harvey reminisced: "Yes, it has been a pleasant world to me."

Hašek, Jaroslav (1883-1923). Czech author and humorist. Dying of tuberculosis, Hašek chastised his physician who refused him a last drink of brandy: "But you're cheating me!"

Hastings, Selina (1707-1791). English religious leader and philanthropist. "My work is done. I have nothing to do but to go to my Father."

Hastings, Warren (1732-1818). British governor of India. Hastings spoke to those assembled around his deathbed: "Surely, at my age it is time to go.

God only can do me good. My dear, why wish me to live to suffer thus? None of you know what I suffer."

Hauff, Wilhelm (1802-1827). German writer and poet. Dying of typhoid, Hauff prayed: "Father, into Thy hands I commend my immortal spirit."

Hauser, Kaspar (c. 1812-1833). A mysterious German youth who claimed that he was kept in a dungeon until his teenage years. Dying of an equally inexplicable stab wound of the chest, possibly self-inflicted, Hauser exclaimed: "Knife... Man stabbed... Gave purse... Look quickly... Go Hofgarten [a public park] ... I didn't do it myself. Many cats are the sure death of a mouse." After speaking to his pastor, Hauser uttered his last words: "Tired, very tired, a long journey to take."

Havelock, Henry (1795-1857). British general who died of dysentery in the Siege of Lucknow during the Indian Mutiny of 1857. Toward the end, Havelock spoke to his comrade James Outram: "For more than forty years, I have so ruled my life that when death came, I might face it without fear." To his son who faithfully nursed him until the end, the general said: "Come, come, my son, and see how a Christian can die."

Alternative: * "Come, my son, and see in what peace a Christian can die."

Haven, Gilbert (1821-1880). American clergyman, educator and abolitionist. Dying of suspected malaria: "It is all bright and beautiful; there is no darkness; there is no river. I am upborne by angels. I am floating away into God."

Havergal, Frances (1836-1879). English poet and hymnodist who wrote "Take My Life and Let It Be." Dying of suspected peritonitis, Havergal managed to say: "There, now it is over! Blessed rest!" She then tried to sing, but only one word emerged: "He..." Some have speculated that she wished to say: "He died for me."

Hawker, Robert (1803-1875). English poet and clergyman. On his deathbed, Hawker spoke: "His banner over me was love." When a fellow clergyman entered his room, Hawker greeted him and carried his hand to his lips; the communication that followed remains: "Sacred to the memory of the dead."

Hawthorne, Nathaniel (1804-1864). American novelist who wrote *House of Seven Gables* and *The Scarlet Letter.* Dying of a painful abdominal ailment, Hawthorne spoke to his friend, the former U.S. President Franklin Pierce (below): "What a boon it would be, if when life draws to a close, one could pass away without a struggle."

Hawthorne, Sophia Amelia (1809-1871). American artist and writer who was the widow of Nathaniel Hawthorne (above). Dying of typhoid fever, Hawthorne told her children: "I only wanted to live for you children, you know. I never wanted anything for myself, except to be with your father." Then: "I am tired... too tired... I am glad to go... I only wanted to live... for you... and Rose. Flowers. Flowers."

Hawtrey, Edward (1789-1862). English educator and linguist. Musing about his last days, Hawtrey spoke of his sister: "My wish would be that we might both drop off the perch together." She may have had different thoughts about that.

Haydn, Joseph (1732-1809): Austrian classical composer who pioneered the development of symphonic and string quartet genres. During the French siege of Vienna in 1809, the aged composer told his staff: "Why this terror? Know that no disaster can come where Haydn is." Dying of advanced heart failure: "Be of good cheer, dear ones, I'm doing fine."

Alternatives: * "My children, have no fear, for where Haydn is, no harm can fall."

* "Children be comforted, I am well."
* "Cheer up, children, I'm all right."
* "God preserve the Emperor!"

Haydon. Benjamin (1786-1846). English artist. Wracked by debt and lack of recognition for his works, Haydon attempted suicide by gunshot at age 60. When this failed, he completed the job by jugulation. He wrote: "No man should use certain evil for probable good, however great the object.

Evil is the prerogative of the Deity..." He ended the note: "God forgive the evil for the sake of the good. Amen." Haydon also left a detailed will, which ended: "… God Almighty, forgive us all. I die in peace with all men, and pray Him not to punish, for the sake of the father, the innocent widow and children he leaves behind. I ask her pardon and my children's for the additional pang, but it will be the last, and released from the burden of my ambition, they will be happier and suffer less. Hoping through the merits of Christ, forgiveness. B.R. Haydon." His final diary entries: "21st [June, 1846]. Slept horribly. Prayed in sorrow, and got up in agitation. 22nd. God forgive me. Amen! Finis of B.R. Haydon."

Hayes, Rutherford (1822-1893). Nineteenth U. S. president. Dying of a heart attack, Hayes spoke of his late wife: "I know that I am going where Lucy is."

Hayne, Isaac (1745-1781). Military officer during the American Revolution. Captured by the British, Hayne was paroled on condition he would not bear arms against them again. He rejoined the revolutionary forces, was recaptured and later hanged by his captors. At the gallows, to his son: "Now, my son, show yourself a man! That tree is the boundary of my life and all of my life's sorrows... Don't lay too much at heart; our separation, it will be short. It was but lately your dear mother died. Today, I die. And you, my son, though still young, must shortly follow us."

Haynes, Lemuel (1753-1833). American clergyman, writer and abolitionist. Haynes laid bare his feelings before he died: "I love my wife, I love my children, but I love my Savior better than all."

Hayward, Susan, born Edythe Marrenner (1917-1975). American film actress. Dying of cancer, Hayward told her son: "I love you."

Hayworth, Rita, born Margarita Carmen Cansino (1918-1987). American film actress. Suffering from dementia during her last years, Hayworth possibly mused about her father, a noted dancer: "He used to do that. He told me how to do that."

Hazen, Richard (1943-1996). American pilot. Hazen was the co-pilot of ValuJet 592 that crashed into the Florida Everglades due to an onboard fire. The last recorded words before his aircraft plunged to earth with the loss of all on board: "Critter five-ninety-two [the aircraft's call sign], we need the, uh, closest airport available."

Hazlitt, William (1778-1830). English author, literary critic, artist and philosopher. Hazlitt spoke to those around his deathbed: "Well, I've had a happy life."

Healy, George (1813-1894). American portrait painter. To his daughter who asked if he were comfortable: "Yes, and happy! So happy!"

Healy, James (1830-1900). American Roman Catholic bishop. Dying of a heart attack, Healy pondered: "I wonder if heaven is worth it all? Yes! Yes! It is worth all this and infinitely more still."

Hearn, Lafcadio (1850-1904). Greek author who wrote extensively about Japan. Dying of heart failure, Hearn lamented about the projected books he would never write: "Ah, because of sickness."

Hearst, William (1863-1951). American newspaper publisher and politician. Hearst was forced to leave his secluded California mansion to seek medical care during his last illness. He asked a friend to: "Please stop at San Simeon and look the place over. I want to be sure everything is all right there." Hearst later died of a heart attack.

Heath, Neville (1917-1946). English criminal, hanged for the brutal murder of two women. When Heath was offered a last whiskey before his execution, he replied: "Yes, please, and while you're about it, sir, you might make that a double."

Alternatives: * "On second thought, ah... you might make that a double."
* "Considering the circumstances, better make it a double."

Hecker, Isaac (1819-1888). American priest and founder of the Paulist Fathers religious society. Dying of cancer, Hecker insisted that he would do his own blessing: "No, I will."

Heckewelder, John (1743-1823). English-born Moravian missionary, primarily to Native Americans in Ohio and Pennsylvania. Heckewelder spoke these words on his deathbed: "Golgotha [where Jesus was crucified]... Gethsemane [a garden where Jesus prayed the night before his crucifixion]..."

Hegel, Georg Friedrich (1770-1831). German philosopher and writer. Dying during a cholera epidemic, Hegel uttered enigmatic and probably apocryphal last words on his deathbed: "Only one of my pupils understood me and even he unfortunately understood me wrongly." Some contend that this utterance actually was made by one of Hegel's rivals, Friedrich von Schelling.

Alternatives: * "Only one man ever understood me. ...And he didn't understand me."
* "Only you have ever understood me. … And you got it wrong..."
* "Only one man ever understood me. ...And he really didn't understand me."

Heine, Heinrich (1797-1856). German poet, writer and literary critic. Dying of a chronic neurologic ailment, Heine was asked if he were in the good graces of the Lord. Smiling, he replied: "Do not trouble yourself. God will pardon me. It's his profession." According to his nurse, Heine's last words were: "I am done for." Others say he probably wished to communicate further: "Write... write... pencil... paper."

Alternatives: * "Set your mind at rest. God will pardon me. It is His profession."
* "God will pardon me, that's his line of work."
* "God will pardon me. It is his trade."
* "God will forgive me, it is his trade."
* "God will forgive me. It is his profession."
* "Of course, God will forgive me. That's his job."
* "I'm dying! I'm dying!"

Helm, Boone (1823-1864). American frontier robber, murderer and cannibal. Helm killed a string of men in the far west during his checkered life. While starving in the mountains, he allegedly killed a family and consumed their remains. Later, Helm and four others were captured and summarily executed by hanging. To one of his dangling comrades, "Three-Fingered Jack" (see Gallagher, Jack above): "Kick away, old fellow. I'll be in hell with you in a minute." Then, avowing his allegiance to the Confederacy, Helm shouted: "Every man for his principles! Hurrah for Jeff Davis. Let her rip!"

Alternative * "Kick away, old Jack. I'll be in hell with you in ten minutes."

Héloïse d' Argenteuil (c. 1101-1164). French prioress, scholar, philosopher and writer. Héloïse successively became the pupil, mistress and wife of the philosopher Pierre Abélard (above). When Abélard was threatened about the affair by Héloïse's uncle, he sent her to a nunnery where she eventually became its prioress. When her demise appeared nigh, Héloïse requested: "In death, at last, let me rest with [the predeceased] Abélard." Héloïse's body subsequently was placed in the tomb beside her husband.

Helper, Hinton (1829-1908). American abolitionist and writer. Despondent over his failed endeavors, Helper committed suicide by asphyxiation: "There is no justice in this world."

Hemingway, Ernest (1899-1961). American writer who won the 1954 Nobel Prize in Literature. The author suffered from chronic depression and other illnesses. The night before committing suicide by a shotgun blast to the head, Hemingway said to his wife: "Goodnight, my kitten."

Henderson, Ebenezer (1784-1858). Scottish missionary, primarily to Scandinavian countries. On his deathbed, Henderson quoted Psalm 73:26: "My flesh and my heart faileth, but God is the strength of my heart and my portion forever."

Hendricks, Thomas (1819-1885). U.S. vice-president in Grover Cleveland's administration. Dying on a trip home to Indianapolis, Hendricks said to his doctor: "At rest at last... now I am free from pain."

Alternative: * "I'm free at last... I mean, at last I'm free from pain."

Hendrix, Jimi (1942-1970). American rock guitarist, singer and lyricist. Hendrix was troubled by drug and alcohol abuse during his career. The concluding lyrics of a song "The Story of Life" written by Hendrix on the eve of his death from the effects of a barbiturate overdose read: "... I wish not to be alone/ so I must respect my other heart./ Oh, the story of Jesus is the story of you and me./ No use in feeling lonely./ I am you searching to be free.

The story of life is quicker than the wink of an eye./ The story of love is hello and goodbye./ Until we meet again."

Henie, Sonja (1912-1969). Norwegian figure skater and actress. Dying of leukemia while on a flight from Paris to Oslo, Henie told her husband: "Oh, Niels, I am so tired."

Henri II de Montmorency, Duc (1595-1632). French military leader and nobleman. Henri was beheaded after his failed rebellion against King Louis XIII's minister, Cardinal Richelieu. At his execution, the condemned man requested: "Give a good stroke. Sweet Savior, receive my soul."

Henrietta Anne, Duchess of Orléans (1644-1670). English-born noblewoman who became a member of the court of French King Louis XIV. Dying of peritonitis from a perforated ulcer (some say poison), Henrietta Anne was asked if she loved God: "With all my heart."

Henrietta Maria de Bourbon (1609-1669). Daughter of French King Henry IV and queen consort of Charles I, King of England. Troubled by insomnia, Henrietta summoned her doctor: "Tell Duquesne that I cannot sleep and that I would like him to take me some new medicine." She died in her sleep from an opiate overdose administered by Duquesne. Some say her medical care was provided by the court physician Antoine Vallot.

Henry IV (1050-1106). German-born Holy Roman Emperor. Remorseful about riches amassed during his reign, Henry remarked on his deathbed: "Oh, how unhappy I am who squandered such great treasures in vain!

How happy I could have been if I had given those things to the poor! But I swear before the eye of the All-Knowing that all my efforts have been only for the advancement of my Church."

Henry II (1133-1189). King of England. During the waning years of his reign, Henry's sons rebelled against him for precedence of ascendancy to the throne. Dying of a bleeding ulcer, he expressed his feelings toward them: "Now let things go as they will. I care no more for myself or for this world…" As he sank into a delirium: "Shame, shame on a conquered king! Cursed be the day I was born! Cursed be the sons I leave!"

Alternatives: * "Let the rest go as it will. Now I care not what becomes of me. Shame, shame on a conquered king!"
* "Now let the world go as it will; I care for nothing more."

Henry IV (1367-1413). King of England. To his son, Henry confessed guilt for his overthrow of his cousin Richard II in 1399: "Well, fair son, what right I had to it, God knoweth. I commit all to God and remember you to do the same." Told that the chamber in Westminster Abbey where he stayed was called Jerusalem, Henry replied: "Lauds be given to the Father of Heaven, for now I know that I shall die here in this chamber, according to the prophesy of me declared, that I should depart this life in Jerusalem."

Henry V (1387-1422). King of England. While on a military campaign in France, Henry was stricken with a fever and dysentery that led to his death. In his final moments, the king appeared to address "an evil spirit:" "Thou liest. Thou liest. My portion is with the Lord Jesus Christ." Henry then prayed: "Into Thy hands, Lord, Thou hast redeemed this life."

Henry VII (1457-1509). King of England. Dying of tuberculosis, Henry told his aides: "If it should please God to send me life, you should find me a new changed man." Then: "We heartily desire our executors to consider how behoofful [useful] it is to be prayed for."

Henry VIII (1491-1547). King of England. Dying of morbid obesity and complications of probable diabetes, Henry exclaimed: "I have abused my life. Yet is the mercy of Christ able to pardon me all my sins, even though they were greater than they be." Advised to take Last Rites, the king replied: "I will first take a little sleep, and then according, as I feel myself, I will advise upon the matter." Immediately before dying, Henry allegedly bemoaned: "All is lost! Monks, Monks, Monks! So, now all is gone - Empire, Body, and Soul!" His last words may reflect his controversial dissolution of monasteries in the late 1530s.

Alternative: * "I trust in the merits of Christ. All is lost! Monks! Monks! Monks!"

Henry II (1519-1559). King of France. Mortally injured during a jousting tournament, Henry spoke to his son and successor Francis II: "My boy, you are going to be without your father, but not without his blessing. I pray God to make you more fortunate than I have been."

Henry III (1551-1589). King of France. During a protracted period of religious strife in France, Henry was stabbed by a fanatical Dominican friar. The mortally-wounded king spoke to his confessor: "I forgive them [his enemies] with all my heart." When asked specifically about those who caused his injury, Henry replied: "Yes, even them. I pray God that He may pardon them their sins as I hope He will pardon mine." To the King of Navarre (the future Henry IV): "I am dying happy in the knowledge that you are by my side. The Crown is yours. I command all the officers to recognize you as King after me... You will have many troubles unless you make up your mind to change your religion. I exhort you to do this!"

Henry IV (1553-1610). King of France. Stabbed in the heart by the religious fanatic François Ravaillac (below), Henry cried: "I am wounded!" Some say he died without further exclamation, but others claim that he spoke further before expiring: "It is nothing."

Henry Christophe (1767-1820). King of Haiti. Henry Christophe's oppressive rule ultimately led to a revolt by his subjects. Before committing suicide by a gunshot to the chest, the king said: "Since the people of Haiti no longer have faith in me, I know what to do!"

Henry Frederick, Prince of Wales (1594-1612). Eldest son of King James I and potential heir to the English throne. Dying of typhoid at age 18, Henry Frederick asked: "Where is my dear sister [Elizabeth]?" When asked if he were in pain: "I would say somewhat, but I cannot utter it."

Henry the Lion (1129-1195). German Duke of Saxony and Bavaria. On his deathbed, Henry prayed: "God be merciful to me a sinner."

Henry, Matthew (1662-1714). Welsh-born English minister. Dying of "apoplexy," Henry announced to a friend: "You have been used to take notice of the sayings of dying men. This is mine: that a life spent in the service of God, and communion with Him, is the most pleasant life that anyone can live in this world."

Alternative: * "A life spent in the service of God, and communion with Him, is the most comfortable and pleasant life anyone can live in this world."

Henry, O.., pen name of William Sidney Porter (1862-1910). American writer and master of the short story genre. As he lay dying of cirrhosis, diabetes and heart failure, O. Henry said: "Don't turn down the light. I'm afraid to go home in the dark." A popular song of his day, "I'm Afraid to Come Home in the Dark," possibly was the inspiration for his statement. Before expiring the following morning, the author asked his physician to: "Send for Mr. Hall," one of his editors.

Alternatives: * "Turn up the lights; I don't want to go home in the dark."
* "Pull up the shades; I don't want to go home in the dark."

Henry, Patrick (1736-1799) American statesman who was a strong backer of independence from England. His stirring speech to the Virginia colonial delegates in 1775 included the exhortation: "Give me liberty or give me death!" Dying of cancer 24 years later, Henry was seen reading his Bible. He allegedly said to a friend: "Here is a book worth more than all others ever printed; yet it is my misfortune never to have found time to read it. I trust in the mercy of God; it is not now too late." When his physician offered a liquid mercury preparation saying it would either cure or kill,

Henry replied: "I am thankful for the goodness of God, which, having blessed me all my life, thus permits me now to die without pain. Behold the benefit and the reality of the Christian religion to one about to die."

Alternative: * "Be thankful for the kind God who allows me to go thus painlessly."

Henry, Philip (1631-1696). English dissenting clergyman. Dying of "colic and stone," Henry said "O death, where is thy..." but death did not allow him to finish his quotation from 1 Corinthians 15:55: "… O death, where is thy victory? O death, where is thy sting?"

Henry, "The Young King" (1155-1183). Second son of English King Henry II. Prince Henry, with other members of his family, rebelled against his father's rule. Dying of dysentery, the contrite Henry asked: "O, tie a rope around my body, and draw me out of bed, and lay me down upon the ashes, that I may die with prayers to God in a repentant manner."

Hepburn, Audrey, born Audrey Ruston (1929-1993). Belgian-born screen actress and humanitarian. Dying of abdominal cancer, to her unmarried sons: "Fellas, your old Ma needs a kiss. Forget the movies- you two are the best work I ever did. I always thought I'd make a wonderful granny. But I guess God had other plans." Commenting about her humanitarian work with UNICEF, she said: "Remember the children when I'm gone. Please make sure those poor starving babies get enough to eat."

Heraclitus of Ephesus (c. 535-c. 475 BCE). Greek philosopher. Dying of "dropsy," Heraclitus asked his physicians for relief from the accumulated body fluids, saying: "Can you turn rainy weather into dry?" Unable to make them understand, the philosopher shut himself in a stable and rubbed dung over his body hoping that it would help extract the abnormal fluids. The remedy failed.

Herbert, Edward (1583-1648). English statesman, soldier, writer, poet and philosopher. When Herbert received an answer about the current time, he replied: "Then an hour hence I shall depart." He turned his head and "expired serenely."

Herbert, George (1593-1633). Welsh-born clergyman and poet. Dying of tuberculosis, Herbert told an acquaintance: "My dear friend, I am sorry I have nothing to present to my merciful God but sin and misery; but the first is pardoned and a few hours will now put a period to the latter, for I shall suddenly go hence and be no more seen." He later said: "I am now ready to die. Lord, forsake me not, now my strength faileth me [perhaps a reference to Psalm 71: 9]; but grant me mercy for the merits of my Jesus. And now Lord, Lord, now receive my soul."

Herbert, Sidney (1810-1861). English statesman. Dying of kidney failure, the 50 year-old Herbert summed-up his life: "Well, this is the end. I have had a life of great happiness. A short one perhaps, but an active one. I have not done all I wished, but I have tried to do my best."

Herder, Johann (1744-1803). German philosopher, clergyman, poet and writer. During his last hours, Herder implored his physician: "My friend, my dearest friend, preserve me still, if that is possible." His last words were: "Refresh me with a great thought."

Hernandez, Jesse (1964-2012). American criminal, executed by lethal injection for the murder of a 10 month-old child: "... God bless everybody. Continue to walk with God." He then shouted: "Go Cowboys! [his favorite professional football team]." As the drugs took effect, Hernandez spoke to the assembled witnesses: "Love y'all, man... Thank you. I can feel it, taste it. It's not bad."

Herndon, William (1813-1857). U.S. naval officer. The steamship SS *Central America*, captained by Herndon, was caught in a severe storm off the North Carolina coast. As the ship sank, he shouted: "I will never leave the ship." A number of passengers were rescued by nearby vessels.

Herrera, Leonel (1947-1993). Hispanic American criminal. Convicted of murders possibly committed by a relative, Herrera spoke before his execution by lethal injection in a Texas prison: "I am innocent, innocent, innocent. Make no mistake about this; I owe society nothing. Continue the struggle for human rights, helping those who are innocent, especially

Mr. [Gary] Graham (above). I am an innocent man, and something very wrong is taking place tonight. May God bless you all. I am ready."

Herrick, Myron (1854-1929). American politician and diplomat. When told by his doctors (some say his wife) that he would be "all right," Herrick replied: "Do you really think so? Well, I will do my best." He died of a heart attack shortly thereafter.

Hervey, James (1714-1758). English clergyman and writer. On his deathbed, Hervey proclaimed: "How thankful am I for death. It is the passage to the Lord and Giver of eternal life. O welcome, welcome death... Lord, now lettest Thou Thy servant depart in peace, for mine eyes have seen Thy salvation!" His last words: "Precious salvation."

Herzl, Theodor (1860-1904). Hungarian-born Zionist leader and journalist. Dying of heart disease and pneumonia, Herzl told his children and mother: "Well, my dear ones, you saw me, and I saw you. Now go back."

Hessus, Helius (1488-1540). German poet and educator. Hessus' last wish: "I want to ascend to my Lord."

Hewart, Gordon (1870-1943). Lord chief justice of England. Disturbed by a bird outside, Hewart exclaimed: "D*** it! There's that cuckoo again!"

Hewitt, Abram (1822-1903). American politician, industrialist and philanthropist. While hospitalized during his last days, Hewitt removed the supplemental oxygen tube and exclaimed: "And now, I am officially dead!"

Hexum, Jon-Erik (1957-1984). American actor who played a role in the TV series *Cover Up*. When filming of a segment was delayed, the actor jokingly said "Can you believe this crap?" He then placed a gun loaded with blanks to his temple and said: "Let's see if I get myself with this one." The blast concussion from the discharge was severe enough to shatter underlying bone, producing a fatal brain injury.

Hey, Wilhelm (1789-1854). German clergyman, hymnodist and poet. Hey wrote a last poem for his two nurses: "So you my nurses dear/ In these last difficult days,/ In bitter parting here,/ Show me your loving ways./ The love so tenderly given/ And yet such strength behind,/ A brief foretaste of heaven,/ Is what it brings to mind."

Heyburn, Weldon (1852-1912). American politician who became a U.S. senator. Dying in office: "I have lived my life as best I could within human limitations. I am worn out in the service of a great cause."

Heylin, Peter (1600-1662). English theologian and church historian. Heylin spoke to his minister: "I know it is church time with you, and I know this is Ascension Day. I am ascending to the Church Triumphant. I go to my God and Savior, unto joys celestial and to hallelujahs eternal."

Hick, Samuel (1758-1829). English clergyman. Realizing the end was near, Hick instructed those at his bedside: "As soon as I die, you must take the body down and lay it out; for you will not be able to get the coffin either down-stairs or out of the windows." As death approached: "I am going; get the sheets ready."

Hickock, Richard (1931-1965). American criminal. In 1959, Hickock and his co-conspirator Perry Smith (below) murdered a Kansas family of four during a robbery. Their heinous crime was highlighted in Truman Capote's book *In Cold Blood*. On the gallows before he was hanged, Hickock said: "I just want to say I hold no hard feelings. You people are sending me to a better world than this ever was." To four of the execution witnesses who were instrumental in his capture: "Nice to see you."

Hickok, James "Wild Bill" (1837-1876). American folk hero, lawman, gunfighter and gambler. In a last letter to his wife, Hickok wrote: "Agnes, darling, if such should be we never meet again, while firing my last shot I will gently breathe the name of my wife- Agnes- and with wishes even for my enemies, I will make the plunge and try to swim for the other shore. Wild Bill." Before he was shot dead in cold blood during a game of poker, Hickok exclaimed about a fellow player: "The old duffer- he broke me on the hand." His last hand of cards contained pairs of black eights and aces, later referred to as the "dead man's hand."

Hicks, Robert (1957-2004). American criminal, executed by lethal injection for the murder of a 28 year-old woman: "I would like to apologize for everything I did. I'm sorry. God forgive me. Come get me, Warden."

Hicks, William "Bill" (1961-1994). American comedian. Dying of pancreatic cancer, Hicks spoke these words on Valentine's Day, 1994: "I've said all I have to say." He remained mute during his last 12 days.

High, Jared (1985-1998). American middle school student. High, a 13 year-old victim of bullying by classmates in his school, committed suicide by gunshot while on the phone with his father. His last word before pulling the trigger: "Dad, I called to say goodbye."

Hilario, Saint Jaime (1889-1937). Martyred Spanish member of the Brothers of Christian Schools. Arrested by anticlerical forces during the Spanish Civil War, Hilario was summarily sentenced to die by firing squad: "To die for Christ, my young friends, is to live."

Hilarion, Saint (died 304). One of the martyrs of Abithina, a Roman province in Africa. When a Roman official ordered Hilarion to renounce Christianity on threats that his nose and ears would be severed, the young man replied: "Do as you please. I am a Christian. Thanks be to God!"

Hilary, Saint (died c. 368). Bishop of Poitiers in west-central France. "Soul, thou hast served Christ these seventy years, and art thou afraid to die? Go out, soul, go out!"

Hill, Ambrose (1825-1865). Confederate general during the U.S. Civil War. In an encounter with Union soldiers, Hill shouted: "Surrender, or I will shoot you. A body of troops are advancing on our left, and you will have to surrender anyway!" He then advanced and demanded: "Surrender your arms!" They declined and shot him dead.

Hill, Benjamin (1823-1882). American politician who became a member of the U.S. senate. Dying of tongue cancer, the hoarse senator was able to articulate his last words clearly: "Almost home!"

Hill, Daniel (1821-1889). Confederate general in the U.S. Civil War and later an educator. Dying of stomach cancer, to his family: "Nearly there."

Hill, Joe, born Joel Hägglund (1879-1915). Itinerant Swedish-American labor leader. Convicted of murdering a Salt Lake City, Utah grocer, Hill was condemned to die by firing squad. Shortly before his execution, he wrote a letter to Bill Haywood, leader of the Industrial Workers of the World: "Goodbye Bill. I will die like a true blue rebel. Don't waste any time in mourning. Organize. It is a hundred miles from here to Wyoming. Could you arrange to have my body hauled to the state line to be buried? I don't want to be found dead in Utah" When the firing squad was given the command: "Ready, aim..." Hill shouted: "Fire... go on and fire!" Instead of Wyoming, his body was shipped to Chicago where it was cremated.

Alternative: * "I will show you how to die. I will show you how to die. I have a clear conscience. I am going now, boys. Goodbye. Goodbye, boys. Fire! Go on and fire!"

Hill, Paul (1954-2003). American pro-life advocate, executed by lethal injection for the murder of an abortion clinic doctor and his bodyguard: "Two of the last things I'd like to say: if you believe abortion is a lethal force, you should oppose the force and do what you have to do to stop it. May God help you to protect the unborn as you would want to be protected."

Hill, Rowland (1744-1833). English revivalist preacher and hymnodist. Hill's reported last words came from one of his hymns: "And when I'm to die, / Receive me, I'll cry; / For Jesus hath loved me, / I cannot tell why…"

Alternative: * "Christ also hath once suffered for sins, the just for the unjust, that he might bring us unto God."

Hill, Ureli Corelli (1802-1875). American musician who was the first conductor of the New York Philharmonic Orchestra. Because of failed business ventures, Hill committed suicide by a drug overdose. In a note left for his wife, he asked: "Why should or how can a man exist and be powerless to earn means for his family?"

Alternative: * "Ha ha! I go, the sooner the better!"

Hillary, Richard (1919-1943). Australian-born British RAF aviator. During WWII, Hillary was shot down by an enemy pilot over the North Sea and subsequently was rescued by a nearby boat. Despite significant burns on his face and hands, he was allowed to return to service. Hillary later died in a crash during a training flight. Asked over the intercom if he were happy, he replied before the fatal plunge: "Moderately, I am continuing to orbit."

Hillman, Sidney (1887-1946). Lithuanian-born American labor leader. Dying of a heart attack, Hillman complained: "I feel like hell. I'm going to lie down again."

Hilton, Conrad (1887-1979). American businessman who founded the Hilton hotel chain. When asked if he had any last words of wisdom, Hilton allegedly quipped: "Leave the shower curtain on the inside of the tub."

Hiltzheimer, Jacob (c. 1729-1798). German-born Philadelphia politician and diarist. Hiltzheimer's final diary entry noted the epidemic of yellow fever that took his life approximately 10 days later: "Deaths today- 66."

Himmler, Heinrich (1900-1945). High-ranking Nazi leader who supervised Adolf Hitler's extermination camps. After his capture by British forces during the last days of WWII, Himmler tried to conceal his identity but eventually revealed his name: "I am Heinrich Himmler." Later, when told to undress, he failed to understand the order, stating: "He [the captor] doesn't know who I am." While being searched, Himmler bit into a concealed cyanide capsule and died before his interrogation could begin.

Hindenburg, Paul von (1847-1934). German military leader and president of the German Republic until Adolf Hitler's ascension to power. Dying of lung cancer, Hindenburg referred to death as his "Friend Hein," a colloquialism for death. At the end he spoke to his doctor: "It's all right, Sauerbruch. Now tell Friend Hein he can come in."

Hinojosa, Richard (1961-2006). American criminal, executed by lethal injection for the rape and murder of a Texas woman: "Kick the tires and light the fire, warden. I'm going home to see my son and my mom."

Hitchcock, Alfred (1899-1980). British-born film director and producer, best-known for his suspense and psychological movies. Dying of kidney failure, Hitchcock pontificated: "One never knows the ending. One has to die to know exactly what happens after death, although Catholics have their hopes."

Hitler, Adolf (1889-1945). Austrian-born Nazi dictator during WWII. Hitler made his Personal Testament shortly before committing suicide: "… My wife and I choose to die in order to escape the shame of overthrow or capitulation. It is our wish for our bodies to be cremated immediately on the place where I have performed the greater part of my daily work during the twelve years of my service to my people." The conclusion of his Political Testament: "… Above all I charge leaders of the nation and those under them to scrupulous observance of the laws of race and to merciless opposition to the universal poisoner of all peoples, international Jewry." When advised to flee in the face of advancing Russian troops, Hitler spoke to his pilot, Hans Baur: "One must have the courage to face the consequences. I am ending it all here! I know that by tomorrow millions of people will curse me. Fate wanted it that way." Then: "I want them to write on my tombstone: 'He was the victim of his generals!'" When told that the wife of the propaganda minister Joseph Goebbels wished to see him, Hitler replied: "I don't want to speak to her anymore." Moments later he shot himself.

Alternative: * To his secretary, Gertraud Junge: "Death for me means only freedom from worries and a very difficult life. I have been deceived by my best friends and I have experienced treason... Now it has gone so far. It is finished. Goodbye."

Hitler, Eva, née Braun (1912-1945). Adolf Hitler's mistress and later his wife. Before she withdrew with her husband and took poison, Braun spoke to a secretary: "Greet Munich [her birthplace] for me. Take my fur coat. I've always liked well-dressed people."

Hobbes, Thomas (1588-1679). English philosopher and political theorist, best-known for his book *Leviathan*. Dying of a stroke, Hobbes stated: "If I had the whole world, I would give it to live one day. I shall be glad to find a hole to creep out of the world at. About to take a leap in the dark."

Alternatives: * "I say again, if I had the whole world at my disposal, I would give it to live one day. I am about to take a leap into the dark."
* "I am taking a fearful leap in the dark."
* "Now am I about to take my last voyage, a great leap in the dark."
* "I am going to take a great leap into obscurity."

Hoche, Lazare (1768-1797). French revolutionary army general. Dying of tuberculosis, Hoche said: "Goodbye, my friends, goodbye. Tell the government to keep a sharp eye in the direction of Belgium. Goodbye, my friends."

Hodge, Charles (1797-1878). American theologian and educator. Toward the end, to his daughter: "Why should you grieve, daughter? To be absent from the body is to be with the Lord, to be with the Lord is to see the Lord, to see the Lord is to be like Him." Later: "My work is done. The pins of the tabernacle are taken out [perhaps a reference to Exodus 35:18]." Shortly before he died, Hodge tried to repeat a stanza from the hymn "Faith in Christ...:" "A guilty, weak, and helpless worm, on Thy kind arms I fall..." His wife had to finish the last lines. As he died: "Say Jesus."

Hodges, Gilbert "Gil" (1924-1972). American major league professional baseball player and manager. Asked about the time for a dinner reservation with one of his coaches, the 47 year-old Hodges replied: "Let's say, 7:30." He then fell dead from a massive heart attack.

Hodgson, Benjamin (1848-1876). American cavalry officer under the command of Major Marcus Reno during the Battle of the Little Big Horn, Montana. Wounded in both legs during Reno's retreat, Hodgson pleaded: "For God's sake, don't leave me here. I am shot through both legs" He grabbed a comrade's stirrup-strap, but was shot dead. His body was recovered and eventually returned to his family.

Hodgson, Francis (1781-1852). English clergyman, writer and close friend of Lord Byron (above). Hodgson's last utterances: "Charming." When asked what was charming: "God's mercy."

Hofer, Andreas (1767-1810). Tyrolean patriot who fought against French and Bavarian forces. Captured during his resistance, Hofer was condemned to die by firing squad. The last lines of a note written before his execution: "... To die is so easy that my eyes have no tears. I write this at five o'clock in the morning. At nine o'clock I will, with the help of all the holy people, arrive before God." Refusing to kneel before the firing squad, he remarked: "I stand in the presence of my Creator and standing I will render back my account to God who gave it. Fire!"

Alternatives: * "I will not kneel. Fire!"
* "Goodbye, wretched world. This death is easy. Fire!"

Hoffa, James "Jimmy" (1913-disappeared 1975). American labor union leader. Released from prison after a conviction for jury tampering and fraud, Hoffa was banned from any union activity. When he ignored this restriction and sought to regain a leadership position in the teamsters union, he mysteriously disappeared. Rumors subsequently circulated that he had been murdered. Some time before his disappearance, Hoffa declared: "I don't need bodyguards." To his wife by telephone while waiting for associates at a suburban Detroit restaurant: "Where the hell is Giacalone [a local mafia member]? I'm waiting for him."

Alternatives: * "I don't need no bodyguards."
* "Has Tony Giacalone called?"
* "I wonder where the hell Tony is? I'm waiting for him."
* "Where the hell is Giacalone? He didn't show."

Hoffmann, E.T.A. (1776-1822). German writer and composer. Hoffmann's stories inspired Offenbach's opera, *The Tales of Hoffmann* and Tchaikovsky's *Nutcracker Ballet.* Having acquired syphilis during his sexually active days, Hoffmann gradually wasted away as the disease progressed. When he lost sensation from the neck down in the late stage of his infection, the writer told his physician: "It will soon be over now; I feel no more pain." He died the next day with these parting words to his wife: "We must, then, think of God also."

Höfle, Hermann (1911-1962). Austrian-born Nazi military leader who participated in the deportation and extermination programs during WWII. Although he escaped punishment immediately after the war ended, Höfle eventually was captured in 1961 and scheduled for trial. He committed suicide by hanging while in prison. His parting words: "Dear Germany."

Hog, James (1799-1858). Scottish esquire. Throughout his life, Hog made it known that he wished to utter the following words on his deathbed: "Lord Jesus, receive my spirit. Thou art my only hope." When the end approached, he was unable to speak. By pointing to a printed alphabet with a reed in his mouth, he spelled: "I am looking to the Savior. My only hope is in Jesus." After indicating that he wanted to return to bed, Hog died peacefully.

Hogg, Ima (1882-1975). American philanthropist and art collector. Dying from complications of an automobile accident, Hogg incorrectly predicted: "It's going to be all right."

Hogg, James (1770-1835). Scottish writer and poet. Commenting on severe hiccuping (singultus) complicating his liver disease, Hogg complained: "It was a reproach to the faculty that they could not cure the hiccup." Seeing that his end was near, he asked his wife to stay at his bedside: "It is likely you may never need to do it again."

Hokusai, Katsushika (1760-1849). Japanese artist. Toward the end, Hokusai lamented: "If only Heaven will give me just another ten years... Just another five more years, then I could become a real painter."

Alternatives: * "If heaven had only granted me five more years, I could have become a real painter."

* "If Heaven would only give me ten more years... if Heaven would only give me five more years of life... I could become a truly great painter."

Holbrooke, Richard (1941-2010). U.S. ambassador to the United Nations. Before surgery for an aortic tear, Holbrooke said to his doctor: "You've got to end this war in Afghanistan." He did not survive the operation.

Holiday, Billie, born Eleanora Fagan (1915-1959). American jazz singer. Dying from complications of cirrhosis and drug abuse, Holiday admonished her medical attendants: "Don't be in such a hurry."

Holliday, John "Doc" (1851-1887). American dentist, gambler and gunslinger who fought alongside the Earp brothers (above) at the O.K. Corral shootout in 1881. Holliday hoped that he would die in a fight or "with his boots on." Instead, he died in a hotel bed from complications of tuberculosis. His last words were uttered after seeing his feet with his boots off: "D*****! Put them back on. This is funny."

Holloway, John (died1807). English murderer. Holloway and a co-conspirator were convicted of the robbery and murder of a wayfarer. On the gallows, he remonstrated: "I am innocent, innocent by God! Innocent, innocent, innocent! Gentlemen, no verdict, no verdict, no verdict! Gentlemen! Innocent, innocent!" A large crowd estimated in the thousands assembled to watch the executions and scores died in the resultant crush.

Holmes, Burton (1870-1958). American traveler and lecturer. Envisioning heaven as the ultimate lecture, Holmes declared: "How I could pack them in with that one."

Holmes, John (1812-1899). American lawyer and brother of the physician Oliver Wendell Holmes, Sr. (below). On his deathbed, Holmes had lain mute and motionless for a long period. When the assembled felt he had expired, his nurse felt his lower extremities and remarked that no one died with warm feet. Holmes roused and referred to the English martyr (below), who was burned at the stake in 1555: "John Rogers did!"

Holmes, John Maurice (died 1933). American criminal. In 1933, the scion of a prominent San Jose, California businessman was kidnapped and later murdered. Holmes and a co-conspirator subsequently were taken into custody for the crime. Before the suspects could be tried, a lynch mob hanged them vigilante-style. As the mob dragged them to the execution site, Holmes pleaded: "For God's sake, give me a chance."

Holmes, Oliver Wendell, Sr. (1809-1894). American physician, educator, poet and author. Holmes spoke to his son who helped him to a favorite chair: "That is better, thank you." Later in the afternoon, he died quietly.

Holmes, Oliver Wendell, Jr. (1841-1935). U.S. Supreme Court justice. In a 1924 letter, Holmes related: "Why should I fear death? I have seen him often. When he comes he'll seem like an old friend. If I were to die, my last words would be: 'Have faith and pursue the unknown end.'" Dying of pneumonia nearly a decade later, Holmes' final words were quite different. Before he was placed in an oxygen tent for the last time, the jurist exclaimed: "Lot of d*** foolery."

Alternative: * "It's a lot of d***** foolery."

Holst, Gustav (1874-1934). English composer, best-known for his orchestral suite *The Planets*. Dying from complications of ulcer surgery, Holst penned his last note: "And I wish myself the joy of your Fellowship at Whitsuntide [the Christian festival seven weeks after Easter]."

Holtby, Winifred (1898-1935). English writer, best-known for her book *South Riding*. Dying of kidney failure, Holtby spoke to her mother about her fiancé. "Mummie, when I'm better, [Harry Pearson] and I are going to get married. It's just an understanding between us- not really an engagement. You don't mind, do you, darling? Not an engagement, just an understanding."

Holton, Daryl (1961-2007). American criminal, electrocuted for the murder of his children. Holton responded to the warden who asked for any last words: "Um, yeah... two words: I do."

Hölty, Ludwig (1748-1776). German poet. Dying of tuberculosis, Hölty foretold his end: "I am very ill. Send for Zimmermann. In fact, I think I'll die today."

Hood, Edwin (1820-1885). English clergyman and writer. Hood's last words: "Oh God! Oh God! My wife! My wife!"

Hood, Thomas (1799-1845). English poet, humorist and editor. Dying of "consumption," Hood humorously commented about a plaster applied to his foot: "There's very little meat for the mustard." To his wife: "Remember Jane, that I forgive all, *all*, as I hope to be forgiven." Hood's last words were: "O Lord, say 'Arise, take up thy cross and follow me [possibly referring to Mathew 16:24].' Dying... dying..."

Hook, Walter (1798-1875). English clergyman and writer. Hook lamented: "I am old, 78, and very infirm. My contemporaries are passing away and I expect soon to receive my summons. Pray for me." Hook miscalculated his age by one year.

Hooker, Richard (c. 1553-1600). English theologian. To his physician: "Good Doctor, God has heard my daily petition, for I am at peace with all men, and He is at peace with me. From that blessed assurance, I feel that inward joy, which this world can neither give, nor take from me. My conscience beareth me this witness, and this witness makes the thoughts of death joyful. I could wish to live to do the Church more service, but cannot hope it, for my days are past as a shadow that returns not."

Hooker, Thomas (1586-1647). English-born Puritan clergyman who settled in America. When told that he would reap the rewards of his labors, Hooker replied: "Brother, I am going to receive mercy."

Hooper, John (1495-1555). English clergyman. Denounced as a heretic for his reformist views, Hooper was condemned to die by burning at the stake. Because the kindling was not properly aged, the flames proved to be inadequate initially. The clergyman responded: "For God's love, good people, let me have more fire." As the flames later consumed him, Hooper cried: "Lord Jesu, have mercy upon me! Lord Jesu, have mercy upon me! Lord Jesus, receive my spirit!"

Hoover, Herbert (1874-1964). Thirty-first U.S. president. Hospitalized for internal bleeding, Hoover responded to his nurse who had announced the visit of a good friend: "Lewis Strauss is one of my best friends."

Hope, Bob, born Leslie Townes Hope (1903-2003). British-born comedian, actor and humanitarian. Sometime before his death, Hope's wife asked where he would like to be buried. The comedian quipped: "Surprise me."

Hope, John (1868-1936). American educator and civil rights activist. Dying of pneumonia, Hope said: "I'd like to live long enough to tell my successor what I'm trying to do."

Hopkins, Gerard (1844-1889). English poet, writer and clergyman. Dying of typhoid fever, Hopkins exulted after receiving Last Rites: "I am so happy, I am so happy. I loved my life."

Hopkins, Harry (1890-1946). Aide to U.S. President Franklin Roosevelt. Dying of stomach cancer, Hopkins remarked: "You can't beat destiny."

Hopkins, John Henry (1792-1868). Irish-born Episcopal bishop of Vermont. "I feel easier."

Hopkins, Johns (1795-1873). American businessman, philanthropist and founder of the university and hospital in Baltimore that bear his name. To his nephew, Hopkins said: "Joe, it is very hard to break up an old habit. I've been living for seventy-eight years now and I find it hard to make a change in my ways."

Hopkins, Samuel (1721-1803). American clergyman, theologian and abolitionist. On his deathbed: "My anchor is well-cast and my ship, though weather-beaten, will outride the storm." To one of the comforters who asked why he groaned: "It is only my body; all is right in my soul." To a visitor: "And now I am going to die, and I am glad of it."

Horn, Thomas "Tom" (1860-1903). American Old West scout, lawman and hired gunman. Convicted of murdering a 14 year-old boy, Horn was sentenced to die by hanging. While waiting for the trap to open, he spoke to an acquaintance: "Joe, they tell me you're married now. I hope you're doing well. Treat her right..."

Horney, Karen (1885-1952). German-born American psychoanalyst. Dying of cancer, Horney expressed her feelings: "I am at last content to be leaving. There is just no point going on."

Hotman, William (died 1781). American Revolutionary War leader. Hotman died of bayonet wounds as he extinguished a fuse lit by the British to blow up Fort Griswold at Groton, Connecticut. To a wounded comrade: "We will endeavor to crawl to this line. We will completely wet the powder with our blood. Thus will we, with the life that remains in us, save the fort and the magazine and perhaps a few of our comrades who are only wounded."

Alternative: * "Let us endeavor to crawl to that train of powder, and wet it with our blood, and thus save the fort and some of our friends who may be only wounded."

Houdetot, Vicomtesse d' (1758-1780). French noblewoman. Summing up her 22 years, Houdetot said: "I regret my life."

Houdini, Harry, born Erik Weisz (1874-1926). Hungarian-born American magician, escape artist and actor. While on tour, Houdini developed peritonitis from a ruptured appendix. Toward the end, he said: "I'm tired of fighting, Dash [his brother's nickname]. I guess this thing is going to get me." Several days before his death, Houdini was struck several times in his abdomen, but opinions differ whether the blows exacerbated his developing illness.

Hough, John (1651-1743). Bishop of Oxford and later Worcester, England. To friends around his deathbed: "We part to meet again, I hope in endless joys."

Houghton, Saint John (c. 1487-1535). Martyred prior of the Charterhouse monastery in London. Houghton was hanged, drawn and quartered for his refusal to sign the Oath of Supremacy and reject his Catholic religion. At the scaffold: "I call Almighty God to witness... that being here to die, I declare that it is from no obstinate rebellious spirit that I do not obey the king, but because I fear to offend the Majesty of God... Rather than disobey the Church, I am ready to suffer. Pray for me and have mercy on my brethren, of whom I have been the unworthy prior." As the executioner prepared to rip out his heart, Houghton cried: "Good Jesu, what will you do with my heart?"

Housman, Alfred (1859-1936). English poet and educator, best-known for his collection of poems *A Shropshire Lad*. Housman spoke to his doctor who had told him a joke: "Yes, that's a good one, and tomorrow I shall be telling it again on the Golden Floor!"

Housman, Robert (1759-1838). English clergyman and theologian. When Housman received a bouquet of violets, he sent his appreciation to the sender: "I shall never again see the spot where those flowers grew. Give him my best thanks for the present."

Houston, Samuel "Sam" (1793-1863). American soldier and politician who played a prominent role in Texas' progression to statehood. Dying of pneumonia, Houston spoke to his son-in-law: "Charlie, have you an American flag? Bring it out. I want to die under its glorious folds. I am sorry that it is the will of God that I cannot see that flag float again. Do you be faithful and true to it forever." A few moments later, he exulted to his wife: "Texas... Texas... Margaret..."

How, William (1823-1897). English bishop and hymnodist. To his family: "Goodnight, I don't want anything, thank you."

Howard, Catherine, Queen of England (c. 1520-1542). Fifth wife of King Henry VIII. Catherine was charged with infidelity to her king, a treasonable offense at the time, and sentenced to death by beheading. On the scaffold, she allegedly said to the executioner: "Pray hasten thy office... I die a Queen, but I would rather die the wife of Culpeper [her supposed former lover]. God have mercy on my soul. Good people, I beg of you pray for me." Catherine's illicit lover later suffered the same fate.

Howard, John (1726-1790). English champion of prison reform and philanthropist. Before dying of typhus while visiting what is now the Ukraine, Howard gave instructions for the interment of his body: "There is a spot near the village of Dauphiny; this would suit me nicely. You know it well, for I have often said that I should like to be buried there. Let me beg of you, as you value your old friend, not to suffer any pomp to be used at my funeral, nor any monument nor monumental inscription whatsoever, to mark where I am laid. But lay me quietly in the earth, place a sundial over my grave, and let me be forgotten." When told that his ailing son was improving: "Is not this comfort for a dying father?" Howard's requests apparently fell on deaf ears. He was buried in an elaborate ceremony on the shore of the Black Sea. Several monuments were erected to his memory in England and elsewhere.

Howard, Joseph "Ragtime Joe" (c. 1896-1924). American gangster. When Howard roughed up one of Al Capones's associates, Capone confronted the gangster who replied: "Aw, g'wan back to your girls, you dago pimp." Capone put a gun to Howard's cheek and shot him dead.

Howard, Moe, born Moses Harry Horwitz (1897-1975). American actor, best-known as a member of the Three Stooges comedy team. Dying of lung cancer, Howard telephoned one of his former partners: "I've been really sick lately, so I'm sorry that I haven't answered yours and Ernie's letters, but I think about you daily."

Howard, Oliver (1830-1909). American military leader during the U.S. Civil War and later, the Western Theater. Suffering a probable heart attack, Howard said to his son (some say his doctor): "Someday it [his heart] will just stop, and I will be on the other shore."

Howard, Robert (1906-1936). American author who created the character Conan the Barbarian. Depression and irresolvable stress led Howard to end his life with a gunshot to the head. His suicide note read: "All fled, all done, so lift me on the pyre; the feast is over, and the lamps expire."

Howard, William, Viscount of Stafford (1614-1680). English nobleman. Howard was accused of plotting to kill King Charles II. Although the charges probably were false, he, nevertheless, was convicted of treason and sentenced to die by beheading. At the place of execution: "This block will be my pillow, and I shall repose there well, without pain, grief or fear." When the executioner asked the condemned man for forgiveness, Howard replied: "I do forgive you."

Howe, Julia Ward (1819-1910). American suffragette, abolitionist, author and poet who wrote the lyrics to "The Battle Hymn of the Republic." Dying of pneumonia, Howe announced: "God will help me. I am so tired."

Hubbard, Elbert (1856-1915). American writer, publisher, artist and philosopher. Hubbard and his wife drowned when the RMS *Lusitania* sank after being torpedoed by a German U-boat near the Irish coast. Before the vessel went down, Hubbard remarked: "Well, Jack, they have got us. They are a d***** sight worse than I ever thought they were."

Hudson, Rock, born Roy Harold Scherer, Jr. (1925-1985). American movie actor. Dying of AIDS, Hudson replied to a friend, Tom Clark, who asked if he wanted another cup of coffee: "No, I don't believe so."

Hügel, Friedrich von (1852-1925). Italian-born theologian of Austrian and Scottish ancestry. Dying, Hügel asked his nurse to: "Pray for me."

Hugh of Lincoln, Saint (c. 1135-1200). French-born English bishop. When someone at his bedside said: "Beg of God to send your widowed church a worthy pastor," Hugh replied: "May God grant it."

Hughes, Charles (1862-1948). U.S. secretary of state and U.S. Supreme Court chief justice. Gravely ill, Hughes opined: "I've been the luckiest man in the world. I've had everything. I've drunk the wine of life to the bottom of the glass. Now only the dregs are left." Immediately before dying, he was asked if he wished to see his children. He replied: "You bet I do!" but changed his mind a few moments later: "I would rather be alone."

Hughes, John (1797-1864). Irish-born Roman Catholic archbishop of New York. When told that his doctors held no hope for recovery: "Did they say so?"

Hugo, Victor (1802-1885). French writer, poet, dramatist and statesman, best-known for his novels *Les Misérables* and *The Hunchback of Notre-Dame*. Dying of pneumonia, Hugo allegedly exclaimed: "This is the fight of day and night. I see black light." He then complained: "Ah, me! How long death is in coming!" Before descending into a mortal coma, Hugo extended a hand to his granddaughter saying: "Goodbye, Jeanne, goodbye."

Alternatives: * "I see the black light."
* "Now day and night are locked in combat. I see black light."
* "Here is the struggle between day and night."

Hull, Isaac (1773-1843). American admiral who commanded the naval vessel "Old Ironsides" during the War of 1812. Hull's last words: "I strike [lower] my flag."

Alternative: * "Bury me in my uniform."

Humbert I, also Umberto I (1844-1900). King of Italy. Mortally wounded by an assassin's gunshot as he left a sporting event, Humbert said to his aides: "It is nothing." He died before medical help arrived.

Humbert II, also Umberto II (1904–1983). Italy's last king. Humbert reigned slightly over a month before the monarchy was abolished. Dying in exile, his last utterance was: "*Italia*."

Humboldt, Friedrich von (1769-1859). German explorer and naturalist who wrote extensively about his travels in Latin America. As the sun streamed into his room, Humboldt remarked: "How grand these rays! They seem to beckon earth to heaven!"

Alternatives: * "How grand is the sunlight. It seems to beckon earth to heaven."
* "How grand those rays. They seem to beckon me to heaven."

Hume, David (1711-1776). Scottish philosopher and historian. During the final days in his struggle with cancer, Hume proclaimed in a letter to a friend: "My distemper is a diarrhœa, or disorder in my bowels, which has been gradually undermining me these two years, but within these six months has been visibly hastening me to my end. I see death approach gradually, without any anxiety or regret. I salute you with great affection and regard for the last time." Near the end, Hume wrote: "I go very fast to decline, and last night had a small fever, which I hoped might put a quicker period to this tedious illness; but unluckily it has in a great measure gone off… Dr. Black can better inform you concerning the degree of strength, which may from time to time remain with me. Adieu." When his physician mentioned an improvement in his condition, the philosopher replied: "Doctor, as I believe you would not choose to tell anything but the truth, you had better say that I am dying as fast as my enemies, if I have any, could wish, and as easily and cheerfully as my best friends could desire."

Humphrey, Hubert (1911-1978). U.S. vice-president in the Lyndon Johnson Administration. Dying of cancer, Humphrey said to a friend: "I feel I have so much to do yet."

Hunt, James (1784-1859). English poet, editor and writer. As he lay dying, Hunt opined: "I don't think I shall get over this." Some say his last utterance was: "Deep dream of peace." These words came from a line in his poem "Abou Ben Adhem:" "Abou Ben Adhem (may his tribe increase!). Awoke one night from a deep dream of peace..."

Hunt, Vincent (1823-1852). English writer, son of the poet James Hunt (above). After taking a cup of cold water, Hunt said: "I drink the morning."

Alternative: "I drink to the morning."

Hunter, William (1535-1555). English Protestant martyr. Because Hunter refused to accept current Catholic dogma, he was condemned as a heretic and sentenced to burn at the stake. Toward the end, his brother said: "William, think of the holy passion of Christ, and be not afraid of death." The doomed man answered: "I am not afraid." As the flames consumed him, Hunter prayed: "Lord, Lord, Lord, receive my spirit!"

Hunter, William (1718-1783). Scottish-born physician and anatomist. On his deathbed, Hunter proclaimed to a friend: "If I had the strength to hold a pen, I would write down how easy and pleasant a thing it is to die."

Huntington, Selena (1707-1791). English Methodist leader. At the end, Huntington proclaimed: "My work is done; I have nothing to do but to go to my Father."

Husband, Richard "Rick" (1957-2003). American commander of the U.S. space shuttle *Columbia* that disintegrated after reentering the earth's atmosphere with the loss of all seven aboard. Moments before the shuttle broke apart, Husband radioed: "And Hous[ton, Texas]... [unintelligible]." An astronaut at ground control in Houston communicated directly with the space shuttle: "... And Columbia, Houston. We see your tire pressure message and we did not copy your last." Husband responded: "And Houston, roger. Bu ..." These were the last words transmitted from the doomed craft.

Huss, John, also Jan or John Hus (c.1369-1415). Martyred Bohemian reformer. Because of his dissention against doctrines of the Catholic Church, Huss was convicted of heresy and condemned to die by burning at the stake. As he approached the execution site: "Lord Jesus, have mercy on me. Into thy hands, O God, I commend my spirit." When asked to recant his views: "No, I never preached any doctrine of an evil tendency; and what I taught with my lips, I now seal with my blood." To his executioner: "You are now going to burn a goose, but in a century you will have a swan whom you can neither roast or boil." As additional brush was added to the fire, he commented: "What holy simplicity" As the flames consumed him, the martyr sang: "Jesus thou Son of David, have mercy on me." Some say Huss died repeating the *Kyrie Eleison* (Lord, have mercy).

Alternative: * "Into Thy hands, Lord, I commit my spirit. Thou hast redeemed me, O most good and faithful God! Lord Jesus Christ, assist me, that with a firm and present mind, by Thy most powerful grace, I may undergo this most cruel death, to which I am condemned for preaching Thy most holy Gospel. Amen." When a chain was placed around his neck:

"Welcome this chain, for Christ's sake!" As the flames consumed him: "Lord Jesus, Thou Son of the living God, have mercy on me!"

Hussein, Saddam (1937-2006). Iraqi dictator, convicted and hanged for crimes committed against humanity during his rule. On the gallows, Hussein began to recite the final Muslim prayer to the effect: "I witness there is no god but Allah and that Mohammed is His messenger. I witness there is no god but Allah and that Mohammed…" At this point, the trap door opened.

Alternatives: * "I bear witness that there is no god but God and I testify that Mohammed is the Messenger of God. I bear witness that there is no god but God and I testify that Mohammed..."
* "Down with the traitors, the Americans, the spies and the Persians."

Husserl, Edmund (1859-1938). German philosopher and educator. Having undergone a religious conversion during his last days, Husserl talked at length about his experience. However, several days before dying, he remained silent. To his nurse before expiring, the philosopher said: "Oh, I have seen something so wonderful! Quick, write it down!" By the time she returned with writing materials, he was dead.

Hutchinson, Thomas (1711-1780). Royal governor of Massachusetts at the time of the Boston Tea Party. Walking toward a coach, Hutchinson appeared to faint, saying: "Help me!"

Huxley, Aldous (1894-1963). English writer, best-known for his novel *Brave New World.* Dying of throat cancer, Huxley wrote on a pad: "LSD- try it- intramuscular- 100 mm [meaning micrograms]." He had used and advocated this psychedelic drug and others before his illness. His wife (some say his doctor) obliged and the writer died peacefully several hours later.

Alternatives: * "LSD, 100 µg, intramuscular."
* "LSD, 100 micrograms I.M."

Huxley, Thomas (1825-1895). British biologist, educator and grandfather of Aldous Huxley (above). Dying of heart and kidney failure, Huxley wrote to a friend: "... At present I don't feel at all like 'sending in my checks!' And without being over sanguine, I rather incline to think that my native toughness will get the best of it- albuminuria [a manifestation of his kidney ailment] or otherwise- Ever your faithful friend, T.H.H."

Hyde, Anne (c. 1637-1671). Wife of English King James II and mother of two future monarchs, Queen Mary II and Queen Anne of England. Dying of breast cancer, Hyde's clergyman asked if she continued in the truth: "What is truth... truth... truth... truth?"

Alternative: * Some say her final words were: "Duke, Duke, death is terrible. Death is very terrible"

Hyde, Edward, Earl of Clarendon (1609-1674). English nobleman. Having fallen out of favor with the English court, Hyde fled to France. Toward the end, he appealed for approval to return home to die: "Since it will be in nobody's power long to prevent me from dying, methinks the desiring a place to die in should not be thought a great presumption." Hyde died in France, but his body was interred in England.

Hyde, John (1865-1912). American missionary to India. Dying of cancer, Hyde proclaimed: "Shout the victory of Jesus Christ!"

Ibsen, Henrik (1828-1906). Norwegian writer and dramatist, best-known for his play *Peer Gynt*. After suffering a series of strokes, Ibsen spent his last few years in bed. Upon receiving a visitor, the playwright overheard his nurse remarking that he was feeling better. Ibsen quickly corrected her: "On the contrary" and later died.

Ignatius of Antioch, Saint (died c. 107). Syrian-born early Christian martyr and supposed follower of the apostle John. Condemned by Emperor Trajan for his Christian beliefs, Ignatius was transported to Rome from Syria and thrown to wild animals in the amphitheater. Before he was killed, the martyr spoke: "Let me enjoy these beasts, whom I wish much more cruel than they are, and if they will not attempt me, I will provoke and draw them by force. I am God's wheat and I am ground by the teeth of wild beasts that I may be found pure bread for Christ."

Alternatives: * "I am the wheat or grain of Christ. I shall be ground with the teeth of wild beasts that I may be found pure bread!"

* "I am the wheat of Christ. May I be ground by the teeth of beasts to become the immaculate bread of Christ."

Ignatius of Loyola, Saint (1491-1556). Spanish knight and priest who founded the Society of Jesus (Jesuits). In a message delivered to the pope by his secretary: "Tell him that my hour has come and that I ask his benediction. Tell him that if I go to a place where my prayers are of any avail, as I trust, I shall not fail to pray for him, as I have indeed unfailingly, even when I had most occasion to pray for myself."

Alternatives: * "Oh, my God."

* "Jesus."

Ilitchewski, Alexander (birth and death dates unclear). Russian poet. Ilitchewski sought the embodiment of feminine beauty during his lifetime. A line of poetry written shortly before his death possibly indicated that he had discovered it: "I have found at last the object of my love!"

Illeppy, Solyman (died 1800). Turkish assassin. The disgruntled student mortally stabbed Jean-Baptiste Kléber who commanded Napoleon's troops in Egypt. To the executioner who burned Illeppy's offending hand and impaled him in a public square: "That is good!"

Imlay, Frances "Fanny" (1794-1816). French-born illegitimate daughter of the English feminist Mary Wollstonecraft (below) and the American businessman Gilbert Imlay. The depressed Fanny left a suicide note before taking an overdose of laudanum: "I have long determined that the best thing I could do was to put an end to the existence of a being whose birth was unfortunate, and whose life has only been a series of pains to those persons who have hurt their health in endeavoring to promote her welfare. Perhaps to hear of my death may give you pain, but you will soon have the blessing of forgetting that such a creature ever existed."

Impey, Elijah (1732-1809). English jurist. Impey apologized for leaning too heavily against his nurse: "Did I hurt you, my dear?"

Ingersoll, Ebon (1831-1879). Member of the U.S. House of Representatives and brother of Robert Ingersoll (below). At the end, his wife remarked: "Why, Papa, your tongue is coated- I must give you some medicine." His response: "I am better now."

Ingersoll, Robert (1833-1899). American lawyer, military officer and politician. Dying of heart failure, Ingersoll responded to his wife's query about how he felt: "Oh, better."

Ings, James (died 1820). British criminal. In 1820, Ings and other members of the "Cato Street Conspiracy" plotted to kill various government members. He and his co-conspirators were arrested before the act could be set in motion. They were convicted of treason and later hanged. Before his execution, Ings stated: "Oh! Give me death or liberty!" To the executioner: "Do it tidy." Then Ings spoke sarcastically to the local vicar: "I hope you'll give me a good character, won't you, Mr. Cotton."

Innocent X (1574-1655). Pope from 1644 until his death. After receiving Last Rites, Innocent told one of his cardinals: "You see where the grandeurs of the sovereign pontiff must end!"

Innocent XI (1611-1689). Pope from 1676 until his death. When told that his relatives would be cared for, Innocent responded: "We have no house or family! God gave us the pontifical dignity, not for the advantage of our kindred, but for the good of the Church and nations."

Innocent XIII (1655-1724). Pope from 1721 until his death. Dying of a strangulated hernia, Innocent was urged to create more cardinals. He refused saying: "We are no longer of this world."

Irenaeus of Sirmium, Saint (died 304). Martyred Serbian bishop. When Irenaeus refused to sacrifice to pagan gods, he was beheaded. "Lord Jesus Christ, who deigned to suffer for the world's salvation, let your heavens open that your angels may take up the soul of your servant Irenaeus, who suffers all this for your name and for the people formed of your catholic church of Sirmium. I ask and implore your mercy to receive me and to strengthen them in your faith."

Irving, Edward (1792-1834). Scottish-born clergyman who was a founding member of the Catholic Apostolic Church. At the end of his life, Irving proclaimed: "If I die, I die unto the Lord. Amen."

Alternative: * "In life and in death, I am the Lord's. Amen"

Irving, Henry, born John Henry Brodribb (1838-1905). English actor, prominent during the Victorian period. While on stage, Irving suffered a stroke and died after reciting Becket's lines in Tennyson's play of the same name: "Into Thy hands, O Lord, into Thy hands."

Irving, Washington (1783-1859). American author, best-known for his short stories "The Legend of Sleepy Hollow" and "Rip Van Winkle." Irving spoke to his niece the night he died of a heart attack: "Well, I must arrange my pillows for another weary night... if this could only end!" Shortly thereafter, he uttered the word "End" and collapsed.

Alternatives: * "I have to set my pillows one more night; when will this end already?"
* "You cannot tell how I have suffered! When will this ever end?"

Irwin, Stephen "Steve" also known as The Crocodile Hunter (1962-2006). Australian adventurer and television personality. While examining a stingray during a snorkeling expedition, Irving remarked to his cameraman: "Don't worry, they usually don't swim backwards." The ray struck him in the chest with its barbed tail, inflicting a mortal injury. Irwin's final remark: "I'm dying."

Isabella I (1451-1504). Queen of Spain who with her husband Ferdinand II sponsored Christopher Columbus' voyages to the Americas. To her family, Isabella admonished: "Do not weep for me nor waste your time in fruitless prayers for my recovery, but pray rather for the salvation of my soul." She stipulated in her will: "... If the king, my lord, should chose a sepulchre in any church or monastery in any other part or place of these my kingdoms, my body may be transported thither, and buried beside the body of his highness, so that the union we have enjoyed while living, and which, through the mercy of God, we hope our souls will experience in heaven, may be represented by our bodies in the earth." Isabella's burial wishes were honored.

Isabella II (1830-1904). Queen of Spain. Dying of a chest ailment, Isabella pleaded with her son-in-law: "Take my hand and pull my right arm as hard as you can. There is something very strange in my chest. I think I am going to faint."

Isaiah (fl. 8th century BCE). Martyred Hebrew prophet. Condemned to die for heresy by the Judean King Manasseh, Isaiah's body was severed by a wooden saw. Before expiring, he spoke to fellow prophets: "Go ye to the country of Tyre and Sidon [cities in present-day Lebanon], for the Lord hath mixed the cup for me alone."

Itō, Hirobumi (1841-1909). Japanese statesman. After serving as Japan's prime minister, Itō became the resident-general of Korea following the Russo-Japanese War. He later was shot dead by a Korean dissident. When told the identity of his assailant, Itō replied: "The fellow is a fool."

Iturbide, Agustin de (see Agustin I of Mexico).

Jackson, Andrew "Old Hickory" (1767-1845). Seventh U.S. president. Dying from complications of heart failure, Jackson, a pious man, proclaimed: "My sufferings, though great, are nothing in comparison with those of my Savior, through whose death I look for everlasting life." He then spoke to those assembled around his deathbed: "What is the matter with my dear children? Have I alarmed you? Oh, don't cry! Be good children and we will all meet in heaven!"

Jackson, Helen (1830-1885). American writer and activist who worked for improved treatment of the Native American "Indian race." Dying of stomach cancer, Jackson remarked: "You know, as I lie here and fancy myself as a ghost, it doesn't seem strange or alarming."

Jackson, James (1959-2007). American criminal, condemned to die by lethal injection for the murder of three family members: "This is not the end but the beginning of a new chapter for you and I together forever. See you all later... See you all on the other side." To the warden: "Warden, murder me... I'm ready to roll. Time to get this party started."

Jackson, Joseph "Shoeless Joe" (1888-1951). American professional baseball outfielder, banned from the sport for his entanglement in the World Series "Black Sox Scandal" of 1919. During successive years, Jackson steadfastly denied any involvement in the matter. Dying of a heart attack, he spoke to his brother: "I don't deserve this thing that's happened to me. I'm about to meet the greatest umpire of all and He knows I'm innocent. Goodbye, good buddy."

Alternative: * "Buddy, I'm going to face the Umpire now. I'm not guilty of the charge."

Jackson, Michael (1958-2009). American recording artist and entertainer. During his last days, Jackson was given the drug propofol to aid in the treatment of his insomnia. This potent anesthetic agent has a white hue that resembles milk. As he left the last rehearsal of his "This Is It" concert, the entertainer prophetically remarked: "This is it... this really is it." The next afternoon, the 50 year-old Jackson died of a drug overdose after he asked his physician for a treatment of "Milk."

Alternative: * "Let me have some milk."

Jackson, Rachel (1767-1828). Wife of U.S. President Andrew Jackson. Mrs. Jackson spoke to her maid about the White House: "I would rather be a doorkeeper in the House of God than live in that palace in Washington."

Jackson, Thomas "Stonewall" (1824-1863). Confederate general during the U.S. Civil War. In the Battle of Chancellorsville in northeastern Virginia, Jackson inadvertently was shot by his own troops. Weakened by the injury, he died of pneumonia eight days later. As the general's condition worsened, he remarked: "It is the Lord's day. My wish is fulfilled. I have always desired to die on Sunday." Several hours later, he deliriously cried:

"Let us go over the river, and sit under the refreshing shadow of the trees." Jackson indeed died on a Sunday.

Alternatives: * In a delirium: "Order A.P. Hill to prepare for action! Pass the infantry to the front rapidly! Tell Major Hawks..."
* "Let us cross the river and rest under the shade of the trees."

Jacob, later known as Israel. Biblical patriarch who was the son of Isaac and Rebekah and grandson of Abraham. After he blessed and charged his sons, Jacob specified his burial plans (Genesis 49:29-32): "I am to be gathered to my people; bury me with my fathers in the cave that is in the field of Ephron the Hittite, in the cave that is in the field at Machpelah, to the east of Mamre, in the land of Canaan, which Abraham bought with the field from Ephron the Hittite to possess as a burying place. There they buried Abraham and Sarah his wife; there they buried Isaac and Rebekah his wife; and there I buried Leah [his wife]- the field and the cave that is in it were purchased from the Hittites."

Jacobi, Johann (1740-1814). German poet and writer. Commenting on a New Year's Eve poem written about New Year's Day, Jacobi reflected: "I shall not in fact see the New Year which I have just commemorated. I hope, at least, it is not apparent in the poem how elderly I am."

Jacobs, Milton (birth and death dates uncertain). American polymath. Before slipping into a coma: "I used to know a lot. Now, I don't know nuttin'."

Jam Master Jay, born Jason Mizell (1965-2002). American rapper and producer. Gunned down in a recording studio by an unknown assailant: "Oh, s***!"

James I (1566-1625). King of England and Ireland as James I and Scotland as James VI. To reconcile various translations of antecedent scriptures, James authorized revision of the Bible, which now bears his name. Dying of dysentery and a stroke, James spoke when offered Absolution: "As it is practiced in the English Church I ever approved it; but in the dark way of the Church of Rome, I do defy it!"

James II (1633-1701). King of England and Ireland as James II and Scotland as James VII. Deposed in 1688, James later fled to France. Dying of a stroke at age 67, to his benefactor, King Louis XIV of France: "Grateful; in peace." To his wife: "Think of it Madam. I am going to be happy." As he died: "Into Thy hands I commend my soul. O Lord, lay not this great sin to their charge."

James V (1512-1542). Scottish king. After a decisive defeat by Henry VIII's army at Solway Moss near the border of Scotland and England, James died unexpectedly of a "marvelous vomit." When told on his deathbed that a daughter of his (Mary Stewart, later Mary, Queen of Scots) had been born, James allegedly reflected: "The Devil go with it! It will end as it began. It came with a lass and it will go with a lass."

Alternatives: * "Adieu, farewell, it came with a lass, it will pass with a lass."
* "It came from a woman, and it will end in a woman."

James the Dismembered, Saint (died 421). Persian Christian martyr. Because of his religious beliefs, James was hacked to death. After his extremities were cut away, he cried to his persecutors who were preparing to decapitate him: "Now the boughs are gone. Cut down the trunk... O Lord of lords, Lord of the living and the dead, give ear to me who am half dead. I have no fingers to hold out to Thee, O Lord, nor hands to stretch forth to Thee. My feet are cut off and my knees demolished, wherefore I cannot bend the knee to Thee, and I am like to a house that is about to fall because its columns are taken away. Hear me, O Lord Jesus Christ, and deliver my soul from its prison!"

Alternative: "O Lord, Father Almighty and Lord Jesus Christ and Most Holy Spirit, I thank Thee that Thou hast enabled me to endure these torments for Thy holy name. But I pray Thee, make me worthy to complete this contest, for the pangs of hell came round about me. They have severed all my limbs. I have no legs to stand on and worship Thy majesty, nor hands to lift up to heaven to pray and call Thy name. They left me neither knees, nor arms, the merciless ones, but I remain as a branchless tree without roots. Therefore, I beseech Thee, O Most Holy King, abandon not Thy servant, but take my soul out of the prison of my body, and place it among Thy holy martyrs, so that we may glorify forever Thy majesty in the ages to come. Amen."

James the Greater, Saint (died 44). Apostle of Jesus Christ. James' execution was ordered by the Judean King Herod Agrippa I. When the man who denounced James suffered remorse for his act and converted to Christianity, he also was condemned to die. On the way to the execution, the informer begged forgiveness. Before their beheading, James replied: "Peace be with you, brother."

Alternative: * "Peace be to thee, brother."

James the Just or James the Less, Saint (died c. 62). Apostle of Jesus Christ. As James was stoned to death for his religious beliefs, he prayed: "I beseech thee, Lord God our Father, forgive them; for they know not what they do."

James, Alice (1848-1892). American diarist and sister of the novelist Henry James, Jr. (below). Dying of breast cancer while in London, James spoke the words she wished to be telegraphed to her family: "Tenderest love to all. Farewell. Am going soon."

James, Henry, Sr. (1811-1882). American theologian, philosopher and father of Henry James, Jr. (below). During his final illness, James confirmed: "I stick by Almighty God. He alone is. All else is death. Don't call this dying- I am just entering on life." Speaking of his late wife, he said: "There's my Mary."

James, Henry, Jr. (1843-1916). American-born writer, son of Henry James, Sr. and brother of William and Alice James. Dying of a stroke and pneumonia: "So here it is at last, the distinguished thing!" The author then spoke to his sister-in-law, also named Alice: "Stay with me, Alice! This is the end."

James, Jesse (1847-1882). American outlaw. James and his brother Frank were wanted for a number of robberies and murders committed over a wide swath of the mid-United States. After returning to Missouri, James rented a house where he hid with several companions. He groused: "If anybody passes, they'll see me." Several months later, the outlaw climbed on a chair to dust a framed picture and exclaimed: "That picture is awful dusty." When he turned around, James was shot in the head by Robert Ford, an associate who hoped to collect a sizable reward.

James, John (1785-1859). English minister and writer. "Attacked by indigestion," the sick man was helped into bed by his physician. The clergyman then quoted a section from Matthew 25:45: "Inasmuch as thou hast done it unto one of the least of these, thou hast done it unto me." The minister then fell into an eternal sleep.

James, William (1842-1910). American philosopher and psychologist, brother of Alice and Henry James (above). Dying of a heart ailment, James spoke to his wife: "It's so good to get home." Toward the end: "I can't stand this again- cruel, *cruel*! It has come so rapidly, rapidly." James then spoke of his brother: "Go to Henry when his time comes."

Janáček, Leoš (1854-1928). Czech composer and conductor. In the throes of an advanced pneumonia, Janáček indignantly spoke to his attendant when she asked if he wished to make peace with God: "Nurse, you probably don't know who I am."

Janeway, Jacob (1774-1858). American clergyman and writer. On his deathbed, to his eldest son: "I am tired of eating. I want to go home!"

Jansen, Ellert (died1549). Martyred Dutch tailor. Persecuted for his Protestant religious beliefs, Jansen and several others were sentenced to die by burning. When offered a chance to escape, he said: "I am now so well satisfied to be offered up, and feel myself at present so happy, that I do not expect to be hereafter better prepared." Before his execution, Jansen exclaimed: "This is the most joyful day in my whole life."

Jara, Saint Cristóbal (1869-1927). Martyred Mexican priest. Because of the government's anticlerical stance during the Mexican Revolution, Jara was accused of inciting rebellion and was summarily executed by soldiers:

"I am innocent and I die innocent. I forgive with all my heart those responsible for my death, and I ask God that the shedding of my blood may bring peace to divided Mexicans."

Jarry, Alfred (1873-1907). French absurdist writer and playwright. Dying of tuberculosis and alcohol abuse, Jarry allegedly said: "I am dying. Please… bring me a toothpick."

Jasper, William (c. 1750-1779). American soldier killed at the Siege of Savannah, Georgia during the Revolutionary War. Jasper lost his life as he planted his regiment's colors during the conflict: "Tell Mrs. Elliott I lost my life supporting the colors she presented to our regiment." Susannah Elliott, a South Carolina matron, had given a pair of embroidered colors to Jasper's unit several years earlier.

Jay, John (1745-1829). First chief justice of the U.S. Supreme Court. Dying of a stroke, Jay requested in his will: "... I would have my funeral decent, but not ostentatious. No scarfs, no rings. Instead, thereof, I give two hundred dollars to any one poor deserving widow or orphan of this town [he died in Bedford, New York] whom my children shall select..."

Jay, William (1769-1853). English clergyman. Jay spoke to those around his deathbed: "Oh, none of you know what it is to die."

Jean Paul, pen name of Johann Paul Richter (1763-1825). German novelist. Dying of "dropsy," Jean Paul responded to a bouquet of flowers presented by his wife: "My beautiful flowers, my lovely flowers."

Jean-Baptiste de La Salle, Saint (1651-1719). French priest and educator. Asked if he accepted his sufferings with joy: "Yes, I adore in all things the designs of God in my regard."

Jeanne d'Albret (1528-1572). Queen of Navarre, a former kingdom straddling the Pyrenees where Spain borders France. Dying of a fever (some say poisoning), d'Albret told her ladies-in-waiting: "Weep not for me, I pray you. God by this sickness calls me hence to enjoy a better life; and now I shall enter into the desired haven toward which this frail vessel of mine has been a long time steering." When asked if she were willing to die: "Yes, more willing than to linger here in this world of vanity." She later said: "As I have lived, so am I resolved to die."

Jeanne d'Arc, Saint (see Joan of Arc, Saint).

Jefferies, Richard (1848-1887). English writer and naturalist. Dying of tuberculosis, Jefferies spoke to his wife: "Yes, yes, that is so. Help Lord, for Jesus' sake. Darling, goodbye. God bless you and the children, and save you all from such great pain."

Jefferson, Thomas (1743-1826). Third U.S. president. Jefferson died of kidney failure and pneumonia on July 4, 1826, within hours of the passing of his colleague John Adams (above). As he became enfeebled, Jefferson told his grandson Thomas Randolph: "... I am like an old watch, with a pinion worn out here and a wheel there, until it can go no longer." He lapsed into a coma on July 2 but roused a day later. To his physician: "Ah, doctor, are you still there. Is it the Fourth?" When awakened for his medication, the dying statesman said: "No, doctor, nothing more." Later that day, he again asked: "This is the Fourth?" When told it would be soon or that it had come: "Ah, just as I wished." During the early hours of the Fourth, he rambled about the Committee of Safety, saying: "Warn the Committee to be on the alert." His grandson recounted: "At four A.M. [July 4] he [Jefferson] called the servants in attendance with a strong and clear voice, perfectly conscious of his wants. He did not speak again." The deaths of Jefferson and John Adams marked the 50th Anniversary of the signing of the American Declaration of Independence.

Alternative: * "I resign my soul to God, my daughter to my Country. Lord, now lettest Thou Thy servant depart in peace." These words probably were spoken in the days prior to his demise. Reports of his praying immediately before death were denied by his physician and other witnesses.

Jeffreys, George (1648-1689). English judge who presided over the "Bloody Assizes" of 1865. Many who participated in the rebellion to overthrow King James II were condemned by Jeffreys' court and executed. Dying of kidney failure, Jeffreys related: "People call me a murderer for doing what at the time was applauded by some who are now high in public favor. They call me a drunkard because I take punch to relieve me in my agony."

Jehoram, also called Joram (died c. 842 BCE). Israeli king who was the son of Ahab (above) and Jezebel (below). When the military commander Jehu was anointed King of Israel, he was charged to kill Jehoram for the "harlotries and sorceries" of his mother Jezebel and atrocities committed during his reign. Before Jehoram was struck by Jehu's arrow, he cried to Ahaziah, King of Judah who was in his presence (2 Kings 9:23): "Treachery, O Ahaziah."

Alternative: * "There is treason, Ahaziah!"

Jenkins, John (c. 1808-1834). Australian murderer. Jenkins and an accomplice shot a doctor who previously had abused him. Refusing to shake hands with his partner in crime, Jenkins said before his hanging: "Let every villain- let every villain shake hands with himself."

Jenner, Edward (1749-1823). English physician who developed a vaccination for smallpox. Dying of a stroke, Jenner allowed: "I do not wonder that men are grateful to me, but I am surprised that they do not feel gratitude to God for thus making me a medium of good."

Alternative: * "I am not surprised that men are not thankful to me; but I wonder that they are not grateful to God for the good which He has made me the instrument of conveying to my fellow creatures."

Jerome of Prague, Saint (c. 1360-1416). Martyred Bohemian religious reformer. Because Jerome criticized aspects of the Catholic religion, he was branded a heretic and condemned to die at the stake. After the sentence was pronounced, his hood was removed and a paper mitre painted with red demons was placed on his head: "Our Lord Jesus Christ, when he should suffer death for me, most wretched sinner, did wear a crown of thorns upon his head; and I for his sake, instead of that crown, will willingly wear this mitre and cap." To the executioner who was lighting wood behind him: "Bring thy torch hither. Perform thy office before my face. Had I feared death, I might have avoided it." As the flames consumed him,

Jerome prayed: "Into Thy hands, O Lord, I commend my spirit. O Lord God, Father Almighty, have mercy upon me, and be merciful unto mine offences, for Thou knowest how sincerely I have loved Thy truth." As the martyr died: "This soul in flames I offer, Christ, to thee."

Alternative: * "Come here and kindle it before my eyes, for if I had dreamed such a sight, I should never have come to this place when I had a free opportunity to escape."

Jerrold, Douglas (1803-1857). English playwright and journalist. As he died, Jerrold told his sons: "This is as it should be."

Alternative: * "I feel like one who is waiting and waited for."

Jesus Christ (c. 6-4 BCE- c. 30-36 CE [age at death c. 33 years]). Biblical spiritual leader, teacher and healer. As Jesus was crucified with two criminals, he said*: "Father, forgive them [his Roman tormentors]; for they know not what they do (Luke 23:34)." When one of the criminals pleaded: "Jesus, remember me when you come into your kingdom," Christ replied: "Truly, I say to you, today you will be with me in Paradise (Luke 23:42-43)." When Jesus saw his mother at the base of the cross, he said: "Woman, behold your son!" Then he spoke to his disciple, the young John who was with her: "Behold, your mother (John, 19:26-27)!" Shortly thereafter, Jesus said: "I thirst." After he was given a sponge filled with sour wine [vinegar] on a hyssop branch [a herbaceous plant found in the eastern Mediterranean], Jesus said: "It is finished," bowed his head and died (John, 19:28-30). The gospel of Luke recounts that Jesus cried out around the ninth hour: "Father, into thy hands I commit my spirit!" Then he "breathed his last (Luke 23:46)." The gospel of Matthew states that Jesus cried out around the ninth hour after being crucified: "My God, my God, why hast thou forsaken me (Matthew 27:46)?" He then cried again and "yielded up his spirit (Matthew 27:46, 50)."

After the resurrection, Jesus appeared to his followers and said: "Thus it is written, that the Christ should suffer and on the third day rise from the dead, and that repentance and forgiveness of sins should be preached in his name to all nations, beginning from Jerusalem. You are witnesses of these things. And behold, I send the promise of my Father upon you; but stay in the city, until you are clothed with power from on high (Luke 24:46-49)." He then led them to Bethany, blessed them and ascended into heaven. Mathew 28:18-20 relates that Jesus met his 11 disciples in Galilee and told them: "All authority in heaven and on earth has been given to me. Go therefore and make disciples of all nations, baptizing them in the name of the Father and of the Son and of the Holy Spirit, teaching them to observe all that I have commanded you; and lo, I am with you always, to the close of the age." Thus ends the gospel of Matthew.

* All quotes above were taken from The New Oxford Annotated Bible with the Apocrypha Revised Standard Version.

Jewel, John (1522-1571). English Anglican bishop of Salisbury. After collapsing at the conclusion of a sermon, Jewel knew what awaited him: "O Lord, confound me not. This is my 'today.' This day quickly let me come unto Thee. This day let me see the Lord Jesus."

Jezebel (died c. 842 BCE). Queen Consort of Ahab, King of Israel. For her promotion of pagan cults and evil deeds, Jezebel was killed by Jehu, an Israelite ruler who earlier murdered her son Jehoram (above). Before she was thrown from a window to her death (defenestration), the queen accosted Jehu: "Did Zimri [an earlier king who killed his predecessor to seize power] have peace, who murdered his master?" Jezebel's body was trampled by horses and her flesh eaten by dogs.

Alternative: * "Is it peace, you Zimri, murderer of your master (2 Kings 9:31)?"

Joachim, Frederick (1546-1608). German Elector of Brandenburg. To his heir, Joachim wisely advised: "Don't blow up what doesn't burn you."

Joan of Arc, Saint, also Saint Jeanne d'Arc (c. 1412-1431). French military leader who helped relieve England's siege of Orléans during the Hundred Year's War. Joan later was tried on trumped-up charges of heresy in Rouen and condemned to die. Before her execution at the stake, the martyr asked a clergyman to hold a crucifix before her: "Oh! My God, go back father, and when the flame rises round me, lift up the cross that I may see it as I die and speak holy words to me to the last." To the Bishop of Beauvais who aided in her downfall: "Bishop! Bishop! You are the cause of my death." To the spectators: "Oh Rouen! I fear you will one day rue my death. Water! Water!" Her last words: "Jesus, Jesus, Jesus!"

Alternatives: * "Hold the cross high so I may see it through the flames."
* "I pray you, go to the nearest church, and bring me the cross, and hold it up level with my eyes until I am dead. I would have the cross on which God hung be ever before my eyes while life lasts in me. Jesus, Jesus."

Jobs, Steven "Steve" (1955-2011). American businessman, inventor and co-founder of the electronics corporation Apple Inc. Following pancreatic cancer surgery and a subsequent liver transplant, Jobs died peacefully in his California home. Before expiring, he said to his sister: "Oh wow. Oh wow. Oh wow."

Jocen (died 1190). English Jewish leader. During the reign of Richard I, a wave of anti-Semitism swept the country. Fearing reprisals, Jocen admonished his fellow Jews: "Brethren, there is no hope for us with the Christians, who are hammering at the gates and walls and who must soon break in. As we and our wives and children must die, either by Christian hands, or by our own, let it be by our own. Let us destroy by fire what jewels and other treasures we have here, then fire the castle, and then perish." He then cut his wife's throat and turned the knife on himself.

Jodl, Alfred (1890-1946). Nazi chief of operations for the German High Command during WW II. Convicted of crimes against humanity, Jodl was sentenced to die by hanging: "My greetings to you, my Germany."

Alternative: * "I greet you, my eternal Germany."

Joffre, Joseph-Jacques (1852-1931). French general. Although Joffre played a significant role during the early fighting of WWI, his influence waned in the latter part of the conflict. To his confessor, before dying: "I have not done much evil in my life, and I have sincerely loved my wife."

Jogues, Saint Isaac (1607-1646). Martyred French priest and missionary. Jogues traveled into Mohawk territory in present-day New York on a peace mission but was killed by Native American militants. Before starting his trek, Jogues penned his concerns: "My heart tells me that if I am the one to be sent on this mission I shall go but I shall not return. But I would be glad if our Lord wished to complete the sacrifice where He began it. Farewell, dear Father. Pray that God unite me to Himself inseparably."

John XXIII (1881-1963). Pope from 1958 to his death. Dying of stomach cancer, John spoke to his family: "Do you remember how I never thought of anything else in life but being a priest? I embrace you and bless you... Pray... I wish to be dissolved and be with Christ... Into Thy hands, O Lord, I commend my spirit."

John Lackland (c. 1167-1216). King of England. After the demise of his brother Richard in 1199, John claimed the throne and ruled until his death. The Barons' War during the latter part of his reign led to the signing of the Magna Carta, a direct challenge to the monarch's absolute authority. Dying of dysentery, John prayed: "To God and St. Wulfstan [the Bishop of Worcester who died in 1095] I commend my body and soul."

Alternative: * "I commit my soul to God and my body to Saint Alstane."

John of Austria, Don (1547-1578). Bavarian-born general who served in the army of his half-brother Philip II of Spain. Dying of a febrile illness, possibly typhus, Don John deliriously cried out: "Aunt! Aunt! My lady Aunt!" Others reported that he quoted from Job 1:21: "Naked I came from my mother's womb, and naked shall I return..."

John of Kronstadt, Saint (1829-1908). Russian Orthodox priest and mystic. Suffering from a painful bladder problem, John said: "I thank God for my sufferings, sent me to purify my sinful soul before death... Holy Communion revives me." When advised of the date, he replied: "Thank God, two more days. We'll have time to do everything." Two days later (some say three), he died, gasping: "I cannot breathe."

John of the Cross, Saint (1542-1591). Spanish priest and poet. The day before his death, John said: "At midnight I will be before God our Lord, saying Matins." When a bell signaled this first office of prayer for the monastic day, he exulted: "Glory be to God! For I must go to say Matins in heaven! Into Thy hands, O Lord, I commend my spirit." His prophesy was fulfilled.

Alternatives: * "It is time for Matins."
* "Glory be to God, for I shall say them in heaven! Into your hands, O Lord, I commend my spirit."

John Paul I (1912-1978). Pope for slightly over a month before dying of a presumed heart attack. The night of his death, John Paul told an aide: "Goodnight. Until tomorrow, if God is willing."

Alternatives: * "I will see you tomorrow, if God wills it."
* Before retiring, John Paul read a newspaper account of the fatal shooting of a Communist youth in Rome: "They kill each other, even among young people."

John Paul II (1920-2005). Second-longest reigning pope (26 years) behind Pius IX (31 years) who died in 1878. Succumbing to complications of a urinary tract infection, John Paul requested: "Let me go to the house of the Father."

Alternatives: * "Allow me to depart to the house of the Father."
* "Let me go to the Lord."
* Dubious: "Amen."

John the Almoner, Saint, also Saint John the Almsgiver (died c. 619). Cyprian-born patriarch of Alexandria, Egypt and philanthropist. When his immediate family died, John gave away his possessions and ministered to the poor. "I thank Thee, O my God, that Thy mercy has granted the desire of my weakness, which was that at my death I should possess naught but a single penny. And now this penny, too, can be given to the poor!"

Alternative: * "I always wanted to possess, at death, nothing but a bed sheet. And now this sheet can be given to the poor."

John the Blind (1296-1346). King of Bohemia. John lost his eyesight to illness around age 40. Led forward by his troops almost a decade later, John was killed while fighting at the Battle of Crécy in northern France. Before dying, he declared: "Let it never be the case that a Bohemian king runs [from a fight]!"

Alternative: * "Never by God will that be that a King of Bohemia flees from the battle."

John the Divine, Saint, also called Saint John the Evangelist and John of Patmos (died c. 100). One of the original 12 disciples of Jesus Christ. John was the only surviving disciple of this group to escape martyrdom. To his followers: "Thou hast invited me to Thy table, Lord, and behold I come, thanking Thee for having invited me, for Thou knowest that I have desired it with all my heart."

Alternative: * "Be with me, Lord Jesus Christ. Peace and grace be with you, my brothers."

John the Dwarf, Saint (died c. 405). Egyptian Christian priest of slight physical stature. To his disciples: "I never followed my own will, nor did I ever teach any other what I had not first practiced myself."

Johns, Stephen (1946-2001). American criminal, executed by lethal injection for the murder of a 17 year-old service station attendant: "... I have, over the past many years, heard many 'last words' of those killed by the State and its citizens. They range from 'I'm sorry' to 'kiss my fat a** ...' I do not forgive those State functionaries who act as 'good Germans' to kill me. I am innocent, but was not given the tools at trial, or on appeal, to make my innocence into a legal reality."

Johnson, Andrew (1808-1875). Seventeenth U.S. president. Johnson succeeded the assassinated Abraham Lincoln and later became the first president to be impeached. In his last days, Johnson spoke prophetically to a friend: "I am winding up my personal affairs. I wish to be my own executor. I have had a bad feeling in my head, which makes me fear apoplexy [stroke], and a man liable to that never knows how suddenly he may be cut off." Several hours later he fell to the floor and mumbled to his daughter: "My right side is paralyzed." When she went for help, he said: "I need no doctor. I can overcome my troubles." Johnson's utterances became incomprehensible and he died the following day.

Johnson, James "Jim" (1949-2002). American criminal, executed by lethal injection for multiple murders: "... The news reports today will say Jim Johnson is dead. Those reports will be untrue... Today I shall meet Jesus my Lord and Savior face to face. When the executioners have done their worst, God will be shown to have done his best. May the God of all grace bring peace to your hearts."

Johnson, John (1861-1909). American politician who became governor of Minnesota. After a long illness, to his wife: "Well, Nora, I guess I am going, but I've made a good fight."

Johnson, John G. (1841-1917). American lawyer and art collector. Johnson spoke his last words before retiring for the night: "Goodnight, I'm going to sleep now."

Johnson, John "Jack" (1878-1946). American-born first African American heavyweight boxing champion. Mortally injured in a car accident in North Carolina, Johnson pleaded with a friend: "Call my wife. Stick by me."

Johnson, Lonnie (1963-2007). American criminal, executed by lethal injection for a double murder: "It's been a joy and a blessing. Give everybody my regards. I love you, and I'll see you in eternity. Father, take me home. I'm gone, baby. I'm ready to go."

Johnson, Lyndon (1908-1973). Thirty-sixth U.S. president. Johnson succeeded the assassinated John F. Kennedy (below). Dying of a heart attack, Johnson telephoned his Secret Service detail: "Send Mike immediately!" By the time help arrived, the former president was dead.

Johnson, Samuel (1709-1784). English writer, poet, critic and lexicographer. Plagued in his last days by the effects of a stroke and gout, Johnson answered his physician who inquired if he were better: "No, sir, you cannot conceive with what acceleration I advance towards death... Give me a direct answer. Tell me plainly, can I recover?" When told that "nothing short of a miracle" would save him, Johnson declared: "Then I will take no more physic- not even my opiates, for I have prayed that I may render up my soul to God unclouded." Shortly before he died, Johnson remarked to a lady visitor who requested his blessing: "God bless you, my dear!" Some say his last words were the Latin phrase: "*Iam moriturus* [Now I am about to die]." Gladiators (see above) used a similar saying before fighting. Others contend that: "… at the very last he had mumbled something (not recorded verbatim, alas) about a cup of warm milk not being handed to him properly." Regardless, Johnson lapsed into a coma and expired shortly thereafter. A portion of his will stated: "… I bequeath to God a soul polluted by many sins, but I hope purified by Jesus Christ…"

Johnson, Stone (1940-1963). American Olympic sprinter and professional football player. Johnson suffered a broken neck in a preseason football game and died 10 days later. Some of his last words were: "Oh my God, oh my God! Where's my head? Where's my head?"

Johnson, Walter "Barney" (1887-1946). American Hall of Fame professional baseball pitcher and manager. Ill with an incurable brain tumor, Johnson partially lost the power of speech several weeks before dying. When a relative asked which team won the World Series that year, he correctly responded: "The [St. Louis] Cardinals."

Johnson, William (1715-1774). Anglo-Irish statesman who was an agent and militia leader of the Iroquois Indians of New York. Dying of a stroke after a long speech, Johnson told a close associate who was a Mohawk chief: "Joseph, control your people. I am going away."

Johnson, William, also "Zip the Pinhead" (c. 1842-1926). Johnson was born with a deformed cranium that gave him the appearance of a microcephalic or "pin head." He was displayed in various circus sideshows most of his life. Although many microcephalics have a diminished mental capacity, Johnsons faculties appeared normal. Dying of a respiratory ailment around age 84, he told his sister: "Well, we fooled 'em for a long time, didn't we?"

Johnston, Albert (1803-1862). Confederate general during the U.S. Civil War. Johnston was shot in the leg during the Battle of Shiloh in southwestern Tennessee. When asked if he were injured, the general replied: "Yes, and I fear seriously." He later died of blood loss.

Johnston, Archibald (1611-1663). Scottish judge and statesman. As a member of the Cromwell government, Johnston was accused of treason after the restoration of the monarchy in 1660. Before his subsequent hanging and beheading, the condemned man prayed: "Abba, Father, accept this, Thy poor sinful servant, coming unto Thee through the merits of Jesus Christ. O pray, pray! Praise, praise!"

Johnston, David (1949-1980). American volcanologist with the United States Geological Survey (USGS). While manning a monitoring station near the Mt. St. Helens volcano in Washington state, Johnston transmitted a warning before he was killed in the May 18, 1980 eruption: "Vancouver [the USGS station in nearby Vancouver, Washington]! Vancouver! This is it! This is..."

Jókai, Mór (1825-1904). Hungarian writer and dramatist. "I want to sleep."

Jolson, Asa "Al" born Asa Yoelson (1886-1950). Lithuanian-born American singer and actor. Shortly after returning from Korea where he entertained American troops, Jolson suffered a heart attack. He quipped to his doctors: "I'm a real important guy. Hell, Truman only had one hour for [General] MacArthur. I got two!" Moments later, he moaned: "This is it! I'm going. I'm going."

Jones, Daniel (1958-1998). A Los Angeles, California resident infected with the human immunodeficiency virus. Jones became disgruntled with the management of his AIDS problem by his Health Maintenance

Organization (HMO). In protest, he spread a banner on a L.A. freeway surface that read: "HMOs are in it for the money. Live free, love safe or die." On live television, Jones set fire to his truck and committed suicide by gunshot.

Jones, Henry (1851-1929). English dramatist. When asked by his niece whether she or the nurse should sit with him, Jones replied: "The prettier. Now fight for it."

Jones, John "Casey" (c. 1863-1900). American locomotive driver. Jones was asked to substitute for an ailing engineer on the Cannonball Express passenger train traveling from Memphis, Tennessee to Canton, Mississippi. Because of the change in engine drivers, the train left the station 95 minutes late. Over the ensuing hours, Jones and his fireman Simeon "Sim" Webb made up most of the lost time. About 35 miles from the end of his run, the engineer encountered another train parked on the tracts ahead. Trying desperately to stop the speeding engine, he yelled to his fireman: "Jump, Sim, jump." The Cannonball Express ploughed into the stopped train killing Jones instantly, the only fatality of the wreck. An inscription on his monument in the Calvary Cemetery, Jackson, Tennessee: "For I'm going to run till she leaves the rail- or make it on time with the southbound mail."

Alternative: * "Jump, Sim, and save yourself."

Jones, Robert (1883-1968). American clergyman and educator. Jones began preaching at age 13 and in 1927 founded the institution that bears his name- Bob Jones University. On his deathbed, to his wife: "Mary Gaston, get my shoes. I must go to preach."

Jones, Robert "Bobby" (1902-1971). American professional golfer who dominated the sport in the 1920s. To please his wife, the golfer converted to Roman Catholicism on his deathbed. Jones admitted to his priest: "You know, if I'd known how happy this had made Mary, I would have done it years ago."

Jones, Warren "Jim" (1931-1978). American cult leader. Jones was responsible for the poisoning deaths of over 900 of his followers in a Jonestown, Guyana encampment. Before shooting himself, Jones left a rambling tape recording explaining his beliefs: "... We said- one thousand people who said, we don't like the way the world is. Take some. Take our life from us. We laid it down. We got tired. We didn't commit suicide, we committed an act of revolutionary suicide protesting the conditions of an inhumane world."

Jones, William "Billy" (1964-2002). American criminal, executed by lethal injection for a murder committed during a robbery: "... My darling Gerti, my wife, I love you endlessly my honeybird. Till we meet again, stay strong. Love, Billy."

Joplin, Janis (1943-1970). American rock music star. Predicting that she would not live past forty, Joplin said: "Maybe I won't last as long as other singers, but I think you can destroy your now by worrying about tomorrow..." After a recording session, the 37 year-old Joplin chatted with the night attendant at her hotel, but her words were not documented. Later, she was found dead from a drug overdose. The clerk who had spoken to Joplin earlier reported that "she seemed perfectly natural" at the time.

Alternative: * To a friend: "Goodnight."

Joram of Israel (see Jehoram).

Jordan, Barbara (1936-1996). American politician and civil rights activist who became a member of the U.S. House of Representatives. Dying from complications of multiple sclerosis and leukemia, Jordan spoke to her physician about her illnesses: "Nothing is a secret anymore."

Jortin, John (1698-1770). English clergyman and church historian. When asked about the publication of his sermons, Jortin replied: "Let them sleep till I sleep." To a servant trying to make him eat: "No, I have had enough of everything."

Joselito, born José Gómez Ortega (1895-1920). Spanish bull fighter. Joselito was fatally gored during a bullfight in Talavera de la Reina near Toledo, Spain. His dying words were: "Mother, I'm smothering."

Joseph (biblical times). Hebrew son of Jacob (above) and the chief advisor to the current Egyptian pharaoh. As told in Genesis 50:24-5, Joseph on his deathbed spoke to his family: "I am about to die; but God will visit you and bring you up out of this land to the land which he swore to Abraham, to Isaac and to Jacob. God will visit you and you shall carry up my bones from here." During the Israelites' subsequent exodus from Egypt, Moses (below) indeed carried Joseph's bones with him.

Joseph II (1741-1790). Holy Roman Emperor and ruler of the Hapsburg Empire. Because his modernizing reforms often were met with opposition, Joseph felt his legacy would reflect failure: "I do not know whether the poet who writes: 'Fearful is the step from the throne to the grave' is right. I do not miss the throne. I feel at peace, but only a little hurt with so much painful effort to have made so few happy and so many ungrateful. But then, such is the fate of men on the throne. Now I see that the Almighty is destroying all my works in my lifetime." He bitterly reiterated his feelings: "[My] epitaph should read: 'Here lies Joseph II, who failed in everything he undertook.'"

Joseph of Cupertino, Saint (1603-1663). Italian Franciscan friar and mystic. When someone at the dying man's beside mentioned God's love, Joseph responded: "Say that again! Say that again! Praised be God! Blest be God! May the holy will of God be done!"

Joshua (died c. 1245 BCE). Leader of the Israelites after Moses' death. Having delivered the Israelites into the Promised Land, Joshua asked his followers to obey the words of the Lord. As recounted in Joshua 24:27-8, he placed a large stone under an oak tree and said: "Behold, this stone shall be a witness against us; for it has heard all the words of the Lord, which he spoke to us; therefore, it shall be a witness against you, lest you deal falsely with your God." He then sent his people away and died.

Joubert, Barthélemy (1769-1799). French general killed by a bullet to the heart while leading his men in battle at Novi, Italy. At the beginning of the skirmish, Joubert exhorted his troops: "Soldiers, march to the enemy!"

Jowett, Benjamin (1817-1893). English theologian, writer and Master of Balliol College, Oxford. On his deathbed, Jowett exclaimed: "I bless God for my life! I bless God for my life! I bless Thee for my life! Mine has been a happy life! I bless God for my life." Before he died, Jowett spoke to a friend: "Bid farewell to the college"

Joyce, James (1882-1941). Irish writer and playwright, best-known for his novel *Ulysses*. Awakening after an operation for a perforated stomach ulcer, Joyce was told that he was receiving a blood transfusion from two soldiers from Neuchâtel, Switzerland. He quipped: "A good omen. I like Neuchâtel wine." His condition worsened over the next two days and he lapsed into a coma. Before dying, Joyce enigmatically asked: "Does nobody understand?"

Alternative: * "Does anybody understand?"

Juárez, Benito (1806-1872). Mexican president. Dying of a heart attack, Juárez queried his physician: "Doctor, is my disease mortal?"

Judas Iscariot (died c. 33). One of the original apostles of Jesus Christ. When he saw Jesus bound and led away by Roman soldiers as a result of his betrayal, Judas lamented (Matthew 27:4): "I have sinned in betraying innocent blood!" He then threw down the 30 pieces of silver given by the priests for his treachery and hanged himself (Matthew 27:5). However, Acts 1:18 chronicles a different demise: "Now this man [Judas] bought a field with the reward of his wickedness and falling headlong he burst open in the middle and all his bowels gushed out."

Judas Maccabaeus (died c. 160 BCE). Jewish warrior. Judas was killed during the Battle of Elasa near modern-day Ramallah, West Bank. Before he died fighting the superior Seleucid army, Judas exclaimed (1 Maccabees 9: 10): "Far be it from us to do such a thing as to flee from them. If our time has come, let us die bravely for our brethren and leave no cause to question our honor." Because of the fierce resistance demonstrated during this battle, Jewish forces eventually repelled the invaders years later.

Alternative: * "God forbid that I should do this thing and flee away from them! If our time be come, let us die manfully for our brethren and let us not stain our honour."

Judd, Sylvester (1813-1853). American clergyman and writer. Judd was afflicted with chills, weakness and sporadic abdominal pains during his last weeks. When told late in his illness that he looked fatigued, the minister replied: "Yes, that is it. Tired to death." Immediately before expiring: "Cover me up warm. Keep my utterance clear. I'm doing well."

Judson, Adoniram (1788-1850). American Baptist missionary to Burma. Late in life, Judson developed a serious lung ailment and was advised to take a long ocean voyage as therapy. Sensing that death was near and disturbed about the effect of the hot climate on his body, he spoke to a fellow missionary on board: "Brother Ranney, will you bury me? Bury me? Quick, quick!" Shortly before expiring, Judson told his servant: "Take care of poor mistress [his wife, Emily below]." He was buried at sea.

Judson, Ann (1789-1826). American-born first wife of the missionary Adoniram Judson (above). Ann who accompanied her husband to Burma also performed missionary work there. Dying of smallpox, she said: "I feel quite well. Only very weak."

Judson, Emily, whose pen name was Fanny Forrester (1817-1854). American writer and third wife of Adoniram Judson. Succumbing to tuberculosis, Emily had expressed a hope that she would die in the month of June. When her sister asked: "Emily, do you know that it is June?" Judson replied: "Yes, my month to die." She expired in her sister's arms.

Judy, Steven (1956-1981). American criminal, executed by electrocution for the murder and rape of a mother and the drowning deaths of her three children: "I don't hold any grudges. This is my doing. Sorry it happened."

Jugurtha (c. 160-104 BCE). King of Numidia or present-day Algeria. Jugurtha was defeated by Roman invaders who took him back to Rome as a prisoner. Incarcerated in a dungeon to starve to death, the crazed king cried: "O Hercules, how cold is your bath!" He died six days later.

Alternatives: * "Heracles [the Greek representation of Hercules], how cold your bath is!"
* "O Romans, you give me a cold bath."

Julian the Apostate (331-363). The last non-Christian emperor of Rome. Because he desired that his empire should embrace paganism, Julian was called the Apostate. Mortally injured during his campaign to conquer Persia, the emperor scooped blood from his wound, flung it into the air and cried: "You have conquered, Galilean! [Christ]." Because of his sun worship, some say Julian's last words were: "Sun, thou hast betrayed me!"

Alternatives: * "Thou hast conquered, O Galilean! Thou hast conquered!"
* "Even here, O Galilean! You pursue me; satiate yourself with my blood, and glory that you have vanquished me!"

Julianus, Didius (c. 137-193). Disgraced Roman emperor. After the assassination of his predecessor, Pertinax, Didius Julianus essentially bought his way to power. Because of his unpopular policies, he was killed shortly after assuming authority. Before dying at the hand of one of his soldiers: "What harm have I done? Have I put anybody to death?"

Julius the Veteran, Saint (255-302). Martyred Roman military veteran. Beheaded for refusing to renounce his Christian beliefs: "Lord Jesus Christ, I suffer this for your name. I beg you to receive my spirit together with your holy martyrs."

Jung, Carl (1875-1961). Swiss psychiatrist and writer. When his domineering attendant left the room, Jung asked his son: "Quick, help me out of bed before she comes back or she will stop me. I want to look at the sunset." Before he died, to his housekeeper: "Let's have a really good red wine tonight."

Justin Martyr, Saint (c. 100-165). Judean Christian martyr and philosopher. Condemned to die by beheading if he did not sacrifice to Roman gods, Justin Martyr responded: "Through prayer we can be saved on account of our Lord Jesus Christ, even when we have been punished, because this shall become to us salvation and confidence at the more fearful and universal judgment-seat of our Lord and Savior."

Alternative: * "We desire nothing more than to suffer for our Lord, Jesus Christ; for this gives us salvation and joyfulness before His dreadful judgment seat."

Ka'ahumanu, Elisabeth (c. 1768-1832). Queen Regent of Hawaii. Elizabeth helped bring Christianity and western culture to Hawaii. At the end of a protracted illness, her spiritual advisor counseled that death was near. She replied: "I am going now" and died several minutes later.

Kafka, Franz (1883-1924). Bohemian-born novelist and poet. Dying of tuberculosis, Kafka asked his friend and fellow writer Max Brod to destroy all of his works, so: "There will be no proof that I ever was a writer." Fortunately, Brod did not carry out his friend's wish. Just before his death, Kafka asked his doctor for a dose of morphine. Shortly after the injection, he said: "Don't try to fool me. You're giving me an antidote. Kill me, or else you are a murderer!" After a second injection: "That's good, but more, more, it's not helping... Don't torture me anymore. Why prolong the agony?" The writer then implored his doctor: "Don't leave me." When reassured that he would not, Kafka said: "But I am leaving you."

Alternative: * Confusing the doctor with his sister whom he did not wish to contaminate with his tuberculosis, Kafka said: "Don't come so close, Elli. Not so close. Yes, this is better."

Kahlo, Frida (1907-1954). Mexican artist and wife of Diego Rivera (below). Chronically ill, Kahlo wrote in her diary several days before her death: "I hope the exit is joyful and hope never to return, Frida." Some have speculated the entry may have been a suicide note, but the writing may signify only that Kahlo foresaw her last days.

Kaiulani, Victoria (1875-1899). Crown Princess of Hawaii. Dying of pneumonia, the delirious princess indistinctly uttered a sound variously interpreted as: "Mama, Papa or Koa [the nickname of one of her cousins]."

Kalakaua, David (1836-1891). King of Hawaii. Comatose from a kidney ailment, the king aroused and said to an aide: "Well, I am a very sick man." He then spoke incoherently in Hawaiian and died.

Alternative: * Less reliably, others say his last words were: "Tell my people I tried to restore our gods, our way of life..."

Kaliayev, Ivan (1877-1905). Russian revolutionary and poet. Kaliayev assassinated the Grand Duke Sergei Alexandrovich of Russia by bombing his carriage. Before his hanging, the anarchist refused a crucifix and absolution saying: "I already told you that I am finished with life and am prepared for death. I consider my death as the supreme protest against a world of blood and tears."

Kaltenbrunner, Ernst (1903-1946). Austrian-born Nazi SS general, executed for war crimes committed during WWII. Before his hanging: "I have loved my German people and my fatherland with a warm heart. I have done my duty by the laws of my people and I am sorry my people were led this time by men who were not soldiers and that crimes were committed of which I had no knowledge. As the hood was placed over his head: "Germany, good luck."

Kamehameha I (c. 1758-1819). King of Hawaii. Credited with conquering and uniting the Hawaiian Islands, the dying king said: "I have given you the greatest good: peace and a kingdom that is all one- a kingdom of all the islands. That is all. It is finished." When asked by assembled chiefs for his counsel: "Move on in my good way and…"

Kamehameha V (1830-1872). King of Hawaii. Dying of a lung ailment, Kamehameha was urged to name his sister-in-law, Queen Emma, as his successor. He refused stating: "She was merely queen by courtesy, having been the wife of a king [Kamehameha IV]."

Kant, Immanuel (1724-1804). German philosopher and writer. Several days before dying, Kant spoke to his physicians and attendants: "I have not yet lost my feeling for humanity." When offered a drink, he said: "It is good."

Alternatives: * "God forbid that I should be sunk so low as to forget the offices of humanity."
* "It is enough."

Kargé, Joseph (1823-1892). Polish-born American Union army general during the U.S. Civil War and a post-war educator. On his way to New York, Kargé remarked to a friend: "I have but one desire concerning it [his death]- that it come suddenly and without warning." As Kargé took a seat on a ferry boat, he suddenly gasped and died.

Karl IX, also Charles IX (1550-1611). King of Sweden. On his deathbed, Karl laid his hand on his son's head and predicted: "He will do it." His son Gustavus Adolphus the Great later would elevate Sweden to great power.

Karl XI, also Charles XI (1655-1697). King of Sweden. Dying of an abdominal malignancy, Karl prayed: "Lord Jesus, receive my spirit."

Karl XII, also Charles XII (1682-1718). King of Sweden. While inspecting his troops during an ill-fated invasion of Norway, Karl was warned by one of his officers about exposing himself to enemy fire: "... Musket-balls and cannon-balls have as little respect for a King as for a common soldier." Karl replied: "Don't be afraid." Shortly thereafter the king sustained a fatal canister shot to the head.

Alternative: * "Fear nothing."

Karl XIV, also Karl Johan and Charles John XIV (1763-1844). King of Sweden and Norway. Dying of a stroke, Karl Johan spoke to his son, the crown prince: "Oscar, Oscar, we shall defend ourselves."

Karl XV, also Charles XV (1826-1872). King of Sweden and Norway. On his deathbed, Karl asked: "Will I be in much pain?"

Karloff, Boris, born William Henry Pratt (1887-1969). English-born actor, best known for his appearances in horror movies. Dying of emphysema and pneumonia, Karloff inexplicably mentioned to his wife the name of a fellow actor whom he had not seen in years: "Walter Pidgeon."

Kath, Terry (1946-1978). American rock musician who founded the band Chicago. At a friend's house, Kath jokingly placed a 9 mm. semiautomatic pistol to his head. Because the gun's magazine was empty, he said: "Don't worry…it's not loaded…" When Kath pulled the trigger, an unobserved bullet in the chamber discharged, killing him instantly.

Katte, Hans Hermann von (1704-1730). Katte, an officer in the Prussian army, was charged with treason for his efforts to help Crown Prince Frederick of Prussia (later Frederick the Great) flee to Great Britain. Before his beheading: "Death is sweet for a Prince I love so well..."

Kauffman, Angelica (1741-1807). Swiss-born artist. While listening to a cousin who mistakenly read a hymn for the dying, Kauffman said: "No, Johann, I will not hear that. Read me the 'Hymn for the Sick' on page 128."

Kaufman, George (1889-1961). Pulitzer Prize-winning American playwright and theater director. On his deathbed, Kaufman allowed: "I'm not afraid anymore."

Kawaguchi, Hirotsugu (died 1985). Japanese airline passenger. The 52 year-old Kawaguchi wrote several notes to his family while aboard Japan Air Lines Boeing 747 Flight 123 that crashed during a domestic flight from Tokyo to Osaka, Japan (see Takahama, Masami below): "Be good to each other and work hard. Help your mother. I'm very sad but I'm sure I won't make it. It's been 5 minutes now. I don't want to take any more planes. To think that our dinner last night was the last time. There was smoke that seemed to come from an explosion in the cabin and we began making a descent. Tsuyoshi [his son] I am counting on you. Mother- to think that something like this would happen. It's too bad. Goodbye. It's 6:30 now. The plane is rolling around and descending rapidly. I am grateful for the truly happy life I have enjoyed until now. Please, Lord, help me." The aircraft crashed into a mountain west of Tokyo at 6:56 P.M. local time with 520 deaths and four survivors. The accident resulted from a catastrophic decompression from a bulkhead failure secondary to an earlier tailstrke on landing.

Kazantzakis, Nikos (1883-1957). Greek writer, best-known for his novel *Zorba the Greek*. When his wife inquired if he were suffering: "No. No. I'm thirsty." Asked if his lips were irritated: "Yes."

Kean, Edmund (c. 1789-1833). English Shakespearean actor. In a note to his estranged wife, Kean pleaded: "Let us be no longer fools. Come home; forget and forgive. If I have erred, it was my head, not my heart, and most severely have I suffered for it. My future life shall be employed in contributing to your happiness; and you, I trust, will return that feeling by a total obliteration of the past. Your wild, but really affectionate husband, Edmund Kean." She heeded his request and the couple reconciled shortly before he expired. Near the end, Kean half-rose from bed and deliriously paraphrased Shakespeare's *Richard III*: "Give me another horse... Howard."

Alternatives: * "A horse! A horse! My kingdom for a horse!"
* Allegedly on his deathbed, Kean's son asked: "Is dying hard, father?" His reply: "Dying is easy; comedy is hard."

Kearny, Philip (1815-1862). American soldier who lost an arm during the Mexican-American War of 1846-7. Kearny later became a general in the Union army in the U.S. Civil War. While inspecting a gap in his defenses, Kearny found himself trapped behind enemy lines. He asked: "Whose troops are these?" Realizing his predicament, he turned his horse to flee but was shot dead.

Alternatives: * When told by a Confederate officer that he could not escape. Kearney's response: "You couldn't hit a barn!"
* "Don't fire. I'm a friend."

Kearns, Jack "Doc" born John McKernan (1882-1963). American fight manager for the World Heavyweight Champion boxer Jack Dempsey and others. Dying in Florida, Kearns spoke to his son about a venture he planned: "We have got to get ready and get on the ball and go to Nevada."

Keating, Lawrence (died 1895). American prison guard at Fort Smith, Arkansas. While incarcerated, the convicted murderer Crawford "Cherokee Bill" Goldsby (above) managed to obtain a pistol and shoot Keating several times. Before dying, the guard implored a fellow officer to: "Kill the dog, Will. He has killed me." Goldsby was hanged the following year.

Keats, John (1795-1821). English Romantic poet. When Keats coughed up blood a year before his death, he remarked: "I know the color of that blood; it is arterial blood. I cannot be deceived in that color; that drop of blood is my death warrant. I must die" His prediction was correct. As he lay suffering from advanced tuberculosis, Keats spoke to a friend, the artist Joseph Severn: "I feel the daisies growing over me." Immediately before expiring, he said: "Severn, I- lift me up- I am dying- I shall die easy; don't be frightened- be firm and thank God it has come." The poet earlier specified that his name should not appear on his tombstone; instead he wished it to read: "Here lies one whose name was writ in water," signifying the transient nature of life.

Alternatives: * "I feel the flowers growing over me."
* "I die of a broken heart."

Keeler, William "Wee Willie" (1872-1923). Hall of Fame American professional baseball player. On New Year's Eve, Keeler said: "I know that I am fighting a losing fight, but I want to live to see 1923 ushered in." At midnight, he sat up in bed and rang a bell to welcome the New Year. He died shortly thereafter.

Keitel, Wilhelm (1882-1946). Supreme Commander of the German Armed Forces during WWII. Keitel was tried for war crimes at the Nuremberg trials and sentenced to die by hanging: "I call on God Almighty to have mercy on the German people. More than two million German soldiers died for the Fatherland before me. I now follow my sons- all for Germany."

Keith, George (c. 1638-1716). Scottish-born American Quaker and missionary. Having disavowed the Quaker movement, Keith spoke to an acquaintance: "I wish I had died when I was a Quaker, for then I am sure it would have been well with my soul."

Kelly, Carl (1959-1993). American criminal, executed by lethal injection for a double murder and robbery: "I'm an African warrior, born to breathe, and born to die." As the drugs took effect: "I feel the poison running now."

Kelly, Edward "Ned" (1855-1880). Australian outlaw, executed for multiple murders and bank robberies. As the hangman adjusted the hood over Kelly's head, the condemned man said: "Ah well I suppose it has come to this… Such is life."

Kelly, George (1887-1974). American playwright and director, best-known for his comedies. At the end, Kelly spoke to a niece trying to give him a farewell kiss: "My dear, before you kiss me goodbye, fix your hair. It's a mess."

Kelly, Michael "King" (1857-1894). Hall of Fame American professional baseball player. During Kelly's career, a song "Slide, Kelly, Slide" was written to commemorate his prowess on the field. On a trip to Boston, he developed pneumonia and remarked on his ride to the hospital: "This is my last slide." Some say he made the remark after he was dropped from a stretcher or slipped on the floor in the hospital. Regardless, Kelly died shortly thereafter.

Alternatives: * "That was my last slide."
* "This is me last ride."

Kelly, Walter "Walt" (1913-1973). American cartoonist who created the *Pogo* comic strip. Dying from complications of diabetes, Kelly slipped in and out of consciousness. When his wife mentioned that she was going for coffee, she didn't know if her husband understood. Kelly clearly remarked: "I wish I could go with you."

Kemble, John (1757-1823). English actor. Kemble reassured his wife: "Don't be alarmed, my dear. I have had a slight attack of apoplexy."

Kennedy, John F. (1917-1963). Thirty-fifth U.S. president. On a visit to Dallas, Texas in November, 1963, Kennedy presciently remarked: "If someone is going to kill me, they will kill me." He later traveled through the city streets in a motorcade with the state's governor John Connelly, his wife Nellie and Mrs. Kennedy. Immediately before Kennedy was shot, Mrs. Connelly remarked: "Well Mr. President, you can't say Dallas doesn't love you!" He replied: "Yes that's obvious." Some say his response was: "No, you certainly can't" or "That's very obvious." As the assassin's bullets struck Kennedy, a Secret Service agent in the vehicle asserted that the president cried: "My God, I've been hit!" Neither the Connellys nor Mrs. Kennedy recalled hearing this exclamation. The president was pronounced dead approximately one half-hour later.

Kennedy, Robert F. (1925-1968). U.S. attorney general and presidential candidate. After winning the California presidential primary, Kennedy addressed a group of supporters in a Los Angeles hotel. As he left the ballroom through an adjoining kitchen, he was gunned down by a Palestinian extremist. Mortally wounded, Kennedy asked his wife Ethel about Paul Schrade, a labor leader who also was shot: "Is Paul okay? Is everybody all right?" Then: "Oh, Ethel, Ethel… Am I all right? Am I going to die?" Some related that he said: "My head" and "Jack… Jack." As Kennedy was transferred to a stretcher: "Oh, no, no, don't. Don't lift me. Don't lift me."

Alternatives: * "No, please don't… don't lift me up."
* "Is it bad? Please, don't. Don't lift me."
* "No, no, no, no, no…"

Kenney, Douglas (1946-1980). American writer and actor who co-founded the *National Lampoon* magazine. Kenney was troubled by depression and substance abuse during his last years. While visiting Hawaii, his lifeless body was found at the bottom of a cliff. Earlier, Kenney had scrawled "I love you," in soap on a mirror in his hotel room and penned a note on a scrap of paper: “These last few days are among the happiest I’ve ever ignored.”

Kenny, Elizabeth (1880-1952). Australian nurse who pioneered a controversial exercise treatment regimen for polio victims. Dying from complications of Parkinson’s disease, Kenny possibly spoke the word “America” on her deathbed, while one witness felt she was trying to say “Mother.” She was buried beside her mother.

Kent, James (1763-1847). American jurist and educator. Kent said to his children: “… Perhaps it would console you to remember, that on this point my mind is clear: I rest my hopes of salvation on the Lord Jesus Christ.”

Kent, John (1766-1843). English hymnodist. Kent’s last words could have been material for a hymn: “I rejoice in hope, I am accepted, accepted!”

Kepler, Johannes (1571-1630). German mathematician and astronomer, best-known for his writings on planetary motion. Asked how he planned to achieve salvation: “Solely by the merits of Jesus Christ, our Savior.”

Ker, Robert (died 1680). Scottish nobleman and Covenanter. During the last part of his life, Ker was incarcerated intermittently for his religious beliefs. On his deathbed, he declared: “This much I can say in humility, that through free grace, I have endeavored to keep the post that God hath set me at. These fourteen years I have not desired to lift one foot before God shewed me where to set down the other.”

Ker, William (1855-1923). Scottish educator, writer and mountaineer. While revisiting the Italian Alps, Ker exclaimed: “I thought this was the most beautiful spot in the world, and now I know it.” Ker then died suddenly of a heart attack.

Kerr, Michael (1827-1876). American politician who became speaker of the U.S. House of Representatives. Dying of tuberculosis, the austere Kerr admonished his son: “I have nothing to leave you, my son, except my good name. Guard it and your mother’s honor and live as I have lived. Pay all my debts, if my estate will warrant it, without leaving your mother penniless.

Otherwise, pay what you can, and then go to my creditors and tell them the truth, and pledge your honor to wipe out the indebtedness."

Kerr, Victor (died 1851). American military officer. Kerr was part of a revolutionary force that attempted to free Cuba from the Spanish. Vastly outnumbered, the invading band was quickly overcome. Before his death by firing squad, Kerr penned a note: "My Dear Friends, I leave you forever, and I go to the other world. I am prisoner in Havana, and in an hour I shall have ceased to exist. My dearest friends, think often of me. I die worthy of a creole, worthy of a Louisianan, and of a Kerr. My dearest friends, adieu for the last time. Your devoted friend, VICTOR KERR." When ordered to reverse his stance before the firing squad, Kerr refused: "No, we look death in the face."

Kershaw, John (1792-1870). English clergyman and cofounder of the Strict Baptists of England denomination. On his deathbed, Kershaw repeated words from a hymnbook: "Yes, I shall soon be landed on yonder shores of bliss; there with my powers expanded, shall dwell where Jesus is." His last utterance was: "God is faithful! God is faithful!"

Ketchel, Stanley "The Michigan Assassin" (1886-1910). Former American middle-weight boxing champion. Ketchel was shot by a disgruntled farmhand whom he had reprimanded. He lived long enough to name his assailant: "It is Hurz [also known as Walter Dipley] who has shot me." Before he died, the boxer said: "Take me home to mom, Pete."

Alternative: * "I'm so tired. Take me home to mother."

Ketchum, Thomas "Black Jack" (1863-1901). American cowboy, robber and murderer. While attempting to rob a train in the New Mexico Territory, Ketchum was wounded and later captured. He was convicted and sentenced to die by hanging. As he climbed the gallows stairs: "I'll be in Hell before you start breakfast, boys!" On the trap, as the noose was placed, Ketchum said: "Goodbye. Please dig my grave very deep. All right, hurry up... Let 'er go, boys, let 'er go!" When the trapdoor fell, the rope decapitated "Black Jack."

Alternative: * "I'll be in Hell before you're finished breakfast, boys! Let her rip!"

Key, Philip (1818-1859). U.S. attorney who was the son of Francis Scott Key, author of "The Star-Spangled Banner." Congressman Daniel Sickles chased down and murdered Key for committing adultery with his wife. Key pleaded: "Don't shoot! Don't shoot me! Don't murder me!" Sickles later was acquitted on the grounds of temporary insanity.

Keyes, Emily (1990-2006). American school girl. Keyes was taken hostage by a disturbed gunman who stormed her school in Bailey, Colorado. Before the teenager was shot to death, she texted her father: "I love U guys." Her assailant then shot himself to death before a SWAT team secured the school.

Keynes, John (1883-1946). English economist whose ideas influenced the economic policies of governments during the 20th Century. Dying of a heart attack, Keynes joked: "I should have drunk more Champagne."

Keyserling, William (1869-1951). Lithuanian-born businessman and philanthropist. Suffering a heart attack at a New York United Jewish Appeal meeting, Keyserling managed to say: "We must save Jewish lives!" before collapsing and dying.

Khan, Abdur Rahman (c. 1844-1901). Emir of Afghanistan. On his deathbed, the emir spoke to his son: "My spirit will remain in Afghanistan, even though my soul will go to Allah. My last words to you, my son and successor, are: 'Never trust the Russians.'"

Khan, Genghis (see Genghis Khan).

Khaury, Herbert (see Tiny Tim).

Kidd, William "Captain Kidd" (1645-1701). Scottish privateer who was accused of murder and piracy on the high seas. After his capture and conviction, Kidd was sentenced to hang. Protesting his innocence to the end, he said: "This is a very fickle and faithless generation." His body was gibbeted (hung for public display) by the Thames River as a deterrent to those who might contemplate similar acts.

Kieft, William (1597-1647). Dutch merchant. Kieft became director of the colonial province of New Netherland, established on the east coast of North America. While sailing back to Holland to answer questions of mismanagement, he perished when his ship foundered near the Welsh coast. Kieft's last words were overheard by survivors: "Friends, I have been unjust toward you; can you forgive me?"

Kierkegaard, Søren (1813-1855). Danish philosopher and theologian. Dying of a progressive paralytic disease in a Copenhagen hospital, Kierkegaard responded to a minister who remarked that he seemed well enough to go home: "Yes, there's just one obstacle, I can't walk. But then there is a different challenge: I can be lifted up. I have had a feeling of becoming an angel, getting wings. It's going to happen, too, sitting astride heaven and singing 'Hallelujah, Hallelujah, Hallelujah!' I know any shepherd's dog can do that; it all depends on how you say it." Asked if his life had progressed satisfactorily: "Yes. That is why I am very happy and very sad, because I cannot share my happiness with anyone." Kierkegaard was unable to speak during the last weeks of his terminal illness.

King, Martin Luther, Jr. (1929-1968). American clergyman, civil rights leader and winner of the 1964 Nobel Peace Prize. In late March, 1968, King traveled to Memphis, Tennessee to support striking African American sanitation workers. On April 4, while standing on the balcony of his motel, a colleague asked King if he remembered Ben Branch, a saxophone player and band leader who would perform at a dinner later that day: "Oh, yes, he's my man. How are you, Ben? Make sure you play 'Precious Lord, Take My Hand' in the meeting tonight. Play it real pretty." When a friend suggested that he wear an overcoat, King responded: "Okay, I will." Moments later King was gunned down by a lone assailant.

Alternative: * "Ben, be sure to sing 'Precious Lord, Take My Hand.' Sing it real pretty."

King, Thomas (1824-1864). American Unitarian minister and fervent supporter of the Union during the U.S. Civil War. Dying of diphtheria and pneumonia, King glanced at his son a last time and said: "Dear little fellow, he is a beautiful boy."

Kingsley, Charles (1819-1875). English clergyman, educator, novelist and historian. Dying of pneumonia, Kingsley told his attendant: "Ah, dear nurse, and I, too, am come to an end; it is all right- all as it should be." On the morning of his death, he recited part of the Episcopal Burial Service: "Thou knowest, O Lord, the secrets of our hearts. Shut not Thy merciful ears to our prayers, but spare us, O Lord most holy, O God most mighty, O holy and merciful Savior, Thou most worthy Judge Eternal, suffer us not at our last hour, from any pains of death to fall from Thee." Kingsley then turned on his side and later died.

Kinnamon, Raymond (1941-1994). American criminal, executed by lethal injection for a murder committed during a robbery: "... I'm not ready to go, but I have no choice; I sent several letters to my family; they'll be very moving when you get them. I want to say goodbye again to my boys. I know I'm missing somebody, but if there's anything I have left to say, it would be that I wish I had a Shakespearean vocabulary, but since I was raised in TDC, I missed out on some of my vocabulary. If my words can persuade you to discontinue this practice of executing people, please do so. If the citizens don't do away with the death penalty, Texas won't be a safe place to be. I have no revenge because hate won't solve anything."

Kipling, Rudyard (1865-1936). Indian-born English writer and poet, author of the novels *Kim* and *Captains Courageous* and the poems "Mandalay" and "Gunga Din." Kipling received the 1907 Nobel Prize in Literature. Dying from complications of a perforated duodenal ulcer, he complained to his doctor: "Something has come adrift inside."

Kirchner, Johanna (1889-1944). German resistance activist during WWII. Kirchner was arrested and condemned for helping Jews and others escape the clutches of the Nazi regime. She was beheaded in Plötzensee

Prison, Berlin. Kirchner wrote a last letter before her death: "Be cheerful and brave, a better future lies before you."

Alternative: * "Don't cry for me. I believe in a better future for you."

Kirkland, Richard (1843-1863). Confederate soldier who served during the U.S. Civil War. Known for his compassion toward wounded of both sides, Kirkland was mortally injured during the Battle of Chickamauga, in contiguous areas of Georgia and Tennessee: "I'm done for... save yourselves and please tell my pa I died right."

Kirkpatrick, William (1838-1921). Irish-American musician and hymnodist. On the evening before his death, Kirkpatrick told his wife he had a melody running though his head and wished to write it down. When she arose the next morning, she found her husband dead at his work table with a newly fashioned hymn before him: "... Just as Thou wilt, Lord, which shall it be?/ Life everlasting, waiting for me?/ Or shall I tarry here at Thy feet?/ Just as Thou wilt, Lord, whatever is meet."

Kitching, J. Howard (1838-1865). Union officer during the U.S. Civil War. Wounded at the Battle of Cedar Creek near Strasburg, Virginia, Kitching died of his injuries months later. Before undergoing an operation, he spoke to his sister: "It will all be over in a few minutes, darling, and we will have such a nice talk about it afterwards."

Kitto, John (1804-1854). English biblical scholar. Words uttered as Kitto died: "I am being choked. Is it death? Pray God to take me soon."

Kivi, Aleksis (1834-1872). Finnish writer and poet. Suffering from mental illness during his last decade, Kivi ironically said before dying: "I live."

Kléber, Jean Baptiste (1753-1800). French military leader who commanded Napoleon's forces in Egypt. A Muslim student studying in Cairo was bribed by countrymen to assassinate the French general. As he lay dying of stab wounds, Kléber cried: "I have been assassinated!"

Kleist, Heinrich von (1776-1811). German dramatist and writer. Overcome by financial difficulties and depression, Kleist shot his terminally-ill lover, Henriette Vogel and turned the gun on himself. The suicide note to his half-sister read: "I cannot die without, contented and serene as I am, reconciling myself with all the world and, before all others, with you, my dearest Ulrike. Give up the strong expressions, which you resorted to in your letter to me: let me revoke them; truly, to save me, you have done all within the strength, not only of a sister, but of a man- all that could be done. The truth is, nothing on earth can help me. And now goodbye: may Heaven send you a death even half equal to mine in joy and unutterable bliss: that is the most heart-felt and profoundest wish that I can think of for you. Your Henry. *Stimmung*, at Potsdam, on the morning of my death."

Klopstock, Friedrich (1724-1803). German poet. Toward the end, Klopstock quoted from one of his odes: "Can a woman forget her child, that she should not have pity on the fruit of her womb? Yes, she may forget, but I will not forget Thee!"

Klopstock, Margareta "Meta" (1728-1758). German writer and wife of the poet Friedrich Klopstock (above). Dying in childbirth, Klopstock spoke to her sister: "It is over! The blood of Jesus Christ cleanse thee from all sin."

Kluge, Günther von (1882-1944). German Field-Marshal during WWII. After the failed assassination attempt on Hitler in July, 1944, von Kluge, who had fallen out of favor with the Führer, feared that he would be implicated in the act. He committed suicide by ingesting cyanide. His suicide note read: "I depart from you, my Führer, as one who stood nearer to you than you perhaps realized in the consciousness that I did my duty to the utmost. Heil, my Führer, von Kluge, Field-Marshal. 18 August 1944."

Knibb, William (1803-1845). English missionary and abolitionist. Dying of a fever, Knibb deliriously imagined that he was addressing his Jamaican congregation: "The service is over. You may go." Immediately before dying, he declared: "All is well."

Knickerbocker, Cholly, born Maury Biddle Paul (1890-1942). New York gossip columnist. Dying of a "heart condition," Knickerbocker spoke to his mom: "Oh, Mother, how beautiful it is."

Knight, Patrick (1968-2007). American criminal, executed by lethal injection for a double murder. Knight had promised to tell a joke at the time of his execution: "... I said I was going to tell a joke. Death has set me free. That's the biggest joke. I deserve this... And the other joke is that I am not Patrick Bryan Knight and y'all can't stop this execution now. Go ahead. I'm finished. Come on, tell me Lord. I love you Melyssa, take care of that little monster for me." Fingerprints confirmed that the correct inmate was executed.

Knorr, Frances (died 1894). Australian criminal. Sentenced to die for the murder of three babies left in her care, Knorr replied to the hangman who asked for last words: "Yes, the Lord is with me. I do not fear what man can do unto me, for I have peace, perfect peace."

Knox, John (c. 1505-1572). Scottish Protestant reformer. Dying of a stroke, Knox asked his colleagues to pray for him. When the clergyman was asked if he heard their prayers, he responded: "I would to God that ye and all men heard them as I have heard them. I praise God of that heavenly sound." In his last moments: "Come, Lord Jesus, sweet Jesus! Into Thy hands I commend my spirit… I have tasted of the heavenly joys where presently I shall be! Now, for the last time I commit soul, body, and spirit into his hands." Uttering a deep sigh, he said: "Now it is come!" His attendant asked the holy man to give a signal that he was at peace. Knox waved his hand, sighed and breathed his last.

Alternative: * Some say his final words were: "Live in Christ, live in Christ, and the flesh need not fear death."

Knox, Ronald (1888-1957). English clergyman, theologian and writer, noted for his translation of the Latin Vulgate Bible. Dying of cancer, Knox was asked if he would care to hear an extract from his translation. He declined saying: "No. Awfully jolly of you to suggest it though."

Koch, Ilse (1906-1967). Convicted German war criminal. Called the "Witch of Buchenwald," Koch was accused of prisoner abuse in the Buchenwald concentration camp near Weimar in east-central Germany. After several trials at the conclusion of WWII, she was sentenced to life imprisonment. On September 1, 1967, while incarcerated in Aichach Prison in Bavaria, Koch hanged herself. Her suicide note read: "I cannot do otherwise. Death is the only deliverance."

Koestler, Arthur (1905-1983). Hungarian-born writer and political activist. Because of long-standing health issues, Koestler and his wife **Cynthia** (below) committed suicide by an overdose of barbiturates. Arthur Koestler's suicide note read: "To whom it may concern. The purpose of this note is to make it unmistakably clear that I intend to commit suicide by taking an overdose of drugs without the knowledge or aid of any other person. The drugs have been legally obtained and hoarded over a considerable period. Trying to commit suicide is a gamble the outcome of which will be known to the gambler only if the attempt fails, but not if it succeeds. Should this attempt fail and I survive it in a physically or mentally impaired state, in which I can no longer control what is done to me, or communicate my wishes, I hereby request that I be allowed to die in my own home and not be resuscitated or kept alive by artificial means. I further request that my wife, or a physician, or any friend present, should invoke habeas corpus against any attempt to remove me forcibly from my house to hospital.

My reasons for deciding to put an end to my life are simple and compelling: Parkinson's Disease and the slow-killing variety of leukaemia [leukemia]. I kept the latter a secret even from intimate friends to save them distress. After a more or less steady physical decline over the last years, the process has now reached an acute state with added complications which make it advisable to seek self-deliverance now, before I become incapable of making the necessary arrangements. I wish my friends to know that I am leaving their company in a peaceful frame of mind, with some timid hopes for a depersonalized afterlife, beyond due confines of space, time and matter and beyond the limits of our comprehension. This 'oceanic feeling' has often sustained me at difficult moments, and does so now, while I am writing this."

What makes it nevertheless hard to take this final step is the reflection of the pain it is bound to inflict on my surviving friends, above all my wife Cynthia. It is to her that I owe the relative peace and happiness that I enjoyed in the last period of my life- and never before."

The note dated June 1982 continued: "Since the above note was written in June 1982, my wife decided that after thirty-four years of working together she could not face life after my death. Cynthia Koestler penned her own note further down the page: "I fear both death and the act of dying that lies ahead of us. I should have liked to finish my account of working for Arthur- a story which began when our paths happened to cross in 1949. However, I cannot live without Arthur, despite certain inner resources. Double suicide has never appealed to me, but now Arthur's incurable diseases have reached a stage where there is nothing else to do."

Kogut, Alexandra (died 2012). American college student. Before Kogut's boyfriend bludgeoned her to death during an argument, she "tweeted" on a social internet site: "Should've known."

Konradin von Hohenstaufen (1252-1268). German (Swabian) nobleman. In 1267, Konradin set forth from Germany to seize the territory of Sicily, which earlier had been granted to the French-born Charles d'Anjou. When Konradin's forces were defeated the following year in central Italy, Charles sentenced the invader to die for his treasonous acts. Before the 16 year-old nobleman was beheaded, he lamented: "Oh my mother, how deep will be thy sorrow at the news of this day?"

Korda, Alexander (1893-1956). Hungarian-born English film director. Dying of a heart attack: "If I say goodnight to you now, will you promise that I won't wake up again?"

Kosinski, Jerzy (1933-1991). Polish-American writer. Depressed by medical issues and criticism of his writing, the 57 year-old Kosinski committed suicide by ingesting barbiturates and alcohol followed by taping a plastic bag around his head. His suicide note read: "I am going to put myself to sleep now for a bit longer than usual. Call the time Eternity."

Kossuth, Lajos (1802-1894). Hungarian statesman. Kossuth was a prominent leader of the 1848-9 Hungarian Revolution but was forced into exile the last four decades of his life. Before dying, he told his sister: "It grieves me that I have to perish in exile." When told he was the most popular Hungarian, Kossuth replied: "Only your vanity holds this."

Kraus, Christian (1753-1807). German philosopher and educator. "Dying is different from what I thought."

Krause, William (1796-1852). Irish clergyman. Dying of "spasms at the heart:" "… I am so restless I can hardly think, but the Lord's hand is not shortened."

Krauth, Charles (1823-1883). American clergyman and educator. Krauth desired solitude during his last days, saying: "I want to be left alone with my God."

Krüdener, Barbara von (1764-1824). Baltic-German religious mystic and writer. Possibly reflecting on a period of early "depravity" in her life, Krüdener mused: "The good I may have done will remain, but what I have done wrong the mercy of my God will blot out."

Kudrinsky, Eldar (died 1994). Fifteen year-old son of a Russian Aeroflot pilot. During a Moscow to Hong Kong flight, Kudrinsky was allowed into the cockpit by his father. The boy accidentally disconnected the aircraft's autopilot, ultimately sending the jet into a fatal dive. Before danger was perceived, Kudrinsky asked: "Why is it turning? When his father questioned if the aircraft were turning by itself, the boy replied: Yes. Is it going off course? I am turning it left!" Despite frantic maneuvering by the crew, flight stability could not be achieved. All 75 people on board perished in the crash.

Kuribayashi, Tadamichi (1891-1945). WWII army general who commanded the Japanese garrison during the Battle of Iwo Jima, an island approximately 650 miles south of Tokyo. Although the circumstances of the general's death remain unclear, Kuribayashi's final transmission to his headquarters quoted the conclusion of a death poem: "... When ugly weeds run riot over this island, my heart and soul will be with the fate of the Imperial nation."

Kurz, Toni (1913-1936). German mountaineer. Caught in an avalanche while attempting to climb the north face of the Eiger in the Bernese Alps, Kurz spoke as he unsuccessfully tried to untie a knot that would allow his rescue: "I can do no more."

Labouchère, Henry Du Pré (1831-1912). English politician and journalist. When an oil lamp at his bedside flared, Labouchère quipped: "Flames? Not yet, I think." Some say a lamp was knocked over causing a fire, thus prompting the possible reference to the underworld.

Labouré, Saint Catherine (1806-1876). French nun, noted for her visions of the Virgin Mary. To a niece who said she would return in the morning to wish a happy New Year: "You shall see me, but I shall not see you, for I won't be here." Catherine died several hours before midnight.

Lacépéde, Comte de Bernard-Germain (1756-1825). French naturalist and writer. Lacépéde asked his son to write on an unfinished manuscript: "Charles, write in large letters the word 'end' at the foot of the page."

Lacordaire, Jean-Baptiste (1802-1861). French theologian. On his deathbed, Lacordaire prayed: "My God, open to me!"

Laden, Osama bin (1957-2011). Saudi Arabian-born terrorist who founded the al-Qaeda group responsible for the September 11, 2001 attacks in New York City, Washington D.C. and Pennsylvania. Sought for a decade, bin Laden eventually was traced to a compound in Pakistan. Before he was shot dead by members of a Navy SEAL team, the fugitive told relatives: "Don't turn on the light."

Laënnec, René (1781-1826). French physician who developed the stethoscope and encouraged its use in the study of chest diseases. Dying of tuberculosis, Laënnec removed his rings, saying: "It would be necessary soon that another do me this service. I do not want anyone to have the bother of it."

Lafayette, Marie-Joseph de (1757-1834). French soldier and statesman who served in the American Revolution. As he lay dying in Paris, Lafayette made the assertion: "What do you expect? Life is like the flame of a lamp. When there is no more oil- zest! It goes out, and it is all over."

La Follette, Robert Sr. (1855-1925). American politician who became a U.S. senator. Dying of atherosclerotic vascular disease, La Follette proclaimed: "I am at peace with all the world, but there is still a lot of work I could do. I don't know how the people will feel towards me, but I shall take to the grave my love for them which has sustained me through life." He later spoke to his son after taking a sip of milk: "It is good."

Lagny, Thomas Fantet de (1660-1734). French mathematician, hydrologist and educator. While barely conscious on his deathbed, Lagny was asked by a colleague to square the number 12. He aroused, quickly answered "144" and fell back dead.

Lagrone, Edward (1957-2004). American criminal, executed by lethal injection for multiple murders: "... Like I said from day one, I didn't go in there and kill them, but I'm no better than the people that did. Jesus is Lord. That's all I have to say."

LaGuardia, Fiorello (1882-1947). American politician who became a member of the U.S. House of Representatives and mayor of New York City. Dying of pancreatic cancer, LaGuardia greeted a judge visiting him: "I'm glad to meet an honest judge."

La Harpe, Jean-François de (1739-1803). French playwright, literary critic, writer and poet. La Harpe's response to hearing the prayer for the sick: "I am grateful to Divine Mercy for having left me sufficient recollection to feel how consoling these prayers are to the dying."

Laing, Ronald (1927-1989). Scottish psychiatrist. Suffering a heart attack while playing tennis, Laing made his wishes clear: "No bloody doctors."

Lakanal, Joseph (1762-1845). French educator and politician. Lakanal perceived his end as he spoke to his doctor: "Your attentions will not save me. I feel that there is no more oil in the lamp."

Lalande, Joseph-Jérôme de (1732-1807). French astronomer. Dying of suspected tuberculosis, Lalande asked his attendants to: "Withdraw. I no longer have need of anything."

Lamar, Lucius (1825-1893). U.S. Secretary of the Interior and associate justice of the Supreme Court. Lamar's parting words: "I am suffocating."

Lamb, Charles (1775-1834). English literary critic, writer and poet. "... My bedfellows are cough and cramp, we sleep 3 in a bed... Don't come yet to this house of pest and age." These often-quoted "last words" found in a letter to his friend Edward Moxon were written 20 months before his death. Ill with a streptococcal infection (erysipelas), Lamb called two names as he died: "Moxon, Proctor."

Lamballe, Marie-Thérèse (1749-1792). Italian-born confidante of French Queen Marie Antoinette. When asked to swear an oath renouncing her king and queen, Lamballe refused. She was dragged into an alley and hacked to death screaming: "Fie on the horror."

Lambert, John (died 1538). Martyred English clergyman. Condemned for heresy because he repudiated various church doctrines, Lambert was burned at the stake. As the flames consumed his body, he proclaimed: "None but Christ, none but Christ."

Lamennais, Hugues-Félicité-Robert de (1782-1854). French clergyman and philosopher. Lamennais commented on sunlight streaming into his bedroom: "Let it come. It is coming for me."

Lamoral, Charles-Joseph, Prince de Ligne (1735-1814). Belgian-born military leader, writer and aristocrat. Deliriously raving before dying: "Back, thou accursed phantom!"

Lamy, Jean-Baptiste (1814-1888). French-born Roman Catholic archbishop of Santa Fe, New Mexico. Dying of pneumonia, Lamy spoke to those assembled at his deathbed: "Thank you. I was able to follow every word of the prayers you came to say for me. Keep praying for me, for I feel that I am going."

Landis, Carole, born Frances Lillian Ridste (1919-1948). American film star. Because of failed love affairs and a declining career, Landis took a fatal dose of the barbiturate Seconal. Her suicide note read: "Dearest Mommie. I'm sorry, really sorry to put you through this. But there is no way to avoid it. I love you darling. You have been the most wonderful Mom ever. And that applies to all of our family. I love each and every one of them dearly. Everything goes to you. Look in the files and there is a will which decrees everything. Goodbye, my angel. Pray for me. Your baby."

Landis, Kenesaw (1866-1944). American jurist and first professional baseball commissioner. When a nurse mentioned that friends had asked how he was doing, Landis replied: "The Judge is doing all right."

Landon, Michael, born Eugene Maurice Orowitz (1936-1991). American actor, writer and producer. Dying of pancreatic cancer, Landon spoke to his dead parents: "Dad, you'll have to wait. I'll be with you in a minute. Oh, Mom, it's so pretty here." When told his parents were waiting, he replied: "Yes, I've got to go." When told that it was time to move on, he responded: "You're right. It's time. I love you all."

Landru, Henri (1869-1922). French criminal. Landru was charged with the serial killing of women lured with the promise of matrimony. Because he skillfully disposed of their bodies, scant evidence was available for examination by the police. Regardless, he was convicted and sentenced to die. When Landru's guards arrived, a priest asked if he wished to offer a last confession: "I am very sorry, but I must not keep these gentlemen waiting." Before he was guillotined, the condemned man observed: "Ah well, it is not the first time that an innocent man has been condemned... I will be brave. I will be brave."

Lang, Cosmo (1864-1945). Scottish-born archbishop of Canterbury. While on his way to catch a train to London, Lang collapsed and died of a heart attack. Before expiring, he exclaimed: "I must get to the station."

Langtry, Lily, born Emilie Charlotte Le Breton (1853-1929). English actress. To a friend: "I know that I am at the end. I shall never get better, dear. I am going, dear. I am very sorry, but I am going."

Lanier, Sidney (1842-1881). American poet and musician. Dying of tuberculosis, Lanier declined further treatment saying "I can't." Some say he refused to drink.

Lannes, Jean (1769-1809). French general. During the French advance on Vienna, Lannes was mortally wounded. When Napoleon saw his injured general, he said "You will live, my friend," Lannes allegedly replied "I trust I may, if I can still be of use to France and your Majesty." Some say Lannes was so grievously wounded that he could only mutter incoherently.

Alternatives: * A recollection by a fellow general: "I am dying for you and for my country. Do not mourn my loss. May you live and save the army."

* A remembrance by a comforting cadet: "I am dying for you, like so many others. You will not mourn my loss any more than the rest. Make peace before it is your turn."

Lansing, Robert (1928-1994). American film and television actor: Dying of cancer at age 66: "You know, I don't mind dying. The thing that p***** me off is that I won't get to be an old man. I was looking forward to that."

Lansky, Meyer, born Meyer Suchowljansky (1902-1983). Russian-born American gangster. Dying of lung cancer, Lansky told his doctors (some say his wife): "Let me go! Let me go!"

Lanza, Mario, born Alfredo Cocozza (1921-1959). American operatic tenor and actor. During a significant portion of his career, Lanza struggled with alcohol abuse and unwanted weight gain. While a patient in a Rome weight loss clinic, he decided to leave the facility. To his chauffeur: "Go to the house. Don't let anyone know what you're up to. Bring me something to wear and let's get the hell out of here before they kill me with all these injections." Before dying, Lanza spoke to his wife by phone: "I love you, Betty... Betty."

Laplace, Pierre-Simon de (1749-1827). French astronomer and physicist. On his deathbed, Laplace allowed: "What we know is very slight. What we don't know is immense." When a friend mentioned that his observations on Jupiter's satellites had been verified by a German observer, Laplace spoke his last words: "Man follows only phantoms."

Alternative: * "What we know is of small amount. What we do not know is enormous."

Larkin, Philip (1922-1985). English librarian, poet and writer. Dying of cancer, Larkin confided to his nurse "I am going to the inevitable."

Larkin, William "Bill" (died 1989). American screenwriter. Larkin and Martin Ragaway were long-standing comedy writers for Bob Hope (above). Several weeks after his good friend Ragaway died, Larkin committed suicide: "I'm so godd*** sick of feeling 98 percent dead that I really want to die. I am lonely but no longer have the patience to be around people. I always say I feel fine. People aren't interested in how you feel, and I don't blame them. Sick people are boring." He continued: "While I had a wonderful life and have done so much more than I ever dreamed of doing, it's over now. I no longer serve any function. There is no reason for me to exist. I'm actually excited about dying. In one instant, I can solve a million little problems." Larkin then shot himself to death.

Laski, Harold (1893-1950). English political scientist, educator and writer. Dying of a virulent case of influenza, Laski mused to his wife: "Isn't this incredible?"

Latimer, Hugh (died 1555). Martyred English Protestant bishop of Worcester. Bishops Latimer and Nicholas Ridley (below) were condemned to die by burning at the stake when they refused to renounce their Protestant faith during the reign of Queen Mary I. As Latimer was consumed by the flames, he admonished his fellow martyr: "Be of good comfort, Master Ridley, and play the man. We shall this day light such a candle, by God's grace, in England, as I trust shall never be put out." As the flames flared, Ridley cried out: "Lord, Lord, receive my spirit." The dying Latimer answered: "O Father of Heaven, receive my soul."

Latrobe, John (1803-1891). American lawyer, philanthropist and writer. Latrobe realized his end was near: "The machine is worn out."

Laud, Hugh (1573-1645). Martyred English Archbishop of Canterbury. Because of his support for King Charles I and opposition to Protestantism, Laud was convicted of treason. On the scaffold, before his beheading, the martyr said: "Lord, I am coming as fast as I can. I know I must pass through the shadow of death before I can come to see Thee. But it is but *umbra mortis*, a mere shadow of death, a little darkness upon nature; but Thou by Thy merits and passion hast broken through the jaws of death. So, Lord, receive my soul and have mercy upon me and bless this kingdom with peace and plenty and with brotherly love and charity, that there may not be this effusion of Christian blood amongst them for Jesus Christ, His sake, if it be Thy will." He prayed for a while and then gave the signal for the axe to fall by saying: "Lord, receive my soul."

Laughton, Charles (1899-1962). English-born actor, producer and director. Succumbing to kidney cancer, Laughton asked: "Am I dying? What's the matter? Am I dying?"

Laurel, Stanley "Stan" born Arthur Stanley Jefferson (1890-1965). English-born American comedian and a member of the Laurel and Hardy comedy act. Before dying of a heart attack, Laurel quipped to his nurse giving him an injection: "I wish I was skiing." When she asked if he were a skier, he replied: "No, but I'd rather be skiing than doing what I'm doing."

Alternatives: * "I'd much rather be skiing than doing this... No, but I'd much sooner be skiing than what I'm doing now."

* "I wish I were skiing now... No, but better be doing that than having those needles stuck into me."

Laurencin, Marie (1883-1956). French painter and printmaker. Laurencin requested: "Let no one come to see me when I am dead."

Laurentius of Rome, Saint, also Lawrence (died 258). Roman Christian martyr. Condemned to die because of his Christian religion, Laurentius allegedly was roasted alive. To his executioner: "Seest thou not, O thou foolish man that I am already roasted on one side, and that, if thou wouldst have me well cooked, it is time to turn me on the other" As he died: "I thank thee, O my God and Saviour, that I have been found worthy to enter into thy beatitude."

Alternatives: * "This side is now roasted enough, turn up, oh tyrant great, assay whether roasted or raw thou thinkest the better meat."
* "This side enough is toasted, so turn me, try and eat, and see whether raw or roasted I make the better meat."
* "My flesh is well-cooked on this one side. Turn the other and eat."
* "I am roasted; now turn me, and eat me."

Laurier, Wilfred (1841-1919). Canadian prime minister. Dying of a stroke, to the nun taking care of him: "Well, it is the bride of the Divine Husband who comes to help a great sinner." When asked if he wished to see a priest: "Very well, but I am not so sick as you think. Only a little weak." After the Last Rites were given, he died saying "It is finished."

Laval, Pierre (1883-1945). French politician who led the Vichy Regime during WWII. Laval was killed by firing squad for his collaboration with Nazi occupiers during the war. Before his execution, he attempted suicide by ingesting poison but was quickly revived. Shortly thereafter, he faced the firing squad, shouting: "*Vive la France*! [Long live France!]"

Lavergne, Madame (died 1794). French noblewoman. When her husband was condemned to die during the French Revolution, Madame Lavergne stood in the assembled crowd and shouted over and over: "*Vive le Roi*! [Long live the king!]" Because utterance of this phrase was considered a treasonous act, she also was condemned to die. On the way to the execution site, she said to her husband who awakened from a faint: "Do not be alarmed. It is your faithful wife who called you. You know I could not live without you, and we are going to die together."

Laverock, Hugh (died 1556). English martyr of the Puritan persecutions during the reign of Queen Mary I. The 68 year-old Laverock was lame and walked with the assistance of a crutch. When he was tied to the stake along with a blind man, he told his fellow martyr: "Be of good comfort, brother, for my Lord of London is our good Physician. He will cure us both shortly- thee of thy blindness and me of my lameness."

Lavry, Aymond de (died 1555). Martyred French Protestant minister. Before being choked and burned at the stake, Lavry spoke these words to his friends: "O Lord, make haste to help me! Tarry not, despise not the work of Thy hands. My friends, I exhort you to study and learn the Gospel, for the word of God abideth forever. Labour to know the will of God and fear not them that kill the body, but have no power over the soul."

Lawrence, David H. "D.H." (1885-1930). English novelist, author of *Lady Chatterley's Lover.* Dying of tuberculosis and possibly malaria, Lawrence said: "I am better now. If I could sweat, I would be better. I am better now." Later: "I think it's time for the morphine."

Alternative: * "Wind my watch."

Lawrence, Ernest (1901-1958). American physicist who was instrumental in the development of the cyclotron. For his endeavors, Lawrence was awarded the 1939 Nobel Prize in Physics. Dying of ulcerative colitis, to his wife: "I'm ready to give up now. Molly, I can't make it."

Lawrence, Gertrude, born Gertrude Dagmar Klasen (1898-1952). English actress and singer. Commenting on the musical *The King and I,* Lawrence said: "About the play, see that Connie Carpenter steps in. She has waited so long for her chance. See that she gets the role. See that Yul [Brynner, her co-star] gets star billing. He has earned it."

Lawrence, Henry (1806-1857). British administrator and military leader in India. Mortally wounded during the Indian Rebellion of 1857, Lawrence requested: "No surrender! Let every man die at his post but never make terms. God help the poor women and children..." To the chaplain: "Let my epitaph be- 'Here Lies Henry Lawrence who tried to do his duty!'" As he died: "Let there be no fuss about me. Let me be buried with the men."

Lawrence, James (1781-1813). U.S. naval captain. During the Battle of 1812 (the actual engagement occurred in 1813), Lawrence took command of the U.S. frigate *Chesapeake* and engaged the British vessel HMS *Shannon* that blockaded Boston harbor. Mortally wounded by a musket ball, he commanded: "Tell the men to fire faster and not give up the ship. Fight her till she sinks." The *Chesapeake* subsequently fell into British hands. A paraphrase of Lawrence's last words "Don't give up the ship" later appeared on Commodore Oliver Perry's battle flag (below).

Lawson, David (1955-1994). American criminal, executed in the North Carolina gas chamber for a murder committed during a robbery: "I'm sorry I killed Wayne Shinn. I hope North Carolina will one day be sorry that they killed me." As the gas took effect: "I'm human! I'm human!"

Le Mesurier, John, born John Le Mesurier Halliley (1912-1983). English television and film actor. Dying from complications of cirrhosis, Le Mesurier reminisced: "It's all been rather lovely."

Lear, Edward (1812-1888). English artist, writer and poet. Dying of heart disease while in Italy, Lear asked his valet to deliver a last message to his friends: "My good Giuseppe. I feel that I am dying. You will render me a sacred service in telling my friends and relations that my last thought was for them... I cannot find words sufficient to thank my good friends for the good they have always done me. I did not answer their letters because I could not write, as no sooner did I take a pen in my hand then I felt as if I were dying."

Leary, Timothy (1920-1996). American psychologist who used and advocated the use of psychedelic drugs. Dying of prostate cancer, Leary commented: "How you die is the most important thing you ever do. It's the exit, the final scene of the glorious epic of your life. It's the third act and, you know, everything builds up to the third act. I've been waiting for this for years." Before he died, he asked over and over: "Why? Why not?"

Alternatives: * "Why not? Why not? Why not? Yeah."
* Some say his last word was: "Beautiful."

Leclerc, Jean (died 1524). French Huguenot martyr. When Leclerc refused to renounce his Protestant faith, he was sentenced to die. After his arrest, the martyr's right hand was severed, his nose was pulled off with pincers and his body was mutilated. Before he died by burning at the stake, Leclerc quoted passages of Psalm 115: "Their idols are silver and gold, even the work of men's hands... They that make them are like unto them; so is every one that trusteth in them... Oh! Israel, trust thou in the Lord. He is their help and shield..."

Lecouvreur, Adrienne (1692-1730). French actress. Taken ill during a performance, Lecouvreur died several days later. When a priest asked if she placed her hope in the God of the Universe, the dying woman told him that her lover Count Maurice de Saxe "... is my Universe, my Hope, my God!" She died unabsolved.

Ledbetter, Huddie "Leadbelly" (1888-1949). American folk and blues singer, composer and guitarist. Terminally ill with amyotrophic lateral sclerosis (Lou Gehrig's disease), Ledbetter told his doctor who advised him to go to bed: "Doctor, don't put me in that bed. You put me in that bed, and I'll never get out."

Alternative: * Playing the guitar during his last hospital stay: "Doctor, if I put this here guitar down now, I ain't never gonna wake up."

Lee, Charles (1731-1782). British-born military leader who fought with George Washington and his Continental Army. Because of poor leadership and insubordination, Lee was drummed out of the service. Dying of pneumonia, he deliriously relived some of his earlier battles: "Stand by me, my brave grenadiers."

Lee, Gideon (1778-1841). U.S. congressman. "I should like to stay with you a little longer to finish some work begun, but if it is the pleasure of God I am ready to go now."

Lee, Gypsy Rose, born Rose Louise Hovick (1911-1970). American burlesque dancer, actress and writer. Dying of lung cancer, Lee was told that her suffering would be over soon. Surprised, she asked: "What do you mean?"

Lee, Robert E. (1807-1870). General-in-chief of Confederate forces during the waning period of the U.S. Civil War. Lee suffered a stroke on September 28, 1870 and died of pneumonia two weeks later. Some accounts state that he was unable to speak during that period. Some biographers, however, allege that Lee relived some of his battlefield encounters immediately before he died: "Tell Hill he *must* come up! Strike [take down] the tent." A.P. Hill was one of Lee's favorite commanders. Later, when asked how he felt, Lee replied "slowly and distinctly:" "I feel better." Refusing his medicine: "It is no use." Some say Lee's last delirious words were: "I will give that sum." This comment, however, was spoken at an earlier church meeting to discuss a minister's salary. Lee generously agreed to make up a deficit in payment to the clergyman.

Alternatives: * "Strike my tent; send for Hill."
* "Strike the tent. Tell Hill he *must* come up!"
* "Have A.P. Hill sent for."

Leeuwenhoek, Antonie van (1632-1723). Dutch scientist, credited with major improvements in the design of the microscope. Toward the end, Leeuwenhoek spoke to a colleague: "Hoogvliet, my friend, be so good as to have those two letters on the table translated into Latin. Send them to London to the Royal Society."

Lefebvre, Eugène (1878-1909). French aviator. Lefebvre was killed when his French-built Wright Flyer crashed at Juvisy in north-central France. Before the doomed flight, he ventured: "Yes I will succeed and I'll make some money, unless I break my neck." The accident gave Lefebvre the dubious distinction of being the first person killed while piloting a powered aircraft.

Leger, Saint (c. 615-678). Bishop of Autun in east-central France. Implicated in the murder of a Frankish king, Leger was condemned to die. As swordsmen led him to his beheading: "There is no need to weary yourselves longer, brothers! Do here the bidding of him that sent you!"

Lehár, Franz (1870-1948). Austro-Hungarian composer and conductor, best known for his operetta *The Merry Widow*. Lehár realized the end was near: "Now I have finished with all earthly business, and high time too. Yes, yes, my dear child, now comes death."

Leibniz, Gottfried von (1646-1716). German philosopher and mathematician. Dying from a painful illness, Leibnitz was asked by his attendant, if he wished to take the sacraments. He replied that he had wronged no one, had nothing to confess and wished to be left in peace. When reminded that he would soon pass from "time to eternity," Leibniz pondered: "Also are other men mortal."

Lekeu, Guillaume (1870-1894). Belgian composer. Dying of typhoid fever, the 24 year-old Lekeu lamented: "So many works unfinished! My quartet!" Possibly, Lekeu referred to his Piano Quartet in B minor, later completed by his mentor, the French composer Vincent d'Indy.

Lenin, Vladimir (1870-1924). Russian communist revolutionary leader. Lenin suffered a number of disabling strokes during his last years. While watching some friends hunt, a retriever returned with a kill. His last words: "Good dog!"

Lennon, John (1940-1980). British-born musician who was a cofounder of The Beatles rock band. As Lennon and his wife walked toward their Manhattan apartment, he was gunned down by a deranged man. Lennon cried: "I'm shot. I'm shot," and collapsed. As he was being transported to a local hospital, a policeman asked if he were John Lennon. The musician allegedly replied: "Yes, I am." Due to the severity of his injury, it is uncertain whether Lennon uttered those last words.

Alternative: * "Yeah."

Leo X (1475-1521). Pope from 1513 until his death. Leo was noted for his challenge of Martin Luther's *Ninety-five Theses* and failure to suppress the Protestant Reformation. Leo probably died of malaria, although rumors of poisoning circulated in response to one of his last statements: "I have been murdered. No remedy can prevent my speedy death." In a turn of direction, he then said: "Pray for me. I want to make you all happy."

Leo XI (1535-1605). Italian-born priest who served as pope less than one month. Dying of a febrile illness: "Do not suggest to us any care for earthly interests; you must speak to us now only about things eternal."

Leo XIII (1810-1903). Pope from 1878 until his death. Awakening from a coma, Leo spoke to his physicians: "This time you will not win your brave fight with death." To one of his cardinals: "To your Eminence, who will so soon seize the reins of supreme power, I confide the church in these difficult times." He then replied to a colleague who asked for a blessing of the court: "Be this my last greeting." To his valet: "My hour has come; farewell. Thanks, my son." Before Leo slipped into his final stupor, he said: "This is the end." When a candle was placed close to his mouth three times with no wavering, the Pope was pronounced dead.

Leonardo da Vinci (1452-1519). Italian polymath- artist, scientist, engineer and inventor who has been called the "Universal Genius" and "Renaissance Man." Leonardo spoke self-effacing last words: "I have offended God and mankind because my work did not reach the quality it should have."

Alternative: * "I have offended God and mankind in not having labored at my art as I ought to have done."

Leopardi, Giacomo (1798-1837). Italian poet, writer and philosopher. Dying during a cholera epidemic, the 38 year-old Leopardi pleaded to a friend: "I am suffocating, Totonno. Give me light."

Alternative: * "I can't see you anymore."

Leopold I (1640-1705). Austrian-born Holy Roman emperor. At the end, Leopold requested: "Let me die to the sound of sweet music."

Leopold I (1790-1865). King of Belgium. On his deathbed, Leopold spoke to his chaplain: "May God pardon all my sins."

Alternative: * "Don't leave me."

Leopold II (1835-1909). King of Belgium. Dying of an "embolism," Leopold complained to his physician: "I am suffocating, doctor! I am suffocating!"

Alternative: * "I am hot."

Lepelletier St. Fargeau, Louis de (1760-1793). French politician. During the French Revolution, Lepelletier was appointed secretary of the National Convention. After voting for Louis XVI's execution, he was assassinated by a member of the king's *Garde du Corps.* Before dying: "I am cold."

Lépine, Marc (1964-1989). Canadian criminal. During a shooting rampage on a Montreal college campus, the deranged man killed 14 women. Before committing suicide by turning the rifle on himself, Lépine said: "Oh, s***."

Leslie, John, Duke of Rothes (c. 1630-1681). Lord Chancellor of Scotland, appointed by King Charles II. In 1680, the Scottish minister Donald Cargill (above) excommunicated King Charles, John Leslie and other government leaders. For his ill-fated action, Cargill was hanged one year later. On his deathbed, Leslie reflected: "We all thought little of what that man Cargill did in excommunicating us, but I find that sentence binding upon me now, and it will bind to eternity!"

Lespinasse, Jeanne-Julie de (1732-1776). French society hostess who owned a prominent Parisian salon. Awakening from a coma, the 43 year-old de Lespinasse asked: "Am I still alive?" She died shortly thereafter.

Lewis, Clive Staples "C.S." (1898-1963). Irish-born British writer, educator and theologian, known for his Christian apologetics and novels *Screwtape Letters* and *The Chronicles of Narnia*. Dying of kidney failure, Lewis exclaimed: "I have done all that I was sent into the world to do, and I am ready to go." When his brother later offered tea, he said: "Thank you" and died moments later.

Lewis, Ellis (1798-1871). American politician who became a Pennsylvania Supreme Court chief justice. Lewis perceived that his end approached: "I believe I am dying now."

Lewis, George (1900-1968). American jazz clarinetist and band leader. Lewis quipped to a friend who handed him a crucifix: "Departings are too hard. I'll be back after you."

Lewis, Helen Joy Davidman (1915-1960). American-born poet and writer. Dying of cancer, to her husband C.S. Lewis (above): "Don't get me a posh coffin. Posh coffins are all rot." Then: "You have made me happy." Finally, she assured her priest: "I am at peace with God."

Lewis, Meriwether (1774-1809). American soldier, politician and explorer who co-led the Lewis and Clark Expedition (1804-1806). Three years after completing his monumental trek, Lewis began a journey from St. Louis to Washington D.C. While on the Natchez Trace southwest of Nashville, Tennessee, he died under suspicious circumstances. After a gunshot rang out at the inn where he stayed overnight, the explorer was found mortally wounded. Lewis allegedly told the innkeeper: "Oh, Lord! Oh, madam! Give me some water, and heal my wounds." Before dying, he exclaimed: "I am no coward, but I am so strong, so hard to die!" Because Lewis exhibited a bizarre behavior in the hours before the shooting, his death was ruled a suicide. Some, however, felt his demise was the result of a botched robbery.

Alternative: * "I am no coward, but it is hard to die… so young… so hard to die."

Lewis, Sinclair (1885-1951). American novelist who was awarded the1930 Nobel Prize in Literature. Dying from complications of alcohol abuse and heart disease, Lewis bid goodbye: "I am happy. God bless you all."

Lewis, Wyndham (1882-1957). English writer and artist. When Lewis' nurse asked about the state of his bowels, he testily replied: "Mind your own business."

Ley, Robert (1890-1945). Nazi war criminal who led the German Labor Front. Indicted at the post-war Nuremburg trials, Ley hanged himself in his cell before his court appearance. His suicide note read in part: "... but the fact that I should be a criminal, that is what I can't stand."

Liaquat Ali Khan (1896-1951). Indian-born first prime minister of Pakistan. Liaquat was assassinated by an Afghan henchman during a public meeting. Before dying of his gunshot wounds: "Allah, save this country! *Pakistan zindabad! Pakistan zindabad!* [Long live Pakistan!]."

Liberace, born Wladziu Liberace (1919-1987). American popular pianist and television personality. Dying from complications of AIDS, Liberace was asked if he would like to attend church: "I wish I could. I'll just stay here and watch my shows."

Liebaut, Albert and Germaine (died 1923). French newlyweds who inexplicably shot themselves to death after their marriage. The couple's suicide note read: "We are killing ourselves because we are too happy... we do not need money, for we are worth over 30,000 francs. We have good health and a wonderful future before us, but we prefer to die now because we are the happiest people in the world. We adore each other but would rather descend into the grave together while we are still so happy."

Lieutand, Joseph (1703-1780). Physician to French King Louis XV. As Lieutand lay dying, he was asked by his confessor if he believed. His reply: "O sir, let me die in peace. I believe in everything except in medicines." Feeling that he was receiving conflicting treatments, Lieutand said: "Ah, I shall die well enough without all that!"

Lieven, Dorothea de (1785-1857). Noblewoman and diplomat, born in present day Latvia. As Lieven's health declined, she sent a note to a friend: "I thank you for twenty years of affection and happiness. Don't forget me. Goodbye. Goodbye."

Liguori, Saint Alphonsus Maria de (1696-1787). Italian bishop. "Give me the picture of Our Lady." Then, Liguori prayed the *Ave Maria* and uttered his last words: "Holy Mary, Mother of God, pray for us sinners, now and at the hour of our death. Amen."

Lilienthal, Otto (1848-1896). German aviation pioneer who experimented primarily with gliders. During his last flight, Lilienthal's craft stalled. The aviator fell from a height of 56 ft, breaking his spine. Not realizing the seriousness of his injuries, he said: "I must rest a little, then we continue."

Liliuokalani (1838-1917). Deposed Hawaiian queen. Dying of a stroke, to a friend: "Thank you. How are you?"

Lincoln, Abraham (1809-1865). Sixteenth U.S. president. While enjoying a play at Ford's Theatre in Washington, D.C., Lincoln took his wife's hand. When Mrs. Lincoln asked what people would think of such an intimate gesture, the president replied: "They won't think anything about it." Some feel Mrs. Lincoln's question referenced the presence of Clara Harris, a guest in the presidential box: "She won't think anything about it." Regardless, moments later, Lincoln was assassinated by John Wilkes Booth, an actor who sympathized with the Confederate cause.

Lincoln, Abraham II (1873-1890). Grandson of U.S. President Abraham Lincoln. Dying of septicemia secondary to a carbuncle under his arm, the 16 year-old Lincoln told his nurse: "It's all right."

Lincoln, Mary (1818-1882). Widow of U.S. President Abraham Lincoln. Residing in a darkened room in her sister's house, Mary requested: "I want to walk across the floor and look out of the window." From the effort, she suffered a stroke that rendered her mute during her last days.

Lincoln, Nancy (1784-1818). Mother of U.S. President Abraham Lincoln. Nancy possibly died of "milk sickness," caused by the ingestion of dairy products produced from cows that consumed the white snakeroot. This plant, found in frontier areas of the U.S., contains the substance tremetol, which can produce a myriad of symptoms including tremors, intense abdominal pain, coma and death. Before expiring, Nancy spoke to her children: "Be good and kind to your father, to one another, and to the world." As the end drew near, to her son: "I am going away from you, Abraham, and shall not return. I know that you will be a good boy, that you will be kind to Sarah [Abraham's sister] and to your father. I want you to live as I have taught you, and to love your Heavenly Father."

Lind, Johanna "Jenny" (1820-1887). Swedish soprano, nicknamed the "Swedish Nightingale." When her daughter opened the blinds of her room, Lind sang the beginning of the German song "To the Sunshine:" "O sunshine! O sunshine!/ How you shine into my heart..." She later prayed: "Dear Lord, You did not let me be made a sacrifice, in any part, in any way. Dear Lord, how beyond all understanding has been Your goodness to me."

Lindbergh, Charles (1902-1974). American aviation pioneer who was the first to fly solo across the Atlantic Ocean. Dying of lymphoma, Lindbergh told his doctors that once he had feared death, but: "This time I am not apprehensive or frightened. Death is a natural process and a part of life. It is one of the events of life." He then spoke to his wife: "It's harder on you, watching me die, than it is on me."

Lindsay, Vachel (1879-1931). American poet. Worried about his finances and health, the delusional Lindsay committed suicide by drinking a bottle of cleaning fluid. Before dying, he enigmatically stated: "They tried to get me! I got them first."

Lindsey, Theophilus (1723-1808). English clergyman, theologian and writer. When asked if he lived by the maxim elaborated by Alexander Pope: "Whatever is, is right?" Lindsey replied: "No. Whatever is, is best."

Alternative: * "God's will is best."

Lippard, George (1822-1854). American writer and social activist. Dying of tuberculosis, Lippard asked his physician: "Is this death?"

Lisle, George (c. 1610-1648). English Royalist officer, taken prisoner during the siege at Colchester during the English Civil War. Condemned to die by his captors, Lisle, along with fellow combatant Charles Lucas (below), faced a firing squad. After Lucas was shot dead, Lisle worried that his distance from the executioners was too great: "I have been nearer to you when you have missed me." The soldiers, however, hit their mark with deadly accuracy.

Liszt, Franz (1811-1886): Hungarian pianist and composer. While visiting Richard Wagner's Bayreuth Festival in July 1886, Liszt was stricken with fever and a productive cough. Disregarding warnings from his physician to rest, he attended a performance of his late son-in-law's opera *Tristan und Isolde* but was too ill to stay for its conclusion. Pneumonia and his underlying chronic cardiopulmonary disease eventually caused his death. Several days before expiring, Liszt called his sleeping valet to bring a chamber pot: "Miska, are you awake?" Returning to bed: "I thank you. Please continue sleeping." Some say his last utterance before dying was "Tristan." Because Liszt essentially was unconscious for his last 20 hours, it is highly unlikely that he spoke that word or any others during his death throes.

Litvinenko, Alexander (1962-2006). Former Russian KGB agent who made unwelcome claims of impropriety against his former superiors. He allegedly was assassinated by radioactive polonium poisoning while in London. In an interview several hours before his death, Litvinenko reportedly said: "The b******* got me, but they won't get everybody." The last portion of his final statement: "... You may succeed in silencing one man but the howl of protest from around the world will reverberate, Mr. Putin [the Russian president], in your ears for the rest of your life. May God forgive you for what you have done, not only to me but to beloved Russia and its people." To his wife: "Marina, I love you so much."

Livingston, Charles (1962-1997). American criminal, executed by lethal injection for the murder of a 38 year-old woman during a robbery. Livingston's parting words: "You all brought me here to be executed, not to make a speech. Get on with it. That's it."

Livingstone, David (1813-1873). Scottish explorer, physician and missionary who spent many years in Africa. Shortly before dying, Livingstone told his servants to: "Build me a hut to die in. I am going home." Later, to an attendant who had given him some water and medications: "All right. You can go out now." He died shortly thereafter, kneeling at his bedside probably in prayer. Livingstone's heart was removed and buried in African soil. His remains were preserved with salt and transported by natives one thousand miles to the coast for shipment to England. The explorer ultimately was buried in Westminster Abbey.

Alternatives: * "I am cold. Put more grass on the hut."

* His last journal entry approximately six days before his death reflected his desperate attempt to obtain milk: "Knocked up quite and remain-recover- sent to buy milch goats. We are on the banks of the Molilamo."

Lloyd George, David (1863-1945). British prime minister during WWI. Dying of cancer, Lloyd George remarked: "I wish I could have the blind faith of the Catholic." To his doctor: "Have you been to chapel?"

Lloyd, Saint John (died 1679). Martyred Welsh priest. Caught up in the Papist Plot, John Lloyd and Philip Evans (above) were convicted of treason and hanged. Evans spoke on the gallows: "Adieu, Father Lloyd! Though only for a little time, for we shall soon meet again." Lloyd replied: "My fellow-sufferer has declared the cause of our death, therefore I need not repeat it; and besides, I never was a good speaker in my life. I shall only say that I die in the true Catholic and Apostolic faith... I forgive all those that have offended me, and if I have offended anybody, I am heartily sorry for it, and ask them forgiveness. I beg the prayers of all, and in particular of the Catholics here present, desiring them to bear their crosses patiently, and to remember that passage of Holy Scripture 'Happy are they that suffer persecution for justice, for theirs is the Kingdom of Heaven.'" After thanking those who had showed him kindness, Lloyd prayed: "Lord, have mercy upon me, a sinner. Into Thy hands, O Lord, I recommend my spirit."

Locke, John (1632-1704). English philosopher, physician and writer. As Locke lay dying, a friend read a Psalm to him. He remarked: "Oh, the depth of the riches of the goodness and knowledge of God." With his last breath, the philosopher said: "Cease now."

Lockhart Timothy "Tim" (1928-1963). American radio disc jockey. While broadcasting, Lockhart suffered a heart attack and attempted to summon his production manager: "Bill, help, help."

Lodge, Henry Cabot (1850-1924). American politician who became a member of the U.S. House of Representatives and later the U.S. Senate. Dying of a stroke complicating gallbladder surgery, Lodge penned a note to President Calvin Coolidge: "The doctors promise prompt recovery. I shall be back in Washington well and strong, and I trust that I shall be able to be of some service to you when I get there."

Lody, Carl (1877-1914). German spy. After moving to Scotland and later, Ireland, Lody reported British military preparations to his homeland during the early stages of WWI. He was arrested and sentenced to die before a firing squad. Before his execution, Lody sent a letter to his family: "My Dear ones, I have trusted in God and He has decided. My hour has come, and I must start on the journey through the Dark Valley like so many of my comrades in this terrible war of nations. May my life be offered as a humble offering on the altar of the Fatherland. A hero's death on the battlefield is certainly finer, but such is not to be my lot, and I die here in the enemy's country silent and unknown, but the consciousness that I die in the service of the Fatherland makes death easy. The Supreme Court Marshal of London has sentenced me to die for military conspiracy. Tomorrow I shall be shot in the Tower [of London]. I have had just judges and I shall die as an officer, not as a spy. Farewell, God bless you, Hans." When the Provost-Marshal arrived to lead him to the execution site, Lody asked: "I suppose that you will not care to shake hands with a German spy?" The Englishman shook his hand.

Loeb, Richard (c. 1905-1936). American criminal. In 1924, Loeb and Nathan Leopold kidnapped and murdered a 14 year-old boy, hoping to collect a sizable ransom and execute the perfect crime. Before any money changed hands, the child's body was found. The two perpetrators were apprehended and brought to trial the same year. Because of an eloquent defense mounted by the lawyer Clarence Darrow, both escaped the hangman's noose but were sentenced to life in prison. In 1936, Loeb was slashed multiple times by a fellow prisoner. Before dying, he said: "I think I'm going to make it!" His wounds proved fatal.

Loewe, Frederick (1901-1988). German-born American composer. Loewe collaborated with lyricist Alan Lerner on a number of musicals including *My Fair Lady*, *Camelot* and *Brigadoon*. Suffering from a heart attack, Loewe complained: "I want to die."

Loft, Robert (1917-1972). American airline pilot. As Eastern Air Lines Flight 401from New York City approached Miami, Florida, the flight crew became distracted by a false landing gear deployment signal. The aircraft inadvertently descended to a dangerously low altitude before the crew realized the imminent peril. When Captain Loft recognized the danger, he responded: "Hey – what's happening here? What's…" Despite efforts to recover altitude, the plane crashed into the Everglades with the loss of 101 of the 176 individuals on board. Loft did not survive the accident.

Logan, Harvey "Kid Curry" (1867-1904). American outlaw who was a member of Butch Cassidy's "Wild Bunch" gang. Although Logan had murdered several men, he was convicted and jailed for robbery. He escaped from prison and eventually was tracked down and wounded by a posse. When one of his cohorts asked if he had been hit, Logan responded: "Yes, and I'm going to end it here." Rather than surrender, he took his life with a gunshot to the head.

Logan, John (1826-1886). Union general and later a U.S. senator. Succumbing to a "congestion of the brain," Logan was told by a visitor:

"General, it would be a mockery to wish you a *merry* Christmas, but I do wish you a quiet and peaceful one" The general replied: "No, not a *merry* Christmas, but I hope a quiet and peaceful one." Dying the day after Christmas, Logan spoke his wife's name: "Mary."

Lombard, Carole, born Jane Peters (1908-1942). American actress and wife of actor Clark Gable. In early 1942, Lombard embarked on a U.S. tour to raise money for the war effort. During her journey, she wired Gable: "Hey, Pappy, you better get yourself into this man's army." At her last stop in Indiana, the actress told a crowd: "Before I say goodbye to you all, come on, join me in a big cheer. V for victory!" To determine her mode of transportation, she flipped a coin to determine whether to take a train or plane back to California. Before boarding a TWA twin-engine aircraft, Lombard confided to a photographer: "When I get home, I'll flop in bed and sleep for twelve hours." The plane crashed near Las Vegas, Nevada, killing all aboard. Shortly after Lombard's death, Gable enlisted in the U.S. Army Air Force.

Lombardi, Vincent "Vince" (1913-1970). American professional football coach, primarily with the Green Bay Packers. Dying of colorectal cancer, Lombardi spoke to a priest: "I'm not afraid to die. I'm not afraid to meet my God now. But what I do regret is that there is so d*** much left to be done here on earth!" Later, he told his conservatively-dressed son: "You look like a lawyer." His last words were spoken to his wife Marie concerning their 30th wedding anniversary: "Happy anniversary Rie. Remember I love you."

London, John "Jack" born John Chaney (1876-1916). American writer, best-known for his novel *The Call of the Wild*. Suffering from a painful kidney ailment, London spoke to his wife the night before his death: "I'm so worn out from lack of sleep. I'm going to turn in. Thank God you're not afraid of anything!" Although morphine vials were found near his body, the official cause of death was listed: "Uraemia following renal colic."

Lonergan, Thomas "Tom" (1964-1998) and **Eileen** (1969-1998). American SCUBA diving enthusiasts. Accidentally abandoned on a diving excursion near Australia's Great Barrier Reef, the couple's bodies were never found. The pair left a message on their diving slate, which was found several months later: "[Mo]nday Jan 26; 1998, 08 am. To anyone [who] can help us; We have been abandoned A[gin]court Reef by MV Outer Edge 25 Jan 98 3 pm. Please help us [come] to rescue us before we die. Help!!!"

Long, Huey "Kingfish" (1893-1935). American politician who was a Louisiana governor and later a U.S. senator. At the time of his death, Long was involved in an attempt to remove a local judge from office. After he was gunned down by the judge's irate son-in-law, Long commented to an associate: "Jimmie, my boy, I'm shot. I wonder why he shot me?" When told the name of his assailant: "I don't know him." Dying two days after unsuccessful surgery, Long complained: "Don't let me die! I have got so much to do!"

Alternative: * "God, don't let me die! I have so much to do!"

Longfellow, Henry Wadsworth (1807-1882). American poet and educator, noted for his epic poems *The Song of Hiawatha* and *Evangeline.* Dying of peritonitis, to his sister who had traveled from Portland, Maine: "Now I know that I must be very ill, since you have been sent for."

Alternative: * "Anne, my dear! If they have sent for you, I know I must be very ill."

Longfellow, Mary (1812-1835). American first wife of Henry Longfellow (above). Dying in Holland after a miscarriage, Mary spoke to her husband: "Dear Henry, do not forget me! Tell my dear friends at home that I thought of them at the last hour." Mary indicated that she would like to see the Episcopal minister, but he arrived too late.

Longley, William "Wild Bill" (1851-1878). American outlaw who committed multiple murders and robberies in Texas. Sentenced to hang for his deeds, Longley confessed: "I deserve this fate. It is a debt I owe for a wild and reckless life. So long, everybody!" As the trap opened, his lanky stature and a long rope allowed the outlaw to land safely on his feet. After several adjustments, the third attempt was successful.

Lope de Vega Carpio, Félix (1562-1635). Spanish playwright, poet and writer. Dying of scarlet fever: "True glory is in virtue. Ah, I would willingly give all the applause I have received to have performed one good action more." When told that the end was near: "All right then, I'll say it: Dante makes me sick."

López, Francisco (1826-1870). President of Paraguay. Killed during a battle with superior Brazilian forces in the northern part of his country, López cried: "I die with my country!"

Alternative: * "I die for my homeland!"

Lord Byron (see Byron, George Gordon, Lord Byron).

Lorenzo de Medici (see Medici, Lorenzo de).

Lorrain, Claude (see Gellée, Claude).

Lothar I (795-885). King of the Franks and Holy Roman Emperor who was the eldest son of Louis I (below). As he lay dying, Lothar bemoaned with hubris: "What manner of king is He above who thus doeth to death such great kings?"

Louis I (778-840). King of the Franks who was the son of Charlemagne (above). During the last part of his reign, Louis was troubled by the bickering of his sons over distribution of portions of his kingdom. Dying, he singled out one of his sons, possibly Louis the German: "I pardon him, but let him know that it is because of him that I am dying." At the end, Louis turned his face to the wall and said "Out! Out!"

Louis VI "The Fat" (1081-1137). King of France. Essentially immobilized by his morbid obesity, one observer wrote that Louis "disappeared in rolls of flesh." On his deathbed, the king gave advice to his son and successor, Louis VII: "Remember, my son, that a kingdom is a public trust, for the exercise of which you must render a strict account after your death."

Alternatives: * "Remember, my son, that kingship is a public charge, for which you will have to render a strict account in another world."

* "Remember, my son, that royalty is but a public employment of which you must render a rigorous account to Him who is the sole disposer of crowns and sceptres."
* "Protect the clergy, the poor and the fatherless. Do justice to every man."

Louis VIII (1187-1226). King of France. As Louis lay dying of dysentery, a young maiden was brought to his bedside with the belief that sex with a virgin would produce a cure. He virtuously declined, saying: "Ah, no! It will not be so, young lady! I will not commit mortal sin for whatever reason!"

Louis IX, also Saint Louis (1214-1270). King of France. While on a Crusade to the Holy Land, Louis took ill with dysentery (some say the plague). On his deathbed, he exclaimed: "Jerusalem. Jerusalem. We will go to Jerusalem." Looking skyward before dying: "O Lord, I shall enter into Thy house and shall worship in Thy holy tabernacle." Louis' flesh was stripped from the bones, which were returned to France.

Alternatives: * "I will enter into Thy temple! I will adore Thee in Thy holy house! I will confess Thy name."

* "I will enter Thy house. I will worship in Thy sanctuary."
* "I will enter Thy house. I will adore in Thy holy temple and will confess Thy name."

Louis XI (1423-1483). King of France. When advised to prepare for death, Louis responded: "I have hope in God that he will aid me; peradventure [perhaps] I am not so ill as you think." He died with words of the *Te Deum* on his lips: "Lord, in Thee have I trusted; let me never be confounded."

Alternative: * "Our Lady of Embrun, my good mistress, have pity upon me; the mercies of the Lord will I sing forever."

Louis XII (1462-1515). King of France. Louis married Mary Tudor, the sister of English King Henry VIII, but died on New Year's Day less than three months following the nuptials. Louis sarcastically said to his bride who was less than thrilled with the marriage: "My Darling, as a New Year's present, I give you my death."

Alternative: * "I am dying. I commend our subjects to your care."

Louis XIII (1601-1643). King of France. Several days before dying of tuberculosis, Louis asked his doctors if there we any possibility of recovery. When there was no response, he said: "Your silence tells me that I must die. God is my witness that I have never liked life and that I shall be overjoyed to go to him." On the day of death, Louis talked to his priest about thoughts of his wife's infidelity. When his confessor rebuked him, the king replied: "In my present state, I ought to forgive her, but I am not obliged to believe her." When his physician said that he only had a few hours to live, Louis said: "Well, my God, I consent with all my heart."

Alternative: * "Dinet [Louis' confessor]! Thoughts arise which trouble me."

Louis XIV "The Sun King" (1638-1715). King of France. Dying of gangrene, possibly from underlying diabetes, Louis saw some of his servants weeping. He responded with a variant of: "Why weep you? Did you think I should live forever? I thought dying had been harder." Asked later that night about any pain, he replied: "No, that's what troubles me. I should like to suffer more for the expiation of my sins." On the day of death after prayers for the dying had been completed, the king said to his clergyman: "These are the last favours of the Church." Several times he repeated: "Now and at the hour of death." Louis' last words: "O, my God, come to my aid; hasten to succour me."

Alternatives: * "Why are you weeping? Did you imagine that I was immortal?"

* "Why are you crying? Did you think I was immortal? I never thought so, and given my age, you should have been prepared to lose me..."
* "These are the last graces of the Church."
* "Those are the last blessings of the Church. O God, come to my help. Please relieve me soon."
* "O God, come unto mine aid; O Lord, make haste to help me."

Louis XV (1710-1774). King of France. Suffering from smallpox, Louis spoke to one of his subjects: "I have been a great sinner, doubtless, but I have ever observed Lent with a most scrupulous exactness; I have caused more than a hundred thousand masses to be said for the repose of unhappy souls, so that I flatter myself I have not been a very bad Christian." After Last Rites were administered: "I have never felt better or more at peace." To Cardinal de La Roche-Aymon who read Louis' apology to subjects for his "occasion for scandal:" "Repeat those words, Monsieur the almoner, repeat them."

Louis XVI (1754-1793). King of France. Louis was condemned to die during the Reign of Terror associated with the French Revolution. On the scaffold, he spoke to the assembled crowd: "Frenchmen, I die innocent. It is from the scaffold and near appearing before God that I tell you so. I pardon my enemies." As he continued his discourse, one of the generals ordered a drum roll, effectively drowning out the monarch: "I desire that France..." The guillotine blade ended Louis' reign and speech.

Alternatives: * "Frenchmen, I die guiltless of the crime imputed to me. I forgive the authors of my death and pray God my blood fall not on France!"

* "Frenchmen, I die innocent of all the crimes which have been imputed to me. I forgive my enemies; I implore God, from the bottom of my heart, to pardon them, and not to take vengeance on the French nation for the blood about to be shed."
* "People, I die innocent! Gentlemen, I am innocent of everything of which I am accused! I wish that my blood may be able to cement the happiness of the French!"
* "I die innocent of all the crimes laid to my charge; I Pardon those who have occasioned my death; and I pray to God that the blood you are going to shed may never be visited on France."

Louis XVII (1785-1795). King of France and the only surviving son of the executed Louis XVI and Marie Antoinette. Louis nominally became king when his father was guillotined in 1793 (above). Dying of tuberculosis, the imprisoned 10-year-old Louis remarked to an attendant who expressed concern about his suffering: "Console yourself. I shall not always suffer." As his pain worsened, the boy asked: "Put me in a place where I shall not suffer so much." In the arms of his attendant, he said: "Oh! Yes! I am still in pain, but not nearly so much. The music is so beautiful!" When asked where it originated: "From above! From amongst all the voices, I have distinguished that of my mother!" Louis then told his keeper: "I have something to tell you!" but died before he could express it.

Louis XVIII (1755-1824). King of France. During his last years, Louis became wheelchair-bound from gout and obesity. Toward the end, he developed gangrene of both feet, possibly secondary to diabetes. When prayers for the dying were read, Louis asked: "Is it as bad as that?" When answered affirmatively, he said: "Well, never mind, go on with it." Immediately before expiring, he tried to get out of bed, saying: "A King should die standing."

Louis I de Bourbon-Condé (1530-1569). French Huguenot leader. Louis sustained injuries to an arm and leg at the Battle of Jarnac during the French Wars of Religion. When it appeared that capture was imminent, a fellow combatant told him "Hide your face:" The injured man replied: "Ah, D'Argence, D'Argence, you will not be able to save me." Louis then was shot dead by an enemy soldier.

Louis François, Duc de Rohan-Chabot (1788-1833). Archbishop of Besançon in eastern France. On his deathbed, Louis François said self-effacingly: "I am nothing, nothing, less than nothing!"

Louis Philippe, Duc de Orléans (1747-1793). French royalty who took the name Philippe Égalité during the Revolution. Beheaded during the Reign of Terror, Louis said to the executioner who asked him to remove his boots: "You can do that more easily to my dead body. Come, be quick!"

Alternative: * "Tush! They will come better off *after*. Let us have done!"

Louis Philippe I (1773-1850). The last king to rule France. On his deathbed, Louis Philippe declared: "Now I go where God calls me."

Louis, Dauphin of France (1729-1765). French royalty, son of King Louis XV (above). The Dauphin died of tuberculosis before he could ascend the throne. Taking the hand of the Bishop of Verdun, Louis said: "Lay it on my heart. You have never left it..." He then remarked to the physician taking his pulse: "Ah! Take the bishop's. What fortitude he has!"

Louis, Joseph "Joe" (1914-1981). American world heavyweight boxing champion, nicknamed the "Brown Bomber." Louis spoke to his doctor: "I'm ready whenever God wants to take me. I've lived my life and done what I needed to do."

Louis, Saint (see Louis IX).

Louisa, Marchioness of Waterford (1818-1891). French-born English artist and philanthropist. On her deathbed, Louisa told a companion: "Oh darling Adelaide, goodness and beauty, beauty and goodness- those are ever the great things!"

Louise Marie, Princess (1737-1787). Daughter of French King Louis XV. Anxious to end her suffering from a "stomach complaint," Louise Marie cried out: "To paradise! Hurry! At the great gallop!"

Alternatives: "Hurry! At a gallop! To paradise!"
* "To heaven! Quickly! At the gallop!"
* "To paradise quickly, quickly at full speed."

Louise of Marillac, Saint (1591-1660). French religious devotee and mystic. Louise, with Vincent de Paul founded the Sisters of Charity, which served the poor, sick and neglected. To the Sisters weeping at her bedside: "Take great care of the poor, live together in great union and cordiality, pray much to the Blessed Virgin; she is your only Mother."

Louise of Mecklenburg (1776-1810). Queen Consort of Frederick William III of Prussia. Weakened by a chest ailment, Louise complained: "I am a Queen, but have no power to move my arms." She then tried to reassure her husband: "Do not fear, dear friend. I am not going to die."

However, after a severe choking spell several minutes later, she exclaimed: "I am dying! Lord Jesus, make it short!"

Louise of Savoy (1476-1531). French noblewoman who was the mother of King Francis I (above). Near the end, Louise's room was brightened by a comet causing her to exclaim: "Ha, there is an omen which appears not for people of low degree. God sends it for us great. Shut the window; it announces my death; I must prepare." Her physicians tried to reassure her, but she persisted: "Unless I had seen the sign of my death, I should have said the same, for I do not myself feel that I am sinking." She died two (some say three) days later.

Alternatives: * "Ah, that is a sign which is not intended to warn people of lowly condition. God sends it to admonish the great ones of the earth. It announces my speedy departure from this world; I must prepare myself, therefore, for death!"

* "If I had not seen the sign of my death, I would believe what you say, for I do not feel that bad."

Louise, Marchioness of Lorne and Duchess of Argyle (1848-1939). Daughter of English Queen Victoria. When flowers were presented to her, Louise realized her end was near: "You will never need to bring any more flowers for me."

Lovat, Simon (see Fraser, Simon).

Lovejoy, Elijah (1802-1837). American abolitionist, clergyman and publisher. Angered by Lovejoy's publication of an African American's lynching, a pro-slavery mob shot him dead and destroyed his printing press. As he expired: "Oh, God, I am shot, I am shot."

Lowder, Charles (1820-1880). English clergyman who founded the Society of the Holy Cross, an organization for Anglo-Catholic priests. Dying from complications of a peptic ulcer, Lowder said to a friend: "You are witness that I die in the faith of the Anglican Church, for they may say that I died a Roman Catholic."

Lowell, Amy (1874-1925). American poet who was awarded a posthumous Pulitzer Prize for her endeavors. Dying of a stroke, Lowell realized her predicament: "My hand is numb. I can't feel the…a stroke, Pete [her companion's nickname]. Get Eastman [her doctor]!"

Alternative: * "My arm hurts. It's numb. I can't use it. Pete, a stroke! Get Eastman!"

Lowell, James (1819-1891). American poet, diplomat and abolitionist. Dying of cancer, to his doctors: "Oh, why don't you let me die?"

Lowry, Robert (1826-1899). American minister and hymnodist. Toward the end, Lowry spoke to a fellow hymn writer, Frances Crosby (above): "Fanny, I am going to join those who have gone before, for my work is now done."

Lucas, Charles (1613-1648). English Royalist commander. Condemned for his participation in the Second English Civil War, Lucas went before a firing squad along with George Lisle (above). His last words as he opened his doublet to expose his chest: "Soldiers, fire!"

Alternatives: * "Fire, rebels!"
* "Now, rebels, do your worst."

Lucas, Joseph (1834-1902). English businessman. Lucas founded Lucas Industries that manufactured electrical components, including headlights for cars. Because of the unreliability of these lamps in the early stages of automobile development, Lucas sarcastically was dubbed: "The Prince of Darkness." Dying of typhoid fever, the businessman admonished: "Never drive at night."

Luciano, Charles "Lucky" born Salvatore Lucania (1897-1962). Italian-born American gangster. While imprisoned during the 1930s, Luciano allegedly cooperated with U.S. authorities to secure Mafia collaboration in the war effort. His contacts supposedly watched for acts of enemy sabotage on the New York waterfront and provided aid to American ground troops invading Sicily. For his assistance, Luciano's sentence was commuted on the condition he accept deportation to Italy. He later met American film producer Martin Gosch in Naples to discuss a film about his life. Suffering a heart attack, the gangster cried out: "Marty..." and died.

Alternative: * "Tell Georgie I want to get in the movies one way or another."

Lully, Jean Baptiste (1632-1687). Italian-born French composer and conductor. While performing his *Te Deum* in early January, 1687, Lully inadvertently drove his conducting staff into one of his toes. Despite medical attention, the toe became infected He died two-and-a half months later from abscess formation and gangrene. Toward the end, his confessor withheld absolution allowing that Lully's illness resulted from his composing music for the theatre. When the composer burned the offending score, the priest relented. Later when a friend expressed horror that the score was destroyed, Lully chuckled: "That's nothing to worry about. You see, I had another copy in my desk." He died repeating words from a hymn he had written on his deathbed: "Sinner, Thou Must Die."

Luna, Álvaro de (c. 1388-1453) Spanish statesman. Implicated in the death of members of the Royal Court, de Luna was condemned to die by beheading. At the block, he was shown the post and hook where his remains would be exhibited. He commented: "It does not matter what they do with my body and head after my death."

Lunalilo, born William Charles Lunalilo (1835-1874). King of Hawaii. Ill with tuberculosis, Lunalilo spoke to an aide: "I am now dying." He closed his eyes and expired.

Luther, Katharina von Bora (1499-1552). German widow of the theologian Martin Luther (below). While fleeing the plague, Frau Luther sustained a serious injury when her horse cart wrecked. Dying, she reassured her children: "I'll cling to Christ like a burr to a topcoat."

Luther, Martin (1483-1546). German clergyman whose break with the Catholic Church led to the establishment of Protestantism. Dying of a probable heart attack (some say a cold or stroke), Luther said: "Dear Lord, I am in much pain and fear I am on my way..." When a friend consoled him,

Luther responded: "Yes, it is a cold, deathly sweat. I shall give up the ghost, because the illness has become more severe." He later recited from Psalms and the Gospel of John. When offered a "restorative" by his physician: "I am dying. I shall render up the ghost." Toward the end, he prayed: "Father, into Thy hands I commend my spirit. For Thou hast redeemed me, God of Truth, O God of truth." When asked if he affirmed Christ and his own teachings, Luther whispered "Yes" and died.

Lux, Walter (died 1979). American airline pilot. On May 25, 1979, American Airlines Flight 191 took off from Chicago's O'Hare International Airport. Moments later the aircraft plummeted to the earth, when the left engine separated from the wing. A total of 258 passengers, 13 crew and two on the ground perished. Captain Lux's last words were: "Ah, American 191 under way."

Lyon, Mary (1797-1849). American educator who founded Mount Holyoke Female Seminary. Dying of erysipelas, Lyon affirmed: "I should love to come back to watch over the seminary, but God will take care of it."

Lyon, Nathaniel (1818-1861). Union officer during the U.S. Civil War. When asked who would lead the troops, Lyon replied: "I will lead you! Onward brave boys of Iowa!" He was killed moments later during the Battle of Wilson's Creek, near Springfield, Missouri.

Lyte, Henry (1793-1847). Scottish-born English clergyman who wrote the hymn "Abide with Me." Dying of tuberculosis, Lyte pointed toward heaven and said: "Peace! Joy!"

Lytteleton, George (1709-1773). English poet and statesman. Lytteleton directed his last words to a friend, Lord Valentia: "Be good, be virtuous, my lord. You must come to this."

Lytton, Edward, whose pen name was Owen Meredith (1831-1891). British statesman and poet. Dying from "a spasm of the heart," Lytton said: "I feel thirsty and I should be glad to drink something."

Mabie, Hamilton (1845-1916). American editor and writer. Dying on New Year's Eve, Mabie allowed: "I have had a quiet but very happy Christmas."

MacArthur, Douglas (1880-1964). American WWII and Korean War Army commander. MacArthur underwent surgery for gallstones, complicated by biliary cirrhosis. After recovering from anesthesia, he spoke to his wife and doctor: "I am going to do the very best I can." Shortly thereafter, he lapsed into a coma and died several days later.

Macaulay, Thomas (1800-1859). English writer, historian, poet and statesman. Suffering from a heart ailment, Macaulay told his butler: "I shall retire early; I am very tired." He died several moments later.

MacDonald, George (1824-1905). Scottish writer and clergyman. Suffering from strokes and dementia, MacDonald spoke very little during his last years. When pushed out in his wheelchair, he aroused and referred to the conveyance: "Whose is this machine?"

MacDonald, George Browne (1805-1868). English clergyman and grandfather of the writer Rudyard Kipling (above). MacDonald spoke on his deathbed: "Lord, what things I lie here and remember."

MacDonald, Jeanette (1903-1965). American singer and actress, best-known for her pairing in musical films with Maurice Chevalier and Nelson Eddy. Dying while awaiting surgery, to her husband: "I love you."

Macdonough, Thomas (1783-1825). U.S. Navy commodore. Sailing from the Mediterranean to the U.S., Macdonough's tuberculosis worsened and he died near Gibraltar. To his physician: "I have an aversion to being thrown into the sea [the traditional burial at sea]. I wish my body taken home for interment." He was buried near his Connecticut home.

MacDowell, Edward (1860-1908): American pianist and composer. During the final stage of a chronic neurological illness, MacDowell uttered seemingly unrelated statements such as: "Beethoven is quite right about some things," "I am going to Rome," "Marian [his wife] in the garden" or "Liszt is here, and I feel that I am going to die."

MacGregor, Robert Roy "Rob Roy" (1671-1734). Scottish outlaw who engaged in cattle rustling and "brigandage." As he lay dying, the 63 year-old MacGregor realized the end was near, saying: "Now all is over. Let the piper play 'We return no more.'" The piper obliged until MacGregor breathed his last.

Machiavelli, Niccolò (1469-1527). Italian political writer, statesman and philosopher. The eponymous term "Machiavellianism" derived from his writings about "the employment of cunning and duplicity in statecraft." Dying, Machiavelli allegedly quipped: "I desire to go to hell, and not to heaven. In the former place I shall enjoy the company of popes, kings, and princes, while in the latter are only beggars, monks, hermits and apostles."

MacKenna, Stephen (1872-1934). Irish writer and translator of ancient works. MacKenna wrote a final letter from hospital to a friend Margaret Nunn: "Dear Peggy, I cannot resist, tho' I mean to see no-one, never no more. But you mustn't bring me anything whatever. I abhor grapes, am worried by flowers, can't read magazines. I'm greatly touched by your goodness, Peggy. Probably you could come any hour, arranging things over the telephone with Sister, you know the ropes... I wept when I got you. S.M.K. [possibly s*** my knickers, a jovial expression]. What a howling swell of an address you have acquired. God save us."

Mackenzie, Morell (1837-1892). English physician, a pioneer in the field of laryngology. On his deathbed, Mackenzie opined: "If I am going to get well, I shall get well anyhow; and if I am not to get well, I may as well stop where I am." To his daughters: "I don't want your mother to do all, but I don't want her to go out of the room much." He later called for his brother, also a physician: "Yes, send for Stephen."

Mackintosh, James (1765-1832). Scottish philosopher, politician and historian. Dying from complications of swallowing a chicken bone, Mackintosh exclaimed: "Happy, happy!"

MacMillan, Daniel (1813-1857). Scottish publisher. Dying, MacMillan spoke to his wife: "Good-bye, kiss me, why don't you speak to me? You will see so much of me come out in the children, dear. It will be a great comfort to you... but you will see the impetuosity."

Macmillan, Harold (1894-1986). British Prime Minister. On his deathbed, Macmillan said: "I think I will sleep now."

Macpherson, James "Jamie" (1675-1700). Scottish criminal. Macpherson, an excellent fiddler, was part of a Scottish gang of marauders and "cattle-lifters." He eventually was captured and sentenced to die by hanging. While awaiting execution, Macpherson composed his own funeral lament, which he sang and played on the violin before he died: "I've spent my time in rioting/ Debauched my health and strength/ I squandered fast as pillage came,/ And fell to shame at length/ But dantonly [? dauntingly] and wantonly and rantingly I'll gae/ I'll play a tune and dance it roun'/ Below the gallows tree." Before the noose was placed, he offered his violin to anyone who would play it at his wake. When no one came forward, he broke the instrument saying: "No one else shall play Jamie Macpherson's fiddle."

Macrina the Younger, Saint (died 379). Cappadocian (present-day Turkey) holy woman. "... O Thou Who hast power on earth to forgive sins, forgive me, that I may be refreshed and may be found before Thee when I put off my body, without defilement on my soul. But may my soul be received into Thy hands spotless and undefiled, as an offering before Thee."

Madison, Dolley Payne, also Dolly or Dollie (1768-1849). Widow of U.S. President James Madison. When her niece (some say nurse) apologized for a minor disturbance: "My dear, do not trouble about it. There is nothing in this world worth really caring for. Yes, believe me, I, who have lived so long, repeat to you, there is nothing in this world here below worth caring for." Madison's last words concerned her son: "My poor boy."

Madison, James (1751-1836). Fourth U.S. president, called "Father of the Constitution." When Madison's niece noticed that he did not look well, she asked what was wrong. He replied: "Nothing more than a change of mind, my dear. I always talk better lying down." After leaving the room for several minutes, she returned and found Madison dead in his chair.

Maeterlinck, Maurice (1862-1949). Belgian-born poet and essayist who won the 1911 Nobel Prize in Literature. Dying of a heart attack, to his wife: "For me this is quite natural. It is for you that I am concerned."

Maginot, André (1877-1932). French politician. Maginot backed the construction of fortifications across portions of France to thwart German military aggression after WWI. Dying before the so-called Maginot Line was completed, he told the French premier: "For me, this is the end, but you- continue."

Magruder, John (1807-1871). American military officer who served in the U.S. Civil War and later, in Mexican Emperor Maximilian I's army. Dying several years after returning to the U.S., Magruder said to his attendant: "I don't think I am long for this world."

Mahan, Alfred (1840-1914). American naval officer and historian. Dying of heart failure, Mahan spoke to his nurse after viewing a tree outside his window: "If a few more quiet years were granted me, I might see and enjoy these things, but God is just and I am content."

Mahler, Gustav (1860-1911): Austrian-born composer and conductor. Dying from complications of bacterial endocarditis, Mahler made conducting movements with his fingers on the bedspread and twice uttered: "Mozartl [Dear little Mozart]."

Alternative: "Mozart."

Mahy, Thomas de, Marquis de Favras (1744-1790). French nobleman who supported the monarchy during the French Revolution. Condemned to die, Mahy criticized the official document outlining his sentence as he was led to the guillotine: "I see that you have made three spelling mistakes."

Mai, Nhât Chi (1934-1967). Vietnamese teacher. Dying of self-immolation to protest the Vietnam War, Mai said in a note she left behind: "I offer my body as a torch to dissipate the dark, to waken love among men, to give peace to Vietnam. The one who burns herself for peace."

Alternative: * "I wish to use my body as a torch to dissipate the darkness, to waken Love among men and to bring peace to Viet Nam."

Main, Sylvester (1817-1873). American musician and music publisher. At the end, Main said to his wife and son: "The dear Lord is about to give me rest. If you love me, do not weep, but rejoice."

Maintenon, Françoise de (1635-1719). Second wife of French King Louis XIV. When asked by her daughters for a blessing, Maintenon replied: "I am not worthy."

Malcolm X, born Malcolm Little (1925-1965). African American minister, revolutionary and human rights activist. After Malcolm left the Nation of Islam organization in 1964, his relations with that group became strained. As he prepared to deliver a speech to his Organization of Afro-American Unity in Manhattan a year later, a commotion broke out in the audience. Malcolm tried to quell the disturbance but was shot dead by three assassins. Several versions of his last words, uttered before the gunfire, include:

* "Hold it! Hold it! Don't get excited… Let's cool it, brothers."
* "Hold it! Hold it! Let's cool it! Let's be cool, brothers!"
* "Brothers! Brothers, please! This is a house of peace!"
* "Now, now, brothers, break it up, be cool, be calm."
* "Brothers and sisters, stay cool!"

Maldonado, Francisco (c. 1592-1639). Argentine-born Jewish physician and writer, killed during the Peruvian Inquisition after refusing to renounce his Jewish faith. Before he was burned at the stake, Maldonado allowed: "This is the will of the Lord. I shall see the God of Israel face to face."

Malherbe, François de (1555-1628). French poet. On his deathbed, Malherbe criticized a priest attempting to describe heaven in "vulgar and trite phrases:" "Ah, for God's sake, say no more of heaven, for your bad style would give me a disgust to it."

Alternatives: * "Hold your tongue; your miserable style puts me out of conceit with heaven."

* "Hold your tongue! Your wretched style disgusts me."
* "Hold your tongue; your wretched style only makes me out of conceit with them."
* "Hold your tongue, father! Your low style entirely makes me out of conceit with them."
* "Hold your tongue! Your wretched chatter disgusts me."
* "Do not speak of it any more. Your bad style leaves me disgusted."
* "Your ungrammatical style is putting me off them."

Malibran, Maria (1808-1836). Parisian-born operatic mezzo-soprano of Spanish ancestry. Falling from a horse, Malibran sustained a head injury that would prove fatal several months later. Before lapsing into a coma, she said to her doctor about earlier therapeutic bloodlettings: "I am a slain woman! They have bled me."

Mancini, Antonio "Babe" (died 1941). English gangster. During an altercation at a local London club, Mancini stabbed a doorman to death. Convicted to die by hanging, the condemned man said "Cheerio" as the noose was placed around his neck.

Mandrin, Louis (1725-1755). French brigand. Mandrin smuggled goods that he sold without paying taxes. When French authorities caught him, the highwayman was sentenced to die "on the wheel." After his extremities and abdomen were beaten with an iron bar, he was hoisted onto a wheel and later strangled. Before he died, Mandrin cried: "Ah, what a moment, great God! And one I ought to have foreseen."

Manet, Édouard (1832-1883). French Impressionist painter. Manet, afflicted with syphilis, required an amputation to treat a gangrenous left foot. He experienced phantom extremity pain, often seen after amputations. When his fellow painter Claude Monet (below) put his hat down on the hospital bed, Manet exclaimed: "Take care! You'll hurt my foot!" Manet died almost two weeks after his surgery.

Mankiewicz, Herman (1897-1953). Hollywood screenwriter and producer. Mankiewicz left instructions for his funeral: "Assuming the ceremony will be held indoors, hats will not be worn, except that Dore Schary [a fellow producer, director and playwright] will wear his hat. You are to go up to Dore Schary and tap him on the shoulder and say: 'Dore, I have a message for you from the deceased: Take off your hat, you're in the house.'"

Alternative: * "Well, that finishes everything I've got to take care of before I go to meet my maker. Or in my case, should I say co-maker?" "Co-maker" referred to his brother who had co-signed a number of Mankiewicz's loans.

Mann, Horace (1796-1859). American politician, educator and member of the U.S. House of Representatives. Mann spoke his last words to his family: "Now I bid you all goodnight."

Manning, Henry (1808-1892). English Roman Catholic cardinal. Manning knew the end was approaching: "I have laid down the yoke. I am at the end of life."

Alternative: * "I have laid down the yoke. My work is done."

Manolete, birth name Manuel Rodríguez Sánchez (1917-1947). Spanish matador. After a fatal goring in the groin by a bull, Manolete agonized to his physician: "I can't feel anything in my right leg! I can't feel anything in my left leg! Doctor, are my eyes open? I can't see."

Mansfield, Edward (1801-1880). American writer, editor and lawyer. "O death, where is thy…" Perhaps Mansfield tried to quote 1 Corinthians 15:55: "... O death, where is thy victory? O death, where is thy sting?"

Mansfield, Katherine, born Katherine Mansfield Beauchamp (1888-1923). New Zealand-born British short-story writer. In the terminal stage of tuberculosis, Mansfield declared during a violent paroxysm of coughing and bleeding: "I believe... I'm going to die."

Alternative: * "I love the rain. I want the feeling of it on my face"

Mansfield, Richard (1857-1907). German-born English actor. When his wife said "God is life," the dying actor replied: "God is love."

Manzoni, Alessandro (1785-1873). Italian poet and writer, best-known for his novel *The Betrothed.* Dying of meningitis, Manzoni was asked by a friend why he was mixing up his words. The writer replied: "If I knew why it was, I wouldn't get them mixed up."

Mao Zedong (1893-1976). Chinese Communist dictator. When a group of Communist Party officials visited during his last illness, Mao said: "Few live beyond seventy, and as I am more than eighty, I should have died already. Are there not some among you who hoped I would go to see Marx sooner?" When they said no, he retorted: "Really? No one? I don't believe it." Later, after suffering a massive heart attack, Mao complained: "I feel very ill. Call the doctors."

Marat, Jean-Paul (1743-1793). Swiss-born French revolutionary, politician and physician. Charlotte Corday (above), a member of a minor French aristocratic family, believed that Marat was partially responsible for the violent turn the French Revolution had taken. Spurred to action, she appeared on Marat's doorstep claiming to have vital information for the revolution. Inexplicably, he consented to an interview over the protests of his wife. After a conversation while Marat sat in his bathtub, Corday stabbed him in the chest. The dying man cried to his wife: "Help, my dear, help!" The murderess was executed by guillotining several days later.

Maravich, Peter "Pistol Pete" (1947-1988). American professional basketball player. Nearly ten years after his retirement, Maravich collapsed during a pickup basketball game. Before dying, he said: "I feel great." The 40 year-old athlete succumbed to an occult congenital heart defect.

Marceau, Marcel, born Marcel Mangel (1923-2007). French actor and mime. Expiring at a race track in Cahors, France, Marceau allegedly said: "Dying is easy... Comedy is hard."

Marcellus the Centurion, Saint (died 298). Martyred Roman centurion from present-day Tangiers, Morocco. When Marcellus refused to worship Roman gods and fight as a centurion, the judge Agricolanus sentenced him to die by beheading: "Agricolanus, may God reward you."

Marconi, Guglielmo (1874-1937). Italian engineer who pioneered wireless telegraphy. Marconi was awarded the 1909 Nobel Prize in Physics. Suffering a massive heart attack, Marconi asked his doctor how he could be alive with no pulse. When he did not receive a plausible answer, the engineer commented that he knew he was dying, saying: "But I don't care. I don't care at all."

Marcus of Arethusa, Saint (fl. 4th century). Martyred Syrian bishop who destroyed a heathen Roman temple. As punishment, Marcus was covered with honey and allowed to be stung to death by bees: "How am I advanced, despising you that are upon the earth!"

Margaret of Antioch, Saint (c. 304). Christian martyr who lived in present-day Turkey. Condemned to die for her Christian religious beliefs, to the executioner: "Brother, draw thy sword now and strike!"

Margaret of Scotland (1424-1445). Scottish-born wife of the future king of France, Louis XI (above). The 20 year-old Margaret died of "inflammation of the lungs" before her husband ascended the throne. Her parting words were: "Fie on life! Speak no more of it to me."

Alternatives: * "Fie on the life of this world! Do not speak to me more about it."
* "Death. Don't talk to me about it anymore."

Maria Theresa of Austria (1717-1780). Holy Roman Empress and queen of Hungary and Bohemia. Asked whether she wanted to sleep, Maria replied: "You want me to sleep? While at any moment I shall be called before my Judge, I am afraid to sleep. I must not be taken unawares. I wish to see death coming." When asked if she were comfortable: "No, but comfortable enough to die." Maria then requested: "Open the windows!" She then lay back and said her final words: "To Thee I am coming."

Alternatives: * "No, I could sleep, but I must not. Death is too near. He must not steal upon me. These fifteen years I have been making ready for him; I will meet him awake."

* "I could sleep, but must not give way to it. Death is so near, he must not be allowed to steal upon me unawares. For fifteen years I have been making ready for him and must meet him awake."
* "I do not sleep. I wish to meet my death awake."

Mariam of Jesus Crucified, Saint, born Mariam Baouardy (1846-1878). Galilean Carmelite mystic. When Mariam entered a cloister in 1867, she took the name Mariam of Jesus Crucified. Dying of gangrene after breaking her arm, Mariam pleaded: "My Jesus, mercy."

Marie Antoinette (1755-1793). Queen consort of Louis XVI of France (above). Accused of treason during the French Revolution, Marie was sentenced to die by beheading. Her husband had been executed earlier on the guillotine. She bade goodbye to her offspring saying: "Farewell, my children, forever. I go to your Father." On her way to the guillotine, Marie accidentally stepped on the foot of the executioner, exclaiming: "Pardon me, sir. I did not do it on purpose." Some say she then uttered "Make haste" before the blade fell.

Alternatives: * "Monsieur, I beg your pardon. I did not do it on purpose."
* "Pardon me sir, I meant not to do it."

Marie Leczinska, also Leszczyńska (1703-1768). Silesian-born queen consort of Louis XV of France (above). Bemoaning the earlier loss of several children and her father, Marie said to her doctor: "Give me back my father and my children and you shall cure me."

Alternatives: * "Give me back my father and my children and I will get well."
* "Give me back my children and you shall cure me."

Marie Louise of Austria (1791-1847). Viennese-born second wife of Napoleon I (below). Dying of "pleurisy," Marie told the bishop at her bedside to: "Go on praying."

Marie of Romania (1875-1938). English-born queen consort of King Ferdinand I of Romania. On her deathbed, Marie admonished her son Carol to: "Be a just and strong king."

Marie Thérèse of France (1778-1851). Duchess of Angoulême and last surviving child of Louis XVI and Marie Antoinette (above). Dying of pneumonia, Marie prayed: "God, I ask pardon for my sins. Assist Thy humble servant in this moment, which will decide her eternity."

Marie Thérèse of Spain (1638-1683). Spanish-born queen consort of Louis XIV of France (above). Dying after a bloodletting and purging for an abscess in her armpit, Marie complained: "Since I have been queen, I have had only one happy day." She then responded to a comment about the inclement weather: "Yes, it is indeed frightful weather for a journey as long as the one before me." Before she died, Marie failed to reveal which single day pleased her. Some say her words actually conveyed more negativity: "Since I became queen, I have not known a single happy day."

Marie-Adélaïde, Princess of Versailles (1685-1712). Italian-born French royalty who married Louis, Dauphin of France. Dying of measles, Marie-Adélaïde responded to a promise that she would be with the Lord: "Yes, Aunt." As she expired: "Goodbye... Today Dauphine, tomorrow nothing. Forgotten tomorrow." Louis died of the same illness six days later.

Marion, Francis (1732-1795). American Revolutionary War officer and politician. Dying, Marion declared to his tearful wife: "My dear, weep not for me. I am not afraid to die; for, thank God I can lay my hand on my heart and say that since I came to man's estate, I have never intentionally done wrong to any."

Maris, Roger (1934-1985). American professional baseball player who set a record of 61 home runs during the 1961 season. Dying of cancer, Maris said: "I want a radio in my room."

Mark the Evangelist, Saint (died c. 68). Martyred North African-born Christian disciple and ascribed author of the New Testament Gospel that bears his name. While residing in Alexandria, Egypt, Mark was condemned for his Christian beliefs and dragged through the streets by a pagan crowd. As he died: "Into Thy hands, O Lord, I commend my spirit."

Alternative: * "I render my spirit into Thy hands, O my God."

Marley, Robert "Bob" (1945-1981). Jamaican singer, songwriter and reggae performer. Dying of cancer, Marley spoke these words to his son: "Money can't buy life."

Marryat, Frederick (1792-1848). English naval officer and writer. The conclusion of Marryat's dictated last thoughts, asserting his faith in Christianity: "... After years of casual, and, lately, months of intense thought, I feel convinced that Christianity is true... and that God is love... It is now half-past nine o'clock. World, *adieu*!"

Mars Phoenix Lander. The NASA Phoenix spacecraft landed on the Martian surface May 25, 2008. The explorer sent back scientific data until November of that year when its batteries failed. Phoenix's last signal to earth was the word "Triumph" transmitted in binary code (01010100 01110010 01101001 01110101 01101101 01110000 01101000 <3). The <3 is an emoticon heart on its side.

Marseille, Hans-Joachim (1919-1942). German fighter pilot ace during WWII. While returning to base, Marseille's cockpit filled with smoke, forcing him to exit the aircraft. He struck a part of the tail section and was killed. His last transmission before jumping: "I've got to get out now. I can't stand it any longer."

Marsh, John (1799-1856). Massachusetts pioneer and physician who settled in California. As he left on a trip to San Francisco, Marsh was accosted by some of his workers over a monetary dispute. He asked the men who were preparing to rob him: "Do you want to kill me?" Marsh was robbed and stabbed to death.

Marsh, Othniel (1831-1899). American paleontologist. Marsh spoke to a colleague, Hugh Gibb, who had prepared many of the scientist's specimens for exhibit: "Goodbye, Gibb."

Marshall, Peter (1902-1949). Scottish-American minister and chaplain of the U.S. Senate. Dying of a heart attack, Marshall asked his wife to contact Clarence Cranford, a fellow clergyman, to substitute for him: "You might ask Cranny to take the Senate prayer tomorrow." Dr. Cranford dutifully read one of Marshall's prayers to the Senate the next day.

Marshall, William (c. 1146-1219). English military leader and politician. On his deathbed, Marshall was invested into the order of the Knights Templar. He spoke his last words to his wife and attendants: "I am dying. I commend you to God. I can no longer remain with you. I cannot defend myself from death."

Marsiglia, Eliza (1799-1856). American matron. Upon hearing word that her son had perished on a trans-Atlantic voyage: "'Tis only a thin gauze veil that holds me from Jesus."

Martí, José (1853-1895). Cuban poet, writer and patriot. Martí was shot by Spanish soldiers during Cuba's War of Independence. An unfinished cryptic letter written by Martí read: "There are some affections which involve such delicate points of honor..."

Martin, Ernest (1960-2003). American criminal, executed by lethal injection for a murder committed during the robbery of a drug store. His final written statement: "Jesus Christ was put to death on the false testimony of those who received money in exchange for the lies they told. Just the same, the state of Ohio has succeeded in its quest for my life by way of perjured testimony and false witnesses who were paid to tell the lies they did. However, there has never been any hate nor desire of revenge in my heart for them, for I know God will repay those for each and every one of their sins that have gone forgotten." While in the death chamber, the felon rambled on for several minutes before saying: "... God bless all of you. That's all I have to say."

Martin, Jerry (died 1980). American ham radio operator who volunteered to help monitor the Mt. St. Helens volcano in Washington state. When the volcano erupted on May 18, 1980, approximately 10 miles from his site, Martin radioed: "Gentlemen, the uh, camper and the car sitting over to the south of me is covered. It's gonna get me too. I can't get out of here..." His body was never found.

Martin, Michael "Captain Lightfoot" (1795-1821). Irish-American criminal. Martin began his career as a highwayman in Ireland and continued the practice when he relocated to the United States. Captured in Massachusetts, the robber was sentenced to die by hanging. He was given the opportunity to signal his own execution: "When shall I drop the handkerchief?" His executioner replied: "When you please."

Martin, R.A.C. (c. 1830-1872). American bank cashier. When the Jesse James gang entered a Columbia, Kentucky bank, Martin shouted: "Bank robbers!" and was shot dead. The outlaws escaped with $600.

Martin, Saint (c. 316-397). Bishop of Tours, France who was born in present-day Hungary. Dying of a fever, Martin envisioned the Devil nearby: "Why standest thou here, horrible beast? Thou hast no share in me. Abraham's bosom is receiving me."

Alternatives: * "Why standest thou here, thou beast of blood? Thou shalt find nothing in me, thou deadly one, for the bosom of Abraham will receive me."

* "What do you have to do with me, evil creature? You cannot do anything more to me, for already I see Abraham, who holds his arms outstretched to me!"

Martindale, Cyril (1879-1963). English biblical scholar. Martindale spoke to a friend: "I'm pretty ill, and, in fact, one night they said prayers for the dying for me. I find it hard to be brought back, but the Lord's will is the most lovable of all."

Martineau, Harriet (1802-1876). English writer, philosopher and activist whose works explored social reform. In her later years, Martineau was plagued by numerous ailments that led to her invalidism. Toward the end, she said: "I have had a noble share of life, and I do not ask for any other life. I see no reason why the existence of Harriet Martineau should be perpetuated."

Marto, Francisco (1908-1919). Portuguese visionary. Marto, his sister (below) and a cousin claimed to have seen angels and the Virgin Mary. Dying of influenza during the great pandemic, Marto cried: "Mother, look at that lovely light there by the door... Now I can't see it anymore."

Alternative: * "Look Mama, what a pretty light there, near the door. Now I don't see it any more. Mama, bless me and forgive me for all the trouble I have caused you in my life."

Marto, Jacinta (1910-1920). Sister of Francisco Marto. Jacinta developed a pulmonary infection and underwent a painful operation to drain fluid from her chest cavity. As she lay dying, she said to her nurse: "I have seen Our Lady. She told me that she was going to come for me very soon and take away my pains. I am going to die. I want the Sacraments." Jacinta expired before Communion could be given.

Marty, Christian (1946-2000). French airline pilot. Marty was the lead pilot of the ill-fated Concorde 4590 flight that crashed on take-off from Paris' Charles de Gaulle Airport in 2000. An air traffic controller warned: "Concorde zero ... 4590, You have flames. You have flames behind you." Marty responded: "Too late... No time, no." All 109 aboard the aircraft and four on the ground perished in the crash.

Martyn, Henry (1781-1812). English clergyman and missionary to India and Persia. Dying of a fever while trying to return to England, Martyn's last journal entry read: "... Oh! when shall time give place to eternity? When shall appear that new heaven and new earth wherein dwelleth righteousness? There, there shall in no wise enter in anything that defileth: none of that wickedness which has made men worse than wild beasts- none of those corruptions which add still more to the miseries of mortality, shall be seen or heard of any more."

Marvell, Andrew, Sr. (c. 1586-1641). English clergyman. After Marvell, boarded a ferry, he apparently had a premonition of doom, shouting "Ho for heaven!" When the vessel floundered, the clergyman perished.

Marx, Julius "Groucho" (1890-1977). American movie and television star who was a member of the Marx Brothers comedy act. Several days before dying of pneumonia, Marx opined: "This is no way to live!" An undated comment on death has circulated widely as Groucho's last statement: "Die, my dear? Why, that's the last thing I'll do!"

Alternative: When a nurse announced she would take his temperature: "Don't be silly. Everyone has a temperature."

Marx, Karl (1818-1883). German-born political and economic theorist who espoused a fundamental philosophy for emerging socialist and communist governments. Dying of a chronic chest ailment, Marx allegedly chided his housekeeper who urged him to speak his final words so they could be recorded for posterity: "Get out of here and leave me alone. Last words are for fools who haven't said enough already."

Alternative: * "Go on, get out - last words are for fools who haven't said enough."

Marx, Leonard "Chico" (1887-1961). American comedian and oldest member of the Marx Brothers comedy act (above). Dying of atherosclerotic vascular disease, Marx reminded his daughter: "Remember, Honey, don't forget what I told you. Put in my coffin a deck of cards, a mashie niblick [a golf club] and a pretty blonde."

Mary I (1516-1558). Queen of England and Ireland who was the daughter of King Henry VIII. In early 1558, France retook Calais from England, an act that disturbed Mary deeply. She lamented: "When I am dead and opened, you shall find Calais lying in my heart." Mortally ill with an influenza-like illness, Mary prayed with her priest before receiving Communion: "Have mercy upon us... Have mercy upon us...Grant us peace." She died moments later.

Alternatives: * To a servant: "When I am dead, you will find Philip [her husband] and Calais engraved on my heart."
* "After I am dead, you will find "Calais" written upon my heart"

Mary II (1662-1694). Queen of England, Scotland and Ireland. Dying of smallpox, Mary received prayers for the dying. When the archbishop paused during the service, the queen asked: "My Lord, why do you not go on? I am not afraid to die." Refusing further medical aid: "I have but little time to live and I would spend it a better way."

Mary Beatrice of Modena (1658-1718). Queen consort of King James II of England (above) and mother of James Francis Edward, "The Old Pretender." Dying of breast cancer, Mary twice said to Countess Molza: "Molza, I pray you, when I am dead, send this crucifix to the king, my son." The countess complied with Mary's wishes.

Mary Frances of the Five Wounds of Jesus, Saint (see Gallo, Saint Maria Francesca).

Mary Magdalene De' Pazzi, Saint (1566-1607). Florentine Carmelite nun and mystic. To the nuns at her deathbed: "I am about to leave you, and the last thing I ask of you- and I ask in the name of our Lord Jesus Christ- is that you love Him alone, that you trust implicitly in Him, and that you encourage one another continually to suffer for the love of Him."

Mary Stuart, Queen of Scots (1542-1587). Scottish queen. Deposed and imprisoned for 19 years, Mary was condemned to die by Queen Elizabeth I for conspiracy to overthrow her monarchy. Mary prayed before her beheading: "Like as Thy arms, Lord Jesus Christ, were stretched out upon the Cross, even so receive me within the stretched out arms of Thy mercy." To her executioner: "I forgive you with all my heart, for now I hope you shall make an end to all my troubles." Mary cried out several times: "In Thee, oh Lord, do I put my trust. Let me never be confounded. Into Thy hands, O Lord, I commend my spirit." When the first axe blow failed to sever her head, Mary moaned: "Sweet Jesus!"

Alternatives: * "Even as Thy arms, O Jesus, were spread upon the Cross, so receive me into Thy arms of mercy, and forgive me all my sins."

* "My God, my God, I have hoped in Thee. I commit myself to Thy hands."

* "Do not cry. I have prayed for you. In You, Lord, I have faith, and You shall protect me forever. Into Thy hands, O Lord, I commend my spirit."

Masaniello, Tommaso (c. 1623-1647). Italian revolutionary. In 1647, Masaniello led a revolt against the Spanish viceroy and his country's influence in Naples. Masaniello was killed either by his own disillusioned followers or Spanish agents. Before dying, he cried to his assailants: "Ungrateful traitors!"

Massenet, Jules (1842-1912). French composer and teacher, best known for his operas. Dying of cancer, Massenet mentioned a fellow composer: "[Camille] Saint-Saëns would wish a grand funeral, but I would be content with a plain hearse and no fuss at all. I have been embraced, right in the theatre, by the Prince of Monaco, but Saint-Saëns has not."

Masterson, William "Bat" (1853-1921). American Old West outdoorsman, lawman and columnist. While writing an article for a New York City newspaper, Masterson suffered a heart attack as he worked. His last written words were: "... Yet there are those who argue that everything breaks even in this old dump of a world of ours. I suppose these ginks who argue that way hold that because the rich man gets ice in the summer and the poor man gets it in the winter, things are breaking even for them both. Maybe so, but I'll swear I can't see it that way..." Immediately before dying, he responded when asked how he felt:"All right."

Alternative: * "... We all get the same amount of ice. The rich get it in the summertime, and the poor get it in the winter."

Mata Hari (her stage name), born Margaretha Zelle (1876-1917). Dutch dancer and WWI German spy. Convicted of espionage by a French military court, Mata Hari was sentenced to die by firing squad. As she prepared for her execution, the condemned woman spoke to a nun: "Don't be afraid, Sister. I'll know how to die." As she dressed, the nun tried to shield her from the wandering gaze of the attending physician: "It doesn't matter, Sister. This is really not the time to be prudish... Death is nothing, nor life either, for that matter. To die, to sleep, to pass into nothingness, what does it matter? Everything is an illusion." When asked if she had any last words: "It is unbelievable." To the officer at the firing line, who offered a blindfold: "Must I wear that?" When told it did not matter: "Thank you, sir."

Mather, Abigail (1670-1702). First wife of the American theologian Cotton Mather. Dying of cancer, Mather said to her father: "Heaven, Heaven will make amends for all."

Mather, Cotton (1663-1728). American clergyman, theologian and writer who was the son of Increase Mather (below). Several hours before dying, Mather affirmed: "Now I have nothing more to do here. My will is entirely swallowed up in the will of God." Later, to his wife: "Is this dying? Is this all? Is this all that I feared when I prayed against a hard death? Oh! I can bear this! I can bear it! I can bear it!" When she wiped tears from his eyes: "I am going where all tears will be wiped away... Grace."

Mather, Increase (1639-1723). American clergyman and writer. Cotton Mather asked his father if he believed he would be in paradise that day: "I do! I do! I do!"

Mather, Richard (1596-1669). English-born American clergyman and father of Increase Mather. When asked how he felt during his terminal illness: "Far from well, yet far better than mine iniquities deserve."

Mathews, Charles (1776-1835). English comic and theatre manager. As he died, Mathews allowed: "I am ready."

Mathewson, Christopher "Christy" (1880-1925). American Hall of Fame professional baseball pitcher. Dying of tuberculosis, Mathewson spoke to his wife: "It's nearly over. I know it's nearly over. It's nearly over, Jane. We've got to face it. This is it. You want to go out and have a good cry, Jane. Go on. But don't make it a long one. This is something we can't help. Are you all right, Jane? Are you sure you're all right?"

Mathis, June (1889-1927). American screenwriter, best-known for her film *The Four Horsemen of the Apocalypse*. While attending a play with her grandmother, the 38 year-old Mathis screamed and clutched her relative: "Oh Mother, I'm dying." She could not be revived.

Matthews, Jeffrey (1972-2011). American criminal, executed by lethal injection for the murder of a relative: "I'm sitting here enjoying my last moments. Enjoy your lives." Referring to a possible reprieve: "I think that governor's phone is broke. He hadn't called yet."

Maturin, Basil (1847-1915). Irish-born clergyman. Maturin drowned when the RMS *Lusitania* liner sank after being torpedoed by a German submarine. He handed over a small child as the last lifeboat was lowered, saying: "Find its mother." Later, his body was found by fishermen.

Maugham, W. Somerset (1874-1965). Parisian-born British novelist and playwright. Toward the end, Maugham jokingly made known his views on the end of life: "Dying is a very dull and dreary affair. And my advice to you is to have nothing whatever to do with it." To his secretary: "Why, Alan! I want to say thank you- and goodbye."

Maupassant, Guy de (1850-1893). French writer, best-known for his short stories. Dying in a demented state from syphilis, de Maupassant allowed: "I don't want to survive myself."

Maurice, Frederick Denison "F.D." (1805-1872). English clergyman, theologian and social activist. On his deathbed, Maurice blessed his family: "... The knowledge of the love of God, the blessing of God Almighty, the Father, the Son and the Holy Ghost be amongst you- amongst us- and remain with us forever."

Maury, Matthew (1806-1873). American naval officer, astronomer and oceanographer. Toward the end, Maury asked his son: "Are my feet growing cold? Do I drag my anchors? All's well."

Maximilian I (1832-1867). Austrian-born Emperor of Mexico. Mexican monarchists, with the backing of Napoleon III, installed Maximilian Emperor of Mexico. When his support from the French waned, he was overthrown and condemned to die by firing squad. Before his execution:

"I forgive everybody. I pray that everybody may also forgive me, and my blood which is about to be shed will bring peace to Mexico. Long live Mexico! Long Live Independence!" Maximilian then commanded: "Fire!" After the volley rang out, some say the condemned leader managed to speak his wife's nickname "Lotte [for Carlota]!" while others say he muttered "*Hombre! Hombre!* [O man! O man!]"

Alternatives: * "I die in a just cause. I forgive all and pray that all may forgive me. May my blood flow for the good of this land. Long live Mexico! ... Men!"

* "... Mexicans! I pray that my blood may be the last to be shed for our unhappy country; and may it insure the happiness of the nation. Mexicans! Long live Mexico!"
* "Poor Carlotta."

Maximilian, Saint (274-295). Martyred Italian Christian pacifist. Refusing to enter prescribed military service under punishment of death, Maximilian told his father: "Give the new uniform you intended for me to the soldier who strikes me." He then was beheaded.

Maximinus II, also Maximinus Daza or Daia (c. 270-313). Roman emperor. Known for his persecution of Christians, Maximinus had a vision on his deathbed: "I see God, with his servants arrayed in white robes, sitting in judgment of me. Christ, have mercy on me!"

Maxwell, C.L. "Gunplay" born James Otis Bliss (1860-1909). American Old West gunfighter, robber and murderer. Confronted by a Utah deputy sheriff, Maxwell was shot dead. Before expiring: "Don't shoot again, Johnstone, you have killed me."

Maxwell, James (1831-1879). Scottish physicist, mathematician and educator. Dying of cancer, Maxwell observed: "I have looked into most philosophical systems and I have seen none that will work without a God."

Mayakovsky, Vladimir (1893-1930). Russian poet and playwright. Despondent over the restrictions of communism, Mayakovsky shot himself. His suicide note read in part: "... Do not blame anyone for my death and please do not gossip. The deceased terribly disliked this sort of thing. Mamma, sisters and comrades, forgive me - this is not a way out (I do not recommend it to others), but I have none other. Lily [a married woman he loved] - love me...Comrades of VAPP [a writers' association] - do not think me weak-spirited. Seriously - there was nothing else I could do. Greetings"

Mayer, Louis, born Lazar Meir (1884-1957). Russian-born American film producer who was a co-founder of the Metro-Goldwyn-Mayer studio. Dying of leukemia, Mayer lamented: "Nothing matters. Nothing matters."

Alternative: * "It wasn't worth it."

Mayhew, Jonathan (1720-1766). American clergyman. On his deathbed, Mayhew responded to a friend who asked if he still held to his theological views: "My integrity I hold fast, and will not let it go."

Mazarin, Hortense née Mancini (1646-1699). Italian-born aristocrat and favorite niece of Cardinal Mazarin (below). Hortense was heavily in arrears at the time of her death, prompting her last word: "Debt." Her creditors held her body for ransom post mortem and released it only after her estranged husband paid off the disputed amount. He kept her remains over a year, even when he traveled. Hortense eventually was buried.

Mazarin, Jules Cardinal, born Giulio Mazzarino (1602-1661). Italian-born French clergyman and statesman who succeeded Cardinal Richelieu as chief minister. Perhaps Mazarin's extravagant lifestyle colored his last words: "O my poor soul, what is to become of thee? Whither wilt thou go? O! were I permitted to live again I would sooner be the humblest wretch in the ranks of mendicants than a courtier." Mazarin then prayed: "Ah, Holy Virgin, have pity on me and receive my spirit."

Alternative: * To the Queen-Mother: "Madam, your favors undid me. Were I to live my life over again, I would be a Capuchin Friar rather than a courtier."

Mazzini, Giuseppe (1805-1872). Italian patriot who helped his country achieve independence and unification. After three days in a coma, Mazzini awoke and exclaimed "Yes, yes, I believe in God." He then fell back dead.

McAuley, Jeremiah "Jerry" (1839-1884). Irish-born American evangelist. McAuley, a convicted thief, converted to Christianity while in New York's Sing Sing prison. After release, he founded the Water Street Mission in New York City that ministered to the downtrodden. Dying of tuberculosis, McAuley spoke to a mission convert as he pointed his hand upward: "It's all right up there."

McCall, Elaine (died 2011). American housewife. During a domestic argument, McCall's husband David fired a shot at her. The 69 year-old housewife then taunted him: "You can't even shoot." David then shot her dead but was unsuccessful in a suicide attempt. He was convicted of second degree murder and sentenced to life in prison.

McCall, John "Jack" (c. 1852-1877). American criminal and frontiersman. McCall was convicted of Wild Bill Hickok's murder (above) and sentenced to hang. When the noose was placed over his neck, McCall requested: "Wait one moment, Marshal, until I pray." Then: "Draw it tighter, Marshal." As the trap was sprung: "Oh, God!"

McCandless, Christopher (1968-1992). American adventurer and writer. In April, 1992, McCandless began a trek into the Alaskan wilderness to live off the land. He wrote a final note August 12 on a page from Louis L'Amour's book, *Education of a Wandering Man*, before dying of starvation: "I have had a happy life and thank the Lord. Goodbye and may God bless all!" McCandless then tacked a note to the back door of an abandoned bus he used for shelter: "SOS, I need your help. I am injured, near death and too weak to hike out of here. I am all alone, this is NO JOKE. In the name of God, please remain to save me. I am out collecting berries close by and shall return this evening. Thank you, Chris McCandless." His body was discovered approximately three weeks later.

McCarty, Henry (see Billy the Kid).

McClellan, George (1826-1885). Union general during the U.S. Civil War and later governor of New Jersey. Dying of a heart attack, to his physician: "Tell her [his wife] I am better now." He expired moments later.

Alternative: * "I feel easy now. Thank you."

McCloskey, John (1810-1885). Archbishop of New York who later became the first American cardinal. When a clergyman said that he hoped McCloskey could meet him in a nearby city later in the year, the cardinal replied: "No, father, I am going on a longer journey. God has been good to me all my life, and I hope He will be good enough now to take me home."

McCormack, John (1884-1945). Irish-born tenor who sang both popular and operatic music. Dying of pneumonia, McCormack joked with his nurse: "So, you're here! In my opinion all women should be strangled at birth!" He lapsed into a coma and died several days later.

McCormick, Cyrus (1809-1884). American inventor who developed the mechanical grain reaper: "It's all right; it's all right. I only want heaven."

McDaniel, Hattie (1895-1952). American television and movie actress. McDaniel was the first African American to win an Academy Award. It was presented for her performance in *Gone with the Wind*. Dying of breast cancer, to a friend: "I'll be all right. I'll soon be up and back into harness."

McDaniel, Sergeant (died 1776). American Revolutionary War soldier. Fighting the British at Fort Sullivan, near Charleston, South Carolina, McDaniel was mortally wounded by a cannon shot: "Fight on, boys. Don't let liberty die with me."

Alternative: * "Fight on, my brave boys. Don't let liberty expire with me today!"

McDuff, Kenneth (1946-1998). American criminal. Although accused of multiple murders, McDuff was executed by lethal injection for the killing of a pregnant woman: "I'm ready to be released. Release me."

McGuffey, William (1800-1873). American educator and author of primary texts widely used throughout the U.S.-the *McGuffey Readers*. Toward the end, he said: "Oh, that I might once more speak to my dear boys! But Thy will be done."

McGuire, Thomas (1920-1945). American fighter pilot ace who scored the second highest number of "kills" during WWII. While leading a group of fighter aircraft, McGuire radioed: "Daddy flight, save your auxiliary [fuel] tanks." While engaging a Japanese plane, he made a low level maneuver that ultimately resulted in a fatal crash. The extra weight of the retained fuel tanks probably played a significant role in McGuire's mishap.

McIntyre, Oscar (1884-1938). American journalist. McIntyre asked his wife Maybelle: "Snooks, will you please turn this way? I like to look at your face."

Alternative: * "Snooks, will you please turn me this way. I like to look at your face."

McKail, Hugh, also MacKail (died 1666). Scottish martyr. After joining the covenanters, MacKail was arrested and sentenced to die by hanging. On the scaffold, he said to the effect: "... And now I begin my intercourse with God, which shall never be broken off. Farewell father and mother, friends and relations. Farewell the world and all delights. Farewell meat and drink. Farewell sun, moon and stars. Welcome, God and Father. Welcome, sweet Jesus, the Mediator of the new Covenant. Welcome, blessed Spirit of Grace and God of all consolation. Welcome, glory. Welcome, eternal life. welcome, death... O Lord, into thy hands I commit my spirit; for thou hast redeemed my soul, O Lord God of truth."

Alternative: * "Farewell moon and stars, farewell world and time, farewell weak and frail body. Welcome eternity, welcome angels and saints, welcome Savior of the world, welcome, God, the judge of all."

McKinley, Ida (1847-1907). Widow of assassinated U.S. President William McKinley. Concerned about measures taken to prolong her life,

Ida pleaded: "Why should I linger? Please God, if it be Thy will, why defer it? He [her husband] is gone and life is dark to me now."

McKinley, William (1843-1901). Twenty-fifth U.S. president, assassinated by an anarchist at the Pan American Exposition in Buffalo, New York. Near the end, McKinley spoke to his doctors: "It is useless, gentleman. I think we ought to have a prayer." He then repeated the Lord's Prayer. Many versions of his last utterances exist, but most convey similar sentiments. When his wife entered the sick room, the president said: "Good-by, all! Good-by! It is God's way; His will be done, not ours." He then repeated a portion of a well-known hymn: "'Nearer, my God, to Thee/ E'en tho' it be a cross...'/ That has been my inextinguishable prayer./ It is God's way." When his wife said she wanted to go [die] with him: "We are all going; we are all going; we are all going... Oh dear!"

Alternatives: * To his wife: "'Nearer, my God, to Thee;/ e'en though it be a cross...'/ has been my constant prayer."

* "'Nearer, my God to Thee, nearer to Thee...'"
* "It is the Lord's way. Good-bye all!"
* "It's God's way. His will, not ours, be done. Nearer, my God, to Thee."

McLain, James (died 1970). American criminal. As he tried to shoot his way out of his own murder trial, McLain cried: "Take lots of pictures! We are the revolutionaries!"

McLaury, Thomas (1853-1881). American outlaw cowboy, killed by the Earp brothers and Doc Holliday (above) during the gunfight at the O.K. Corral in Tombstone, Arizona. Two of his companions in the shootout carried weapons, but McLaury apparently was unarmed. He pulled open his coat and said: "I have got nothing." When the shooting stopped, McLaury was dead.

Alternative: * "I'm not armed."

McNeil, Hugh (1830-1862). Union officer during the U.S. Civil War. Spurring his men on in a battle near Sharpsburg, Maryland, McNeil shouted: "Forward, Bucktails, forward!" He immediately was felled by a

Confederate's shot. Bucktails was the nickname of McNeil's Pennsylvania infantry regiment.

McPherson, Aimee (1890-1944). Canadian-American evangelist. McPherson died of an apparent accidental overdose of sleeping pills. Before retiring to bed, she remarked on hearing an airplane: "I wonder if we'll be flying around in airplanes when we die?"

McQueen, Steven "Steve" (1930-1980). American film actor. Dying of a chest malignancy, McQueen asked for: "Ice cubes... ice cubes... I want more ice cubes." Later he spoke the names of his daughter, son and wife: "Terry... Chad... Barbara..."

McSorley, Ernest (1912-1975). The Canadian-born McSorley was captain of the 729-foot Great Lakes freighter SS *Edmund Fitzgerald* that was caught in a severe November storm on Lake Superior. His last radio communication stated: "We are holding our own." Soon after he said those words, the ship sank and all 29 men aboard drowned.

McVeigh, Timothy (1968-2001). American terrorist, convicted of the 1995 bombing of a federal building in Oklahoma City that killed 168 individuals. Before his execution by lethal injection, McVeigh quoted lines from British poet William Henley's "Invictus:" "I am the master of my fate;/ I am the captain of my soul."

Mead, Margaret (1901-1978). American cultural anthropologist. Dying of cancer, Mead remarked: "Nurse, I think I'm going." When her attendant said that all must pass some day, Mead replied: "Yes, but this is different."

Meade, George (1815-1872). Union general during the U.S. Civil War who defeated Robert E. Lee's Confederate forces at the Battle of Gettysburg. Dying of pneumonia, Meade realized the end was near: "I am about crossing a beautiful wide river and the opposite shore is coming nearer and nearer."

Meanes, James (1956-1998). American criminal, executed by lethal injection for a murder committed during a robbery. Before dying, Meanes philosophically said: "As the ocean always returns to itself, love always returns to itself. So does consciousness, always returns to itself. And I do so with love on my lips. May God bless all mankind."

Medici, Catherine de (1519-1589). Franco-Italian consort of King Henry II of France (above). Catherine was one of the instigators of the St. Bartholomew's Day massacre that resulted in the slaughter of many Huguenots. Dying of "pleurisy," Catherine exclaimed: "Ah, my God, I am dead!"

Medici, Lorenzo de (1449-1492). Florentine political and cultural leader who died of a fever that was "eating away the whole man, the arteries and veins, the limbs, intestines, nerves, bones and marrow." When reminded that he must meet death with fortitude, de Medici corrected his admonisher: "With cheerfulness, if such be the will of God." Asked how he liked a bite of proffered food: "As a dying man always does." He expired reciting passages from scriptures.

Alternative: * "If it is God's will, nothing can be more pleasant to me than death."

Medill, Joseph (1823-1899). Canadian-born American politician and newspaper publisher who was a friend and supporter of Abraham Lincoln. To his physician: "My last words shall be 'What is the news?'" Medill was true to his word; he died 10 minutes later without further utterance.

Medina, Javier (1969-2002). Mexican-born American criminal, executed by lethal injection for the murder of an undercover police officer. After thanking Mexican citizens for their help trying to spare his life and apologizing to the victim's family, Medina began singing "Amazing Grace" but lost consciousness at the phrase "I once was lost, but now am found..."

Medina, Pedro Luis (1957-1997). Cuban-born American criminal, executed by electrocution for the murder of a Florida woman: "I am still innocent."

Medley, Samuel (1738-1799). English clergyman, best-known for his hymn "I Know that My Redeemer Lives." When Medley realized the end was near, he commented: "I am a poor shattered bark, just about to gain the harbor, and oh how sweet will be the port after the storm." Before his last breath, he continued: "Dying is sweet work, sweet work! My Father, my heavenly Father, I am looking up, I am looking up to my dear Jesus, my God, my portion, my all in all. Glory, Glory, Home, Home!"

Alternatives: * "I am now a shattered bark, just about to gain the blissful harbour, and oh how sweet will be the port after the storm."

* "… I am looking to my dear Jesus, my portion, my all in all. Home, home, Hallelujah"

Meir, Golda, born Golda Mabovich (1898-1978). Russian-born Israeli prime minister. Dying of cancer, Meir said to her nurse: "See, even steel sometimes weakens." Asked by her son what she was thinking, Meir replied: "About the afterworld."

Melanchthon, Philip (1497-1560). German religious reformer who collaborated with Martin Luther (above). Dying of a respiratory infection, Melanchthon frequently quoted Romans 8:31: "If God be for us, who can be against us?" When asked if he needed anything: "Nothing but heaven. Let me rest and pray. My end is near." Later, the beginning of Psalm 31:5 was quoted to him: "Into Thy hand I commit my spirit…" When asked if he heard it, Melanchthon replied with a resounding: "Yes!"

Alternative: * "Nothing but heaven. And, therefore, do not ask me such questions anymore."

Melba, Nellie, born Helen Mitchell (1861-1931). Australian operatic soprano. Dying of a blood stream infection complicating facial surgery, Melba told a friend: "John, why must I be subjected to a lingering death?" Later, she attempted to sing Bach-Gounod's "Ave Maria" but was only able to produce a few words.

Melchior, Lauritz (1890-1973). Danish-American operatic tenor. Melchior spoke his last words to his granddaughter: "Have a good life."

Mellon, Richard (1858-1933). American industrialist and philanthropist. The multimillionaire Mellon and his brother Andrew enjoyed playing practical jokes on each other. Dying of pneumonia, the weakened Richard beckoned Andrew to his bedside saying: "Closer." As his brother leaned nearer, the dying man brushed his shoulder, hissed "Last tag" and died. His brother Andrew was left permanently "it."

Melville, Herman (1819-1891). American author who wrote the novel *Moby Dick*. Dying of heart disease, Melville quoted the last words of the hero in his novella *Billy Budd*: "God bless Captain Vere."

Mencken, Henry Louis "H.L." (1880-1956) American journalist, editor, critic and satirist. Mencken jokingly composed his own epitaph, which does not appear on his tombstone: "If after I depart this vale, you ever remember me, and have thought to please my ghost, forgive some sinner and wink your eye at some homely girl." Near the end, he spoke to James Farrell, a fellow writer: "Remember me to my friends. Tell them I'm a hell of a mess." Later Mencken confided to a friend: "Louis, this is the last time you'll see me." He was found dead in bed the next day.

Mendeleev, Dmitri (1834-1907). Russian chemist who devised the periodic table of elements. Dying of pneumonia, to his physician: "Doctor, you have science, I have faith." The same phrase appeared in Jules Verne's novel *A Journey to the North Pole* published three decades earlier.

Mendelssohn, Felix (1809-1847). German pianist, conductor and composer. After suffering a series of strokes in late October-early November 1847, Mendelssohn briefly regained consciousness. When his wife asked if he had pain, he replied in the negative. When she inquired if he were tired, he said: "Yes, I am tired, terribly tired." The 38-year-old composer then lapsed into a coma and died November 4 from "the Curse of the Mendelssohns."

Alternative: * "Weary, very weary."

Menelik II (1844-1913). King and founder of modern-day Ethiopia. Dying from complications of a series of strokes: "God, help my people!"

Mercier, Désiré-Félicien (1851-1926). Belgian clergyman and philosopher. Toward the end, Mercier said: "I thirst to lead souls unto Thee, O Lord!" After receiving the Last Rites, he decided: "Now there is nothing more to be done except to wait."

Mercury, Freddie, born Farrokh Bulsara (1946-1991). African-born British rock musician. Dying from complications of AIDS, Mercury allegedly asked for help to the bathroom to: "Pee pee."

Meredith, George (1828-1909). English writer and poet. Meredith spoke about his doctor: "I am afraid Sir Thomas thinks very badly of my case."

Mergenthaler, Ottmar (1854-1899). German-born inventor of the linotype machine used in newspaper printing. Dying of tuberculosis, to his family and friends: "Emma, my children, my friends, be kind to one another."

Mérimée, Prosper (1803-1870). French writer and dramatist, best-known for his novella *Carmen*, the basis of Georges Bizet's opera of the same name. His last words: "Goodnight now. I want to go to sleep."

Merman, Ethel, born Ethel Zimmermann (1908-1984). American singer and film actress. Dying of a brain tumor, Merman acerbically responded to a friend who mentioned an unflattering story being told about her: "A**holes!"

Merry del Val, Rafael (1865-1930). British-born clergyman of Spanish ancestry who became Papal Secretary of State during Pope Pius X's tenure. Dying of heart failure complicating an appendectomy: "I'm too heavy, doctor. Isn't it true? I know it."

Meslier, Jean (1664-1733). French Catholic priest who secretly espoused atheism and anarchy. Meslier wrote in his will: "I should like to see, and this will be the last and most ardent of my desires, I should like to see the last king strangled with the guts of the last priest." This quotation resembles a line in Denis Diderot's poem "Les Éleuthéromanes," written later: "His hands would plait the priest's guts, if he had no rope, to strangle kings."

Messner, Tammy Faye Bakker (1942-2007). Former wife of the disgraced American televangelist Jim Bakker. Dying of colon cancer, Messner told her second husband: "I'm in the hands of Jesus…"

Mesurier, John le, born John le Mesurier Halliley (1912-1983). British actor. Dying from complications of cirrhosis, Mesurier spoke to his wife before lapsing into a coma: "It's all been rather lovely."

Metastasio, Pietro, born Pietro Antonio Trapassi (1698-1782). Italian opera librettist, poet and writer. After Last Rites were administered, Metastasio allowed: "I offer to Thee, O Lord, Thy own Son, who already has given the pledge of love, inclosed in this thin emblem; turn on Him thine eyes; ah! behold whom I offer to Thee and then desist, O Lord! if Thou canst desist from mercy."

Metchnikoff, Élie (1845-1916). Russian bacteriologist who won the 1908 Nobel Prize in Medicine. Metchnikoff spoke to his physician immediately before he died: "You remember your promise? You will do my postmortem and look at the intestines carefully, for I think there is something there now." Metchnikoff died of heart failure, which caused fluid to accumulate in his abdominal cavity.

Metternich, Klemens von (1773-1859). German-born foreign minister and chancellor of the Austrian Empire. Toward the end, Metternich spoke to a friend about his career: "I was a rock of order!"

Mew, Charlotte (1869-1928). British poet and writer. Depressed in her last years, Mew committed suicide by drinking a caustic chemical. She told the doctors attempting to save her: "Don't keep me. Let me go."

Meyerbeer, Giacomo, born Jacob Liebmann Beer (1791-1864). German-born composer whose works embodied the grand style of French opera. Before retiring for the night, to visitors: "I will see you in the morning. I bid you goodnight." He was found dead in bed.

Meynell, Alice (1847-1922). English poet, writer and women's rights activist. At her end, Meynell allowed: "This is not tragic. I am happy."

Michelangelo, born Michelangelo di Lodovico Buonarroti Simoni (1475-1564). Italian artist, sculptor and poet. His will read: "My soul I resign to God, my body to the earth, and my worldly possessions to my relations; admonishing them that through their lives and in the hour of death they think upon the sufferings of Jesus Christ. And I do desire that my body be taken to the city of Florence for its last rest." Michelangelo's body eventually was moved from Rome to Florence, fulfilling his last request. Some say his last words were directed to those at his deathbed: "Through life remember the suffering of Jesus."

Alternative: * "I commit my soul to God, my body to the earth, my possessions to my nearest relatives. I die in the faith of Jesus Christ and in the firm hope of a better life."

Michelet, Jules (1798-1874). French historian and writer. When his physician ordered a change in bed linen, Michelet replied deliriously: "Linen, doctor, you speak of linen? Do you know what linen is?... The linen of the peasant, of the worker... linen, a great thing... I want to make a book of it."

Michelson, Albert (1852-1931). Prussian-born American physicist who pioneered measurement of the speed of light. Michelson was awarded the 1907 Nobel Prize in Physics. While dictating, the 78 year-old physicist interrupted his recording: "The following is a report on the measurement of the velocity of light made at the Irvine Ranch, near Santa Ana, California, during the period of September, 1929 to..." He fell asleep and never awoke.

Middleton, Frank (1963-1996). American criminal, executed by lethal injection for the rape and murder of a woman. "What are you people looking at? I'm going to the Promised Land! Ha, ha, ha!"

Milborne, Jacob (1640-1691). American son-in-law and secretary of Jacob Leisler who led an insurrection against colonial New York landowners. Convicted of treason, both men were hanged. Milborne's last words were directed toward a man whom he perceived had led to his conviction: "Robert Livingston, for this I will implead [accuse or plead a case against] thee at the bar God!"

Alternative: * "You have caused my death. Before God's tribunal I will impeach you for the same."

Miles, Dixon (1804-1862). Union officer during the U.S. Civil War. In the battle at Harpers Ferry, Miles surrendered his garrison to the Confederates, the largest capitulation of combatants during that war. In the process of the hasty surrender, Miles was wounded by an artillery shell. To one of his subordinate officers: "Captain, I have done my duty to my country and I am ready to die. God bless you."

Milholland, Inez (1886-1916). American suffragette and lawyer. Dying of pernicious anemia, Milholland's last public words were directed to President Woodrow Wilson: "Mr. President, how long must women wait for liberty?"

Mill, John (1806-1873). English philosopher and economist. When told he had no chance of recovery from a severe skin infection (erysipelas), Mill answered: "My work is done... You know that I have done my work."

Millay, Edna St. Vincent (1892-1950). American writer and poet who won the1923 Pulitzer Prize for Poetry. Millay was found dead from a fall down a flight of stairs, possibly after a heart attack. She had written a note to her maid before the fatal event: "The iron is set too high. Don't put it on where it says 'Linen' or it will scorch the linen. Try it on 'Rayon' and then perhaps on 'Woolen.' And be careful not to burn your fingers when you shift it from one heat to another. It is 5:30 and I have been working all night. I am going to bed. Good morning."

Miller, Glenn (1904-1944). American trombonist and band leader. To aid the war effort, Miller organized a jazz band that entertained various Allied troops in Europe. Before departing England for a trans-channel flight to Paris, he seemed to have a premonition about the trip. He spoke to George Simon, an American jazz writer and musician: "Christ, I don't know why I spend my time making plans like this. You know, George, I have an awful feeling you guys are going to go home without me, and I'm going to get mine in some godd*** beat-up old plane." Looking around the aircraft, he asked a companion, Colonel Norman Baesell (above): "Where the hell are the parachutes?" Miller's plane disappeared over the English Channel without a trace.

Miller, Hugh (1802-1856). Scottish geologist and writer. Miller suffered a deep depression that led to his suicide by gunshot. He left this note for his wife: "Dearest Lydia, My brain burns, I must have walked; and a fearful dream rises upon me. I cannot bear the horrible thought. God and Father of the Lord Jesus Christ, have mercy upon me. Dearest Lydia, dear children, farewell. My brain burns as the recollection grows. My dear, dear wife, Farewell, Hugh Miller."

Miller, Joaquin (c. 1837-1913). American poet. Miller was a well-rounded man who lived with Native Americans for a period, wrote poetry, edited newspapers, managed a pony express service and practiced law. His dying words were: "Take me away! Take me away!"

Millet, Jean-François (1814-1875). French artist. Observing a deer wounded by hunters and savaged by dogs outside his window, Millet prophesied: "It is an omen. This poor beast, which comes to die beside me, warns me that I too am about to die."

Milligan, Terence "Spike" (1918-2002). Indian-born Irish comedian, musician, playwright and writer. Dying of kidney failure, Milligan composed his own epitaph: "I told you I was ill," but his headstone ultimately read: "Love, light, peace." His last words: "Come on out."

Milne, Walter, also Mill (died 1558). Scottish martyr. Milne was the last Protestant martyr to be condemned to the stake prior to the Scottish Reformation. Before he was burned, the 82 year-old man addressed the crowd: "Dear friends, the reason why I am to suffer this day is not because I have committed any crimes, although I consider myself a most miserable sinner before God- but it is for the defense of the faith of Jesus Christ as set forth in the Old and New Testament for us. It is the faith for which godly martyrs have offered themselves gladly before, being assured of eternal happiness... Therefore, if you wish to escape the second death, do not be seduced with the lies of priests, monks, friars, priors, abbots, bishops and the rest... Depend only upon Jesus Christ and His mercy..." As the flames flared, Milne prayed: "Lord, have mercy on me! Pray, people, while there is yet time!"

Milnes, Richard, Baron of Houghton (1809-1885). English politician, poet and writer. Toward the end, Milnes quipped: "My exit is the result of too many entrées."

Milton, John (1608-1674). English poet and writer, best-known for his epic poem *Paradise Lost*. Dying of kidney failure, Milton remarked: "Death is the great key that opens the palace of eternity."

Alternative: * Some say Milton's last words were spoken to his wife: "Make much of me as long as I live, for thou knowest I have given thee all when I die at thy disposal," but these words were uttered well before his fatal illness.

Mineo, Salvatore "Sal" (1939-1976). American film and theater actor, best-known for his role in the movie *Rebel Without a Cause*. Mineo was stabbed in the heart during a suspected robbery attempt. Before dying, he cried: "Oh God! No! Help! Someone help!" A neighbor tried to revive him but was unsuccessful.

Alternative: * "Help! Help! Oh, my God!"

Mirabeau, Honoré, Comte de (1749-1791). French politician who briefly served as president of the National Assembly during the French Revolution. Succumbing to a sudden painful illness, Marabeau predicted: "I shall die today. When one is in that situation, there remains but one thing more to do; and that is to perfume me, to crown me with flowers, to environ me with music, so that I may enter sweetly into that slumber wherefrom there is no awakening." Later: "I carry in my heart the dirge of the monarchy, the ruins whereof will now be the prey of the factious." At that point, he lost his voice and scrawled on a scrap of paper: "TO SLEEP!" Having regained his speech, Mirabeau asked for laudanum: "My sufferings are intolerable. I have within me a hundred years of life but not a moment's courage." When the medication failed to arrive: "You are deceiving me." When reassured that the draught had been requested, he spoke to Cabanis, one of his physicians: "Were not you my doctor and my friend? And did you not promise to spare me the pains of such a death? Must I carry with me the regret of having confided in you?" When another healer entered, Mirabeau told a companion: "Swear to me that you will not tell Petit what you are preparing for me!" When the concoction arrived, he drank it down, turned on his side and died.

Alternatives: * "To die is to sleep."

* "Give me more laudanum, that I may not think of eternity and of what is to come. I have an age of strength, but not a moment of courage."
* As the sun shone into his room, Mirabeau commented: "If that is not God himself there, it is his cousin at least... Let me fall asleep to the sound of delicious music."
* "Surround me with perfumes and the flowers of spring; dress my hair with care, and let me fall asleep amid the sound of delicious music."
* "Crown me with flowers. Intoxicate me with perfumes. Let me die to the sound of delicious music."
* As a cannon fired in the distance: "Are those already the Achilles' funeral?"

Mirande, Henri (1877-1955). French artist and illustrator. Seeing himself in the mirror, Mirande commented: "Yes, I have the appearance of death!"

Misawa, Mitsuharu (1962-2009). Professional Japanese wrestler. During a match, Misawa took a hit that incapacitated him. When a referee asked whether or not he could move, the injured man replied: "Cannot move..." He lost consciousness and was taken to a hospital where he died.

Mishima, Yukio, pseudonym of Kimitake Hiraoka (1925-1970). Japanese social reformer, writer, poet, playwright and actor. When postwar Japan seemed to conflict with his values, Mishima tried to take over a civil defense camp in an effort to restore the emperor to power. When the officers there mocked him, he shouted: "Long Live the Emperor!" Returning to his comrades, Mishima fumed: "I don't think they [the soldiers] even heard me." He then performed ritual *seppuku* (self-disembowelment). To conclude the ceremony, a comrade attempted to perform a decapitation but was unsuccessful. Another member was able to complete the beheading. Later, a note was found on Mishima's desk stating the belief: "Human life is limited, but I would like to live forever."

Alternative: * "Long live his imperial Majesty!"

Mitchell, Aaron (1930-1967). American criminal, executed in the San Quentin, California gas chamber for the murder of a policeman. "I am Jesus Christ. Look what they have done to me."

Mitchell, Margaret (1900-1949). American writer, best-known for her novel *Gone with the Wind.* Mitchell was struck by an automobile, which resulted in a skull fracture and internal injuries. Before dying in hospital, she would arouse and speak short phrases: "It hurts," "It tastes bad [in response to a drink of orange juice]" and "I'll take care of that in the morning."

Mitchell, Maria (1818-1889). First American professional astronomer. Dying of a "brain disease," Mitchell remarked: "Well, if this is dying, there is nothing unpleasant about it."

Mitchell, Martha (1918-1976). Former wife of John Mitchell, the U.S. attorney general under President Richard Nixon. Dying essentially alone, Mitchell complained to her nurse about her society friends: "Those people sure let me down when I needed them most. I never did like them anyhow. I always felt more comfortable with plain, ordinary folks."

Mitchell, Silas (1829-1914). Union Army surgeon in the U.S. Civil War. During his last moments, Mitchell deliriously relived an operation performed on a battlefield: "That leg must come off. Save the leg- lose the life!"

Mitchell, William "Billy" (1879-1936). American Army general, called the father of the U.S. Air Force for his advocacy of military air superiority. Thinking about his burial, Mitchell decided: "Although I should like to be with the pilots and my comrades in Arlington, I feel that it is better for me to go back to Wisconsin, the home of my family."

Mitchell, William (1952-1987). American criminal, executed by electrocution for the murder of a 14 year-old boy during a robbery: "A few hours ago, Wayne Snow [chairman of the Georgia State Pardons Board] said I had no redeeming qualities. The only thing I've got to say to Wayne Snow is kiss my a**. Bye."

Mitford, Mary Russell (1787-1855). English writer. Mitford's life was cut short from complications of a carriage accident. Her final letter to a friend read in part: "... Today I am better, but if you wish for another cheerful evening with your old friend, there is no time to be lost. God bless you, my dear friend! Ever affectionately yours, M.R. Mitford."

Mizell, Jason (see Jam Master Jay.)

Mizner, Wilson (1876-1933). American playwright and entrepreneur. When a priest asked Mizner if he wished to speak to him, the playwright quipped: "Why should I talk to you? I've just been talking to your boss." He then told his physician: "Well doc, I guess this is the main event."

Mocenigo, Tommaso (1343-1423). Venetian doge (leader) and statesman. On his deathbed, Mocenigo mentioned the names of several potential successors. He then warned against Francesco Foscari saying in part: "... If he is made Doge, you will be at war continually... You will lose your money and your reputation. You will be at the mercy of a soldiery! I have found it impossible to forebear expressing to you thus my opinion. May God help you to make the wisest choice! May He rule your hearts to preserve peace!" Regardless, Foscari was elected doge, and Mocenigo's predictions were borne out.

Modigliani, Amedeo (1884-1920). Italian artist and sculptor who worked primarily in France. Dying of meningeal tuberculosis, Modigliani allowed:

"I have only a fragment of brain left." He died saying: "Italy! Dear, dear Italy!"

Moffat, Robert (1795-1883). Scottish missionary to Africa. Moffat spoke on his deathbed: "It is all a mystery. Will not the Judge of all the earth do right?" After repeating the Scotch version of Psalm 103, the missionary stopped and said: "There is nothing like the original."

Mohaupt, Juliana (died 1859). Orphaned niece of the Austrian writer and painter Adalbert Stifter. The 18 year-old Mohaupt ran away from home and was found dead weeks later in the Danube River. Her suicide note read: "I am going to my mother in the great Service."

Moir, David (1796-1851). Scottish physician, poet and writer. Moir prayed: "May the Lord my God not separate between my soul and body until He has made a final separation between my soul and sin, for the sake of my Redeemer."

Molière, born Jean-Baptiste Poquelin (1622-1673). French actor and playwright. After one of his performances, Molière died of a massive hemorrhage complicating his tuberculosis. Earlier, he prophesied: "I see that it cannot last. I can no longer bear up against the misery which never ceases one instant to oppress me... and I feel that I am going." At the end, Molière said to a pupil: "Don't be frightened. You have seen me throw up a great deal more [blood] than this and to spare. Nevertheless, go and tell my wife to come up." By the time she arrived, the actor was dead.

Molineux Thomas, also Molyneux (died 1387). English Constable of Chester. Surrounded by enemies during the Battle of Radcot Bridge, Oxfordshire, England, Molineux plunged into the water in an attempt to escape. When his foes demanded that he come to shore, the constable asked: "If I come, will ye save my life?" Told that no guarantees could be given, Molineux replied: "Well then, if there be no other remedy, suffer me to come up, and let me try with hand blows, either with you or some other, and so die like a man." He was dispatched forthwith.

Moncey, Bon Adrien (1754-1842). Distinguished French officer who served during the French Revolution and Napoleonic Wars. Moncey gave this advice at his death: "Let everyone fulfill and close his course like me."

Monet, Claude (1840-1926). French Impressionist painter. Two weeks before dying of lung cancer, Monet told the former French Prime Minister Georges Clemenceau about some seedlings in his garden: "You will see all that in the spring, but I won't be here anymore." At a second visit, Clemenceau asked if the painter were suffering. Monet answered "No" and died moments later.

Monge, Luis José (1918-1967). Puerto Rican-born American criminal, executed in the Colorado State Penitentiary gas chamber for the murder of his wife and three children. Before dying, Monge inquired: "Will that gas bother my asthma?"

Monica, Saint (c. 331-387). Algerian-born pious woman, the mother of St. Augustine of Hippo (above). Dying in Italy, Monica was asked if she wished she were in her native Africa: "Nowhere is far from God." To her children: "Lay this body wherever it may be. Let no care of it disturb you; this only I ask of you that you should remember me at the altar of the Lord wherever you may be... In peace I will sleep with Him and take my rest."

Monime (died c. 72 BCE). Greek Macedonian noblewoman who was one of the wives of Mithridates VI, king of a region that is modern-day Turkey. After his defeat by the Roman army, Mithridates sent his eunuch to prepare his queen for death in the least offensive way. Monime took her crown and tried to hang herself, but the straps broke. She cried: "O wretched head-band! Not able to help me in this small thing!" She spat on the crown and presented her neck to the eunuch's knife.

Monod, Adolphe (1802-1856). Danish-born French Protestant minister and writer. Dying of cancer, Monod proclaimed: "This oppression is altogether physical: God is not the less with me. I am waiting for Him in the faith of Jesus Christ and of the Holy Spirit."

Monroe, James (1758-1831). Fifth U.S. president. Dying of heart failure and tuberculosis, Monroe spoke to a friend concerning James Madison, the immediate past president: "I regret that I should leave this world without again beholding him." Monroe died on Independence Day, July 4, as had two of his predecessors, Presidents John Adams and Thomas Jefferson.

Monroe, Marilyn, born Norma Jeane Mortenson [later changed to Baker] (1926-1962). American actress and presidential favorite. Before dying, Monroe spoke to the actor Peter Lawford, brother-in-law of President John Kennedy: "Say goodbye to Pat [Patricia Kennedy Lawford], say goodbye to the president [John Kennedy] and say goodbye to yourself, because you're a nice guy... I'll see... I'll see." She was found dead several hours later of a suspected drug overdose, "a probable suicide."

Alternative: * "Say goodbye to Pat, say goodbye to Jack [President John Kennedy] and say goodbye to yourself, because you're a nice guy."

Montagu, Mary (1689-1762). English aristocrat, poet and writer. Dying of breast cancer, Montagu allowed: "It has all been most interesting."

Montaigne, Michel de (1533-1592). French writer and statesman. Montaigne died of a severe throat abscess, allegedly saying: "I submit myself to Nature, confident that she is armed with claws and teeth to defend us against the assault of maladies." Because of the extensive swelling in his throat, it is unlikely that he articulated those words. A similar quote appeared in his *Essays* 12 years before his death.

Montcalm, Louis (1712-1759). French military commander during the French and Indian War. After sustaining a gunshot injury during the Battle of Quebec, Montcalm was told that his wound was mortal. He replied: "I am glad of it." When told that his time was short, he said: "So much the better. I am happy that I shall not live to see the surrender of Quebec." When his officers asked for further orders, Montcalm allowed: "I will neither give orders nor interfere any further. I have much business that must be attended to, of greater moment than your ruined garrison and this wretched country. My time is very short; therefore, pray leave me. I wish you all comfort, and to be happily extricated from your present perplexities." Although he lingered several hours more, no further dialog was recorded.

Montesquieu, Charles-Louis (1689-1755). French political and social philosopher. An uninvited clergyman asked the dying Montesquieu if he were aware of the greatness of God: "Yes, and of the littleness of man."

Montessori, Maria (1870-1952). Italian educator and physician whose method of study for young children bears her name. To her son shortly before suffering a stroke: "Am I no longer of any use, then?"

Montez, Lola, stage name of Eliza Gilbert (1821-1861). Irish-born actress, dancer and one-time mistress of King Ludwig I of Bavaria and the composer Franz Liszt (above). Dying of pneumonia, Montez said to a clergyman reading from the Bible: "Tell me, tell me more of my dear Savior!" Toward the end, she complained: "I am very tired."

Montezuma II, also Moctezuma II (c. 1466-1520). Aztec emperor. Montezuma was stoned by his own people because of his friendly dealings with the Spaniards led by Hernán Cortés. As he died, the Aztec ruler spoke to a priest who tried to convert him to Christianity: "I have but a few moments to live and will not at this hour desert the faith of my fathers." He then sought to entrust the welfare of his daughters to the Spanish leader Cortés: "I confide to your care my beloved children, the most precious jewels I can leave you. The great monarch beyond the ocean will interest himself to see that they come into their inheritance, if you present before him their just claims. I know your master will do this, if for no other reason, than for the kindness I have shown the Spaniards, though it has occasioned my ruin. For all my misfortunes, I bear you no ill will."

Montfort, Simon de (c. 1208-1265). French-born English political and military leader. In 1264, Montfort led an attempt to overthrow King Henry III and one year later was mortally wounded during the Battle of Evesham in Worcestershire, West Midlands. When he found his men surrounded: "By the arm of St. James, they [the adversarial forces] have not learnt that from themselves, but from me. Commend your souls to God, for our bodies are theirs." When ordered to surrender: "Never will

I surrender to dogs and perjurers; but to God alone." He was killed by a blow from behind, crying: "It is God's grace!"

Alternatives: * "By the arm of St. James, it is time to die!"

* "By the arm of St. James, they come on skillfully. It is not from themselves, but from me, that they have learned that order. Now let us commend our souls to God; for our bodies are our enemies."
* "Let us commend our souls to God, for our bodies are [belong to] the foe's."
* As Montfort died: "Thank God."

Montgomery, Bernard "Monty" (1887-1976). British field marshall during WWII. Several weeks before dying, Montgomery remembered the costly North African Battle of El Alamein, Egypt, which he led: "I couldn't sleep last night. I had great difficulty. I can't have very long to go now. I've got to meet God and explain all those men I killed at Alamein." Those were his last coherent words before dying.

Alternative: * "Well, now I must go to meet God and try to explain all those men I killed at Alamein."

Montgomery, James (1771-1854). Scottish-born poet, hymnodist and journalist. The day before dying, Montgomery placed a hand over his heart and remarked to a friend: "I feel considerable oppression here." Before retiring, he told a servant: "Goodnight" and died of a heart attack during the night.

Montgomery, James R. (died 1864). Confederate Army private during the U.S. Civil War. Mortally wounded in the Battle of Spotsylvania Court House, Virginia, Montgomery sent a farewell blood-stained letter to his father in Mississippi: "Death is inevitable. This is my last letter to you. I write to you because I know you would be delighted to read a word from your dying son." He expired several days later.

Montgomery, Richard (1736-1775). Irish-born Continental Army general during the American Revolutionary War. Leading his men during the ill-fated Battle of Quebec, Montgomery exhorted: "Come on, my good soldiers, your General calls upon you to come on." He was cut down by the first enemy volley.

Alternative: * "Men of New York, you will not fear to follow where your general leads. Forward!"

Montherlant, Henri de (1895-1972). French novelist and dramatist. On the day of his suicide, Montherlant dined in his usual restaurant. When served his customary decaffeinated coffee, the writer instructed: "Today I'll have a real coffee." Later, Montherlant swallowed a cyanide capsule and shot himself in the head.

Montmorency, Anne, Duc de (1493-1567). French soldier and statesman who became Marshal of France. Sustaining a fatal injury during the Battle of Saint-Denis near Paris, Montmorency misspoke about his true age of 74: "Do you think a man who has known how to live honorably for eighty years does not know how to die for a quarter of an hour?"

Moody, Arthur (1902-1954). American newspaper correspondent and member of the U.S. Senate. Before dying of pneumonia and a heart attack, Moody commented: "I feel better."

Moody, Dwight (1837-1899). American evangelist and educator who founded Moody Bible Institute. Dying of a heart ailment, Moody told his family: "Earth recedes; heaven opens before me. No, this is no dream... It is beautiful. It is like a trance. If this is death, it is sweet. There is no valley here. God is calling me, and I must go." He then gave instructions to his followers for the continuation of his ecclesiastical work and spoke of his deceased grandchildren: "Dwight, Irene! I see the children's faces." Then: "Give my love to them all." To his wife: "Mamma, you have been a good wife to me." Toward the end, Moody lost consciousness, but his physicians were able to revive him. He angrily responded: "What does all this mean? What are you all doing here? This is a strange thing. I have been beyond the gates of death and to the very portals of heaven, and here I am back again! It is very strange." Later he began to worsen and told one of his physicians who was preparing an injection: "Doctor, I don't know about this. Do you think it is best? It is only keeping the family in anxiety." At that point, all resuscitative efforts ceased and he died quietly.

Moody, Vaughn (1869-1910). American dramatist and poet. Dying of a brain tumor, Moody repeated lines from Shakespeare's comedy *Measure for Measure*: "Reason thus with life: If I do lose thee, I do lose a thing that none but fools would keep."

Moon, Keith (1946-1978). British musician who was a drummer in the rock group The Who. When Moon's girlfriend refused to cook him a meal, he responded: "If you don't like it, you can f*** off!" He then went into a bedroom, took an overdose of a medication used to treat the effects of alcohol withdrawal and died.

Moore, James (died 1875). American criminal, hanged for the murder of a deputy marshal. Moore exclaimed on the scaffold: "There are worse men here than me." Some have attributed this statement to Daniel Evans. Evans was convicted of the robbery and murder of a riding companion and was executed the same day; he remained mute when asked for last words.

Alternative: * "I have lived like a man, and I will die like a man. I am prepared… I think I see men here who are worse than I have ever been. I hope you may make peace with God before brought to my condition."

Moore, John (1761-1809). Scottish-born British general. Moore led his troops to victory over the French during the Battle of Corunna in the Peninsular War. Mortally injured by a cannon shot, his sword hilt became entangled in his chest wound. When an officer tried to extract it: "It is well as it is. I would rather have my sword to go out of the field together with me." To his surgeons: "You can be of no service to me. Go to the soldiers, to whom you can be useful. I am beyond your skill." Later, Moore asked: "Are the French beaten?" When told in the affirmative, he spoke to a comrade: "I feel myself so strong. I fear I shall be long dying. It's great uneasiness. It's great pain. Everything François says is right. I have great confidence in him." Later, seeing one of his men: "Stanhope, remember me to your sister."

Alternative: * "I hope the people of England will be satisfied, and that my country will do me justice."

Moore, Jonathan (1974-2007). American criminal, executed by lethal injection for the murder of a police officer during a robbery. To the victim's widow: "... It was done out of fear, stupidity and immaturity. I'm sorry. I did not know the man but for a few seconds before I shot him. It wasn't until I got locked up and saw that newspaper, I saw his face and his smile and I knew he was a good man. I am sorry for all your family and for my disrespect — he deserved better...We're done, Warden"

Moore, Thomas (1779-1852). Irish poet, singer and songwriter, best-known for his poem "The Last Rose of Summer." Moore's last words were directed to his wife: "Lean upon God, Bessie, lean upon God."

Moorhouse, Henry (1840-1880). British evangelist. Moorhouse's last words reflected his faith: "All is well. God is love."

Moran, Patrick (1876-1924). American professional baseball player and manager. Hospitalized with Bright's disease, Moran spoke to a fellow manager: "Hello John. Take me out of here."

Moran, Thomas (died 1971). American pickpocket extraordinaire. Dying in a Miami, Florida rescue shelter, Moran groused: "I've never forgiven that smart-alecky reporter who named me 'Butterfingers'- to me it's not funny."

Morant, Harry "Breaker" born Edwin Henry Murrant (1864-1902). Anglo-Australian soldier, accused of killing prisoners during the Boer War. Despite claiming that he was only following orders, Morant was court-martialed and sentenced to die. Accounts of his last words vary. The condemned man admonished the firing squad: "Shoot straight, you b*******! Don't make a mess of it!"

Alternative: * Because he refused a blindfold, others say he remarked: "Take this thing [the blindfold] off. Be sure and make a good job of it!"

Morata, Olympia (1526-1555). Italian-born holy woman, scholar and writer. Morata married a German physician, moved to his home country and converted to Protestantism. When her husband read passages from the Bible to console her, the dying woman replied: "I long to be dissolved, and to be with Christ. I am all joy- full of joy. And now, dear husband, I know you no more. I feel an inexpressible tranquility and peace with God, through Jesus Christ!"

Alternatives: * "I can scarcely see you my friends, but all around me there seem to be beautiful flowers."

* "For the last seven years Satan has not ceased to use every means to induce me to relinquish my faith, but now it would appear that he has lost his darts, for I have no other sensation in this hour of my departure than of undisturbed repose and tranquility of soul in Jesus."

More, Saint Thomas (1478-1535). English statesman, philosopher and author of the novel *Utopia*. More opposed the divorce of King Henry VIII from Catherine to marry Anne Boleyn. He also refused to sign the Act of Supremacy backed by Henry VIII that would have severed relations with the pope. For his actions, More was sentenced to die for treason. When he felt the scaffold shake, he told his executioner: "I pray you, Sir, see me safe up, and for my coming down let me shift for myself." When the axe man begged forgiveness, More said: "Thou wilt do me this day a greater benefit than ever any mortal man can be able to give me. Pluck up thy spirit man, and be not afraid to do thine office. My neck is very short; take heed, therefore, that thou strike not away, for saving thy honesty." When a blindfold was offered, More said: "I will cover them myself." He then put his neck on the block and moved his beard aside saying: "Stay friend till I put aside my beard, for that never committed treason."

Alternatives: * "I pray you, I pray you Mr. Lieutenant, see me safe up. And for my coming down let me shift for myself."

* "I can manage to get down alone. Courage my good man, don't be afraid. But, take care for I have a short neck, and you have to look your honor."

* "Master Lieutenant, give me thine hand, I pray thee see me safe up; for my coming down let me shift for myself."
* "Give me a hand going up; I shall fend for myself coming down."
* "Thou art to do me the greatest benefit I can receive."
* "My beard has never committed treason; pity that should be cut"
* "Pity that should be cut that has never committed treason."
* "This hath not offended the king."
* "[I die] the king's good servant, but God's first."

Moreau, Jean (1763-1813). French general. Moreau once fought under Napoleon I but later turned against his leader. Banished to the United States, he later returned to Europe to fight against the French. During the 1813 Battle of Dresden, the general was fatally wounded by cannon shot: "What? I, Moreau! I to die among the enemies of France, struck down by a French ball!"

Morecambe, Eric, stage name of John Eric Bartholomew (1926-1984). British comedian. Following a performance in a Tewkesbury, Gloucestershire theatre, Morecambe collapsed from a fatal heart attack, saying: "I'm glad that's over."

Morehead, John (1867-1936). American Lutheran minister. Referring to his late wife, Morehead inquired: "Will you do me a favor? Will you kindly ask my physician how long before I shall join my Nellie?"

Morelos, José (1765-1815). Mexican independence fighter and clergyman. Morelos helped lead Mexico in its bid for independence from Spain. He was captured and later placed before a Spanish firing squad: "Lord, if I have done well, thou knowest it; if ill, to thy infinite mercy I commend my soul."

Morgan, John Pierpont (1837-1913). American financier and philanthropist. Toward the end, Morgan requested: "Don't baby me so!"

Alternatives: * Others claim his last words were: "I've got to get to the top of the hill..." or "I've got to get up the hill..."

Moriale, Fra (1303-1354). French-born mercenary in the service of the king of Hungary and the pope. For his pillaging, Moriale was arrested by Italian authorities and sentenced to die. Moriale spoke to the crowd before his beheading: "I die for your poverty and my wealth!"

Morris, Gouverneur (1752-1816). American statesman who wrote portions of the U.S. Constitution. Morris died after inserting a piece of whale bone into his urinary tract in an unsuccessful attempt to relieve an obstruction. On his deathbed: "Sixty-four years ago it pleased the Almighty to call me into existence, here, on this spot, in this very room, and now shall I complain that He is pleased to call me hence?" When told that the weather was fine, Morris replied: "A beautiful day, yes, but..." and then recited lines from Thomas Gray's "Elegy Written in a Country Churchyard."

Morris, William (1834-1896). English craftsman, writer, poet, artist and social activist. Realizing that his life was coming to an end, Morris wrote to a friend: "Come soon, I want a sight of your dear face." He later spoke to his physician: "I want to get mumbo-jumbo out of the world."

Morrison, George (1866-1928). Scottish Presbyterian preacher. Morrison probably referred to his celestial destination: "It's an ever open door, never closed to anyone. It is wide open now, and I'm going through."

Morrow, Victor "Vic" (1929-1982). American television and film actor. Before shooting a scene for *Twilight Zone: The Movie* that involved a helicopter, Morrow said "I should have asked for a stunt double!" During filming, the aircraft malfunctioned and fell on the actors. Morrow and one of the two children in the scene were decapitated while the other child was crushed by the falling helicopter.

Morse, Samuel (1791-1872). American inventor and painter who pioneered development of the single-wire telegraph and Morse code. When told God had been good to him, Morse replied: "Yes, so good, so good, and the best part of all is yet to come." Later, Morse's physician tapped (percussed) the dying man's chest saying: "This is the way we doctors telegraph." The inventor then spoke his last words: "Very good."

Morton, Oliver (1823-1877). American politician and U.S. senator. After suffering a series of strokes, Morton spoke to a Dr. Thompson who held his hand at bedside: "I am dying. I am worn out."

Alternative: * "I am so tired; I am worn out."

Mosedale, Ken (1950-2000). Australian pilot. On a trans-Australian flight with seven passengers, Mosedale was asked to verify his aircraft's altitude. He spoke his call sign: "Sierra Kilo Charlie- um-standby." Without further radio transmissions, the plane plummeted to earth five hours later. The presumed cause of the crash was oxygen starvation due to a failure of cabin pressurization.

Moses (fl. 13th century BCE). Hebrew prophet and leader. Although Moses realized he would not enter the Promised Land with the tribes he had led from bondage in Egypt, he, nevertheless, gave them his blessing (Deuteronomy 33:29): "Happy are you, O Israel! Who is like you, a people saved by the Lord, the shield of your help and the sword of your triumph! Your enemies shall come fawning to you and you shall tread upon their high places!" He then ascended nearby Mt. Nebo, viewed the Promised Land and died.

Moses, Anna "Grandma" (1860-1961). American artist. Upset at her placement in a nursing home, the 101 year-old Moses hid her doctor's stethoscope. When he inquired about it, she replied: "That's what I won't tell you! I hid it. It's a forfeit. You take me back to Eagle Bridge [her home], and you'll get back your stethoscope." She died in the nursing home.

Mostel, Samuel "Zero" (1915-1977). American stage, screen and television actor. Hospitalized for a fainting episode, possibly related to an aortic aneurysm, Mostel said: "I feel dizzy. You better call a nurse."

Motley, John (1814-1877). American diplomat and historian. Dying of a possible cerebral hemorrhage, Motley had a premonition of what would transpire: "I am ill, very ill. I shall not recover."

Mott, James (1788-1868). American abolitionist and philanthropist, husband of Lucretia Mott (below). Dying of pneumonia while visiting his daughter in Brooklyn, to his wife: "I would like to go home, but I suppose I shall die here, and then I shall be at home; it is just as well."

Mott, Lucretia (1793-1880). American abolitionist and suffragette. Dying of pneumonia, Mott pleaded: "Let me go! Do take me! Oh, let me die! Take me now, this little standard bearer! The hour of my death!" Before losing consciousness, she put her hands to her head in pain, crying: "O my! My! My!"

Moyse, Frédéric (died 1938). French criminal, sentenced to die for killing his son: "What! Would you execute the father of a family?" Moyse was the 390th man dispatched by the famous French executioner Anatole Deibler.

Mozart, Wolfgang Amadeus, born Joannes Chrysostomus Wolfgangus Theophilus (a variant of Amadeus) Mozart (1756-1791). Austrian composer, conductor and pianist. As Mozart died from complications of probable rheumatic fever, his sister-in-law Sophie Haibel commented: "... As I approached his bed, he called to me: 'It is well you are here; you must stay to-night and see me die.' I tried as far as I was able to banish this impression; but he replied: 'The taste of death is already on my tongue, I taste death; and who will be near to support my Constance [Constanze, his wife] if you go away?' [Franz] Süssmayer [his favorite pupil] was standing by the bedside, and on the counterpane lay the *Requiem*, concerning which Mozart was still speaking and giving directions. He now called his wife and made her promise to keep his death secret for a time from everyone but [Johann] Albrechtsberger, that he might thus have an advantage over other candidates for the vacant office of capellmeister to [Vienna's] St. Stephen's [Cathedral]. His desire in this respect was gratified, for Albrechtsberger received the appointment. As he looked over the pages of the *Requiem* for the last time, he said, with tears in his eyes: 'Did I not tell you I was writing this for myself?'" In a delirium immediately before his death, Mozart reportedly made the sound of drums heard in his *Requiem*, but this noise probably was only his labored breathing. He became unconscious after a blood-letting session and died. His biographer, Georg Nissen, wrote that

Mozart's wife had a different memory of his death: "[Mozart said] 'now I must die, when I could care for you and the children. Ach, now I leave you unprovided for.' Suddenly he began to vomit— it spat out of him in an arch— it was brown, and he was dead."

Alternatives: * "I have the flavour of death on my tongue. I taste death; and who will support my dearest Constanze if you do not stay with her?"

* "The taste of death is upon my lips. I feel something that is not of this earth."
* "You spoke of refreshment, my Emilie [his daughter]. Take my last notes, sit down to my piano here, sing them with the hymn of your sainted mother; Let me hear once more those notes, which have so long my solacement and my delight." She sang several stanzas of his *Requiem*, concluding with: "... Thy home it will be with thy Savior and God,/ Their loud hallelujah to sing."

Mudgett, Herman, also known as Dr. H.H. Holmes (1861-1896). American serial killer. Mudgett confessed to the murder of numerous individuals, perhaps as many as 200, mainly for their life insurance money. To the executioner: "Take your time; don't bungle it." Before he was hanged: "As God is my witness, I was responsible for the death of only two women. I didn't kill Minnie Williams! Minnie killed her..." Ironically, his neck did not snap when the trap opened, and he spent an agonizing number of minutes strangling to death.

Muhammad, born Abu al-Qasim Muhammad ibn Abd Allah ibn Abd al-Muttalib ibn Hashim (c. 570-632). Arabian prophet and founder of the Islamic religion. Sensing his approaching death, Muhammad spoke to his followers: "I have heard that a rumor of the death of your prophet filled you with alarm; but has any prophet before me lived forever that ye think I would never leave you? Everything happens according to the will of God, and has its appointed time, which is not to be hastened nor avoided. I return to him who sent me and my last command to you is that you remain united, that ye love, honor and uphold each other, that ye exhort each other to faith and constancy in belief and to the performance of pious deeds... Death awaits us all. Let no one seek to turn it aside from me. My life has been for your good. So will be my death." As his terminal suffering increased: "O God, help me overcome the agonies of death." Resting his head on his wife's lap: "Rather, God on High and paradise." The prophet then turned his eyes skyward and said: "O God, pardon my sins. Yes, I come... among my fellow-citizens on high."

Alternatives: * "God be with me in the death struggle."

* "O God, pardon my sins. Yes, I come... among my fellow-labourers on high."
* "Lord, pardon me and place me among those whom thou hast raised to grace and favor."
* "Lord, grant me pardon... I have chosen the most exalted company in paradise."
* "... O Allah, with the supreme communion; O Allah, with the supreme communion; O Allah, with the supreme communion."
* "... O Allah, the highest companions. O Allah, the highest companions. O Allah, the highest companions."
* "O Allah, be it so! Henceforth among the glorious hosts of paradise."
* "O Allah, be it so! Among the glorious associates in paradise!"

Mukasa, Saint Joseph (1860-1885). Ugandan Roman Catholic martyr. When Mukasa criticized King Mwanga's execution of Christian missionaries in his country, the monarch ordered his beheading: "Tell Mwanga I have forgiven him for putting me to death without a reason. But let him repent, otherwise I shall accuse him in God's court."

Mukhtar, Omar, also Omar al Mukhtar (1862-1931). Leader of the Libyan resistance movement against Italian colonization of his country. Captured by Italian forces, Mukhtar was sentenced to die by hanging. He told his captors: "I shall over live my executioner." The condemned man then said: "Believing soul, return to your maker satisfied."

Alternative: * "We surely belong to Allah and to Him we shall return."

Muller, Franz (1840-1864). German-born criminal. Muller robbed and killed a London banker while traveling on a British train, the first murder committed on this mode of transportation in England. Before his hanging, the condemned man who steadfastly had declared his innocence spoke to the minister at his side: "I did it."

Müller, George (1805-1898). Prussian-born English evangelist, orphanage director and educator. When his son-in-law suggested a change in activity for the following day, Müller replied: "We will say nothing about tomorrow." He was found dead beside his bed the following day.

Müller, Max (1823-1900). German-born British writer who specialized in Indian studies. On his deathbed, Müller remarked: "I am so tired."

Mulligan, James (1830-1864). Union officer during the U.S. Civil War. Mortally wounded in the Battle of Kernstown, near Winchester, Virginia, Mulligan told his troops: "Lay me down and save the flag!"

Mumford, William (c. 1820-1862). American Confederate sympathizer. When Union forces overran New Orleans, Louisiana, the American flag was raised to the chagrin of Confederate supporters. Mumford, a local resident, lowered the flag and paraded it through the streets. He was arrested, accused of treason and sentenced to die by hanging: "I consider that the manner of my death will be no disgrace to my wife and child; my country will honor them."

Muni, Paul, born Meshilem Meier Weisenfreund (1895-1967). Ukrainian-born American movie actor. Dying of a heart ailment, Muni looked at his father's picture and said: "Papa, I'm hungry."

Muniz, Pedro (1956-1998). American criminal, executed by lethal injection for the rape-murder of a college student. Muniz's last remarks were directed to the victim's brother: "I know you can't hear me now but I know that it won't matter what I have to say. I want you to know that I did not kill your sister. If you want to know the truth, and you deserve to know the truth, hire your own investigators. That is all I have to say."

Muñoz Seca, Pedro (1879-1936). Spanish playwright. After the outbreak of the Spanish Civil War in 1936, Muñoz Seca was arrested and sentenced to die for his criticism of the government in power. A humorist to the end, he quipped: "I am starting to believe you are not intending to count me amongst your friends." As he stood before a firing squad, Muñoz Seca exclaimed: "You can take my hacienda, my land, my wealth, even, as you are going to do, my life. But there is one thing that you cannot take from me- my fear!"

Munro, Hector, whose pen name was "Saki" (1870-1916). Burmese-born British humorist and short-story writer. Munro enlisted in the army at the outbreak of WWI and fought during the French campaign. When a comrade lit a cigarette on the battlefield, he exclaimed: "Put that bloody cigarette out!" A German sniper then shot Munro dead.

Alternative: * "Put that d***** cigarette out!"

Munson, Thurman (1947-1979). American professional baseball player. Munson owned a jet aircraft that he frequently used for travel between New York City and his home in Ohio. While practicing takeoffs and landings, his plane crashed. Trapped in the cockpit, Munson asked his two traveling companions: "Are you guys okay?" They replied: "Yeah, how about you?" He answered: "I don't know. I can't move, I can't move." Munson perished in the ensuing fire.

Münsterberg, Hugo (1863-1916). German-born American psychologist and educator. Shortly before delivering a lecture to his Radcliffe students, Münsterberg made a prediction about WWI to his wife: "By spring we shall have peace." He later collapsed and died as he began his lecture.

Murat, Joachim (1767-1815). King of Naples and Marshal of France under Napoleon I, his brother-in-law. When Bonaparte fell, Murat was captured and condemned to die. He refused a blindfold, saying: "I have braved death too often to fear it." Murat then told the firing squad: "Soldiers! Do your duty! Straight to the heart but spare the face. Fire!" As he fell: "*Vive la France*!"

Alternatives: * "Spare my face; aim at my heart. Fire!"

* "Soldiers, do your duty. Aim for the heart but, spare the face; I have too often faced death to fear it!"

* "Soldiers, save my face; aim at my heart. Farewell!"

Murger, Louis-Henri (1822-1861). French writer, known for his portrayal of Bohemian life: On his deathbed, the chronically-ill Murger reflected: "No more music! No more commotion! No more Bohemia!"

Murillo, Esteban (1617-1682). Spanish Baroque painter. Murillo died from complications of a fall from a scaffold while painting an altarpiece. Earlier, he had chosen his epitaph: "*Vive moriturus* [Live as though about to die]."

Murphy, Francis "Frank" (1890-1949). American politician and associate justice of the U.S. Supreme Court. Dying of a heart attack, Murphy asked: "Have I kept the faith?"

Murphy, Mario (1972-1997). Mexican-born criminal, convicted for the contract killing of a Virginia man for insurance money. Before dying by lethal injection, Murphy said: "Today is a good day to die. I forgive all of you. I hope God does too."

Murray, William, Lord Mansfield (1705-1793). Scottish-born barrister and politician. Several days before he died, Murray complained of insomnia: "Let me sleep. Let me sleep."

Murrieta, Joaquin (c. 1829-1853). Mexican criminal. Murrieta and Manuel "Three Fingered Jack Garcia (above) committed numerous robberies and murders in California during the Gold Rush. Cornered and shot dead by a band of rangers: "It is enough. Shoot no more. The job is finished. I am dead."

Murrow, Edward "Ed" (1908-1965). American radio and television broadcaster, best-known for his coverage of WWII action. Dying of lung cancer, to his wife: "Well Jan, we were lucky at that."

Musset, Alfred de (1810-1857). French poet and writer. Dying of a heart ailment, de Musset exclaimed: "What a splendid thing peace is! People are certainly wrong to be afraid of death., which is no more than its highest expression." When he placed his hand over his heart, he was asked if there were pain. de Musset then closed his eyes and said: "Sleep! At last I am going to sleep!"

Mussolini, Benito "Il Duce" (1883-1945). Italian dictator who allied with Germany during WWII. While attempting an escape to Spain, the deposed Mussolini and his mistress Claretta Petacci (below) were captured near Lake Como and executed by Italian communist partisans. Before the first shot rang out, Il Duce sputtered: "But, but, Mister Colonel..." Then, he cried: "Shoot me in the chest!" The bodies were moved to Milan and hung from hooks on the roof of a gas station for public viewing.

Mussorgsky, Modest (1839-1881): Russian composer, best-known for his opera *Boris Godunov*, the suite *Pictures at an Exhibition* and the orchestral piece *Night on Bald Mountain*. Mortally ill from chronic alcohol abuse, Mussorgsky cried out in his last minutes to the effect: "It's the end! Woe is me!"

Alternatives: * "All is over! Woe is me!"
* "Everything is finished. Ah, how miserable I am!"

Mutton, Andrew (birth and death dates unclear). American mobster. Mutton's car was notoriously difficult to start. When the vehicle effortlessly purred to life one morning, he replied to an associate: "Well, this is certainly a pleasant surprise." Moments later a bomb wired to the ignition system exploded, dispatching Mutton and injuring his friend who later gave an account of the gangster's last words.

Nabokov, Vladimir (1899-1977). Russian-born American writer and noted lepidopterist, best-known for his novel *Lolita*. Dying of a bronchial ailment, Nabokov said to his son: "A certain butterfly is already on the wing."

Nadir Shah (1688-1747). Persian warrior-king. Because of his despotic rule and the fear he instilled in his soldiers, Nadir was assassinated by a group of disgruntled countrymen. Before he died, the ruler shouted at one of the assailants: "Thou dog!"

Napoleon I, born Napoleone di Buonaparte (1769-1821). Corsican-born French emperor. Dying of suspected stomach cancer while exiled on the South Atlantic island of St. Helena, Napoleon deliriously spoke: "France... Army... Head of the army... Josephine."

Alternatives: * "France, army, Josephine"
* "My God! The French nation! Head of the army."

Napoleon II, born Napoleon François Bonaparte (1811-1832). King of Rome and son of Napoleon I. Dying of tuberculosis, Napoleon told his valet: "I am going under... I am going under... Call my mother... Take the table away... I don't need anything anymore." As the attendant left the room, Napoleon clutched his arm and cried: "Packs! Blisters [which were used to treat various ailments]!"

Alternative: * "Call my mother! Call my mother! Take the table away... I don't need anything anymore. Poultices"

Napoleon III, born Louis-Napoleon Bonaparte (1808-1873). French emperor and nephew of Napoleon I. At the conclusion of the Franco-Prussian War in 1870, Napoleon was compelled to surrender when his troops were defeated by Prussian forces at Sedan in northeastern France. Reliving the battle during his last moments three years later, the exiled emperor asked his physician: "Were you at Sedan?"

Napoleon IV, born Napoleon Eugène Bonaparte (1856-1879). French prince and military officer who was the son of Napoleon III. Napoleon emigrated to England, became a member its armed forces and participated in the Anglo-Zulu War in South Africa. During a lull in the fighting, the prince and his men took a brief respite. He then gave the order: "Prepare to mount." When he commanded: "Mount," the detachment was ambushed by Zulus and Napoleon was speared to death.

Naruszewicz, Adam Stanislas (1733-1796). Polish nobleman, educator, historian and writer. Referring to a history of Poland he was writing, Naruszewicz asked: "Must I leave it unfinished?"

Narváez, Ramón (1800-1868). Spanish general and politician. On his deathbed, a priest asked Narváez if he had forgiven his enemies. The general pointedly replied: "I do not have to forgive my enemies. I have had them all shot."

Alternative: * "I do not have to forgive my enemies, because I killed them all."

Nasser, Gamal (1918-1970). Egyptian president who helped establish regional Arab solidarity and modernization during his 14 years in power. Dying of a heart attack, Nasser told his wife: "I don't think I could eat a thing."

Nast, Thomas (1840-1902). German-born American political cartoonist and statesman. Dying of yellow fever contracted while serving as Consul-General to Ecuador, Nast allowed: "I feel much better."

Nation, Carry Amelia (1846-1911). American temperance leader in the pre-prohibition era. The 64 year-old Nation collapsed while giving a speech and died shortly thereafter. Before passing, she summed up her efforts: "I have done what I could."

Navratil, Michel (1880-1912). Czech tailor. Navratil took his two sons from his estranged wife and attempted to immigrate to the U.S. aboard the ocean liner *Titanic*. As the vessel sank, he allegedly told his four year-old son: "My child, when your mother comes for you, as she surely will, tell her that I loved her dearly and still do. Tell her I expected her to follow us, so that we might all live happily together in the peace and freedom of the New World." Both children survived and were reunited with their mother.

Neander, Johann, born David Mendel (1789-1850). German theologian and church historian. Toward the end, Neander allowed: "I am weary; let us go home! Good night!"

Alternative: * "I am weary; I will now go to sleep. Good night!"

Nehru, Jawaharlal (1889-1964). Indian prime minister and father of Indira Gandhi (above). Dying of a heart attack, Nehru told a servant: "I think the pain will pass, so you need not awaken the doctor."

Alternative: * "I have disposed of all my files."

Nehru, Motilal (1861-1931). Indian politician who became a leader of his country's independence movement. Awaking from a coma, Nehru spoke to his colleague Mohandas Gandhi (above): "Bapu [Gandhi's nickname], if you and I happened to die at the same time, you, being a saintly man, would presumably go to heaven right off. But, with due deference, I think this is what would happen: you would come to our river of death; you would stand on the bank and then, most probably, you would walk across it, perhaps alone or maybe holding onto the tail of a cow. I would arrive much later. I'd get into a fast new motor boat, shoot past you and get there ahead of you. Of course, being very worldly, I might not be allowed into heaven- if there is one."

Nelson, Earle (1897-1928). American serial killer. Nelson left a string of bodies in the U.S. and Canada. He eventually was captured in Manitoba and sentenced to hang. Before his execution: "I am innocent. I stand innocent before God and man. I forgive those who have wronged me and ask forgiveness of those I have injured. God have mercy!"

Nelson, George "Baby-Face" born Lester Gillis, (1908-1934). American bank robber and murderer. When FBI agents caught up with Nelson in a small town outside Chicago, he shouted: "Come on, you yellow-belly son of a b****! Come get it!" Although the gangster was shot multiple times, he was able to reach a nearby car. He told an accomplice: "You'll have to drive. I'm hit pretty bad." Later as his wounds were cleaned and a blanket was placed over him: "That's better." To his wife as he died: "It's getting dark, Helen. I can't see you anymore."

Nelson, Horatio (1758-1805). British Vice Admiral. On October 21, 1805, an outnumbered British fleet under the command of Admiral Nelson defeated the combined Franco-Spanish armada off Cape Trafalgar near the Strait of Gibraltar. Before engaging the enemy, Nelson told his signalman:

"Mr. Pasco, I wish to say to the fleet 'England confides that every man will do his duty.' You must be quick, for I have one more signal to make, which is for close action." For the ease of signal transmission, "confides" was changed to "expects." As the battle raged, Nelson told Thomas Hardy, the captain of his ship: "This is too warm work, Hardy, to last long." Shortly thereafter, Nelson suffered a gunshot wound through the chest that injured his spine: "They have done for me at last, Hardy. Yes, my back bone is shot through." As he was taken below decks, Nelson told the ship's surgeon: "Ah, Mr. Beatty, you can do nothing for me. I have but a short time to live. My back is shot through." To Hardy who had returned below deck: "I am a dead man, Hardy... I am going fast. It will all be over with me soon. Come nearer to me. Let my dear Lady Hamilton [his mistress] have my hair and all other things belonging to me." To the surgeon: "You know I am gone. I know it." As he laid his hand on his left side: "I feel something rising in my breast, which tells me so." When asked about pain: "So much that death would be a relief. Nevertheless, everybody wishes to live a little longer." When Hardy again returned, Nelson requested: "Don't throw me overboard... take care of my dear Lady Hamilton, Hardy; take care of poor Lady Hamilton. Kiss me, Hardy." As his cheek (some say forehead) was kissed, Nelson said: "Now I am satisfied; Thank God, I have done my duty... God bless you, Hardy" Later, he complained: "I wish I had not left the deck, for I shall soon be gone." To the chaplain: "Doctor, I have not been a great sinner. Remember that I leave Lady Hamilton and my daughter Horatia as a legacy to my country." Some say at this point he spoke: "Fan, fan ... rub, rub ... drink, drink..." as his thirst increased. Then: "Thank God, I have done my duty. I praise God for it" Nelson's body was preserved in a barrel of brandy and returned to England for burial. The impoverished Lady Hamilton died of dysentery 14 years later.

Alternatives: * "England expects every man to do his duty."

* "Send out the challenge: 'England expects every man this day to do his duty.'"
* "Drink, drink, fan, fan, rub, rub."
* Some say the ship's chaplain recorded Nelson's last utterance as: "Thank God, I have done my duty. God and my country."

Nelson, William (1824-1862). Union general who served during the U.S. Civil War. Nelson was shot by an angry fellow officer whom he had offended: "Send for a clergyman, I wish to be baptized. I have been basely murdered." To a friend who came to his aid: "Tom, I am murdered." Although indicted, Nelson's assailant was never jailed for his offence.

Nengapeta, Sister Anuarite (1939-1964). Belgian Congolese nun. During the 1960-4 Congo Civil War, rebels arrived at Nengapeta's convent and attempted to rape her. She was beaten, stabbed and shot by soldiers but refused to accede to their demands: "I don't want to commit this sin! If you want to, kill me. I forgive you because you don't know what you are doing. It is thus that I would have it end."

Neri, Saint Philip (1515-1595). Italian priest who ministered to the sick and poor. After a day of strenuous activities, Neri remarked as he prepared for bed: "Last of all, we must die."

Nero (37-68). Roman emperor who was the son of Agrippina (above). Facing a revolution and assassination, Nero contemplated suicide. Possibly referring to his earlier attempts at poetry and singing, he reflected: "Oh, what an artist to perish!" Unable to perform the act of self-destruction with a dagger, the emperor bemoaned his ineptitude: "Fie, Nero, fie! Courage man! Come, rouse thee!" As horsemen approached, Nero repeated a line from Homer's *Iliad*: "Sound of swift-footed steeds strikes on my ears." Finally, the emperor was able to end his life with a servant's help. When a centurion sent to arrest him tried to control the bleeding, Nero expired, saying: "It is now too late! Is this your fidelity?"

Alternatives: * "What an artist dies in me! It is now too late."
* "What an artist the world is losing in me!"
* "Jupiter, what an artist perishes in me!"
* "What an artist is dying! How ugly and vulgar my life has become!"
* "The galloping of speedy steeds assails my frightened ears."
* "In my ears resounds the gallop of fury-footed steeds."
* "Hark, the sound I hear! It is the hooves of galloping steeds!"
* "Too late! This is fidelity?"

Nevin, Ethelbert (1862-1901). American pianist and composer. Nevin spoke his last words to his wife: "Anne, I am dying, and I do not wish to leave you."

Newell, Arthur (1854-1912). American banker and RMS *Titanic* victim. As the stricken vessel began sinking, Newell helped his family into a lifeboat, saying: "It does seem more dangerous for you to get into that boat than to remain here with me here but we must obey orders." He was last seen helping others into lifeboats.

Newell, Harriet (1793-1812). American missionary to India and Burma. Dying of tuberculosis, Newell asked: "Oh, the pain, the groans, the dying strife. How long, oh Lord, how long?"

Newman, Ernest (1868-1959). English music critic and biographer. When asked by his wife if he needed anything: "Yes, I want my cup of tea."

Newman, John (1801-1890). English cardinal, theologian and educator. Dying of pneumonia: "I am not capable of doing anything more- I am not wanted- now mind what I say, it is not kind to me to wish to keep me longer from God. I feel bad. I hope to go to sleep."

Newman, Samuel (1602-1663). English-born American clergyman. Seemingly in good health, Newman had a premonition of death. Asking a deacon to pray with him, the clergyman then said: "Angels, do your office" and expired.

Newport, Francis (1620-1708). Debauched English nobleman who was head of the English Infidel Club. When asked if he wished to have a prayer offered for him, the dying Newport replied: "Tigers and monsters! Are ye also become devils, to torment me and give me a prospect of heaven, to make my hell more intolerable?" He then cried out: "Oh, the insufferable pangs of hell and damnation" and died.

Newton, Huey (1942-1989). African American political activist who co-founded the Black Panther Party. To an assassin who shot him on an

Oakland, California street corner: "You can kill my body, but you can't kill my soul. My soul will live forever!"

Newton, Isaac (1642-1727). British mathematician, physicist and philosopher. Newton's studies laid the groundwork for the understanding of gravity and classical mechanics. Toward the end, Newton mused: "I don't know what I may seem to the world. But as to myself I seem to have been only like a boy playing on the seashore and diverting myself in now and then finding a smoother pebble or a prettier shell than ordinary, whilst the great ocean of truth lay all undiscovered before me."

Newton, John (1725-1807). English slave trader who later became an abolitionist and priest. Newton wrote the lyrics for the ever-popular hymn "Amazing Grace." Toward the end, he told a friend: "I am like a person going on a journey in a stage coach, who expects its arrival every hour, and is frequently looking out of the window for it... I am packed and sealed, and ready for the post." Asked if his mind were comfortable: "I am satisfied with the Lord's will."

Alternatives: * "I am still in the land of the dying; I shall be in the land of the living soon."

* "My memory is almost gone, but two things I remember: that I am a great sinner and that Christ is a great Savior."

Newton, Richard (1676-1753). English educator and writer. On his deathbed, Newton proclaimed: "Christ, Jesus, the Saviour of sinners and the life of the dead. I am going, going, going to Glory! Farewell sin! Farewell death! Praise the Lord!"

Ney, Michel (1769-1815). French general who was active during the Napoleonic Wars. After Napoleon I's defeat at Waterloo, Ney was arrested and charged with treason. When the condemnation article was read the night before his execution, Ney dismissively replied: "To the point- what is the use of all that? Say simply- Michel Ney, soon a little dust; that is all." Before the firing squad, he refused a blindfold, saying: "Do you not know, sir, that a soldier does not fear death?... Frenchmen, I protest against my condemnation. My honor..." Some say Ney was shot dead without further ado. Others allege Ney asked if he could give the order for the squad to shoot: "Soldiers, when I give the command to fire, fire straight at my heart. Wait for the order. It will be my last to you. I protest against my condemnation. I have fought a hundred battles for France, and not one against her... Soldiers! Fire!"

Alternatives: * "My comrades, fire on me!"
* "Comrades, straight to the heart, fire!"

Nezahualcoyotl (1402-1472). Ruler of the city-state Texcoco in pre-Columbian Mexico. "The fleeting pomp of the world is like the green willow... but at the end a sharp axe destroys it, a north wind fells it..."

Nicholas I (1796-1855). Emperor of Russia. Dying of pneumonia as his country was being defeated by England and France in the Crimean War, Nicholas asked his son and heir to inform the army: "Tell them that in the other world I shall continue to pray for them. I have always tried to work for their good. If I failed in that, this was not because of a lack of goodwill, but because of a lack of knowledge and ability. I beg them to pardon me." To his son: "I wanted to take everything difficult, everything heavy upon myself and to leave you a peaceful, orderly and happy realm. Providence determined otherwise. Now I shall ascend to pray for Russia and for you. After Russia, I loved you above everything else in the world. Serve Russia."

Nicholas II (1868-1918). Last emperor of Russia. Forced to abdicate in 1917, Nicholas was imprisoned and later executed with his family. When told by his captors that he would be shot, the deposed emperor stammered: "What..."

Alternative: * Some say he uttered words similar to those Christ spoke on the cross: "Father, forgive them, for they know not what they do."

Nichols, John (1841-1863). Confederate guerilla fighter during the U.S. Civil War. After a series of robberies in northwest Missouri, Nichols was apprehended by Union forces and sentenced to die. On the scaffold, he placed the noose around his neck, saying: "Gentlemen, I am going to show you how a Confederate soldier dies." Then, Nichols responded to a priest who encouraged him to forgive those that had wronged him: "Yes, I have shot at soldiers and they have shot at me. I have threatened people, and they have threatened me." As the hood was placed over his head: "Goodbye, boys, everybody."

Nicholson, John (1821-1857). Irish-born British military leader. During the 1857 Indian Rebellion, Nicholson was mortally wounded during the Siege of Delhi. Hearing that one of his officers spoke of retreat, he exclaimed: "Thank God, I have strength yet to shoot him, if necessary." Later: "... Tell my mother that I do not think we shall be unhappy in the next world. God has visited her with a great affliction, but tell her she must not give way to grief." Nicholson's last words were directed to a colleague who had apologized for his absence: "No; I knew that your duty to the service required your being at head-quarters, and I was glad to think that you were there to give your counsel."

Nicoll, William (1851-1923). Scottish theologian and writer. At the end, Nicoll proclaimed: "I believe everything I have written about immortality."

Niebuhr, Barthold (1776-1831). German historian, writer and statesman. Niebuhr asked about the proffered medicine that normally was reserved for extreme cases: "What essential substance is this? Am I so far gone?"

Nietzsche, Friedrich (1844-1900). German philosopher, poet and writer, well-known for his novel *Also Sprach Zarathustra*. Insane during his last decade from an undefined illness, Nietzsche called the name of his sister who had cared for him in the last stages of his decline: "Elisabeth."

Nijinsky, Vaslav (1890-1950). Russian ballet dancer and choreographer. Nijinsky suffered from schizophrenia during his last years but succumbed to acute kidney failure. As he died, he called out: "Mamasha! [Mother]."

Nilsson, Harry (1941-1994). American pop-rock singer and songwriter. Nilsson died of heart failure complicating a massive heart attack suffered one year earlier. To his wife: "I love you so much."

Nimitz, Chester (1885-1966). Commander of the U.S. Pacific naval fleet during WWII. Dying of complications from a stroke, to a visitor who was sipping sherry: "Jack, you can have something stronger if you like."

Nixon, Richard (1913-1994). Thirty-seventh U.S. president. After suffering a massive stroke, the 81 year-old Nixon desperately called to his housekeeper for help.

Nixon, Thelma "Pat" (1912-1993). Wife of U.S. President Richard Nixon. Dying of lung cancer, Pat related: "I've had a wonderful life!"

Nobel, Alfred (1833-1896). Swedish chemist who invented dynamite and endowed the annual prizes that bear his name. Dying of a stroke, the only word he could utter was "Telegram."

Noble, Margaret "Nivedita" (1867-1911). Irish-born activist who served the poor and sick of Calcutta, India. Dying of dysentery, Noble expressed her optimism: "The ship is sinking, but I shall see the sun rise."

Nodier, Charles (1780-1844). French writer, noted for his gothic novels. At the end, Nodier spoke to his family: "It is very hard, my children. I no longer see you. Remember me. Love me always."

Nolan, Lewis, also Louis (1818-1854). Canadian-born British officer, killed at the Charge of the Light Brigade during the Crimean War. Nolan delivered the ill-fated message to a superior officer who was hesitant to obey the order to charge Russian troops: "There, my Lord, is your enemy; there are your guns." The brigade suffered heavy casualties during the engagement and was forced to retreat.

Nordica, Lillian, born Lillian Norton (1857-1914). American operatic soprano. Dying of pneumonia, Nordica spoke to her long-dead parent: "I am coming, Mother."

North, Frederick (1732-1792). English prime minister during the American War of Independence. Before dying, North was asked about discomfort: "I feel no pain, nor have I suffered any."

Norton, Katherine (died 1746). Scottish woman, betrothed to a condemned Jacobite rebel. Determined to attend his execution, Norton spoke at its conclusion: "My dear, I follow thee, I follow thee! Sweet Jesus, receive both our souls together!" She fell into the arms of a companion and died.

Nostradamus, born Michel de Notre Dame (1503-1566). French soothsayer and apothecary, best-known for his book *The Prophesies*. Dying of "dropsy," Nostradamus prophesized to his assistant: "Tomorrow, at sunrise, I shall no longer be here." The seer was found dead the next morning.

Nothnagel, Hermann (1841-1905). German physician. Nothnagel described his own cardiac symptoms the day before he died: "Paroxysms [bouts] of angina pectoris, with extremely violent pains. Pulse and attacks... completely different, sometimes slow, about 56-60, entirely regular, very intense, then again accelerated, 80-90, rather even and regular, finally completely arrhythmic, entirely unequal, now palpitating, now slow, with differing intensity. The first sensations of these attacks date several- three or four- years back, in the beginning rather weak, becoming slowly more and more definite. Properly speaking attacks with sharp pains have appeared only within the last five or six days. Written on July 6, 1905, late in the evening, after I had three or four violent attacks."

Nott, Eliphalet (1773-1866). American clergyman, educator and inventor. "One word, one word, Jesus Christ!" Then: "My covenant God."

Novalis, pseudonym of Georg Friedrich Freiherr von Hardenberg (1772-1801). German poet, writer and philosopher. Dying of tuberculosis, Novalis asked his brother to: "Play a little to me on the harpsichord."

Noyes, John (died1557). Protestant martyr, condemned for his religious beliefs. Noyes spoke to a fellow sufferer tied to the stake: "We shall not lose our lives in this fire but change them for a better. And for coals have pearls." As the flames grew, Noyes prayed: "Lord, have mercy upon me! Christ, have mercy upon me! Son of David, have mercy upon me!"

Oates, Lawrence (1880-1912). British explorer. Oates was a member of Robert Scott's ill-fated 1912 expedition to the South Pole (below). Suffering from severe frostbite after reaching the pole, Oates felt that he would be a hindrance to his comrades on their return trip. Before leaving their tent during a raging blizzard, he said: "I am just going outside and may be some time." Despite his self-sacrifice, none of the explorers made it back to base camp alive.

Oates, Titus (1649-1705). English conspirator. Oates hatched the "Popish Plot," which alleged that Catholic authorities had plotted to kill King Charles II. This fabricated conspiracy resulted in the death of a number of innocent individuals. He eventually was convicted of perjury and imprisoned for a period. At the end of his life, Oates reflected: "It is all the same in the end."

O'Banion, Dion (1892-1924). Chicago florist, bootlegger and alleged murderer. Because of turf disputes in the bootlegging racket, a contract was put on O'Banion. When confronted by assailants in his flower shop, he said: "Hello boys. Are you from Mike Merlo's [a rival gangster]?" O'Banion was killed by multiple gunshots.

Oberon, Merle, born Estelle Merle Thompson (1911-1979). Anglo-Indian actress. Dying of a stroke, Oberon said to her husband: "Darling, I love you so much. Thank you for the happiest years of my life."

Obregón, Álvaro (1880-1928). Mexican politician. Obregón was re-elected president of Mexico in 1928 but was assassinated before he could assume office. While sitting in a restaurant, the politician asked: "*Más totopos* [more tortilla chips]," moments before he was shot dead by a Catholic fanatic.

O'Brien, William (1852-1928). Irish nationalist, social reformer and member of Parliament. When his wife asked if he should sleep: "Well, the night is so long and dreary, I think I will wait up a little longer."

Ocampo, Melchor (1814-1861). Mexican liberal politician, known for his anticlerical views. Because of friction with the conservative government, the 47 year-old Ocampo was seized by rebels and sentenced to die. When the executioner told him to kneel before the firing squad, he replied: "Why? I'm right at the height of the rifles."

O'Carolan, Turlough (1670-1738). Irish composer, singer and harpist. At the end, O'Carolan wished for a last drink of whiskey (some record wine), saying: "It would be hard indeed if we two dear friends should part after so many years, without one sweet kiss."

Ochs, Philip "Phil" (1940-1976). American folk singer, songwriter and social activist. Troubled by alcohol abuse and depression, Ochs passed a message at his last concert: "One day you'll read about it. Phil Ochs- A suicide at 35." He later hanged himself in his 35th year.

O'Connell, Daniel (1775-1847). Irish nationalist and political leader. While on a pilgrimage to Rome, O'Connell became ill in Genoa. He told his attendant: "Send my heart to Rome and my body to Ireland." To a priest: "I am dying, my dear friend." Then: "Jesus! Jesus!" O'Connell's request for the disposition of his remains was fulfilled.

Alternative: * "I hope my soul will pass through Ireland."

O'Connell, William (1859-1944). American clergyman who became archbishop of Boston. Suffering from pneumonia, O'Connell spoke to a priest reading to him: "You need not read anymore. Run along. Jerry will be here soon. I would like to sit here and think." He died shortly thereafter.

Oecolampadius, Johannes (1482-1531). German Protestant reformer. On his deathbed: "I shall presently be with my Lord Christ!" When asked if the light bothered him, Oecolampadius put his hand on his breast and said: "Here is [an] abundance of light." After reciting Psalm 51, he prayed "Oh Christ, save me!" and died.

Oei Tjie Sien (1835-1900). Wealthy Chinese emigrant who founded a trading company in Indonesia. At his wife's deathbed, Oei promised that he would join her when their oldest child had been raised. When this task was accomplished, he insisted it was time to die. On his deathbed, a ginseng root was placed in his mouth as a stimulant. Oei removed it and said: "This is no use. Your mother has come for me and I must go."

Offenbach, Jacques (1819-1880): German-born French cellist and composer of operettas and operas. Offenbach prophesied immediately before his death from a cardiac arrest: "I think tonight will be the end." Later, an old friend, the comic actor Léonce, visited the composer's apartment. When Offenbach's manservant answered the door, Léonce asked: "How is he?" "Monsieur Offenbach is dead; he died quite peacefully, without knowing anything about it." Léonce rejoined: "Ah!- he will be very surprised when he finds out."

O'Folliard, Tom (c. 1858-1880). American outlaw who was a member of Billy the Kid's gang. O'Folliard was cornered at Fort Sumner, New Mexico and mortally wounded by Pat Garrett's posse. O'Folliard responded to Garrett who advised him to stop cursing so close to death: "Aw, go to hell, you long-legged son-of –a- b****."

Ohad, Arnon (died 1992). El Al Airlines first officer. On October 4, 1992 an Israeli Boeing 747 cargo aircraft, El Al Flight 1862, took off from Amsterdam's Schiphol Airport but crashed into a nearby apartment complex when two right-sided engines fell from the wing. As the plane plummeted, Ohad radioed: "Going down, eh... 1862, going down, going down, copied, going down." The flight crew of four and 39 souls on the ground perished in the disaster.

O'Hara, Miles (1851-1876). American soldier. O'Hara was attached to a cavalry unit under the command of Marcus Reno in the Battle of Little Big Horn. While on the skirmish line, O'Hara was mortally wounded. When his unit began a retreat, he implored: "For God's sake, don't leave me."

Ohlin, Per Yngve (see Dead).

O'Keeffe, Georgia (1887-1986). American artist, best-known for her floral and southwestern U.S. landscape paintings. Asked how she felt, O'Keeffe realized the end was near: "It's time for me to go."

O'Kelley, Edward (1858-1904). American murderer. In 1892, O'Kelley killed Robert Ford who had murdered the outlaw Jesse James (above) a decade earlier. He was sentenced to life in prison but was released after serving eight years. In early 1904, O'Kelley quarreled with a policeman who had arrested him earlier: "You come with me. I'll arrest you, you son-of-a-b****." As they struggled, a friend tried to intervene, prompting O'Kelley to shout: "We will murder this fellow!" The policeman freed his hands and was able to shoot his assailant dead.

Old Joseph, also Tuekakas (1785-1871). Native American chief of the Pacific Northwest Nez Perce tribe. Old Joseph spoke to his son and successor, Young Joseph: "… A few more years and the white men will be all around you. They have their eyes on this land. My son, never forget my dying words. This country holds your father's body. Never sell the bones of your father and mother." Years later, Joseph's grave was desecrated and his skull was removed as a souvenir by local landowners.

Oldenbarnevelt, Johan van (1547-1619). Dutch statesman who fought for the independence of his country from Spain. Because his views on the status of Holland clashed with his opponents, Oldenbarnevelt was accused of treason and sentenced to beheading. To his executioner: "Make it short, make it short."

Olgiati, Girolamo (1453-1477). Milanese slayer of Galeazzo Sforza, the Duke of Milan (below). Because of his tyrannical and cruel nature, Sforza was marked for assassination. After the deed was accomplished, Olgiatti and his associates were quickly captured and executed. Before dying, Olgiatti declared: "My death is untimely, my fame eternal, the memory of the deed will last for aye [ever]."

Alternative: * "Death is bitter, but glory is eternal. The memory of my deed will endure."

Olinger, Robert (c. 1841-1881). American lawman who served under Sheriff Pat Garrett (above). While incarcerated in Olinger's care, Billy the Kid managed to escape and kill a fellow deputy. As Olinger approached the outlaw, he was felled by a shotgun blast. When told that his associate also had been murdered: "Yes, and he's killed me too."

Oliphant, Laurence (1829-1888). South African-born British writer, traveler and mystic. As he died, Oliphant requested: "More light."

Oliphant, Margaret (1828-1897). Scottish writer. At her death, Oliphant proclaimed: "I seem to see nothing but God and Our Lord."

Oliver, François (1497-1560). Chancellor of France. On the orders of Cardinal Lorrain, Oliver had condemned many innocent people to die because of their faith. Filled with contrition on his deathbed, he lamented: "Ah! cardinal, you are getting us all damned!"

Olivier, Laurence (1907-1989). Knighted British actor who starred on stage and screen. When a nurse attempted to moisten the dying Olivier's lips, she inadvertently spilled water (some say juice) on his face. He sarcastically alluded to Shakespeare's *Hamlet* where the main character's sleeping father was killed by poison dripped into the ear: "This isn't *Hamlet*, you know. It's not meant to go in my bloody ear."

Alternative: * "My dear, we are not doing f****** *Hamlet*!"

Omar Khayyám (c. 1048-1131). Persian astronomer, mathematician and poet, best-known for the English translation of his poems in the *Rubáiyát of Omar Khayyám*. During evening prayers, Omar Khayyám bowed his head to the ground and said: "O God, verily I have known Thee to the extent of my power. Forgive me, therefore. Verily, my knowledge of Thee is my recommendation to Thee." Then he died.

Onassis, Jacqueline Kennedy (1929-1994). American editor and widow of U.S. President John F. Kennedy. Dying of lymphoma, Kennedy spoke of her deceased children: "My little angels- I'll be with you soon." She then said to her two surviving children: "Don't cry for me. I'm going to be with your father now."

Oneby, John (c. 1674-1727). English criminal. Oneby killed a man in a tavern brawl and was condemned to die. To escape the gallows, the murderer slashed his wrist while waiting execution. The suicide note left for his jailers: "… Give Mr. Akerman, the turnkey below stairs, half a guinea, and Jack who waits in my room five shillings. The poor devils have had a great deal of trouble with me since I have been here."

O'Neill, Eugene, Sr. (1888-1953). American playwright who won the 1936 Nobel Prize in Literature. Of note, O'Neill was born in a New York City hotel room. Throughout his adult life, the writer battled depression and alcohol abuse. Before expiring in a Boston hotel from a chronic neurological ailment and pneumonia, O'Neill requested: "When I'm dying, don't let a priest or a Protestant minister or a Salvation Army captain near me. Let me die in dignity. Keep it as simple and brief as possible. No fuss, no man of God there. If there is a God, I'll see him and we'll talk things over." As he lay dying, O'Neill lamented: "I knew it! I knew it! Born in a godd** hotel room and dying in a hotel room!"

Alternative: * "I knew it. I knew it. Born in a hotel room - and God d*** it - died in a hotel room."

O'Neill, Eugene, Jr. (1910-1950). American Greek literary scholar and son of playwright Eugene O'Neill (above). O'Neill, like his father, was plagued by depression and alcohol abuse. At age 40, he took his life by slitting his wrists and ankles, leaving a suicide note beneath an empty whiskey bottle: "Never let it be said of an O'Neill that he failed to empty a bottle. *Ave atque vale* [Hail and farewell]."

O'Neill, James (1847-1920). Irish-born American actor. O'Neill spoke to his son Eugene, Sr. (above): "Glad to go, boy... a better sort of life... another sort... somewhere. This sort of life... froth! Rotten! All of it... no good!"

O'Neill, William (1860-1898). American military officer who fought in Teddy Roosevelt's Rough Riders regiment during the Spanish-American War. Before the charge up San Juan Hill, near Santiago, Cuba, O'Neill casually strolled before his crouching men while calmly smoking a cigarette. When told that he easily could be shot, O'Neill scoffed: "Sergeant, the

Spanish bullet isn't made that will kill me." Shortly thereafter, he was killed instantly by a stray bullet to the head.

Opie, Amelia (1769-1853). English writer and poet. Opie replied to those who asked how she was doing: "Tell them I have suffered great pain, but I think on Him who suffered for me. Say that I am trusting in my Savior and ask them to pray for me." When told that many prayers were said for her: "It were worthwhile to be ill, to have the prayers of our friends." As she died: "All is peace… All is mercy…"

Oppenheimer, J. Robert (1904-1967). American physicist who helped develop the atomic bomb. Suffering from throat cancer, Oppenheimer wrote a note several days before he died: "I am in some pain... my hearing and my speech are very poor."

Orbeeck, van (birth and death dates uncertain). Dutch painter. On his deathbed, van Orbeeck spoke to his physicians: "Gentlemen, have no regard for my forty-six years. You must count them *double*, for I have lived day and night."

O'Reilly, John (1844-1890). Irish-American journalist and poet. Dying from a possible overdose of a soporific, O'Reilly said to his wife: "Yes, Mamsie dear, I have taken some of your sleeping medicine. I feel tired now, and if you will let me lie down on that couch, I will go to sleep right away... Yes, my love! Yes, my love!"

O'Rourke, Heather (1975-1988). American child actress who played in the *Poltergeist* films. The 12 year-old O'Rourke succumbed from complications of a congenital intestinal disorder. When her mother said: "I love you," the dying child replied: "I love you too."

Orsini, Felice (1819-1858). Italian revolutionary who attempted to assassinate the French Emperor Napoleon III. To an agitated co-conspirator on the scaffold: "Try to be calm, my friend, try to be calm."

Ortega y Gasset, José (1883-1955). Spanish philosopher and writer. At the end, Ortega y Gasset said to his wife: "I have a great confusion in my head. I would like you to clear it up for me."

Orwell, George, pen name of Eric Blair (1903-1950). Indian-born British, writer of the futuristic novel *Nineteen Eighty-Four.* Dying from complications of tuberculosis at age 46, Orwell wrote: "At fifty, everyone has the face that he deserves."

Oscar II (1829-1907). King of Sweden. Dying of a heart ailment, Oscar requested: "Don't let them shut the theatres for me." He then said to his doctors: "Thank you."

Osler, William (1849-1919). Canadian-born physician, writer and educator. Through numerous editions, Osler's book *The Principles and Practice of Medicine* has been utilized by generations of physicians. Dying during the Spanish influenza epidemic, he spoke to his wife: "Nighty-night, a darling."

Osman I (1258-1326). Founder of the Ottoman dynasty. Dying of old age, to his son and successor: "Cultivate justice and thereby embellish the earth. Rejoice my departed soul with a beautiful series of victories... Propagate religion by thy arms."

Alternative: * "Rule mercifully and justly and uphold the law of Islam."

Oswald, Lee Harvey (1939-1963). American assassin who allegedly shot President John F. Kennedy during his visit to Dallas, Texas (above). As Oswald was transported to a county jail, an escort quipped that he hoped anyone shooting at the prisoner would be as good a marksman. Oswald replied: "Oh, you're being melodramatic. Nobody's gonna shoot at me." When told to "hit the floor" if there were any problems: "... I'll do whatever you do." Moments later he was shot at close range and killed by a nightclub operator, Jack Ruby. Oswald loudly moaned "Ohhhh," before dying.

Alternatives: * "Aw, there ain't going to be anybody shooting at me, you're just being melodramatic."

* "There ain't nobody gonna shoot me."

Oswald, Saint (c. 604-642). King of Northumbria (northern England) who was killed and dismembered at the Battle of Maserfield in west-central England. Praying for his soldiers and people: "May the Lord, have mercy on their souls."

Otho, Marcus (32-69). Roman emperor. Defeated by Vitellius' army in a power and territorial struggle, Otho told his followers: "If you love me in reality, let me die as I desire and do not compel me to live against my will, but make your way to the victor and gain his good graces." Before falling on his sword, the deposed emperor told his attendant: "Go then and show yourself to the soldiers, lest they should cut you to pieces for being accessory to my death."

Oughtred, William (1574-1600). English mathematician and clergyman who devised the slide rule. When told that Charles II had been restored as king, Oughtred retorted: "And are ye sure he is restored? Then give me a glass of sack [wine] to drink his Sacred Majesty's health!"

Ouida, pen name of Louise de la Ramée (1839-1908). English writer. Dying of pneumonia: "I have been very ill these days and my maid is of the opinion that I shall never get well. The weather is intensely cold and at St. Remo it is so warm and brilliant. It is odd that there should be so great a difference. Excuse this rough word- I am ill and cannot write well."

Outlaw, Sebastian "Bass" (c. 1854-1894). American gunfighter. During an altercation, Outlaw, a former Texas Ranger, shot and killed a fellow lawman. He was tracked down and mortally wounded by a constable. Before expiring, Outlaw exclaimed: "Go gather my friends around me, for I know that I must die."

Owen, John (1616-1683). English clergyman, theologian and writer. When told by the Reverend William Payne that the theologian's book *Meditations on the Glory of Christ* was being printed, Owen responded: "I am glad to hear it. But, oh Brother Payne, the long-wished for day is come at last, in which I shall see that glory in another manner than I have ever done or was capable of doing in this world." He died later that day.

Owen, Robert (1771-1858). Welsh social reformer and philanthropist who founded several utopian societies in the U.S. Dying of bronchitis, to his son: "Very easy and comfortable." Then: "Relief has come!"

Owen, Wilfred (1893-1918). English poet and frontline military officer. Before he was killed in WWI action, Owen spoke to one of his men: "Well done... You are doing that very well, my boy."

Owens, John, also called Bill Booth (died1886). American criminal, condemned to hang for the murder of a settler over a $5 dispute. At his execution, Owens asked: "What time is it?" When told eleven o'clock, he replied: "I wish you'd hurry up. I want to get to hell in time for dinner."

Ozanam, Frédéric (1813-1853). French scholar and co-founder of the Society of Saint Vincent de Paul charity. On his deathbed, Ozanam prayed: "My God, my God, have mercy on me."

Packer, Alfred (1842-1907). American gold-prospector who allegedly shot and cannibalized several of his companions during the severe winter of 1873-4. Originally sentenced to die by hanging, Packer's punishment was commuted to a 40 year imprisonment. Eventually paroled, he maintained to the end of his life: "I'm not guilty of the charge."

Pætus, Arria (died 42). Wife of Roman senator Caecina Pætus. Condemned to die for alleged disloyalty to Emperor Claudius, Caecina Pætus decided on suicide by dagger as the proper remedy but balked at carrying out the act. Arria took the weapon and did the deed to herself, encouraging her husband to follow suit: "It does not hurt, Pætus."

Paganini, Niccolò (1782-1840): Italian virtuoso violinist and composer. Paganini allegedly conveyed his last wishes to the servant girl who was preparing to buy food for his supper: "Twelve sous, that is too much money, Julietta. Try to get one for eight sous, but be careful, a pigeon which costs eight sous may have too much bone." A friend later described

Paganini's death scene: "Out of curiosity, I stepped into the room. The famous violinist, whom I had applauded with great enthusiasm in Germany, England and France, lay in a dilapidated bed, a napkin round his neck, and next to him was a plate on which were the remains of a pigeon." During his last years, Paganini often communicated by conversation books, because a chronic throat ailment limited phonation. One of his last entries concerned a question about a concoction for his long-standing digestive disorder: "I don't know the laxative 'Red Roses.'"

Page, Elijah (1981-2007). American criminal, convicted of a murder committed during a robbery. Asked if he had any last words before his execution by lethal injection: "Yes, no last words."

Pahlavi, Mohammad Reza (1919-1980). Deposed Shah of Iran. Suffering from advanced cancer, Pahlavi's valet asserted he would get better. The shah responded: "No, you don't understand. I'm dying." To his physicians: "I am fed up with living artificially. I don't want to live like Tito [the Yugoslavian dictator who died from protracted complications of atherosclerosis].

Pahlavi, Reza (1878-1944). Persian soldier and later Shah of Iran. Deposed by the Allies during WWII in favor of his son (above), Pahlavi died of a heart ailment while in exile. At the end, he spoke to his son: "Do not fear the difficulties. Go forward to meet them. Never try to avoid them. One must confront difficulties face to face in order to remove them."

Paine, Saint John, also Payne (1532-1582). English Catholic martyr. A disreputable informer accused Paine of plotting to kill Queen Elizabeth I. Convicted of treason, he was condemned to die by hanging and quartering. On his dying breath, Paine proclaimed his innocence: "My feet never did tread, my hands never did write, nor did my wit ever invent any treason against her Majesty."

Paine, Lewis (see Powell, Lewis).

Paine, Thomas (1737-1809). English-born American revolutionary, philosopher and pamphleteer, author of *Common Sense*, *Rights of Man* and *The American Crisis*. During his last days, Paine seemed to have misgivings about his criticism of organized religion: "I would give worlds, if I had them, if *The Age of Reason* had never been published. O Lord, help me! O Christ, help me! O God what have I done to suffer so much? But there is no God! But if there should be, what will become of me hereafter? Stay with me, for God's sake! Send even a child to stay with me, for it is hell to be alone. If ever the devil had an agent, I have been that one." When a priest attempted to convert the revolutionary to Christianity, Paine angrily replied: "Let me have none of your popish stuff! Get away with you! Good morning! Good morning!" He then turned to his nurse (some say housekeeper) and said: "Don't let 'em come here again. They trouble me." When Paine's rotund physician remarked that his patient's abdomen had diminished, the activist retorted: "And yours augments." Later, a friend asked the dying man if he believed Jesus Christ was the Son of God. Paine replied: "I have no wish to believe on that subject!" When asked if he had received good care, he said: "Oh, yes!"

Alternative: * "Taking a leap into the dark. O mystery!"

Pallotti, Saint Vincent (1795-1850). Italian Roman Catholic priest. Suffering from pneumonia, Pallotti's uttered his last prayer: "Jesus, bless the Congregation: a blessing of goodness, a blessing of wisdom." When a colleague asked Pallotti to pray for a prolongation of his life, the dying man replied: "Let me go, where God wants me."

Palm, Johann (1768-1806). German book dealer whose firm circulated a criticism of Napoleon I. For his trouble, Palm was shot by a French firing squad. A final letter to his family before the execution: "To you my dear wife, I say a thousand thanks for your love. Trust in God and do not forget me. I have nothing in the world to say but farewell, you and the children. God bless you and them... Once more, farewell. Yonder we shall meet again. Your husband and children's father, Johann Palm. Braunau, in prison, August 26, 1806, a half hour before my death."

Palmer, Courtlandt (1843-1888). American founder of the free-thinking Nineteenth Century Club, where a variety of social and scientific issues were debated. Dying of peritonitis, Palmer asserted: "I want you to say that you have seen a free-thinker die without fear of the future and without changing his opinion."

Alternative: * "The general impression is that Freethinkers are afraid of death. I want you one and all to tell the whole world that you have seen a Freethinker die without the least fear of what the hereafter may be."

Palmer, John (1742-1798). English actor. Palmer died suddenly on stage after reciting a line from August von Kotzebue's play *The Stranger*: "There is another and a better world."

Palmer, Raymond (1808-1887). American minister and hymnodist. Palmer died reciting words from one of his hymns "Jesus, These Eyes Have Never Seen:" "When death these mortal eyes shall seal,/ And still this throbbing heart,/ The rending veil shall Thee reveal,/ All glorious as Thou art!"

Palmer, Roundell, Earl of Selborne (1812-1895). British lawyer, politician and writer. At the end, Palmer asked: "Lord, show me what Thou wouldst have me to do and help me to do it faithfully and well."

Palmer, William (1824-1856). English physician, convicted of poisoning a friend for monetary gain. When he stepped on the gallows and looked at the trapdoor, Palmer inquired: "Are you sure this is safe?"

Pambo the Hermit, Saint (c. 303-375). Egyptian Christian holy man who lived a recluse's life. On his deathbed: "I thank God that not a day of my life has been spent in idleness; never have I eaten bread that I had not earned with the sweat of my brow. I thank God that I do not recall any bitter speech I have made, for which I ought to repent now."

Pancras, Saint, also Pancratius (c. 290- c. 304). Roman Christian martyr. Beheaded at age 14 for his religious beliefs, Pancras spoke to Emperor Diocletian: "In body I am a child, but I bear a man's heart. And by grace of my Master Jesus Christ, thy threats seem as vain to me as this idol which stands before me. And as for the gods whom thou desirest me to adore, they are naught but imposters, who sully the women of their own household, and spare not their own kin. If thine own slaves today behaved as these gods, thou wouldst be in haste to put them to death. And it wonders me much that thou dost not blush to adore such gods!"

Pantazopoulos, Maria (died 2012). Canadian real estate agent. Immediately following her wedding, the 30 year-old Pantazopoulos posed for pictures on the bank of a rapidly flowing river. She fell in and drowned, crying: "I'm slipping, I'm slipping; I'm slipping."

Panzram, Carl (1891-1930). American serial killer, condemned to die by hanging. Before his execution, Panzram expressed his views on the situation: "In my lifetime, I have murdered twenty-one human beings. I have committed thousands of burglaries, robberies, larcenies, arsons and, last but not least, I have committed sodomy on more than 1000 male human beings. For all these things, I am not the least sorry. I have no conscience, and so that does not worry me. I don't believe in man, God nor devil. I hate the whole d*** human race, including myself." At the end, Panzram was unhappy with the progress of his execution saying: "I wish the human race had one neck and I had my hands around it… Let's get going! What are we stalling around for?" When the hangman asked for any last words, he said: "Yes, hurry it up, you Hoosier b******! I could hang a dozen men while you're fooling around!"

Alternatives: * "Hurry it up, you Kraut b******! I could kill a dozen men while you're screwing around!"

* "Hurry up, you Hoosier b******; I could kill ten men while you're fooling around!"

Pape, Klaus von (1904-1923). German businessman. Pape, an early member of the Nazi Party, was killed with 15 others in the abortive Beer Hall Putsch that attempted to propel Adolf Hitler to power: "Is Hitler alive? Is Ludendorff? Then I gladly die for my fatherland."

Park, Mungo (1771-1806). Scottish explorer. In 1805, Park embarked on an expedition to Africa, seeking to explore the Niger River. A last letter penned to Mrs. Park: "... I think it not unlikely but I shall be in England before you receive this. You may be sure that I feel happy at turning my face towards home. We this morning have done with all intercourse with the natives; and the sails are now hoisting for our departure for the coast." Park and his companions drowned when their canoe came under attack by hostile natives.

Parker, Bonnie (1910-1934). American criminal. Parker and her sidekick Clyde Barrow robbed a number of banks and were responsible for a series of murders in the central U.S. A short time before they were gunned down by Louisiana and Texas lawmen, Parker composed a poem entitled "The Trail's End:" "... Some day they will go down together/ And they will bury them side by side/ For a few it means grief/ For the law it's relief/ But it's death to Bonnie and Clyde." The felons were buried in separate cemeteries.

Parker, Dorothy (1893-1967). American satirist, writer and poet. Parker spoke to her friend Beatrice Ames shortly before dying of a heart attack: "I want you to tell me the truth. Did Ernest [Hemingway] really like me?"

Parks, Robyn (died 1992). American criminal, sentenced to die by lethal injection for a murder committed during a robbery. As the lethal cocktail was administered, Parks said "I'm still awake." Before dying, he told his girlfriend goodbye: "I love you too, Debra."

Parnell, Charles (1846-1891). Irish nationalist who worked for Ireland's home rule. Dying of a heart attack (some say a "rheumatic heart"), Parnell spoke to his wife: "Kiss me, sweet wife, and I will try to sleep a little."

Parr, Kenneth (1980-2007). American criminal, executed by lethal injection for the rape and murder of a 28 year-old woman: "I just want to tell my family I love y'all, man. ... Keep your head up, y'all. I'm ready."

Parry, William (1790-1855). British arctic explorer. On his deathbed, Parry requested: "Mind, let there be no deathbed scene." When asked if he wished to have his children present: "Yes, but take care, take care." Foreseeing that the end was near: "The chariots and horses!"

Parsons, Albert (1848-1887). American anarchist and labor union activist. Parsons and seven other labor union leaders were accused of inciting a deadly 1866 riot at Haymarket Square in Chicago. Parsons, along with George Engel, Adolph Fischer (both above) and August Spies (below) were hanged at the same time. Prior to his execution, Parsons asked: "Will I be allowed to speak, O men of America? Let me speak, Sheriff Matson! Let the voice of the people be heard! O..." The hangman ended his speech.

Parsons, Theophilus (1750-1813). American jurist and politician who strongly supported ratification of the U.S. Constitution. On his deathbed, after a considerable period of silence, Parsons revived and deliriously said: "Gentlemen of the jury, the case is closed, and in your hands. You will please retire and agree upon your verdict."

Pascal, Blaise (1623-1662). French mathematician, scientist, writer and philosopher. Pascal, among other scholarly endeavors, pursued studies of calculating machines and the physical properties of fluids. At the end, Pascal prayed: "May God never abandon me."

Alternative: * "My God, forsake me not."

Pascin, born Jules Pincas (1885-1930). Bulgarian-born French artist. Wracked by depression and alcohol abuse, Pascin cut his wrists and wrote in blood on his wall (some say toilet door) to Cecile "Lucy" Vidal Krohg, a former lover: "Adieu Lucy." He then hanged himself.

Pasternak, Boris (1890-1960). Russian writer, best-known for his novel *Doctor Zhivago*. Pasternak was awarded the 1958 Nobel Prize in Literature but was pressured to decline it by the Soviet government. Dying of lung cancer, to his wife: "I can't hear very well. And there's a mist in front of my eyes. But it will go away, won't it? Don't forget to open the window tomorrow." As he died: "Good-bye . . . why am I hemorrhaging?"

Pasteur, Louis (1822-1895). French scientist, known for his pioneering work in microbiology and vaccination. Pasteurization, a process to halt the spoilage of perishable food and beverages, bears his name. Dying from complications of a stroke, Pasteur refused a proffered glass of milk, saying: "I cannot."

Patmore, Coventry (1823-1896). British poet and literary critic. Dying of pneumonia, Patmore said to his wife: "I love you, dear, but the Lord is my life and my light."

Paton, John (died 1684). Martyred Scottish Covenanter and military leader. Because of his defiance of the monarchy and Catholic doctrine, Paton was condemned to die. On the scaffold before his hanging, the martyr said: "... Farewell sweet scriptures, preaching, praying, reading, singing and all duties. Welcome Father, Son and Holy Spirit. I desire to commit my soul to Thee in well-doing. Lord, receive my spirit."

Pattison, Dorothy, also known as Sister Dora (1832-1878). British nun and nurse. Dying of breast cancer, Sister Dora related: "I see Him standing there! The gates are open wide!" Later she sent those in her room away, saying: "I have lived alone. Let me die alone. Let me die alone."

Patton, George (1885-1945). American general who commanded allied forces in North Africa and the European Theater during WWII. While on a hunting trip prior to his planned rotation from Germany to the U.S., Patton was severely injured in an automobile accident. Realizing the seriousness of the situation, he commented: "This is a hell of a way to die." Toward the end, to his wife: "It's too dark, I mean, too late."

Paul I (1754-1801). Emperor of Russia. Paul was assassinated by angry courtiers for his attempts to reduce the privileges of the nobility: "Gentlemen, in heaven's name spare me! At least give me time to say my prayers!"

Paul I (1901-1964). King of Greece. Dying of cancer, Paul had a vivid vision of eternity, saying to his wife: "When you have known the road on the other side, you don't want to struggle along it on this side anymore..." Rejecting further means to prolong his life, he declared: "The injections will separate you [his queen] and me, and the drip feedings will hold me back. I want to be quite conscious when I go." Immediately before dying, Paul commented: "I see the light! It is much larger now, and the peace is getting stronger! Now we go!"

Paul III (1468-1549). Pope from 1534 until his death. Toward the end, Paul prayed the words of Psalm 19:13: "Keep back thy servant also from presumptuous sins; let them not have dominion over me! Then I shall be blameless and innocent of great transgression."

Paul the Apostle, Saint, also Paul of Tarsus (died c. 67). Martyred Roman Christian missionary. Paul founded a number of Christian churches and wrote the epistles found in the Bible's New Testament. The mode of Paul's death remains obscure, but he probably was beheaded by his Roman persecutors. While jailed in Rome (2 Timothy 4:6-8, 22), he wrote to his disciple Timothy in Ephesus: "For I am already on the point of being sacrificed; the time of my departure has come. I have fought the good fight, I have finished the race, I have kept the faith. Henceforth there is laid up for me the crown of righteousness, which the Lord, the righteous Judge, will award to me on that Day: and not only to me but also to all who have loved His appearing..." Later in the chapter (2 Timothy 4:21-2), Paul requested: "Do your best to come before winter. Eubulus sends greetings to you, as do Pudens and Linus and Claudia and all the brethren. The Lord be with your spirit. Grace be with you." Some say his last uttered word was: "Jesus!"

Paul, Maury (see Knickerbocker, Cholly).

Paulinus, Saint (c. 354-431). French-born, poet, writer and politician who became bishop of Nola in southern Italy. On his deathbed, Paulinus quoted Psalm 119:105: "Thy word is a lamp to my feet and a light to my path."

Paulus, Julius (fl. 2nd to 3rd century). Roman jurist who declared as he died: "There is another life... though my life be gone, I pray God that my students might find the truth."

Pausch, Randolph (1960-2008). American computer scientist and educator. Dying of pancreatic cancer, Pausch responded to a friend who said it was okay to let go: "I'll get back to you on that."

Pavarotti, Luciano (1935-2007). Italian operatic tenor. Dying of cancer, to his manager: "I believe that a life lived for music is an existence spent wonderfully, and this is what I have dedicated my life to."

Pavese, Cesare (1908-1950). Italian writer, poet, translator and critic. Suffering from depression and disillusionment, Pavese committed suicide by a drug overdose. His last diary entry read: "The thing most feared in secret always happens. All it needs is a little courage. The more the pain grows clear and definite, the more the instinct for life asserts itself and the thought of suicide recedes. It seemed easy when I thought of it. Weak women have done it. It needs humility, not pride. I am sickened by all of this. Not words. Action. I shall write no more."

Pavlova, Anna (1881-1931). Russian prima ballerina. Succumbing to a painful chest ailment, Pavlova spoke about one of her signature roles where she played a dying swan: "I'm dying. Give me something to ease my pain… Bring me my swan costume... Play that last measure [of "The Dying Swan" melody] softly."

Alternative: * "Get my swan costume ready."

Paxton, Elisha (1828-1863). American lawyer and Confederate officer in the U.S. Civil War. Paxton was felled by a gunshot to the chest during the skirmish at Chancellorsville, Virginia. As he extended his arms to a subordinate: "Tie up my arm."

Payne, John (1842-1916). English poet. Payne asked a last minute question: "Have you got the sheets? Did you get the pillow-cases?"

Payson, Edward (1783-1827). American Congregational preacher. Dying of a painful chest ailment, Payson was heard to say "These are God's arrows, but they are all sharpened with love." At the time of death, he told his wife and children: "Faith and patience, hold out! I feel like a mote in a sunbeam" Prior to his demise, Payson had prepared a placard to be placed on his body while it lay in repose: "Remember the words, which I spake unto you while I was yet present with you."

Payton, Walter (1954-1999). American professional football player and member of the Pro Football Hall of Fame. Dying of a liver ailment, to his son who had entered the room: "Where have you been?"

Peabody, Everett (1830-1862). Union officer in the U.S. Civil War. Peabody tried to rally his men in the face of a Confederate advance during the Battle of Shiloh, Tennessee: "Stand to it yet." He was killed by a gunshot to the head.

Peabody, George (1795-1869). American-born businessman and philanthropist. After his last prayer: "It is a great mystery, but I shall know all soon."

Peace, Charles (1832-1879). English burglar and murderer, executed by hanging. Peace allegedly said on the way to the gallows: "What is the scaffold? A short cut to heaven."

Alternative: * Others say he asked for a glass of water, which was refused.

Peacock, Thomas (1785-1866). English writer, playwright and poet. During a house fire, Peacock attempted to salvage books from his library. When admonished to flee, he responded: "By the immortal gods, I will not move!" He later died from injuries sustained during the conflagration.

Peale, Charles (1741-1827). American artist, naturalist and patriot. At the end, Peale asked his daughter to feel his pulse. When she replied that she couldn't feel one, he remarked: "No, it is gone. The law makes my will." He died moments later.

Alternative: * "I thought so. The law makes my will."

Pearson, Henry (1830-1894). English-born Australian politician. "My life has been faulty, but God will judge me by my intentions."

Peckham, Rufus (1809-1873). American jurist and U.S. congressman. Peckham, his wife and over 200 passengers on the steamer *Ville du Havre* perished in the North Atlantic Ocean after colliding with a Scottish vessel. Peckham reflected: "If we must go down, let us die bravely."

Alternative: * "Wife, we have to die. Let us die bravely."

Peel, Robert (1788-1850). English prime minister. Dying of injuries sustained during a horse-riding accident, Peel said to his wife before his outing: "Julia, you are not going without wishing me goodbye or saying those sweet words 'God bless you.'"

Peerson, also Pierson, Anthony (died 1543). English Protestant martyr. Because of Peerson's reformist preaching, he was condemned as a heretic and sentenced to be burned. Approaching the execution site, he embraced the stake, saying: "Now welcome, mine own sweet wife; for this day shalt thou and I be married together in the love and peace of God." Peerson then arranged the straw around his legs and placed some atop his head, saying: "This is God's hat. Now I am dressed like a true soldier of Christ, by whose merits only I trust this day to enter into His joy."

Péguy, Charles (1873-1914). French writer, poet and military officer during WWI. When one of his men objected to exposing himself because he did not have a helmet, Péguy exclaimed: "That doesn't matter in this tempest. Look, I haven't mine, either! Go on firing!" Moments later, Péguy suffered a mortal head wound.

Alternative: * "Keep firing."

Pelletier, Louis Michel de (1760-1793). French politician. Because he voted for the death of Louis XVI, de Pelletier was assassinated by one of the king's supporters. Before he died, de Pelletier moaned: "I am cold."

Pellico, Silvio (c. 1788-1854). Italian writer and patriot, imprisoned nearly a decade for his anti-Austrian views. While incarcerated under harsh conditions, he penned memoirs of his experience there. On his deathbed almost 24 years later, Pellico placed his hands over his heart and declared: "Here my God is." He then said: "In two or three hours I shall be in paradise. If I have sinned, I have also atoned. When I wrote *My Prisons*, I had the vanity to believe myself a great man; but then I saw it was not true and repented my conceit."

Alternative: * "O Paradise! O Paradise! At last comes to me the grand consolation. My prisons disappear; the great of earth pass away; all before me is rest."

Penfield, Wilder (1891-1976). American-born Canadian neurosurgeon. Dying of cancer, Penfield remarked about his cane: "I won't need this anymore, but maybe I'll keep it anyway, just for while I'm in the hospital."

Penn, Gulielma (1644-1694). English-born first wife of William Penn (below). To a relative: "I have cast my care upon the Lord… My dear, love to all friends. May the Lord preserve and bless us."

Penn, Springett (1674-1696). English-born Quaker son of Gulielma and William Penn. Dying of tuberculosis: "Let my father speak to the doctor and I'll go to sleep." He died shortly thereafter in his father's arms.

Penn, William (1644-1718). English-born Quaker who founded the Province of Pennsylvania. After sustaining a series of strokes, Penn offered his thoughts: "Son William, if you and your friends keep to your plain way of preaching and keep to your plain way of living, you will make an end of the priests to the end of the world. Bury me by my mother. Live all in love. Shun all manner of evil, and I pray God to bless you all; and He will bless you all."

Alternative: * "To be like Christ is to be a Christian."

Penrose, Boies (1860-1921). U.S. senator and lawyer. Dying of a respiratory ailment, Penrose spoke to his valet: "See here, William. See here. I don't want any of your d***** lies. How do I look? Am I getting any better? The truth now... All right, William. When you go to church tomorrow, pray for me too." Penrose died the following day.

Penruddock, John (1619-1655). English cavalier. For his efforts to restore Charles II to the English throne, Penruddock was sentenced to die by beheading. Kissing the axe, he said: "I am like to have a sharp passage of it, but my Savior hath sweetened it unto me. If I would have been so unworthy as others have been, I suppose I might by a lie have saved my life, which I scorn to purchase at such a rate. I defy temptations and them that gave them me. Glory be to God on high, on earth peace, goodwill towards men, and the Lord have mercy upon my poor soul. Amen."

Penry, John (1559-1593). Martyred Welsh preacher. Because of his separatist views, Peary was condemned by the Church of England and hanged for heresy. On the gallows: "… I come with the rope about my neck to save you. Howsoever it goeth with me, I labor that you may have the Gospel preached among you. Though it cost my life, I think it well bestowed."

Peponila (died 79). Wife of the Gallic rebel Sabinus. Pleading with Emperor Vespasian to spare her children: "These little ones, Caesar, I bore and reared in the monument that we might be a greater number to supplicate you." Her plea fell on deaf ears.

Pepys, Samuel (1633-1703). English statesman and diarist whose writing uniquely chronicled contemporary English life. To his nephew and his housekeeper: "Be good friends. I do desire it of you." Later, Pepys was asked if the nephew should be called: "Yes." He died several hours later.

Perceval, Spencer (1762-1812). British Prime Minister. Perceval was assassinated by a disgruntled citizen. His last utterance was: "Oh! I am murdered!"

Alternatives: * "Murder!"
* "O my God!"

Percy, Walker (1916-1990). American writer of philosophical novels. Percy won the 1962 U.S. National Book Award for Fiction for his novel *The Moviegoer*. Dying of prostate cancer: "Don't ask the Lord to keep me here. Ask him to have mercy." When asked by his nurse if his wife should be called: "No. She understands."

Pericles of Athens (c. 490-429 BCE). Athenian statesman and military leader. To those assembled at his deathbed: "I have never caused any citizen to mourn on my account."

Alternatives: * "No Athenian ever put on black through me."
* "For no Athenian, through my means, ever wore mourning."

Perko, Ivanka (died 2006). Slovenian migrant. Perko survived Nazi and Communist regimes but died from complications of a falling banana that scraped and ultimately infected her leg: "I can't believe, after all this time, it was a bloody banana that killed me."

Perón, Eva (1919-1952). Argentine first lady, actress and social activist. Dying of cancer, Perón spoke to her maid: "I never felt happy in this life. That is why I left home. My mother would have married me to someone ordinary, and I could never have stood it, Irma. A decent woman has to get on in the world." Before she lost consciousness, she remarked to her sister: "Eva is leaving."

Alternative: * "Eva is going."

Perón, Juan (1895-1974). President of Argentina and husband of Eva Perón. Dying of a heart attack, Perón spoke to his physician: "Taina, I'm leaving this world- my people- my people."

Perpetua, Saint (died 203). Carthaginian pious woman, condemned to die in the arena with her servant Felicitas for their Christian beliefs. After being mauled by a wild cow, Perpetua tied her hair up saying: "It is not becoming for a martyr to suffer with disheveled hair, lest she appear to be mourning in her glory." Not realizing the extent of her injuries, she asked: "When am I going to be taken out to the cow?" Perpetua then spoke to her fellow martyrs: "Continue firm in the faith, love one another and be not distressed at our sufferings." She then was beheaded.

Alternatives: * "I cannot tell when we are to be led out to that cow."
* "Stand fast in the faith, and love one another. Do not let our sufferings be a stumbling block to you."

Perrin, Abner (1827-1864). Confederate brigadier general during the U.S. Civil War. While leading his brigade at Mule Shoe, near Spotsylvania, Virginia, Perrin remarked: "I shall come out of this fight a live major general or a dead brigadier." Seven bullets ended his military career.

Perry, Oliver (1785-1819). U.S. naval hero of the Battle of Lake Erie during the War of 1812. After accepting the British surrender, he informed his superior: "We have met the enemy and they are ours." Dying of yellow fever almost six years later aboard his ship in the Caribbean Sea: "Few persons have greater inducements to make them wish to live than I, but I am perfectly ready to go if it pleases the Almighty to take me. The debt of nature must be paid!" Preparing to make his will, Perry procrastinated: "But tomorrow will do." He died before completing the document.

Perugino, Pietro (c. 1446-1523). Italian Renaissance painter. Dying of the plague, Perugino refused to see a priest: "I am curious to see what happens in the next world to one who dies unshriven [without confession]."

Pessoa, Fernando (1888-1935). Portuguese poet, writer and philosopher. Dying of cirrhosis: "I know not what tomorrow will bring."

Pestel, Pavel (1793-1826). Russian revolutionary. Because his social and economic reforms clashed with those of the government, Pestel was convicted of treason and sentenced to die by hanging. When the hangman's rope broke on the first attempt, Pestel contemptuously said: "Stupid country, where they do not even know how to hang."

Petacci, Claretta (1912-1945). Mistress of the Italian dictator Benito Mussolini (above). Before she and the dictator were shot by partisans, Petacci cried: "Mussolini must not die!"

Pétain, Henri-Philippe (1856-1951). WWI French military hero who was imprisoned for life for his involvement with the Vichy Republic during WWII. To his wife: "Do not weep. Do not grieve."

Peter I, also Peter the Great (1672-1725). Russian czar. Peter, through a succession of wars, transformed Russia into a major European power. After receiving the Last Rites: "Lord, I believe. I hope. I hope God will forgive me my many sins because of the good I have tried to do for my people." While attempting to write his will, Peter was able to scrawl only: "Give back everything to..." He then called his daughter's name "Anna" but fell unconscious before she arrived.

Alternatives: * "Give back all to..."
* "I believe, Lord, and confess, help my unbelief."

Peter II (1715-1730). Russian czar. With his final thoughts disordered by smallpox, Peter commanded: "Get my sledge ready; get my sledge ready! I want to go to my sister." His sister Natalya had predeceased him by 14 months.

Peter III (1728-1762). German-born Russian emperor. Because he lacked support by Russian society and the military, Peter's wife crowned herself Czarina as Catherine II and had the dethroned ruler killed. As he died, Peter supposedly lamented: "It was not enough then to prevent my reigning over Sweden and to tear from my head the crown of Russia! They must have my life besides!"

Peter of Alcantara, Saint (1499-1562). Spanish Franciscan mystic. As he died, Peter repeated the first verse of Psalm 122: "I was glad when they said to me; 'Let us go into the house of the Lord.'"

Peter of Lampsacus, Saint (died c. 250). Christian martyr from present-day Turkey. To test his faith, Peter was commanded to sacrifice to the goddess Venus. He refused saying: "I am astonished that you should command me to worship a woman, who according to your own history was a vile and licentious character, and guilty of such crimes as your own laws now punish with death. No, I shall offer to the one only living and true God the sacrifice of prayer and praise." For his defiance, his bones were pulled apart, his head was severed and his body was consigned to the dogs.

Peter the Martyr, Saint (1206-1252). Italian Catholic priest. Because Peter denounced a group of Milanese heretics, a faction of this band conspired to kill him. As he died from an axe wound to the head, the martyr supposedly wrote in the dirt with his blood: "I believe in one God."

Alternative: * "Lord, into Thy hands I commend my spirit."

Peter, Prince of Portugal (1392-1449). Portuguese nobleman and warrior. Peter was killed at the Battle of Alfarrobeira, near Lisbon while fighting King Alfonso V's army: "Oh, body of mine! I feel that you can do no more; and you my spirit, why should you tarry here?" As he fell to the ground: "Fight on, comrades! And you, you villains, do your worst!"

Peter, Saint (died c. 64). One of Jesus Christ's 12 original apostles. Peter became the first pope and was martyred for his Christian beliefs. Before his crucifixion, Peter spoke to his wife who apparently suffered a similar fate: "... My dear, remember the Lord."

Peters, Hugh (1598-1660). English clergyman and political advisor. Peters was implicated in the regicide of English King Charles I and subsequently sentenced to die. Before he was hanged, drawn and quartered, Peters was forced to watch the execution of a co-conspirator John Cook. After a bystander implored him to repent, he replied: "Friend, you do not well to trample on a dying man." When the bloodied hangman mockingly asked what he thought of the proceedings, Peters said: "I am not, I thank God, terrified at it; you may do your worst." As he ascended the ladder: "Sir, you have here slain one of the servants of God before mine eyes; and have made me to behold it, on purpose to terrify and discourage me: but God hath made it an ordinance to me for my strengthening and encouragement." As he prepared to die: "What flesh, art thou unwilling to go to God through the fire and jaws of death? Oh, this is a good day. He is come that I have long looked for, and I shall be with Him in glory."

Petrarch, Francesco (1304-1374). Italian scholar and poet whose humanist philosophy laid the groundwork for the birth of the Renaissance period. Discovered dead in his library, the conclusion of Petrarch's last letter read: "Adieu, my friends; adieu my correspondence."

Pettit, Roger (died 1982). American first officer on Air Florida Flight 90, bound from Washington D.C. to Ft. Lauderdale, Florida, on January 13, 1982. Because of inadequate deicing before takeoff and other pilot errors, the jet crashed into a bridge on the Potomac River moments after it became airborne. Pettit's last words were directed to the plane's captain, Larry Wheaton: "Larry, we're going down, Larry!" The pilot replied: "I know it!" Four motorists on the bridge and 74 of 79 on the aircraft perished.

Pheidippides (530-490 BCE). Greek messenger. When the Persian army landed at the Bay of Marathon, Greece in 490 BCE with plans to attack Athens, Pheidippides, a long-distance runner, was dispatched to seek aid from the Spartans. The messenger returned with disappointing news that help would not be forthcoming. Regardless, the Greek army prevailed without assistance and quickly marched home to Athens, apparently bringing the story to an end. However, over the years, the tale morphed into a legend of courage and endurance. Supposedly, at the conclusion of the Battle of Marathon, Pheidippides ran 26 miles to Athens to pass word of the Greek victory: "Rejoice, we are victorious!" Upon delivering the message, he collapsed and died. In the interim, writers from Herodotus to Robert Browning embellished the story and gave it a life of its own. Browning concluded his poem *Pheidippides*: "... He flung down his shield,/ Ran like fire once more: and the space 'twix the Fennel-field/ and Athens was stubble again, a field, which a fire runs through,/ Till in he broke: 'Rejoice, we conquer!'/ Like wine through clay,/ Joy in his blood bursting his heart,/ he died- the bliss!" When plans were made to revive the ancient Olympic Games in the early 1890s, suggestions were made to include a 26 mile foot race, which would be called the Marathon. Some authors feel that a Greek soldier actually delivered the message of victory (see Eucles above): "Rejoice! For we rejoice!"

Alternatives: * "Joy. We win!"
* "Joy to you. We've won!"

Philby, Harry St. John (1885-1960). Ceylonese-born British intelligence officer, Arabic scholar and writer who was the father of the spy Kim Philby. Dying of a heart attack, Philby complained to his son: "God, I'm bored!"

Philip II (1527-1598). King of Spain. Philip succumbed to a "cancer" that caused his skin to "consume away on his bones by incurable ulcers, which sent forth swarms of worms, so that nobody could approach without fainting." To his son and successor: "I meant to save you this scene, but I wish you to see how the monarchies of the earth end. You see that God has denuded me of all the glory and majesty of a monarch in order to hand them to you. In a very few hours I shall be covered only with a poor shroud and girded with a coarse rope. The king's crown is already falling from my brows and death will place it on yours... This crown will someday fall away from your head as it now falls from mine... My days are numbered and draw to a close..." Asking for Extreme Unction, Philip said: "Father, give it to me now, for now is the time... I die like a good Catholic, in faith and obedience to the Holy Roman Church."

Philip III (1578-1621). King of Spain. Perhaps Philip's extravagant spending and neglect of his kingdom's economic needs colored his final words: "Oh would to God I had never reigned! Oh, that those years I have spent in my kingdom I had lived a solitary life in the wilderness! Oh, that I had lived a life alone with God! How much more secure should I now have died! With how much more confidence should I have gone to the throne of God! What doth all my glory profit, but that I have so much the more torment in my death?"

Alternatives: * "Ah, how happy would it have been for me had I spent these twenty-three years that I have held my kingdom, in retirement."

* "Oh, if it should please heaven to prolong my life, how different should my future be from my past conduct."
* "What an account I shall have to give to God! Oh, why did I ever reign? Ah! If it pleased the Lord to prolong my life, how I should like to live otherwise than I have hitherto lived."

Philip IV (1605-1665). King of Spain. When told that an illegitimate son wished to see him: "Tell him to go back to Consuegra [a municipality in the province of Toledo]. It is now time for nothing but death."

Philip the Apostle, Saint (died c. 90). One of the original 12 apostles of Jesus Christ. Martyred for his Christian conversions in Greece, Syria and parts of present-day Turkey, Philip prayed: "... Clothe me in Thy glorious robe and Thy seal of light that ever shineth, until I have passed by all the rulers of the world and the evil dragon that opposeth us."

Philippa of Hainault (1314-1369). Queen consort of English King Edward III. When Philippa developed "dropsy," she realized the end was near. She made these requests of the king: "Sir, we have in peace and joy and great prosperity passed all our time together. Sir, now I pray you at our parting to grant me three requests. Sir, I ask, first of all, that all the people I have dwelt with on this side of the sea and the other, that it may please you to pay everything I owe them. And next, sir, all such intentions and promises as I have made to the churches, as well of this country as beyond the sea, where I have paid my devotions, that you will fulfill them. And thirdly, I ask that it may please you to take none other sepulture, whensoever it shall please God to call you out of this transitory life, but beside me in the church of Westminster." The king assured her that the requests would be honored. She died in prayer shortly thereafter.

Phillips, David, whose pen name was John Graham (1867-1911). American novelist and muckraker journalist. Phillips was shot multiple times by an eccentric paranoid violinist, Fitzhugh Goldsborough (above) who believed his family had been libeled by one of the author's novels: "It is of no use. I could have won against two bullets but not against six."

Phillips, John "Jack" (1887-1912). British wireless operator on HMS *Titanic*. Prior to the vessel's ill-fated maiden voyage, Bruce Ismay, the director of the White Star Line, told the manager of the shipyard building the vessel: "Control your Irish passions, Thomas [Andrews]. Your uncle here tells me you proposed 64 lifeboats and he had to pull your arm to get you down to 32. Now, I will remind you just as I reminded him: these are my ships. And, according to our contract, I have final say on the design. I'll not have so many little boats, as you call them, cluttering up my decks and putting fear into my passengers." After striking an iceberg in the North Atlantic Ocean, Phillips repeatedly sent SOS messages before the vessel sank: "Have struck iceberg. Badly damaged. Rush aid" The last recorded message: "SOS SOS CQD CQD [the distress call] MGY [*Titanic's* call sign]. We are sinking fast. Passengers are being put into boats. MGY." As the wireless failed, a final transmission was sent: "CQ..." He then told his assistant, Harold Bride: "Come on, let's clear out." Bride survived, but Phillips' body was never recovered. Of the 2,224 persons on board, 1,514 perished. Ironically Ismay was saved by a lifeboat and died 25 years later of a stroke.

Phillips, Philip (1834-1895). American evangelist called "The Singing Pilgrim." A letter to a friend read: "You see that I am still in the land of the dying. Why I linger so long is to me a problem... Often during the night seasons I have real visions. I am walking on the banks of the Beautiful River and getting glimpses of the bright Beyond... Blessed be God! I shall soon know! What a singing time we will have when we get there!"

Phillips, Ulrich (1877-1934). American historian and educator who wrote about the antebellum South and slavery. Dying of cancer: "In body I'm down but not out; in mind, as lively as ever- a cricket!"

Phillips, Wendell (1811-1884). American abolitionist and social reformer. Dying of a heart attack, Phillips remarked to his physician: "I have no fear of death. I am as ready to die today as at any time." At the end, he remembered his wife: "What will become of poor Ann?"

Philopoemen (253-183 BCE). Greek warrior. Captured by his enemy Dinocrates, Philopoemen was imprisoned and sentenced to die. To avoid a possible backlash of sentiment if the conquered general should be executed, the vanquished man was offered a cup of poison in his cell. When told that most of his cavalry had escaped, Philopoemen said: "It is well that we have not been in every way unfortunate." He drank the poison and died.

Phipps, Thomas, elder and younger (died 1789). English father and son, accused of forgery. Both were convicted of "uttering a note of hand for twenty pounds." Leaving the jail, the younger Phipps confessed: "It was I alone who committed the forgery; my father is entirely innocent and was ignorant of the note being forged when he published it." Regardless, they were driven to the place of execution where the father remarked: "Tommy, thou hast brought me to this shameful end, but I freely forgive thee." At the scaffold, the father spoke again: "You have brought me hither, do you lead the way?" After devotions were completed, they embraced and died by hanging.

Phocas (died 610). Byzantine Emperor. Defeated in a civil war, the victor Heraclius asked Phocas: "Is this how you have ruled, wretch?" His reply: "And will you rule better?" Phocas lost his head shortly thereafter.

Phocion (c. 402-c. 317 BCE). Athenian military leader and statesman. Accused of treason for supposedly disobeying an order, Phocion spoke to a friend about the ingratitude of the city: "Yes, but not surprising. This is what usually happens at Athens to her great men." Before hemlock was proffered, Phocion was asked if he had any message for his son: "I bid him cherish no resentment against the Athenians." When the dose of poison proved insufficient to kill, the executioner refused to prepare an additional aliquot until he was paid. Phocion sarcastically remarked: "In Athens, it is hard for a man even to die without paying for it."

Phoenix, River, born River Jude Bottom (1970-1993). American movie actor, musician and social activist. Dying of a drug overdose, Phoenix allegedly spoke to a nightclub doorman: "I'm gonna die, Dude!"

Alternative: * "No paparazzi. I want anonymity."

Piaf, Édith, born Édith Gassion (1915-1963). French popular singer and actress. Dying of cancer, Piaf remarked to her sister: "I can die now... I've lived twice. Be careful, Momome... All the d***** fool things you do in life you pay for."

Picasso, Pablo (1881-1973). Spanish-born artist and sculptor. Dying of a heart attack, Picasso spoke to his doctor, a bachelor, while holding the hand of his second wife: "You are wrong not to marry. It's useful."

Alternative: * "Drink to me. Drink to my health. You know I can't drink anymore."

Piccolo, Brian (1943-1970). American professional football player. Dying of cancer, to his wife: "Can you believe it, Joy? Can you believe this s***?"

Pickford, Mary, born Gladys Smith (1892-1979). Canadian-born American movie actress. Dying of a cerebral hemorrhage, Pickford pointed to nearby pictures: "There's Mama and Papa. And there's Jesus."

Pike, Albert (1809-1891). American lawyer, journalist, poet, Freemason and Confederate officer during the U.S. Civil War. Dying of an ailment that robbed him of speech, Pike wrote on a piece of paper the Hebrew word for peace: "*Shalom. Shalom. Shalom.*"

Pike, James (1913-1969). American bishop. While traveling in the Judean Desert, Pike's car developed mechanical trouble. He said to his wife who prepared to seek aid: "Diane... Tell them to bring lots of water- and yell 'help me' all the way along." When she returned with aid, Pike had wandered away and died of heat-related injuries.

Pike, Zebulon (1779-1813). American military officer and explorer for whom Pike's Peak in Colorado was named. During the War of 1812, Pike was mortally wounded taking Fort York near present-day Toronto. When lifted aboard a nearby naval vessel, the dying Pike asked about the "huzza of the troops:" "What does it mean?" His subordinate replied: "Victory," and related that the Stars and Stripes had replaced the Union Jack.

Pilkington, George (1865-1897). Irish-born writer and missionary to Uganda. Pilkington was mortally wounded while accompanying Ugandan soldiers sent to suppress a rebellion in the eastern part of the country: "Thank you my friends, you have done well to take me off the battlefield. Now give me rest."

Pinochet, Augusto (1915-2006). Chilean dictator. Pinochet led the coup that ousted President Salvatore Allende and later directed the purge that led to the deaths of thousands of his countrymen. Dying from complications of a heart attack, Pinochet spoke his wife's nickname: "Lucy..."

Pio of Pietrelcina, Saint (1887-1968). Italian Capuchin priest, scarred by stigmata. Gazing at a picture of his mother: "I see two mothers!" When told that only one woman was visible: "Do not worry; I see very well. I see two mothers there." As he worsened, Pio admonished his colleague: "Do not wake anybody up." At the end: "Jesus! Mary!"

Pirandello, Luigi (1867-1936). Sicilian-born dramatist and writer who won the 1934 Nobel Prize in Literature. Pirandello's burial instructions: "When I am dead, do not clothe me. Wrap me naked in a sheet. No flowers on the bed and no lighted candle. A pauper's cart. Naked. And let no one accompany me, neither relatives nor friends. The cart, the horse, the coachmen, *e basta* [enough]. Burn me." To his physician: "No need to be so scared of words, doctor. This is called dying." Contrary to his wishes, Pirandello was given a state funeral and buried in his native Sicily.

Alternatives: * "The hearse, the horse, the driver, and- enough!"

* To his son about visions he experienced the previous night: "I look forward to writing down, in a few days, all I imagined in those few hours."

Pissarro, Lucien (1863-1944). French-born Impressionist artist and publisher. At the end: "What's the use?"

Pistorius, Johannes, also called Jan de Bakker (1499-1525). Dutch martyr. Because he refused to recant his Protestant beliefs, Pistorius was condemned to die. As he was burned at the stake, he recited a passage from Corinthians I 15:55: "... O death, where is thy victory? O death, where is thy sting?"

Pitman, Isaac (1813-1897). English educator who devised a widely-used phonic shorthand system. Dying of "congestion of the lungs:" "To those who ask how Isaac Pitman passed away, say: 'peacefully and with no more concern than passing from one room to another to take up some further employment.'"

Pitoëff, Georges (1884-1939). Russian-born French actor and producer. To his wife: "I am going to die in a half-hour... Ludmilla, Ludmilla, you know that there are only 1500 francs left."

Pitt, William, the Elder (1708-1778). British prime minister. Standing to speak in the House of Lords, Pitt suffered a seizure that led to his death. To his son (below): "Go, my son, go whither your country calls you. Let her engross all your attentions. Spare not a moment which is due to her service in weeping over an old man who will soon be no more."

Pitt, William, the Younger (1759-1806). British prime minister. Dying of a stomach ailment, Pitt possibly reflected on the poor turn of events in the current conflict with France: "Oh, my country! How I leave my country!" Some authors have substituted "love" for "leave." Others contend, however, that Pitt's last thoughts dwelled on food: "I think I could eat one of Bellamy's veal pies" or "I think I could eat one of Nicholls' veal pies." At the time of Pitt's death, John Bellamy managed the House of Commons refreshment room and Nicholls served as its butler.

Alternatives: * "Oh, my country! How I love my country!"

* "Oh my country, how I leave thee! Oh my country, how I love thee! My country, oh my country... I think I could eat one of Bellamy's pork pies."
* "Give me one of Bellamy's meat pies."
* "My country! How I love my country! I could do with one of Bellamy's veal pies."

Pius II (1405-1464). Pope from 1458 until his death. Speaking disparagingly to his physician: "One of the miseries of princes is to have flatterers even around their deathbed."

Pius IV (1499-1565). Pope from 1599 until his death. "Lord, now lettest Thou Thy servant depart in peace."

Alternative: * "God's will be done."

Pius V, Saint (1504-1572). Pope from 1566 until his death. "Lord, increase the suffering, but, if it please Thee, increase the patience also."

Pius VI (1717-1799). Pope from 1775 until his death. When Napoleon's army conquered the Papal States in 1798, Pius refused to relinquish his powers and subsequently perished in prison: "Lord, forgive them."

Pius VII (1742-1823). Pope from 1800 until his death. Exiled by Napoleon I to Savona, a city near Genoa, and later Fontainebleau, Pius' last words reflected those places: "Savona... Fontainebleau..."

Pius IX (1792-1878). Pope from 1846 until his death. To his physician: "Death wins this time, doctor." To the cardinals at his bedside: "Guard the church I loved so well and sacredly." When the prayer "Go forth Christian soul," was offered, Pius whispered: "Yes, go forth!" When the Act of Contrition was reiterated: "With the assistance of Thy Holy Grace."

Pius X, Saint (1835-1914). Pope from 1903 until his death. Depressed by the outbreak of WWI, Pius refused to bless the armies of the Holy Roman Empire and dismissed an emissary of Emperor Franz Joseph: "Get out of my sight! Away! Away! We grant blessings to no one who provokes the world to war." As he died, to his confessor: "I resign myself completely."

Alternative: * "I am dying for all the soldiers on the battlefield... I give myself entirely to God's holy will."

Pius XI (1857-1939). Pope from 1922 until his death. Pius XI died of a heart attack and was somewhat inarticulate at the end. Several disparate versions of the pope's last words survive:

* "My soul parts from you all in peace."
* "My soul is in the hands of God."
* "... God is merciful. May his will be done."
* "I still have so many things to do."
* "Jesus and Mary. Peace to the world."

Pizarro, Francisco (c. 1471-1541). Spanish conquistador who subdued the Incan nation. Pizarro was attacked by comrades of a fellow explorer whom he had recently murdered: "What ho! Traitors! Have you come to kill me in my own house?" After his throat was slashed, he managed to mutter: "Jesu!" As he lay dying, he traced a cross with his own blood and kissed it.

Plato (c. 427-c. 347 BCE) Greek philosopher who was a follower of Socrates (below) and teacher of Aristotle. Plato helped lay the groundwork for the development of western philosophy. At the end: "I thank the guiding providence and fortune of my life, first, that I was born a man and a Greek, not a barbarian or a brute; and next, that I happened to live in the age of Socrates."

Platt, Orville (1827-1905). U.S. senator. Dying of pneumonia, to his physician: "You know what this means, doctor, and so do I."

Plotinus (c. 205-270). Egyptian-born Roman philosopher. "I am making my last effort to return that which is divine in me to that which is divine in the universe."

Alternative: * "... Even now I am laboring to return that which is divine in us, unto that Divinity which informs and enlivens the whole universe."

Plowman, Max (1883-1941). English writer, poet and pacifist. A letter to his magazine editor read: "Good wishes to you very sincerely. Do come and see us here someday- even tho' we are bunged up at the moment. And let me know if the enclosed needs revisions. Yours ever, Max P."

Plumb, Preston (1837-1891). Union officer during the U.S. Civil War and later a U.S. senator. A letter to his former secretary read: "Dear Frank, Please come to my room tomorrow (Sunday) about ten o'clock. Yours truly, P.B.P." Plumb died of a stroke shortly thereafter.

Plummer, Henry (1832-1864). American sheriff, suspected of robbery and murder. Strung-up by vigilantes: "You wouldn't hang your own sheriff, would you?" The lynch mob had no problem doing so.

Poe, Edgar Allan (1809-1849). American writer and poet, best-known for his mystery stories and tales of the macabre. Admitted to hospital in a delirious state, Poe called the name "Reynolds" throughout the night. Weakened by his exertions, he said: "Lord, help my poor soul" and died.

Alternative: * In R.H. Stoddard's memoir: "Doctor, it's all over; write 'Eddy is no more.'" As the end neared: "His mind wandered, and his words grew wild, as the waves of life and death kept swaying to and fro in his breast."

Poisson, Jeanne, Madame de Pompadour (1721-1764). Member of the French court and mistress of King Louis XV. Dying of tuberculosis, Madame de Pompadour spoke to her confessor who was departing: "Wait one moment, Monsieur le Curé, and we will both leave together."

Alternative: * Some say Poisson addressed God in her last minutes as she painted her cheeks with rouge: "Wait a second." Regardless, she died shortly thereafter.

Pole, Margaret, Countess of Salisbury (1473-1541). English noblewoman. Because of her family's antagonistic relations with King Henry VIII, Pole was imprisoned in London's Tower and accused of treason. At the scaffold, she was told to yield her head to the block with dignity. Some say she complied and uttered: "Blessed are they who suffer persecution for justice's sake for theirs is the Kingdom of Heaven." However, most accounts relate that Pole put up strong resistance shouting: "No, my head never committed treason, and if you will have it, you must take it as you can." She was dragged to the block and the executioner made a butchery of his work. Multiple blows were required to dispatch the unfortunate noblewoman.

Polk, James (1795-1849). Eleventh U.S. president. Dying of cholera, to his wife: "I love you Sarah. For all eternity, I love you."

Polk, Sarah (1803-1891). Widow of U.S. President James Polk. On her deathbed, Polk asked for "Ice." When her niece tried to feed it with a spoon, she said: "I am *not* a baby, my dear!" Polk died minutes later.

Polo, Marco (1254-1324). Venetian merchant and writer who traveled extensively in Asia. Many felt that the stories of his oriental experiences were fabrications. On his deathbed, Polo told a priest who urged him to recant his tales: "I have not told half of what I saw, for I knew I would not be believed!"

Polycarp, Saint (c. 69-c. 155). Martyred Bishop of Smyrna, Asia Minor. Polycarp refused to renounce his Christian faith when faced with the threat of death: "For eighty six years I have been his servant and he has never done me wrong; how can I blaspheme my King who saved me? I am a Christian; if you wish to study the Christian doctrine, choose a day and you will hear it." To avoid being nailed to the stake: "Let me alone as I am: For he who has given me strength to endure the Fire, will also enable me, without your securing me by nails, to stand without moving in the pile." Before Polycarp was bound to the stake, he spoke to the proconsul: "Thou threatenest me with fire which burns for an hour, and so is extinguished; but knowest not the fire of the future judgment, and of that eternal punishment, which is reserved for the Ungodly. But why tarriest thou? Bring forth what thou wilt!" As he was tied to the stake, Polycarp prayed: "O Father of Thy beloved and blessed Son Jesus Christ, through whom we have attained the knowledge of Thee, O God of angels and principalities, and of all creation, and of all the just who live in Thy sight, I bless Thee that Thou hast counted me worthy of this day, and this hour, to receive my portion in the number of the martyrs, in the cup of Christ for the resurrection to eternal life both of soul and body in the incorporation of the Holy Ghost, among whom may I be received before Thee this day as a sacrifice well-savored and acceptable, which Thou, the faithful God, hast prepared, promised beforehand, and fulfilled accordingly. Wherefore I praise Thee for all these things; I bless Thee, I glorify Thee, by the eternal High Priest, Jesus Christ, Thy well-beloved Son, through whom, with him, in the Holy Spirit, be glory to Thee, both now and forever. Amen." When the flames failed to consume him, Polycarp was slain by the sword.

Pompadour, Madame de (see Poisson, Jeanne Antoinette).

Pompey, Gnaeus (106-48 BCE). Roman military and political leader. Defeated in a power struggle with Julius Caesar, Pompey fled to Egypt and was assassinated on orders of the sitting king. To the man who stabbed him: "I am not mistaken, surely, in believing you to have been formerly my fellow-soldier."

Pompidou, Georges (1911-1974). French prime minister. Dying of cancer, to a friend: "You cannot know what I am suffering."

Poniatowski, Prince Józef (1763-1813). Polish military leader who participated in Napoleon's Russian campaign. While providing aid to retreating French troops, a bridge crucial to Poniatowski's escape was destroyed: "Gentlemen, it now behooves us to die with honor." Severely wounded, he plunged into the river and died.

Ponselle, Rosa (1897-1981). American operatic soprano. Dying of cancer, Ponselle spoke about one of her favorite operas, Verdi's *La Forza del Destino*: "...It's ironic. It's as if my whole life has been the *Force of Destiny*."

Poole, William "Bill the Butcher" (1821-1855). American gang leader who was a butcher by trade. Poole became a member of the Know Nothing political party that tried to limit German and Irish immigration. Gunned down by a rival: "Goodbye, boys! I die a true American. What grieves me most is thinking that I have been murdered by a set of Irish."

Alternative: * "I think I am a goner. If I die, I die a true American."

Pope, Alexander (1688-1744). English poet and writer, best-known for his poem *Rape of the Lock*. Dying of "a dropsy in the breast," Pope was asked if he wished to see a priest: "I do not think it is essential, but it will be very right, and I thank you for putting me in mind of it." To a friend who inquired about his health: "Here am I, dying of a hundred good symptoms." Reportedly, Pope's last statement was: "There is nothing meritorious but virtue and friendship, and indeed, friendship itself is only a part of virtue!"

Pope, William (died 1797). Leader of an English atheist cult that often kicked a Bible around the floor during meetings. On his deathbed: "I have no contrition. I cannot repent. God will damn me. I know the day of grace is past. You see one who is damned forever. Oh, Eternity! Eternity! Nothing for me but hell. Come eternal torments... Do you not see? Do you not see him? He is coming for me. Oh, the burning flame, the hell, the pain that I feel. Eternity will explain my torment" Asked if he wished a prayer said for him, Pope cried: "No."

Alternatives: * "I have done the damnable deed. The horrible damnable deed. I cannot pray. God will have nothing to do with me. I will not have salvation at His hands. I long to be in the bottomless pit, the lake which burneth with fire and brimstone. I tell you I am damned. I will not have salvation. Nothing for me but hell. Come eternal torments. Oh God, do not hear my prayers for I will not be saved. I hate everything God has made!"

* "I long to die that I may be in the place of perdition that I may know the worst of it. My damnation is sealed!"

Porter, Henry (1941-1985). Mexican American criminal, executed by lethal injection for the murder of a police officer: "... This is America's equal justice. A Mexican's life is worth nothing. When a policeman kills someone, he gets a suspended sentence or probation. When a Mexican kills a police officer, this is what you get. From there you call me a cold-blooded murderer. I didn't tie anyone to a stretcher. I didn't pump any poison into anybody's veins from behind a locked door. You call this justice? I call this and your society a bunch of cold-blooded murderers... I hope that God will be as merciful to society as he has been to me. I'm ready, warden."

Porter, Katherine (1890-1980). American writer who was awarded the 1966 Pulitzer Prize for her collected stories. To the nun caring for her: "Death is beautiful. I long to die. I love God. I know that He loves me." When told that eternity would be a far better place than her earthly existence: "Oh yes, I know that."

Porter, Noah (1811-1892). American minister, educator and lexicographer. To his daughter: "Go, call your mother. Wake her up. I want to consult with her."

Porter, William Sidney (see Henry, O.).

Porteous, Beilby (1731-1808). Bishop of London, chaplain to King George III and abolitionist. "Oh, that glorious sun."

Pot, Pol, born Saloth Sar (1925-1998). Cambodian dictator who led the notorious Khmer Rouge during the last quarter of the 20th century. Due to the brutality of his totalitarian regime, an estimated quarter of the Cambodian population perished. Dying in captivity, Pot responded to a reported who asked if the dictator regretted his bloody actions: "No, I want you to know. Everything I did, I did for my country."

Potamiaena, Saint (died c. 205). Egyptian martyr. Condemned to die because of her Christian faith, Potamiaena said to the executioner who had poured boiling pitch over her body to prevent gang-rape: "When I am in heaven, I will ask the Lord to repay you for all that you have done for me."

Pothinus, Saint (c. 87-c. 177). French Bishop of Lyon. Persecuted and imprisoned by the Romans, Pothinus was asked by his guards (some say the governor) about the Christian God. He replied: "If you are worthy, you shall know." He then was beaten unconscious and died in his prison cell several days later.

Potter, Beatrix (1866-1943). English writer and illustrator, best-known for her children's books that featured animals such as Peter Rabbit. To the caretaker of her estate: "I'm dying. Stay on and maintain the farm for Mr. Heelis [her husband] when I am gone." Her last letter: "Dear Joe Moscrop [her master shepherd], Still some strength in me. I write a line to shake you by the hand; our friendship has been entirely pleasant. I am very ill with bronchitis. With best wishes for the New Year."

Powell, Adam Clayton, Jr. (1908-1972). U.S. congressman, civil rights activist and clergyman. Dying from complications of prostate surgery, to a female reporter who entered his hospital room requesting an interview: "Sweetheart, I don't feel up to it now. Come back later."

Powell, Lewis, also called Lewis Paine (1844-1865). One of the American co-conspirators in the Abraham Lincoln assassination. Powell failed to assassinate U.S. Secretary of State William Seward during the unfolding of the conspiracy. Before his hanging, Powell asserted: "If I had two lives to give, I'd give one gladly to save Mrs. Surratt [also hanged for her alleged participation (below)]. I know that she is innocent and would never die in this way if I hadn't been found in her house. She knew nothing about the conspiracy at all and is an innocent woman." To the hangman who wished him a quick death: "You know best, captain. I thank you; goodbye"

Power, Tyrone (1914-1958). American film and stage actor. After collapsing from a heart attack while filming *Solomon and Sheba*, Power told a friend: "Don't worry. The same thing happened about a week ago."

Preble, Edward (1761-1807). U.S. naval officer who distinguished himself during the North African 1st Barbary War. Dying from a wasting illness, to an old shipmate: "To die on a bed of glory would be something, but to die of a stinking consumption is too bad." Later, to his brother: "Give me your hand, Enoch! I'm going. Give me your hand."

Prentiss, Elizabeth (1818-1878). American writer, poet and hymnodist. To her husband: "Darling, don't you think you could ask the Lord to let me go?" On her bedroom wall, she had hung the motto: "Patience, my heart! Be still, my will."

Prescott, William (1796-1859). American historian. Because of his long-standing poor eyesight, Prescott's secretary read from a book on Russia. When the historian asked about a certain diplomat, neither could recall his name. When his wife supplied the name, Prescott inquired: "How came *you* to remember?" He retired to another room, suffered a stroke and died.

Presley, Elvis (1935-1977). American actor and singer, popularly called "The King of Rock and Roll." On the day of his death, Presley told a female companion that he was going to the bathroom to read. She asked him not to fall asleep, and he replied: "Okay, I won't." Presley later was found dead from a suspected drug overdose.

Alternatives: * "Precious, I'm going to go into the bathroom and read."
* "I'm going to the can, Ginger."

Preston, John (1587-1628). English minister and writer. When asked if he feared death: "No... Blessed be God. Though I change my place, I shall not change my company, for I have walked with God while living and now I go to rest with God." At the end: "I feel death coming to my heart; my pain shall now be turned into joy."

Priestley, Joseph (1733-1804). English chemist, theologian and political theorist who discovered the element oxygen. To his grandchildren and attendants the day before he expired: "I am going to sleep like you, but we shall all awake together, and I trust to everlasting happiness." After finishing some corrections to his work *The Doctrines of Heathen Philosophy*: "That is right. I have now done." He died within the hour.

Alternative: * "I am going to sleep as well as you; for death is only a good long sound sleep in the grave, and we shall meet again."

Prinze, Freddie, born Frederick Pruetzel (1954-1977). American comedian and actor. Before committing suicide by a gunshot to the head, the depressed Prinze telephoned his estranged wife: "I love you, Kathy. I love the baby, but I need to find peace. I can't go on." His suicide note read: "I must end it. There's no hope left. I'll be at peace. No one had anything to do with this. My decision totally- Freddie Prinze P.S. I'm sorry. Forgive me. Dusty's here [his business manager]. He's innocent. He cared."

Prisca, Saint, also Priscilla (birth and death dates uncertain). Early Roman Christian martyr. Prisca was tortured extensively and later beheaded for her religious beliefs. "My courage and my mind are so firmly founded upon the firm stone of my Lord Jesus Christ that no assault can move me. Your words are but wind, your promises are but rain, your menaces are passing floods and however hardly these things hurtle at the foundation of my courage, they cannot change me."

Pro Juárez, Miguel (1891-1927). Mexican Catholic priest falsely accused of sedition. Standing before the firing squad: "Long live Christ the King!"

Probus, Saint (died c. 304). Christian martyr from present-day Turkey. Probus refused to renounce his Christian religion and was imprisoned with two fellow martyrs, Andronicus (above) and Tarachus (below). A proconsul urged Probus to deny Christ, promising him honors from the Emperor and his own friendship: "I neither desire imperial honors nor seek your friendship." The martyrs were tortured and later hacked to death.

Alternative: "I expect nothing from you [the proconsul] but a cruel death; and I ask of God only the grace to persevere in the confession of his holy name to the end."

Protasius, Saint (fl. 1st or 2nd century). Italian holy man, son of Saint Vitalis and Saint Valeria and brother of Saint Gervasius. The brothers were martyred for their Christian beliefs by order of the war-monger Count Astasius: "I am not angry with you, Count, because I expect the eyes of your heart to be blind; but I pity you, because you do not know what you are doing! Finish what you have begun, then, so that the loving-kindness of our Savior may embrace me with my brother!" Both were beaten. Gervasius succumbed to his wounds, and Protasius was beheaded.

Proust, Marcel (1871-1922). French novelist, author of *Remembrance of Things Past.* Dying of pneumonia and a lung abscess, Proust was asked by his brother if he were causing pain: "Yes, Robert dear, you are."

Puccini, Giacomo (1858-1924). Italian composer, best-known for his operas *La Bohème, Madame Butterfly* and *Tosca.* Dying from complications of throat cancer, Puccini whispered: "My poor Elvira, my poor wife."

Alternative: * To his stepdaughter: "Remember that your mother is a remarkable woman."

Puglisi, Pino (1937-1993). Sicilian priest, shot dead because of his opposition to the local Mafia. To his assassin: "I expected it to happen."

Alternative: * "I've been expecting you."

Pulitzer, Joseph (1847-1911). Hungarian-born American newspaper publisher whose awards for meritorious writing and photography bear his name. Because of a hypersensitivity to sound, Pulitzer admonished a friend reading to him: "Softly, quite softly, quite softly."

Pusey, Edward (1800-1882). English Anglican priest and Hebrew scholar. To friends gathered at his deathbed: "By His authority committed unto me, I absolve thee from all thy sins." He then said "My God!" and died.

Pushkin, Alexander (1799-1837). Russian poet and writer, best-known for his play *Boris Godunov.* Mortally wounded in a duel over his wife's honor, Pushkin addressed his books: "Farewell, my friends." To his wife: "Try to be forgotten. Go live in the country. Stay in mourning for two years, then remarry, but choose somebody decent." When a friend adjusted his position, Pushkin exclaimed: "Life is finished!" The friend misunderstood and commented: "Yes, it is finished. We have turned you round." Pushkin replied distinctly: "I can't breathe! I am stifling!" and died.

Alternatives: * "It is over with life. Breathing becomes difficult. It suffocates me."
* "I said *life* is over. I can't breathe. Something is crushing me."

Pushmataha (c. 1764-1824). Native American Choctaw chief. Pushmataha persuaded his Choctaw tribe to fight on the American side during the War of 1812. Dying of pneumonia nearly a decade later, to his companions: "I shall die, but you will return to our brethren. As you go along the paths you will see the flowers and hear the birds sing but Pushmataha will see and hear them no more. When you shall come to your home, they will ask you, where is Pushmataha? And you will say to them He is no more. They shall hear the tidings like the sound of the fall of a mighty oak in the stillness of the wood."

Putnam, Israel (1718-1790). American Revolutionary War officer. A stroke ended his military career in 1779, and he died 11 years later: "I am resigned to the will of God and am willing to die now."

Pyle, Ernest "Ernie" (1900-1945). American war correspondent who won a Pulitzer Prize in 1944 for his reporting in both European and Pacific combat theaters. While on an island near Okinawa, Pyle's jeep was hit by enemy fire. He asked a companion: "Are you all right?" Moments later, Pyle was mortally wounded by a gunshot to the head.

Pythagoras (c. 570-c. 495 BCE). Greek philosopher and mathematician. An apocryphal account allows that Pythagoras supposedly angered certain members of society when they were denied entry into his exclusive circle. In retribution, they set fire to a house where he and his students were staying. Escaping the conflagration, they came to a field of beans. Pythagoras refused to trample through the crop stating: "It is better to perish here than to kill all these poor beans." He and most of his students were massacred when the assassins caught up with them.

Quarles, Francis (1592-1644). English poet and writer, best-known for his book *Emblems*. As he died, Quarles prayed: "O sweet Savior of the world, let thy last words upon the cross be my last words in this world: Into Thy hands, Lord, I commend my spirit. And what I cannot utter with my mouth, accept from my heart and soul."

Quattrocchi, Fabrizio (1968-2004). Italian security officer, taken hostage by militants in the early stage of the Iraq War. When his captors came to execute him, Quattrocchi defiantly shouted: "Now I will show you how an Italian dies!" He was shot dead.

Quezon, Manuel (1878-1944). Exiled President of the Philippines. When told that American forces had landed in New Guinea and were preparing to liberate the Philippines, Quezon said: "Just six hundred miles!"

Quick, John (1748-1831). English actor and comedian, favored by King George III. "Is this death?"

Quijano, Alfredo (1890-1927). Mexican revolutionary, condemned to die for his rebellious acts against the government. To observers at his execution: "Goodbye, goodbye." To the firing squad: "You are too far away. Come closer." After they moved a few steps, he urged: "You are still too far away. You had better come still closer." When asked if he desired a blindfold, Quijano defiantly said: "No!"

Quin, James (1693-1766). English actor and comedian. Dying of a fever: "I could wish that the last tragic scene were over, and I hope I may be enabled to meet and pass through it with dignity."

Alternative: * "I could wish this tragic scene were over, but I hope to go through it with becoming modesty."

Quisling, Vidkun (1887-1945). Norwegian politician and WWII Nazi sympathizer who was shot as a traitor. To those at his execution: "I'm convicted unfairly, and I die innocent." To members of the firing squad: "Do not allow your conscience to trouble you in later years, not on my account. You are acting under orders, and are only doing your duty as soldiers, like myself."

Quitman, John (1798-1858). American military leader, Mississippi governor and U.S. congressman. When Quitman's daughter urged the ailing man to put his trust in the Lord, he replied: "I *do*, my child."

Alternative: * "Yes, yes. I know it. He is my trust."

Rabelais, François (c. 1494 -1553). French Renaissance writer, satirist, doctor, monk and scholar, best-known for his collection of novels *The Life of Gargantua and Pantagruel.* On his deathbed, Rabelais supposedly replied to an inquiry about his condition made by a cardinal's page: "Tell my lord the state in which you find me. I am off in search of a great may-be. He is up at the top of the tree; tell him to keep there. As for you, you'll never be aught but a fool. Let the curtain fall, the farce is played out." After wrapping himself in a domino, a hooded garment, Rabelais made a Latin pun: "*Beati qui in domino moriuntur* [Blessed are those who die in the Lord, or Blessed are those who die wearing a cloak]."

Variations of his last words:

* "Tell my lord in what circumstances thou findest me. I am just going to leap into the dark. He is up in the cock-loft; bid him keep where he

is. As for thee, thou'lt always be a fool. Let down the curtain, the farce is done." Calling for his hooded cloak: "Put me on my domino, for I am cold. Besides, I will die in it, for *Beati qui in domino moriuntur*."

* "I am going to seek the great perhaps."
* "I am off in search of the great perhaps."
* "I am going to the great perhaps."
* "I am going to seek a great purpose. Draw the curtain. The farce is played."
* "I am going to seek a grand perhaps; draw the curtain, the farce is played."
* "I am going to seek a great perhaps. Bring down the curtain, the farce is played out."
* "Ring down the curtain; the farce is over. I go to seek the great perhaps."
* "Let down the curtain, the farce is over."
* "Draw the curtain. The farce is ended."
* Possibly alluding to the oil used for the Sacraments of Extreme Unction: "My boots have been greased for the long journey."

Variations of his will:

* "I owe much. I have nothing. I give the rest to the poor."
* "I have nothing, I owe a great deal, and the rest I leave to the poor."
* "I have nothing. I owe much. The rest I leave to the poor."

Rachel, Mademoiselle, born Élisa Rachel Félix (1820-1858). Swiss-born French actress. Dying of tuberculosis: "I am happy to die on a Sunday. It is sad to die on a Monday." She indeed died on a Sunday.

Alternative: * "My poor Rebecca, my dear sister, I am going to see thee! I am indeed happy."

Rachmaninoff, Sergei (1873-1943). Russian-born pianist, conductor and composer. Shortly before dying of metastatic melanoma, Rachmaninoff remarked that he heard music close by. When told none was being played, he said: "A-a-ah... that means it's playing in my head."

Racine, Jean (1639-1699). French dramatist and poet. To his friend Nicolas Boileau (above): "I look upon it as a great blessing for me to have died before you." When told by his son that his doctors felt he was improving: "Let them have their say. We are not going to contradict them. But, my son, would you, too, deceive me? Are you, too, in the conspiracy? Believe me that God alone is master of the event. And I can assure you that, did He grant me the option- living or dying at choice- I should not know which to choose. But I have paid the price of death."

Radcliffe, Ann (1764-1823). English writer and poet. Dying of a respiratory ailment, to her husband who was feeding her: "There is some substance in that." Radcliffe died several hours later.

Radcliffe, James (1689-1716). English Jacobite rebel who was accused of treason. To the executioner before his beheading: "I am but a poor man. There's ten guineas for you. If I had more, I would give it to you. I desire you to do your office so as to put me to the least misery as you can."

Radcliffe, John (c. 1650-1714). English physician, politician and philanthropist. The conclusion of a letter to his sister Millicent read: "… I have nothing further than to beseech the Divine Being who is the God of the living to prosper you and all my relations with good and unblameable lives, that when you shall change the world you are now in, for a better, we may all meet together in glory and enjoy these ineffable delights which are promised to all that love Christ's coming. Till then, my dear, dear Milly, take this as a last farewell from your Affectionate and Dying Brother, J. Radcliffe. N.B. The Jewels and Rings in my gilt cabinet, by my Great Scrutore [a writing desk], not mentioned in my will, I hereby bequeath to you."

Ragaway, Martin (1923-1989). American film and television writer. Dying of cancer and unable to speak, Ragaway wrote: "Game's over, we all lose."

Raleigh, Walter (c. 1552-1618) English courtier, soldier and explorer. Although a favorite of Queen Elizabeth I, Raleigh later came afoul of King James I for "intrigues against the crown" and aggressive acts against the Spanish in South America. Accused of treason under sentence of death, Raleigh contemplated his fate: "... I have a long journey to take, and must bid the company farewell. I have been a man of many ventures, and now

I embark on the last and longest. So, I take my leave of you, making my peace with God." When the condemned man approached the executioner, he saw a bald man and threw him his cap saying: "Thou hast more need of this than I." At the scaffold: "Now I am going to God." After feeling the edge of the executioner's axe: "Dost thou think that I am afraid of it? This is that that will cure all sorrows." When Raleigh was asked to place his head a certain way on the block, he said: "What matter, which way the head lie, so the heart be right." Refusing a blindfold: "Think you that I fear the shadow of the axe when I fear not the substance." To the assembled people: "Give me heartily your prayers." Urging the reluctant executioner to commence: "Strike, man, strike! What dost thou fear?" Lady Raleigh retained her husband's embalmed head until her death.

Alternatives: * "Do you think I am a babe to fear steel? 'Tis a sharp medicine, but 'tis a sure cure for all diseases."

* "This is a sharp Medicine, but it is a Physician for all diseases and miseries."
* "This is a sharp medicine, but a sure remedy for all evils!"
* "Tis a sharp remedy, but a sure one for all ills."
* "This is a sharp, but sure remedy against all miseries and disease."
* "Show me the axe, show me the axe. This gives me no fear. It is a sharp medicine to cure me of all my diseases."
* "Tis a sharp medicine, but a sound cure for all diseases."
* "This is a sharp medicine to cure all my diseases."
* "It matters not how the head lies provided the heart be right. Now I am going to God."
* "No matter how the head lies, so that the heart be right."
* "What matter how the head lies, so the heart be right."
* "So that the heart be right, it is no matter which way the head lieth"
* "Why dost thou not strike? Strike, man!"

Ralston, William "Billy" (1826-1875). American businessman, financier and founder of the Bank of California. After the collapse of his financial empire, Ralston drowned in San Francisco Bay: "Keep these [clothes] for me. There are valuable papers in my pocket." It is unclear whether his death resulted from natural causes or a suicide.

Ramakrishna, born Gadadhar Chatterjee (1836-1886). Indian-born Hindu philosopher and religious leader. Before dying of cancer, Ramakrishna called the name of the Hindu goddess: "Kali! Kali! Kali!"

Ramdass, Bobby (1963-2000). American criminal, executed by lethal injection for the murder of a convenience store worker during a robbery: "Redskins are going to the Super Bowl." Ramdass' prediction was wrong.

Rameau, Jean-Philippe (1683-1764). French composer and keyboard artist, prominent during the Baroque era. To his confessor: "What the devil do you mean singing to me, priest? You are out of tune."

Alternatives: * "Why the devil do you have to sing to me, *Monsieur le Curé*? Your voice is out of tune!"

* "What the devil are you trying to sing, *monsieur le curé*? Your voice is out of tune!"

Ramée, Louise de la (see Ouida).

Ramsay, David (1749-1815). American physician, politician and Revolutionary War historian. Ramsay was shot and killed by a criminal he examined and deemed deranged. "I know not if these wounds be mortal. I am not afraid to die; but should that be my fate I call on all here present to bear witness that I consider the unfortunate perpetrator of this deed a lunatic and, free from guilt."

Ramseur, Stephen (1837-1864). Confederate general in the U.S. Civil War. Mortally wounded during the Battle of Cedar Creek in northern Virginia, Ramseur dictated a farewell letter to his wife: "Bear this message to my precious wife. I die a Christian and hope to meet her in Heaven."

Alternative: * "I have a firm hope in Christ, and I trust to meet you hereafter."

Randolph, John (1773-1833). American statesman who became a member of the U.S. House of Representatives and Senate. Succumbing to tuberculosis and an erratic mind, to an attendant: "Remorse, remorse,

remorse! Let me see the word. Get a dictionary. Let me see the word." When no dictionary could be found, the word "remorse" was written on one of Randolph's engraved calling cards: "Remorse! You have no idea what it is… It has contributed to bring me to my present situation; but I have looked to the Lord Jesus Christ and hope I have obtained pardon." Referring to the card: "Put it in your pocket. When I am dead, look at it." Later: "I cast myself on the Lord Jesus Christ for mercy." Before expiring, Randolph penned a rambling note to his children: "Dying. Home... Randolph and Betty, my children, adieu! Get me to bed at Chatham or elsewhere, say Hugh Mercer's or Minor's. To bed I conjure you all!"

Rank, Otto, born Otto Rosenfeld (1884-1939). Austrian psychoanalyst and colleague of Sigmund Freud (above). Dying from complications of a kidney infection, Rank referred to death as: "Comical."

Raphael, born Raffaello Sanzio da Urbino (1483-1520). Italian Renaissance artist and architect, best-known for his Madonnas and large figure compositions. Dying of an acute febrile illness: "Whence comes the sunshine?" His last word: "Happy..."

Rappe, Virginia (1895-1921). Hollywood actress. Rappe died under suspicious circumstances after attending a party given by the actor Roscoe "Fatty" Arbuckle. A witness at Arbuckle's subsequent murder trial testified that the actress said: "I'm dying. I'm dying... he [Arbuckle] hurt me!" Later the witness recanted, alleging that Rappe only said: "I'm dying. I'm dying." Arbuckle eventually was acquitted of any wrongdoing.

Rasputin, Grigori (c. 1871-1916). Siberian-born faith-healer and mystic. A number of noblemen in the court of Tsar Nicholas II (above) resented Rasputin's influence over the tsar and tsarina and subsequently devised a plan to eliminate him. Poisoned, shot and mutilated by a group of these men, Rasputin cried: "May God forgive you... What do they want of me? What do they want?"

Alternative: * After Felix Yusupov, a Russian aristocrat, shot Rasputin in the chest, the mystic ran through the palace yard screaming: "Felix,

Felix, I'll tell the tsarina everything." He was shot again and his body was dumped into a nearby river.

Rathbone, Basil (1892-1967). South African-born British stage and film actor. Dying of a heart attack, Rathbone spoke to his wife: "You know, I'm not afraid to die, but I just wish it didn't have to be!"

Ravachol, born François Koenigstein (1859-1892). French anarchist and murderer. Ravachol was sent to the guillotine for bombing houses belonging to two French officials. Before the blade fell: "Goodbye, you pigs! Long live anarchy."

Ravaillac, François (1578-1610). Assassin of French King Henri IV. Before his execution, Ravaillac was told that that absolution could be given only if he disclosed his accomplices: "I have none. It is I alone that did it. Give me a conditional absolution. You cannot refuse this." When told that eternal damnation would follow if any abettors were discovered: "I receive absolution upon this condition." The assassin then had his flesh torn by hot pincers, his wounds flooded with hot metal and oil and his body drawn and quartered.

Alternative: * "Give it me conditionally upon condition that I have told the truth."

Ravel, Maurice (1875-1937). French composer and pianist. Following an operation for a suspected brain tumor, Ravel rallied briefly and was asked if he would like to see his brother: "Ah! Yes indeed." After viewing his bandaged head in a mirror, the musician quipped: "I look like a Moor." He lapsed into a coma and died nine days later.

Ray, John, also Wray (1627-1705). English naturalist and writer. The conclusion of Ray's farewell letter to a friend read: "... When you happen to write to my singular friend, Dr. Hotton [a botany professor], I pray tell him I received his most obliging and affectionate letter, for which I return thanks, and acquaint that I am not able to answer it."

Read, Thomas (1822-1872). American poet and portrait painter. "Sweet are the kisses of one's friends."

Récamier, Jeanne (1777-1849). French socialite. Dying of cholera, to her niece: "We shall meet again, we shall meet again."

Red Jacket, also called Sagoyewatha (c. 1758-1830). Native American Seneca chief and orator. Red Jacket took his name from a favored coat given to him by the British. Dying of cholera, to his family: "I am going to die. I shall never leave this house again alive... When I am dead, it will be noised [talked about] abroad through all the world. They will hear of it across the great waters and say: 'Red Jacket, the great orator, is dead.' And white men will come and ask you for my body. They will wish to bury me. But do not let them take me. Clothe me in my simplest dress, put on my leggings and my moccasins and hang the cross, which I have worn so long, around my neck and let it lie on my bosom. Then bury me among my people. Neither do I wish to be buried with pagan rites. I wish the ceremonies to be as you like, according to the customs of your new religion [some family members converted to Christianity], if you choose. Your ministers say the dead will rise. Perhaps they will. If they do, I wish to rise with my old comrades. I do not wish to rise among pale faces. I wish to be surrounded by red men. Do not make a feast according to the custom of the Indians. Whenever my friends chose, they could come and feast with me when I was well, and I do not wish those who have never eaten with me in my cabin to surfeit at my funeral feast." Red Jacket then asked for the local minister: "I do not hate him. He thinks I hate him, but I do not. I would not hurt him." When told that the minister could not come: "Very well, the Great Spirit will order it as He sees best, whether I have an opportunity to speak with him." Of the missionary: "He accused me of being a snake and trying to bite somebody. This was true and I wish to repent and make satisfaction." As he died, to his family: "Where is the missionary?" Red Jacket initially was buried in a Native-American cemetery, but his remains were transferred later to a grave in Buffalo, New York.

Reed. John (1887-1920). American journalist and communist activist who covered the 1917 Bolshevik Revolution. Dying of typhus, to his wife: "You know how it is, when you go to Venice. You ask people: 'Is this Venice?' just for the pleasure of hearing the reply."

Reed, Thomas (1839-1902). American politician who became speaker of the U.S. House of Representatives. Dying of a heart attack, Reed experienced periods of delirium. To his physician who had administered a "remedy:" "Doctor, you have no legal right to do that! It is the third time you have taken the liberty. I will have you to understand that the citizen is not obliged to submit to the dictation of the man with the hoe."

Reed, Major Walter (1851-1902). American Army physician, best-known for his work, which helped control mosquito-borne yellow fever. Dying after surgery for a ruptured appendix: "I leave so much." On hearing the recommendation of his promotion to colonel, Reed frowned and said: "I care nothing for that now."

Rees, John (birth and death dates unclear). English clergyman. To a fellow minister who asked about his state of mind: "Christ in his person, Christ in the love of his heart, and Christ in the power of his arm, is the rock on which I rest; and now, death, strike!"

Reeves, George, born George Keefer Brewer (1914-1959) American actor, best-known for his Superman role in the television series. Depressed because of difficulty finding work, Reeves spoke to friends before shooting himself in the head: "I'm tired. I'm going back to bed." His death was ruled a suicide, but some have challenged that conclusion.

Remington, Frederic (1861-1909). American artist and sculptor, best-known for his old American West depictions. When told he needed an appendectomy, Remington quipped: "Cut her loose, Doc!" He died of postoperative peritonitis.

Rénan, Joseph-Ernest (1823-1892). French philosopher, philologist, historian and writer. To his wife: "Courage, little one, one must submit to the laws of nature, of which we are the manifestation. We all pass on.

The heavens alone remain." Later, he shouted several times: "Have mercy on me!" Rénan then ranted about architecture and said: "Take away this sun from above the Acropolis!" When asked for a clarification, his last utterance was: "I know what I'm saying, but my words are dense."

Alternatives: * To his wife: "Why are you sad? Be calm and resigned. We undergo the laws of that nature of which we are a manifestation. We perish, we disappear; but heaven and earth remain and the march of time goes on forever."

* "I have done my work. I die happy. It is the most natural thing in the world to die; let us accept the Laws of the Universe the heavens and the earth remain."
* "Let us submit to the Laws of Nature of which we are one of the manifestations. The heavens and the earth abide."

Reno, Jesse (1823-1862). Union officer during the U.S. Civil War. On a reconnoitering mission near South Mountain, Maryland, Reno was mortally wounded by Confederate troops. Carried to a rear area, he spoke to a colleague, General Samuel Sturgis: "Hallo, Sam, I'm dead!" When Sturgis remarked that the wounded man must be joking, Reno replied: "Yes, yes, I'm dead. Goodbye." As he was tended by surgeons: "Tell my command that if not in body, I will be with them in spirit."

Renoir, Pierre (1841-1919). French Impressionist artist. Severely limited by arthritis in his later years, Renoir claimed after completing his last painting: "I think I am beginning to understand something about it... Today I learned something."

Alternative: * "I am still progressing."

Renslow, Marvin (1961-2009). American pilot of a commercial turboprop airplane inbound to Buffalo Niagara International Airport on a cold evening. Moments before losing control of the aircraft, First Officer Rebecca Shaw (below) commented on icing conditions affecting the flight. As the plane plunged toward the ground, Renslow shouted: "Jesus Christ... [unintelligible]... ther bear... gear up oh (expletive)... we're down!" All 49 aboard the aircraft and one person on the ground perished.

Renwick, James (1662-1688). Scottish martyr. Refusing to acknowledge the divine right of the Scottish king, Renwick was condemned to die by hanging. On the scaffold: "Lord, into Thy hands I commend my spirit, for Thou hast redeemed me, Lord God of truth."

Retzins, Jahan (1742-1821). Swedish naturalist and chemist. On his deathbed, Retzins made note of his dissolution: "Now the legs are dead. Now the muscles of the bowels cease their functions. The last struggle must be heavy, but for all that, it is intensely interesting."

Revel, Bernard (1885-1940). Lithuanian-born rabbi and scholar. Dying of a stroke: "I hope you have lived long enough with me not to resent the fact that I shall not live long. You don't measure life by the yardstick of years, but by accomplishments and achievements. It was my privilege to serve God, the Torah and the children of the Torah."

Reynolds, John (1820-1863). Union general who served during the U.S. Civil War. As Reynolds led his troops at the Battle of Gettysburg, Pennsylvania, he sustained a mortal wound to the head: "Forward, men, forward for God's sake and drive those fellows out of those woods!"

Alternative: * "Forward, forward men! Drive those fellows out of that! Forward! For God's sake, forward!"

Reynolds, Joshua (1723-1792). English artist, best-known for his portraits. Dying from "an enlargement of the liver:" "I have been fortunate in long good health and constant success, and I ought not to complain. I know that all things on earth must have an end, and now I am come to mine."

Rhodes, Cecil (1853-1902). English-born South African businessman, politician and philanthropist who helped colonize Rhodesia (present-day Zimbabwe). Dying of heart failure: "When I am dead, let there be no fuss. Lay me in my grave. Tread down the earth and pass on. I shall have done my work." As death neared: "So much to do; so little done." Before Rhodes expired, he asked one of his secretaries to: "Turn me over, Jack."

Alternative: * "So little done, so much to do."

Ribbentrop, Joachim von (1893-1946). German Nazi foreign minister during WWII. Hanged as a war criminal for offences against humanity: "God protect Germany. May I say something else?" When told he could: "My last wish is that Germany realize its entity and that an understanding be reached between the East and the West. I wish peace to the world." Before the hood was placed over his head, to a chaplain: "I'll see you again."

Alternatives: * "God save Germany! My last wish is that Germany rediscover her unity and that an alliance be made between East and West and that peace reign on earth."

* "God protect Germany. God have mercy on my soul. My final wish is that Germany should recover her unity and that, for the sake of peace, there should be understanding between East and West. I wish peace to the world."

Rice, James (1828-1864). American lawyer and Union officer who served in the Forty-fourth New York Infantry Regiment during the U.S. Civil War. Mortally wounded at Spotsylvania, Virginia: "Tell the Forty-fourth I am done fighting. Turn me over and let me die with my face to the enemy."

Rice, John (1777-1831). American clergyman, writer and educator. To his wife: "Mercy is triumphant." As Rice spoke his last word, his voice fell, prompting a friend to ask: "Was it 'great?'" When his wife replied: "No, it was a longer word," Rice repeated the word "Triumphant" and died.

Rich, Bernard "Buddy" (1917-1987). American jazz musician, billed as the "Best Drummer in the World." Before surgery for a brain tumor, his nurse asked if he were allergic to anything: "Yeah, country music." Rich died postoperatively.

Alternative: * "Only two things- country and western."

Rich, James (1972-1999). American criminal, executed by lethal injection for the murder of a fellow inmate: "All praise and glory be to Allah ... may he bless this whole world with peace and his utmost blessings and may he bless this world with his utmost mercy."

Rich, Mary, Countess of Warwick (1625-1678). Irish aristocrat and writer. On her deathbed, Mary spoke to her attendants: "Well, ladies, if I were one hour in heaven, I should not wish to be again with you, much as I love you."

Richard I, The Fearless (933-996). French nobleman who led the feudal state of Normandy. Richard decreed in his will that his body be placed under the chapel eaves so: "... that the dripping of the rain from the holy roof may wash my bones as I lie, and may cleanse them of the spots of impurity contracted during a negligent and neglected life."

Richard I, The Lionhearted (1157-1199). English king and commander during the Third Crusade. Later, while besieging a castle in the Limousin province of France, Richard was shot in the left shoulder by a young archer. When the defender was captured, the king magnanimously said: "Live on, and by my bounty behold the light of day... Young man, I forgive you my death. Let him go, but not empty handed; give him a hundred pieces and free him from these chains." Dying in his mother's arms from complications of his gangrenous wound: "I place all my trust, after God, in thee, that thou wilt make provision for my soul's welfare with motherly care, to the utmost of thy power."

Alternative: * "Youth, I forgive thee! Take off his chains, give him 100 shillings and let him go."

Richard III (1452-1485). King of England. At the Battle of Bosworth Field against Henry Tudor, Richard was unhorsed and mortally wounded: "I will die King of England. I will not budge a foot." Because some of his men had defected, he shouted before dying: "Treason, treason!" Contrary to popular belief, the king probably did not utter the famous Shakespearian quote from *Richard III*: "A horse! A horse! My kingdom for a horse," as his final statement.

Richard, Michael (1959-2007). American criminal, executed by lethal injection for the rape and murder of a Texas woman: "I'd like my family to take care of each other. I love you, Angel. Let's ride. I guess this is it."

Richelieu, Cardinal, born Armand du Plessis (1585-1642). French clergyman, statesman and chief minister of Louis XIII. The priest attending Richelieu on his deathbed asked if he forgave his enemies: "Absolutely, and I pray God to condemn me, if I have had any other aim than the welfare of God and the state." Others record that he stated his belief more succinctly to the effect: "I have no enemies save those of the state." On the evening of Richelieu's death, the queen sent a messenger to inquire about his health: "I am very ill, and tell her majesty that if, in the course of my life, she has considered that I have given her cause of complaint, I most humbly beg her to pardon me." He died moments later.

Alternative: * To his niece who showed him a relic with supposed mystical powers: "Niece, there are no truths but those in the Gospels. One should believe in them alone." Further: "I beg you to retire. Do not allow yourself to suffer the pain of seeing me dead."

Richmond, Legh, also Leigh (1772-1827). English clergyman and writer. "It will be all confusion." When his wife asked for clarification: "The church! There will be such confusion in my church!"

Richter, Johann Paul (see Jean Paul).

Richthofen, Manfred von (1892-1918). WWI German fighter pilot ace, known as the "Red Baron." Before his last combat flight, Richthofen was asked for an autograph: "What's the hurry? Are you afraid I won't come back?" Mortally wounded during a subsequent encounter, he was able to land his aircraft. Before dying, Richthofen managed to tell those assisting him: "*Kaputt*… [dead or broken]."

Rickey, Branch (1881-1965). American major league baseball player and executive. Collapsing during a banquet speech: "… I don't believe I'm going to be able to speak any longer…"

Riddle, Granville (died 2003). American criminal, executed by lethal injection for a murder committed during a robbery: "... I would like to say to the world, I have always been a nice person. I have never been mean-hearted or cruel. I wish everybody well."

Ridley, Nicholas (c. 1500-1555). English Protestant martyr. Condemned for heresy, Ridley was burned at the stake with fellow martyr Hugh Latimer (above). When the flames burned only the lower part of his body, Ridley exclaimed: "Let the fire come unto me, I cannot burn. Lord, have mercy upon me." As he died: "Lord, Lord, receive my spirit." The dying Latimer answered: "O Father of heaven, receive my soul."

Rigaut, Jacques (1898-1929). French Surrealist poet whose works often dealt with suicide. Before shooting himself in the heart, Rigaut professed in an article: "Suicide is a vocation."

Riggs, Christina (1971-2000). American criminal who attempted suicide after she murdered her two children. Before her execution by lethal injection: "No words can express just how sorry I am for taking the lives of my babies. No way I can make up for or take away the pain I have caused everyone who knew and loved them... I love you, my babies."

Alternative: * "There is no way words can express how sorry I am for taking the lives of my babies. Now I can be with my babies, as I always intended. I love you, my babies."

Riker, John (1822-1862). American lawyer and Union officer in the U.S. Civil War. Riker was killed while exhorting his troops in the Battle of Fair Oaks, Virginia during the Peninsular Campaign: "Boys, we're surrounded-give them the cold steel!"

Riley, James Whitcomb (1849-1916). American poet and writer who wrote the poem "Little Orphan Annie." Paralyzed by a stroke, Riley was taken for a car ride by his brother-in-law. Worried about the July heat, his relative described an old method of keeping cool by wearing a cabbage leaf in a hat. Riley replied: "That reminds me of an old... man who used to wear a cabbage leaf in the seat of his pants to keep his brains cool." Later that evening, Riley asked his nurse for "Water." When she returned with it, she found the poet dead.

Rilke, Rainer (1875-1925). Bohemian-born poet and writer. Dying of leukemia, to a friend: "Help me to my own death. I don't want the doctor's death. I want to have my freedom." To his physician: "You won't tell me how I am, will you? If I'm asleep when you come into the room, don't speak to me. But press my hand to let me know that you are there, and I will press your hand in return…like this. Then you will know that I'm awake. If I don't press your hand, promise that you will sit me up and do something to make me regain consciousness."

Rimbaud, Jean (1854-1891). French poet. Dying of cancer, Rimbaud penned a note from his hospital bed in Marseilles to the manager of a steamship company seeking a passage to Suez: "... I'm completely paralysed, so I wish to embark in good time. Tell me at what time I must be carried on board." Rimbaud died before he could be transferred.

Ripley, Robert (1890-1949). American entrepreneur, cartoonist and television personality who created the series of curiosities called *Ripley's Believe It or Not.* During a broadcast of his television show, Ripley suffered a heart attack and was hospitalized. Later, he telephoned a friend from his hospital room: "I'm just in for a checkup, and I'll be out to the farm to see you tomorrow." He died of his ailment shortly thereafter.

Rita of Cascia, Saint (1381-1457). Italian nun and mystic. Dying of tuberculosis, to her fellow nuns: "May God bless you and may you always remain in holy peace and love with your beloved Spouse, Jesus Christ."

Rittenhouse, David (1732-1796). American astronomer, mathematician and educator who helped survey part of the Mason-Dixon line. Dying of cholera, to his nephew: "Yes, you have made the way to God easier."

Rivarol, Antoine de (1753-1801). French writer and supporter of the Royalists during the French Revolution. Dying in Berlin from an "inflammation of the chest:" "My friends, behold the great shadow approaches. These roses are about to change into poppies. It is time to contemplate eternity."

Rivera, Diego (1886-1957). Mexican artist and muralist. Dying of heart failure, Rivera was asked if he would prefer his hospital bed raised: "On the contrary, lower it."

Rizal y Alonso, José (1861-1896). Philippine writer, physician and nationalist, executed by the Spanish for his alleged revolutionary activities. To his confessor: "Oh, Father, how terrible it is to die! How one suffers! Father, I forgive everyone from the bottom of my heart. I have no resentment against anyone. Believe me, Your Reverence." Before the firing squad: "It is finished."

Rizzo, Francis "Frank" (1920-1991). American politician who became mayor of Philadelphia, Pennsylvania. To his secretary: "Hello there, Jodi!" Rizzo entered a bathroom and died suddenly of a heart attack.

Rob Roy (see MacGregor, Robert Roy).

Robert I, also Robert the Bruce (1274-1329). King of Scotland. Robert fought the English until Scotland was recognized as an independent nation. Realizing that his death approached, Robert spoke to Sir James Douglas (above) about his unachievable desire to go on a Crusade: "My dear friend Douglas, you know that I have had much to do, and have suffered many troubles during the time I have lived to support the rights of my crown. At the time I was most occupied, I made a vow, the non-accomplishment of which gives me much uneasiness. I vowed that if I could finish my wars in such a manner that I might have quiet to govern peaceably, I would go and make war against the enemies of our Lord Jesus Christ, and the adversaries of the Christian faith. To this point my heart has always leaned; but our Lord was not willing, and gave me so much to do in my lifetime, and this last expedition has lasted so long, followed by this heavy sickness, that, since my body cannot accomplish what my heart wishes, I will send my heart, in the stead of my body, to fulfill my vow. And as I do not know any one knight so gallant or enterprising, or better formed to complete my intentions than yourself, I beg and entreat of you, dear and special friend, as earnestly as I can, that you would have the goodness to undertake this expedition for the love of me, and to acquit my soul to our Lord and Saviour; for I have that opinion of your nobleness and loyalty, that if you undertake it, it cannot fail of success, and I shall die more contented. But it must be executed as follows: I will that, as soon as I shall be dead, you take my heart from my body and have it well embalmed; and you will also take as much money from my treasury, as will appear to you sufficient to perform your journey, as well as for all those whom you may choose to take with you in your train; you will then deposit your charge at the Holy Sephulchre of our Lord, where he was buried, since my body cannot go there… And wherever you pass, you will let it be known, that you bear the heart of King Robert of Scotland, which you are carrying beyond seas by his command, since his body cannot go thither." The king then thanked Douglas and said: "Thanks be to God! For I shall die in peace, since I know that the most valiant and accomplished knight in my kingdom will perform that for me, which I am unable to do for myself." Douglas was killed fighting the Moors in southern Spain, but the casket containing Robert's heart survived and was returned to Scotland for burial there.

Roberts, Douglas (1962-2005). American criminal, executed by lethal injection for a murder committed during a robbery: "… I've been hanging around this popsicle stand way too long, I want to tell you all. When I die, bury me deep, lay two speakers at my feet, put some headphones on my head and rock 'n' roll me when I'm dead. I'll see you in heaven some day. That's all, warden." As the drugs took effect, he mouthed: "I love you all. I've got to go."

Robertson, Frederick (1816-1853). English minister and theologian. Dying of a painful illness, to the nurse who was turning him in bed: "I cannot bear it. Let me rest. I must die. Let God do his work."

Robertson, Thomas (1829-1871). English actor and playwright. To his son: "Goodbye, my boy, and God bless you. Come and see me tomorrow. If I don't speak to you, don't be frightened and don't forget to kiss your father."

Robertson, W. Graham (1866-1948). British artist and writer. Robertson left funeral and burial instructions: "I should like the ashes to be buried or otherwise disposed of at the crematorium, with no tombstone nor inscription to mark the place of burial. No funeral, no mourning, no flowers. By request. If these arrangements are carried out, one may perhaps manage to die without making a public nuisance of oneself. W. Graham Robertson."

Robespierre, Maximilien (1758-1794). French revolutionary leader who was overthrown during the Reign of Terror and condemned to die. In a suicide attempt, Robespierre tried to shoot himself in the head but only succeeded in wounding his jaw. Taunted at the guillotine about his involvement in the death of Georges-Jacques Danton (above): "Cowards! Why did you not defend him then?" When a spectator wiped blood from the condemned man's injured jaw: "Thank you, sir." Some say he spoke those words to the executioner who loosened a constricting belt.

Robinson, Edwin (1869-1935). Pulitzer Prize-winning American poet. Dying of cancer, Robinson was asked by a friend if he were allowed to smoke: "What difference does it make? We'll have our cigarettes together."

Robinson, Henry (1775-1867). English diarist and lawyer. Robinson's final diary entry read: "... He [fellow writer Matthew Arnold] thinks of Germany as he ought, and of Goethe [whom Robinson had met] with high admiration. On this point I can possibly give him assistance, which he will gladly- but I feel incapable to go on."

Robinson, William (died 1659). English-born American Quaker who was one of the so-called Boston martyrs. Robinson, along with Marmaduke Stevenson (below) and Mary Dyer (above) refused to change their religious beliefs in accordance with those of the Massachusetts Bay Colony and were sentenced to die by hanging: "I suffer for Christ, in whom I live, and for whom I die."

Robota, Rosa (1921-1945). Polish prisoner in the Auschwitz-Birkenau concentration camp. Robota helped smuggle black powder into the facility that eventually was used to blow up one of the crematoria. She and three accomplices were sentenced to die by hanging for their deed. To the assembled inmates: "Be strong. Have courage."

Rochambeau, Jean-Baptiste (1725-1807). French general who aided America during the Revolutionary War. To his wife, discussing a party he missed due to a cold: “You must agree that I would have cut a pretty figure at the marriage yesterday.”

Rockefeller, John, Sr. (1839-1937). American businessman and philanthropist who founded the Standard Oil Company. Dying from complications of atherosclerosis, to his valet: “Raise me up a little bit higher. That’s better”

Rockefeller, Michael (1938-1961). American explorer and fourth-generation member of the Rockefeller dynasty. While on an expedition to New Guinea, Rockefeller’s boat capsized. He called to a companion as he tried to swim to shore: “I think I can make it.” His body was never found.

Rockne, Knute (1888-1931). Norwegian-born University of Notre Dame football coach. After boarding a plane, to a fellow passenger: “I suggest you buy some reading material. These plane engines make an awful racket and just about shut off most conversation.” Rockne perished when the plane crashed en route to California.

Rockwell, George Lincoln (1918-1967). Founder of the American Nazi Party. Leaving a laundromat in Arlington, Virginia: “I forgot my bleach.” Moments later, Rockwell was gunned down by a disgruntled former member of his party.

Alternative: * “I forgot something.”

Rodgers, James “Jimmie” (1897-1933). American country and blues singer. Dying of tuberculosis, Rodgers collapsed complaining of shortness of breath: “Let me take a blow.”

Rodgers, James W. (1910-1960). American murderer, put to death by a firing squad. Asked if he had any final words: “Why yes, a bulletproof vest, please.” When offered a coat at the execution site: “Don’t worry, I’ll be where it’s warm soon.”

Alternative: * “I done told you my last request ... a bulletproof vest.”

Rodgers, John (1772-1838). American naval officer in the War of 1812. Dying of a chronic ailment, Rodgers spoke to his valet: "Butler, do you know the Lord's Prayer?" When answered in the affirmative: "Then repeat it for me." Rodgers died in his companion's arms.

Rodin, Auguste (1840-1917). French sculptor and artist who created the bronze sculpture *The Thinker*. Dying of influenza: "And people say that Puvis de Chavannes [a French painter] is not a fine artist."

Rodin, Rose (died 1917). Wife of the French sculptor Auguste Rodin. "I don't mind dying, but it's leaving my man. Who will look after him? What will happen to the poor thing?" The sculptor died almost nine months later.

Rodney, George (1718-1792). British admiral who saw service during the American War of Independence. To his physician who asked how he felt: "I am very ill indeed!"

Rodosovich, Michael (died 1991). American airline pilot. As Continental Express Flight 2574 began its descent into a Houston, Texas airport, first officer Rodosovich said: "Push'n this descent making like the space shuttle." Shortly thereafter, the left leading edge of the horizontal stabilizer detached, sending the aircraft into a fatal dive. All 14 aboard perished in the crash. The separation resulted from improper maintenance on the tail section at an earlier inspection.

Rodriguez, Blas de (died 1597). Martyred Spanish missionary to Native Americans in the present-day state of Georgia. Because Rodriguez publically censured one of the tribe members for his polygamy, it was decreed that the missionary should die. Rodriguez spoke to the assembled armed warriors: "My children, I do not care about my dying. Even though you may kill me, the death of this body is inevitable. We have to be always prepared because we all have to die one day; but what pains me more is that the Evil-one has persuaded you to do such a grave thing against God your creator. Moreover, even it hurts me more than you [who] are so oblivious of what we missionaries have done for you, teaching you the way to happiness and life eternal. Look, my sons, you are still on time, if you wish to reject your evil intentions, God our master, is very merciful and will forgive you." His captors allowed a two day reprieve but then crushed his skull with a tomahawk.

Rodriguez, Manuel (see Manolete).

Rogers, John (c. 1500-1555). English Protestant martyr. Condemned because of his denunciation of Catholicism, Rogers was sentenced to die at the stake. As the flames rose, he prayed: "Lord, receive my spirit."

Rogers, William "Will" (1879-1935). American humorist, stage and motion picture actor, newspaper columnist and cowboy. Rogers once quipped: "Lord, let me live until I die." In a radio broadcast announcing a flight from Washington state to Alaska with veteran pilot Wiley Post, Rogers said: "Well, Wiley's got her warmed up. Let's go." Both perished when the aircraft crashed in Alaska.

Rohan-Chabot, Louis (1788-1833). French cardinal. Proclaiming his unworthiness: "I am nothing, nothing, less than nothing!"

Röhm, Ernst (1887-1934). German military officer who commanded the Nazi SA storm troopers. To curb the power of the SA, Adolf Hitler ordered the assassination of Röhm and some of his associates in a purge known as "Night of the Long Knives:" "If I am to be killed, let Adolph do it himself."

Roi, Charles de la (died 1946). American criminal, executed in the San Quentin, California gas chamber for the murder of a fellow inmate. "Warden, I'd like a little bicarb because I'm afraid I'm going to get gas in my stomach right now."

Roland de la Platière, Jean (1734-1793). French statesman and a leader of the French Revolution. Running afoul of the revolutionaries, Roland fled Paris, but his wife was captured and executed on the guillotine. When he learned of her death, he committed suicide by a sword through his heart. A note at his feet: "Whoever thou art that findest me lying, respect my remains; they are those of a man who consecrated all his life to being useful and who has died, as he lived, virtuous and honest... Not fear, but indignation, made me quit my retreat, on learning that my wife had been murdered. I wished not to remain longer on an Earth polluted with crimes."

Alternative: * "... After my wife's murder, I would not remain any longer in a world so stained with crime."

Roland de la Platière, Marie-Jeanne (1754-1793). French author, supporter of the French Revolution and wife of Jean Roland de la Platière (above). When the Rolland de la Platières fell out of favor with the revolutionaries, Madame Roland failed to flee Paris and was condemned to die. On her way to the guillotine, she turned to a statue of Liberty and famously said: "O Liberty! O Liberty! What crimes are committed in thy name!" She then spoke to a man who seemed frightened of his own execution: "Go first. I can at least spare you the pain of seeing my blood flow."

Romaine, William (1714-1795). English clergyman and theologian. When asked if Christ's salvation were precious to him: "He is a precious Savior to me now." As he died: "Holy, holy, holy blessed Jesus. To Thee be endless praise."

Romanes, Francis, also Francisco de san Roman (died c. 1542). Spanish martyr. Because of his conversion to Protestantism, the Inquisition condemned Romanes to die at the stake. Refusing to kneel before a wooden cross: "It is not for Christians to worship wood." As the flames consumed him, the martyr turned his head to the side, which was interpreted as a sign of repentance. After he was pulled from the fire, Romanes asked: "Did you envy my happiness?" His executioners promptly threw him back into the fire, where he repeated the seventh Psalm until he died.

Romanes, George (1848-1894). Canadian-born British biologist and physiologist. An agnostic for part of his professional life, Romanes confided to his wife after taking Communion: "I have now come to see that faith is intellectually justifiable. It is Christianity or nothing."

Romanov, Olga (1882-1960). Last surviving daughter of Czar Alexander III of Russia. Comparing her life to a sunset: "I can see every event in my life in the light of a setting sun. The sunset is over."

Romero, Óscar (1917-1980). Salvadorian archbishop who spoke against government repression and killing of dissenters. Romero was shot while celebrating mass in a hospital: "May God have mercy on the assassins."

Rommel, Erwin, "The Desert Fox" (1891-1944). German Field-Marshal during WWII. For his alleged involvement in the Count von Stauffenberg plot to kill Adolf Hitler, Rommel was ordered to commit suicide or face trial and hanging. To his wife: "I have come to say goodbye... in a quarter of an hour I shall be dead. They suspect me of having taken part in the attempt to kill Hitler. It seems my name was on Goerdeler's list to be President of the Reich ... I have never seen Goerdeler in my life... The Fuehrer has given me the choice of taking poison or being dragged before the People's Court. They have brought the poison. They say it will take only three seconds to act." When his wife begged him to stand trial, Rommel replied: "No. I would not be afraid to be tried in public, for I can defend everything I have done. But I know that I should never reach Berlin alive." Goerdeler, a politician, possibly would have been chosen chancellor if the plot to assassinate Hitler had succeeded. Later, Rommel spoke to his son at their home: "I have just had to tell your mother that I shall be dead in a quarter of an hour. To die by the hand of one's own people is hard. But the house is surrounded and Hitler is charging me with high treason. In view of my services in Africa, I am to have the chance of dying by poison. The two generals have brought it with them. It is fatal in three seconds. If I accept, none of the usual steps will be taken against my family- that is, against you. They will also leave my staff alone..." Rommel then spoke to his aide Hermann Aldinger: "It is all prepared down to the last detail. I am to be given a state funeral. I have asked that it take place at Ulm [a city near his home]. In a quarter of an hour you, Aldinger, will receive a phone call from the Wagnerschule Hospital in Ulm to say that I have had a brain seizure on the way to a conference. I must go. They only gave me ten minutes." Before leaving with the two generals to meet his fate, Rommel realized he had left money in his wallet: "There's still 150 marks in there.

Shall I take the money with me?" When his pet dachshund frolicked close by, the field marshal told his son: "Shut the dog in the study, Manfred." Shortly thereafter, he took cyanide and later was buried with full honors.

Rook, John (1959-1986). American criminal, executed by lethal injection for the rape-murder of a nurse: "Freedom. Freedom at last, man! It's been a good one."

Roosevelt, Eleanor (1884-1962). American activist, politician and widow of President Franklin Roosevelt. At the end, Eleanor said to her nurse: "I wish to die." When the nurse answered that God would call her when her work on earth was finished, she replied: "Utter nonsense!"

Roosevelt, Franklin (1882-1945). Thirty-second U.S. president. While sitting for a portrait, Roosevelt complained: "I have a terrific headache." When the president slumped forward, his cousin asked if he had dropped his cigarette. Roosevelt looked up and said: "I have a terrific pain in the back of my neck." He lost consciousness and died of a stroke.

Alternative: * "I have a terrific pain in the back of my head." As he was carried to bed: "Be careful."

Roosevelt, Theodore, Sr. (1831-1878). American businessman, philanthropist and father of President Theodore Roosevelt. Dying of cancer, Roosevelt summoned his physician, daughters and wife: "Call the doctor! Bamie! Corinne! Mother, come here- for God's sake- quick!"

Roosevelt, Theodore "Teddy" (1858-1919). Twenty-sixth U.S. president. Before dying in his sleep, Roosevelt spoke to his valet, James Amos: "James, will you please put out the light?"

Root, Elihu (1845-1937). American lawyer and statesman who became U.S. secretary of state and later a U.S. senator. Asked if he believed in God: "I have devoted considerable thought to the question with the result that, while as a lawyer I cannot prove a case for the existence of God, as an individual I firmly believe that there is a God and I have no fear of death."

Rosa, Salvatore (1615-1673). Italian Baroque artist and poet. When asked by a friend how he was doing: "Bad, bad! To judge by what I now endure, the hand of death grasps me sharply."

Rosenberg, Alfred (1893-1946). Estonian-born Nazi party ideologue who was convicted of war crimes. At the gallows, when asked if he had any last words: "No."

Rosenberg, Ethel (1915-1953). American spy who was convicted of passing atomic bomb secrets to the Soviet Union. She and her husband Julius (below) were executed by electrocution. The conclusion of a note written before her death: "... My husband and I must be vindicated by history... We are the first victims of American fascism! Love you, Ethel."

Rosenberg, Julius (1918-1953) American spy executed with his wife Ethel for passing information about the atomic bomb to the Soviet Union. In a post script to a letter to his lawyer: "Ethel wants it made known that we are the first victims of American fascism."

Ross, Harold (1892-1951). American journalist who founded and edited *The New Yorker* magazine. Ross' last telephone conversation from his hospital bed: "I'm up here to end this thing [cancer] and it may end me too. But that's better than going on this way. God bless you, I'm half under the anesthetic now." Ross died during chest surgery.

Ross, Michael (1959-2005). American criminal, executed by lethal injection for the murder of eight young women. When asked if he wished to say any last words: "No thank you."

Ross, Robert "Robbie" (1869-1918). French-born English writer and long-time companion of Oscar Wilde (below). Possibly reflecting on the pair's stormy relationship, Ross paraphrased John Keats' epitaph (above) "Here lies one whose name was writ in water." to: "Here lies one whose name was writ in hot water."

Rossetti, Christina (1830-1894). English poet and sister of Dante Rossetti (below). Dying of breast cancer: "I love everybody! If ever I had an enemy, I should hope to meet and welcome that enemy to heaven."

Rossetti, Dante (1828-1882). English poet and artist. In the terminal stage of kidney failure, Rossetti was told that his brother would visit the following day: "Then you really think that I am dying? At last you think so! But I was right from the first." Shortly before he expired: "I believe I shall die tonight. Yesterday I wished to die, but today I must confess that I do not." Rossetti's prediction was correct.

Rossini, Gioachino (1792-1868). Italian composer, best-known for his operas *The Barber of Seville*, *Cinderella* and *William Tell*. Suffering from the effects of chronic bronchitis and emphysema, the 76-year-old Rossini underwent two operations for rectal cancer that resulted in a virulent infection with severe pain. As he lay dying, the composer screamed: "What are you doing, Blessed Virgin? Here am I suffering the torments of hell and I have been calling you since nightfall. You hear me! You can do it if you like; it all depends on you. Come on, now, be quick..." The last sounds he uttered before drifting into unconsciousness were the names of the Virgin, St. Anne and his wife: "Santa Maria... Sant'Anna... Olympe."

Rothschild, Mayer (1744-1812). German financier who was the patriarch of the Rothschild banking dynasty. On his deathbed, Rothschild told his five sons to obey Moses' law, remain united and consult their mother before embarking on any action. "Observe these three points, and you will soon be rich among the richest, and the world will belong to you." Obviously, they listened carefully.

Rothstein, Arnold "Mr. Big" (1882-1928). American mobster and gambler who allegedly fixed the 1919 baseball World Series. Rothstein supposedly was shot because he reneged on a gambling debt (some say during a poker game). To his wife in the hospital: "I want to go home. All I do is sleep here. I can sleep home... I feel fine. Besides I've got to. Don't go away. I need you. I don't want to be alone. I can't stand being alone.

I've got to get home." When asked by the police to name his assailant: "Me mudder did it. You stick to your trade. I'll stick to mine."

Rousseau, Jean-Jacques (1712-1778). Swiss-born French philosopher, political theorist and writer, best-known for his book *The Social Contract* and treatise *Emile*. Dying of a stroke, to his wife: "You weep; is it for my happiness? I die in peace. I never wished to injure anyone, and may safely count on God's mercy." Then: "Throw up the window, that I may see once more the magnificent scene of nature... Being of Beings, God! See how pure the sky is! There is not a single cloud! Do you see that its gates are open and that God awaits me?"

Alternatives: * "See the sun, whose smiling face calls me, see that immeasurable light. There is God! Yes, God himself, who is opening His arms and inviting me to taste at last that eternal and unchanging joy that I had so long desired."

* "I go to see the sun for the last time."
* "How pure and lovely is the sky. There is not a cloud in it. I hope the Almighty will receive me there."

Royer-Collard, Pierre-Paul (1763-1845). French statesman and philosopher. "There is nothing solid or substantial in the world but religious ideas. Never give them up, or, if you do, come back to them."

Rubens, Peter Paul (1577-1640). Flemish Baroque painter. Succumbing to heart failure, Rubens realized: "Death will soon close my eyes forever."

Rubinstein, Anton (1829-1894). Russian pianist, composer and conductor who founded the St. Petersburg Conservatory. Dying of heart disease, to his wife: "I am suffocating! A doctor! Quick! A doctor!"

Rubinstein, Arthur (1887-1982). Polish-born pianist, best-known for his interpretation of Chopin's music. Several days before his death, to a friend about another pianist: "I've always said that if I'm ever going to miss a note, I'd commit suicide. Well, I wish to God he would miss one!"

Rubinstein, Helena, born Chaya Rubinstein (1870-1965). Polish American businesswoman who founded a world-famous cosmetic empire. Asked if she were afraid of death: "Not in the least now. But I've waited too long. It should be an interesting experience."

Rubinstein, Nikolay (1835-1881). Russian pianist, composer, conductor, and founder of the Moscow Conservatory. Dying of abdominal tuberculosis, to his caretaker: "Oysters! Nothing, Helen Andreyevna, will do me so much good as a dozen cold oysters and an ice afterwards." After Rubinstein began eating, he developed severe cramps, vomited and died several hours later.

Rudolf, Crown Prince of Austria (1858-1889). Son of Austrian Emperor Franz Joseph I. Rudolf committed suicide with his mistress Marie (Mary) Vetsera (below) during a period of "mental unbalance." The note to his wife read: "Dear Stephanie, You are freed henceforward from the torment of my presence. Be happy, in your own way. Be good to the poor little girl [their daughter] who is the only thing I leave behind. Give my last greetings to all my acquaintances... I face death calmly. Death alone can save my good name. With warmest love from your affectionate Rudolf."

Ruffini, Ernesto (1888-1967). Archbishop of Palermo, Sicily. "I am dying, but I am tranquil. I am with the Madonna."

Ruloff, Edward (c. 1820-1871). Canadian-born philologist and serial killer. Ruloff was executed for the slaying of a store clerk. Before his hanging: "Hurry it up! I want to be in hell in time for dinner."

Alternative: "I can't stand still."

Runyon, Damon (1884-1946). American author, best-known for his short stories. Dying of throat cancer: "You can keep the things of bronze and stone and give me one man to remember me just once a year."

Rupert, Jacob "Jake" (1867-1939). American beer executive, politician and owner of the New York Yankees baseball team. The day before he died, Rupert extended his hand to the visiting Babe Ruth (below) and said: "Babe!" He spoke his last words to his secretary: "Good morning."

Rush, Benjamin (1746-1813). American physician and politician, one of the signatories of the Declaration of Independence. Dying of typhus, Rush admonished his son: "Be indulgent to the poor."

Rush, Harold (died 1915). Trooper in the Australian Light Horse Regiment. During the disastrous Battle of the Nek in the Gallipoli Campaign of WWI, Rush spoke to a comrade [cobber] immediately before he was killed: "Goodbye, cobber. God bless you."

Russell, Charles A. (1832-1900). Irish-born Lord Chief Justice of England. "My God, have mercy upon me."

Russell, Charles M. (1864-1926). American artist and sculptor who specialized in works of the Old American West. Dying of heart failure, to his physician: "Doc, I guess I ain't going to make the grade for you this time."

Russell, George, whose pen name was Æ or A.E. (1867-1935). Irish writer, poet, painter and nationalist. Dying of cancer, to a friend: "Yes, I am not in pain. I have realized all my ambitions. I have had an astounding interest in life. I have great friends. What more can a man want?"

Alternative: * "Yes, I am not in pain. I have realized most of my ambitions. I have had an outstanding interest in life. I've got friends. What more can a man want?"

Russell, Jerome (died 1539). Scottish Franciscan monk, martyred for his religious faith and "heresy." To a fellow martyr before their burning at the stake: "... Brother, fear not... Death cannot destroy us, for it is destroyed already by Him for Whose sake we suffer."

Russell, John (1842-1876). English politician and writer, father of the philosopher Bertrand Russell. Dying of bronchitis (some say tuberculosis): "It is all done. Goodbye my little dears forever."

Russell, William (1639-1683). English politician and nobleman. Russell opposed the succession of King James II of England and subsequently was sentenced to die for his beliefs. During his time, prisoners often bribed the executioner for a clean cut. When the axe man initially botched the execution: "You dog, did I give you ten guineas to use me so inhumanly?" Eventually, Russell's head rolled.

Russert, Timothy "Tim" (1950-2008). American television journalist who hosted NBC's *Meet the Press*. After greeting a colleague with the phrase "What's happening?" Russert collapsed and died of a heart attack.

Ruth, George "Babe" (1895-1948). American major league baseball homerun king, called "The Sultan of Swat." Dying of throat cancer, Ruth struggled to his feet. His nurse (some say his doctor) asked where he was going: "Not far. I'm going over the valley." After returning to bed, he prayed: "My Jesus, mercy... My Jesus, mercy... My Jesus..."

Rutherford, Samuel (c. 1600-1661). Scottish clergyman, theologian and writer. Because of his non-conformist leanings, Rutherford was accused of treason but died in jail before going to trial. To a messenger: "Tell the Parliament that I have received a summons to a higher bar. I must needs answer that first; and when the day you name shall come, I shall be where few of you shall enter." To the ministers at his deathbed: "There is none like Christ. O, dear brethren, pray for Christ, preach for Christ, do all for Christ; feed the flock of God. And, O, beware of men-pleasing... Having recovered from a fainting episode: "... Glory shines in Immanuel's land. O, for arms to embrace Him! O, for a well tuned harp."

Alternatives: * "If he should slay me ten thousand times, ten thousand times I'll trust. I feel, I feel, I believe in joy and rejoice. I feed on manna. Oh for arms to embrace him. Oh for a well-tuned harp."

* To his child: "I have again left you upon the Lord; it may be you will tell this to others, that the lines are fallen to me in pleasant places, I have a goodly heritage; I bless the Lord that gave me counsel."

Rutherford, Thomas (1712-1771). English clergyman and educator. "He has, indeed, been a precious Christ to me and now I feel Him to be my rock, my strength, my rest, my hope, my joy, my all in all."

Ruthven, Alexander (c. 1580-1600). Scottish nobleman who was accused of conspiring to murder King James VI of Scotland. As Ruthven was stabbed by the king's men: "Alas! I had na wyte [blame] of it."

Ryan, Cornelius (1920-1974). Irish-born journalist and writer, best-known for his WW II books. Dying of prostate cancer, to his wife: "Katie, I'm so d***** tired!"

Ryland, John (1753-1825). English Baptist minister and hymnodist. "No more pain."

Sabatier, Raphaël (1732-1811). French consulting surgeon to Napoleon I. Ashamed of his deteriorating condition, Sabatier advised his son: "Contemplate the state into which I am fallen and learn to die."

Sacco, Nicola (1891-1927). Italian-born anarchist. Sacco with Bartolomeo Vanzetti (below) allegedly killed two men during a Massachusetts robbery. Although many questioned the pair's guilt, they were convicted and executed by electrocution. Sacco's parting words: "Long live anarchy! Farewell, my wife and child and all my friends!" Before the switch was thrown, he muttered: "Good evening, gentlemen; farewell my mother."

Sa'di, born Musharrif al-Dīn ibn Muṣlih al-Dīn (c. 1213-1291). Persian poet. "Better is the sinner who hath thoughts about God than the saint who hath only the show of sanctity."

Saint-Edme, Bourg (see Bourg, Edme-Théodore).

Saint-Gaudens, Augustus (1848-1907). Irish American sculptor, known for his statues commemorating U.S. Civil War heroes. Dying of cancer, on viewing the sunset: "It is very beautiful, but I want to go farther away."

Saint-John, Henry (see Bolingbroke, Henry St. John).

Saint-Pierre, Charles Abbé de (1658-1743). French philosopher, writer and reformer. To the priest who had administered Last Rites to appease his family: "I am only to be reproached for this action. I do not believe a word of all this. It was a vile concession for the family and for the house, but I wanted to be the confessor of the truth all my life."

Saint-Saëns, Camille (1835-1921). French pianist, organist and composer. Dying after a voyage to Algiers: "This time I think it's really the end."

Saint-Simon, Claude-Henri, Comte de (1760-1825). French social scientist and philosopher. To his followers: "Remember, that to accomplish grand deeds you must be enthusiastic. All my life is comprised in this one thought- to guarantee to all men the freest development of their faculties. The future is ours!"

Alternative: * "The future belongs to us. In order to do great things, one must be enthusiastic."

Sakharov, Andrei (1921-1989). Russian nuclear physicist, dissident and member of the Congress of People's Deputies. Sakharov was awarded the 1975 Nobel Peace Prize but was not allowed to accept it. Preparing for a debate in the Congress, to his wife: "Tomorrow there will be a battle!" Several hours later, Sakharov died of a heart attack.

Saki (see Munro, Hector Hugh).

Sakuma, Tsuhmu (died 1910). Japanese submarine officer who drowned with his crew during a diving exercise in southwestern territorial coastal waters. A note found in the sunken vessel read: "…"I have no words to beg pardon for losing His Majesty's boat and for killing my men, owing to my carelessness. But all the crew have well discharged their duties till their death, and have worked with fortitude. Our only regret is that this accident may, we fear, cause a hindrance to the development of the submarine… I am greatly satisfied. I have always been prepared for death on leaving home. I humbly ask Your Majesty, the Emperor, to be so gracious as not to let the bereaved families of my men be subjected to destitution. This is the only anxiety which occupies my mind at present... 12.30 o'clock.

Respiration is extraordinarily difficult. I mean I am breathing gasoline. I am intoxicated with gasoline. Captain Nakano... It is 12.40 o'clock." All 14 men aboard the submarine perished.

Saladin (c. 1137-1193). Kurdish general and sultan of Egypt. Dying of a "virulent fever:" "When I am buried, carry my winding-sheet [burial cloth] on the point of a spear, and say these words: 'Behold the spoils which Saladin carries with him! Of all his victories, realms, and riches, nothing remains to him but this.'" When a divine read the Holy Word: "... He is God, than whom there is no other God, who knoweth the unseen and the seen, the Compassionate, the Merciful," Saladin replied "True" and died.

Alternatives: * "This [his winding-sheet] is all that remains to the mighty Saladin, the conqueror of the East."

* "After I am dead, carry a sheet on the spear's point to the grave, and say these words: 'These are the glorious spoils which Saladin carries with him! Of all his victories and triumphs, of all his riches and realms, nothing remains but this winding-sheet.'"

Salieri, Antonio (1750-1825). Italian-born composer, conductor and teacher. During the last three decades of his life, Salieri lived under the unjustified suspicion that he poisoned his fellow composer, Wolfgang Mozart (above). He was institutionalized in his last years for senile dementia and a failed suicide attempt. When a former student visited him near the end, Salieri spoke in one of his more lucid moments: "In spite of this being my last illness, I can declare in good faith that there is nothing to that absurd rumor; you know what I mean- Mozart, they say I poisoned him. But I didn't! It's malice, sheer malice. Tell everyone for me, dear [Ignaz] Moscheles, old Salieri, who is about to die, has told you himself."

Alternative: * "Although this is my last illness, I can in all good faith swear that there is no truth to the absurd rumor; you know – I'm supposed to have poisoned Mozart. But no, it's spite, nothing but spite, tell that to the world, my dear Moscheles; old Salieri, who's going to die soon, told you that."

Salmasius, Claudius (1588-1653). French scholar. "I have lost an immense portion of time! Time, that most precious thing in the world! Had I but one year more, it should be spent in studying David's Psalms and Paul's Epistles."

Alternative: * "I have lost a world of time! Had I one year more of life, it should be spent in perusing David's Psalms and Paul's Epistles. I would mind the world less, and God more."

Salomon, Haym (1740-1785). Polish-born merchant who was a prominent backer of the American Revolution against Great Britain. Dying bankrupt, to a friend: "Take care of them [his family], McCrae. There will be very little, very little for them."

Salt, Titus (1803-1876). British businessman, politician and philanthropist. Concerning a proposed memorial statue, Salt possibly referred to the fate of Lot's wife (Genesis 19: 26): "So they wish to make me into a pillar of Salt!" Toward the end: "How kind He is to me."

Salvini, Tommaso (1829-1915). Italian actor, known for his Shakespearian roles. "I do not will [want] to die- absolutely."

Samson (fl. 12th century BCE). Israelite leader and judge. When delivered to his Philistine enemies by the temptress Delilah (Judges 16:28, 30), the blinded Samson prayed: "O Lord God, remember me, I pray Thee and strengthen me; I pray Thee, only this once, O God, that I may be avenged upon the Philistines for one of my two eyes." As he pulled down the pillars where his enemies were assembled: "Let me die with the Philistines."

San Martín, José de (1778-1850). Argentine liberator of the southern portion of South America from Spanish rule. Suffering chest pains, San Martín spoke to his daughter and son-in-law: "Mercedes, this is the exhaustion of death! Mariano, back to my room!"

Sánchez, Manuel Rodríguez **(see Manolete).**

Sanctus, Saint (died 177). Martyred Gallic deacon from Vienne (west-central France). Sanctus was arrested during the reign of Roman Emperor Marcus Aurelius (above) who attempted to suppress the Christian religion. As Sanctus was roasted alive with hot brass plates, he repeatedly cried: "I am a Christian! I am a Christian!"

Sand, George, pseudonym of Aurore Dupin (1804-1876). French writer and one-time partner of Fryderyk Chopin (above). Her burial instructions: "*Laissez la verdure*," loosely translated: "Leave the green," i.e. "Do not cover [the] tomb with anything, but let the grass grow there." To her grandchildren: "Farewell, I am going to die! Goodbye, Lina. Goodbye, Maurice. Goodbye, Lolo. Good..."

Sanders, George (1906-1972) Russian-born British television and film actor. Depressed about his health, Sanders' wrote a suicide note before taking an overdose of drugs: "Dear World, I am leaving you because I am bored. I feel I have lived long enough. I am leaving you with your worries in this sweet cesspool. Good luck." Signed "George Sanders."

Sanders, Harland "Colonel" (1890-1980). American founder of a fast-food chicken franchise. Dying from complications of leukemia, to his doctor: "I just want to rest."

Sanderson, Frederick (1857-1922). English headmaster. Suffering a heart attack after delivering a speech, Sanderson was asked if he were tired for questions: "No... no."

Sanderson, Ricky (1959-1998). American rapist and murderer. Before his execution in the gas chamber, Sanderson decried abortion by refusing his final meal: "Yeah, about the last meal I do. I didn't take that because I have very strong convictions about abortion and with 33 million babies that have been aborted in this country, died for no reason, I'm dying for a deed I did and I deserve death for it and I'm glad Christ forgave me. Those babies never got a first meal and that's why I didn't take the last, in their memory. I'm just thankful God has been gracious to me. That's it." As he waited for the gas: "Thank you Jesus, I'm going home."

Sanderson, Robert (1587-1663). English theologian and chaplain to King Charles I. "My heart is fixed, Oh God! My heart is fixed where true joy is to be found."

Sandoz, Jules (1858-1928). Swiss-born American pioneer who settled in the Sandhills of Nebraska. "The whole d*** Sandhills is deserted. The cattlemen are broke, the settlers about gone. I got to start all over, ship in a lot of good farmers in the spring, build up, build, build..."

Sandri, Sandro (1895-1937). Italian war correspondent, killed in an American-flagged vessel by Japanese warplanes while covering the Sino-Japanese War. "They've killed me this time. What an end. In another nation's ship in this country [China]."

Sanger, Margaret (1879-1966). American nurse and birth control activist who founded the Planned Parenthood organization. Dying of heart failure, to her friends who brought refreshments: "A party! Let's have a party!"

Sankey, Ira (1840-1908). American gospel singer and hymnodist. As Sankey slipped into unconsciousness, he sang the first stanza of his favorite Fanny Crosby hymn "Saved by Grace:" "Some day the silver cord will break/ And I no more as now shall sing./ But, O, the joy when I awake/ Within the palace of the King!"

Santa Anna, Antonio López de (1794-1876). Mexican military and political leader who served as president of his country multiple times. To his wife: "Leave me alone, so I can get some rest."

Alternative: * "God bless, God d***!"

Santayana, George (1863-1952). Spanish-American philosopher, poet, writer and educator. Although not his last utterance, Santayana is best-known for a quote from his 1905-1906 book *The Life of Reason*: "Those who cannot remember the past are condemned to repeat it." Near death, Santayana was asked if he were suffering: "Yes, my friend. But my anguish is entirely physical. There are no more difficulties, whatsoever."

Sappho (died c. 570 BCE). Greek poet. Sappho's farewell words to her daughter Cleïs: "For it is not right that there should be lamentation in the house of those who serve the Muses. It would not be seemly for us."

Alternative: * "For it is not right that in the house of song there be mourning. Such things befit us not."

Sarber, Jesse "Jess" (1886-1933). American county sheriff. When gunmen freed the gangster John Dillinger (above) from a jail run by Sarber, the lawman was mortally wounded by machine gun fire. Before dying, he said: "Oh, men, why did you do this to me?" To his wife: "Mother, I believe I'm going to have to leave you."

Saro-Wiwa, Kenule "Ken" (1941-1995). Nigerian environmental activist and writer. Saro-Wiwa led a nonviolent organization that protested pollution by multinational oil companies. To silence his group, he and eight others were falsely accused of murder and hanged: "Lord, take my soul, but the struggle continues."

Saroyan, William (1908-1981). Pulitzer Prize-winning American writer. Before he died of cancer, Saroyan quipped: "Everybody has got to die, but I have always believed an exception would be made in my case. Now what?" His last words, spoken to his son Aram: "It's the most beautiful time of my life... and death."

Alternative: * "I know everybody has to die sooner or later, but I thought an exception would be made in my case."

Sarpi, Paolo (1552-1623). Venetian scholar, writer, patriot and statesman. "Be thou [Venice] everlasting."

Alternative: * "May she endure forever."

Sarsfield, Patrick, Earl of Lucan (c. 1650-1693). Irish general who perished fighting for France at the Battle of Landen in present-day Belgium. Withdrawing a bloody hand from his wound: "Would to God this were shed for Ireland." He died several days later.

Sartre, Jean-Paul (1905-1980). French existentialist philosopher, political activist and writer. Sartre declined the 1965 Nobel Prize in Literature, because he eschewed public honors. Dying of a lung ailment, to his companion, Simone de Beauvoir: "I love you very much, my dear Beaver."

Sasaki, Sadako (1943-1955). Hiroshima atomic bomb victim. Dying of radiation-related leukemia a decade after the event, the 12 year-old Sasaki responded after tasting her tea: "It's good."

Satank, also Sitting Bear (died 1871). Native American Kiowa chief. Satank conducted a raid on a wagon train in Texas that resulted in seven deaths. As the chief was being transported to stand trial, he tore away his wrist manacles and stabbed a guard, chanting: "O sun, you remain forever, but we Kaitsenko [society of the bravest Kiowa warriors] must die. O, earth, you remain forever, but we Kaitsenko must die." He was killed in the ensuing scuffle.

Sauckel, Fritz (1894-1946). German director of Nazi slave labor during WWII. Before he was hanged as a war criminal, Sauckel said: "I pay my respects to American officers and American soldiers, but not to American justice... I die innocent. My sentence is unjust. God protect Germany!"

Sauer, Taylor (died 2012). American college student, killed while using her telephone to "facebook" while driving. After posting "I can't discuss this now. Driving and facebooking is not safe! Haha..." the 18 year-old Sauer fatally crashed her speeding car into a slow-moving truck.

Saul (died c. 1007 BCE). First king of Israel. Wounded by the Philistines in the Battle of Gilboa in central Israel (1 Samuel 31:4), Saul commanded his armor-bearer: "Draw your sword and thrust me through with it, lest these uncircumcised come and thrust me through and make sport of me." When his attendant would not comply, Saul fell on his sword.

Alternative: * "Stand, I pray thee, upon me, and slay me; for anguish is come upon me, because my life is yet whole in me."

Saunders, Laurence (1519-1555). English Protestant martyr. For his unfavorable remarks made against the Catholic Church, Saunders was convicted of heresy and burned at the stake. Before dying, he embraced the stake, saying: "Welcome the cross of Christ. Welcome ye faggots and ye flames destined to consume my mortal body; but which, in place of hurting, shall only serve to raise this immortal spirit to the mansions of glory and life everlasting."

Alternative: * "Welcome the cross of Christ. Welcome everlasting life."

Saunderson, Nicolas (1682-1739). British mathematician. Various sources have reported that Saunderson's last words were: "... Time, matter and space are perhaps but a point." However, after uttering this statement, he drifted into a delirium, revived several hours later and exclaimed: "O thou God of Clarke and Newton, have mercy on me!" Saunderson then expired.

Savage, Richard (c. 1697-1743). English poet and playwright. In 1727, Savage stabbed a man to death in a coffeehouse brawl, was convicted of murder and subsequently pardoned. Incarcerated at age 46 for an insignificant debt, Savage told his jailer: "I have something to say to you, sir." He paused but lost the thought: "'Tis gone." Shortly thereafter, he also was gone.

Savalas, Aristotle "Telly" (1922-1994). Greek-American film and television actor. Dying from complications of cancer, to his son: "I love you, son."

Savina of Milan, Saint (died 311). Italian martyr, killed for the aid she gave to Christian prisoners. "O Lord, who hast ever preserved me in chastity, suffer me not longer to be wearied with journeying! Command me not to go beyond this place! Let my body here find rest! I commend to Thee my servant, who has borne so much for me, and let me be worthy to see my brother in Thy kingdom, whom I have not seen here!"

Savio, Saint Dominic (1842-1857). Italian student of Saint John Bosco of the Salesian Order (above). Dying of a respiratory ailment, to his distraught parents: "Surely you're not crying, Mom, at seeing me go to heaven? Look, Dad, look! Can't you see? The wonderful! The beautiful!"

Alternative: * "Goodbye, Dad, goodbye . . . what was it the parish priest suggested to me ... I don't seem to remember . . . Oh, what wonderful things I see ..."

Savonarola, Girolamo (1452-1498). Martyred Italian preacher and reformer. Because Savonarola attempted to purge the Catholic church of its vices and reform the government, he was branded a heretic and condemned to die by hanging. Before the ruling tribunal: "My Lord died innocent of all crime, for my sins; and shall not I willingly give my soul for the love of Him." When the throng praised Savonarola: "A sinful man stands not in need of human praise or glorification, nor is this life a time for praise." On the scaffold: "At the last hour God alone can give mortals comfort. The Lord hath suffered as much for me." After his death, the martyr's body was burned and his ashes were scattered.

Alternatives: * "O Florence, what hast thou done today?"
* "My Lord was pleased to die for my sins. Why should I not be glad to give up my poor life out of love to Him."

Saxe, Maurice de (1696-1750). German-born French military officer. Dying of a "putrid fever," to his physician: "Doctor, life is but a dream. Mine has been a bright, but a short one."

Alternatives: * "I see that life is but a dream; mine has been a beautiful one and a short one."
* "The dream has been short, but it has been beautiful."

Scarron, Paul (1610-1660). French writer, dramatist and poet, known for his comedies. To his family: "Ah! My children, you cannot cry as much for me as I have made you laugh in my time!" Some say that a few moments later he added: "I could not have supposed it is so easy to make a joke of death."

Alternative: * "I never thought that it was so easy a matter to laugh at the approach of death."

Schaft, Jannetje "Hannie" (1920-1945). Dutch resistance member who fought against the Germans during WWII. Captured and shot at the end of the war, to the soldier who failed to kill her with the first bullet: "I shoot better than you!"

Schiele, Edith (died 1918). Austrian wife of Egon Schiele (below). Mortally ill with influenza, Schiele wrote her husband a note as he made a deathbed sketch: "I love you eternally and love you more and more infinitely and immeasurably." Her husband died three days later.

Schiele, Egon (1890-1918). Austrian expressionist artist. Dying of influenza near the end of WWI, to his sister-in-law: "The war is over and I must go. My paintings shall be shown in all the museums of the world." He wrote a last note to his sister, saying: "Edith Schiele is no more."

Schiller, Johann Friedrich von (1759-1805). German writer, playwright, philosopher and poet, known for the dramas *William Tell* and *The Maid of Orleans*. Dying of tuberculosis, Schiller was asked how he felt: "Calmer and calmer." Later, arousing from sleep, he allegedly said: "Many things are growing plain and clear to my understanding. One look at the sun..." Before dying, Schiller tried to ask for medicinal "naphtha" but was unable to speak the last syllable of the word.

Alternatives: * "Many things are growing plain and clear to me."
* "Many things are growing clearer and clearer to me."

Schimmelpenninck, Mary (1778-1856). English writer and abolitionist. Awakening from a coma: "Rejoice with me! Rejoice with me! I am entering my Father's house! Do you not hear the voices, and the children's are the loudest!"

Alternative: * "Oh, I hear such beautiful voices, and the children's are the loudest!"

Schlageter, Albert (1894-1923). German WWI veteran and saboteur. In the post-war period, Schlageter carried out sabotage against the French who had occupied the Ruhr region. He was captured and sentenced to die before a firing squad: "I find some satisfaction in dying. Perhaps I can help through my example. From 1914 until this day, I have sacrificed all of my strength and labor, out of love and loyalty, to my German homeland. Where it was in need, I sought to help. Greet my parents, brothers and sisters, relatives, my friends, and my Germany."

Schleiermacher, Friedrich (1768-1834). German theologian and philosopher. Dying of an "inflammation of the lung," to his wife: "My dear, I seem to be really in a state which hovers between consciousness and unconsciousness, but in my soul I experience the most delightful moments. I must ever be in deep speculations, but they are united with the deeper religious feelings…" Requesting a change in position: "Now I can hold out here no longer. Lay me in a different posture."

Schlieffen, Alfred von (1833-1913). German field marshal during the pre-WWI era. "It must come to a fight. Keep the right wing strong."

Schmidt, Hans-Theodor (1899-1951). German Nazi adjutant at the Buchenwald concentration camp during WWII. Condemned to die by hanging for his war crimes: "Like me, you are obeying orders. I am dying innocent."

Schmidt, Hans-Thilo (1888-1943). WWII German spy who passed information on the Nazi's Enigma coding machine to the French. Before his execution by gunshot: "My death will consummate everything and my cause, crowned by my death, will emerge irreproachable and perfect."

Schmitt, Aloysius (died 1941). U.S. Navy chaplain. After assisting sailors through a porthole in the bombed USS *Oklahoma* during the WWII Japanese raid on Pearl Harbor: "Go ahead boys, I'm all right." Schmitt perished, because he was too large to fit through the porthole.

Schmitz, Aron Ettore, whose pen name was Italo Svevo (1861-1928). Italian writer, best-known for his novel *Confessions of Zeno*. At the end, a friend asked Schmitz if he wished to pray: "When you haven't prayed all your life, there's no point at the last minute."

Schnorr von Carolsfeld, Ludwig (1836-1865). German operatic tenor. A favorite of Richard Wagner, Schnorr died from complications of a virulent infectious illness. On his deathbed, Schnorr mentioned the role that Wagner was writing for him: "Farewell, Siegfried! Console my Richard!"

Schoenberg, Arnold (1874-1951): Austrian-born composer and conductor, known for his revolutionary atonal works. Inquiring about his son's tennis match: "Has Ronny won?" His last word immediately before dying from complications of hardening of the arteries: "Harmony."

Scholl, Arthur "Art" (1931-1985). American acrobatic pilot. Moments before his plane crashed into the Pacific Ocean while filming for a movie sequence: "I have a problem... I have a real problem."

Scholl, Hans (1918-1943). German founding member of the White Rose anti-Nazi resistance movement. Arrested by the Gestapo and later beheaded with his sister Sophie (below): "Long live freedom!"

Scholl, Sophie (1921-1943). German member of the anti-Nazi White Rose movement, executed for treason with her brother Hans. Before dying on the guillotine: "God, you are my refuge into eternity."

Alternatives: * "Your heads will fall as well."
* "The sun still shines."

Schreiner, Olive (1855-1920). South African writer and pacifist. Schreiner's last letter read: "I long to see the stars and the veldt. One day I will go up to Matjesfontein [about 150 miles northeast of Cape Town where she once lived] just for one day, if I can find anyone to take me. It doesn't seem to me that this is Africa. A Happy New Year, my dear one."

Schreuder, William (see Veldhuyzen van Zanten, Jacob).

Schrödinger, Erwin (1887-1961). Austrian physicist who was awarded the 1933 Nobel Prize in Physics. Dying of tuberculosis, to his wife: "Annikin, stay with me- so that I don't crash."

Schubert, Franz (1797-1828). Austrian composer and pianist. Delirious from the effects of typhoid fever, Schubert responded to consoling words from his brother and a physician: "Here, here is my end." Later, he asked to be placed in his own bed. When assured that he already was there: "No, no. It is not true. Beethoven is not laid here."

Alternatives: *"No, no, here is my end."
* "Oh! This is the last of all."
* "This is not Beethoven lying here."

Schultz, Dutch, born Arthur Flegenheimer (1902-1935). American gangster. Gunned down by rival mobsters in a Newark, New Jersey restaurant, Schultz underwent surgery but died one day later. At the end, he deliriously raved: "... Look out! Mamma, mamma! Look out for her. You can't beat him. Police, mamma! Helen, mother, please take me out. Come on, Rosie. O.K. Hymes would do it. Not him. I will settle... the indictment. Come on, Max, open the soap duckets. Frankie, please come here. Open that door, Dumpey's door. It is so much, Abe that... with the brewery. Come on. Hey, Jimmie! The Chimney Sweeps. Talk to the sword. Shut up, you got a big mouth! Please help me up, Henry. Max, come over here... French-Canadian bean soup... I want to pay; let them leave me alone..." After these last words, Schultz became comatose and died.

Schulz, Charles (1922-2000). American cartoonist who created the comic strip *Peanuts.* Dying of colon cancer, Schulz remembered the cartoon characters he had created in his strip: "... Charlie Brown, Snoopy, Linus, Lucy... How can I ever forget them..."

Schumann, Clara (1819-1896). German piano virtuoso, composer and wife of Robert Schumann (below). Dying of a stroke, to her daughters who lived with her at the time: "Poor Marie, you two must go to a beautiful place this summer."

Schumann, Robert (1810-1856). German pianist, conductor and composer. Dying insane in an asylum, Schumann had not seen his wife Clara for two years. During her visit at the end, the failing composer mumbled: "My…I know." Possibly he meant: "My Clara, I know you."

Schumann-Heink, Ernestine (1861-1936). Bohemian-American contralto. Dying of leukemia, to her family: "I die without fear or regret." Informed that a newsboy had sent his regards: "God bless him."

Schurman, Anna van (1607-1678). German-born Dutch scholar, artist and poet. "I have proceeded one step farther toward eternity, and if the Lord shall be pleased to increase my pains, it will be no cause of sorrow to me."

Schurz, Carl (1829-1906). Prussian-born American soldier and politician who served in the Union army during the U.S. Civil War. Schurz later was elected to the U.S. Senate. "It is so simple to die."

Schwarzenberg, Prince Felix of Austria (1800-1852). Bohemian-born Austrian prime minister. When told by his physician that a stroke was imminent if he continued his current lifestyle: "That manner of death has my full approval." Schwarzenberg died suddenly of a stroke.

Schweitzer, Albert (1875-1965). German-born French physician-missionary, musician and theologian. For his humanitarian work, Schweitzer won the 1952 Nobel Peace Prize. Schweitzer died in current-day Gabon, west-central Africa, where he had operated a hospital over five decades. To his daughter: "I'm tired, very tired."

Schwerin, Kurt von (1684-1757). Prussian military officer, killed by a cannonball during the Battle of Prague in the Seven Years' War: "Let all brave Prussians follow me!"

Scipio Nasica (c. 100-46 BCE). Roman consul and military leader. Scipio sided with Pompey in the civil war against Julius Caesar. When his army was defeated, Scipio committed suicide by stabbing himself to avoid capture by his enemies: "All is well with the general!"

Scobee, Richard "Dick" (1939-1986). American commander of the space shuttle *Challenger* that exploded during launch. Scobee's last words affirmed the command to "throttle-up:" "Roger, go at throttle-up." As the shuttle soared skyward, a faulty seal on an external fuel tank caused an explosion that resulted in the loss of all onboard

Scott, James (1649-1685). Dutch-born English nobleman. English King James II sentenced Scott to die for his rebellion against the crown. Fearing the executioner's axe would not sever his head cleanly: "Here are six guineas for you; pray do your business well. Do not serve me as you did my Lord [William] Russell (above). I have heard you struck him three or four times." To his servant: "Here, take these remaining guineas and give them to him if he does his work well." Again, to the executioner: "If you strike me twice, I cannot promise you not to stir." Scott continued: "Prithee, let me feel the axe. I fear it is not sharp enough." When assured it was sharp and heavy enough, he spoke no further. Ironically, several blows were required to sever the condemned man's head.

Alternatives: * "Here are six guineas for you and do not hack me as you did my Lord Russell. I have heard you struck him four or five times; if you strike me twice, I cannot promise you not to stir."

* "There are six guineas for you, and do not hack me as you did my Lord Russell. I have heard that you struck him three or four times. My servant will give you more gold if you do your work well."

Scott, John, Lord Eldon (1751-1838). English barrister who became Lord Chancellor of England. When informed that the weather was cold outside, Scott responded: "It matters not to me, where I am going, whether the weather here be hot or cold."

Scott, Robert Falcon (1868-1912). English Antarctic explorer. Scott's expedition struggled to be the first to reach the South Pole but found that Norwegian Roald Amundsen's group had achieved the goal one month earlier. The final diary note written by Scott before he and his men froze to death on their abortive return from the South Pole: "… Had we lived, I should have had a tale to tell of the hardihood, endurance, and courage of my companions which would have stirred the heart of every Englishman. These rough notes and our dead bodies must tell the tale, but surely, surely, a great rich country like ours will see that those who are dependent on us are properly provided for. R. Scott."

Alternative: * "For God's sake, look after our people."

Scott, Thomas (1535-1594). English member of Parliament. To a priest attempting to comfort him: "Begone, you and your trumpery; until this moment I believed that there was neither a God nor a hell! Now I know and I feel that there are both, and I am doomed to perdition by the just judgment of the Almighty!"

Scott, Thomas (1747-1821). English minister and writer. To his wife and children: "... This is heaven begun. I have done with darkness forever! Satan is vanquished! Nothing remains but salvation with *eternal glory, eternal glory*!"

Scott, Walter (1771-1832). Scottish writer and poet, best-known for his historical novels *Rob Roy* and *Ivanhoe.* Dying of a stroke, Scott replied to his son-in-law and biographer John Lockhart who asked which book he wished to have read: "There is but one book; bring me the Bible." Again, to his son-in-law: "Lockhart, I may have but a minute to speak to you. My dear, be a good man. Be virtuous. Be religious. Be a good man. Nothing else will give you any comfort when you come to lie here." Asked if his wife and daughter should be called: "No, don't disturb them. Poor souls, I know they were up all night. God bless you all."

Scott, Walter "Death Valley Scotty" (1872-1954). American prospector, con man and recluse. Despite his checkered life, Scott's epitaph offers sound advice: "I got four things to live by: don't say nothin' that will hurt anybody; don't give advice- nobody will take it anyway; don't complain; don't explain."

Scott, Winfield (1786-1866). U.S. Army general and unsuccessful presidential candidate. To his groom: "Peter, take good care of my horse."

Alternative: * "Take good care of him, James."

Scriabin, Alexander (see Skryabin, Alexander).

Scripps, Edward (1854-1926). American newspaper publisher and philanthropist. Dying of a heart ailment, Scripps ruminated: "Too many cigars this evening, I guess."

Seberg, Jean (1938-1979). American actress who starred in Hollywood and European films. Dying from an overdose of barbiturates, the depressed Seberg's suicide note to her son asked: "Forgive me. I can no longer live with my nerves. Understand me. I know that you can and you know that I love you. Be strong. Your loving mother, Jean."

Sedgwick, John (1813-1864). Union general in the U.S. Civil War. When fired on by Confederate forces at the Battle of Spotsylvania, Virginia, one of Sedgwick's men flinched when a bullet came near: "Why, my man, I am ashamed of you, dodging that way. They couldn't hit an elephant at this distance." When told that dodging shells had saved his life, the general replied: "All right, my man; go to your place." Shortly thereafter, Sedgwick fell dead from a bullet to the head.

Alternatives: * "What, what men, this will never do, dodging for single bullets! I tell you they could not hit an elephant at this distance."
* "Pooh, men. Don't duck. They couldn't hit an elephant at that distance."
* "Nonsense, they couldn't hit an elephant at this dist..."

Segrave, Henry (1896-1930). British motorboat and motorcar driver. After Segrave's craft disintegrated during an attempt to break the world water speed record, he asked: "Did we do it?" Moments before dying, Segrave was told that he had achieved his goal.

Selznick, David (1902-1965). American movie producer, best-known for his Academy Award-winning *Gone with the Wind* production. Dying of a heart attack: "Mind if I sit down?"

Senancour, Étienne (1770-1846). French writer and philosopher. Senancour composed his own epitaph: "Eternity, be thou my refuge."

Seneca, Lucius (c. 4 BCE-65 CE). Roman philosopher and statesman. For his alleged complicity to kill Emperor Nero, Seneca drank poison and slit veins in his arms in an attempt to commit suicide. He then stepped into a hot bath and sprinkled his slaves with water before dying: "I offer this liquid as a libation to Jupiter the Liberator."

Alternative: * "I offer this liquid as a libation to Jupiter the Deliverer."

Senna Da Silva, Ayrton (1960-1994). Brazilian Formula One race driver. During a Grand Prix race in Italy, Senna remarked: "The car seems OK..." Later, his steering column cracked, precipitating a fatal crash.

Seraphim of Sarov, Saint (1759-1833). Russian Orthodox priest and mystic. Seraphim recited an Easter chant the day before his death: "O Passover, great and most Holy, O Christ, O Wisdom, Word, and Power of God! Grant that we may more perfectly partake of You in the day that knows no end, in Your Kingdom." He was found dead the following day in a position of prayer.

Şerbănescu, Alexandru (1912-1944). Romanian fighter pilot who flew missions for Germany during WW II. After taking hits from Allied warplanes: "My boys, I'm going down."

Serling, Rodman "Rod" (1924-1975). American television writer and producer, best-known for his series *The Twilight Zone*. His thoughts about dying: "… That's what I anticipate death will be: a totally unconscious void in which you float through eternity with no particular consciousness of anything. I think once around is enough. I don't want to start it all over again…" Before his unsuccessful coronary bypass surgery: "You can't kill this tough Jew."

Serra, Junípero (1713-1784). Spanish Franciscan priest who founded a number of missions in present-day California: "I promise, if the Lord in His infinite mercy grants me eternal happiness, which I do not deserve because of my sins and faults, that I shall pray for all and for the conversions of so many whom I leave unconverted… Now I shall rest."

Servetus, Michael (c. 1511-1553). Martyred Spanish theologian, physician and scholar. Because his views clashed with current religious doctrine, Servetus was convicted of heresy and sentenced to die at the stake. As the flames consumed him: "Jesus Christ, Thou son of the eternal God, have mercy upon me!"

Seso, Don Carlos (1516-1559). Spanish martyr. Condemned to die at the stake for his adherence to a faith contrary to the Church of Rome: "I could demonstrate to you that you ruin yourselves by not imitating my example. But there is no time. Executioners, light the pile that is to consume me."

Seton, Anna (1795-1812). A member of the American Sisters of Charity, an organization founded by her mother, Saint Elizabeth Seton (below): "Can it be for me? Should you not rejoice? It will be but a moment- and-reunited for eternity! A happy eternity with my mother! What a thought! Laugh, Mother! Jesus!"

Seton, Saint Elizabeth (1774-1821). Founder of the American Sisters of Charity and first native-born American saint in the Roman Catholic Church. Dying of tuberculosis: "At the hour of death, call me and bid me come to Thee, that with Thy saints I may praise Thee, forever and ever! Jesus." Later: "Soul of Christ, sanctify me; body of Christ, save me; blood of Christ, inebriate me; water out of the side of Christ, strengthen me." A few moments after she spoke these words Elizabeth murmured; "Jesus, Mary, Joseph" and died.

Seton, William (1768-1803). American merchant. Dying of tuberculosis, Seton spoke to his wife, Elizabeth (above): "I want to be in heaven. Pray, pray for my soul. My dear wife and little ones... my Christ Jesus, have mercy and receive me. My Christ Jesus." When Elizabeth asked if he thought he would go to his Redeemer, he answered "Yes."

Seume, Johann (1763-1810). German writer and traveler. To a friend who asked if he needed anything: "Nothing, dear Weigel. I only wanted to tell you that you shouldn't be annoyed if I should say some things I wouldn't say in a different situation. I take a guilt with me. You I cannot repay. My eyes grow dim."

Severus, Saint (died c. 348). Bishop of Ravenna, Italy. Near the end, Severus opened the family mausoleum where his wife and daughter were buried: "My dear ones, with whom I lived so long in love, make room for me, for this is my grave and in death we shall not be divided." He lay down between the remains of his family and died.

Severus, Septimus (145-211). Roman emperor who became mortally ill on a campaign to modern-day Scotland. "I have been everything, and everything is nothing. A little urn will contain all that remains of one for whom the whole world was too little."

Alternatives: * "I have been all things and it has profited me nothing."

* "Little urn, thou shalt soon hold all that will remain of him whom the world could not contain."
* "Hurry, if anything remains for me to do."
* "Come, give it to me, if we have anything to do."

Sévigné, Marguerite de (1646-1705). French aristocrat and letter writer. Dying of a fever, to a priest who said her beauty would return to dust and ashes: "Yes, but I am not yet dust and ashes."

Seward, William (1801-1872). American politician who arranged the purchase of Alaska from Russia in 1867, the so-called "Seward's Folly." While serving as Abraham Lincoln's secretary of state, Seward was attacked as part of the presidential assassination but survived his injuries. Seven years later, to his daughter-in-law when asked for a last message: "Nothing. Only 'Love one another.'"

Seymour, Edward (c. 1506-1552). English military leader, Lord Protector of England and brother of Jane Seymour, wife of King Henry VIII. Sentenced to die for mismanagement of power, Seymour pleaded before his beheading,: "… I desire you all to bear me witness that I die here in the faith of Jesus Christ, desiring you to help me with your prayers that I may persevere constant in the fame to my life's end... Lord Jesus, save me!"

Seyss-Inquart, Arthur (1892-1946). Czech-born German Nazi officer. Seyss-Inquart was responsible for deportation of Jews and others in occupied Holland to concentration camps in the east. He was hanged as a war criminal: "I hope that this execution is the last act of the tragedy of the Second World War and that the lesson taken from this world war will be that peace and understanding should exist between peoples. I believe in Germany." His execution was not the last in the post-war period.

Sforza, Galeazzo (1444-1476). Italian nobleman, the Duke of Milan. Because of his cruel and tyrannical behavior, Sforza was assassinated by several disgruntled officials of the Milanese court: "Oh God!"

Shackleton, Ernest (1874-1922). Irish-born explorer, best-known for his journeys to Antarctica. While on an expedition to Antarctica and South Georgia Island, Shackleton asked his doctor when he suffered a back pain: "You are always wanting me to give up something. What do you want me to give up now?" The doctor answered: "Chiefly alcohol, boss. I don't think it agrees with you." Shackleton replied: "I can feel the pain coming again. Give me the medicine quickly." The explorer died of a heart attack shortly thereafter.

Shah, Nadir (1688-1747). Despotic Persian leader who conquered territories ranging from Afghanistan to the Russian Caucasus. Because members of his army felt threatened by his power, Shah was stabbed to death. To his assassin: "Thou dog!"

Shaka Zulu (c. 1787-1828). African Zulu leader, bludgeoned to death because of his autocratic rule. To one of his assassins: "Hau! You too, Mbopa, son of Sitayi, you too are killing me."

Shakespeare, William (1564-1616). English poet and arguably one of the world's foremost dramatists. Shakespeare decreed in his last will and testament: "... I gyve [give] unto my wief [wife] my second best bed with the furniture. Item, I gyve and bequeath to my saied [said] daughter Judith my broad silver gilt bole. All the rest of my goodes [goods], Chattel, Leases, plate, Jewels, and household stuffe whatsoever, after my Dettes [debts] and Legacies paid, and my funerall expences discharged, I gyve, devise, and bequeath to my Sonne-in-Lawe, John Hall [a physician], gent. and my Daughter Susanna his wife, whom I ordaine and make of this my last will and testament... In witness whereof, I have hereunto put my hand, the daie and yeare first abovewritten. By me, William Shakespeare."

His epitaph: "Good frend for Iesvs sake forbeare,
To digg the dvst encloased heare.
Bleste be ye man yt spares thes stones,
And cvrst be he yt moves my bones."

["Good friend, for Jesus' sake forbear,
To dig the dust enclosed here.
Blessed be the man that spares these stones,
And cursed be he that moves my bones."]

Shakur, Tupac "2 Pac" born Lesane Parish Crooks (1971-1996). American rapper and actor. Shakur was shot assassination-style while driving to a Las Vegas nightspot. When asked if he were shot: "I'm hit... I can't breathe." As he was transported to hospital: "I'm dying, man." He expired on life-support six days later.

Sharbil, also Charbel (died c.113). Christian martyr from Edessa, Mesopotamia. Refusing to sacrifice to the Roman gods during Trajan's rule, Sharbil was tortured after condemning the deities "... For one had intercourse with boys, which is not right; and another fell in love with a maiden who fled for refuge into a tree, as your shameful stories tell..." Before he died: "Forgive me, Christ, all the sins I have committed against Thee... let Thy death, which was for the sake of sinners, restore to life again my slain body in the day of Thy coming." He then was beheaded.

Sharp, Cecil (1859-1924). English composer, musicologist and folk music collector. Dying of cancer, Sharp was told that he would feel no further pain after an injection. His reply: "Never again."

Sharp, William, whose pen name was Fiona Macleod (1855-1905). Scottish writer and poet. Sharp spoke to his wife using his term for the fairy life or realm where he would return at his death: "Oh, the beautiful 'Green Life' again! Ah, all is well."

Shastri, Lal (1904-1966). Indian prime minister and philanthropist. Dying of a heart attack: "*Mere Baap. Hai Ram* [My Father. Oh God!]."

Shave Head, also Charles Kashlah (died 1890). Native American Bureau of Indian Affairs officer. Shave Head was part of a group of lawmen detailed to arrest Sioux chief Sitting Bull (below) who had resisted the U.S. government's encroachment on Native American rights. Shave Head suffered a mortal wound during the skirmish and expired hours later: "I will die in the faith of the white man and to which my five children already belong, and be with them. Send for my wife that we may be married by the Black Gown before I die." To a priest: "Did I do my duty?" When answered in the affirmative: "It is well." Sitting Bull also died of injuries received during the encounter.

Shaw, George Bernard (1856-1950). Irish dramatist, writer and socialist who won the 1925 Nobel Prize in Literature. Dying from complications of a fall: "Well, it will be a new experience anyway." To his last visitor, Lady Astor (above), two days before his death: "Oh, Nancy, I want to sleep... sleep." When she tried to persuade him to take some soup: "Good Lord, no. Take it away." Later, to his nurse: "Sister, you're trying to keep me alive as an old curiosity. But I'm done. I'm finished. I'm going to die."

Shaw, Henry, whose pen name was Josh Billings (1818-1885). American writer, humorist and lecturer. Dying of a probable heart attack, to a physician: "My doctors East ordered rest of brain, but you can see I do not have to work my brain for a simple lecture- it comes spontaneously."

Shaw, Rebecca (died 2009). American copilot on a commercial turboprop aircraft inbound to Buffalo Niagara International Airport, New York on an icy evening. From the cockpit voice recorder, Shaw exclaimed: "I've never seen icing conditions. I've never deiced... I've never experienced any of that. I don't want to have to experience that and make those kinds of calls. You know I'd've freaked out. I'd've have like seen this much ice and thought oh my gosh we were going to crash..." Immediately before impact, Shaw said "We're..." and screamed. All 49 aboard the aircraft and one person on the ground perished.

Shaw, Robert (1837-1863). Union officer in the U.S. Civil War. Shaw led the all-black Fifty-fourth Regiment Voluntary Infantry unit at the Battle of Fort Wagner, South Carolina. He was mortally wounded as he urged his troops onward: "We shall take the fort or die there. Now I want you to prove yourselves men! Forward, Fifty-fourth!"

Shaw, Samuel (1754-1794). American consul to Canton, China. Returning to the U.S. to recover his health, Shaw spoke to the ship's surgeon: "God's will be done." When the doctor shed a tear that fell on Shaw's hand: "My dear friend, you know I am dying. Speak comfort to me."

Sheed, Francis (1897-1981). Australian-born publisher of religious books. Refusing to eat his last hospital meal of "a flabby piece of fish," Sheed groused as he pushed the morsel around on his plate: "I fancy I'll let it live."

Sheppard, Jack (1702-1724). English burglar and "gaol-breaker." After many arrests and subsequent escapes, Sheppard finally kept his date with the hangman: "Of two virtues, I have ever cherished an honest pride: never have I stooped to friendship with Jonathan Wild [a notorious English criminal], or with any of his detestable thief-takers; and, though an undutiful son, I never damned my mother's eyes."

Sheppard, William (died 1854). American criminal. Sheppard was condemned to hang for the murder of a man who refused his daughter's hand in marriage. The response to a query about how he felt: "I feel like an innocent man."

Sheridan, Philip (1831-1888). Union army general who saw action in the U.S. Civil War. Commenting on the completion of his memoirs as he died of a heart attack: "I hope that some of my old boys will find the book worth the purchase."

Sheridan, Richard (1751-1816). Irish-born dramatist and politician, best-known for his play *The School for Scandal.* On his deathbed, Sheridan directed a message to a friend: "Tell Lady Besborough [a former lover] that my eyes will look up to the coffin-lid as brightly as ever." As he died: "Did you know Burke [Edmund Burke, the Irish statesman]?"

Sherman, John (1823-1900). American lawyer and politician who held multiple positions in the U.S. government. "I think you had better send for the doctor. I am so faint."

Alternatives: * Awakening from sleep, Sherman recognized his secretary and daughter: "Why Babcock... Oh, Mamie."

* When told that some friends were paying their respects: "You must show them hospitality."

Sherman, William (1820-1891). Union general who devastated large portions of the South with his "scorched earth" policy during the U.S. Civil War. Asked by his daughter what he would like on his monument: "Faithful and honorable, faithful and honorable."

Sherwood, Mary (1775-1851). English author, best-known for her books for children. To her family: "God is very good. Remember this, my children, that God is love. He that dwelleth in love dwelleth in God and God in him."

Shirley, Lawrence, 4th Earl Ferrers (1720-1760). English aristocrat and criminal. The eccentric Shirley shot a family steward over a disagreement in the disbursement of some money owed his estranged wife and for evidence given on her behalf. To the hangman who asked him for forgiveness: "I freely forgive you as I do all mankind, and I hope myself to be forgiven." Inquiring about his position on the scaffold: "Am I right?"

Shore, Dinah, born Frances Rose Shore (1916-1994). American singer, actress and television personality. Dying of ovarian cancer, to her family: "You all have brought such joy to my life. I love every one of you."

Sibelius, Jean (1865-1957). Finnish composer and violinist, known for his symphonies and symphonic poem *Finlandia*. Dying of a stroke, to his wife: "I think that the cranes have taken leave of me. I was on my usual walk. The cranes were flying low over Ainola [his home near Helsinki]- I have never seen them fly that low before. Straight above Ainola one of them parted with a sad cry and banked in a steep curve around the hill, almost as if it meant to say goodbye."

Sickingen, Franz von (1481-1523). German nobleman and soldier. Fatally wounded while defending his castle, to a priest who tried to administer the Last Rites: "I have confessed God in my heart. He is the one to give absolution and administer the Sacrament."

Sidney, Algernon (1622-1683). English jurist and politician. Sidney was charged with treason and beheaded for his involvement in the Rye House Plot against the rule of King Charles II. When the condemned man placed his head on the block, the executioner asked, as was the custom: "Are you ready, sir? Will you rise again?" Sydney replied: "Not till the general resurrection. Strike on!"

Sidney, Philip (1554-1586). English soldier, statesman and poet. Fighting against the Spanish at the Battle of Zutphen in the Netherlands, Sidney sustained a gunshot to the leg that progressed to gangrene over the following three weeks. Offering his water to a fallen comrade: "Thy necessity is yet greater than mine." Near death: "I do with trembling heart and most humbly entreat the Lord that the pangs of death may not be so grievous as to take away my understanding... I would not change my joy for the empire of the world." To his brother at bedside: "Love my memory, cherish my friends. Their faith to me may assure you they are honest. But above all, govern your will and affections by the will and word of your Creator, in me beholding the end of this world with all her vanities."

Alternative: * "Give the water to him; his sufferings are greater than mine."

Simeon, Charles (1759-1836). English clergyman. A visiting minister quoted James 1:4: "... Let steadfastness have its full effect, that you may be perfect and complete, lacking in nothing." The guest then repeated one of his colleague's expressions: "All is ordered in infinite wisdom and unbounded love." Simeon replied "And that is quite sufficient for me." His visitor recited a benediction and the dying man, with his last breath, said "Amen!"

Simon of Sudbury (c. 1316-1381). Archbishop of Canterbury and later Lord Chancellor of England. Because Simon was held responsible for an oppressive poll tax, he was hacked and beheaded by a mob during the 1381 Peasants' Revolt: "My children, take heed what ye do. Would you murder your Primate, your pastor? I pray ye commit not such a crime, lest all England be laid under the curse of an interdict." Laying his head on the block: "O Lord, lay not this deed of blood to the charge of my erring flock." After an inexperienced rioter failed to sever his head on the first swing, Simon cried: "Oh my God, this is Thy hand!" He raised his hand to his neck and the next blow severed his fingers. After six more swings (some say a total of eight), the deed was done.

Alternatives: * "... Oh, take heed, lest for the act of this day all England be laid under the curse of the interdict."
* "Ah! Ah! It is the hand of God!"

Simon of Swineshead (died 1216). English Roman Catholic monk. Because of displeasure with the rule of English King John, the monarch allegedly was poisoned by Simon of Swineshead. As the monk drank tainted wine to induce John to follow suit, he said: "If it shall like your princely majesty, here is such a cup of wine as ye never drank better before in all your lifetime. I trust this wassail shall make all England glad." John possibly died from a preexisting case of dysentery rather than poisoning.

Simpson, Charles (died 1931). American criminal, condemned to hang for the murder of a shopkeeper: "Make it snappy."

Simpson, Tom (1937-1967). British road racing cyclist. Collapsing from dehydration and the effects of stimulants administered during a stage of the Tour de France, Simpson was told that his cycling for the day was over. He responded incoherently: "No, no, no, no, no, get me up, up. I want to go on, on, get me up, get me straight." When righted and placed on his bicycle: "Me [toe] straps, Harry, me straps." As he started off: "On, on, on." Simpson again collapsed and died.

Alternative: * Although a newsman reported the cyclist's last words were: "Put me back on my bike," those close to Simpson denied the claim.

Sinatra, Francis "Frank" (1915- 1998). American radio, television, stage and screen star. Dying of a heart attack: "I'm losing it."

Sisera (fl. 12th to11th centuries BCE). Hated Canaanite military commander. When Sisera's army was defeated by the Israelites, he fled to the tent of Heber the Kenite. He told Heber's wife Jael to: "Stand at the door of the tent, and if any man comes and asks you: 'Is any one here?' say no." As he slept, Jael took a tent peg and spiked it through Sisera's temple into the ground (Judges 4: 20).

Sitting Bull (c. 1831-1890). Lakota Sioux leader who resisted the U.S. government's encroachment on Native American rights. Sitting Bull was instrumental in the defeat of George Custer's army regiment at the Battle of Little Bighorn (above). Arrested later by the Indian agency police as a troublemaker, Sitting Bull shouted in the Sioux language: "I am not going. Do with me what you like. I am not going. Come on! Come on! Take action! Let's go!" In the ensuing struggle, he was shot dead.

Sitts, George (c. 1913-1947). American criminal. Sitts escaped from prison while serving a life term for murder and killed two lawmen before his recapture. At his electrocution: "This is the first time authorities helped me escape prison."

Sitwell, Edith (1887-1964). English writer and poet. Dying of a cerebral hemorrhage: "I'm afraid I'm being an awful nuisance."

Siward (died 1055). Scandinavian-born Earl of Northumbria who led a victorious force against the Scottish King Macbeth in 1054. Dying of dysentery a year later, Siward allegedly complained: "Shame on me that I did not die in one of the many battles I have fought, but am reserved to die with disgrace of the death of a sick cow! At least put on my armor of proof, gird the sword by my side, place the helmet on my head, let me have my shield in my left hand and my gold-inlaid battle-axe in my right hand, that the bravest of soldiers may die in a soldier's garb."

Sixtus II, Saint (died 258). Pope from 257 until his death one year later. By command of the Roman Emperor Valerian, Sixtus was condemned to die by beheading for his Christian faith. When his deacon, Laurentius, asked: "Whither goest thou father, without thy son?" Sixtus replied: "I am not forsaking thee, my son; greater combats await thee. Cease to weep; after three days thou wilt follow me, the Levite, his priest." Indeed, three days later, Laurentius himself (above) was roasted to death over a slow fire.

Alternatives: * "My son, don't think that I'm abandoning you, but greater battles still await you in behalf of the faith of Christ. In three days you will follow me, as the Levite follows the priest. While you are awaiting, take the treasures of the Church and distribute them to whom you think best."

* "I am not deserting you, my son, nor abandoning you, but greater trials for the faith of Christ await you! Three days from now, you the Levite, will follow me, the priest! Meanwhile, take the church's treasure and distribute it as you see fit."

Skryabin, Alexander, also Scriabin (1872-1915). Russian composer and mystic. Dying of a facial infection: "I am convinced that suffering is necessary, because of its *contrast*..." Then, pointing to his chest: "I hurt here. What does that mean?" Suddenly he cried out: "This pain is unbearable... If this lasts, I won't be able to *live*... I can't bear it... This means the end! But this is a catastrophe..." In a delirium before dying: "Who is there?"

Alternative: * "Suffering is necessary. It is good. I have a sense of well-being in suffering."

Slovik, Edward "Eddie" (1920-1945). U.S. Army private who served during WWII. Slovik was the only American soldier executed for desertion since the U.S. Civil War. Before the firing squad: "They're not shooting me for deserting the United States Army, thousands of guys have done that. They just need to make an example out of somebody and I'm it because I'm an ex-con. I used to steal things when I was a kid, and that's what they are shooting me for. They're shooting me for the bread and chewing gum I stole when I was 12 years old." When the chaplain asked Slovik to say a prayer for him, the condemned man replied: "Okay, Father. I'll pray that you don't follow me too soon."

Alternative: * "... They're shooting me for that brass I stole when I was 12 years old..."

Słowacki, Juliusz (1809-1849). Polish romantic poet. Dying of tuberculosis: "What time is it?"

Smalridge, George (1663-1719). English minister who became Bishop of Bristol. Dying of apoplexy (some say a chest disorder): "God be thanked I have had a very good night."

Smeaton, Mark (c. 1512-1536). English musician in the court of King Henry VIII. Accused of adultery with Queen Anne Boleyn, Smeaton was beheaded: "Masters, I pray you all to pray for me, for I have deserved the death."

Smedley, Edward (1788-1836). English clergyman and writer. To his wife: "Be always thankful."

Smith, Abigail Adams (1765-1813). American matron who was the daughter of President John Adams (above). Dying of breast cancer, Smith sang her favorite hymn "Longing for Heaven:" "O, could I soar to worlds above,/ That blessed state of peace and love!/ How gladly would I mount and fly/ On angels' wings to joys on high!"

Smith, Adam (1723-1790). Scottish political economist and philosopher. To his visiting friends: "I love your company, gentlemen, but I believe I must leave you to go to another world."

Alternative: * Some recount a slightly different phrasing: "I believe we must adjourn this meeting to some other place."

Smith, Alfred "Al" (1873-1944). American politician who was a New York governor and unsuccessful presidential candidate in1928. Dying of a heart attack, to his priest: "Start the Act of Contrition."

Smith, Bessie (1894-1937). American blues singer. Smith was fatally injured in a car wreck: "I'm going, but I'm going in the name of the Lord."

Smith, Donald (1820-1914). Scottish-born Canadian business and political leader. Before dying, Smith repeated verses from the hymn "O God of Bethel:" "O God of Bethel, by whose hand Thy people still are fed..."

Smith, Edward (1850-1912). English captain of the RMS *Titanic* that sank April 15, 1912 after colliding with an iceberg in the North Atlantic Ocean. Captain Smith perished with his ship. Numerous accounts of his last words exist, but their authenticity is questionable:

Alternatives: *To crewmembers: "Well boys, you've done your duty and done it well. I ask no more of you. I release you. You know the rule of the sea. It's every man for himself now, and God bless you."

* As the ship sank: "Be British boys, be British!"
* To oarsmen in nearby life boats: "Good boys, good lads… Don't mind me, men. God bless you."
* Before drowning: "Good-bye boys, I'm going to follow the ship!"
* "Let me go!"

Smith, Ellen (see DeGraff, Peter).

Smith, Elliott (1969-2003). American rock singer and songwriter. Suffering from depression and substance abuse, Smith apparently stabbed himself to death. His undated suicide message found on a Post-it note read: "I'm so sorry- love, Elliott. God forgive me."

Smith, Erasmus "Deaf" (1787-1837). American scout and spy in the Texas War of Independence. At the end, the hearing-challenged Smith facetiously requested: "When I die, bury me standing on my head, because I came into this world feet first and I've had bad luck ever since

Smith, Frederick (1872-1930). English statesman who rose to the rank of Lord Chancellor. Dying from complications of cirrhosis, to his clerk: "I'm afraid, Peteil!"

Smith, Hyrum (1800-1844). American religious leader and brother of Joseph Smith (below). Shot by a riot mob while awaiting trial for treason, Smith declared: "I'm a dead man!"

Smith, Jefferson "Soapy" (1860-1898). American con artist and crime boss whose nefarious activities extended from Colorado to Alaska. While in Alaska, a meeting was organized on a Skagway wharf to address a grievance against Smith. When his path was blocked by four guards, a gunfight ensued. Before Smith died of a wound to the chest, he tried to resist: "My God, don't shoot!"

Smith, John (1930-1983). American criminal, electrocuted for the murder of two individuals for insurance money: "Well, the Lord is going to get another one."

Smith, Joseph (1805-1844). American religious leader who founded the Church of Jesus Christ of Latter-day Saints. While awaiting trial for "treasonous acts" against a contentious newspaper, Smith and his brother Hyrum were shot and killed by a lynch mob in Illinois. Leaning over his wounded brother: "Oh! My poor, dear brother Hyrum!" Near death, Smith spoke to a colleague who survived the ordeal: "That's right, Brother Taylor, parry them off as well as you can... Oh, Lord! My God!"

Smith, Michael (1945-1986). American astronaut aboard the ill-fated space shuttle Challenger. As the shuttle roared skyward, Smith exclaimed 73 seconds into the flight: "Uh, oh!" A faulty seal on an external fuel tank caused an explosion that resulted in the loss of all onboard.

Smith, Perry (1928-1965). American criminal. Smith and Richard Hickock (above) murdered a Kansas family of four during a robbery. The crime was sensationalized in Truman Capote's book *In Cold Blood*. Before his execution by hanging, Smith opined: "I think it's a helluva thing to take a life in this manner. I don't believe in capital punishment, morally or legally. Maybe I had something to contribute, something... It would be meaningless to apologize for what I did. Even inappropriate. But I do. I apologize."

Alternative: * "I think it is a hell of a thing that a life has to be taken in this manner. I say this especially because there's a great deal I could have offered society. I certainly think capital punishment is legally and morally wrong. Any apology for what I have done would be meaningless at this time. I don't have any animosities toward anyone involved in this matter. I think that is all."

Smith, Robert Weston (see Wolfman Jack).

Smith, Sydney (1771-1845). English clergyman, humorist and writer. Searching for a medicine bottle, his nurse (some say wife) came across a half-filled container of ink. When she joked that he had taken a dose of ink by mistake, Smith quipped: "Then bring me all the blotting paper there is in the house!"

Smith, Thomas (1513-1577). English scholar and trusted advisor of Queen Elizabeth I. "It is a matter of lamentation that men know not for what end they were born into the world until they are ready to go out of it."

Smith, William (1727-1803). Scottish-born American clergyman and educator. To his physician: "By the Lord God, if you don't stay longer with me, I will send for another doctor."

Smoker Mankiller (died 1875). Native American criminal, convicted of the fatal shooting of a neighbor. Mankiller was tried at Fort Smith, Arkansas before "The Hanging Judge" Isaacs Parker. The condemned man's last comments were spoken in his native language and translated for the crowd: "I am prepared to die. I did not kill Short; I would acknowledge it if I had. I have never been guilty of a mean act in my life. I killed a Cherokee; but I killed him in self-defence. My conviction was caused by prejudice and false testimony."

Smollett, Tobias (1721-1771). Scottish writer and poet. Dying of an intestinal ailment, Smollett jokingly wrote to a friend, the surgeon John Hunter: "With respect to myself, I have nothing to say but that, if I can prevail upon my wife to execute my last will, you shall receive my poor carcase in a box after I am dead to be placed among your rarities. I am already so dry and emaciated, that I may pass for an Egyptian mummy, without any other preparation than some pitch and painted linen..." He spoke his last words to his wife: "All is well, my dear." Smollett died in Italy and was buried there.

Snow, Catherine (c. 1793-1834). Canadian criminal, executed by hanging for the alleged murder of her husband. Pregnant at the time of conviction, her execution was delayed until the birth of her baby. On the scaffold: "I was a wretched woman, but as innocent of any participation in the crime of murder as an unborn child."

Snow, Edgar (1905-1972). American journalist who wrote about the Chinese Communist Revolution. As two friends entered his room, Snow said: "Well, we three old bandits!" He then became comatose and died without speaking further.

Snyder, Adam (1799-1842). American politician who became a member of the U.S. House of Representatives. To a friend: "Thompson, is it not hard that now I am prepared to live and serve my country, I must die."

Snyder, Ruth (1895-1928). American criminal who was electrocuted for the murder of her husband: "Oh, Father, forgive them for they know not what they do... Father, forgive me! Oh, Father, forgive me! Father, forgive them, Father, forgive them..."

Sobhuza II (1899-1982). King of Swaziland, Africa. During a meeting with advisors concerning political relations with other African states, Sobhuza told his minister of health: "I am going." When asked where, the king smiled, waved goodbye and died.

Sobieski, John III (1629-1696). King of Poland. Possibly lamenting his difficulty establishing domestic policies: "... For God's sake, do not suppose that any good thing can come out of this age when vice has increased to such an enormous degree as almost to exclude all hopes of forgiveness from the mercy of the Deity... My orders are not attended to while I am alive; can I expect to be obeyed when I am dead? Where corruption universally prevails... the voice of conscience is not heard and reason and equity are no more... What can you say to that, Mr. Will-maker?"

Socrates (c. 469-399 BCE) Greek philosopher who ran afoul of the Athenian hierarchy for some of his teachings and contrary views. Forced to ingest hemlock, Socrates spoke to one of his disciples as he lay dying: "Crito, we ought to offer a cock to Asclepius [the Greek god of medicine, also spelled Asclepois and Aesculapius]. See to it, and don't forget."

Alternatives: * "Crito, we owe a cock to Asclepois; pay it and do not forget."
* "Crito, I owe a cock to Aesculapius; do not forget to pay it."
* "Crito, we owe a rooster to Asclepius. Please, don't forget to pay the debt."

Sonnier, Elmo "Pat" (1950-1984). American criminal, executed by electrocution for a double murder. Sonnier spoke to the father of one of his victims: "Mr. LeBlanc, I can understand the way you feel. I have no hatred in my heart, and as I leave this world, I ask God to forgive what... I have done. I ask you to have forgiveness." Sister Helen Prejean, a Roman Catholic nun, became Sonnier's spiritual advisor and was present at his execution. Sonnier was one of the felons featured in Prejean's book *Dead Man Walking.*

Soo, Jack, born Goro Suzuki (1917-1979). Japanese-American actor and comic. Dying of esophageal cancer: "It must have been the coffee." In one of his television roles, Soo had the reputation for making terrible coffee.

Sophia Charlotte (1744-1818). German-born Queen Consort of George III, King of Great Britain and Ireland. Thinking that Charlotte was comatose, one of her attendants remarked: "This is a life of toil and trouble, but there is another life beyond it, in which none shall know trouble." The Queen who had heard every word replied: "*Very true.*"

Sophie Charlotte, Duchesse d'Alençon (1847–1897). Bavarian-born philanthropist. Sophie Charlotte perished in a fire at a Parisian charity bazaar, refusing rescue until others were evacuated: "Because of my title, I was the first to enter here. I shall be the last to go out."

Sophonisba (fl. around 200 BCE). Carthaginian noblewoman who was married to Masinissa, a North African Numibian leader. Because of her Carthaginian sympathies, the Romans ordered Masinissa to surrender Sophonisba for transport to Rome. Instead, he offered her a draft of poison: "I accept this nuptial present; nor is it an unwelcome one, if my husband can render me no better service. Tell him, however, that I should have died with greater satisfaction had I not married so near upon my death."

Alternative: * "If my husband has for his new wife no better gift than a cup of death, I know his will and accept what he bestows. I might have died more honorably if I had not wedded so near to my funeral."

Soubirous, Saint Bernadette (1844-1879). French nun who reported multiple visions of the Virgin Mary. Dying of tuberculosis, Bernadette agonized: "Oh! Oh! Oh! My God, I love Thee with all my heart and with all my soul and with all my strength." Later, she implored: "Mother of God, pray for me, poor sinner! Mother of God, pray for me, poor sinner!" When asked what could be done for her, Bernadette replied: "I want you to help me." As she died: "Poor sinner."

Alternative: * "All this is good for heaven! Blessed Mary, Mother of God, pray for me a poor sinner. A poor sinner."

Soucek, Karel (1947-1985). Czech-born Canadian stunt man. In 1984, Soucek successfully plunged over Niagara Falls in a specially designed barrel. The following year, he arranged a similar extravaganza where he and his barrel would be dropped 180 feet into a tank of water to finance a planned Niagara Falls museum. Earlier, he responded to a question about the afterlife: "There is no heaven or hell; there is no God. It's all a myth. You're born, you live, one day you die and that's it." As the barrel fell, it accidentally struck the side of the tank, mortally injuring Soucek.

Sousa, John Philip (1854-1932). American conductor and composer who was known as the "March King." Over his career, Sousa wrote 136 marches and 15 operettas. Dying of a heart attack while on tour, to those attending him: "Oh, I don't need a doctor."

Sousley, Franklin (1925-1945). American soldier who was one of the six U.S. Marines captured in the iconic flag raising photograph taken on Iwo Jima Island during WWII. Sousley later was shot by a Japanese sniper. When asked how he was doing: "Not bad. I can't feel a thing." Some say he was killed instantly.

Southcott, Joanna (1750-1814). English religious fanatic and mystic. Southcott died convinced of her supernatural powers: "If I have been deceived, doubtless it was the work of a spirit. Whether the spirit was good or bad I do not know."

Southey, Robert (1774-1843). English poet laureate and writer. Before his dementia deepened: "Memory, memory, where art thou gone?"

Spafford, Horatio (1828-1888). American lawyer, religious leader and hymnodist. Spafford wrote the hymn "It Is Well with My Soul" following multiple personal tragedies including the deaths of his four daughters in a maritime accident. Dying of malaria, to his wife: "Annie, I have experienced a great joy! I have seen wonderful things!"

Speaker, Tristram "Tris" (1888-1958). American major league baseball player. Dying of a heart attack, Speaker told a doctor: "My name is Tris Speaker."

Speijk, Jan van (1802-1831). Dutch naval officer. During the Belgian War of Independence, Speijk's vessel inadvertently entered an enemy port. Rather than surrender, he detonated onboard explosives saying: "Rather to blow up, then!"

Spellman, Francis (1889-1967). Roman Catholic archbishop of New York. To his physician: "Now don't you worry about anything."

Spencer, Diana, Princess of Wales (see Diana, Princess of Wales).

Spencer, Henry (died 1914). American criminal who murdered a dance teacher. On the scaffold: "What I got to say is that I'm innocent of the murder of Allison Rexroat! I never killed her! It's a lie! You're all dirty b*******! You got no right! I never touched her! So help me, God, I never harmed a hair on her head! So help me God!"

Spencer, Herbert (1820-1903). English philosopher, biologist and sociologist. Spencer's concepts of evolution preceded those of Charles Darwin (above). "Now I take this step for the benefit of those who are to be my executors: my intention being that after death this my body shall be conveyed by sea to Portsmouth." His remains were cremated and interred in a London cemetery.

Spencer, Stanley (1891-1959). English artist. Dying of cancer, to the nurse who had given him an injection: "Beautifully done."

Spengler, Peter (died c. 1525). German Protestant martyr. Because of his conflict with the Catholic Church, Spengler was condemned to die by drowning. "It is all one, for shortly I must have forsaken this skin, which already scarcely hangeth to my bones. I know well that I am a mortal and a corruptible worm, and have nothing in me but corruption. I have long time desired my latter day, and have made my request that I might be delivered out of this mortal body, to be joined with my Savior Christ. I have deserved through my manifold sins committed against my Savior Jesus Christ, my cross, and my Savior Christ hath borne the cross, and hath died upon the cross, and for my part I will not glory in any other thing, but only in the cross of Jesus Christ."

Spenkelink, John (1949-1979). American criminal, electrocuted for the murder of a traveling companion: "Capital punishment- them without the capital get the punishment."

Spies, August (1855-1887). German-American anarchist and labor union activist. Eight union leaders, including Spies, were condemned to hang for their involvement in Chicago's Haymarket Square riot where a number of people were killed or injured. Spies spoke prior to his execution: "There will come a time when our silence will be more powerful than the voices you strangle today!"

Spinoza, Baruch (1632-1677). Dutch philosopher. Dying of tuberculosis, to friends departing for church: "God willing, we shall resume our conversation after the sermon." Later: "God have mercy upon me and be gracious to me, a miserable sinner." A physician present at the time of death failed to provide a record of Spinoza's actual last words.

Spruance, Raymond (1886-1969). American naval leader of the U.S. Pacific Fleet during WWII and later, ambassador to the Philippines. To his nurse: "I want to say goodnight to my wife."

Spurgeon, Charles (1834-1892). English clergyman and writer. Awakening temporarily from a coma, to his wife: "Oh, Wifie, I have had such a blessed time with my Lord!"

Squanto, also called Tisquantum (died 1622). Native American member of the Pawtuxet tribe who aided the newly-arrived Pilgrim settlers in Plymouth, Massachusetts. Dying of "Indean feavor," to William Bradford, the Pilgrim leader: "Please pray for me, Governor, that I might go to the Englishmen's God in heaven." As he died, Squanto bequeathed his possessions to his English friends.

Stack, Andrew Joseph "Joe" (1956-2010). American software engineer. Because of an ongoing dispute with the Internal Revenue Service, Stack piloted his single-engine aircraft into the Austin, Texas tax bureau building, killing himself and one agent while injuring thirteen others. As he took-off, he told the control tower: "Going southbound, sir... Thanks for your help. Have a great day." Stack's suicide note read in part: "… I saw it written once that the definition of insanity is repeating the same process over and over and expecting the outcome to suddenly be different. I am finally ready to stop this insanity. Well, Mr. Big Brother IRS man, let's try something different; take my pound of flesh and sleep well."

Staël-Holstein, Anne de (1766-1817). French writer, self-exiled for her opposition to Napoleon I. During her last illness: "I have always been the same, ardent and sad; I have loved God, my father and liberty." After receiving a dose of opium, she was asked if she could sleep: "Yes, heavily, like a big peasant woman." She died without waking.

Alternative: * "Soundly and sweetly."

Stahl, Charles "Chick" (1873-1907). American major league baseball player and manager. Complaining about the stress of his job and personal problems, Stahl drank carbolic acid and left a suicide note that read: "Boys, I just couldn't help it. You drove me to it."

Alternative: * Some say he staggered into a teammate's room and said: "I couldn't help it. I did it, Jim. It was killing me and I couldn't stand it."

Staley, Layne (1967-2002). Member of the American band, Alice in Chains. After arguing with a friend, the drug-addicted Staley pleaded: "Not like this. Don't leave like this. Not like this." The musician's decomposed body was discovered several weeks later.

Stalin, Joseph (1878-1953). Soviet Union dictator. Suffering a massive stroke, Stalin mumbled a response to a query whether a physician should be called: "Dz... dz..." The dictator realistically was unable to communicate in the hours before his death, although some contend that he deliriously asked: "Where am I...What the hell? Oh God d***** no! I couldn't find the left foot sock. Is it under the chair?"

Stallings, George (1867-1929). American major league baseball player and manager who urged his pitchers to avoid walking batters. On his deathbed, when asked what caused his bad heart: "Oh, those bases on balls!"

Stambolov, Stefan (1854-1895). Bulgarian prime minister. Assassinated by political enemies, Stambolov was ambushed while on a carriage ride. To his wife as he died: "... You were a good wife. Be a good mother to the children. God preserve you and Bulgaria!"

Stanford, Jane (1828-1905). American philanthropist. Stanford and her husband co-founded Stanford University in California. Dying of strychnine poisoning: "My jaws are stiff. This is a horrible death to die." Her murderer was never identified.

Stanhope, Philip, Fourth Earl of Chesterfield (1694-1773). English statesman and writer. On the visit of his godson Solomon Dayrolles: "Give Dayrolles a chair."

Stanislas I (1677-1766). King of Poland. Stanislas commented on his bathrobe, which caught fire and caused mortal burns: "You gave it to me to warm me, but it has kept me too hot!"

Stanislavsky, Konstantin (1863-1938). Russian actor and director of the Moscow Art Theatre. Asked if he wished to send a letter to his sister: "I've lots to say to her, not just something. But not now. I'm sure to get it all mixed up."

Stanley, Arthur (1815-1881). English clergyman who became Dean of Westminster Abbey. "The end has come in the way in which I most desired it should come. I could not have controlled it better. After preaching one of my sermons on the beatitudes, I had a most violent fit of sickness, took to my bed, and said immediately that I wished to die at Westminster. I am perfectly happy, perfectly satisfied; I have no misgivings." His last recorded words were: "I wish Vaughan to preach my funeral sermon, because he has known me longest."

Stanley, Henry (1841-1904). Welsh explorer and journalist who found the missing missionary David Livingstone in Africa ("Dr. Livingstone, I presume?"). Toward the end, Stanley's mind wandered: "... Oh, I want to be free!. I want to go into the woods and be free! I want- I want- to go home." To his wife: "Goodnight, dear; go to bed, darling." Hearing Big Ben chime: "Four o'clock. How strange! So that is the time. Strange!" When offered a stimulant, he refused saying: "Enough!"

Stanton, Charles (1811-1846). American explorer and member of the ill-fated Donner Party expedition traveling from Missouri to California.

Stanton died in the Sierra Nevada mountain range when he became too weak to travel further. When asked by a fellow traveler if he were coming: "Yes, I'm coming soon."

Stanton, Edwin (1814-1869). American politician who served as President Lincoln's Secretary of War. Dying of a respiratory ailment (some say a heart attack), Stanton asked for a clergyman: "Send for Dr. Starkey."

Stanton, Elizabeth (1815-1902). American women's rights activist. To her doctor the day before dying of heart failure: "Now, if you can't cure this difficulty of breathing, and if I am not to feel brighter and more like work again, I want you to give me something to send me pack-horse straight to heaven." On the day of her death: "Now I'll be dressed." Stanton later died in her sleep.

Stanton, Louise (died 1933). American aviator and adventurer. Mourning the recent loss of her husband, Stanton flew her plane toward the Atlantic Ocean in an apparent suicidal act: "I'm just going out into space to find out what it's all about; if there isn't anything, that will be OK too."

Starkweather, Charles (1938-1959). American serial killer. Starkweather and his accomplice Carol Fugate murdered 11 people over a two month period during the winter of 1957-58. Before his execution by electrocution, Starkweather was asked if he would donate his eyes to an organ bank: "Hell no! No one ever did anything for me. Why in the hell should I do anything for anyone else?"

Starr, Myra Maybelle "Belle" (1848-1889). American outlaw, branded the "Bandit Queen" of the Old West. Ambushed by an unknown assailant, to her daughter: "Baby, your brother Eddie shot me. I turned and seen him cross the fence, after he cracked down on me the second time." Some claim that Starr died without speaking. The murder was never solved.

States, Edward (died 2001). Pilot of American Airlines Flight 587 that crashed after takeoff from John F. Kennedy International Airport in New York City. "Get out of it. Get out of it." All 260 on board and five on the ground perished. The accident was attributed to overuse of rudder controls to counteract turbulence. These actions resulted in loss of the aircraft's vertical stabilizer and subsequent airworthiness.

Stauffenberg, Claus von (1907-1944). WWII German army officer. Seconds before his execution by a Nazi firing squad for his involvement in the 1944 attempt on the life of Adolf Hitler: "Long live our holy Germany!"

Stedman, Edmund (1833-1908). American poet, essayist and businessman. Looking at accumulated mail shortly before he died: "Twenty-seven letters! What is the use?"

Steele, Anne (1716-1778). English hymn writer. On her deathbed, Steele thought of words from Job 19:25: "I know that my Redeemer liveth."

Stein, Gertrude (1874-1946). American-born writer and poet. Before surgery for stomach cancer, to her companion Alice Toklas: "What is the answer?" When there was no response, she laughed and asked: "In that case, what is the question?" She died several days postoperatively.

Stein, Heinrich (1757-1831). Prussian statesman. To his agent: "As I believe firmly in an enduring communion between the living and the dead, it will be a joy to me to see from above that you serve my children with the same true devotion that you have shown to me." Stein admonished a young man at his bedside, should war break out: "Fight like a good Prussian for king and country."

Steinbeck, John (1902-1968). Nobel and Pulitzer Prize-winning American writer, best-known for his novel *The Grapes of Wrath*. When Steinbeck's wife asked: "What is it?" he referred to a friend, Shirley Fisher: "I seem to hear the sound of distant drums... Maybe it's just Shirley playing the bagpipes."

Steinberg, Milton (1903-1950). American rabbi, philosopher and writer. To his nurse: "I have to apologize to my wife and children for leaving them in such a spot."

Steiner, Rudolf (1861-1925). Austrian philosopher and social reformer. To a friend: "Why do modern poets feel such a fear of supersensible wisdom?" When his companion answered: "Because there are no poets," Steiner rejoined: "Yes, but it must be a poet who says that."

Steinmetz, Charles (1865-1923). German-born American electrical engineer and mathematician who pioneered the development of alternating current. Dying of heart failure, Steinmetz was advised to stay in bed: "All right, I will lie down again." He expired moments later.

Stengel, Charles "Casey" (1890-1975). American major league baseball player and manager. While watching a game on television, the National Anthem was played. Stengel, dying of cancer, stood, placed his hand over his heart and spoke his last words: "I might as well do this one last time."

Stephen of Jerusalem, Saint (died c. 35). Stephen, a follower of Jesus Christ, ran afoul of the Jewish hierarchy in Jerusalem and was stoned to death for his "blasphemous" preaching (Acts 7: 56-60). "Behold, I see the heavens opened and the Son of Man standing at the right hand of God... Lord Jesus, receive my spirit." Stephen then knelt down and said: "Lord, do not hold this sin against them."

Sterne, Laurence (1713-1768). Irish-born novelist and clergyman, best-known for his novel *The Life and Opinions of Tristram Shandy, Gentleman.* Dying of tuberculosis, Sterne held up an arm as if he were warding off a blow and said: "Now it has come."

Stevens, Thaddeus (1792-1868). American politician, abolitionist and member of the U.S. House of Representatives. To his attendant who asked if he needed anything: "Nothing more in this world."

Stevenson, Adlai (1900-1965). American politician who twice ran unsuccessfully for the U.S. presidency. Dying of a heart attack: "I feel faint."

Stevenson, Marmaduke (died 1659). Martyred English-born American Quaker. Because he refused to alter his religious beliefs in accordance with the Massachusetts Bay Colony, Stevenson was sentenced to die by hanging: "Be it known unto you all this day that we suffer not as evil-doers, but for conscience's sake. This day shall we be at rest with the Lord."

Stevenson, Robert Louis (1850-1894). Scottish author, best-known for his novels *Treasure Island* and *Dr. Jekyll and Mr. Hyde*. Dying of a cerebral hemorrhage, to his wife: "I have a strange pain in my head." Some say he spoke words to the effect: "What's that? Do I look strange?"

Alternatives: * "What's that! Does my face look strange?"
* "My head, my head!"

Stewart, James "Jimmy" (1908-1997). American film and stage actor. Speaking of his late wife: "I'm going to go be with Gloria now."

Stewart, Robert, Viscount Castlereagh (1769-1822). Irish-born British foreign secretary and leader of the House of Commons. Severely depressed, Stewart committed suicide by cutting his throat (jugulation). To his physician: "I have done for myself. I have opened my neck."

Alternative: * "Bankhead, let me fall into your arms. It is all over."

Stillwell, Joseph "Vinegar Joe" (1883-1946). American commander of U.S. forces in the China-Burma-India Theater during WWII. Dying of stomach cancer: "Say, isn't this Sunday?" He expired on a Saturday.

Stoker, David (1959-1997). American criminal, executed by lethal injection for the murder of a convenience store clerk during a robbery: "I have a statement prepared that I have given to the Chaplain that I want released to the media. I am ready, Warden." In his written statement, Stoker steadfastly proclaimed his innocence but concluded his message: "... Let's rock 'n roll. The End. David Stoker."

Stolberg, Friedrich von (1750-1819). German poet. To his physician: "Will it be over with me tomorrow or the day after tomorrow?" When answered affirmatively: "God be praised! I thank you! I thank you with all my heart! *Praised be Jesus Christ*!" He died moments later.

Stone, Harland (1872-1946). Chief justice of the U.S. Supreme Court. Stricken with a cerebral hemorrhage moments before he was to deliver a decision: "The case should be stayed; we decided to send this case back to conference for reconsideration."

Stone, John (died 1840). American criminal, hanged for the murder of Lucretia Thompson, a farmer's wife: "I swear to you, sheriff, I am an innocent man. I have never been to the Thompson house, and I never saw Mrs. Thompson on the day that she was murdered. I believe that there were two of them- two men- who did the murder that I've been wrongly accused of... Even if I did know their names, I'd swing before I'd have their blood upon me."

Stone, Lucy (1818-1893). American abolitionist and suffragist. Dying of stomach cancer, to her daughter: "Make the world better."

Stone, Samuel (1602-1663). Anglo-American Puritan clergyman. Discussing several deceased associates: "Heaven is the more desirable for such company as Hooker and Shepherd and Haynes who are got there before me"

Stonhouse, James (1716-1795). English physician and clergyman. "The great conflict is over; now all is done... Precious salvation!"

Stowe, Calvin (1802-1886). American biblical scholar and educator who was the husband of Harriet Beecher Stowe (below). Dying of kidney failure: "Peace with God! Peace with God!"

Stowe, Harriet Beecher (1811-1896). American abolitionist and writer, best-known for her novel *Uncle Tom's Cabin*. To her nurse: "I love you."

Strachey, Lytton (1880-1932). English biographer and critic. Succumbing to cancer: "If this is dying, then I don't think much of it."

Straus, Oscar (1870-1954). Austrian composer, primarily of operettas, songs and film scores. When asked how he was doing: "Well, good."

Straus, Rosalie (1849-1912). German-American wife of the businessman and politician, Isidor Straus. Refusing to enter a lifeboat on the sinking RMS *Titanic*, to her husband: "We have been together for 40 years, and we will not separate now." His body was recovered but Rosalie's remains were not found.

Alternative: * "We have lived together for many years. Where you go, I go."

Strauss, David (1808-1874). German theologian, best-known for his book *Life of Jesus*: "My philosophy leaves me utterly forlorn! I feel like one caught in the merciless jaws of an automatic machine, not knowing at what time one of its great hammers may crush me."

Strauss, Johann, Jr. (1825-1899). Austrian conductor and composer, best-known for his waltzes, polkas, marches and operettas. Terminally ill from pneumonia and pleurisy, "The Waltz King" roused from sleep and sang a few words of a song written by his former music teacher Joseph Drechsler: "... es muss geschieden sein," loosely translated "... it is time to part." When his wife asked him to rest, Strauss replied: "I will, whatever happens." He then died peacefully in his sleep.

Strauss, Richard (1864-1949): German classical composer and conductor, best-known for his tone poems and operas. To his daughter-in-law: "Funny thing, Alice, dying is just the way I composed it in *Tod und Verklärung* [his tone-poem *Death and Transfiguration*]." Strauss died peacefully in his sleep shortly thereafter.

Stravinsky, Igor (1882-1971). Russian-born conductor and composer who scandalized the Parisian musical scene with his 1913 modernistic ballet and concert piece *The Rite of Spring*. To a nurse wheeling him through his new Manhattan apartment: "How lovely! This belongs to me. It is my new home." He died of heart failure later that night.

Streicher, Julius (1885-1946). German Nazi propagandist and publisher, convicted of crimes against humanity during WWII. Before Streicher was hanged: "Now it goes to God..." He then faced the witnesses and screamed: "Purim Fest [a Jewish commemoration of deliverance] 1946...

The Bolsheviks will hang you one day. I am with God." As the hood was lowered over his head: "Adele, my dear wife!"

Alternative: * "Heil Hitler! This is my Purim celebration 1946. I go to God. The Bolshevists will one day hang you, too."

Stresemann, Gustav (1878-1929). German chancellor and foreign minister of the Weimar Republic. Stresemann was awarded the 1926 Nobel Peace Prize for his efforts to reconcile Germany and France in the post- WWI period. Before dying of a heart attack: "I'm all right, perfectly all right."

Strindberg, August (1849-1912). Swedish dramatist, writer and artist. Dying of cancer: "Everything is atoned for." To his nurse who arose to adjust his pillow: "No, lie where you were before. Don't bother about me. I no longer exist."

Stritch, Samuel (1887–1958). Archbishop of Chicago. Celebrating mass for the first time after having an arm amputated for a blood clot: "Well, I feel like a priest again." Later, he suffered a stroke and remained speechless except for his reply of "Yes" when asked if he were all right.

Stroheim, Erich von (1885-1957). Austrian director and film star. Dying of cancer, to a friend: "This isn't the worst. The worst is that they [Hollywood] stole twenty-five years of my life."

Strong, Nathan (1748-1816). American clergyman and hymnodist. To an acquaintance: "Death is to me but as going into the next room; and to that next room most of my friends have already gone, many more than are here among the living."

Strozzi, Filippo (1488-1538). Florentine plotter against the Medici dynasty. Imprisoned by Cosimo de Medici, Strozzi left a note before he died: "If I have not hitherto known how to live, I shall know how to die." Some say he scratched a line from Virgil's *Aeneid* with his sword on the prison wall: "From my blood an avenger will arise to others." Strozzi then committed suicide by falling on his sword.

Alternatives:* "But from my bones, may some avenger rise!"
* "May some Avenger from my ashes rise!"

Stuart, Anne (see Anne Stuart, Queen of England).

Stuart, James (died 1851). Australian-born American robber and murderer. Before his hanging: "I die reconciled; my sentence is just."

Stuart, James "Jeb" (1833-1864). Confederate general during the U.S. Civil War. Mortally wounded during the Battle of Yellow Tavern (an abandoned inn north of Richmond, Virginia), Stuart said: "I am resigned, if it be God's will, but I would like to see my wife... but God's will be done." Then, to his physician: "Doctor, I suppose I am going fast now. It will soon be over. But God's will be done. I hope I have fulfilled my destiny to my country and my duty to my God..." After making provisions for disposal of his worldly possessions, Stuart sang several verses of the hymn "Rock of Ages." Again, to his doctor: "I am going fast now. I am resigned. God's will be done."

Stuart, Jesse (1907-1984). American writer, poet and educator. Finishing a prayer with his wife and a friend, Stuart concluded with "Amen" and suffered a massive stroke.

Suárez, Francisco (1548-1617). Spanish Jesuit theologian and philosopher. "I would have never believed it so sweet to die."

Sucre, Antonio José de (1795-1830). Venezuelan military leader who allied with Simón Bolivar (above) in the liberation of South American states from Spain. Shot by an assassin while riding his horse in the Colombian jungle: "D***! A bullet!"

Sulayman II (died 1016). Caliph of Córdoba, Spain. When the vanquished Suleiman appeared with his father and brother before the victorious Berber force that overran his empire, he implored "Strike me only; these are innocent." Regardless, the three were beheaded.

Suleiman I, the Magnificent, also Suleyman (1494-1566). Ruler of the Ottoman Empire. Dying before concluding a battle in Hungary: "The drum of victory had not yet beat."

Sulla, Lucius (c. 138-78 BCE) Roman consul and military leader. "No friend ever served me, and no enemy ever wronged me, whom I have not repaid in full."

Sullivan, Arthur (1842-1900): British composer who collaborated with librettist William Gilbert (above) to produce a series of comic operas, including *The Pirates of Penzance*, *H.M.S. Pinafore* and *The Mikado*. Sullivan's last diary entry several weeks before his death read: "Lovely day... I am sorry to leave such a lovely day." Succumbing to heart failure and bronchitis, he moaned: "My heart! My heart!"

Sullivan, Jack (died 1936). American criminal, executed in the Arizona gas chamber for the murder of a railroad worker. Sullivan responded to a query if he needed anything "Yes, you might get me a gas mask."

Sullivan, John (1858-1918). American champion professional heavyweight boxer. Dying of a heart attack: "I'll be all right in a little while."

Sumner, Charles (1811-1874). American lawyer and abolitionist who was elected to the U.S. Senate. Dying of a heart attack, to a colleague: "... The Civil Rights Bill, don't let it be lost- don't let it fail, my bill, The Civil Rights Bill!" To a friend who was a neighbor of the poet Ralph Waldo Emerson: "Judge, tell Emerson how much I love and revere him." To another friend entering his room: "Sit down."

Sun Yat-sen (1866-1925). Chinese liberator and first president of the newly-formed Republic of China. Dying of cancer: "Peace, struggle, save China."

Sunday, William "Billy" (1862-1935). American professional baseball player and evangelist. Suffering chest pains, Sunday was told by a physician that nothing was wrong. As the doctor left, Sunday said: "Don't forget me, Doc." Later, as he died, to his wife: "I'm getting dizzy, Ma."

Surratt, Mary (c. 1820-1865). American innkeeper, hanged for her alleged part in the conspiracy to assassinate President Abraham Lincoln. Surratt was the first woman executed by the United States federal government. To a priest: "Holy Father, can I not tell these people before I die that I am innocent of the crime for which I have been condemned to death." Her request was denied. To a guard moving her to the spot of execution: "Please don't let me fall."

Susann, Jacqueline (1918-1974). American writer, best-known for her novel *Valley of the Dolls*. Dying of cancer, to her husband: "Let's get the hell outta here [the hospital], doll." To a friend: "Goodbye, my darling."

Sutter, Johann "John" (1803-1880). German-born American pioneer. Sutter's discovery of gold on his property sparked the 1849 California Gold Rush. When told that the U.S. House of Representatives had failed to act on a land claim he had made: "Next year... they will surely..."

Svevo, Italo (see Schmitz, Aron Ettore)

Swedenborg, Emanuel (1688-1772). Swedish scientist, theologian, mystic and writer, best-known for his book on the afterlife *Heaven and Hell*. His response when told the time: "It is well. I thank you. God bless you."

Sweeney, Brian (1963-2001). American business consultant. Sweeney was a passenger on the hijacked United Airlines Flight 175 that crashed into the South Tower of the World Trade Center during the September 11, 2001 attacks. Telephone message to his wife Julie: "Hey, Jules. It's Brian. I'm on a plane that's been hijacked. It doesn't look good. I just want to tell you how much I love you. I hope that I call you again. But if not, I want you to have fun. I want you to live your life. I know I'll see you someday."

Swetchine, Anne-Sofia (1782-1857). Russian-born Parisian hostess, writer and mystic. A devout Roman Catholic, Swetchine replied when told the time: "It will soon be time for mass. They must raise me."

Swift, Anne (1843-1922). American teetotaler and widow of Gustavus Swift (below). To her physician who advised sherry as a stimulant: "Well, doctor, I'm your patient and it's my duty to cooperate with you and I will- *even to the extent of drinking sherry.*"

Swift, Gustavus (1839-1903). American philanthropist and industrialist who founded one of the largest meat-packing firms in the world. While recovering from an operation, to his wife: "I like to hear you read." Swift died suddenly as she read.

Swift, Jonathan (1667-1745). Anglo-Irish writer, satirist and poet, best-known for his book *Gulliver's Travels.* During his last years, Swift's mind became unsound. On his deathbed, he was visited by the composer George Handel (above): "Ah! A German and a genius! A prodigy- admit him!" Later, to his nurse: "I am dying like a poisoned rat in a hole. I am what I am! I am what I am!"

Swift, Rigby (1874-1937). British Member of Parliament and jurist. Before succumbing to a heart attack, Swift penned a last letter: "My dear Chief, Your most kind and sympathetic letter has been a wonderful tonic and already I feel much better. Yours very faithfully, Rigby Swift."

Switzer, Carl "Alfalfa" (1927-1959). American child star of the *Our Gang* film series. Switzer was shot to death during an argument over a debt. "I want that fifty bucks you owe me and I want it now."

Sylvester I, Saint (died 335). Pope from 314 until his death. To his followers: "Love one another, govern your churches diligently and protect your flocks from the teeth of wolves."

Symons, William (1843-1899). British army officer, mortally wounded in the Boer War during the Battle of Talana Hill, Natal, South Africa. Surveying the battle scene from a rampart, Symons ignored his subordinates' warning to take cover: "I am severely- mortally- wounded in the stomach." To his attending doctor: "Tell everyone I died facing the enemy. Tell everyone I died facing the enemy."

Synge, John (1871-1909). Irish dramatist. Dying of cancer: "It's no use fighting death any longer."

Tabor, Horace (1830-1899). American prospector, businessman and politician. Dying from complications of appendicitis, to his wife, the notorious Baby Doe: "Hold on to the Matchless Mine. It will make millions again when silver comes back." Tabor probably did not own the mine at the time of his death; his wife died in poverty 35 years later.

Tacitus, Publius (56-117). Roman senator and historian who left directions for his burial: "... At my funeral let no token of sorrow be seen, no pompous mockery of woe. Crown me with chaplets [prayer beads], strew flowers on my grave, and let my friends erect no vain memorial to tell where my remains are lodged."

Taft, Robert (1889-1953). U.S. congressman who was the son of President William Taft. Dying of cancer and a cerebral hemorrhage, to his wife: "Well, Martha... Glad to see you looking so well."

Tait, Archibald (1811-1882). Scottish-born Archbishop of Canterbury. To relatives and friends at his deathbed: "And now it is all over. It isn't so very dreadful after all." When they offered to pen a response to a letter of affection sent by the queen: "No, I will write it myself. Give me pen and paper." His note read: "A last memorial of twenty-six years of devoted service: with earnest love and affectionate blessing on the Queen and her family." Shortly before Tait died: "It is coming. It is coming."

Takahama, Masami (died 1985). Japan Airlines pilot. On August 12, 1985 Japan Airlines Flight 123 departed Tokyo International Airport for Osaka. Approximately 12 minutes into the flight, the aircraft suffered a massive decompression that resulted in a crash 32 minutes later. Immediately before striking a mountain, Captain Takahama ordered: "Raise nose. Raise nose. Power…" Only four of 524 on board survived.

Talleyrand, Henri de, Comte de Chalais (1599-1626). French soldier and aide to King Louis XIII. Condemned for his involvement in the conspiracy against Cardinal Richelieu, Talleyrand was beheaded. To his executioner: "Do not keep me in suspense." Because the executioner was inexperienced, multiple blows were required to sever Talleyrand's head. Until the bitter end, the condemned man uttered Jesus' name.

Talleyrand-Périgord, Charles-Maurice de (1754-1838). French statesman and bishop. When told that the Archbishop of Paris wished that he could die in his place: "He can find a better use for it." Toward the end, King Louis Philippe asked Talleyrand how he felt. The statesman replied: "I am suffering, Sire, the pangs of the damned." After the King left his bedside, Talleyrand remarked: "It is beautiful to die in this house, where the king has paid a visit." When a priest tried to anoint Talleyrand's hands at the conclusion of the Last Rites, the dying man said: "No, no, *Monsieur L'Abbé.* You forget that I am a bishop [of Autun, France]." By custom, the priest then anointed the top of his hands.

Alternative: * "Sire, you have come to witness the sufferings of a dying man; and those who love him can have but one wish, that of seeing them shortly at an end... Sire, our house has received this day an honour worthy to be inscribed in our annals, and one which my successors will remember with pride and gratitude."

Talma, François-Joseph (1763-1826). French actor and theatrical manager. Complaining of a visual problem: "The worst is, I cannot see."

Alternative: * "Voltaire... like Voltaire... always like Voltaire... The hardest thing of all is not to see."

Tamerlane, also called Timur (1336-1405). Mongol leader who conquered a large swath of Asia. Dying during a bitterly cold winter while leading his troops against the Chinese: "Never has death been frightened away by screaming." To his sons and grandsons: "Do not forget the precepts I gave you for the good of the people. Keep yourselves informed about the condition of the common people, sustain the weak and, above all, restrain the avarice and ambition of the powerful. May justice and kindness constantly direct your conduct. Know how to wield your sword with wisdom and valor, if you want to enjoy a long reign and a strong empire. Beware of discord among yourselves, for your courtiers and your enemies will never cease to exploit your reverses of fortune. Faithfully observe the rules of government I left you in my political testament. Finally, always remember the last words of a dying father."

Taney, Roger (1777-1864). U.S. Supreme Court justice. Perceiving the end was approaching: "Lord Jesus, receive my spirit."

Tanner, Henry (1859-1937). American-born artist who worked in France most of his adult life. To a friend: "How beautiful spring-time is in Paris. The earth is awakening once more."

Tarachus, Saint (died c. 304). Christian martyr from present-day Syria. Tarachus refused to renounce his Christian religion and was imprisoned with two fellow martyrs, Saint Andronicus and Saint Probus (above). When the proconsul asked Tarachus his name three times, the holy man replied to each query: "I am a Christian." When told he could save himself by sacrificing to idols: "Away, thou minister of Satan, and keep thy advice for thy own use... O God of heaven, look down upon me and be my judge." The three Christians were tortured and later hacked to death.

Tarbell, Ida (1857-1944). American journalist. Dying of pneumonia over the Christmas holidays, Tarbell was asked by a group of carolers visiting her hospital room which carol she would like to hear: "Hark, the Herald Angels Sing." She then lost consciousness and died a few days later.

Tarkovsky, Andrei (1932-1986). Russian filmmaker and theatre director. Dying of lung cancer: "It is time for a new direction..."

Tasso, Torquato (1544-1595). Italian poet who died of mental illness shortly before he was to receive a crown of laurels from the pope: "This is the crown with which I hoped to be crowned. It is not the glory of the poet's laurel, but the glory of the blessed in heaven." As he died: "Lord, into Thy hands I commend my spirit."

Alternatives: * "This is the chariot on which I hope to go crowned, not with laurel as a poet into the capitol, but with glory as a saint into heaven."

* "This is the crown with which I hoped to be crowned, not as a poet in the Capitol, but with the glory of the blessed in heaven."

Tate, Sharon (1943-1969). American actress, stabbed to death by a member of the Charles Manson gang. The pregnant Tate begged her assailant: "Please — please don't kill me — I don't want to die. I just want to have my baby."

Tatum, Arthur "Art" (1909-1956). American jazz pianist. Dying of kidney failure, Tatum telephoned his sister who agreed to visit him: "I'll be looking for you."

Taylor, Bayard (1825-1878). American travel writer and poet. Dying of a liver ailment, to his wife and doctor: "I want- I want, oh, you know what I mean, that stuff of life."

Taylor, Jane (1783-1824). English writer of books for children who penned the lyrics: "Twinkle, Twinkle, Little Star." Dying of breast cancer: "Are we not children, all of us?" Before she expired: "Well, I don't think now I shall see Ann [her older sister] again; I feel I am dying fast."

Taylor, Jeremy (1613-1667). English theologian, Bishop of Down and Connor, and later Dromore, Northern Ireland. Dying of a fever: "My trust is in God... Bury me at Dromore."

Taylor, John (1580-1653). English poet and Thames waterman. Because of his avocation and occupation, Taylor called himself "The Water Poet." At his death: "How sweet it is to rest."

Taylor, Robert, born Spangler Arlington Brugh (1911-1969). American film and television actor. Dying of lung cancer, Taylor asked his friend Ronald Reagan: "I only have one request right now. Tell Ursula [his second wife], be happy."

Taylor, Rowland (1510-1555). English Protestant martyr. Branded a heretic for his words against the Roman Catholic Church, Taylor was sentenced to burn at the stake. As he was transferred back to Hadley, his place of rectory, the condemned man said: "I shall this day deceive the worms in Hadley churchyard." Asked to explain his statement: "I am as you see, a man that hath a very great carcass, which I thought should have been buried in Hadley churchyard, if I had died in my bed, as I well hoped I should have done. But herein I see I was deceived. And there are a great number of worms in Hadley churchyard, which should have had jolly feeding upon this carrion which they have looked for many a day. But now I know we be deceived, both I and they; for this carcass must be burnt to ashes, and so shall they lose their bait and feeding that they looked to have had of it." When he came within two miles of Hadley, Taylor remarked: "… I lack not past two styles to go over, and I am even at my Father's house." At the stake, a piece of wood was thrown at him drawing blood from his face. He mildly rebuked the offender by saying: "O friend, I have harm enough. What need of that?" As the flames burned higher, he prayed: "Merciful Father of heaven, for Jesus Christ my Savior's sake, receive my soul into Thy hands."

Taylor, Zachary (1784-1850). Twelfth U.S. president. Ill with gastroenteritis, to his wife: "I am about to die. I expect the summons soon. I have endeavored to discharge all my official duties faithfully. I regret nothing, but am sorry that I am about to leave my friends." He expired shortly thereafter.

Alternatives: * "I am not afraid to die: I am ready: I have endeavored to do my duty."
* "I am prepared to die. I have faithfully endeavored to do my duty."

Tchaikovsky, Pyotr (1840-1893): Russian composer, best-known for his symphonies, concertos, tone poems and ballets. When Tchaikovsky became delirious from complications of cholera, he repeated the feminine word "*proklyatya*" or "accursed one," possibly referring to his former benefactress Nadezhda von Meck. The word also could have alluded to his fatal disease cholera, which also is feminine in the Russian language. Some say he actually spoke von Meck's name. In the hours before his death, the composer was asked if he wanted something to drink. The weakened Tchaikovsky could respond only with affirmative or negative grunts.

Alternatives: * "Hope... accursed..."
* When given a drink: "That's enough."
* "I believe it's death."

Tecumseh (1768-1813). Native-American leader of the Shawnee confederacy. Killed fighting Americans during the War of 1812, to his men: "Be brave! Be strong! Be brave!... Brother warriors, we are now about to enter into an engagement from which I shall never come out. My body will remain on the field of battle." Handing his sword to a fellow combatant: "When my son becomes a noted warrior and able to wield a sword, give this to him." Before dying, Tecumseh commented: "One of my leg [*sic*] is shot off! But leave me one or two guns loaded. I am going to have a last shot. Be quick and go!"

Alternative: * "I am shot."

Teilhard de Chardin, Pierre (1881-1955). French theologian and paleontologist. Dying of heart disease: "I go to meet Him who comes!" When told that he had had a heart attack: "I can't remember anything. This time I feel it's terrible."

Tekakwitha, Saint Kateri (1656-1680). Christian Algonquin Native American holy woman. "Jesus! Mary! I love you." Facial disfigurations from childhood smallpox were said to have disappeared immediately after her death.

Teller, Edward (1908-2003). Hungarian-born American physicist who was instrumental in the development of the hydrogen bomb. Dying of a stroke, Teller inexplicably said: "I should have been a concert pianist."

Temple, Henry, 3rd Viscount Palmerston (1784-1865). British statesman who held many government positions including that of prime minister. To his physician who commented on the politician's imminent death: "Die, my dear doctor? That's the last thing I think of doing."

Alternative: * Others state that his final thoughts were on a document: "That's article 98; now go to the next."

Ten Boom, Elisabeth (1885-1944). Dutch citizen, arrested by the Nazis for sheltering Jews in her house during WWII. As she died in a concentration camp: "So much work to do..."

Tennent, William (1705-1777). American Presbyterian minister. When told of the severity of his illness: "I am very sensible of the violence of my disorder; that it has racked my constitution to an uncommon degree, and beyond what I have ever before experienced, and that it is accompanied with symptoms of approaching dissolution. But, blessed be God, I have no wish to live if it should be His will and pleasure to call me hence." Collecting his thoughts: "Blessed be God, I have no wish to live, if it should be His will and pleasure to call me hence, unless it should be to see a happy issue to the severe and arduous controversy my country is engaged in; but even in this, the will of the Lord be done."

Tennyson, Alfred Lord (1809-1892). English poet laureate. To his physician: "What a shadow this life is and how men cling to what is, after all, but a small part of the great world's life." Later, he asked: "Death?" When the doctor nodded, Tennyson said: "That's well." After his last meal, the poet enigmatically repeated: "I have opened it," possibly referring to an opened copy of Shakespeare in his hand. At the end, to his son: "Hallam, Hallam..." and then to his wife: "God bless you, my joy!"

Teresa Benedicta of the Cross, Saint, born Edith Stein (1891-1942). German philosopher and nun. Although Stein had converted from Judaism to Catholicism, she was deported to the Auschwitz concentration camp, where she perished. On the journey there, her train stopped briefly in Breslau, her birthplace. She commented: "This is my home. I'll never see it again." When asked what she meant: "We are going to our death." When asked if her fellow prisoners were aware of their fate: "It's better for them not to know." When offered food: "No, thank you. We won't take anything."

Teresa of Ávila, Saint (1515-1582). Spanish Roman Catholic nun, theologian and mystic. Before receiving Extreme Unction: "O my Lord and my Spouse! This is the longed-for hour. It is time now that we should see each other, my Beloved and my Lord. It is time now that I should go to Thee. Let us go in peace, and may Thy holy will be done. Now the hour has arrived for me to leave this exile, and to enjoy Thee Whom I have so much desired." When asked if she wished to be buried at Ávila: "Have I anything mine in this world? Or will they not afford me here a little earth?" To a weeping companion: "Do not cry, it is the Lord's will." Some say her last words were from Psalm 51:17: "The sacrifice acceptable to God is a broken spirit; a broken and contrite heart, O God, Thou wilt not despise."

Alternatives: * "O my Lord, and my spouse, the desired hour is now come. It is now time for me to depart hence. Thy will be done."
* "Over my spirit flash and float in divine radiancy the bright and glorious visions of the world to which I go."
* "My Lord, it is time to move on. Well then, may your will be done. O my Lord and my Spouse, the hour that I have longed for has come. It is time to meet one another."
* "... a contrite and humble heart, O God, Thou wilt not despise."

Teresa, Mother, born Anjezë Gonxha Bojaxhiu (1910-1997). Albanian-born Roman Catholic nun who founded the Calcutta-based Missionaries of Charities foundation. Mother Teresa died of heart-related issues saying. "I cannot breathe."

Alternative: * "Jesus, I love you. Jesus, I love you."

Terhune, Albert (1872-1942). American writer and dog breeder, best-known for novels about his canine friends. At the end, Terhune spoke to his wife about their home: "I shall come back. I shall be here at Sunnybank with you always. I promise you that when you walk in the rose garden, I shall be with you. When you wander around the place, when you sit by the pool, when you sit on the veranda and watch our 'Light at Eventide,' I shall be with you. I shall surely be here. You must believe me."

Terrail, Pierre de Bayard (see Bayard, Chevalier Pierre de).

Terriss, William, born William Lewin (1847-1897). English actor, best-known for his swashbuckling roles. Terriss was stabbed to death at London's Adelphi Theatre by a deranged actor. As he died: "I shall come back. Can any man be so foolish as to believe that there is no Afterlife?" Terriss' ghost supposedly haunts the theatre where he was slain.

Terry, Ellen (1847-1928). English Shakespearean actress. Dying of a cerebral hemorrhage: "Up to the skies... down to the..." Terry wrote this last word in the dust on her bedside table: "Happy."

Teyte, Maggie (1888-1976). English operatic soprano. "I have not lived like a Catholic, but I hope I shall die like one."

Tezuka, Osamu (1928-1989). Japanese cartoonist and animator. Dying of cancer: "I'm begging you, let me work!"

Thackeray, William Makepeace (1811-1863). English writer and satirist, noted for his novel *Vanity Fair.* In pain from a stroke, to his daughter: "It can't be helped, darling. I didn't take enough medicine last night. I have taken some more. I shall be better presently." Anecdotally, two days after Thackeray's death, his daughter, while sleeping, imagined that her father asked: "Are you sick my child?"

Thalberg, Irving (1899-1936). American film producer. Dying of pneumonia, Thalberg spoke to a friend: "I'm not going to make it this time..." He then spoke of a popular hymn: "Nearer My God to Thee." Later he asked a colleague: "What are the grosses... at the Astor? *Romeo and Juliet.* What were the weekend grosses?" To his wife: "Don't let the children forget me."

Thanos, John (1949-1994). American robber and killer of three teenagers. Before his execution by lethal injection: "*Adios.*"

Thayer, William (1864-1932). American physician who was a close associate of Dr. William Osler (above). Dying of a heart ailment: "This is the end, and I am not sorry."

Theodore, Saint (died c. 287). Italian Christian martyr. When ordered by Roman authorities to offer sacrifices to pagan gods, Theodore refused. As his flesh was torn from his ribs in punishment, his tormenters asked if he wanted to be with them or his Christ: "With my Christ I was and am and will be!" Theodore then was burned to death.

Theodoric the Goth (died 526). A ruler born in present-day northeastern Austria. During his reign, Theodoric controlled Italy and large tracts of surrounding territories. Legend holds that he jumped on a black horse and chased a stag saying: "I am ill-mounted. This must be the foul fiend on which I ride. Yet will I return, if God wills and Holy Mary." Theodoric was never seen again.

Theodosia, Saint (died c. 308). Lebanese Christian martyr. Arrested in nearby Caesarea for speaking to condemned Christians, Theodosia was tortured and eventually drowned: "By your cruelty you procure me that great happiness which it was my grief to see deferred. I rejoice to see myself called to this crown, and return hearty thanks to God for vouchsafing me such a favour."

Alternative: * "Don't you see that I am experiencing what I have prayed for- to be found worthy of joining the company of the martyrs of God!"

Theophrastus (c. 372-c. 287 BCE). Greek philosopher, scientist and student of Aristotle. To his disciples: "Farewell, and may you be happy. Either drop my doctrine, which involves a world of labor, or stand forth its worthy champions, for you will win great glory. Life holds more disappointment than advantage. But, as I can no longer discuss what we ought to do, do you go on with the inquiry into the right conduct." Toward the end: "We die just when we are beginning to live."

Theramenes (died c. 404 BCE). Athenian military leader and statesman. Because his policies conflicted with the ruling hierarchy headed by Critias, Theramenes was condemned to die. Drinking a hemlock concoction, Theramenes mockingly toasted his accuser: "This to the health of the lovely Critias!"

Thérèse of Lisieux, Saint (1873-1897). French Carmelite nun. Dying in severe pain from tuberculosis, to her prioress: "Mother, isn't this the agony? Am I not going to die?" When told she might linger a few more hours: "Well, all right! All right! Ah! Oh, I would not want to suffer a shorter of time. Oh, I love Him! My God, I love You!"

Thistlewood, Arthur (1774-1820). English conspirator. Thistlewood and a small group of activists were involved in the Cato Street Conspiracy that planned to murder members of the British cabinet. Convicted of treason, he was sentenced to die by hanging followed by beheading. On the scaffold: "I have now but a few moments to live, and I hope the world will think that I have at least been sincere in my endeavors."

Thomas of Lancaster (c. 1278-1322). English nobleman. Fighting with the Scots against King Edward II, Thomas was taken prisoner at the Battle of Boroughbridge. Sentenced to die, locals pelted him with stones and mud as he was taken for execution. Before his beheading, Thomas turned his eyes skyward and said: "King of heaven, have mercy on me, for the king of earth hath forsaken me!" To his confessor: "Fair father, abide with me until I am dead, for my flesh quaketh for dread of death." When ordered to face his accusers: "Now, fair lords, I shall have done all you wish."

Thomas the Apostle, Saint also Thomas the Twin, also Doubting Thomas (died late 1st century). One of Jesus Christ's original 12 apostles. While spreading the gospel in India, Thomas was struck down by the spear of a dissenter: "See, I adore, but not this idol; I worship, but not this metal; I adore, but not this graven image. I adore my Lord Jesus Christ, in whose name I command you, O demon lurking inside, to destroy the idol." Before he died: "Lord, I thank Thee for all Thy mercies. Into Thy hands I commend my spirit."

Alternative: * "I adore, but not this metal; I adore, but not this graven image; I adore my Master Jesus Christ in Whose name I command thee, demon of this idol, to destroy it forthwith."

Thomas, Dylan (1914-1953). Welsh poet and writer, best-known for his poem "Do Not Go Gentle into That Good Night" and his drama *Under Milk Wood.* After a drinking marathon while visiting New York City, Thomas allegedly commented: "I have just had eighteen whiskeys in a row. I do believe that is a record." Told later that his delirium tremens would stop, he said: "Yes, I believe you." To make conversation, a friend related that an acquaintance with tremors saw white mice and roses. Thomas responded: "Roses pleural or Rose's roses with an apostrophe?" He lapsed into a coma and died.

Alternatives: * "I just had eighteen straight scotches. I think that's the record! After thirty-nine years, this is all I've done."
* "I've had 18 full whiskeys; I think that's a record."

Thomas, George (1816-1870). Union general during the U.S. Civil War. Dying of a stroke (some say a heart attack): "I want air!"

Thomas, Olive, born Olive Duffy (1894-1920). American model and silent-screen actress. Thomas accidentally ingested a cleaning chemical and died several days later, despite intensive treatment. When asked how she was: "Pretty weak, but I'll be all right in a little while, don't worry, darling."

Thomas, Shannon (1971-2005). American robber and murderer. At his execution, Thomas made a rambling statement before the lethal drugs were injected. As they took effect, he asked: "Is the mic [microphone] still on?" He died without further comment.

Thomas, Theodore (1835-1905). German-born violinist and classical orchestral conductor. Dying of pneumonia: "I have had a beautiful vision, a beautiful vision."

Thompson, Francis (1859-1907). English poet and writer. Dying of tuberculosis, Thompson repeated the last line from one of his poems "The Poppy:" "My withered dreams... my withered dreams..."

Thompson, Hunter (1937-2005). American author and originator of "gonzo" journalism. Before dying of a self-inflicted gunshot wound, Thompson left a suicide note entitled "Football Season Is Over:"

"No More Games. No More Bombs. No More Walking. No More Fun. No More Swimming. 67. That is 17 years past 50. 17 more than I needed or wanted. Boring. I am always bitchy. No Fun — for anybody. 67. You are getting Greedy. Act your old age. Relax — This won't hurt."

Thompson, John (1844-1894). Canadian prime minister. During his induction into Queen Victoria's Privy Council at Windsor Castle, Thompson suffered a fatal heart attack: "I have a pain in my chest." When offered aid: "I am all right, thank you."

Thompson, Thomas (1955-1998). American criminal, executed by lethal injection for a rape-murder: "For seventeen years the AG [Attorney General] has been pursuing the wrong man. In time he will come to know this. I don't want anyone to avenge my death. Instead I want you to stop killing people. God bless."

Thompson, William "Big Bill" (1869-1944). American politician who became mayor of Chicago. Known for his corruption while in office, to a friend who reassured him that affairs were in order: "Everything is all set, Jim... that's right, that's right."

Thoreau, Henry (1817-1862). American writer, poet, naturalist and philosopher, known for his novel *Walden, or Life in the Woods* and his essay "Resistance to Civil Government." Dying of tuberculosis, to his aunt, who asked if he had made peace with God: "I didn't know we'd ever quarreled." When she (some say a friend) asked if he had concerns about the next world: "One world at a time." At the end: "Now comes good sailing." He then mumbled: "Moose... Indian…" and died.

Alternative: * "I never quarreled with my God."

Thorn, Martin (died 1898). American criminal, electrocuted for murdering his landlady's former lover: "I have no fear. I am not afraid. I am positive God will forgive me."

Thorndike, Edward (1874-1949). American psychologist and educator. To a friend: "Poff [a dismissive term], you are looking at a tired old man."

Thrale, Hester (1741-1821). English writer and diarist. Thrale succumbed to complications of a fall. After the arrival of her children: "Now I shall die in state." Another acquaintance related that her last words were: "I die in the trust and fear of God."

Three Fingered Jack (see Gallagher, Jack and Garcia, Manuel).

Thring, Edward (1821-1887). English schoolmaster and writer. In response to a compliment on his life's work: "I do not think much of the greatness of the work I have done, but I should be glad if, when I am gone, someone in the other world should touch me on the shoulder and say 'Mr. Thring, I have been a better man for having known you.' Believe me, a life lived in earnest does not die. It goes on forever." His last diary entry read: "And now to bed. Sermon finished and a blessed feeling of Sunday coming." Thring later died as he read the Communion Service in his school's chapel.

Thurber, James (1894-1961). American humorist, writer and cartoonist. Dying from complications of a stroke and pneumonia, to his wife: "God bless... God d***..."

Thurlow, Edward (1731-1806). English lawyer and statesman. "I'll be shot if I don't believe I'm dying!"

Thurner, Josef (died 1991). First officer on Austrian Lauda Air Flight 004. While flying from Bangkok to Vienna, one of the Boeing 767's flight reversers inadvertently deployed, resulting in a fatal stall. All 223 on board perished. Thurner's last transmission: "Oh, reverser's deployed!"

Tibbles, Susette (1854-1903). Native American writer and champion of her people's rights. To a friend with whom she had spoken in her native Omaha dialect: "Sorry, dear. Forgot you don't know our language."

Tiberius (42 BCE-37 CE). Roman military leader and emperor, known for his cruelty and tyrannical rule. The dying Tiberius spoke contemptuously to attendants leaving his room: "You know when to abandon the setting and hasten to the rising sun!"

Tidd, Richard (1775-1820). English boot maker and conspirator. Tidd was a member of the Cato Street Conspiracy that planned to assassinate members of the British cabinet. He was convicted of treason and sentenced to be hanged and beheaded. On the scaffold, to John Ings, a fellow conspirator: "How are you, my hearty?"

Tilden, Samuel (1814-1886). American politician and unsuccessful candidate for the U.S. presidency. A final request: "Water!"

Alternative: * "Drink."

Tillich, Paul (1886-1965). German-American theologian and philosopher. Dying of a heart attack, to his doctor after consulting with a dietician: "All my hard work. All my work in vain. I am eating nothing at all... absolute asceticism."

Tillman, Patrick "Pat" (1976-2004). American professional football player and soldier. Before he died from "friendly fire" while serving in Afghanistan, Tillman shouted to the unit shooting at him: "Cease fire, friendlies! I am Pat f****** Tillman, d*** it..."

Timrod, Henry (1829-1867). American poet, teacher and Confederate soldier during the U.S. Civil War. Dying of tuberculosis, Timrod failed to swallow a drink at his bedside: "Never mind. I shall soon drink of the river of eternal life."

Timur (see Tamerlane).

Tindal, Matthew (c. 1657-1733). English deist and writer. "If there be a God, I desire him to have mercy on me!" From his deathbed upon observing a portrait of Christ: "How is it possible that I shou'd ever believe that fellow to be [the] Son of God."

Tiny Tim, born Herbert Khaury (1932-1996). American musician, music historian and ukulele player. Tiny Tim suffered a heart attack while playing his signature tune "Tiptoe Through the Tulips" at a gala benefit. When asked if he were okay, he replied: "No, I'm not!" The musician then collapsed and died.

Tiptaft, William (1803-1864). English minister. "What a mercy, my last moments are my best... Thy love is better than wine. Praise God! Grace shall have all the praise."

Titus (39-81). Roman military leader and emperor. Titus was the brother of Domitian (above) and son of Vespasian (below) whom he succeeded. Dying of a fever, he spoke words to the effect: "I deserve not death, but I repent nothing else in my life except for one thing." Although he did not elaborate, it is speculated that Titus failed to eliminate the threat of his brother whom he suspected of plotting against him.

Alternatives: * "I have made but one mistake."
* "My life is taken from me though I have done nothing to deserve it. For there is no action of mine which I should repent but one."

Todd, D'Arcy (1808-1845). English military leader. A day before he died from a head wound during the Anglo-Sikh War, Todd wrote to his brother: "… 'Be ye also ready' [possibly referring to Matthew 24:44] sounds in my ears, and I only wish to live that the grace of God and the love of Christ may prepare me to leave a world in which there can be no joy for me... Oh, my brother and friend, pray for me! I cannot write more. Dearest Jane, accept my best love. May the God of love be with you both. Ever, my dearly loved brother, your affectionate and attached D'Arcy."

Tojo, Hideki (1884-1948). Japanese prime minister during WWII. Convicted of war crimes, Tojo and colleagues were sentenced to die by hanging: "My execution is some consolation, although it certainly cannot compensate for my responsibility to the nation. But internationally, I declare myself innocent. I only gave in to superior force... I now walk to the gallows, happy to shoulder my responsibility." As the condemned men neared their execution, they responded with the Japanese salutes: "*Banzai*!" and "*Dai-Nippon*!"

Toklas, Alice (1877-1967). American-born writer and companion of Gertrude Stein (above). When asked by her maid if she wanted food or drink: "No" to both. When asked if she wanted to die: "Yes!"

Toland, John (1670-1722). Irish-born British writer and philosopher. Toland's response to a friend who hoped he was better: "Sir, I have no hopes but in God." Asked if he needed anything: "I want nothing but death."

Toler, John, Lord Norbury (1740-1831). Irish-born jurist and politician. Toler asked an attendant to take a message to a friend, also near death: "James, run round to Lord Erne and tell him, with my compliments, that it will be a dead heat between us."

Toler, Martin (1955-2006). American coal miner. Toler and 11 other men were trapped when an explosion ripped through a West Virginia coal mine. His farewell note: "Tell all I'll see them on the other side. It wasn't bad. Just went to sleep. I love you." A lone survivor reported that Toler led a prayer for "individual forgiveness" before he died.

Tolkien, John (1892-1973). British author who wrote the fantasy works *The Hobbit* and *The Lord of the Rings.* Dying of pneumonia, to a friend: "I feel on top of the world."

Tolstoy, Leo (1828-1910). Russian philosopher and writer, best-known for his novel *War and Peace.* Dying of pneumonia, friends urged Tolstoy to reconcile himself with the Russian Orthodox Church: "Even in the valley of the shadow of death, two and two do not make six." As his condition worsened: "So this is the end! And it's nothing..." After an injection and application of supplemental oxygen: "Ah, what a bother. Let me go somewhere, where nobody can find me. Leave me alone..." To his physicians: "This is all foolishness! What's the point in taking medicine?" Slowly Tolstoy muttered: "The truth... I care a great deal. How they..."

Alternatives: * "To escape... I must escape... Truth... I love much."
* "But the peasants...how do peasants die?"

Tone, Theobald (1763-1798). Irish independence leader who was one of the founding members of the Society of United Irishmen. Tone was captured by the British and sentenced to die for his rebellious ideas. When told that he could not choose his mode of execution, the rebel managed to slit his throat (jugulation) to avoid a public hanging. When a surgeon reported that the wound did not appear mortal, Tone replied: "I find, then, I am but a bad anatomist." After the surgeon warned that any movement or speech could result in the prisoner's death, the condemned man retorted:

"I can yet find words to thank you, sir: it is the most welcome news you could give me. What should I wish to live for?" Tone then fell back dead.

Tonks, Henry (1862-1937). English artist and surgeon. To his attendant: "You may as well say goodbye, as I shall not be here in the morning." He was correct.

Toombs, Robert (1810-1885). American politician who supported the Confederacy during the U.S. Civil War and opposed post-war reconstruction. When told that prohibitionists were staging a rally: "Prohibitionists are men of small pints." As the end neared, to a friend: "I am sorry the hour is come. I hope we shall meet in a better place."

Toplady, Augustus (1740-1778). English Anglican clergyman and composer of the hymn "Rock of Ages." Dying of tuberculosis, when asked about pain: "It is delightful." Then to his friends: "Oh, what a blessing that you are made willing to give me over into the hands of my dear Redeemer, and part with me, for no mortal can live after the glories which God has manifested to my soul."

Alternatives: * "Sickness is no affliction, pain no curse, death no dissolution. The sky is clear; there is no cloud; come, Lord Jesus, come quickly!"
* "Come, Lord Jesus, come quickly! No mortal can live after the glories which God has manifested to my soul!"

Toral, José de León (1900-1929). Mexican Roman Catholic militant who assassinated president-elect Álvaro Obregon (above). Sentenced to die before a firing squad, Toral cried: "Long live..." Perhaps he was trying to shout the battle cry of the Cristero movement: "Long live Christ the King!"

Torres-Acosta, Saint Maria (1826-1887). Spanish Christian woman who devoted her life to helping the poor and ill. On her deathbed, to her fellow Sisters: "Children, live together in peace and unity."

Toscanini, Arturo (1867-1957). Italian classical conductor. Dying of a stroke, Toscanini imagined he was conducting a rehearsal: "No, not like that, more smoothly, please more smoothly. Let's repeat. More smoothly. That's it, good, now it's right."

Touhy, Roger "Terrible" (1898-1959). American gangster and bootlegger. Having made many enemies in the course of his career, Touhy was gunned down while entering his sister's house: "I've been expecting it. The b******* never forget."

Toulouse-Lautrec, Henri (1864-1901). Post-impressionist French artist. Suffering from a congenital disease of the skeletal system and alcoholism, to his priest: "Monsieur le Curé, I am happier to see you now than I shall be in a few days, when you come with your little bell." To his father: "I knew, papa, that you wouldn't miss the death." As his father flicked at flies with Toulouse's shoelaces, the artist remarked: "Old fool."

Touro, Judah (1775-1854). American businessman and philanthropist. Touro's burial instructions: "When I am dead, carry me to the spot of my birth, and bury me by the side of my mother."

Toussaint L'Ouverture, François (c. 1746-1803). Haitian revolutionary leader. Having led an antislavery rebellion against the French, Toussaint later was arrested on his home soil and sent to France. His appeal to Napoleon I: "... First Consul, father of all French soldiers, upright judge, defender of the innocent, pronounce a decision as to my destiny. My wound is deep; apply a remedy to it. You are the physician. I rely entirely on your wisdom and skill" To his servant: "Carry my last farewell to my wife, my children and my niece. Would I could console thee under this cruel separation. Be assured of my friendship and the remembrance which I shall always preserve of thy services and thy devotedness." He died while in prison.

Toussaint, Pierre (1766-1853). Haitian-born American philanthropist. Toussaint, an emancipated slave, performed many charitable acts for the poor of New York City. To a friend: "God is with me." When asked if he needed anything: "Nothing on earth."

Traubel, Horace (1858-1919). American writer, poet, publisher and social activist. "I am tired, d***** tired. God d***** tired." As he died, Traubel murmured to those at his bedside: "Laugh, for God's sake, laugh."

Travis, William (1809-1836). American soldier who commanded the defenders at the Alamo, San Antonio, Texas. Travis sent a letter by his courier dated February 24, 1836 requesting help during the siege:

"To the People of Texas & all Americans in the world. Fellow citizens & compatriots;

I am besieged, by a thousand or more of the Mexicans under Santa Anna. I have sustained a continual Bombardment & cannonade for 24 hours & have not lost a man. The enemy has demanded a surrender at discretion, otherwise, the garrison are to be put to the sword, if the fort is taken. I have answered the demand with a cannon shot, & our flag still waves proudly from the walls. I shall never surrender or retreat. Then, I call on you in the name of Liberty, of patriotism & everything dear to the American character, to come to our aid, with all dispatch. The enemy is receiving reinforcements daily & will no doubt increase to three or four thousand in four or five days. If this call is neglected, I am determined to sustain myself as long as possible & die like a soldier who never forgets what is due to his own honor and that of his country. Victory or Death.

William Barret Travis Lt. Col. Comdt.

P.S. The Lord is on our side. When the enemy appeared in sight we had not three bushels of corn. We have since found in deserted houses 80 or 90 bushels and got into the walls 20 or 30 head of beeves [a pleural of beef]."

He and his compatriots were killed during the final siege on March 6. Travis' last known order: "The Mexicans are upon us. Give 'em hell."

Tree, Herbert (1853-1917). English actor and theater manager. Contemplating a forthcoming role: "I shall not need to study the part at all. I know it already."

Tresckow, Herrmann "Henning" von (1901-1944). German officer who was one of Claus von Stauffenberg's associates in the Operation Valkyrie plot to assassinate Adolf Hitler. Before committing suicide by exploding a grenade: "… The worth of a man is certain only if he is prepared to sacrifice his life for his convictions."

Alternative: * "A man's moral worth is established only at the point where he is ready to give his life in defense of his convictions."

Trexler, Samuel (1877-1949). American clergyman and writer. To a friend: "I'm feeling fine. Let me see the papers."

Tristan, Flora (1803-1844). French writer and social activist. Dying of typhoid fever while in Bordeaux, France: "If I should die, tell everyone who has loved me that I too love them- immensely, religiously." Somewhat befuddled, she later said: "The sea, isn't it beautiful, so shining... but am I not in Bordeaux?"

Trobriand, Regis de (1816-1897). French-born American writer and Union army general during the U.S. Civil War. Letter to a former aide: "… You will understand, dear [Sylvester] Bonnaffon, that in such condition it is out of the question for me to receive any visit, or even to designate any possible time of meeting, as by that time it is as likely that I may be underground as on it. Farewell then, or '*au revoir*' as the case may turn. Anyhow, I remain, Yours faithfully, R. de Trobriand."

Trollope, Anthony (1815-1882). English writer. From the conclusion of his autobiography: "Now I stretch out my hand, and from the further shore I bid adieu to all who have cared to read any among the many words I have written." Dying of a stroke, the only word Trollope could speak was "No."

Trollope, Frances (1780-1863). British writer and mother of Anthony Trollope (above). Speaking of her daughter: "Poor, Cecilia."

Tromp, Maarten (c. 1597-1653). Dutch admiral. Mortally wounded in a battle with English warships off the Dutch coast, to his men: "Take courage, children! My career has closed with glory."

Alternative: * "Take courage, children! Act so that my end will be glorious, as my life has been."

Trotsky, Leon, born Lev Davidovich Bronstein (1879-1940). Russian revolutionary who ran afoul of Joseph Stalin (above) and took refuge in Mexico. Attacked by an assassin on the orders of Stalin, Trotsky was struck in the head with an axe. To his protectors, who prepared to kill the assassin: "Do not kill him! This man has a story to tell." To a bodyguard who made lightly of his wound: "No, I feel here. This time they succeeded. Take care of [my wife] Natalia. She has been with me many, many years." In hospital, to his wife as nurses tried to undress him for surgery: "I do not want them to undress me. I want you to undress me." Before he slipped into a coma and died postoperatively: "... Please say to our friends that I am sure of the victory of the Fourth International [Communist organization]. Go forward!"

Alternative: * "I will not survive this attack. Stalin has finally accomplished the task he attempted unsuccessfully before."

Trujillo, Rafael (1891-1961). Dominican Republic dictator, assassinated by rebels who wished to topple his repressive regime: "Ay, ay, ay, ay!"

Truman, Harry (1884-1972). Thirty-third U.S. president. Dying of pneumonia: "I feel all right." Asked if he were experiencing any pain: "No." Some say his last words were unrecorded.

Trumpeldor, Joseph (1880-1920). Russian-born Zionist activist. Mortally wounded while protecting a Jewish settlement in his adopted Israel: "Never mind; it is good to die for our country."

Alternative: * "It is alright; it is better to die for our country."

Truth, Sojourner, born Isabella Baumfree (c. 1797-1883). African American abolitionist, former slave and preacher. Speaking earlier of death: "Stepping out into the light, oh, won't that be glorious? Oh, I'm not going to die! I'm just going home like a shooting star." Her last words: "Be a follower of the Lord Jesus."

Tubman, Harriet, born Araminta Ross (c. 1820-1913). African American escaped slave who helped others to freedom on the Underground Railroad. Dying of pneumonia, to her friends and family: "Now, a song." She then sang: "Swing low, sweet chariot/, Coming for to carry me home..." Her parting words: "I go to prepare a place for you."

Tucker, Karla Faye (1959-1998). American criminal, convicted of a double murder committed during a robbery. Before dying of a lethal injection: "Yes sir, I would like to say to all of you – the Thornton family and Jerry Dean's family [the murder victims' relatives] that I am so sorry. I hope God will give you peace with this. [To her husband] Baby, I love you. Ron [the brother of one of the victims], give Peggy a hug for me. Everybody has been so good to me. I love all of you very much. I am going to be face to face with Jesus now. Warden Baggett, thank all of you so much. You have been so good to me. I love all of you very much. I will see you all when you get there. I will wait for you."

Tucker, Richard (1913-1975). American operatic tenor and cantor. Before dying of a heart attack while on tour, to his wife by telephone: "Anyway, how about you? What are you up to today? Tell me so I can call you after Bob [Merrill, a fellow singer] and I get done rehearsing."

Tuekakas (see Old Joseph).

Tuggle, Lem (died 1996). American criminal, executed by lethal injection in mid-December for the rape and murder of a middle-aged woman. Tuggle's last words were appropriate for the season: "Merry Christmas."

Tukhachevsky, Mikhail (1893-1937). Marshal of the Soviet Union. To a fellow prisoner about spurious charges of treason brought against him by the Stalin regime: "Have you been dreaming about all this?" Tukhachevsky later was executed by a gunshot.

Alternative: * "I feel I'm dreaming."

Túpac Amaru (1545-1572). Last of the indigenous Incan rulers. Francisco de Toledo, the Viceroy of Peru, decreed that the young chief should die by decapitation. On the scaffold, Túpac declared: "Let it be proclaimed to all the world that I have done no wrong, and that I die only because it is the pleasure of the tyrant." He then knelt down, saying: "Oh God, behold how mine enemies rob me of my blood."

Turenne, Henri Vicomte de (1611-1675). French military officer who fought during the Battle of Salzbach in present-day Germany. Urged to seek cover: "Then I will gladly come, for I particularly wish not to be killed just now." As he redirected his firepower, Turenne was killed by a cannon shot.

Alternative: * "I do not mean to be killed to-day."

Turgenev, Ivan (1818-1883). Russian writer and poet. To his family: "Come nearer... nearer. Let me feel you all near me. The moment of parting has come. Goodbye, my darlings."

Turgot, Anne-Robert (1727-1781). French economist and statesman. Accused of ruining his health from overwork, Turgot died of "gout" at age 53: "You blame me for attempting too much, but you know that in my family we die of gout at fifty."

Turner, Edward (1798-1837). Jamaican-born British chemist. During his waning days, Turner told friends: "O happy I am! How kind everyone is to me! It is worthwhile being sick to see how kind everyone is to me..." Later, when told that his pulse was perfectly calm: "Then what can make it so, at such an hour? What, but the power of religion? What, but the Spirit of God?" Near the end: "... Pray for me, that my struggle will not be long. Pray that I may have peace… I could not have believed that I could be happy on my death-bed. I am content my career should close." When asked if Christ were as good as his word: "Yes, quite." Turner then closed his eyes and died.

Turner, Frederick (1861-1932). Pulitzer Prize-winning American historian, essayist and educator. Dying of a heart attack, to his wife (some say his doctor): "I know this is the end. Tell Max [Farrand, his agent] that I am sorry I haven't finished my book [on American history]."

Turner, Joseph (1775-1851). English landscape artist. To his physician when informed that death was near: "Go downstairs, take a glass of sherry and then look in on me again... Well, I suppose I am a nonentity now." Some say his last words were: "The sun, my dear, the sun is God."

Alternative: * "Silence!"

Turner, Nathaniel "Nat" (1800-1831). American slave. Turner led a slave rebellion in Virginia that resulted in multiple deaths. Before his hanging, flaying and beheading: "It's in God's hands now."

Tussaud, Anne Marie (1761-1850). French-born English artist who created death masks of some of the heads that rolled during the French Revolution. To her two sons: "I divide my property equally between you and implore you, above all things, never to quarrel." Madame Tussaud's Wax Museums continue to entertain curious spectators worldwide.

Twain, Mark (see Clemens, Samuel).

Tweed, William "Boss" (1823-1878). American politician, jailed for stealing millions of dollars from taxpayers through political corruption. Dying in prison of pneumonia, Tweed spoke of those responsible for his incarceration: "I guess Tilden and Fairchild have killed me at last. I hope they will be satisfied now." Before he expired, to the matron's daughter: "Mary, I have tried to do good to everybody, and if I have not, it is not my fault. I am ready to die, and I know God will receive me." To his physician: "Doctor, I've tried to do some good, if I haven't had good luck. I am not afraid to die. I believe the guardian angels will protect me." As he died: "I have tried to right some great wrongs. I have been forbearing with those who did not deserve it. I forgive all those who have ever done evil to me, and I want all those whom I have harmed to forgive me."

Tyler, John (1790-1862). Tenth U.S. president. To a physician who prescribed brandy and mustard plasters at the end: "Doctor, I think you are mistaken." To another physician: "Doctor, I am going…" When told that he hoped not: "Perhaps it is best."

Tynan, Kenneth (1927-1980). British drama critic and writer. Dying of emphysema, to his wife: "Please come back soon."

Tyndale, William (c. 1492-1536). English Protestant martyr. Because Tyndale's religious views conflicted with those of England's King Henry VIII, he was branded a heretic and sentenced to die. Before his strangulation and burning at the stake: "Lord, open the King of England's eyes."

Alternative: * "Lord, open the ears of England's King."

Tyndall, John (1820-1893). Irish-born English physicist. After his wife accidentally gave him an overdose of a sleep medication: "Yes, my poor darling, you have killed your John! Let us do all we can. Tickle my throat! Get a stomach pump... Yes, I know you are all trying to rouse me."

Tyng, Dudley (1825-1858). American clergyman and abolitionist. While standing near a piece of farm machinery, Tyng's arm became entangled and was badly mangled. Before the clergyman died, he said to the effect: "Stand up for Jesus!" These words became the inspiration for George Duffield's hymn "Stand Up, Stand Up for Jesus." Toward the end, Tyng was asked by his father if he were happy: "Oh! Perfectly, perfectly."

Tyson, James (1819-1898). Australian millionaire who bragged that: "[I have] never entered a church, theatre or public house..." Asked if he had a happy life: "Sufficiently so. I am persuaded that attainment is nothing. The pleasure is in the pursuit, and I have been pursuing all my life. Yes, I consider that I have been happier than most men." Asked about religion: "Theology ain't my business. I do what I think seriously right: I stand to take my chance, and I have no fear..."

Tzu-Hsi, also called Cixi (1835-1908). Chinese empress dowager who was a virtual ruler for three decades. Dying of a stroke: "Never again allow any woman to hold the supreme power in the state. It is against the house-law of our dynasty and should be strictly forbidden. Be careful not to allow eunuchs to meddle in government matters. The Ming dynasty was brought to ruin by eunuchs, and its fate should be a warning to my people."

Uemura, Naomi (1941-1984). Japanese adventurer. Uemura climbed Denali (formerly Mt. McKinley) in Alaska but faltered in perilous weather on the way down. A support plane picked up a last transmission: "I am lost." His body was never found.

Umberto I (see Humbert I).

Umberto II (see Humbert II).

Underhill, Wilber "The Tri-State Terror" (1901-1934). American robber and murderer. Mortally wounded while trying to escape from lawmen: "Tell the boys I'm coming home."

Urban V (1310-1370). Pope from 1362 until his death. To his aides: "Leave the doors open, so that everyone may enter and see how a pope dies."

Urquhart, Thomas (1611-c. 1660). Scottish writer and revolutionary. Urquhart allegedly died "in a fit of excessive laughter" when told about the Restoration of King Charles II to the English throne.

Ussher, James (1581-1656). Irish archbishop, educator and writer. On his deathbed: "Lord, forgive my sins, especially my sins of omission."

Alternative: * "O, Lord, forgive me, especially my sins of omission. God be merciful to me a sinner!"

Ustinov, Jonah (1892-1962). Palestine-born writer and father of the actor Peter Ustinov. "I will remember you in my dreams."

Vaché, Jacques (1895-1919). French artist. Vaché killed himself and two friends with an opium overdose: "I shall die when I want to die. And then I shall die with someone else. To die alone is boring. I should prefer to die with one of my best friends." Vaché had expressed this sentiment at an earlier time.

Valdés, Gabriel de la Conceptión (1809-1844). Cuban poet, convicted of participating in a slave rebellion. Before a firing squad: "Goodbye, O world; here there is no pity for me. Soldiers, fire." Numerous shots hit Valdes but failed to kill him. Pointing to his heart, the poet then cried: "Will no one have pity on me? Here! Fire here!" The resulting volley found its mark.

Valentich, Frederick (1958-1978). Australian pilot who described a UFO flying around his airplane. Before he disappeared, Valentich radioed: "Ah, Melbourne, that strange aircraft is hovering on top of me again… It is hovering and it's not an aircraft."

Valentino, Rudolph, born Rodolfo Alfonso Raffaello Pierre Filibert Guglielmi di Valentina D'Antonguolla (1895-1926). Italian silent film actor. Following emergency surgery for a ruptured appendix: "I just want to see what I look like when I'm sick, so that if I ever have to play the part in pictures, I'll know how to put on the right makeup." Delirious ramblings recorded by his nurse after peritonitis set in: "*Mama mia*. I didn't mean it... Maria, your turn... George, last night, remember, we were lost in the woods... *Je t'aime*, Freckle Nose... Indian Chief Black Feather... I took all the bugs out of the rose bushes... Babykins... On the other hand, the other hand- I love you- you!" During a lucid period before he died, to his nurse: "Don't pull down the blinds. I feel fine. I want the sunlight to greet me!"

Alternative: "Please raise the shade. I want to see the sunlight."

Vallée, Hubert "Rudy" (1901-1986). American popular singer, entertainer and bandleader. Watching a telecast of the centennial celebration of the Statue of Liberty, to his wife: "I wish we could be there. You know how I love a party." He died of advanced cancer moments later.

Van Buren, Martin (1782-1862). Eighth U.S. president. Dying of heart failure, to his pastor (some say his sons): "There is but one reliance, and that is upon Christ, the free Mediator of us all."

van Gogh, Theodoor "Theo" (see Gogh, Theodoor "Theo" van).

van Gogh, Vincent (see Gogh, Vincent van).

Vanderbilt, Alfred (1877-1915). American businessman and philanthropist who was the son of Cornelius Vanderbilt II (below). Vanderbilt spoke to his valet before perishing on the RMS *Lusitania*, torpedoed by a German submarine: "Find all the kiddies you can, boy." He then offered his life vest to a female passenger.

Alternative: * "Come and let us save the kiddies."

Vanderbilt, Cornelius "Commodore" (1794-1877). American railroad and shipping tycoon, owner of the New York Central line. To his son: "Keep the money together, hey! Keep the Central our road. That's my boy Bill!" For his funeral: "No flowers at my funeral, not one! No costly badges of mourning. No crape for showing off!" After hearing an attending clergyman's prayer: "That's a good prayer. I shall never give up trust in Jesus: how could I let that go?"

Vanderbilt, Cornelius II (1843-1899). American businessman and philanthropist who was the son of William Vanderbilt (below). Suffering a stroke, to his wife: "I think I am dying."

Vanderbilt, William (1821-1885), American businessman and philanthropist who was the son of Commodore Vanderbilt. Commenting earlier on his wealth: "The care of 200 millions of dollars is too great a load for any brain or back to bear. It is enough to kill a man. There is no pleasure to be got out of it as an offset- no good of any kind. I have had no real gratification or enjoyment of any sort more than my neighbor on the next block who is worth only half a million." While discussing business matters with a colleague, Vanderbilt died suddenly.

Vane, Henry (1613-1662). English statesman who became colonial governor of Massachusetts. After returning to England, Vane was arrested for treason following the restoration of King Charles II. On the scaffold before his beheading, Vane prayed: "Father, glorify Thy servant in the sight of men, that he may glorify Thee in the discharge of his duty to Thee and to his country."

Vanini, Lucilio (1585-1619). Italian philosopher, clergyman and writer. Condemned by a French council for witchcraft and his atheist views, Vanini had his tongue cut out and was strangled and burned at the stake: "There is neither God nor devil: for were there a God, I would entreat him to consume this Parliament with his thunder, as being altogether unjust and wicked; and were there a devil, I would also pray him to swallow it up in some subterranean place; but since there is neither the one nor the other, I cannot do it."

Alternative: * "There is neither God nor devil: for if there were a God, I would pray him to send a thunderbolt on the Council, as all that is unjust and iniquitous, and if there were a devil, I would pray him to engulf it in the subterranean regions; but since there is neither one nor the other, there is nothing for me to do."

Vanzetti, Bartolomeo (1888-1927). Italian-born fish monger and suspected anarchist. Vanzetti and Nicola Sacco (above) were executed by electrocution for the alleged murder of a paymaster and guard at a factory. Before his death, the condemned man spoke in a low voice: "I wish to tell you that I am an innocent man. I never committed any crime, but sometimes some sin." To the warden: "Thank you for everything you have done for me. I am innocent of all crime, not only this one, but all crime. I am an innocent man… I wish to forgive some people for what they are now doing to me."

Vargas, Getúlio (1882-1954). Brazilian president. Despondent because of eroding faith in his leadership, Vargas shot himself in the chest. His suicide note read: "I have fought against the looting of Brazil. I fought against the looting of the people. I have fought bare-breasted. The hatred, infamy, and calumny did not beat down my spirit. I gave you my life! Now I offer you my death. Nothing remains. Serenely, I take the first step on the road to eternity and I leave life to enter history."

Vaughan, Sarah (1924-1990). American jazz singer. Dying of lung cancer, Vaughan did not wish to remain hospitalized: "I want to go home! Take me home!" Her wish was granted and she died shortly thereafter.

Veblen, Thorstein (1857-1929). American economist, best-known for his book *The Theory of the Leisure Class.* His farewell note read: "It is also my wish, in case of death, to be cremated, if it can be conveniently done, as expeditiously and inexpensively as may be, without ritual or ceremony of any kind; that my ashes be thrown loose into the sea, or into some sizable stream running to the sea; that no tombstone, slab, epitaph, effigy, tablet, inscription or monument of any name or nature, be set up in my memory or name in any place or at any time; that no obituary, memorial, portrait or biography of me, nor any letters written to or by me be printed or published, or in any way reproduced, copied or circulated." Veblen's ashes were scattered over the Pacific Ocean.

Vega Carpio, Félix Lope de (see Lope de Vega Carpio, Félix.)

Veigel, Eva (1724-1822). Austrian dancer and wife of the actor David Garrick (above). To a servant offering her a cup of tea: "Put it down, hussy! Do you think I cannot help myself?" She took a sip and died.

Veldhuyzen van Zanten, Jacob (died 1977). Dutch captain on KLM Flight 4805. Recorded cockpit conversation moments before KLM and Pan American Boeing 747 jumbo jets collided on a fog-shrouded Canary Island runway with the loss of 583 lives:

The Dutch flight engineer William Schreuder asked about the Pan American aircraft: "Did he not clear the runway then?"

Veldhuyzen: "What do you say?"

Schreuder: "Is he not clear, that Pan American?"

Veldhuyzen: "Oh, yes," and initiated the fatal take-off while the Pan American aircraft was still on the runway. Veldhuyzen uttered a scream moments before impact.

Vélez, Lupe (1908-1944). Mexican-born Hollywood actress. Depressed after becoming pregnant out of wedlock, Vélez killed herself with an overdose of drugs. Her suicide note written to the baby's father, actor

Harald Maresch, read: "To Harald, May God forgive you and forgive me too, but I prefer to take my life away and our baby's before I bring him with shame or killing him, Lupe." On the reverse side of the note: "How could you, Harald, fake such a great love for me and our baby when all the time you didn't want us. I see no other way out for me so goodbye and good luck to you. Love, Lupe."

Note to her secretary, Beulah Kinder: "My Dear Mrs. Kinder: My faithful friend, you and only you know the facts for the reason I am taking my life. May God forgive me and don't think bad of me. I love you many. Take care of my mother, so, goodby and try to forgive me. Say goodby to all my friends and the American press that were always so nice to me. Lupe"

On the reverse side of the note, Vélez asked for safekeeping of her dogs: "Take care of Chips and Chops."

Vercellis, Comtesse de (1669-1728). French noblewoman. After passing flatus: "Good. A woman who can fart is not dead." She expired moments later.

Verdi, Giuseppe (1813-1901). Italian composer, primarily of operas. While sitting on the side of the bed trying to button his vest, Verdi spoke to his attendant: "What does it matter, one button more or less." He fell back unconscious from a massive stroke and died six days later.

Vergniaud, Pierre (1753-1793). French statesman who was condemned to die by the guillotine during the French Revolution. While imprisoned, Vergniaud engraved (some say wrote with his blood) on his cell wall: "Death before dishonor."

Alternatives: * "Rather death than crime."
* "The revolution is like Saturn: It will devour all its children."

Verlaine, Paul (1844-1896). French poet. When a friend whispered that the poet was dying: "Don't sole the dead man's shoes yet." Verlaine expired speaking the names of two friends: "Lepelletier! François! François! Coppée! Coppée! Come, come to me"

Verne, Jules (1828-1905). French writer, best-known for his science-fiction novels. Dying from complications of diabetes, to his family: "Honorine, Michel, Valentine, Suzanne- are you here? Good, you're all there. Now I can die." After receiving the Last Rites, to his priest: "You have done me good. I feel regenerated."

Versalle, Richard (1932-1996). American operatic tenor. Versalle fell from a ladder as he sang a line from Leoš Janáček's opera *The Makropulos Case*: "... Too bad you can only live so long." He died shortly thereafter of an apparent heart attack.

Vespasian (9-79). Roman emperor. Near death from a fever, Vespasian referred to the post mortem custom of deifying Roman emperors: "Oh dear! I think I'm turning into a god…" Later as he was helped to his feet: "An emperor ought to die standing." He expired shortly thereafter.

Vetsera, Mary (1871-1889). Austrian aristocrat. Vetsera apparently committed suicide in a pact with her lover Prince Rudolf of Austria (above). Her suicide note to Countess Marie Larisch, an intermediary between the two lovers: "Dear Marie, Forgive me all the trouble I have caused. I thank you so much for everything you have done for me. If life becomes hard for you, and I fear it will after what we have done, follow us. It is the best thing you can do. Your Mary." Larisch declined the request.

Vianney, Jean-Marie, Saint (1786-1859). French clergyman. In his later years, Vianney would greet up to 20,000 pilgrims yearly. Asked where he would like to be interred: "At Ars [his parish], but my body is not much."

Vicars, Hedley (1826-1855). Mauritian-born British soldier, killed at Sevastopol during the Crimean War. As he advanced against Russian forces: "Men of the 97th [Regiment], follow me." Mortally wounded by a Russian soldier: "Cover my face, cover my face."

Vichy-Chamrond, Marie Anne, Marquise du Deffand (1697-1780). French hostess and literary figure. "... I accuse myself of having violated the Ten Commandments of God and of having committed the seven mortal sins." Regardless, she refused a priest as confessor: "I shall confess to my friend, the Duc de Choiseul."

Vicious, Sid, born John Simon Ritchie (1957-1979). English musician who was a member of the Sex Pistols band. The heroin-intoxicated Vicious committed suicide in early February, 1979. Nancy Spungen, his girlfriend, died of a stab wound three-and-a-half months earlier, possibly by the hand of the musician. Vicious' suicide note read: "We had a death pact. I have to keep my half of the bargain. Please bury me PTO [please turn over, because the note was written in two parts] next to my baby. Bury me in my leather jacket, jeans and motorcycle boots. Goodbye."

Victoria, Empress (1840-1901). Daughter of English Queen Victoria and widow of German Emperor Frederick III. Dying of cancer, to her aides as she was moved from a garden to her room: "Stop, so that I can take a last look at the garden I made in memory of a great and undying love."

Victoria, Alexandrina (1819-1901). Queen of the United Kingdom of Great Britain and Ireland. To her daughter: "I don't want to die yet. There are several things I want to arrange." Possibly referring to the Boer War: "Oh, that peace may come. Bertie! [her son Edward, heir apparent to the throne]."

Vidocq, Eugène-François (1775-1857). French criminal who reformed and became a noted detective. Because of the crime-fighting techniques he developed, Vidocq has been called the Father of Criminology. Near death, to his doctor and priest: "You... my only physician... How great is the forgiveness for such a life?"

Vigny, Alfred-Victor de (1797-1863). French poet, writer and playwright. Dying of cancer: "Pray for me. Pray to God for me."

Villa, Francisco "Pancho" (1878-1923). Mexican revolutionary. Gunned down despite his retirement from the revolutionary scene: "Don't let it end like this. Tell them I said something!" Because of the magnitude of Villa's injuries, it is unlikely he uttered these requests.

Villars, Claude-Louis (1653-1734). French military leader. When reminded by his confessor of an English commander killed in battle, Villars replied: "I always deemed him more fortunate than myself."

Villecerf, Madame de (died 1712). French noblewoman. Villecerf died following a bloodletting when an artery was opened instead of a vein. Fearing that the surgeon might suffer as a result of his mistake, she magnanimously tried to comfort him: "I do not look upon you as a person whose error has cost me my life, but as a benefactor who advances my entry into a happy immortality. As the world may judge otherwise, I have put you in a situation, by my will, to quit your profession."

Villiers, George, 1st Duke of Buckingham (1592-1628). English military leader and statesman. Stabbed by a disgruntled military officer passed over for promotion, Villiers cried: "God's wounds, the villain hath killed me!"

Alternative: * "Traitor, thou killest me!"

Villiers, George, 2nd Duke of Buckingham (1628-1687). English statesman and courtier. Finding himself in declining health and financial straits, Villiers bemoaned his condition in a last letter to a friend: "... I am forsaken by all my acquaintances, neglected by the friends of my bosom and dependants on my bounty; but no matter! I am not fit to converse with the former and have no abilities to serve the latter. Let me not however be forsaken by the good. Favour me with a visit as soon as possible. I am of opinion this is the last visit I shall ever solicit from you. My distemper is powerful. Come and pray for the departing spirit of the poor unhappy Buckingham."

Vincent, Gene, born Vincent Eugene Craddock (1935-1971). American rock and roll singer. Dying from alcohol abuse and a bleeding stomach ulcer: "Mama, if I get through this, I swear I'll be a better man."

Vitellius, Aulus (15-69). Roman emperor. Deposed by his rival Vespasian (above), Vitellius was murdered by Roman troops: "Yet I was once your Emperor."

Voltaire, born François-Marie Arouet (1694-1778). French philosopher who became one of his country's most prominent Enlightenment writers. Voltaire's supposed last utterances differ significantly:

* To his valet: "Adieu my dear Maraud; I am dying."
* To a servant: "Take care of [my niece] Maria."
* To his nurse: "For all the wealth in Europe, I would not see another infidel die."
* When asked by a priest whether he would renounce Satan: "Now, now my dear man, this is no time to make new enemies."
* Others contend that Voltaire reacted to the mention of Jesus Christ's divinity, which he had previously denied: "In the name of God, Sir, do not speak to me any more about that man, and let me die in peace."
* When a lamp flared at his bedside: "The flames already?"
* Some relate that Voltaire spoke to his physician of abandonment by God and his date with Satan: "I am abandoned by God and man! I will give you half of what I am worth if you will give me six months' life. Then I shall go to hell; and you will go with me. O Christ! O Jesus Christ!"

Waddell, George "Rube" (1876-1914). American major league baseball player. Dying of tuberculosis, Waddell quipped about his wasted condition to some of his teammates: "I'll be over tomorrow to show you guys how to run. I've got my weight down now."

Wade, Benjamin (1800-1878). American lawyer and U.S. senator. Whispering to his wife: "I cannot speak at all."

Wagner, Cosima (1837-1930). Italian-born daughter of the Hungarian pianist Franz Liszt and wife of the composer Richard Wagner. "Glorious... sorrow..."

Wagner, Richard (1813-1883): German composer and conductor, best-known for his heroic operas. In the throes of a fatal heart attack, Wagner asked his maid to: "Call my wife and the doctor." As he was being moved to a couch, a watch given by his wife fell from his pocket. He exclaimed: "My watch!" and died.

Waiblinger, Wilhelm (1804-1830). German romantic poet. Dying of consumption, Waiblinger spoke to his loved ones: "Farewell."

Alternative: "Addio!"

Wainwright, Henry (1828-1875). English criminal who murdered his mistress. To the crowd that had assembled to watch his hanging: "You curs! Come to see a man die, have you!"

Walker, Madam C.J., born Sarah Breedlove (1867-1919). African American entrepreneur, social activist and philanthropist. Walker was president of a company that made beauty and hair products for African American women. She became the first of her race in the U.S. to become a millionaire. To her nurse: "I am not going to die, because I have so much work to do yet. I want to live to help my race."

Walker, Charles (1940-1990). American criminal, executed by lethal injection for a double murder committed during a robbery: "I'm guilty. I can accept my punishment. I'm sorry I done it, yeah, but it's done."

Walker, James Alexander (1832-1901). Confederate general during the U.S. Civil War who later became a U.S. congressman. To his daughter Willie: "The sun is setting, daughter. I can't wait. Once more I want to stand up by the window and watch the sun set. Help me to get up, Will. I want to stand on my feet again and die like a man and a soldier."

Walker, James John (1881-1946). American Democratic politician who became mayor of New York City. Walker later resigned from office because of corruption. To his nurse who ordered him back to bed: "Am I not the master of my own house? Oh, you must be a good Democrat!" When she answered yes, he said: "In that case I shall abide by the wishes of a fair constituent."

Walker, Richard (1679-1764). English academician and philosopher. To his nurse who exclaimed: "Ah, poor gentleman, he is going:" "Going, going! Where am I going? I'm sure I know no more than the Man in the Moon."

Walker, Robert (1918-1951). American actor, best-known for his role in the Alfred Hitchcock film *Strangers on a Train.* Before the administration of a sedative by his psychiatrist: "I feel terrible, doc. Do something quick!" Walker died shortly thereafter.

Walker, William (1824-1860). American physician and mercenary. Arrested while attempting to establish an English-speaking colony under his control in Central America, Walker was condemned to die. To a priest before facing a Honduran firing squad: "I am a Roman Catholic. The war which I made upon Honduras, in accordance with the suggestions of certain Ruatanoes [people of Roatán Island, Honduras], was unjust. Those who accompanied me are not to blame. I alone am guilty. I ask pardon of the people. I receive death with resignation. Would that it may be for the good of society."

Wallace, Lewis "Lew" (1827-1905). American diplomat, U.S. Civil War Union general and author of *Ben-Hur: A Tale of the Christ.* Dying of a stomach ailment: "Thy will be done."

Wallace, William (1821-1862). Union general in the U.S. Civil War. Wounded during the Battle of Shiloh in Tennessee, Wallace was reunited with his wife and died in her arms, saying: "We meet in heaven."

Wallenda, Karl (1905-1978). German-born high-wire artist, killed while performing in Puerto Rico. Before stepping on a wire suspended between two hotels: "Don't worry about it. The wind is stronger on the street than up here." Buffeted by a gust of wind, Wallenda lost his balance and fell approximately 120 feet to his death.

Waller, Thomas "Fats" (1904-1943). American jazz musician and composer. Shortly before dying of pneumonia on a train headed cross-country, Waller spoke to a friend who complained about the coldness of his compartment: "You'll be okay when you get into bed."

Walton, William (1902-1983): British classical composer. To his wife Susana shortly before he died from an unspecified "cardiac crisis:" "Don't leave me, please don't leave me."

Warburton, John (1776-1857). English clergyman. On his deathbed, Warburton feebly spoke: "Hal... Hal..." Mustering his strength, he clearly articulated "Hallelujah!" and expired.

Ward, Mary "Maisie" (1889-1975). British writer and publisher. "I still have enthusiasm. But what use is enthusiasm without energy?"

Ward, Samuel "Sam" (1814-1884). American statesman, lobbyist and brother of Julia Ward Howe (above). "I think I am going to give up the ghost."

Warham, William (c. 1450-1532). Archbishop of Canterbury, England. On his deathbed, Warham was told that he still had a small sum of money left: "That is enough to last till I get to Heaven."

Warner, Charles (1829-1900). American writer and essayist who co-authored the 1873 book *The Gilded Age* with Samuel Clemens (above). To his host: "I am not well and should like to lie down. Will you call me in ten minutes? Thank you. You are very kind. In ten minutes, remember?" At the appointed time, Warner was found dead.

Warren, Earl (1891-1974). Chief justice of the U.S. Supreme Court who retired from his post in 1969. When told by Justice William Brennan that the Court had ordered President Richard Nixon to surrender the Watergate tapes to a district court, Warren replied: "Thank God! Thank God! Thank God! If you don't do it this way, Bill, it's the end of the country as we have known it." He died of a heart attack shortly thereafter.

Warren, Joseph (1741-1775). American Revolutionary War officer. Warren exhorted his troops after he was mortally wounded by a British soldier during the Battle of Bunker Hill: "I am a dead man. Fight on, my brave fellows, for the salvation of your country."

Warren, Leonard, born Leonard Warenoff (1911-1960). American operatic baritone. While performing at the Metropolitan Opera House in Verdi's *La Forza del Destino*, Warren concluded the recitative that began "*Morir! Tremenda cosa!* [Die! How terrible!]" and the aria "*Urna fatale* [Fatal urn]."

Failing to sing his next lines, Warren pleaded with a cast member: "Help me! Help me!" He fell to the stage floor and died of a presumed cerebral hemorrhage.

Alternative: * Some say Warren sang the beginning of the next aria: "*Oh, gioia! Oh, gioia!* [Oh, happiness! Oh, happiness!]" before he collapsed.

Wart, Rudolf von der (died 1308). German nobleman. Wart was condemned to die for his alleged complicity in the murder of German King Albrecht (Albert) I. While stretched on the torture wheel, Wart's wife gave comfort throughout the ordeal: "Gertrude, this is fidelity till death."

Washakie (died 1900). Native American Shoshoni chief. In the 1860s, Washakie helped negotiate a treaty creating a reservation that provided schools, churches and hospitals for his people. On his deathbed, to his family: "You now have that for which we have so long and bravely fought. Keep it forever in peace and honor. Go now and rest. I shall speak to you no more."

Washington, Booker (1856-1915). American educator, writer and social activist. Stricken with heart failure in New York, Washington pleaded: "Take me home. I was born in the South. I have lived and labored in the South, and I wish to die and be buried in the South." When he arrived home in Alabama, he asked about his infant grandson: "How is Booker?" He died shortly thereafter.

Washington, George (1732-1799). American military leader and first president of the independent United States. Dying of an acute severe respiratory infection, Washington spoke to his secretary: "I find I am going; my breath cannot last long. I believed from the first that the disorder would prove fatal..." He then asked that his affairs should be put in order. When an attendant helped to raise him in bed: "I am afraid I fatigue you too much." When answered to the contrary, he said: "Well, it is a debt we must pay to each other, and I hope when you aid of this kind you will find it." To one of his physicians: "Doctor, I die hard, but I am not afraid to go. I believed from my first attack that I should not survive it. My breath cannot last long." Later, to other attending doctors: "I feel I am going. I thank you for your attentions, but I pray you take no more trouble about me, but let me go off quietly. I cannot last long." About five hours later, again, to his secretary: "I am just going. Have me decently buried, and do not let my body be put into the vault in less than three [some say two] days after I am dead [Washington had a fear of being buried alive]. Do you understand me?" When answered in the affirmative, Washington uttered his last words: "'Tis well."

Alternatives: * "... Let me die without further interruption. I feel myself going. I thank you for your attention. You had better not take any more trouble about me, but let me go off quietly. I cannot last long."

* "Doctor, I have been dying a long time; my breath cannot last long- but I am not afraid to die."

Washington, Martha (1731-1802). Widow of U.S. President George Washington. Dying of a fever, to her grandchildren: "I am now undergoing my final trial, but I have been prepared for a long time." After Last Rites were given, Washington asked for her burial gown: "Bring me my white gown, the one I have laid by as my last dress."

Waters, Ethel (1896-1977). American blues, jazz and gospel singer. In an interview before her death, Waters said: "I'm not afraid to die, honey. In fact I'm kind of looking forward to it. I know the Lord has his arms wrapped around this big, fat sparrow." At the end: "Merciful Father! Precious Jesus!"

Watson, Thomas (1856-1922). American politician who became a member of the U.S. House of Representatives and Senate. Dying of a stroke: "It's my finish. I am not afraid of death. I am not afraid of death."

Watt, James (1736-1819). Scottish inventor and scientist whose refined steam engine energized the Industrial Revolution. To friends: "All will be well in the end. We must do the best we can on earth and look for the rest in heaven." Then: "I am very sensible of the attachment you show me, and I hasten to thank you for it, as I feel that I am now come to my last illness."

Watteau, Antoine (1684-1721). French artist. Dying of tuberculosis, to the priest who proffered an ill-carved crucifix: "Remove that crucifix; it grieves me to see it. Is it possible that my master is so ill served?"

Alternative: * "Take this crucifix away from me! How could an artist dare to portray so grossly the features of a God?"

Watts, George (1817-1904). British artist and sculptor. "Now I see that great book! I see that great light!"

Watts, Kevin (1981-2008). American criminal, executed by lethal injection for a triple murder: "I'm out of here, man. I'm gone. Keep me in your hearts." Before losing consciousness, he asked: "Can I say something? I'm dying but..."

Wayne, Anthony "Mad Anthony" (1745-1796). American Revolutionary War leader and member of the U.S. House of Representatives. While returning from an inspection of frontier posts: "This is the end... I am dying... I cannot bear up much longer... Bury me here on the hill- by the flagpole [Fort Presque Isle, near present-day Erie, Pennsylvania]."

Wayne, John, born Marion Robert Morrison (1907-1979). American film actor, producer and director. Dying of cancer, Wayne was asked if he recognized a companion: "Of course I know who you are. You're my girl. I love you." One of Wayne's popular quotes: "Life's hard; it's even harder if you're stupid."

Webb, Mary (1881-1927). English writer and poet. When informed that tea would be brought to her: "That will be nice."

Webb, William "Chick" (1905-1939). American jazz drummer and band leader. Dying of tuberculosis, to his mother: "I'm sorry. I've got to go."

Weber, Carl Maria von (1786-1826): German composer, pianist and conductor. Dying of tuberculosis, to an attendant: "Now let me sleep."

Webern, Anton von (1883-1945): Austrian composer and conductor. At the close of WWII, Webern was fatally wounded by an American soldier. His final words: "I've been shot. It is over."

Webster, Daniel (1782-1852). American statesman who became a member of the U.S. House of Representatives and Senate. On his deathbed, Webster drifted in and out of consciousness. After awakening: "Life! Life! Death! Death! How curious it is!" Toward the end: "Life till death. I wish to retain my senses till I die." Webster then said: "Poetry- Gray." When several stanzas of Gray's *Elegy* were repeated for him: "That is poetry, all right." When a portion of Psalm 23 was repeated: "The fact! The fact! That is what I want! Thy rod! Thy rod! Thy staff! Thy staff!" Unconscious for a period, Webster again awoke, speaking his last words: "I still live."

Alternative: * "Well, children, doctor. I trust on this occasion I have said nothing unworthy of Daniel Webster. Life, death; death, death. How curious it is."

Webster, Noah (1758-1843). American lexicographer and writer. Webster compiled the first American English dictionary. When advised to prepare for the end: "I'm ready to go. My work is all done. I know in whom I have believed. I have struggled with many difficulties. Some I have been able to overcome and by some I have been overcome. I have made many mistakes, but I love my country and have labored for the youth of my country, and I trust no precept of mine has taught any dear youth to sin."

Weed, Stephen (1834-1863). Union officer during the U.S. Civil War. While holding his position on Little Round Top, Gettysburg, Pennsylvania, Weed exclaimed as he fell mortally wounded: "I would rather die here than that the rebels should gain an inch of this ground."

Weed, Thurlow (1797-1882). American politician and journalist. Confused during his last hours, Weed thought that he had finished a meeting with long-deceased President Lincoln and General Winfield Scott (some say Secretary of State William Seward): "I want to go home."

Weil, Simone (1909-1943). French philosopher, writer, mystic and social activist. Suffering from tuberculosis, Weil was urged by her doctor to eat: "When I think of my fellow citizens who are dying of hunger in France, I cannot eat."

Weiss, Emanuel "Mendy" (1906-1944). American murderer. Weiss was an associate of Louis Buchalter who led the Murder, Inc. organization. Before Weiss' execution in the electric chair: "Can I say something? All I want to say is I'm innocent. I'm here on a framed-up case. And Governor Dewey knows it. I want to thank Judge Lehman. He knows me because I am a Jew. Give my love to my family ... and everything."

Weizmann, Chaim (1874-1952). Russian-born first Israeli president. To his nurse: "I am going on a very, very long journey. Prepare everything."

Welch, John (c. 1568-1622). Scottish clergyman. While preaching in France, Welch died unexpectedly: "It is enough, O Lord, it is now enough. Hold thy hand. Thy servant is a clay vessel and can hold no more!"

Weld, Angelina (1805-1879. American abolitionist, women's rights activist and educator. Fearing the end was near: "Death! Death! Life eternal! Eternal life!" Trying to quote James 5:4, she babbled: "The hire of the laborers kept back by fraud crieth, and the cries are in the ear of the Lord." The Bible passage reads: "Behold, the wages of the laborers who mowed your fields, which you kept back by fraud, cry out; and the cries of the harvesters have reached the ears of the Lord of hosts."

Welles, Orson (1915-1985). American actor, writer, director and producer, best-known for his film *Citizen Kane* and the radio adaptation of H.G. Wells's novel *The War of the Worlds.* Welles left a message on the telephone answering machine of his close friend Henry Jaglom: "This is your friend. Don't forget to tell me how your mother is." Welles died of a heart attack later that day.

Wellesley, Arthur, Duke of Wellington (1769-1852). British general who defeated Napoleon I at Waterloo in 1815. Asked if he wanted tea: "Yes, if you please." Wellesley then inquired: "Do you know where the apothecary lives?" When told in the affirmative: "Then send and let him know that I should like to see him. I don't feel quite well and I will lie still till he comes." Later in the day "a fit came on," and Wellesley died.

Wells, Brian (1956-2003). American pizza deliveryman. Wells was involved in a plot to rob a bank using an explosive device placed around his neck by two co-conspirators. Before the bomb squad could intervene, the device detonated, killing Wells instantly. Words variously spoken by Wells to the police before the explosion:

* "Why is nobody trying to get this thing off me? It's going to go off. I'm not lying."
* "I don't have a lot of time."
* "It's gonna go off."
* "He pulled a key out and started a timer. I heard the thing ticking when he did it."
* "Can you at least take these freaking handcuffs off so I can hold this thing up? It's killing my neck."
* "I didn't do it."
* "Did you call my boss?"

Wells, Herbert "H.G." (1866-1946). British novelist, best-known for his science fiction creation *The War of the Worlds*. Wells spoke impatiently to his relatives (some say a friend) at the deathbed: "Don't interrupt me. Can't you see I'm busy dying?" Later, to his nurse: "Go away. I'm all right." He died minutes later.

Wenceslas, Saint (c. 907-c. 929). King of Bohemia. Wenceslas was murdered by his brother who wished to ascend the throne in his place: "May God forgive you, brother."

Wentworth, Thomas, Earl of Strafford (1593-1641). English statesman. Because of alleged mismanagement in the service of King Charles I, Wentworth was accused of treason and sentenced to die. Before his beheading: "That block must be my pillow, and here I shall rest from all my labours. No thoughts of envy, no dreams of treason, nor jealousies, nor cares, for the king, the state, or myself, shall interrupt this easy sleep."

Wentworth then asked to be remembered to a number of relatives and friends. As he gazed at the block: "I do as cheerfully put off my doublet at this time as ever I did when I went to bed." When the executioner asked for forgiveness: "I forgive you and all the world." Declining a blindfold: "Nay, for I will see it done."

Alternatives: * "I know how to look death in the face and the people too. I thank God I am no more afraid of death, but as cheerfully put off my doublet at this time as ever I did when I went to bed."

* "All will soon be over. One blow will render my wife a widow, my children orphans, and deprive my servants of their master. God be with them and you. Thanks to the internal strength that God has given me, I take this [his doublet] off with as tranquil a spirit as I have ever felt when taking it off at night upon retiring to rest."

Wesley, Charles (1707-1788). English clergyman and hymnodist who became a leader in the newly-formed Methodist movement with his brother John (below). To his wife and family at the bedside: "My Lord, my heart, my God!"

Alternative: * "I shall be satisfied with Thy likeness. Satisfied! Satisfied!"

Wesley, John (1703-1791). English evangelist, theologian and missionary who founded the Methodist movement. After giving burial instructions, Wesley admonished: "Pray and praise." To friends who came to pay their last respects, he proclaimed: "The best of all is: God is with us." Throughout the night, he repeated: "I'll praise! I'll praise!" Wesley's last word before expiring was: "Farewell."

Alternative: * "The best of all is: God is with me."

Wesley, Martha (1706-1791). English Methodist supporter who was the sister of Charles and John Wesley (above). Asked by her niece if she were in pain: "No, but a new feeling. I have the assurance which I have long prayed for. Shout!"

Wesley, Samuel (1662-1735). English clergyman and patriarch of the Wesley clan (above). To his family: "Now let me hear you talk about heaven." When his son Charles asked how he was feeling: "Oh, my Charles, I feel a great deal. God chastens me with strong pain, but I praise Him for it; I thank Him for it; I love Him for it." When asked if he were near heaven: "Yes, I am." After the prayers for the dying: "Now you have done all."

Wesley, Samuel Sebastian (1810-1876): English organist and composer who was the grandson of Charles Wesley. Dying of Bright's disease, to his sister: "Let me see the sky."

Wesley, Sarah (1726–1822). English wife of Charles Wesley. During her last night, Sarah asked before falling asleep: "Open the gates! Open the gates!" Upon awakening, she was asked if she found Christ precious: "O yes!" When queried if she were happy, Sarah answered "Yes" and died.

Wesley, Susanna (1669-1742). English matriarch of the Wesley clan of clergymen and musicians (above). To her family: "Children, as soon as I am released, sing a psalm of praise to God."

Wessel, Gansfortius (died 1489). German theologian and mystic. "I know only Jesus the crucified."

Westerfield, Roy (died 1988). American comptroller for Pacific Engineering Production Company of Nevada, a supplier of chemical propellants for the U.S. space program. Moments before a massive explosion, Westerfield was reporting to a dispatcher by telephone when he spoke to a fellow worker guiding other employees out of the building: "Get 'em all out of here." Both men perished in the explosion.

Whale, James "Jimmy" (1889-1957). English-born Hollywood film and theater director. Suffering from the effects of a stroke and depression, Whale killed himself by drowning. The last words of his suicide note: "... The future is just old age and illness and pain. Goodbye and thank you for all your love. I must have peace and this is the only way. 'Jimmy.'"

Whately, Richard (1787-1863). English theologian and writer who was Archbishop of Dublin. Plagued by a partial paralysis and leg ulcer, Whately professed: "I wish for nothing but death." Shortly before he died, a chaplain quoted a portion of Philippians 3: 21from the English Bible: "... who shall change our vile body..." The archbishop interrupted him and asked for his own translation: "This body of our humiliation." Whately responded: "That's right, not vile- nothing that He made is vile."

Wheaton, Lawrence "Larry" (died 1982). Aircraft captain on Air Florida Flight 90 bound from Washington D.C. to Ft. Lauderdale, Florida. Because of inadequate deicing before takeoff and other errors, the jet crashed into a bridge on the Potomac River shortly after it became airborne. First Officer Roger Pettit's last words were directed to the pilot: "Larry, we're going down, Larry." Wheaton replied: "I know it!" Four motorists on the bridge and 74 of 79 on the aircraft perished.

Wheelock, Eleazar (1711-1779). American clergyman and educator who founded Dartmouth College. To his relatives: "Oh, my family, be faithful unto death."

Whistler, James (1834-1903). American-born artist, best-known for his *Portrait of the Artist's Mother* popularly called *Whistler's Mother.* When offered some chicken broth: "Take the d***** thing away." As a friend prepared to leave: "But why do you go so soon?"

Whitaker, William (1548-1595). English theologian and educator. When told what to expect with his coming "dissolution:" "Life or death is welcome to me, and I desire not to live but so far as I may be serviceable to God and His church."

White, Barry, born Barry Eugene Carter (1944-2003). American popular singer-songwriter. Dying of kidney failure: "Leave me alone – I'm fine."

White, Clifton (1958-2001). American criminal, executed by lethal injection for the rape and murder of a North Carolina woman: "I just hope everything goes all right. I hope the Lord takes me home. Thank you, warden."

White, Henry (1785-1806). English poet who died of tuberculosis while a student at the University of Cambridge. Conclusion of a last letter to his brother that was never delivered: "... Our lectures begin on Friday, but I do not attend them until I am better. I have not written to my mother, nor shall I while I remain unwell. You will tell her, as a reason, that our lectures began on Friday. I know she will be uneasy, if she does not hear from me, and still more so if I tell her I am ill. I cannot write anymore at present, than that I am your truly affectionate brother, H.K. White."

White, Joseph, born José Blanco Crespo (1775-1841). Spanish-born British theologian and poet. Rousing from a somnolent state: "Now I die."

White, Melvin (1950-2005). American criminal, executed by lethal injection for the rape and murder of a nine year-old girl. After apologizing to the murdered girl's family: "... All right, warden, let's give them what they want."

White, Walter (1893-1955). American civil rights leader. When asked by his daughter if he liked her dress: "I plead the Fifth Amendment." Dying of a heart attack shortly thereafter, White fell to the floor knocking over a table: "I knew that darned table was going to tip!"

Whitefield, George (1714-1770). English clergyman who became one of the leaders of the newly-formed Methodist religion. To a companion: "I am almost suffocated. I can scarce breathe. My asthma quite chokes me… *I am dying.*"

Whitman, Walter "Walt" (1819-1892). American poet, best-known for his works *O Captain! My Captain!* and *Leaves of Grass.* Referring to his friend Thomas Donaldson: "O, he's a dear, good fellow."

Alternatives: * "Oh, I feel so good!"

* Requesting a change in bed: "Shift, Warry [Frederick Warren Fritzinger, Whitman's nurse]."
* "Hold me up; I want to s***."

Whitney, William (1841-1904). American financier and statesman. To the nurse who informed his children that he was too sick for visitors: "Don't get angry, nurse. I love my son and daughter. It does me good to chat with them."

Whitrick, Kevin (1965-2007). British electrical engineer. The depressed Whitrick announced online that he intended to hang himself: "I've had it. You want it on cam? I'll do it. You think I am full of s***? Well, not this time, mate." Some viewers encouraged him to proceed while others tried to dissuade him. Whitrick documented his suicide live via webcam.

Whittier, John Greenleaf (1807-1892). American poet and abolitionist. To his physicians: "You have done all that love and human skill could do. I thank you. It is of no use. I am worn out." When his nurse tried to close the blinds, Whittier said: "No! No!" When his niece asked if he knew who she was: "I have known thee all the time."

Alternative: * "Give my love to the world."

Whittington, John (died 1875). American criminal. Whittington clubbed a drinking companion, cut his throat and robbed him of "a large sum of money." He was tried for murder at Fort Smith, Arkansas before "The Hanging Judge" Isaacs Parker. Unwilling to speak, Whittington's last statement was read by a clergyman "How I Came to the Gallows... My father taught me to be honest... but he did not teach me to be religious... He showed me how to drink whiskey... and that is what brought me to the gallows... Oh! That men would leave off drinking altogether! And O parents! I send forth this dying warning to you today, standing on this gallows. Train up your children in the way they should go, my father's example brought me to ruin. God love us all. Farewell! Farewell!"

Whittle, Daniel (1840-1901). American evangelist and hymnodist. The dying Whittle spoke to a concerned friend: "It is all right. The Lord knows best and all will result in my good. All sorrow will fade away and all pain depart as dew before the morning sun."

Wieland, Christoph (1733-1813). German writer and poet. Wieland quoted from Shakespeare's *Hamlet*: "To be or not to be..."

Alternative: * "To sleep- to die..."

Wiggins, Thomas "Blind Tom" (1849 –1908). American blind autistic savant. Born a slave, the lad was able to mimic on the piano virtually any tune played for him. At the end of a half century of touring as a piano virtuoso, Blind Tom suffered a stroke. Later, as he tried to play Stephen Foster's "Old Folks at Home," he sobbed saying: "I'm done, all gone missus" and fell dead.

Wilberforce, Samuel (1805-1873). English Bishop of Winchester and son of William Wilberforce (below). Dying after a fall from his horse: "There is no such thing as sudden death to a Christian."

Wilberforce, William (1759-1833). English abolitionist, evangelist and statesman. After hearing that parliament had passed an anti-slavery bill: "Thank God that I have lived to see the day when England is willing to give twenty millions for the abolition of slavery." Several days later on his deathbed, to a friend: "I am in a very distressed state." His companion tried to reassure by saying that the great man had his "feet on the rock." Wilberforce responded "I do not venture to speak so positively, but I hope I have." To his family: "I now feel so weaned from earth, my affections so much in heaven, that I can leave you all without regret; yet I do not love you less, but God more." Some say his last word was: "Heaven."

Wild, Jonathan "Thief-Taker General" (c. 1682-1725). English thief who specialized in the fencing of stolen goods. Wild's alleged last request before his hanging: "Lord Jesus receive my soul."

Wilde, Oscar (1854-1900). Irish writer, playwright and poet, best-known for his novel *The Picture of Dorian Gray* and comedy *The Importance of Being Earnest*. In the days preceding his death, Wilde suffered from an ear infection that progressed to meningitis and delirium. In his semi-comatose state, he could only mumble unintelligible words. Despite Wilde's altered mental state, many authors have attributed a plethora of last words that may or may not have been uttered in the days leading up to his death.

Alternatives: * To a friend who wanted to apply mustard plasters: "You ought to be a doctor, as you always want people to do what they don't want to."

* Wilde referred to a play he was writing, comparing it to a French coin worth a hundredth of a franc: "It's worth fifty centimes."
* In his Parisian hotel, Wilde spoke about his surroundings: "It's the wallpaper or me- one of us has to go."
* "My wallpaper and I are fighting a duel to the death. One or the other of us has to go."
* "These curtains are killing me; one of us has got to go."
* After ordering a last bottle of champagne: "I am dying, as I lived, beyond my means."
* "Ah, well, then I suppose I shall have to die beyond my means."

Wilde, William (1815-1876). Irish surgeon, writer and father of Oscar Wilde (above). Referring to his rowdy sons: "Oh those boys, those boys!"

Wilkerson, Wallace (c. 1834-1879). American criminal, convicted of murder stemming from a card game. Wilkerson chose a firing squad as his means of execution. When the bullets failed to hit a vital organ, he screamed: "Oh, my God! Oh, my God! They have missed [a white target placed over his heart]!" In agony, he died minutes later.

Wilkes, John (1725-1797). English statesman, journalist and activist for civil liberties. Toasting his daughter with a glass of water she handed him: "I drink to the health of my beloved and excellent daughter!"

Willard, Domonic (date of birth and death unclear). American criminal. Willard apparently was a mobster during the U.S. Prohibition era. Before his execution by firing squad, he was asked if he had any last requests: "Why, yes, a bulletproof vest."

Willard, Frances (1839-1898). American temperance and women's suffrage leader. Dying of influenza, to her physician who said there was no hope for recovery: "It is well, for I am very weary. How beautiful to be with God!"

William I, also Kaiser Wilhelm I (1797-1888). Emperor of Germany. To his chancellor, Otto von Bismarck: "I've always been pleased with you. You've done everything well."

William II, also Kaiser Wilhelm II (1859-1941). Emperor of Germany. Deposed after WWI, William was exiled to Holland. At the time of his death, an invasion of England by Nazi troops seemed imminent. To his daughter: "Are we still going to attack England? Should that really happen- and should we win- we must immediately stretch out our hand to England and go together. Without England, we cannot endure." Dying of "an embolism in the lungs," William told his relatives: "This is the end of me. I am sinking! I am sinking!"

William I, also William the Conqueror (c. 1027-1087). King of England. Realizing that he would not survive an injury sustained during his last conquest: "I commend myself to Mary, the Holy Mother of God, my heavenly lady, that by her intercession I may be reconciled to her Son, Our Lord Jesus Christ."

Alternatives: * "Then to our blessed Lady Mary, the mother of God, I commend myself. May she, by her holy intercessions, reconcile me to our Lord and Savior, Jesus Christ. God be merciful to..."
* "I commend my soul to Mary, the Holy Mother of God."

William II (c. 1056-1100). King of England. To his hunting partner Walter Tirel after a deer appeared close by: "Shoot, you devil! Shoot, in the devil's name! Shoot, or it will be the worse for you!" An arrow fired by his companion or a member of the party mortally wounded the king.

Alternatives: * "Shoot, Walter, shoot as if it were the devil!"
* "Shoot, Walter! Shoot in the Devil's name, shoot!"

William III (1650-1702). King of England, Scotland and Ireland. Dying of complications after a fall from his horse, to his doctors: "I know that you have done all that skill and learning could do for me, but the case is beyond your art, and I submit." Toward the end, he asked: "Can this last long?" When told that death was near: "I do not die yet. Hold me fast." William later expired in the arms of one of his pages.

William IV (1765-1837). King of Great Britain and Ireland. Remembering Britain's victory over Napoleon I at Waterloo, William spoke to his doctors "I know that I am going, but I should like to see another anniversary of Waterloo. Try if you cannot tinker me up to last over that date." Wishing to hold the tricolored banner brought by the Duke of Wellington: "Unfurl it and let me feel it... Glorious day..." He died shortly after celebrating the Waterloo anniversary, saying: "The Church! The Church!"

William of Orange, also William the Silent (1533-1584). Revolutionist Dutch ruler. William was assassinated by a Spanish sympathizer, Balthazar Gérard (above), for his military engagements against Spain: "I am wounded... God have mercy on me and on my poor people!" To his sister, who asked if he commended his soul to the Lord: "I do." Some say his last word to his sister's query was a simple "Yes."

Alternatives: * "God pity me, I am sadly wounded! God have mercy on my soul, and on this unfortunate nation."

* "O my God, have mercy upon my soul. O my God, have mercy upon this poor people."

William, Duke of Hamilton (1616-1651). Scottish nobleman. Wounded at the Battle of Worcester in central England while fighting for Charles II, William professed: "I believe that though in the last hour of the day I have entered into my Master's service, yet I shall receive my penny."

Williams, Alfred (1877-1930). Impoverished British poet and writer. To his wife Mary who was dying of cancer: "My dear, this is going to be a tragedy for us both." Mary expired several weeks later.

Williams, Alice (died1924). Wife of Daniel Williams, a prominent American surgeon (below). When it was suggested that a prayer be said, the agnostic Mrs. Williams replied: "A little late, don't you think?"

Williams, Charles (1886-1945). English theologian, writer and poet. To a priest: "Will you say a Mass for anyone I have ever loved in any way?"

Williams, Daniel (1856-1931). American surgeon who pioneered chest operations. Dying of a stroke, Williams mentioned his estate in the town of Idlewild, Michigan: "Take me to Idlewild to die."

Williams, Edward (1920-1988). American lawyer and owner of professional baseball and football teams. Dying of cancer, to his physician: "Have I put up a good fight? Have I tried? Do I have to keep fighting? Can I quit?"

Williams, Egbert "Bert" (1874-1922). Bahamian-born American Vaudeville comedian and singer. Dying of pneumonia, to his physician: "I feel eighty percent better."

Williams, Frederick (1972-2004). Liberian-born American deacon. While being led into an Atlanta, Georgia detention center for "violent behavior," Williams was shot multiple times with a Taser device: "Don't kill me! I have a family to support. I've calmed down." He died shortly thereafter.

Alternative: * "Please don't kill me!"

Williams, Hiram "Hank" (1923-1953). American country music singer and songwriter. During a long journey to a concert venue, William's chauffeur asked if he wished to have a meal: "No. I just want to get some sleep." Later, when the driver stopped for fuel, he found Williams dead.

Williams, James (1740-1780). American pioneer and military leader during the American Revolutionary War. Mortally wounded fighting the British during the Battle of Kings Mountain, South Carolina: "I die contented, since we have gained the victory."

Williams, John (1854-1932). American statesman who became a member of the U.S. House of Representatives and Senate. "I've done things that seemed at the time worth doing. I think that if a man can get to my age and, looking back, believe a majority of the things he did were worth the effort, he has nothing to regret."

Williams, Kenneth (1926-1988). British actor and comedian. Dying of a drug overdose, Williams' final diary entry: "Oh, what's the bloody point?"

Williams, Stanley "Tookie" (1953-2005). American criminal. Convicted of multiple murders, Williams' executioners had difficulty inserting the needle for his lethal injection: "You guys doing that right?"

Williams, Wendy (1949-1998). American punk rock performer with the Plasmatics band. After several earlier attempts to end her life, Williams succeeded with a self-inflicted gunshot wound. Her suicide note explained: "The act of taking my own life is not something I am doing without a lot of thought. I don't believe that people should take their own lives without deep and thoughtful reflection over a considerable period of time. I do believe strongly, however, that the right to do so is one of the most fundamental rights that anyone in a free society should have. For me much of the world makes no sense, but my feelings about what I am doing ring loud and clear to an inner ear and a place where there is no self, only calm. Love always, Wendy."

Williams, William, Jr. (1956-2005). American criminal, executed by lethal injection for multiple murders: "I'm not going to waste no time talking about my lifestyle, my case, my punishment. Mom, you've been there for me from the beginning. I love you. To my nieces, nephew and uncle I love you very much. Y'all stick together. Don't worry about me. I'm OK."

Williamson, John "Sonny Boy" (1914-1948). American blues musician. Beaten during a robbery, Williamson told his wife: "Lord have mercy." When she asked what happened, he replied: "I'm dying."

Willie, Robert (1958-1984). American criminal, electrocuted for the rape and murder of a young woman. "I would just like to say, Mr. and Mrs. Harvey, that I hope you get some relief from my death. Killing people is wrong. That's why you've put me to death. It makes no difference whether it's citizens, countries or governments. Killing is wrong." Willie asked the warden to remove his hood, so he could wink at his spiritual adviser Sister Helen Prejean, a Roman Catholic nun. Willie was one of the felons featured in Prejean's book *Dead Man Walking.*

Willkie, Wendell (1892-1944). American politician who unsuccessfully mounted a U.S. presidential run. Dying of a heart attack, Willkie responded to a nurse who asked how he was doing while swabbing his throat: "How can I talk with my mouth full of that stuff?" Asked later if he would like to have a scotch and water: "Okay, if you make it warm." Willkie died moments later.

Wilmot, John, Earl of Rochester (1647-1680). English poet and libertine. Dying from a debauched lifestyle: "The only objection against this Book [the Bible] is a bad life!" Hearing of a companion's departure: "Has my friend left me? Then I shall die shortly."

Wilson, Alexander (1766-1813). Scottish-American ornithologist, naturalist and poet. "Bury me where the birds will sing over my grave."

Wilson, Edward (1872-1912). English polar explorer and physician who perished on Robert Scott's ill-fated Antarctic expedition (above). Last letter to his wife: "God knows I am sorry to be the cause of sorrow to anyone in the world, but everyone must die and at every death there must be some sorrow. All the things I had hoped to do with you after this Expedition are as nothing now, but there are greater things for us to do in the world to come. My only regret is leaving you to struggle through your life alone, but I may be coming to you by a quicker way. I feel so happy now in having got time to write to you. One of my notes will surely reach you... Your little testament and prayer book will be in my hand or in my breast pocket when the end comes. All is well."

Wilson, Ellen (1860-1914). First wife of U.S. President Woodrow Wilson. Dying of kidney failure, to her physician: "Doctor, if I go away, promise me that you will take good care of my husband."

Wilson, Jack "Jackie" (1934-1984). American popular singer. Wilson suffered a presumed massive heart attack (some say a stroke) while performing the song "Lonely Teardrops." He sang: "My heart is crying, crying..." and collapsed. Wilson remained in a semi-comatose state until his death eight years later.

Wilson, Margaret (died 1685). Scottish martyr. When Wilson refused to vow allegiance to the reigning monarch and renounce the Covenant, she was tied to a stake in the Solway Firth lying between Scotland and England: "I will not [abjure the Covenant]. I am one of Christ's children. Let me go." She then sang and recited scripture before drowning.

Wilson, Michael (1975-2014). American criminal, executed by lethal injection for a murder committed during a robbery. As the drugs took effect, Wilson complained: "I feel my whole body burning." Because a standard lethal drug cocktail was not available at the time, the substitute mixture used in Wilson's execution was called into question.

Wilson, Robert A. (1932-2007). American writer, philosopher and mystic. A last posting on his internet "group mind:" "Hi there, Various medical authorities swarm in and out of here predicting I have between two days and two months to live. I think they are guessing. I remain cheerful and unimpressed. I look forward without dogmatic optimism but without dread. I love you all and I deeply implore you to keep the lasagna flying. Please pardon my levity, I don't see how to take death seriously. It seems absurd. RAW."

Wilson, Woodrow (1856-1924). Twenty-eighth U.S. president. Two days before his death from complications of a stroke, Wilson was told that several specialists would visit him. His response: "Be careful. Too many cooks spoil the broth." The next day, he said: "I am a broken piece of machinery. When the machinery is broken... I am ready" To his physician: "You have been good to me. You have done everything you could." On the day of death, the president called the name of his second wife: "Edith."

Alternative: * "The machinery is just worn out. I am ready."

Windsor, Duchess of, born Bessie Wallis Warfield (1896-1986). American divorcée for whom Edward VIII of England gave up his throne to wed. Demented in her last years: "Look at the way the sun is lighting the trees! You can see so many colors! Tell David [the name she called her late husband] to come in. He wouldn't want to miss this!"

Winkelried, Arnold von (died c. 1386). Swiss patriot. Legend relates that von Winkelried broke through the Austrian line at the Battle of Sempach, near Lucerne, Switzerland by pushing against the spears of enemy combatants, declaring: "Friends, I am going to lay down my life to procure you victory. All I request is that you provide for my family. Follow me and imitate my example."

Alternatives: * "I will open a passage into the line; protect, dear countrymen and confederates, my wife and children..."
* "Make way for liberty."

Winne, George (1947-1970). American college student. To protest the Vietnam War, Winne set himself ablaze next to a sign that read: "In God's name, end this war." To his mother before he died: "I believe in God and the hereafter and I will see you there."

Winthrop, Frederick (1839-1865). Union officer during the U.S. Civil War. Wounded at the Battle of Five Forks, near Petersburg, Virginia, Winthrop was told that the attack had been successful: "Thank God, I am now willing to die." Delirious before expiring two hours later, he relived the battle, commanding: "Straighten the line."

Winthrop, John (1588-1649). English-born Puritan leader and first Massachusetts Bay Colony governor. Pressured on his deathbed to sign an order banishing a religious heretic: "I have done too much of that work already."

Wirz, Heinrich "Henry" (1823-1865). Swiss-born Confederate officer who commanded a prison camp for Union soldiers during the U.S. Civil War. Convicted of prisoner mistreatment and murder, Wirz was sentenced to be hanged: "I have nothing to say, only that I am innocent, and will die like a man, my hopes being in the future. I go before my God, the almighty God, and he will judge between me and you." Before the trap fell, to the prison commandant, Captain Walbridge: "Goodbye Captain. I thank you and the other officers of the prison, for you have all treated me well."

Alternative: * "This is too tight, loosen it a little. I am innocent. I will have to die sometime. I will die like a man. My hopes are in the future."

Wise, Stephen (1874-1949) Hungarian-born American Reform rabbi. To his children: "Take my hand, darlings. I am entering the Valley."

Wishart, George (c. 1513-1546). Scottish martyr. Because of his preaching for the Reformation, Wishart was branded a heretic and sentenced to die by the flames: "For the sake of the true gospel, given one by the grace of God, I suffer this day with a glad heart. Behold and consider my visage. Ye shall not see me change color. I fear not this fire." As he kneeled at the stake: "O thou Savior of the world, have mercy upon me! Father of Heaven, I commend my spirit into thy hands!" When the executioner asked for forgiveness, Wishart replied: "Come hither to me." Kissing him on the cheek, the condemned man said: "Lo! Here is a token that I forgive thee, my heart; do thine office."

Witt, Cornelis de (1623-1672). Dutch politician and brother of Jan de Witt (below). Having run afoul of the government, both brothers were accused of treason. de Witt pleaded with the mob that tortured and killed them: "What do you want me to do? Where do you want me to go?"

Witt, Jan de (1625-1672). Dutch politician. To the mob that killed him and his brother: "What are you doing? This is not what you wanted."

Wittgenstein, Ludwig (1889-1951). Austrian-born British philosopher, writer and educator, best-known for his posthumously published papers *Philosophical Investigations.* Dying of cancer, to the wife of his physician: "Tell them I've had a wonderful life."

Wolcot, John, whose pen name was Peter Pindar (1738-1819). British satirist and poet. On his deathbed, when asked if he wanted anything: "Give me back my youth."

Wolf, Hugo (1860-1903): Austrian composer, best-known for his many art songs (Lieder). Demented by syphilis, Wolf uttered these words, possibly reflecting about his works or those of his contemporaries: "Loathsome music!"

Wolfe, Arthur (1739-1803). Irish jurist and politician. During an insurrection in Dublin, Wolfe was dragged from his carriage and nailed to a door by a pike: "Put me out of pain."

Wolfe, Charles (1791-1823). Irish poet and clergyman. Dying of tuberculosis, Wolfe repeated a part of the Lord's Prayer and said to a relative: "Close this eye. The other is closed already. And now, farewell." Wolfe resumed the prayer and then fell into the eternal sleep.

Wolfe, James (1727-1759). British military leader. Mortally wounded during the Battle of Quebec, Wolfe was asked if he wanted a surgeon: "There's no need; it's all over with me." When told that his army was victorious over the French who were running (retreating): "Who run?" Wolfe then issued orders to cut off the fleeing French. "Now God be praised; I will die in peace!" At the end: "Lay me down. I am suffocating."

Alternatives: * "What! Do they run already? Then I die happy."
* "Support me. Let not my brave soldiers see me drop; the day is ours! Oh! Keep it!"

Wolfe, Thomas (1900-1938). American writer, best-known for his novel *Look Homeward Angel.* Dying of tuberculous meningitis, to his brother: "Fred, I've had a dream. We were riding in a big car, a big shining car, out in the country. And we had a lot of good things to eat and drink in the car. You were all dressed up, Fred. You looked pretty good. And I looked pretty good too." Wolfe's last word allegedly was: "Scotch."

Alternative: * "All right, Mabel [his sister], I am coming."

Wolfit, Donald (1902-1968). British stage actor and theatrical director. When a young protégée commented that dying must be difficult for such a successful man: "Dying is easy. Comedy is hard."

Wolfman Jack, born Robert Weston Smith (1938-1995). American veteran radio disc jockey. After returning from a tour promoting his autobiography, Wolfman Jack spoke to his wife: "Oh, it is so good to be home!" He then collapsed and died of a heart attack.

Wollstonecraft, Mary (1759-1797). English writer and feminist. Dying in childbirth, Wollstonecraft's husband tried to prepare her for the eventuality: "I know what you are thinking of, but I have nothing to communicate upon the subject." Before she lost consciousness: "He [her husband] is the kindest, best man in the world."

Wolsey, Thomas (c. 1473-1530). English Lord Chancellor and Archbishop of York. Arrested for treason because of his opposition to Henry VIII's plan to divorce Catherine of Aragon, Wolsey took ill with the "bloody flux" before he could be escorted to London. To William Kingston (also Kyngston), Constable of the Tower of London: "Well, well, master Kingston, I see how the matter against me is now framed; but if I had served my God as diligently as I have done the king, He would not have given me over in my grey hairs." Immediately before dying: "... Forget not what I have said; and when I am gone, call it often to mind."

Alternatives: * "And, Master Kyngston, had I but served my God as diligently as I have served my King, He would have not given me over in my grey hairs. But this is the just reward that I must receive for my indulgent pains and study, not regarding my service to my God, but only to my prince."

* "Master Kingston, farewell. I can no more, but wish all things to have good success. My time draweth on fast. I may not tarry with you. And forget not, I pray you, what I have said and charged you withal. For when I am dead ye shall, peradventure [perchance], remember my words much better."

Wood, Frederick (died1963). American criminal, electrocuted for a double murder: "Gentlemen, observe closely as you witness the effect of electricity on Wood."

Alternatives: * "Gents, this is an educational project. You are about to witness the damaging effect electricity has on Wood."
* "I'm going to prove conclusively that wood conducts electricity."

Wood, Grant (1891-1942). American artist, known for his painting of Midwest scenes. Dying of cancer, Wood spoke his sister's name: "Nan." Nan Wood Graham was the model for his painting *American Gothic.*

Wood, Henry (1869-1944). British conductor and composer, known for his association with the Promenade Concerts. "I am not afraid to die."

Wood, John (1827-1889). British naturalist and writer. Wood's last request: "Give me a large cup of tea." He died after drinking the beverage.

Wooden, Timothy (died 1849). American settler. While logging in Wisconsin, Wooden contracted cholera and was told the end was near. His terse response: "I ain't doin' anything else."

Woodhull, Nathaniel (1722-1776). American Revolutionary War officer. Woodhull fought in the Battle of Long Island, New York and was taken prisoner. He was struck with a sword multiple times by a British officer when he refused to swear allegiance to the king. Before dying of his wounds: "Please supply the wants of the American prisoners from the provisions brought from my farm."

Woodruff, David (1959-2002). American criminal, executed by lethal injection for a murder committed during a robbery. When asked for last words, Woodruff replied: "We're not here for a social event, we're here for a killing… Let's get this show on the road."

Woodville, William (1752-1805). English physician and botanist. To the carpenter measuring him for his coffin: "I shall not live more than two days, therefore, make haste."

Woolf, Virginia (1882-1941). English writer, best-known for her novels *Mrs Dalloway* and *To the Lighthouse* and the essay *A Room of One's Own*. Dogged by depression, Woolf killed herself by drowning in a river. The suicide note left for her husband read: "Dearest, I feel certain I am going mad again. I feel we can't go through another of those terrible times. And I shan't recover this time. I begin to hear voices, and I can't concentrate. So I am doing what seems the best thing to do. You have given me the greatest possible happiness. You have been in every way all that anyone could be. I don't think two people could have been happier till this terrible disease came. I can't fight any longer. I know that I am spoiling your life, that without me you could work. And you will I know. You see I can't even write this properly. I can't read. What I want to say is I owe all the happiness of my life to you. You have been entirely patient with me and incredibly good. I want to say that—everybody knows it. If anybody could have saved me it would have been you. Everything has gone from me but the certainty of your goodness. I can't go on spoiling your life any longer. I don't think two people could have been happier than we have been. V."

Woollcott, Alexander (1887-1943). American journalist and radio personality. Woollcott commented during his last radio broadcast: "Germany was the cause of Hitler just as much as Chicago is responsible for the *Chicago Tribune* [newspaper]." Shortly thereafter, he suffered a heart attack, exclaiming: "I am dying! Where are my tablets? Get my [nitro] glycerin tablets!"

Woolman, John (1720-1772). American Quaker preacher and abolitionist. Dying of smallpox while traveling in England: "I believe my being here is in the wisdom of Christ; I know not as to life or death."

Woolston, Thomas (c. 1670-1733). English theologian, jailed for his anti-Christian writings. On his impending death while imprisoned: "My time is come. This is a struggle which all men must go through, and which I bear not only patiently, but with willingness."

Woolton, John (c. 1535-1594). English clergyman who became Bishop of Exeter. Paralleling Roman Emperor Vespasian's last words (above),

Woolton maintained that he would die standing up: "A Bishop ought to die on his legs."

Wordsworth, William (1770-1850). English Poet Laureate, best-known for his poem *The Prelude*. Dying of pleurisy, Wordsworth was asked if he wished to have the Sacrament: "That is just what I want." When his niece walked into the room, the disoriented poet mistook her for his late daughter: "God bless you. Is that Dora?"

Wormer, Eden (died 2012). American student. Wormer, a 14 year-old schoolgirl, endured bullying from classmates over a two year period. After telling her father "I love you, daddy. Goodnight," she hanged herself.

Wotton Henry (1568-1639). English writer, poet and diplomat. To a colleague before dying of a "feverish distemper:" "... And, my dear friend, I now see that I draw near my harbor of death- that harbor that will secure me from all the future storms and waves of this restless world. And I praise God I am willing to leave it, and expect a better- that world wherein dwelleth righteousness, and I long for it."

Wright, Joseph (1855-1930). English philologist and writer. Dying of pneumonia, his last word appropriately was: "Dictionary."

Wright, Orville (1871-1948). American aviation pioneer. Orville and his brother Wilbur built and successfully flew the first heavier-than-air, controlled, powered airplane. Dying of a heart attack, Orville asked his nurse to defer to his housekeeper about preparing his meal: "You had better let Carrie do that, Miss. She knows all my cranky little ways."

Wuornos, Aileen (1956-2002). American criminal, executed by lethal injection for multiple murders: "Yes, I'd just like to say I'm sailing with the Rock and I'll be back like Independence Day with Jesus, June 6, like the movie, big mother ship and all. I'll be back."

Wyatt, Thomas (c. 1521-1554). English leader of a rebellion protesting Queen Mary's decision to marry Philip of Spain. Convicted of treason and sentenced to die by beheading, Wyatt spoke about a confession made under duress: "Whereas it is said abroad that I should accuse my Lady Elizabeth's grace and my Lord Courtenay [a suspected conspirator]; it is not so, good people, for I assure you that neither they nor any other now yonder in hold or durance [imprisonment] was privy of my rising a commotion before I began." When accused of saying otherwise to the council that convicted him, Wyatt responded before he lost his head: "That which I said then, I said. But that which I say now is true."

Wycherley, William (c. 1640-1716). English playwright. To deprive a "disagreeable" nephew of his inheritance, the septuagenarian Wycherley married a young woman 11 days before he died. His request to her: "My dear, it is only this: that you will never marry an old man again."

Wylie, Elinor (1885-1928). American poet and writer. As she proofed her latest volume of verses, Wylie asked her estranged husband to bring a glass of water. When he complied, she said: "Is that all it is?" and died of a massive stroke.

Wythe, George (1726-1806). American politician, jurist and abolitionist who signed the U.S. Declaration of Independence. Supposedly poisoned by a disgruntled great-nephew, Wythe exclaimed: "I am murdered!" Later before he expired: "Let me die righteous."

Xavier, Saint Francis (1506-1552). Spanish-born missionary to India and Asia. Dying of a fever: "Jesus, Son of David, have mercy on me. O Virgin Mother of God, remember me." Shortly before expiring: "In Thee, O Lord, have I hoped; I shall not be confounded forever..."

Alternative: * "Jesus, Son of David, have mercy on me. O most Holy Trinity." Addressing the Blessed Virgin: "Queen of Heaven, show thyself a mother!"

Ximénes de Cisneros, Francisco (c. 1437-1517). Spanish Grand Inquisitor. "In Thee, O Lord, have I trusted."

Yakir, Iona (1896-1937). Member of the Russian army general staff. Before the firing squad during one of Stalin's purges: "Long live the Party! Long live Stalin!"

Yamashita, Tomoyuki (1885-1946). Japanese military officer during WWII. Yamashita was convicted of atrocities committed in the Philippines against civilians and prisoners of war. At his hanging: "I will pray for the Japanese emperor and the emperor's family and national prosperity. Dear father and mother, I am going to your side. Please educate my children well." While on the scaffold, through the disordered syntax of an interpreter: "As I said in Manila Supreme Court that I have done with all my capacity, so I don't ashame in front of God for what I have done when I have died. But if you say to me, 'you do not have any ability to command Japanese Army,' I should say nothing for it, because it is my nature. Now, our war criminal trial going on in Manila Supreme Court, so I wish be justify under your kindness and right. I don't blame my executioners. I will pray God bless them."

Yancey, Robert (1855-1931). American attorney and politician. Dying of a probable heart attack, to his daughter: "I will just lie here for a few minutes. I will stay here a little while, just to please you. Don't leave me, little lady. I love to watch your bright young face. Two things in this world I have always loved- a bright young face and walking in the sunshine."

Yancey, William (1814-1863). American politician, secessionist and member of the U.S. House of Representatives. Ailing from kidney failure, to his wife: "I am dying... All is well... It is God's will... Sarah."

Yeats, John "Jack" (1839-1922). Anglo-Irish artist and father of the poet William B. Yeats (below). To a friend: "Remember, you have promised me a sitting in the morning."

Yeats, William B. (1865-1939). Irish poet who was awarded the 1923 Nobel Prize in Literature. Discussing burial plans: "If I die here, bury me up there [at Roquebrune near the French border with Monaco] and then in a year's time when the newspapers have forgotten me, dig me up and plant me in Sligo [Ireland where he spent his childhood]... I want to be buried as a poet, not as a public man." The transfer of his remains actually occurred almost a decade later.

Alternative: * "If I die here, bury me up there on the mountain, and then after a year or so, dig me up and bring me privately to Sligo."

Yellow Wolf, also He-Mene Mox Mox (c. 1855-1935). Native American Nez Perce warrior. In his autobiography, Yellow Wolf detailed his participation in skirmishes with whites and the atrocities committed against his people. On his deathbed, he told his family that he would die at dawn the next morning: "as the sun rested on the edge of the horizon." He continued: "My old friends have come for me! There they are! Do you not see them?"

Yesenin, Sergei (1895-1925). Russian lyrical poet. Troubled with alcohol abuse and depression, Yesenin committed suicide by hanging. He wrote in his own blood: "Goodbye, my Friend. Goodbye... In this life there's nothing new in dying. But, nor, of course, is living any newer."

Yi Sun-sin (1545-1598). Korean naval commander. Mortally wounded during a naval engagement with the Japanese off the Korean coast: "The war is at its height- wear my armor and beat my war drums. Do not announce my death."

Young, Brigham (1801-1877). American leader of the Church of Jesus Christ of Latter Day Saints (the Mormon Church). Dying from complications of appendicitis, Young said "Amen" after receiving the Last Rites. As he expired, he whispered the given name of the Mormon Church founder Joseph Smith: "Joseph! Joseph! Joseph!"

Alternative: "I feel better."

Young, Francis (1884-1954). English writer and poet. To his wife: "Let me go now, darling. I can't go on suffering like this."

Young, Whitney (1921-1971). American civil rights leader and educator. During a visit to Lagos, Nigeria, Young suffered a cardiovascular event while swimming. Before he was stricken, he called to a friend: "This is great!"

Ysaÿe, Eugène (1858-1931). Belgian violinist, conductor and composer. Listening to a violinist play one of his compositions: "Splendid, the finale just a little too fast."

Yvart, Victor (1764-1831). French agronomist, writer and administrator. "Nature, how lovely thou art."

Zaharias, Mildred "Babe" (1911-1956). American athlete who was proficient in many sports. Dying of cancer, to her husband: "Bye, bye, honey. I'm going to go now. I love you and thank you for everything."

Zane, Giacomo (1529-1560). Italian poet. "I should like to live."

Alternative: * Some, however, say his last words actually were: "I should not like to live."

Zangara, Giuseppe (1900-1933). Italian-born assassin who attempted to shoot President-elect Franklin D. Roosevelt but inadvertently killed Chicago Mayor Anton Cermak (above). Angered that no photojournalists were present at his execution by electrocution: "You give me electric chair. I no afraid of that chair! You one of capitalists. You is crook man too. Put me in electric chair. I no care! Get to hell out of here, you son of a b**** [spoken to the attending minister]... I go sit down all by myself... Viva Italia! Goodbye to all poor peoples everywhere! Lousy capitalists! No picture! Capitalists! No one here to take my picture. All capitalists lousy bunch of crooks. Go ahead. Pusha da button!"

Zapata, Emiliano (1879-1919). Leader of the 1910 Mexican Revolution. Shot by federal troops, Zapata's last words closely paralleled those allegedly uttered by another Mexican revolutionary Pancho Villa four years later (above): "Don't let me die like this; say I said something."

Zeisberger, David (1721-1808). Moravian missionary to Native American tribes. Dying from a slow, painful illness: "I am going, my people, to rest from all my labors and to be at home with the Lord. He has never forsaken me in distress and will not forsake me now. I have reviewed my whole life and found that there is much to be forgiven." He then uttered his last words: "The Savior is near. Perhaps He will soon call and take me home."

Alternative: * "Lord Jesus, I beseech Thee; come and take my spirit to Thyself... Thou hast never forsaken me in any of the severe trials of my life; Thou wilt not forsake me now."

Zeno of Citium (c. 334-262 BCE). Cyprian-born philosopher who founded the Greek sect of the Stoics. Accidentally breaking a toe in a fall (some say a finger), the septuagenarian Zeno took this as an omen that death was near. He struck the ground with his hand and said: "Earth, dost thou demand me? I am ready." Zeno then strangled himself (some say he died by holding his breath).

Alternative: * "I come, I come, why dost thou call for me?"

Zenzaburo, Taki (died 1868). Japanese military officer. Zenzaburo was forced to commit suicide by hara-kiri to atone for a misguided order he gave: "I, and I alone, unwarrantably gave the order to fire on the foreigners at Kobe [Japan], and again as they tried to escape. For this crime I disembowel myself, and I beg you who are present to do me the honor of witnessing the act."

Zeppelin, Ferdinand von (1838-1917). German general and builder of dirigible airships. Dying of pneumonia, to his daughter: "I have perfect faith."

Zhou Enlai (1898-1976). Chinese statesman who was premier of the People's Republic of China under Mao Zedong (above). Dying of cancer, to his wife: "Little Chao, there are so many things, so many things I have not told you, and now it is too late."

Ziegfeld, Florenz "Flo" (1867-1932). American impresario who created the Broadway theatrical *Ziegfeld Follies*. Dying of "pleurisy," the delirious

Ziegfeld cried: "Curtain! Fast music! Light! Ready for the last finale! Great! The show looks good, the show looks good!"

Zimmermann, Johann von (1728-1795). Swiss physician, writer and philosopher. "Leave me alone. I am dying."

Zinzendorf, Nicolaus von (1700-1760). German theologian who founded the Moravian Church. Dying of a fever, to his son-in-law: "Now, my dear son, I am going to the Savior. I am ready. I am quite resigned to the will of my Lord. If He is no longer willing to make use of me here, I am quite ready to go to Him, for there is nothing more in my way."

Zip the Pinhead (see Johnson, William Henry).

Žiźka, Jan (c. 1360-1424). Bohemian military leader. Succumbing to the plague, Žiźka commanded: "Make my skin into drumheads for the Bohemian cause," so he could continue leading his troops after he died.

Zola, Émile (1840-1902). French novelist and political activist. In a room filled with carbon monoxide from a blocked chimney: "I feel sick. My head is splitting. No, don't you see the dog is sick too. We are both ill. It must have been something we have eaten. It will pass away. Let us not bother them."

Zook, Samuel (1821-1863). Union officer during the U.S. Civil War. Zook was shot multiple times while leading his men in the Battle of Gettysburg, Pennsylvania. When told that the Confederate forces had been beaten: "Then I am satisfied and am ready to die."

Zrinyi, Miklós (1508-1566). Croatian military leader and nobleman. Choosing his best sword to lead his men at the Battle of Szigeth at the Hungarian-Croatian border: "With this good sword gained I my first honours, and with this will I pass forth to hear my doom before the judgment seat of God." Zrinyi perished during the fighting.

Zweig, Stefan (1881-1942). Austrian writer. Disillusioned by the turmoil in Europe under fascism, Zweig and his wife immigrated to Brazil. He and his partner later committed suicide by a drug overdose: "Before parting from life of my own free will and in my right mind, I am impelled to fulfill a last obligation: to give heartfelt thanks to this wonderful land of Brazil... With every day I have learned to love this country more and more, and nowhere else would I have preferred to rebuild my life from the ground up, now that the world of my own language has been lost and my spiritual homeland, Europe, has destroyed itself. But after one's sixtieth year, unusual powers are needed in order to make another wholly new beginning. Those that I possess have been exhausted by the long years of homeless wandering. So I hold it better to conclude in good time and with erect bearing a life for which intellectual labor was always the purest joy and personal freedom the highest good on this earth. I salute all my friends! May it be granted them yet to see the dawn after the long night! I, all too impatient, go on before."

Alternative: * "... I believe it is time to end a life which was dedicated only to spiritual work, considering human liberty and my own as the greatest wealth in the world. I leave an affectionate goodbye to all my friends."

Zwingli, Ulrich (1484-1531). Swiss Protestant reformist. During the Battle of Kappel in north-central Switzerland between Protestant and Catholic factions, Zwingli was mortally wounded while aiding an injured soldier: "What does it matter? They may kill the body, but they cannot kill the soul!"

Alternative: * "Can this be considered a calamity? Well, they can, indeed, kill the body, but they are not able to kill the soul."

Bibliography

An expanded bibliography arranged by individual names can be found at: LastWordsBibliography.blogspot.com

Alford, H. How to Live. New York, NY, Hachette Book Group, 2009.

Andrews, R. The Concise Columbia Dictionary of Quotations. New York, NY, Columbia University Press, 1992.

Baring-Gould, S. The Lives of the Saints, 2nd ed. London, UK, John Hodges, 1874.

Barrett, E., Mingo, J. It Takes a Certain Type to Be a Writer. York Beach, ME, Conari Press, 2003.

Barrett, E., Mingo, J., eds. W.C. Privy's Original Bathroom Companion. New York, NY, St. Martin's Press, 2003.

Bega. Last Words of Famous Men. London, UK, Williams & Norgate, Ltd., 1930.

Bennett, B., Harte, N., eds. The Crabtree Orations 1954-1994. London, UK, The Crabtree Foundation, 1997.

Bent, S.A. Short Sayings of Great Men. Boston, MA, James R. Osgood and Co., 1887.

Billington, J.H., ed. Respectfully Quoted A Dictionary of Quotations. Mineola, NY, Dover Publications, Inc., 2010.

Bisbort, A. "Famous Last Words" Apt Observations, Pleas, Curses, Benedictions, Sour Notes, Bons Mots, and Insights from People on the Brink of Departure. San Francisco, CA, Pomegranate Communications, Inc., 1953.

Boller, P.F. Jr. Presidential Anecdotes. New York, NY, Oxford University Press, 1996.

Boller, P.F., Jr., George, J. They Never Said It A Book of Fake Quotes, Misquotes & Misleading Attributions. Oxford, UK, Oxford University Press, 1989.

Bonar, A, R., ed. The Last Days of Eminent Christians. Edinburgh, UK, T. Nelson, 1841.

Botham, A. The Ultimate Book of Useless Information. New York, NY, Perigee Books, 2007.

Brahms, W.B. Last_Words of Notable People. Haddonfield, NJ, Reference Desk Press, Inc., 2010.

Brandreth, G.D. 871 Famous Last Words and Put-downs, Insults, Squelches, Compliments, Rejoinders, Epigrams, and Epitaphs of Famous People. New York, NY, Bell Publishing Co., 1979.

Brennan, S., ed. Murderers, Robbers, & Highwaymen. New York, NY, Skyhorse Publishing, 2013.

Breverton, T. Immortal Last Words History's Most Memorable Dying Remarks, Deathbed Declarations and Final Farewells. London, UK, Quercus Publishing Plc., 2010.

Brewer, E.C. Dictionary of Phrase and Fable: Giving the Derivation, Source, or Origin of Common Phrases, Allusions, and Words That Have a Tale to Tell. Cambridge, UK, Cambridge University Press, 2014.

Brodhead, M.J. Isaac C. Parker Federal Justice on the Frontier. Norman, OK, University of Oklahoma Press, 2003.

Brownlee, W. C., King, A. Saint Patrick and the Western Apostolic Churches. New York, NY, American and Foreign Christian Union, 1857.

Butler, A. The Lives of the Fathers, Martyrs and Other Principal Saints, Vol. II. Dublin, IE, James Duffy, 1866.

Cameron, K., Comfort, R. The School of Biblical Evangelism. Alachua, FL, Bridge-Logos, 2004.

Ceilán, C. Thinning the Herd Tales of the Weirdly Departed. Guilford, CT, Lyons Press, 2008.

Clark, D.W., ed. Death-Bed Scenes. New York, NY, Lane & Scott, 1851.

Cornelius, J.K. Literary Humor. Mumbai, IN, Better Yourself Books, 2005.

Cousineau, P. Deadlines A Rhapsody on a Theme of Famous and Infamous Last Words. San Francisco, CA, Sisyphus Press, 1994.

Crawford, B., ed. Texas Death Row Executions in the Modern Era. New York, NY, The Penguin Group, 2008.

Derby, G., ed. A Conspectus of American Biography. New York, NY, James T. White & Co., 1906.

D'Israeli, I.C. Curiosities of Literature. New York, NY, D. Appleton & Co., 1846.

Dymock, J., Dymock, T. Bibliotheca Classica: or, A Classical Dictionary. London, UK, Longman, Rees, Orme, Brown, Green & Longman, 1833.

Egbert, W.R. Last Words of Famous Men and Women. Norristown, PA, Herald Printing and Binding Rooms, 1898.

Elder, R.K. Last Words of the Executed. Chicago, IL, The University of Chicago Press, 2010.

Encarta Book of Quotations. New York, NY, St. Martin's Press, 2000.

Englebert, O. Lives of the Saints. New York, NY, Barnes & Noble, Inc., 1994.

Fadiman, C., ed. The Little, Brown Book of Anecdotes. New York, NY, Little, Brown and Co., Inc., 1985.

Fadiman, C., Bernard, A., eds. Bartlett's Book of Anecdotes. Boston, MA, Little, Brown and Co., 2000.

Fedele, G., ed. Golden Thoughts of Mother, Home & Heaven. Gainesville, FL, Bridge-Logos, 2003.

Feldman, M. Whad'ya Know? Test Your Knowledge with the Ultimate Collection of Amazing Trivia, Quizzes, Stories, Fun Facts and Everything Else You Never Knew You Wanted to Know. Naperville, IL, Sorcebooks, Inc., 2009.

Forbes, M., Bloch, J. They Went That-a-Way... New York, NY, Simon and Schuster, 1988.

Foster, E. New Cyclopædia of Prose Illustrations Adapted to Christian Teachings. New York, NY, Funk & Wagnalls Co., 1872.

Fox, J. A History of the Lives, Suffering, and Triumphant Deaths of The Primitive as well as the Protestant Martyrs. Detroit, MI, Kerr, Doughty & Lapham, 1853.

Fox, J. History of Christian Martyrdom. New York, NY, J.P. Peaslee, 1834.

Francis, J.R. The Encyclopædia of Death and Life in the Spirit-World, Vol. I. Chicago, IL, The Progressive Thinker Publishing House, 1906.

Glynne-Jones, T. The Book of Words. London, UK, Arcturus Publishing Ltd., 2008.

Gould, L.L., ed. American First Ladies. New York, NY, Routledge, 2001.

Gould, S.C., Gould, L.M., eds. Miscellaneous Notes and Queries, Vol. II. Manchester, NH, S.C. & L.M. Gould, 1885.

Green, J. Famous Last Words. London, UK, Omnibus Press, 1979.

Green, J., Corcoran, A. You Know You Need a Vacation if… Kansas City, MO, Andrews McMeel Publishing, LLC, 2008.

Grounds, E., ed. The Bedside Book of Final Words. Gloucestershire, UK, Amberley Publishing, 2014.

Guthke, C.S. Last Words: Variations on a Theme in Cultural History. Princeton, NJ, Princeton University Press, 1992.

Hamilton, L. The Future State and Free Discussion; Four Sermons Preached in the First Presbyterian Church of Oakland. San Francisco, CA, J.H. Carmany & Co., 1869.

Harmon, L. Fragments on the Deathwatch. Boston, MA, Beacon Press, 1998.

Harrington, F.H. Hanging Judge. Norman, OK, University of Oklahoma Press, 1996.

Hartston, W. The Encyclopedia of Useless Information. Naperville, IL, Sourcebooks, Inc., 2007.

Hessenmueller, E.L. Best Thoughts of Best Thinkers. Cleveland, OH, Best Thoughts Publishing Co., 1904.

Hewitt, M.E., ed. Lives of Illustrious Women of All Ages. Philadelphia, PA, G.G. Evans, Publisher, 1860.

Hom, S.K., ed. R.I.P. Here Lie the Famous Last Words, Epitaphs, Morbid Musings, and Fond Farewells of the Famous and Not-so-Famous. New York, NY, Sterling Publishing Co. Inc., 2007.

J.M.H., ed. Last Words of Remarkable Persons. London, UK, Partridge & Co., 1876.

Keyes, R. The Quote Verifier. New York, NY, St. Martin's Press, 2006.

Knowles, E., ed. The Oxford Dictionary of Quotations, 5th ed. Oxford, UK, Oxford University Press, 2001.

Knox, V. Elegant Extracts: or, Useful and Entertaining Passages in Prose. London, UK, C. and J. Rivington, 1824.

Latham, E. Famous Sayings and Their Authors. London, UK, Swan Sonnenschein & Co., Ltd., 1906.

Lawrence, J.W. The Seven Laws of the Harvest God's Proven Plan for Abundant Life. Grand Rapids, MI, Kregel Publications, 1995.

Larson, C.B., Elshof, P.T., eds. 1001 Illustrations that Connect. Grand Rapids, MI, Zondervan Publishing House, 2008.

Lewis, J.W., Jr. What Killed the Great and Not So Great Composers. Bloomington, IN, AuthorHouse, 2010.

Lockyer, H. Last Words of Saints and Sinners. Grand Rapids, MI, Kregel Publications, 1969.

Marvin, F.R. Last Words (Real and Traditional) of Distinguished Men and Women. New York, NY, Fleming H. Revell Co., 1902.

May, H.G, Metzger, B.M., ed. The New Oxford Annotated Bible with the Apocrypha Revised Standard Version. New York, NY, Oxford University Press, 1977.

McKenzie, C. Wise Women Wit and Wisdom from Some of the World's Most Extraordinary Women. Edinburgh, UK, Mainstream Publishing, 2013.

Miller, K.E. Last Laughs Funny Tombstone Quotes and Famous Last Words. New York, NY, Sterling Publishing Co., Inc., 2006.

Morson, G.S. The Words of Others From Quotations to Culture. New Haven, CT, Yale University Press, 2011.

Nash, J.R. Encyclopedia of Western Lawmen & Outlaws. Lanham, MD, M. Evans, 1992.

Newton, M. The Encyclopedia of Serial Killers, 2nd ed. New York, NY, Facts On File, Inc., 2006.

O'Kill, B. Exit Lines Famous (and Not-so-Famous) Last Words. Essex, UK, Longman Group Ltd., 1986.

O'Neal, B. Encyclopedia of Western Gunfighters. Norman, OK, University of Oklahoma Press, 1979.

Petrucelli, A.W. Morbid Curiosity The Disturbing Demises of the Famous and Infamous. New York, NY, Penguin Group, 2009.

Pierce, C. Famous Last Words. Philadelphia, PA, Saturnalia Books, 2008.

Power-Waters, B. Is It Safe? Lincoln, NE, iUniverse, 2008.

Pritchard, M. I Told You I Was Ill. London, UK, RW Press Ltd., 2014.

Richardson, M. The Royal Book of Lists British Royal History. Toronto, ON, Dundurn Press, 2001.

Robertson, C., ed. Dictionary of Quotations, 3rd ed. Hertfordshire, UK, Wordsworth Editions Ltd., 1998.

Robinson, R., ed. Famous Last Words Fond Farewells, Deathbed Diatribes, and Exclamations Upon Expiration. New York, NY, Workman Publishing Co, Inc., 2003.

Rosser, D. A Smattering of Stuff. Bloomington, IN, Xlibris, 2012.

Ruffin, C.B. Last Words A Dictionary of Deathbed Quotations. Jefferson, NC, McFarland & Co., Inc., Publishers, 1995.

Sarat, A., Shoemaker, K., eds. Who Deserves to Die? Boston, MA, University of Massachusetts Press, 2011.

Scott, D. Famous Last Words. New York, NY, Carlton Press, Inc., 1992.

Seinfelt, M. Final Drafts Suicides of World-Famous Authors. Amherst, NY, Prometheus Books1999.

Shaw, K. 5 People Who Died during Sex and 100 Other Terribly Tasteless Lists. New York, NY, Broadway Books, 2007.

Shields, D. The Thing about Life Is that One Day You'll Be Dead. New York, NY, Alfred A. Knopf, 2008.

Shriner, C.A., ed. Wit, Wisdom and Foibles of the Great. New York, NY, Funk & Wagnalls Co., 1920.

Stephen, L., ed. Dictionary of National Biography. London, UK, Smith, Elder & Co., 1885.

Swainson, B., ed. Encarta Book of Quotations. New York, NY, St. Martin's Press, 2000.

The Quiver: An Illustrated Magazine for Sunday and General Reading. Vol. XI. London, UK, Cassell, Petter & Galpin, 1876.

The Wordsworth Dictionary of Phrase and Fable. Ware, Hertfordshire, UK, Wordsworth Editions, Ltd., 2001.

Thomas, D.A. Revelation 19 in Historical and Mythological Context. New York, NY, Peter Lang Publishing, Inc., 2008.

Thompson, A.C. Last Hours, or Words and Acts of the Dying. Boston, MA, Perkins & Whipple, 1851.

Tsouras, P.G. The Book of Military Quotations. St. Paul, MN, Zenith Press, 2005.

Wagman-Geller, M. And the Rest Is History. New York, NY, Perigee Books, 2011.

Wallechinsky, D., Wallace, A., Basen, I., et al. The Book of Lists The Original Compendium of Curious Information. Toronto, ON, Seal Books/ Random House of Canada, 2005.

Ward, L. Famous Last Words The Ultimate Collection of Finales and Farewells. New York, NY, Sterling Publishing Co. Inc., 2004.

Wilson, R.M. Legal Executions in the Western Territories, 1847-1911. Jefferson, NC, McFarland & Co., Inc., Publishers, 2010.

Index

A

B

C

D

F

G

H

I

J

K

L

M

N

O

P

S

T

U

V

W

X

Y

Z

Printed in the United States
By Bookmasters